WRONGS AND CRIMES

Wrongs and Crimes

VICTOR TADROS

Professor of Criminal Law and Legal Theory, University of Warwick

OXFORD
UNIVERSITY PRESS

OXFORD
UNIVERSITY PRESS

Great Clarendon Street, Oxford, OX2 6DP,
United Kingdom

Oxford University Press is a department of the University of Oxford.
It furthers the University's objective of excellence in research, scholarship,
and education by publishing worldwide. Oxford is a registered trade mark of
Oxford University Press in the UK and in certain other countries

First published 2016
First published in paperback 2019

Published in the United States of America by Oxford University Press
198 Madison Avenue, New York, NY 10016, United States of America

British Library Cataloguing in Publication Data
Data available

Library of Congress Cataloging in Publication Data
Data available

ISBN 978–0–19–957137–6 (Hbk.)
ISBN 978–0–19–884159–3 (Pbk.)

Acknowledgements

I hate this book. I have failed to write it for a long time, and not for want of trying. One reason is that views about criminalization depend on views about punishment. As I didn't know what to think about punishment, my views about criminalization stalled. So I agreed to write a short introductory book about punishment, which I intended to call 'Retribution and Security'. The aim was to find the most plausible and humane version of retributivism—roughly, the view that punishment ought to be inflicted because it is deserved—and to show the relationship between retributivism and the state's responsibility to make people secure from wrongdoing.

The book that emerged, *The Ends of Harm: The Moral Foundations of Criminal Law,*[1] did not achieve this aim. It was not short, not introductory, and attacked rather than defended retributivism. It was concerned with security—providing security to citizens from wrongdoing, is, I argued, the main legitimate aim of a system of punishment. It aimed to show how, through wrongdoing, wrongdoers could be liable to be harmed in service of that aim in the light of the enforceable protective duties that they incur through wrongdoing.

This book examines the relationship between wrongdoing and criminalization more deeply. It concerns the nature and sources of wrongdoing, personal and interpersonal responses to it, and the response that the state should make, through the criminal law, to wrongdoing. In a sense, it is a companion to *The Ends of Harm*—although most people now accept the duty view of punishment I defended there (chuckle!), I thought it worth deepening and extending my view. I also depart from some of my earlier views. I mostly leave it to others (as though anyone could be bothered!) to find the inconsistencies.

It also considers the scope of the criminal law, in the light of my views about the general relationship between wrongs and crimes. No readable book could consider all of the issues relevant to the scope of the criminal law. This unreadable book does not do so either. But it does consider some of the central and most interesting questions.

Many people have helped me in ways large and small. I have not acknowledged particular suggestions that influenced the content, sometimes very directly—there would have been far too many footnotes were I to have done so. I hope those whose ideas I stole are happy to find them mangled here, even unacknowledged.

The book emerged from a four-year collaborative project on criminalization, funded by the Arts and Humanities Research Council, to whom I am grateful. In the latter stages of the project I have also benefited from a Major Leverhulme Research Fellowship, which allowed me to work on the chapters related to the project on war that I have been conducting, especially Chapters 2, 3, 5, and 17. I am grateful to the Leverhulme Trust. My co-investigators on the AHRC project, as well as the two doctoral students who were involved, provided a constant stream of support and stimulation that I now miss. They are Andrew Cornford, Antony Duff, Lindsay Farmer, Christine Kelly, Sandra Marshall, and Massimo Renzo. Without them, there would be no book.

The project involved meetings, workshops, and conferences, in the UK and beyond. We discussed a wide range of topics, with an extremely wide range of people, drawing

[1] (Oxford: OUP, 2011).

on diverse disciplines. This both advanced my own thinking, and confused me, no end. Many audiences listened to and discussed earlier drafts of the work here, and papers that did not make it into the book. Those I remember are Cornell, Edinburgh, Essex, Helsinki, King's College London, London School of Economics, Oxford, Pennsylvania Pompeu Fabra, Queen's Kingston, Harvard, Hull, Stirling, Tufts, Uppsala, University College London, Warwick, Yale, York Toronto, and York York.

Warwick University provided me with the ideal institutional environment to write the book: rigorous, collegiate, relaxed, fun, and free. I should especially acknowledge two centres that help to make Warwick my intellectual home: the Criminal Justice Centre and the Centre of Ethics, Law and Public Affairs.

Three workshops were held on part of the manuscript, at the London School of Economics, at Warwick University, and at King's College London. These workshops helped me to improve the book a great deal. I am especially grateful to my commentators—James Edwards, Tim Fowler, Zosia Stemplowska, Patrick Tomlin, Maria Alvarez, Richard Holton, David Owens, and Laura Valentini—who produced brilliant and detailed responses to several chapters.

I had many helpful comments and suggestions beyond these events. I am especially grateful for these to Mitch Berman, Paul Bouhabib, Kim Brownlee, Paula Casals, Matthew Clayton, Sharon Cowan, James Edwards, David Enoch, Cécile Fabre, Lindsay Farmer, Kim Ferzan, Andrew Gold, John Goldberg, Bob Goodin, Doug Husak, Erin Kelly, Seth Lazar, Jeff McMahan, Anton Markoc, Michael Moore, Dana Nelkin, Serena Olsaretti, Tom Parr, Derk Pereboom, Amit Pundik, Massimo Renzo, Jacob Ross, Laura Roth, Tim Scanlon, David Shoemaker, Matthew Stephenson, Jens Damgaard Thaysen, Patrick Tomlin, Daniel Viehoff, Andrew Williams, and Gideon Yaffe. Without their messing things up, the book would have been much better.

There is a vast literature discussing the wide range of issues that this book is concerned with. I have not remotely done justice to that literature. The literature is so vast that doing so would have been impossible. I can only express my gratitude to the whole community of scholars in moral, political, and legal philosophy from whom I have learned.

I have drawn on previous published work in several places in this book: 'Punishment and the Appropriate Response to Wrongdoing',[2] 'Harm, Sovereignty, and Prohibition',[3] 'Wrongness and Criminalization',[4] 'What Might Have Been',[5] 'Consent to Harm',[6] 'Orwell's Battle with Brittain: Vicarious Liability for Unjust Aggression',[7] 'Wrongful Intentions Without Closeness',[8] and 'The Wrong and the Free'.[9] I am also grateful to the team at Oxford University Press with their stellar support from beginning to end.

Once again, I am grateful to my family for the good things in my life: none would be nearly as good without them, and most would not exist. I thank Emily, for loving, lying, and laughter; Bruno, without whom I would be lost; and Lola, for exemplary illustrations of the will to power. Most of all, I send my love to Rafi, to whom this book is dedicated: small boy; big heart; loud voice!

[2] *Criminal Law and Philosophy*, forthcoming. [3] (2011) 17 *Legal Theory* 35.

[4] In A Marmor *The Routledge Companion to Philosophy of Law* (London: Routledge, 2012).

[5] In J Oberdiek *Philosophical Foundations of the Law of Torts* (Oxford: OUP, 2014).

[6] (2011) 64 *Current Legal Problems* 23.

[7] (2014) 42 *Philosophy and Public Affairs* 42.

[8] (2015) 43 *Philosophy and Public Affairs* 52.

[9] In K K Ferzan and S J Morse *Legal, Moral, and Metaphysical Truths: The Philosophy of Michael S Moore* (Oxford: OUP, 2016)

Table of Contents

1
Introduction

Young Genghis
A Two Scene, One Act Morality Play.

Scene 1

1172: a hut on the outskirts of Ulaanbaatar.

Genghis: Mum, I don't want to be a blacksmith just like grandpa.

Mrs Khan: Well, what do you want to be, son?

Genghis: I want to do something I'll be remembered for.

Mrs Khan: We just want you to do whatever makes you happy.

Scene 2 …

I. Wrongdoing and Blighted Lives

Wrongdoing can blight the lives of the victims. No one disagrees. It also blights the lives of wrongdoers. If wrongdoers are punished for their wrongdoing, their lives can be blighted by the consequences of their wrongdoing. But their lives can also be blighted simply by the wrongdoing itself.

Mrs Khan's response makes me chuckle for more than one reason. The obvious reason is that we should consider other people in deciding what to do. The less obvious reason has to do with Mrs Khan's mistaken view about what she should want for her son. Imagine Mrs Khan reflecting (perhaps from on high) about her son's life at its conclusion. She shouldn't think: my advice was bad for others, so I shouldn't have given it, but at least things went well for Genghis. A happy life has not gone well if the person is happy at systematic violent wrongdoing.

Here's another way to see the same thing. Suppose that you discover that your child was involved in serious wrongdoing. You don't know, yet, whether she was the wrongdoer or the victim. If she is a serious harmful wrongdoer she will not be caught and punished, let us suppose, and her wrongdoing will not make her unhappy. If she is the victim, the crime will make her very unhappy. Thinking just about her, does her life go better if she is the criminal or the victim?

I have asked many people this question. Many people prefer that she is the victim of the wrongdoing. This preference may not extend to wrongdoing that causes death or permanent brain injuries. People may prefer her to be a murderer than to be murdered. A similar thing is true for injuries that destroy central features of personhood. But somewhere short of serious brain injuries, people tend to prefer that their child is the victim of serious harmful wrongdoing than that she is the wrongdoer. Even those who reject this judgement find it a tough call. As it is terrible for a person to be the victim of serious harmful wrongdoing, it is also terrible for a person to be a wrongdoer—it is not only a terrible thing, it is terrible for the wrongdoer.

In what way is it terrible for the wrongdoer? Wrongdoers can be perfectly happy, even happy at their wrongdoing. But there is an important aspect of the wrongdoer's life that she has reason to disvalue. Now suppose that she does not disvalue it—despite the fact that she has acted wrongly, she is happy, perhaps even happy at her wrongdoing. All the worse! She has reason to disvalue acting wrongly; it is regrettable for her that she fails to disvalue what she has reason to disvalue. She compounds the disvalue of acting wrongly with her failure to recognize it. This is why we do not think that it is worse in itself for a wrongdoer that she comes to recognize that she has done something wrong, though, of course, recognition will inevitably be painful for her.

II. Responses to Wrongdoing

My interest in this book is in the relationship between moral wrongs and crimes. It goes without saying that there is an important relationship of some kind between these things. At least the most famous crimes—such as murder, rape, serious assaults, theft, and fraud—are also moral wrongs. Surely they are criminalized because acting in the relevant way is wrong; or at least, the facts that make acting in these ways wrong are also reasons to criminalize them. And it seems, at least at first blush, that conduct that is not wrong ought not to be criminalized: singing, painting, and joking, for example, ought not to be criminalized, even if people do not like the particular songs, paintings, or jokes.

Of course, there are many more difficult cases. Some things that are wrong do not seem to warrant criminalization: this seems true of many cases of lying. And the state might seem justified in criminalizing some conduct that does not seem wrong: although it is a controversial example, this might be true of possession of certain drugs or firearms. People disagree about both kinds of case.

Theories of criminalization tend to focus on the periphery: controversial cases where we are unsure, or disagree, about whether the conduct should be criminalized. But it is just as important to focus on the core cases of serious wrongdoing: why should murder, rape, serious assault, and burglary be criminalized? In the light of our views about that, we are in a better position to appreciate why controversial cases are controversial, and perhaps also to understand how to resolve them.

My opening remarks indicate one puzzle about the relationship between core wrongs and crimes. It is this: wrongdoing makes the lives of wrongdoers go worse. Just as virtue is its own reward, vice is its own punishment (of course, I don't mean this literally). Actual punishment normally makes the lives of those punished go even worse. If so, how can we justify punishment? And if we cannot justify punishment, we cannot justify criminalization either—at least if by criminalizing conduct the state warrants punishment for it.

Of course, punishing wrongdoers can also be good—it can protect people by deterring wrongdoing. But even if punishment is good for others, it is not good for the wrongdoer. What needs justifying is harming wrongdoers in order to protect other people. Merely pointing to the benefits of punishment does not fully justify it. It points to a reason to punish, but it has to be shown why wrongdoers are not wronged when they are harmed to achieve these benefits.

Here is one answer: the wrongdoer may have reason to disvalue his life in virtue of his wrongdoing, but that is his own fault. And if we make his life go even worse by punishing him, that is also his own fault. Given that he could have avoided the disvalue and the punishment that goes with it simply by doing what he was required to do, he is responsible for the disvaluable effects of his wrongdoing on his own life, and we thus have less reason to be concerned at his life going badly.

Part of this answer is part of the truth. The responsibility of the wrongdoer for his wrongdoing makes a difference to the permissibility of harming him. But even this is only a superficial part of the truth. There are deep and difficult questions why responsibility is important, and the sense in which it is important. Once we reflect on the more complete causal history of wrongdoing, there is at least an important sense in which his wrongdoing was not avoidable. So we need to investigate whether our convictions about the importance of responsibility survive scrutiny and why.

But much of the answer is either false, or misleading, or both. The lives of wrongdoers have the same importance as the lives of everyone else. It is no less important that their lives, like the lives of everyone else, are as close to what a person's life ought to be like, given their qualities and abilities. They may be far away from such a life if they are acting wrongly. They are still further away if they suffer for it. When a person acts wrongly we have powerful reasons to help them bring their lives closer to what their life ought to be like.

The idea that there is less reason to care about the lives of wrongdoers seems to me false in the light of this. A person who cares as much or more about the lives of wrong doers than others does not make a moral mistake; indeed, such a person seems especially praiseworthy, given that we are understandably repulsed by serious wrongdoing.

This brings me to my own answer to the justification of punishment, or at least a sketch of that answer. It builds on this basic idea: respect for other people requires us, in our dealings with them, to consider their reasons to respond to the circumstances that they are in. A central part of the justification of the treatment of others, especially the disadvantageous treatment of others, depends on the fact that a person has a life to lead for herself, where she judges for herself what is important to her. This explains why the treatment of others can depend on what they choose, or consent to.

But there are limits to the importance of choice and consent in the treatment of others. One important limit depends on their duties. Consent is less important in the justification of treating a person in a certain way if that person has a duty to accept the treatment. And the person can have a duty to accept the treatment if she has certain underlying duties, such as the duty to further the goals that affecting her serves.

In the light of this, first consider how a wrongdoer herself can come closer to what a human life should be like in the face of serious wrongdoing: she can do so by responding to that wrongdoing in the appropriate way. The appropriate way to respond to one's wrongdoing is to set oneself certain ends. These ends include full and deep recognition of the wrongdoing, apology, and compensation. It also includes the end of protecting the victim against further wrongdoing of a similar kind, and protecting others.

This helps to justify certain responses that others, including the state, may make to wrongdoers in virtue of their wrongdoing. The fact that wrongdoers have stringent duties to serve certain ends because of their wrongdoing helps to justify the state harming wrongdoers in service of those ends. This, I argue, is central to the justification of punishment. I call this theory of punishment *the duty view*: the view that the duties that offenders incur through their wrongdoing are central to the justification of punishment. I partly defend this view elsewhere.[1] My aim in this book is to deepen that defence, and to explore its implications for the relationship between wrongdoing and criminalization.

[1] See *The Ends of Harm: The Moral Foundations of the Criminal Law* (Oxford: OUP, 2011). I have further defended and developed the argument there in 'Replies' (2012) 5 *Jerusalem Review of Legal Studies* 89; 'Responses' (2013) 32 *Law and Philosophy* 241; 'Answers' (2015) 9 *Criminal Law and Philosophy* 73.

III. Exploring Criminalization

Central debates in the philosophy of criminalization revolve around principles that would restrict the scope of the criminal law, or provide reasons to criminalize conduct. Some of these principles suggest a direct relationship between wrongs and crimes. For example, some think that we have a reason to criminalize all morally wrongful conduct. Some think that we ought not to criminalize conduct unless that conduct is wrongful independently of it being criminalized. Some think that it is wrong to criminalize conduct unless that conduct is either wrong independently of it being criminalized, or because of its being criminalized.

Many people endorse principles that are less directly connected with wrongdoing. For example, some think that it is permissible to criminalize conduct only if that conduct is harmful, or if it risks harm, or if criminalizing the conduct prevents harm. Still others think that it is permissible to criminalize conduct only if the conduct violates the rights of others, or if criminalizing the conduct would prevent rights violations. Some think that more than one thing is necessary: that the conduct criminalized must be both wrongful and harmful, for example, or that it must involve a harmful rights violation.

Accounts of criminalization tend to proceed by example. Is some version of the harm principle valid? But then we would not be able to criminalize harmless wrongdoing. And some harmless wrongdoing is very serious. In response, either abandon the harm principle or revise it in a way that can accommodate the case.

This way of proceeding is fine as far as it goes, but it does not go too far, or too deep. It leaves untouched the more fundamental questions concerning the relationship between wrongdoing and criminalization. To grasp both the value of criminalizing conduct and its limits, we must understand the nature and sources of wrongdoing, the reasons for criminalizing wrongdoing, an explanation why wrongdoers are liable to punishment, and the proportionality principles that determine both the scope of that liability, and when it is permissible to act on it. Thus, this book is as much about wrongs as it is about crimes.

IV. The Structure

This book is about wrongs, crimes, and the relationship between them. It begins with wrongdoing in general, and ends at the farthest reaches of the criminal law.

Part A explores moral wrongdoing and personal, interpersonal, and punitive responses to it. Chapters 2 and 3 discuss the importance of moral wrongdoing. This cannot be grasped by examining the semantics of wrongdoing. It requires an understanding of the role that wrongdoing plays in our lives, both as people deciding how to act and as judges who evaluate and respond to wrongdoing.

Theories of wrongdoing differ along two dimensions. One concerns the relationship between wrongdoing and responses to it. A response-dependent view prioritizes the judges: an act is wrong because of the response that it is appropriate to make to that act. In contrast, an action-guiding view prioritizes the role of wrongdoing in practical reasoning, where some of the acts that might be done are wrong. In contrast with the response-dependent view, this view explains the responses that it is apt to make to wrongdoing in the light of the nature of wrongdoing.

A second dimension involves the distinction between first-personal and interpersonal ideas. A first-personal view prioritizes the perspective of those who might act wrongly. An interpersonal view prioritizes the relationship between the wrongdoer and others. Of course, all plausible accounts of wrongdoing must explain the central case of wrongdoing: the case where one person wrongs another. But not all views explain the general nature and importance of wrongdoing interpersonally. Either of these views could be action-guiding or response-dependent. I defend a first-personal action-guiding account of wrongdoing.

Whilst Chapter 2 is critical of the idea that wrongdoing should be understood in a response-dependent way, it defends the idea that there are responses that are distinctively appropriate to wrongdoing. Chapter 4 is concerned with the relationship between first-personal responses to wrongdoing and state punishment. The idea that certain responses are appropriate to wrongdoing is a central part of a theory of responsibility, and helps to support the infliction of punishment. This chapter develops, and to some extent revises, some arguments developed in *The Ends of Harm*.

Chapter 5 aims to show that the aptness of the relevant first-personal responses to wrongdoing can survive a difficult challenge: that we are not responsible for acting wrongly. The challenge is closely related to the challenge that Derk Pereboom poses to the idea that we can deserve blame for wrongdoing.[2] I show that Pereboom's argument against desert is not decisive: we have other reasons to reject desert. More importantly, I show that even if it is, we are responsible in a different sense: we have distinctive reasons to respond to our own wrongdoing in virtue of fulfilling certain conditions of responsibility for it. By showing this, I reinforce the idea that wrongdoers have reasons to accept certain burdens being inflicted on them due to their responsibility for it.

Part B discusses general questions about the relationships between wrongs and crimes. Many people defend restrictive principles of criminal law. These principles can be either content-focused or effect-focused. Content-focused principles claim that only certain kinds of conduct can be criminalized. Effect-focused principles claim that conduct can be criminalized only if doing so has certain effects. I show that such principles are either false, or do not significantly advance our understanding of criminalization.

Other principles are justificatory: they aim to show that we uniformly have reasons or duties to criminalize certain conduct. Like restrictive principles, such principles can be either content-focused or effect-focused. Again I show that such principles are either false, or do not significantly advance our understanding of criminalization. These arguments are developed in chapters 6 and 7.

Chapter 8 is concerned with the idea that there is a close relationship between wrongs and crimes. The criminal justice system is an arm of the state, and thus the philosophy of criminal law is part of political philosophy. But, I argue, this should not lead to scepticism about the deep relationship between wrongs and crimes. I show this is false by focusing on the most plausible version of the view that political philosophy is *sui generis*: political liberalism. I claim that the most plausible version of this view leaves the relationship between wrongs and crimes intact in central cases.

This chapter also highlights the importance and limits of two senses of autonomy: authenticity and independence. A person's life is authentic insofar as she lives it according to her own values, decisions, and judgements, by exercising her own

[2] Originally in *Living Without Free Will* (Cambridge: CUP, 2001) and further developed and defended in *Free Will, Agency, and Meaning in Life* (Oxford: OUP, 2014).

practical and theoretical capacities. A person's life is independent insofar as others do not shape her life against her will.

Chapter 9 draws together and develops the ideas in Part B to offer a general theory of criminalization. That theory structures our thinking about criminalization by explaining the role of both wrongdoing and the effects of criminalization in the decision to criminalize.

Parts C and D explore particular questions about the relationship between wrongs and crimes. Part C is concerned with core ideas of harm and autonomy that shape our understanding of central cases of interpersonal wrongdoing.

Chapters 10 and 11 are concerned with the relationships between three central ideas that structure our thinking about wrongs and crimes: harm, autonomy, and consent. Chapter 10 is concerned with harm. I defend the idea that harm is primarily concerned with well-being, and explore some central features of well-being. I then defend a complex counterfactual view of harm: the view that whether a person is harmed depends on comparisons between a being's current state of well-being and states of well-being that she might have been in.

Chapter 11 is concerned with the importance of consent. It shows that harm is not the only source, or even the central source, of wrongdoing. People owe each other consent-sensitive duties: roughly, duties not to do things unless the person to whom we will do them consents. Harm plays a role in explaining which consent-sensitive duties exist, but it is only part of a more complex explanation of such duties. The two senses of autonomy introduced in Chapter 8 are central to the importance of consent.

As consent is central to the criminal law, the next three chapters, 12, 13, and 14, are concerned with the conditions under which valid consent is undermined. Chapter 12 is concerned with threats and coercive offers and Chapter 13 is concerned with mistake and deception. The validity of consent, in both cases, has been explained by considering what a person would have done were the threat or error not to have occurred. I show that this way of thinking is mistaken in both cases, and suggest an alternative that explores how the meaning of acts can be altered by threats and errors. This gives rise to a more plausible account of when threats and errors make consent invalid, and of the gravity of wrongdoing when they do.

Chapter 14 is concerned with whether consent can be made invalid by the content of what is consented to: in particular, whether consent to be harmed, or otherwise negatively affected, is invalid simply because of what is consented to. It defends the view that consent can be invalid in this way because people have self-regarding duties not to consent to certain treatment.

Part D is concerned with some of the outer reaches of the criminal law. Chapter 15 explores acts that are often discussed in the context of the offence principle: the principle that conduct can be criminalized because it is offensive. I argue that offensiveness is not fundamental. Acts are offensive because of independent facts that make them wrong, and these facts can sometimes justify criminalization. I then consider the nature of impersonal value, and show how value of that kind bears on wrongs and crimes.

Chapters 16 and 17 are concerned with the criminalization of inchoate wrongs and crimes. Chapter 16 is concerned with the nature of inchoate wrongdoing. It focuses on a central case of incomplete inchoate wrongdoing, arguing for the significance of intentions in explaining wrongdoing of that kind. This chapter also offers further defence of an idea that I have explored elsewhere: that intentions non-derivatively make certain acts wrong.

Chapter 17 is concerned with inchoate crime, focusing on an important case: the criminalization of firearms possession. This chapter explains why it is permissible to criminalize inchoate wrongdoing, and also some conduct that is not wrong. It thus provides a further challenge to the idea that only wrongdoing can be criminalized. Whilst there is a deep relationship between wrongs and crimes, there are wrongs that cannot be criminalized, and, more controversially, crimes that criminalize conduct that is not wrong.

PART A
PUNISHING WRONGS

2

Wrongness and Response

A minimal view of the relationship between wrongs and crimes is that the facts that make some acts wrong are contingent reasons to criminalize those acts. Consider the view that the criminal justice system is justified solely by good consequences. The main good consequence is harm prevention. And the main way harm is prevented is by deterrence. On this view, harming others is wrong because harm is bad. The criminal justice system ought to criminalize harmful wrongdoing because doing so deters people from harming others by providing them with prudential reasons not to harm others. Thus, the criminal law ought to be concerned with wrongdoing: harm makes conduct wrong, and thus harmful wrongdoing ought to be criminalized.

On this view, the relationship between wrongs and crimes is contingent. Criminalizing wrongful conduct is wrong if doing so does not have good consequences, such as harm prevention. Criminalizing permissible conduct is right if doing so has good consequences, such as harm prevention. In the real world, the criminal law should focus on harmful wrongdoing, but not because of any deep relationship between wrongs and crimes.

It is not very plausible that the relationship between wrongs and crimes is simply contingent in this way. At least when considering core crimes, such as murder, rape, serious assault, and theft, we punish people for their crimes. This immediately suggests a deeper relationship between wrongs and crimes. Any plausible theory of the criminal justice system should capture this idea.

This chapter provides the foundations for exploring one idea to support a less contingent relationship between wrongs and crimes: that the relationship between wrongs and crimes arises because of the responses that are owed to wrongdoing.

Section I is concerned with public blame for wrongdoing, explaining possible connections between the communicative or expressive roles of the criminal justice system and the nature of wrongdoing. Section II distinguishes and clarifies questions about the nature of wrongness, fixes the focus of this chapter, and sketches the answer to the question that I am focused on, an answer defended in Chapter 3. Section III explores a distinction that is a central focus of this chapter and the next: the distinction between having a decisive reason for action and its being all things considered wrong not to act in that way. Section IV outlines one way to draw that distinction: that wrongness is distinct because of the responses that it is apt to make to it. This is the response-dependent view of wrongdoing. It also distinguishes versions of that view. Section V explores and rejects one objection to the response-dependent view: that the aptness of the relevant responses does not track wrongdoing. Section VI offers a different, and decisive, objection to response-dependent views: that they provide the wrong order of explanation between wrongness and response. I support this objection by considering the phenomenology of deciding to act, where some acts that the person might perform seem wrong. This paves the way for the first-personal action-guiding account of wrongdoing that I offer in Chapter 3.

I. Public Blame for Wrongdoing

One way to defend the non-contingent relationship between wrongs and crimes focuses on the expressive or communicative functions of the criminal justice system. One reason why we convict and punish wrongdoers, and not the innocent, is that criminal justice officials publicly blame people for their conduct. Public blame is warranted only if the person is blameworthy. It is apt to blame a person for wrongdoing, and only for wrongdoing. Therefore, only wrongdoing ought to be criminalized. Otherwise, state officials will blame those who are not blameworthy.

Whilst this argument fails, it points at something true. The criminal justice system has a role in publicly blaming wrongdoers, at least on some interpretation of what blame is. The justification for doing this is not limited to its deterrent effects; there is value in itself in communicating the fact that the conduct was wrong, to the victim, to the wrongdoer, and to others. If blame, or at least a certain kind of blame, is reserved for wrongdoers in response to their wrongdoing, we have one reason to focus the criminal justice system on wrongdoing.

But this view is not fully responsive to the problem of punishment. The central problem of punishment is how to justify a systematic state practice of intentional harm infliction. It is powerfully intuitive that this practice ought to focus primarily on wrongdoers. But why? The answer that blame is warranted only if the person has acted wrongly does not answer this question.

It might be argued that the only way of adequately publicly blaming a person involves the intentional infliction of harm. I doubt this: intentionally inflicting harm on wrongdoers is an odd way to express blame. But even if it was true, public blame is insufficiently important to justify the kind and magnitude of harm that is inflicted by any plausible system of state punishment.

Furthermore, it is not *inevitable* that the criminal justice system blames. The state could intentionally inflict harm on people without blaming them, simply for reasons of deterrence. Indeed, it sometimes does so. Not all crimes have a blaming function; some simply have the function of securing compliance with the law because of the good consequences of doing so. But even in that case, it seems that there are strong reasons against punishing the innocent. These reasons may not always be decisive—we will see in Chapters 6 and 17 that they are not—but they are normally decisive. It is not very plausible that a criminal justice system that eschewed public blame would only have contingent reasons to focus its attentions on wrongdoers.

The view that gives central importance to public blame, or other forms of communication, also fails to respond adequately to this problem: the main reason for retaining the criminal justice system, given all of the horrors it causes, is surely that retaining it prevents even greater horrors—the horrors that would arise from the increased prevalence of serious wrongdoing that would result from abolition.

Relatedly, it is worth noting that criminal justice is necessary to secure all other state institutions and many private practices. The systems of private law, public law health and safety law, family law, that underpin financial institutions, educational institutions, military institutions, family stability and security, and the political system depend on the criminal law to enforce the decisions taken in these other branches of law.[1] To take only one example, the damages that a court orders in the case of breach of contract will often be paid only if punishment is threatened for a failure to do so.

[1] See, especially, V Chiao 'What is the Criminal Law For?' (2016) 35 *Law and Philosophy* 137. As we will see in Chapter 8, this is not to say that criminal law lacks an inherently backward looking dimension, as Chiao seems to suggest.

The idea that wrongdoers ought to be blamed is not responsive to the more central functions of the criminal law. We need to show why wrongdoers, in particular, may be harmed to prevent the greater prevalence of serious wrongdoing, where innocent people may not. That seems to have little to do with the value of blame.

The central question of the criminal justice system, then, is this. How is it that a person becomes liable to have harm intentionally inflicted upon her in order to secure the ends of punishment, where the central end is prevention of serious wrongdoing? Any plausible answer to this question should explain why a person becomes liable to be harmed in this way by having acted wrongly.

A more complete answer to the central problems of punishment, then, relies on the importance of wrongdoing. Why is it wrongdoing, and not something else, that makes a person liable to the intentional infliction of harm? An answer requires us to understand what is distinctive about wrongdoing, and the role that it plays in our lives, both as people who might act wrongly, and as people who respond to wrongdoing. Yet even if the blaming function does not adequately respond to the central problems of punishment, it is important. Focusing on the relationship between wrongdoing and blame deepens our understanding of this function.

In this chapter and the next, I focus on the general nature of wrongdoing. In the two chapters that follow I offer a general account of the personal and interpersonal responses that it is appropriate to make to wrongdoing. This helps us to understand the role of the criminal law, as a distinctive, and especially harsh, response to serious wrongdoing.

II. The Questions of Wrongdoing

What is moral wrongness? That question is ambiguous. One ambiguity is that it might refer either to *pro tanto* or all things considered wrongness. Sometimes *pro tanto* wrongdoing is all things considered permissible. For example, taking your fire hydrant is *pro tanto* wrong, but all things considered permissible if it is done to put out a dangerous fire. I am interested only in all-things-considered moral wrongness. For short, I will simply call it 'moral wrongness', but bear in mind the 'all things considered' epithet that restricts my focus.

A full account of moral wrongness explains three things, and the relationships between them. First, there is the concept of moral wrongness. Second, there are the facts that can make particular acts wrong. Third, there is a more general explanation of the role that moral wrongness has in our practical and critical deliberations.[2]

My main focus is on the third element of a theory of wrongness. But a theory of the role that wrongness plays in practical and critical deliberation relies on an account of the way that facts make acts wrong. A good explanation of the role of wrongness in practical and critical deliberation thus provides a natural explanation of the way that certain facts, but not others, make particular acts wrong.

[2] For a similar idea, see T M Scanlon *What We Owe to Each Other* (Cambridge, Mass: Harvard UP, 1998) 391, fn 21. For further exploration in the context of Scanlon's contractualism, see P Hieronymi 'On Metaethics and Motivation: The Appeal of Contractualism' in R Jay Wallace, R Kumar, and S Freeman *Reasons and Recognition: Essays on the Philosophy of T M Scanlon* (Oxford: OUP, 2011) especially 113–5.

In this chapter and the next, I outline and defend a view of wrongness that explains the contrast between wrongness and irrational action by pointing to the limits that wrongness puts on our freedom. Roughly, when we decide that an action is wrong, we are unfree to perform that action. The relevant unfreedom occurs not from external sources, but within practical deliberation itself. Deliberating about wrongness involves deliberating about whether we are free in this way.

This view is controversial in two ways. First, it prioritizes the action-guiding role of wrongdoing rather than its role in critical deliberation. That is, it treats as most fundamental the role that moral wrongness has in the mind of a person deliberating what to do, where some of the acts that she could perform might be wrong. It is a secondary matter to determine the appropriate way that we, and others, have to react to our wrongdoing. A good account of the reactions to wrongdoing depends on a proper account of the role that it has in practical reasoning, not the other way around.

The second feature, that will play a larger role in the next chapter, is that moral wrongdoing is fundamentally first-personal rather than interpersonal. Interpersonal relationships are not fundamental to an account of wrongdoing. Furthermore, explaining the special motivational force that wrongdoing has in the practical reasoning of those who are committed to living morally relies primarily on personal rather than interpersonal facts—a proper explanation why wrongdoing has the role that it has in our practical reasoning does not draw on the idea that moral wrongdoing governs our interactions with each other. Overall, then, I will defend a first-personal deliberative account of wrongdoing.

Here is a summary of my arguments for prioritizing the role of wrongdoing in deliberation. First, it provides a more natural account of the phenomenology of the role that wrongness plays in practical reasoning. At least for those who are morally motivated, in deciding what to do, we consider which acts it would be wrong for us to perform. The appropriateness of the reactions that others would have to our conduct does not play a fundamental role in our reasoning about wrongness. At most it offers us a heuristic device for working out what it would be wrong for us to do. We do not determine what is wrong by reflecting on what others would have reason to hold us accountable for; things are the other way around.

Second, it provides us with a better account of the relationship between wrongness and accountability practices. An investigation into our reactions to wrongdoing relies on an account of wrongness rather than the other way around. Our accountability practices are to be justified as appropriate (or not) in virtue of the way that we ought to respond to wrongdoing of certain kinds (or perhaps of all kinds). If so, we rely on a conception of wrongdoing in critically scrutinizing our accountability practices. It is much less plausible that we justify a set of judgements about what is wrong by considering whether it is appropriate to hold people accountable for these things.

To orient readers, here is a sketch of my argument for prioritizing the first-personal role of wrongdoing. Whether an action is wrong depends in part on what we owe to others. Other people have rights that we act or refrain from acting in certain ways. And of central importance in an account of such rights is the fact that people have the capacity to reason for themselves and to determine for themselves how to act. Any account of wrongness must naturally explain this personal way in which actions can be wrong.

But wrongful actions do not always wrong other people. Other facts can make an action wrong. Acts that are wrong in virtue of these facts are wrong impersonally.

Actions can be wrong because they destroy, erode, or fail to advance things of value, even if there is no person who can complain about these acts, and even if the relevant values are not values of persons. A proper account of wrongdoing must be able to explain how these facts make actions wrong.

And even if these facts do not make acts wrong, that is not true because of the nature of wrongdoing, but because these facts lack the significance that makes acts wrong. A theory of wrongness should at least explain why it is debatable whether these acts are wrong, and not rule them out prior to debate. Friends and enemies of such wrongs are having a debate about what is wrong, not about the nature of wrongdoing.

Furthermore, a good account of wrongdoing should be unified in the following sense. Certain properties of moral wrongdoing exist uniformly across wrongs, regardless of whether the facts that make these acts wrong are personal or impersonal. The basic role that wrongness plays in practical reasoning does not depend on whether the values that are engaged by the act under consideration are personal or impersonal. Furthermore, at least at a most general level, the appropriate way to respond to wrongdoing, both for the wrongdoer herself and by others who hold that person responsible for the wrongdoing, does not depend on whether the wrong is personal or impersonal.

Interpersonal accounts of wrongdoing fail to account for this very general unity in the realm of wrongdoing. They provide an unattractive hybrid picture of the role that personal and impersonal value plays in wrongdoing. Interpersonal accounts of wrongdoing treat the idea that we owe it to others that we accommodate their concerns in our actions as central to an account of what wrongdoing is. But as a result, these accounts of wrongdoing fail naturally to explain the way in which personal and impersonal value can be engaged in our deliberations about the same actions. And they fail to provide a uniform account of the motivational force of conclusions about wrongness.

III. Wrongness, Rationality, and Reasons

Moral wrongness is a kind of wrongness. But not all wrongness is moral wrongness. An answer to a question can be wrong. A bath may be the wrong size to fit in a bathroom. I might play the wrong notes in a Mozart sonata. This jacket may look wrong on me, or it may be the wrong jacket to go with these trousers. A football player might have the wrong attitude to play a particular role in a team. None of these things is typically morally wrong.

Some might doubt that we have a special and distinctive idea of moral wrongness. Compare reasons. Some think that there is no special kind of reason that is a 'moral reason'. The general class of reasons, it is claimed, is not divided into moral and non-moral kinds. This may be thought true because anything that might count as a good moral reason—giving money to help others, for example—also makes the person for whom it is a reason better off when she acts on it. Charitable giving is one way to make one's life go better, so the relevant reasons are always both moral and prudential.[3] Or it might be thought true because any fact that can contribute to the moral wrongness

[3] See J Raz 'Morality and Self-Interest' in *Engaging Reason: On the Theory of Value and Action* (Oxford: OUP, 1999) 304–10.

of an act can also provide a reason for action that is unrelated to moral wrongness. For example, the fact that acting in a certain way will save a life can make it morally wrong not to act in that way. But this fact can also provide a reason for action even where refraining from acting in that way is not morally wrong—for example, if saving the life is supererogatory.

There is a weak sense in which there are distinctively moral reasons. A moral reason is a reason that can make a contribution to a moral requirement. This leaves open the possibility that there are non-moral reasons—reasons that cannot contribute to moral requirements. I suspect that there are such reasons—I can have a reason to scratch an itch, but this reason cannot contribute to a moral requirement to scratch. And it leaves open the possibility that facts that give rise to moral reasons have practical significance in other ways.

Whatever the right view about reasons, the idea that moral wrongness is distinctive is powerful. A terrible dress sense offends against taste, not morality. Moral wrongness has a special stringency and importance that needs explaining. Even trivial wrongs, such as turning up late for a meeting, have a different character from offences against taste. This character needs explaining.

Whilst moral wrongness is distinct from other kinds of wrongness, all kinds of wrongness have something in common. Here is a first stab: if it is wrong to *v*, *v*ing is ruled out. This character of wrongness implies that we can express wrongness claims as requirements of a kind. Don't give that answer; don't wear that jacket, or at least not with those trousers; don't put that bath in that bathroom; don't play that note; don't have that attitude if you want that role in the team. An account of wrongness aims to characterize the 'ruling out' that wrongness implies. An account of moral wrongness aims to characterize the distinctive kind of requirement involved in moral wrongness.

It might be thought that only the requirements of morality are categorical, where non-moral demands are hypothetical. When one person says to another 'don't play that note' in virtue of the fact that it is the wrong note in a Mozart sonata, the claim is best filled out as follows (on this view): 'if you want to play the Mozart sonata correctly, don't play that note'.

But non-moral demands can be categorical. Consider irrational acts. The term 'rationality' is used in many ways. Here I mean simply that an act is irrational if there is a decisive reason against performing it. Not all irrational acts, in this sense, are morally wrong, but requirements of rationality are not hypothetical. There can be decisive reasons against performing a non-wrongful act that are categorical. Not all decisive reasons are decisive 'given the aims of the person to whom they apply'. They can be decisive independently of a person's goals.

Even in the musical case above, it is not clear that the demand not to play the note is best understood as hypothetical—a person may have a decisive reason to play a Mozart sonata, and not to play the wrong notes, regardless of whether she is motivated to do so. This claim is consistent with the idea that the rational requirement is not moral.

Nevertheless, moral wrongness has a special status and force. An act may be wrong in some non-moral sense, but if it is morally wrong not to perform that act, there is a decisive reason to perform it, as we will see more clearly in Chapter 3. If the murderer at the door asks the whereabouts of the person he wants to kill, I am morally required to give the wrong answer. If I do, I have a decisive reason to give him that answer. In this sense, moral wrongness dominates other kinds of wrongness in practical deliberation.

IV. Response-Dependent Accounts of Wrongdoing

If it is morally wrong for me to *v*, I have a decisive reason not to *v*. But I can have a decisive reason not to *v* without it being morally wrong to *v*. Let us call such acts 'merely irrational acts'. Good accounts of moral wrongness explain the contrast between acts that are morally wrong and merely irrational acts. We can call the problem they are trying to solve the parsing problem.

One tempting solution to the parsing problem, which has a long pedigree, focuses on the appropriate responses to the relevant acts. Such views are response-dependent views about wrongness.[4] They solve the problem as follows. Consider those actions that there is a decisive moral reason not to perform. When a person performs some of these actions, but not others, certain responses are apt. Actions are morally wrong because such responses are apt. They are merely irrational when such responses are not apt.

For example, murder is morally wrong, on this view, because it is apt to respond to those who have murdered in certain ways. It is not apt to respond to those who have played the wrong notes in a Mozart sonata in these ways, and because of that playing these notes is not morally wrong.

The 'because' aspect of response-dependent views needs emphasizing. Suppose that there are distinct responses that it is apt to make to wrongdoing. Wrongdoing is a necessary and sufficient condition for the aptness of certain responses. A response-dependent view of wrongdoing does not follow. Certain responses may be uniquely apt for wrongdoing because of unique characteristics of wrongdoing, and not the other way around. Response-dependent views are distinctive in claiming that wrongness is explained by the appropriate responses, and not the other way around.

This is not always noticed. For example, Alan Gibbard claims that an act is wrong 'if and only if it violates standards for ruling out actions, such that if an agent in a normal frame of mind violated those standards because he was not substantially motivated to conform to them, he would be to blame'.[5] Gibbard intends a response-dependent account of wrongdoing, but his formulation does not capture this. The order of explanation might go either way to make Gibbard's formulation true.[6] Response-dependent accounts of wrongdoing, then, are distinctive in their aim to explain the contrast between wrongdoing and merely irrational action by showing that certain responses explain what is distinct about moral wrongdoing.

There are many response-dependent views. Here are two dimensions of such views. First, they differ about the person whose reactions are treated as central. Are the responses of the wrongdoer herself paramount, or the responses of the victim of the wrongdoing, or the responses of all rational agents? For example, Stephen Darwall emphasizes the importance of accountability, which he understands as a second-personal idea. Thus, he defends an interpersonal response-dependent account of

[4] See, for example, J S Mill 'Utilitarianism' in J Gray (ed), *On Liberty and Other Essays* (Oxford: OUP, 1991) 184; S Darwall *The Second-Person Standpoint: Morality, Respect and Accountability* (Cambridge, Mass: Harvard UP, 2006) ch 5 and M Bedke 'Passing the Deontic Buck' in R Schafer-Landau *Oxford Studies in Metaethics* vol 6 (Oxford: OUP, 2011). See, also, Hieronymi 'On Metaethics and Motivation', 116–8.

[5] *Wise Choices, Apt Feelings: A Theory of Normative Judgement* (Oxford: OUP, 1990) 45.

[6] See, more generally, K Fine 'Ontological Dependence' (1995) 95 *Proceedings of the Aristotelian Society* 269.

wrongdoing. As he puts it: 'It is part of the very idea of a moral demand that we are accountable for complying.'[7]

In contrast, a first-personal view prioritizes the responses of the wrongdoer herself. For example, some might claim that acts are wrong because it is apt for people to feel guilty about them. As should now be clear, first-personal views are consistent with the idea there are distinct interpersonal practices that apply to wrongdoing, but they don't explain wrongdoing by referring to these practices.

Second, different views prioritize different reactions to wrongdoing. Different views prioritize the emotions, such as guilt, resentment, or indignation; or accountability practices, such as blaming or demanding; or practical responses, such as the duty to repair or the right to impose sanctions.

The appropriateness of a reaction does not imply that the relevant person ought to have that reaction all things considered. There may be strong reasons to have an inappropriate reaction, and strong reasons against having an appropriate reaction. For example, I ought to blame a person for her non-wrongful actions if blaming her will save many lives. But blaming her is nevertheless inappropriate. Similarly, I ought not to blame a wrongdoer for her wrongful actions if doing so would cost many lives. But blaming her is nevertheless appropriate. A great deal of ink has been spilled attempting to clarify what the 'right kinds of reasons' are that make attitudes, beliefs, and so on apt. I will not add to the ink-spill here.

V. Tracking Challenges

One objection to response-dependent views is that there is no distinctive response that is warranted to all wrongful conduct, and only to wrongful conduct: all candidate reactions, it might be argued, fail accurately to track wrongdoing in particular. All plausible candidate responses are appropriate even when a person has not acted wrongly. And all plausible candidate responses are not appropriate for some instances of wrongdoing.

This challenge is difficult to assess. One reason is that it is difficult to characterize the responses without referring to wrongdoing. It is hard to see how a response-dependent view of wrongdoing can be true if the distinctive character of the response relies on a grasp of the thing it is supposed to explain. I leave this objection aside, though I suspect it has some force, because a wide range of responses might be considered, and it would be difficult to show that none is independent of wrongdoing. Subject to that concern, I think that this challenge can be met.

In outlining challenges to such views it helps to have in mind a particular view. I pick a view where the relevant response is blame, and it is apt for third parties, as well as victims, to do the blaming. Consider:

> *Blame (first draft)*: It is wrong for D to *v* because it is apt for other people to blame D for *v*ing.

As the nature of blame is disputed, this view is vague, but it is sufficiently precise to help us understand different arguments for and against response-dependent views.[8]

[7] See *The Second-Person Standpoint*, 99. Darwall is not always clear in distinguishing the idea of interpersonal demands from interpersonal practices of accountability. Sometimes he seems to endorse a view that I examine in the next chapter: the *interpersonal demand view*.

[8] To see some of the variety, see the essays in D J Coates and N A Tognazzini *Blame: Its Nature and Norms* (Oxford: OUP, 2013).

Here are three tracking challenges to *Blame* that I discuss in turn. First, we blame people not, or not only, for their actions, but for their attitudes. Second, not all wrongdoing is blameworthy: that which is excused is not.[9] Third, blame is sometimes appropriate between people with shared commitments, and in some such cases, as the norm violated is local to their relationship, the conduct is not wrong.

i) The target of blame

We do blame people for certain attitudes: racist attitudes or self-important attitudes, for example. Blame can be appropriate, in such cases, without the person acting on their attitudes.[10] If their actions reveal their attitudes, they are blamed directly for those attitudes. For example, a person who inadvertently reveals racist attitudes in conversation is blamed for his attitudes, not for the conversation that reveals them. Furthermore, people are blamed for doing the right thing for the wrong reason because of the attitude they display. For example, it is wrong for a professor to give his student a high mark for an essay because he finds her attractive, even if the mark is warranted for other reasons.

Here is a response: just as it is wrong to perform certain actions, it is wrong to have certain attitudes. Similarly, where a person does the right thing for the wrong reason she wrongly acts for the wrong reason. For example, even if the professor gives the right mark, he wrongly assigns her mark because she is attractive. So *Blame* can be revised as follows:

> *Blame (Second Draft)*: D's acts, motivations, or attitudes are wrong because it is apt to blame D for those acts, motivations, or attitudes.

This revision does not seem satisfactory in some cases where it has been argued that the person does the right thing for the wrong reason. In some such cases, blame is directed at the action, not the attitude. If some such acts are permissible, *Blame* fails. T M Scanlon argues for a view of this kind. He suggests that if a permissible action is performed for a bad reason, we blame the person for her action and not her attitude, because the attitude alters the meaning of the action.[11]

To illustrate, consider:

> *Bad Trolley*: A trolley is heading towards five people who it will kill if nothing is done. Duncan, a bystander, can divert the trolley towards Vera. Duncan does this, but only in order to kill Vera, whom Duncan hates, and not to save the five.

Scanlon believes that if it would be permissible to turn the trolley with a good intention it is permissible to turn it with a bad intention.[12] But, he argues, the action is blameworthy because Duncan's bad intention affects its meaning. This view improves

[9] For this challenge to Darwall's response-dependent account of wrongdoing, see M Smith and J T Strabbing 'Moral Obligation, Accountability, and Second-Personal Reasons' (2010) 81 *Philosophy and Phenomenological Research* 237, 240–2.

[10] See P Graham 'A Sketch of a Theory of Moral Blameworthiness' (2014) 88 *Philosophy and Phenomenological Research* 388.

[11] *Moral Dimensions: Permissibility, Meaning, Blame* (Cambridge, Mass: Harvard UP, 2008) ch 4.

[12] For doubts see, for example, J McMahan 'Intention, Permissibility, Terrorism, and War' (2009) 23 *Philosophical Perspectives* 345; V Tadros *The Ends of Harm: The Moral Foundations of Criminal Law* (Oxford: OUP, 2011) ch 7; R Wedgwood 'Defending Double Effect' (2011) 24 *Ratio* 384. I support the relevance of intentions to permissibility further in Chapter 16.

on the starker view that Duncan is *only* criticized for being a bad person, or for being at fault for acting for bad reasons,[13] or for his attitudes.[14] Scanlon rightly argues that views that do not refer to the action performed seem incomplete: our criticisms focus on the killing, and not only on the attitude behind it.[15] Scanlon does not conclude that he acts wrongly, but that he is blameworthy for his permissible action because of the meaning of the act.

It is not clear what changes in meaning make acts blameworthy in Scanlon's view. In standard cases where a person does the right thing for the wrong reason, the meaning of an act is changed, but it is not blameworthy. Consider:

> *Bad Rescue*: Mitt saves Petra from drowning, but only because he wishes to persuade her to change her will so that he will inherit from her.

Mitt may be criticized for his attitudes and the reasons for which he acts, and the meaning of his act is altered: it is not benevolent, but selfish. But Mitt is not blameworthy for saving Petra. This contrasts with *Bad Trolley* where the appropriate target of blame is the act itself.

Perhaps it might be argued that *Bad Trolley* and *Bad Rescue* are different, because Vera is harmed whereas Petra is benefited. But it is not clear why this matters given that Vera would also have been harmed if Duncan had acted with good attitudes. The better view is that Duncan's intentions make his act in *Bad Trolley* wrong, whereas that is not true of Mitt's act in *Bad Rescue*, in which case *Blame (Second Draft)* survives.

Suppose that Scanlon is right that Duncan is blameworthy for permissibly harming Vera in *Bad Trolley*, as many people believe. That still does not show that *Blame* is wrong. Even if it was permissible for Duncan to turn the trolley, it was wrong for Duncan to be guided by Vera's death. This might explain why blame is warranted for the death. Even if Duncan can be blamed for a permissible act, this is derived from the fact that Duncan was wrongly guided in performing it.

Those sympathetic to *Blame*, but who are persuaded by Scanlon's analysis of *Bad Trolley*, can further revise the view by referring to permissible acts that are performed for the wrong motivations. As I think that the relevant acts are wrong, I find this revision unnecessary.

ii) Responsibility, excuse, and blame

The second challenge concerns the fact that wrongness is insufficient for blameworthiness because wrongdoing can be excused. This view relies on the familiar contrast between justifications and excuses. If a person is fully justified for a *pro tanto* wrongful act, she acts permissibly. If she is fully excused, though, she is not blameworthy for her all things considered wrongful act. For example, an involuntarily intoxicated person who insults a friend may not be blameworthy, but she still wrongly insults the friend.

The *Blame View* meets this challenge by adding further conditions to the aptness of blame, the most important of which concern responsibility for wrongdoing. People

[13] See J J Thomson 'Self-Defense' (1991) 20 *Philosophy and Public Affairs* 283, 294–5.

[14] See P Graham 'A Sketch of a Theory of Moral Blameworthiness'.

[15] Thomson also notes that a person who acts on a bad intention in cases of this kind might act badly, but nevertheless permissibly. See 'Physician-Assisted Suicide: Two Arguments' (1999) 109 *Ethics* 497, 517.

are aptly blamed for wrongdoing, but only on condition that they are responsible for it. People may be blamed for wrongly insulting others, for example, but only on condition that they are responsible for their insults, and this explains why blaming the involuntarily intoxicated person is not apt.

This response is not ad hoc. The distinction between the apt target of certain responses and enabling and disabling conditions is significant across contexts. For example, jokes are the apt target of laughter—we laugh at jokes. But the aptness of laughing at a joke can be disabled, for example, if it is told at a funeral. Similarly, blame might be an appropriate response to wrongdoing only if it is enabled by responsibility, and not disabled by excuses.

Hence *Blame* can be further revised:

> *Blame (Third Draft)*: D's acts, motivations, or attitudes are wrong because it is apt to blame D for those actions, motivations, or attitudes, on condition that D is responsible for those acts, motivations, or attitudes, and is not excused for them.

Furthermore, we can provide an attractive rationale for this revision. We blame *a person* for her wrongdoing. To do this, an act must have been performed which provides the appropriate target for blame, but that act must also be properly attributable to the person who is blamed. A person with a complete excuse for her wrongful conduct has performed an act that is the appropriate target of blame, but blaming her is inappropriate because the act is not properly attributable to her.

iii) Blame and commitment

Blame sometimes seems appropriate for non-wrongful conduct in contexts where certain commitments and activities are shared. Here are three examples. A manager of a football team might blame a player for the loss of a game if he fails to score, but it is not morally wrong to fail to score. A musician might appropriately blame a member of his band for a bad performance, even if it is not morally wrong to perform badly. One friend may blame another for a breakdown of their friendship, but this need not imply that it is morally wrong to let it break down.

Some might argue that all of these cases are cases of moral wrongdoing. The football player owes it to his teammates to score. The band member owes it to the other members to play well. Friends owe it to each other not to allow their friendship to break down. Hence, these acts are all wrong. Blame, it might be argued, is inappropriate in these cases because those outside the relevant activity lack standing to blame these people for their wrongdoing.

Although these people do owe these things to others, though, I doubt that these are necessarily cases of moral wrongdoing. The conduct is not wrong, roughly speaking, because the norm violated is local: it governs only the shared activity or commitments, and is not one that those outside that activity or commitment have reason to care about. In contrast with standard cases where a person lacks standing to blame, those who are outside the activity have no reason to blame the person, even as a private matter.

If this is right, defenders of a response-dependent account of wrongdoing might revise their view further:

> *Blame*: D's acts, motivations, or attitudes are wrong because it is apt for anyone with standing to blame D for those actions, motivations, or attitudes, on condition that D is responsible for those acts, motivations, or attitudes, and is not excused for them.

Although I will ultimately reject *Blame*, it is important to recognize that it is not vulnerable to tracking challenges. By responding to these challenges, we see that there are distinctive responses that it is appropriate to make to wrongdoing, subject to certain conditions. That helps us to understand the character and scope of interpersonal norms and practices of accountability.

VI. The Order of Explanation

The fact that *Blame* is not vulnerable to tracking challenges does not show that it is true. It shows only that it is a necessary and sufficient condition of the wrongness of an act, motivation, or attitude that (under certain conditions) it is apt to blame a person for it. This idea is neutral between two views: the view that the aptness of these responses explains wrongness and the view that wrongness explains the aptness of these responses. I argue that response-dependent views have the order of explanation wrong. We grasp wrongness independently of the responses we owe to it, and this independent idea of wrongness explains why certain responses to it are apt.

i) The felicity conditions of blame

We blame people for things—primarily wrongful actions. Let us focus on them to simplify our discussion. As blaming has propositional content, the aptness of blaming depends on whether the propositions that partly constitute blame are true. If I blame a person for her actions, I imply that she has acted wrongly and that explains why blame is not (or at least not normally) apt for permissible acts. Other personal and interpersonal reactions to wrongdoing, such as guilt and resentment, are similar.

This fact might be thought decisively to count against any response-dependent account of wrongness. As David Brink puts it in criticizing John Stuart Mill's response-dependent account of wrongness, Mill's view that acts are wrong in virtue of being blameworthy makes the wrongness of an act depend upon the appropriateness of sanctioning it. But this inverts what many would regard as the usual dependency between wrongness and sanction. Many think that sanctions are appropriate for wrong acts because they are wrong. This requires grounding their wrongness in some independent account; it is not the suitability for sanction that makes an act wrong. Perhaps one ought to sanction wrong acts, but it doesn't seem that they are wrong because one ought to sanction them.[16]

Even if responses such as guilt, blame, and resentment do not involve sanctions, this criticism seems to have force. I find it ultimately decisive. But Brink does not show that it is. Consider this very general argument against response-dependent values of any kind:

1) It is apt to respond to some fact, *f*, with some response, *r*, because of some property of *f*, *p*.
2) If so, *p* explains the aptness of *r* to *f*.
3) If *p* explains the aptness of *r* to *f*, the aptness of *r* to *f* cannot explain *p*.
4) Therefore, the aptness of *r* to *p* cannot explain *p*.

[16] *Mill's Progressive Principles* (Oxford: OUP, 2013) 107.

This general argument fails.

To see this, fill out the argument for funniness:

1) It is apt to respond to some fact, *f*, by laughing at it only if *f* has certain properties that make it funny.
2) If so, the properties of *f* that make it funny explains the aptness of laughing at *f*.
3) If the properties that make *f* funny explain the aptness of laughing at *f*, the aptness of laughing at *f* cannot explain funniness.
4) Therefore, the aptness of laughing at *f* cannot explain funniness.

Both 1) and 2) seem true. But 3) is false. It seems very hard to explain funniness without referring to the aptness of laughter.

Admittedly, there are felicity conditions for funniness that makes laughing at certain things apt. Things are not funny simply because some people tend to find them funny. Some people find things funny that are not funny. Furthermore, a community could realize that something was funny when previously they had failed to find it funny and vice versa. So things are not funny simply because of the responses we tend to have to them. But this does not show that the aptness of laughter is irrelevant to explaining funniness. We can see this from the fact that people who lack all of the responses that it is apt to make to funniness cannot understand funniness at all.[17]

Defenders of *Blame* might claim a similar thing about the relationship between wrongness and blame. Even though there are independent felicity conditions for blame—we appropriately blame people only for acts which have certain properties and not others—the appropriateness of certain responses, such as blame, is essential to a complete account of wrongness.

ii) Aptness and the parsing problem

Although the fact that there are felicity conditions for blaming does not show that response-dependent views are false, it does undermine one argument that has been given for them.

It has been argued that response-dependent views should be favoured because they uniquely solve the parsing problem: they distinguish wrongdoing from merely irrational acts. Consider Stephen Darwall's argument. A person might have a decisive reason to perform a supererogatory act; but by definition, it is not wrong to do so. Some argue that morality would be too demanding were it to require us to perform supererogatory acts. To make sense of this, Darwall claims, we necessarily rely on the idea that people can hold each other to account only for some of the acts that reason requires of them. Hence, wrongdoing is a response-dependent ideal.[18]

But if the aptness of responses to morally wrongful acts depends on certain felicity conditions being fulfilled we need an independent account of these felicity conditions to solve the parsing problem. It is true that blame, for example, is apt only for wrongful acts and not for supererogatory acts, even if there is a decisive reason to perform such acts. But we cannot determine which acts are wrongful amongst the acts that there is a decisive reason not to perform simply by focusing on this fact. For blaming is apt only if certain felicity conditions are fulfilled, and we need an account of what these conditions are.

[17] See, further, C Wright *Truth and Objectivity* (Cambridge, Mass: Harvard UP, 1992) 100–7.

[18] *The Second-Person Standpoint*, 96–7.

But once we recognize this, we see that response-dependence is not uniquely placed to solve the parsing problem. Any view of wrongness relies on distinctions between facts that make acts wrong and facts that do not. These facts determine whether blame is apt on any view. Response-dependent views aim to guide judgements about these distinctions by focusing on the responses that it is apt to make to them. But they are not uniquely placed to perform this task. Any theory of wrongness, response-dependent or otherwise, first-personal or interpersonal, relies on independent judgements about the moral salience of certain facts.

So Darwall is wrong to think that substantive claims, such as the claim that there are supererogatory acts that we have a decisive reason to perform, assume response-dependence. They assume that there is some theory of wrongness that provides a principled explanation of the distinction between facts that support decisive reasons and facts that support moral requirements, without assuming any particular theory.

iii) Judging wrongness

How, then, do we determine whether some normative idea, such as wrongness, is response-dependent? We do so by reflecting on our experience of determining whether that normative idea is satisfied.

Recall funniness. The response we make to something being funny is plausibly involved in our reflections about whether and why something is funny. Suppose that I am told a joke. It doesn't make me laugh, but I am assured that this is because of my bad sense of humour, and not because it is unfunny. Reflecting on the kind of laughter that is appropriate in response to good jokes does seem to guide me in determining whether the joke is funny, and hence whether my failure to laugh at it is a result of me having a bad sense of humour, or rather because the joke is unfunny. This supports the response-dependent view of funniness.

This, though, seems less plausible in the case of wrongness. Suppose that I am unsure whether it would be wrong to perform some action that I am inclined to perform. In determining whether this action is wrong, I do not focus on responses that would be made to it. Whether those responses are apt depends on my conclusions about the wrongness of the conduct. Rather, we focus on whether we are free to do it. If I am free to act in a certain way, I will feel indignant at being blamed for it, even if I had a decisive reason not to act thus. If I was not free to do it, I will conclude that blaming me for it is apt. Of course, this idea, that we distinguish wrongdoing from merely irrational acts by focusing on freedom, needs explication. I claim only that this account has greater fidelity to our experience of deciding whether our acts are wrong.

For example, suppose that I can save a person's life, but only at great cost to myself. In determining whether it would be wrong for me to refrain from saving the person, I do not primarily focus on whether others would be warranted in blaming me for failing to save the person, or whether I would appropriately feel guilty were I not to do so. I focus primarily on whether the harm that the other person will suffer is sufficiently important to compel me to save them, given the harm I will suffer if I do. I have not explained the idea that wrongdoing is compelling in a way that rationality is not; I only rely on our experience that this is so.

It is true that if I do something that I am unfree in the relevant sense to do I will feel guilty. I will also see it as appropriate for others to blame me. A proper understanding of guilt and blame depend on the idea that a person has done or refrained from doing what they were not free to do or refrain from doing. But the primary question that

I ask myself in determining whether it would be wrong for me to act in a certain way is a question about my freedom.

Here is another way to support the same conclusion. We are especially motivated not to act wrongly. But in standard cases, the source of that desire is not to avoid the responses that will be made to wrongdoing. The source of my motivation not to act wrongly is not the avoidance of guilt or blame, at least in standard cases.[19] A person who is motivated in this way seems to require a prop for complying with her moral demands that she should not require, ideally at least.

And these responses do not seem sufficient to motivate compliance with morality in standard cases. Suppose, for example, that I can save myself from a lethal threat only by killing you. It is very costly to me to refrain from killing you. Now suppose that what we mean when we say that this is wrong is that it would be apt for other people to blame me for killing you. It would be difficult to see why I would avoid killing you in that case. I can see that it would be bad for me that others blame me, and even worse that it is apt for them to do so. But it is difficult to see how these facts could be sufficient to motivate compliance with moral demands—better to be blameworthy than dead, I might think.

Finally, where some normative idea is response-dependent, that idea has no role in case the response fails. Suppose that it was never apt to laugh at jokes. Funniness would then have no action-guiding role. We normally have no reason to tell a joke that does not make laughter apt. This helps to support a response-dependent account of funniness.

Now compare wrongdoing. Suppose that free-will sceptics are right that standard responses to wrongdoing, such as guilt, blame, resentment, and indignation, are never apt.[20] This view does not deprive wrongdoing of any role. Such sceptics could still think it important to distinguish between acts that are wrong and acts that are merely irrational. Such a person could think it permissible to order an ice cream that she has decisive reason not to eat, whilst thinking it wrong to tell a lie, because she is free to do the former but not to do the latter. Making this judgement seems important independently of judgements about the warranted responses to such conduct.

Overall, then, response-dependent accounts of wrongdoing fail to capture the role that deliberations and judgements about moral wrongdoing play in our lives. Blame is typically apt for moral wrongdoing, and only for moral wrongdoing, at least under certain conditions. I doubt that this explains what wrongdoing is.

VII. Conclusion

Response-dependent accounts of wrongness are not incoherent. Furthermore, defenders of response-dependent accounts can respond adequately to a range of tracking problems. The main doubt that I have offered against these views is that they fail to account for our experience of judging whether an act is wrong, and our motivation to act on that judgement. When we consider whether it would be wrong to act in a certain way, the responses that others will be warranted in making to our conduct typically does not figure in our deliberations. This is in contrast with, for example, an

[19] This kind of concern is also expressed in D Owens *Shaping the Normative Landscape* (Oxford: OUP, 2012) 72–3.

[20] See, for an excellent defence of this view, D Pereboom *Free Will, Agency, and Meaning in Life* (Oxford: OUP, 2014). I discuss this view in Chapter 5.

investigation into whether a joke is funny, where the warranted responses do play a central role in such deliberations.

We have good reason to look for an independent theory of wrongness; one that explains the experience that we have that we are free to act in a way that is merely irrational, but not when our acts are wrong. Freedom seems to play a more fundamental role in deciding whether our acts are wrong. But freedom is also a vague idea, and it needs explaining.

3

Wrongdoing and Respecting Value

Morally wrongful conduct is a subclass of conduct that conflicts with our decisive reasons. The parsing problem is how to explain this subclass. We should not hope to explain wrongness by completely reducing it to other ideas. Rather, I am to explain the importance of wrongness in practical reasoning and practices of responsibility.

The previous chapter rejected response-dependent views by showing that they do not best explain the experience of deciding whether an act is wrong. This suggests that wrongness is action-guiding. Such a view can be first-personal or interpersonal. Interpersonal views claim that what is distinctive about moral wrongness is their source in our relations with others. The idea is not that certain decisive reasons for action arise because others are valuable—all views accept this. The idea is rather that the distinction between wrongful and merely irrational acts is itself explained interpersonally.

In contrast to such views, I defend a particular first-personal view: the *Respecting Value* view. This view aims to explain the idea that we are free to act irrationally but not wrongly. It grounds this idea in the way in which certain values undermine the value of autonomy. Respect for these values makes it inappropriate for us to value the free performance of these acts. This explains why we are constrained not to perform these acts. And that explains why they are morally wrong.

This view, I will show, is superior to rival views in explaining the scope, unity, and motivational force of wrongdoing. It also helps to explain why distinctive responses to wrongdoing are, in general, appropriate, whilst accommodating the fact that different kinds of wrong demand different responses.

Section I develops an idea that we began to explore at the end of the previous chapter: that understanding wrongness involves understanding the role that it has in making decisions and practical reasoning. It also defends the idea that it is conceptually true that we have a decisive reason not to act morally wrongly. Section II explores interpersonal views, focusing especially on T M Scanlon's contractualist account of moral wrongdoing. Section III shows that we should reject such views. Section IV explores practical reasoning to provide a framework for thinking about the role of moral wrongdoing in decision-making. Section V outlines and defends the *Respecting Value* view.

I. Wrongdoing, Motivation, and Conflicts

A good account of moral wrongdoing explains the special motivation that we have not to act wrongly. We are motivated not to act in conflict with our decisive reasons. But we are especially motivated not to act wrongly. We see this from the fact that a person who properly understands that some act is morally wrong understands that she is not free to perform it. Our question is what this means and why it is important.

i) Constraining valued outcomes

Suppose that a person recognizes that it is wrong to perform some act. If she is well-motivated, she is motivated not to do it. How is this motivation best understood?

The motivation is not a mere impulse like repulsion. A moral person may be repelled from acting wrongly, but this is not the crucial distinguishing marker of moral motivation. A moral person who judges her act to be wrong understands the normative force of the moral wrongness of the action. But the normative force of moral wrongness is not simply the moral force of having a decisive reason; it is normatively compelling in a way that mere decisive reasons are not.

The reasons that make acts wrong need not always motivate. Even those who are morally good might refrain from acting wrongly because the act repels them, or because they are threatened with punishment, or simply out of habituation. But the normative force of moral wrongdoing is sufficient to guide morally well-motivated people.

The normative force of morality explains our reaction to acting morally wrongly, when we recognize that we have. We reflect on the decision to act wrongly. We now feel the normative force of the facts that make the act wrong: something that we either failed to recognize or that failed to move us. We desire to turn the clock back and act differently in the light of this normative force, but, of course, we cannot do so. The resulting frustration helps to explain guilt.[1] It also helps to explain the frustration we feel with wrongdoers. When we reflect on another person's wrongdoing, we see things from their perspective. We feel the motivational force of the facts that did not move the person. We then feel compelled to get the other person to recognize the force of these facts.

Morality, though, is not distinguished simply by the strength of our motivations. Failure to finish an important project, for example, can also be met with frustration, even if such failure is not wrong. Regret rather than guilt is the resulting feeling. And we can feel this pressure interpersonally as well—we feel frustrated at imprudent acts of others, especially if the imprudent person is seriously harmed as a result. At the end of a life, the failure to achieve one's most important goals, and one's gravely imprudent acts, can provide a much greater source of regret than less serious instances of moral wrongdoing, even if the person judges well. The special motivational force of moral wrongdoing, this suggests, is a difference in quality, not quantity.

I have already suggested a first pass as the distinct motivational quality of morality: that it constrains. It is tempting to see this constraint as law-like—morality commands just like the law does. But this gets things back to front. Legal commands are intended to be moral demands. We understand them only because we understand moral demands. So the analogy with law does not help to explain moral wrongdoing.[2]

One dimension of understanding morality as a constraint involves understanding what it constrains. One idea is that morality holds us back from doing what we want. If a person concludes that it is wrong to act in a certain way, and she is morally motivated, she feels constrained from doing what she wants (if, of course, she wants to do what it is wrong for her to do).

In the light of this, it may seem that morality does not constrain the virtuous. Here is why this might seem true. Certain facts make *v*ing wrong. But these facts also make *v*ing undesirable. Were I ethical, I would not desire to *v*. So wrongness does not constrain the virtuous. For example, your suffering can make it wrong for me to hit you.

[1] See, further, V Tadros *The Ends of Harm: The Moral Foundations of Criminal Law* (Oxford: OUP, 2011) 47–8.

[2] Oh no! I said something about general jurisprudence! If you have fallen asleep, please wake up now.

But it also makes hitting you undesirable. So the wrongness of me hitting you is not constraining.

But morality does feel constraining, even to the virtuous. An example will help to explain why:

> *Sinking Ship*: A ship is sinking. There is not enough room in the lifeboats for every child. The Captain has responsibility for allocating places on the lifeboats, and uses what appears to be a fair lottery system to do so. His child is on the ship, and is included in the lottery. He could rig the lottery in his child's favour, but he does not do this. His child's name is drawn and she is saved. Later, he finds out that the First Officer interfered with the lottery to ensure that the Captain's child was saved. Had he not done this, the child would have died.

Suppose that it would have been wrong for the Captain to rig the lottery to save his child. This seems true. Although we have a duty to save our children rather than the children of others, in this case the Captain must respect the equal claim that each child has to a place on the lifeboat. Conducting a fair lottery does this.

This does not imply that the Captain fails in being glad that his child was saved. Furthermore, had the First Officer not interfered, he would have good reason for regret; he may even reasonably regret that the First Officer did not act wrongly. He may also reasonably regret being required to perform an action that results in his child's death. He would not have reason to regret performing the action—that implies that he wishes that he would have acted differently, and that is inconsistent with properly respecting the demands of morality. But he may regret both the fact that he is required to perform the action, and the outcome of performing it.

Even though the Captain values the outcome, it is nevertheless appropriate for him to criticize the First Officer for acting wrongly, even if he is glad that he did so. If he does so, his attitudes are not inconsistent. He can rightly claim that he would not have acted in the same way, as demonstrated by the fact that he did not rig the lottery, and he can criticize the First Officer as a result. This does not conflict with his being glad that the action was performed.

This is one very general challenge to consequentialism: the idea that moral requirements are to be explained by the value of the consequences of complying with them. Our attitudes about wrongdoing and our attitudes about its consequences come apart. A person who is constrained by morality is not committed to preferring the outcome where wrongdoing does not occur.

This conflict between action and outcome also helps to explain the psychological conflict that morality seems to give rise to. The Captain's commitment to his child compels him to prefer the outcome where his child is saved, impelling him to save his child. But whilst this psychological pull is powerful he is constrained from acting on it. He recognizes this by conducting the lottery fairly.

This makes vivid the sense in which morality constrains the virtuous: it constrains them from achieving outcomes they have reason to value. Even though the Captain is psychologically conflicted, there is no practical conflict between the demands that arise from his relationship with his child and the demands of morality. The demands of morality constrain him not to govern his actions by his commitment to his child. The demands of morality thus deprive his preferred outcome from having reason-giving force.[3]

[3] There is some relationship between the idea outlined here and both Frances Kamm's idea of an 'irrelevant utility' in *Morality, Mortality vol. 1: Death and Whom to Save From It* (Oxford: OUP, 1993) ch 8, and Joseph Raz's account of exclusionary reasons in *Practical Reasons and Norms* (Oxford: OUP, 1999). Exactly what relationship depends on the answers' difficult interpretative and moral questions that I leave aside.

ii) Does reason conflict with morality?

I claimed that there is no normative conflict, only a psychological conflict, in *Sinking Ship*. What I mean is that the conclusion that it is wrong for the Captain to rig the lottery resolves any conflict of normative reasons about whether to rig the lottery. There is no further judgement to be made about what the Captain has a decisive reason to do.

There are two ways of understanding this view. One possibility is:

> *The Overriding View*: Reasons supplied by morality are always decisive reasons all things considered, and thus override any reasons that are in conflict with morality.

This view implies that morality supplies a reason for action that is in conflict with other reasons that the person may have, but that morality always defeats these other reasons.

Here is a contrasting view:

> *The Conclusion View*: The fact that it is all things considered wrong for a person to act in a certain way concludes any conflicts of reason.

On this view, the reasons that favour acting wrongly have already been considered and found wanting in the conclusion that the act is wrong. There is no further conflict to be resolved to determine whether reason requires a person to refrain from acting thus, even one that will be defeated by moral reasons.

Even on this view the person faces a psychological conflict. And the person who refrains from acting wrongly has something to regret: the failure to satisfy the reasons for the wrongful act that were found wanting in the conclusion that the act was wrong. But once the conclusion is correctly reached that the act is wrong, there is no room for further consideration of the reasons for acting wrongly: the conclusion that the act is wrong is drawn because these reasons are defeated by reasons against performing the action.

The Conclusion View seems the better view. Suppose that the Captain knows that he is required to conduct the lottery fairly. There seems no room for a further judgement, even one that we know will be resolved in favour of morality, about whether to conform to the requirement.

One reason why this seems right is that it seems necessary to provide a plausible explanation of what the Captain does in *Sinking Ship*. Those who favour the *Overriding View* might argue as follows: the Captain gives some weight to his all things considered duty to provide everyone with a fair opportunity to be saved. He also gives some weight to the value to him that his child in particular is saved. The fact that he does not rig the lottery implies that he gives morality greater weight than saving his child. But this does not seem psychologically plausible. The idea that morality is more important to a person than her children seems hard to believe, at least for most parents.

Furthermore, the idea of practical dilemmas between moral wrongdoing and other values is hard to understand. Clearly there are conflicts between *pro tanto* wrongdoing and other reasons—*pro tanto* moral demands can be defeated. But once we see this, it is difficult to see how there could be a further role for conflicts between all things considered moral demands and other reasons.

Everyone recognizes that it is sometimes permissible to violate *pro tanto* duties. This is familiar where we have conflicting duties: if the only way for me to fulfil a promise to take my kids to the zoo involves running a pedestrian over, I should violate the duty to fulfil the promise.

Pro tanto duties can also be overridden by other considerations. Consider Frances Kamm's case:

> *Kidney*: Elizabeth has promised to meet Joan for lunch. On the way, she comes across a car-crash. As a result, Carlo needs a kidney transplant, and Elizabeth is the only person who can donate one. If she gives Carlo the kidney, she will miss lunch.[4]

Suppose that Elizabeth does not have a *pro tanto* duty to give Carlo the kidney. There is then a conflict between Elizabeth's duty to go to lunch and her reason to give Carlo the kidney. But it is permissible all things considered for Elizabeth to give Carlo the kidney.

Susan Wolf doubts this, suggesting that it is wrong for Elizabeth to breach her promise, even though she has a decisive reason to do this. We need not draw the further conclusion that it is permissible for her to breach the promise, she suggests.[5] But it is hard to believe that Elizabeth acts wrongly all things considered. We naturally contrast her *pro tanto* duty and her all things considered duty in this case.

Morality already makes room for conflicts between *pro tanto* duties and non-moral reasons for action, then. Given this, what role does the idea of an all things considered duty have in practical reasoning? The *Conclusion View* is that determining whether a person has an all things considered duty involves whether a person ought, all things considered, to comply with her *pro tanto* duties. The conclusion that it is all things considered wrong for X to *v* is warranted when other considerations do not defeat the practical force of our *pro tanto* duties. Without this, it is difficult to understand the familiar contrast between *pro tanto* duties and all things considered duties that shapes our practical reasoning.

Even though she understands this view, Wolf nevertheless thinks that we can have a decisive reason to act wrongly all things considered. She draws this conclusion by reflecting on cases such as:

> *Heroine*: Bell, an academic, has office hours on a Tuesday. She finds out that Courtney, her philosophical heroine is on a rare visit nearby. If she goes to attend Courtney's lecture, she will fail to attend her office hours, and her students will not have that opportunity to discuss their grades.

Bell has a *pro tanto* duty to attend her office hours. She is not required to attend Courtney's lecture. The *Conclusion View* implies that if she has an all things considered duty to attend her office hours, she has a decisive reason to do so. If she does not have such a duty, she may lack a decisive reason to do so. Wolf, in contrast, thinks that she may have an all things considered duty to attend her office hours and lack a decisive reason to do so.

In response, first note that our judgement about whether Bell has a decisive reason to attend her office hours or to go to the lecture is not clear. That judgement depends on the importance of the office hours for the students and on the importance of the lecture for her. In this respect, *Heroine* is not an ideal case to establish the existence, or not, of practical conflicts between morality and other values—we are not even clear about how to resolve her conflict of reasons.

Furthermore, it is not clear that Bell has an all things considered duty to attend her office hours. Wolf is inclined to think that she has, I think, because the value of

[4] *Morality, Mortality II: Rights, Duties, and Status* (Oxford: OUP, 1996) 313–4.

[5] See 'Above and Below the Line of Duty' in *The Variety of Values: Essays on Morality, Meaning, and Love* (Oxford: OUP, 2015).

attending the lecture and dinner is primarily self-regarding. This distinguishes *Heroine* from *Kidney*. I think that Wolf believes that even those who think that *pro tanto* duties can be overridden by other-regarding goals, as in *Kidney*, will believe that they cannot be overridden by self-regarding goals.[6]

But self-regarding goals can sometimes override *pro tanto* duties, supporting an all things considered permission to infringe those duties. For example, Bell would lack a decisive reason to attend her office hours if she needed to go to hospital for a broken leg (*Broken Leg*). She nevertheless lacks a duty to go to the hospital—attending her office hours would be unwise, but it would not be wrong. Yet Bell is permitted to go to hospital rather than attending her office hours in that case. The view that we cannot have decisive self-regarding reasons to violate a *pro tanto* duty implausibly implies that her failure to attend her office hours is all things considered wrong.

In *Heroine*, the importance of the lecture and dinner to Bell might be sufficient to render it permissible for her to breach her duty to attend her office hours. If it is, *Heroine* is just like *Kidney* and *Broken Leg*—she is permitted to breach her *pro tanto* duty in all three cases even though she lacks a conflicting duty.

If the lecture is insufficiently important, what further room is there for the idea that Bell could lack a decisive reason to attend her office hours? We can accommodate the idea that the lecture might be sufficiently important to defeat her *pro tanto* duty to attend the office hour—*Broken Leg* suggests that we must accommodate that idea. If it is, she is permitted to attend the lecture. If not, she is not. It is difficult to find a role for the idea that the lecture is sufficiently important for Bell to have a decisive reason to attend it, or even a sufficient reason to attend it, and yet that it is wrong for her to do so.

This suggests that we should favour the *Conclusion View*. That view explains practical conflicts between morality and non-moral reasons: there are conflicts between *pro tanto* duties and such reasons. Non-moral reasons can sometimes be decisive in resolving such conflicts. The *Conclusion View* attractively explains how *pro tanto* duties are converted into all things considered duties—they do so when conflicting reasons are defeated by *pro tanto* duties. The *Overriding View*, in contrast, cannot explain the idea that *pro tanto* duties and all things considered duties have different roles in practical reasoning.

II. Interpersonal Views of Wrongdoing

People have a decisive reason not to act morally wrongly. But people can also have a decisive reason not to perform some permissible acts. The difference between *merely* having a decisive reason not to *v* and it being wrong to *v* has to do with the special motivational qualities of wrongness, I have suggested. Morality constrains the pursuit of the things that we value most, including things that we value most for good reason. This difference is a difference in kind, not in degree—moral wrongness makes an act compelling in a distinctive way. Yet the way that wrongness is compelling is normative rather than psychological: when an act is wrong a person is compelled not to perform it in virtue of the reasons against performing the action.

Although we have learned several things about wrongness, we are still fully to capture the sense of the difference in kind between wrongness and mere decisive reasons.

[6] I draw this conclusion from her discussion in 'Above and Below the Line of Duty', 209.

This section explores interpersonal accounts of this difference. Here is a more succinct account of the problem of wrongness: if X has a decisive reason not to *v*, there is some fact, or set of facts, *f*, that supply this reason. The value of *f* makes any countervailing reasons insufficient to justify X *v*ing. A subclass of such acts is wrong. The problem is to explain this subclass.

One explanation is that acts are wrong because we can demand of each other that they are not performed:

> *Interpersonal Demand*: when *f* makes it morally wrong for X to *v*, it does so because other people legitimately demand of X that he refrains from *v*ing because of *f*.

This is not a response-dependent view. The interpersonal dimension is action-guiding.[7]

A closely related view emphasizes our ability to justify ourselves to each other rather than the demands that we can make on each other:

> *Interpersonal Justification*: when *f* makes it wrong for X to *v*, it does so because X cannot justify *v*ing to others because of *f*. This is because others have a reason to reject X *v*ing (or, perhaps, a principle that permits X *v*ing) because of *f*. X has such a reason if *f* conflicts with things that X has reason to want for his own sake.

These views are similar in that they are action-guiding interpersonal views. They come apart in the source of that guidance: the right to make demands on the one hand and, on the other, the obligation to justify ourselves to others.

As my argument against interpersonal action-guiding views is general, we need not concern ourselves with the best such view, but it helps to have a particular candidate in mind. The most plausible and fully developed view is T M Scanlon's contractualism, which is a version of the second view.[8]

Scanlon suggests the following test for wrongness:

> *Scanlon's Test*: an act is wrong if and only if any principle that permitted it would be one that could reasonably be rejected by people with the motivation of finding principles for the general regulation of behaviour.[9]

Our reason to ensure that we are able to have certain kinds of relationships with all other people provides a powerful motivation to ensure that we regulate our conduct according to principles that can be accepted by those people. This, Scanlon argues, explains why when we consider whether to act in a certain way, we give priority to reasons that they have to object to us acting thus.

Scanlon only intends contractualism to explain a narrow but centrally important part of morality—the part that is concerned with what we owe to each other. One way to understand this is that Scanlon provides an account of what it is to wrong a person all things considered.[10] As Scanlon suggests, acts can be morally wrong in a wider sense even though they do not satisfy *Scanlon's Test*.[11]

[7] Because he does not always distinguish interpersonal and response-dependent views, Stephen Darwall sometimes expresses his view a bit like this. See, for example, *The Second-Person Standpoint: Morality, Respect and Accountability* (Cambridge Mass: Harvard UP, 2006) 92. This may be because he sees demands as essentially tied to the responses that we make if we fail to comply. His view, though, is probably best characterized as a response-dependent interpersonal view.

[8] Defended in *What We Owe to Each Other* (Cambridge, Mass: Harvard UP, 1998).

[9] *What We Owe to Each Other*, 4.

[10] See, also, F M Kamm *Intricate Ethics: Rights, Responsibilities, and Permissible Harm* (Oxford: OUP, 2007) 468.

[11] See *What We Owe to Each Other*, 171–87.

Outlining three attractions of Scanlon's view will help to clarify it.[12] First, most wrongdoing sets back the interests of other people. Serious wrongs, such as murder, rape, lying, cheating, and stealing, are clear examples. When these wrongs are perpetrated, the victims are wronged. An attractive explanation is that these acts are wrong because they involve a failure adequately to respond to objections that victims can make to them. Such failures demonstrate a lack of respect for those wronged.

In contrast, many facts that give me decisive reasons for action, but that do not ground moral wrongs, do not significantly affect others. The source of my decisive reason to finish the book I am writing, or to order the tastiest dish on the menu, is not the interest that others have in my doing these things. This plausibly explains why failure to do them is not wrong.

Second, we often have good reason to require others not to act wrongly—to express that they are required to do so, and sometimes to reinforce that expression with force. This is not normally warranted to ensure that the person does not act in a way that is merely irrational. This suggests that interpersonal views plausibly track the scope of moral wrongdoing. This is because the underlying explanation they offer why an act is wrong accords with social responses to wrongdoing, and to the prospect that others might act wrongly.

In the light of this, interpersonal views can also plausibly explain why distinct interpersonal responses are warranted in the case of moral wrongdoing. When a person acts wrongly, she violates a norm that has its source in the interests of others. This explains why those others are warranted in making distinct and powerful responses to those acts.[13]

Third, there is an initially appealing explanation of the distinctive motivational force of morality that supports interpersonal action-guiding moral views. Earlier, I suggested that moral motivation is normative and qualitatively distinct. The value of complying with moral requirements is not completely reducible to the facts that give rise to those requirements. This value might be thought of as social. Respect for others requires us to take seriously reasons that they can offer to us for or against our actions. If these reasons are decisive respect for the special value of those who offer them requires us to conform to them.

A group of people who comply with a set of legitimate interpersonal reasons constitutes what we might call a community of mutual respect. The value of such a community plausibly explains the distinctive motivational force of moral wrongness. Living with others on this basis gives rise to a valuable moral community where each person acts in accordance with the distinctive value of others, a value that they have because of general and morally significant features of persons. Such a community is something that we all have reason to care a great deal about. Hence, the value of such a community is normative, and it is compelling in a distinct way.

Of course, such a community may not be possible in fact, either because some people violate or fail to respond to interpersonal reasons, or because some people fail to recognize that others are due the respect that gives those reasons their special force. But the ideal of a community of mutual respect can guide us even if it cannot be realized.

[12] The sketch in the following paragraphs is drawn in part from Scanlon's account, *What We Owe to Each Other*, ch 4.

[13] As we saw in the previous chapter, this is not Scanlon's view, for Scanlon thinks that our reasons to alter the relevant relations depend on the meaning of actions rather than on wrongness. *Moral Dimensions: Permissibility, Meaning, Blame* (Cambridge, Mass: Harvard UP, 2008) ch 4.

By complying with morality, we ensure that we do our part in the project of furthering such a community, so responsibility for the failure to realize such a community is not ours.

There is a great deal that is attractive about interpersonal action-guiding views. The underlying value of a community of mutual respect does, I think, have an important role to play in understanding both the source and motivational force of certain moral demands.

III. Rejecting Interpersonal Views of Wrongdoing

Nevertheless, I doubt that interpersonal views properly explain the general class of moral wrongdoing. They are better seen as complementing a more general view.

i) The order of explanation

One concern is that interpersonal action-guiding views, like response-dependent views, explain moral wrongness by referring to something that is explained by moral wrongness. Interpersonal views explain wrongness by the failure to justify our acts to each other. But, it might be argued, we cannot justify ourselves to each other because our acts are wrong. Wrongness thus explains why certain acts are inconsistent with an ideal of moral community rather than being explained by such an ideal.

Others can legitimately demand of us that we do not act in certain ways, or reject our doing so, only if we are required not to do so. It is wrong to demand of another person that she does not do something, or to reject her doing it, unless her doing it is wrong. But this suggests that we make an independent judgement of the wrongness of an act to draw conclusions about interpersonal action-guiding judgements.

For example, the fact that my conduct will harm you provides a reason against me acting in that way. If there is no countervailing reason to act in that way, the fact that my conduct will harm you makes it wrong. This also gives you a reason to reject me acting in that way, and founds a demand that you can make on me not to act in that way. The fact that you will be harmed seems to explain why it is wrong for me to act directly, without relying on the idea that you have reasons to reject me acting in that way, or to make demands on me.

ii) Motivation and the scope of wrongdoing

A second problem is more complex. The fact that the interpersonal views only plausibly explain a narrow part of morality makes them unsuitable as a solution to the problem of moral motivation. As I noted above, interpersonal views most plausibly explain when we wrong others all things considered. They explain only the duties that we owe to each other—what are sometimes called 'directed duties'—and the wrong that we do to others when we violate these duties.

They do not plausibly explain all wrongs, not even all wrongs that are explained by the value of other sentient beings. But the distinctive motivational qualities of morality are more general—they feature in all moral requirements. Hence, we should doubt that interpersonal views properly explain these qualities.

To clarify this objection, I first clarify the distinction between directed and non-directed moral duties. I then explore two responses to non-directed duties. Directed duties are duties owed to others. X owes Y a duty not to *v* if Y's interests explain why X is under a duty not to *v*. The normal way to explain Y's interest in X being under such a duty is Y's interest in X not *v*ing.[14] For example, X owes Y a duty not to physically assault her because of Y's interest in X being under such a duty. Her interest in this being so is her interest in not being assaulted.

This also explains why Y can demand of X that he does not assault her. Anyone else can demand of X that he does not assault Y, but Y is especially well placed to make this demand given that her interests explain the duty that X is under. And this also explains why Y can release X from the duty that he is under by consenting, subject to certain conditions—because Y's interests are at stake, Y should have control over X's conduct.[15]

But some beings whose interests explain duties that others are under cannot evaluate those interests or the impact they should have on the conduct of others. They include very small infants, those who are severely cognitively disabled, and non-human animals. The fact that these beings cannot evaluate the significance of their interests for others, or offer reasons or objections in the light of such evaluations, does not significantly affect the quality of the duties that they are owed. If they have interests that explain duties that others are under, these duties have the same character as duties owed to those with greater evaluative and cognitive capacities.

Furthermore, though this is controversial, some duties are not owed to others at all. They include duties not to destroy things of natural beauty and duties to secure the well-being of future generations. The fact that the latter duty does not have its only source in the difference it makes to particular human beings is clear from the now well-known non-identity problem—the duty to secure the well-being of future generations exists even when our actions affect the identities of those people who come into existence.[16] But even if such duties do not exist, we can surely understand them as moral duties. They should not be ruled out in advance by a particular view of the nature of morality.

The main challenge to interpersonal views that I am concerned with here is not the most familiar challenge—to show that we can explain the existence of the wider range of duties just identified. Rather, the fact that such duties exist suggests that interpersonal views do not provide a suitable solution to the general problem of distinguishing wrongness from mere decisive reasons against action. As the problem of moral motivation arises for all duties, the solution provided by interpersonal views is insufficiently general.

Here are two ways for those sympathetic to interpersonal views to explain such duties. The first, which is Scanlon's proposal, divides morality into two parts—narrow morality and wide morality. Narrow morality is the part of morality governed by *Scanlon's Test*. It concerns what we owe to those who are capable of having judgement-sensitive attitudes about us. Wide morality includes the range of duties that are not owed to those with the relevant capacities and attitudes.[17]

There are, of course, important differences in the content of our duties that depend on the facts that explain them. Whether the duty is owed to a person who is capable of assessing reasons and values makes this kind of difference. For example, we owe a

[14] As we will see in Chapter 11, there are exceptions.

[15] We will explore this idea in greater depth in Chapters 11, 12, and 13.

[16] See, especially, D Parfit *Reasons and Persons* (Oxford: OUP, 1984) Part IV. We will consider these duties in Chapter 15.

[17] See *What We Owe to Each Other*, 171–87.

duty not to affect a person in certain ways without her consent partly because of her interest in having control over her life. That interest depends on her capacity to judge, to evaluate, and to execute plans. Obviously, no such duty is owed to those who lack the relevant capacities. But this does not support interpersonal views of wrongdoing. These differences in capacity ground differences in the content of duties, not in the general character of duties.

The motivational force that duties have, and that gives them their distinct role in practical reasoning, does not depend on whether those duties are owed to rational agents. Consider Scanlon's own example: suppose that there it would be wrong to flood the Grand Canyon, because doing so would destroy something of awe-inspiring beauty.[18] Scanlon seems tempted by the view that all that this claim amounts to is that there is a very weighty reason not to do it.[19] But this fails adequately to characterize the view that the conduct is wrong. Moral demands are different in kind, rather than merely in degree, from decisive reasons, and this is as true in cases where wrongdoing is grounded in impersonal values as it is in cases where duties are owed to others. The view that there is simply a very powerful reason against harming non-human animals is even less plausible. Their interests press on us in broadly the same way as the interests of other human beings.

This suggests that the right solution to the problem of moral motivation is unified in the following sense: it should capture the qualitative difference between acting wrongly and acting in a way that there is a decisive reason not to act across the full range of duties, including duties that we owe to others who can make demands of us, duties that are directed to beings with interests but who cannot make demands of us, and duties that have their source in impersonal value.

iii) Extending interpersonal views

For this reason, some might favour a more general solution that Derek Parfit proposes. Parfit thinks that contractualism would be more plausible if reasons that could be offered to reject a principle could be impersonal as well as personal.[20] On this view, the distinctive quality of wrongness is explained by the reasons that others have to object to us acting in certain ways. But these objections are not restricted to facts about those making the objections. They can object on the basis of a wider range of values, including both impersonal values and the values of those who lack judgement-sensitive attitudes. Were contractualism to be understood in this way, and were it defensible, Parfit argues, it would 'unify, and help to explain, all of the moral particular facts that can make acts wrong'.[21]

To make progress with this suggestion, it would need to be shown that the aim to live in a community of mutual respect can plausibly explain the distinctive qualities of moral motivation in the broader range of cases that we have been considering. The special quality of motivation that we find in all cases of wrongness, on this view, is explained by the fact that in all such cases, were we to act, we would undermine a community of mutual respect. Parfit does not show that a satisfactory explanation of this kind can be developed.

18 *What We Owe to Each Other*, 219. 19 *What We Owe to Each Other*, 220.

20 Compare, also, Darwall's suggestion that violations of the norms of a moral community need not depend on the interests of members of that community being threatened. See *The Second Person Standpoint*, 95.

21 *On What Matters* vol 2 (Oxford: OUP, 2011) 217.

Nevertheless, Parfit's suggestion might seem attractive. Perhaps we can demand of each other that we show adequate respect for a wide range of values. A failure to do this may erode the aim to live in a community of mutual respect. We all have reason to care about beings without the capacity for judgement, and things of impersonal value. Because we care about these things, we also care that others respond appropriately to them, and certain relationships with others may depend on their doing so.

But the special motivational force of morality is not best explained by these interpersonal ambitions. The explanation of the wider range of duties that we are considering is more direct. Our ambition for a certain valuable kind of interpersonal community supplements rather than supplies the source of these duties.

Consider a person who recognizes that it is wrong to bring about the suffering of non-human animals. She feels constrained, and not simply in the way that she is constrained not to do what she has decisive reason not to do. It does not seem plausible that her motivation arises because harming them would set back the possibility of living in a community of mutual respect with other people. The suffering of the animal constrains her directly. The effects of her conduct on the relationships that it is possible for her to have with other people is derived from this constraint, and does not explain it.

To reinforce this view, consider:

> *Just Fido and I*: Fido, my dog, and I are the only two sentient beings left in the universe. I am the last person who will ever exist.

It seems wrong for me to torture Fido. If I recognize this, I do not plausibly have in mind the fact that torturing him would make it impossible to share a community of mutual respect with other people who have judgement-sensitive attitudes—there is no one to form such a community with.[22]

Scanlon suggests that a central reason for accepting contractualism is that it accurately captures the role that wrongdoing plays in our deliberations. He writes:

> When I reflect on the reason that the wrongness of an action seems to supply not to do it, the best description of this reason I can come up with has to do with the relation to others that such acts would put me in: the sense that others could reasonably object to what I do (whether or not they would actually do so).[23]

But *Just Fido and I* suggests that our relations with others do not adequately explain the duty not to harm non-human animals. This is a reason to reject interpersonal views more generally, at least insofar as they are intended to solve the problem of moral motivation. The explanation underlying such views cannot adequately explain the scope of morality.

iv) Reasons to be moral: Their weight and their quality

Here is a third doubt. I noted earlier that the distinction between what we have decisive reason not to do and what it is wrong to do is a difference in kind and not merely in

[22] In *Death and the Afterlife* (Oxford: OUP, 2013) Samuel Scheffler suggests that we would be much less motivated to advance our projects were we to know that we were the last generation of people ever to exist. I doubt that Scheffler is generally right about this—if we fail to achieve certain goals, people will never have achieved these goals. This fact can give us greater motivation to achieve these goals. But even were Scheffler's view right, we would surely still have good reasons to be powerfully motivated not to harm others, including non-human animals.

[23] *What We Owe to Each Other*, 155.

degree. When an act is wrong, we do not simply have a very weighty reason not to do it; we are constrained.

We have a powerful reason to value being in a community of mutual respect, and this gives us a reason to govern our actions in a way that is consistent with living in such a community, even when that community cannot be realized. But this reason cannot explain the qualitative difference between moral constraints and decisive reasons for action. The ideal of a community of mutual respect would only explain why we have weighty reasons to be moral, not the distinctive role that wrongness plays in practical reasoning.

Consider the contrast that we noticed in exploring *Sinking Ship*: a person can have a good reason to value the outcome of an act that it is wrong to perform. In such cases, a person can be motivated not to act wrongly. For example, the Captain rightly values the outcome where his child is wrongly saved, yet he is constrained from bringing that outcome about. How is this to be explained? Scanlon might suggest that the Captain values saving his child but values the ideal of a community of mutual respect more.

This suggestion seems suspiciously like the view of morality that we rejected earlier: the view that morality provides us with one set of reasons amongst others with which it competes. And it is not very plausible that the Captain does value the relevant ideal more than he values his child. After all, were he required to choose between saving his child and setting back the ideal of moral community, he would surely choose the former. The values behind the interpersonal view that Scanlon defends cannot adequately explain why anyone in the Captain's position ever does what morality requires of them. But yet some people do act rightly even when this is at great cost to the things they value most.

These concerns do not show, and are not aimed at showing, that the ideal of a community of moral respect is morally irrelevant. The ideal may be valuable, and it may be an ideal that we set back when we act wrongly. But I doubt that the ideal of a moral community can explain the special role that wrongness plays in practical reasoning.

IV. Decisions, Actions, and Practical Reasoning

The last discussion invites an explanation of the distinctive character of wrongdoing that explains constraints more directly. Such an explanation does not appeal simply to certain values that will be set back if the person does not act wrongly. As action-guiding views focus on the role that wrongdoing plays in practical deliberation, it will help to have a better sense of the elements of practical deliberation. This will make clearer the role that freedom has in deliberation, and hence the source of the limits that wrongdoing places on it.

i) Judging, deciding, and acting

Here is a simple model of practical deliberation. We weigh the strength of our desires for and against performing a range of acts. Our strongest desire wins, and when it does, we act.

There are many problems with this simple idea. The one I focus on here is its failure to explain the experience of choosing. Christine Korsgaard mounts the objection this way:

> It may be that what actually happens when you make a choice is that the strongest of your conflicting desires wins. But that is not the way you think of it when you deliberate. When you

deliberate, it is as if there were something over and above all your desires, something that is *you*, and that *chooses* which one to act on.[24]

Korsgaard concludes with a familiar idea: that when we deliberate we consider reasons, including reasons that we have for our desires, and for acting on them. She writes:

The idea that you choose among your conflicting desires, rather than just waiting to see which one wins, suggests that you have reasons for or against acting on them. And it is these reasons, rather than the desires themselves, which are expressive of your will. The strength of a desire may be counted *by you* as a reason for acting on it; but this is different from *its* simply winning. This means that there is some principle or way of choosing that you regard as expressive of *yourself*, and that provides reasons that regulate your choices among your desires.[25]

Korsgaard correctly diagnoses a problem with the idea that we practically deliberate simply by the competition of conflicting desires, and she rightly thinks that this does not give a proper role for choice in our practical deliberations.

Her solution, though, is incomplete. Just as deciding to *v* is not reducible to one's desire to *v* being strongest, it is also not reducible to the judgement that one has the strongest reason to *v*. A person who recognizes the rational requirement to *v* need not automatically *v*. Her decision to *v* intercedes between her recognition that she has the strongest reason to *v* and her *v*ing. Furthermore, after she has decided to *v*, she must still execute her intention to *v*.

Of course, there are intentional actions where deliberation does not occur, and also actions where forming and executing intentions are not separate events. Some intentional actions are spontaneous. When they are, a person acts spontaneously in the light of reasons for action that she accepts. But at least where deliberation and judgement occur, the judgement that *v* is to be done, forming the intention to *v*, and executing that intention, are distinct stages in the process of *v*ing intentionally. For this reason, a person's judgement that she has a decisive reason to *v* does not fully express her will to *v*.

Intentional action, then, expresses a person's agency beyond desiring or judging. It also explains why actions are the appropriate subject of moral evaluation, over and above the judgement that lies behind them. The person who judges that a certain act is to be done may or may not act on her judgement. When she acts, she may affirm her judgement. But a complete moral assessment of an action is not reducible to an assessment of the judgement that lay behind it. We evaluate not only judgements, but also decisions, intentions, and actions that affirm or conflict with those judgements.

That supports the view defended in the previous chapter that we appropriately blame people for their actions, and not simply for the judgements that lead to those actions. The fact that a person judged badly can be the subject of moral criticism in itself. But further stages of the process where judgement results in action are also evaluated—not only did the person judge badly, she expressed that judgement through an exercise of her will.

When things go well, we value certain actions as willed expressions of our judgements. These actions can be valued as our own. They are our own not simply because they reflect our judgements, but also because our judgements are made effective in our actions through our agency. Deciding and executing intentions makes our judgements effective in action.

[24] *Creating the Kingdom of Ends* (Cambridge: CUP, 1996) 370.
[25] *Creating the Kingdom of Ends*, 370.

Suppose that I perform an admirable action—for example, I spontaneously help a person in need. I value having performed the action in part because of the values that give me decisive reason to perform it—the person's need is met. I also value it because it reflects my judgement that it is valuable. But beyond that, I value it as an expression of my will. This explains why we value autonomous action more than an equivalent bodily movement that is caused by our judgements: it is better to save a person intentionally than to cause the person to be saved by one's judgement causing a muscle spasm.

V. Wrongdoing, Value, and Freedom

It is valuable to express our judgement through decision and action if things go well, I have suggested. Which such expressions are valuable?

i) Freedom and respect: The basic idea

Suppose that I act on the mistaken judgement that I have a decisive reason to *v*, where I have a decisive reason to refrain from *v*ing. What I value in *v*ing is not valuable, or insufficiently valuable to justify *v*ing. Some, but only some, such cases involve wrongdoing. We are concerned here with those that do not involve wrongdoing. In at least some such cases the action can be valued as an expression of my will.

Suppose that I consider two mutually exclusive options, *a* and *b*, where *a* is best, but *b* is acceptable. Although I have a decisive reason to *a*, and thus a decisive reason not to *b*, it may be appropriate to value *b*ing as an expression of my will. Here is one quick explanation: I may not have done the best thing, but I did *my* thing. This can be valuable. My overall argument does not depend on this being true, I should say. But recognizing the value of the free performance of suboptimal actions as expressions of our agency helps us to grasp a converse idea: the idea that the expression of our agency is not valuable, or disvaluable, in other cases. This is true of wrongdoing, and helps to explain the distinctive role that wrongdoing has in practical reasoning.

Here is the main idea. Certain actions are not valuable as free expressions of agency because of the significance of the reasons against acting in that way. Respect for these values makes valuing one's free performance of such actions inappropriate. This explains the idea that these values constrain. And this explains wrongness. I call this the *Respecting Value* view of wrongdoing.

To grasp the view, it helps to consider an example. Compare the decisive reason that a novelist has not to give a facile ending to a great book that he has almost completed with the decisive reason that he has not to harm another person against her will. In both cases, the value that grounds the person's decisive reason for action may be very important—the book will be great only if it has the right ending, and if it does have the right ending it will be a very important expression of the novelist's creative talents; the harm that he will do to the person he assaults will be significant, and the affront to her ability to determine for herself how others treat her is grave. Yet it seems that the novelist is morally required not to assault the other, but not to give the novel the right ending. This might seem true because another person is the victim of an assault, but not of a book having a bad ending. We have already seen the inadequacy of this explanation.

Here is how *Respecting Value* explains the contrast. Suppose that the novelist chooses to give the novel a facile ending. He sets back the value of the book, and he has a powerful reason to regret having done this. But the value of the book does not undermine the value of the novel as an expression of his agency. As the novel is his, he is free to finish it in whatever way he wants. Here is what this means. If he finishes it badly, the value that the novel would have had if he had finished it better does not undermine the value of the novel as an expression of his autonomous agency.

Here is one rough way to see this. Compare his finishing the novel badly, but as a free expression of his agency, with it being finished slightly better by a computer program. Because the novel is an expression of his agency in the first case, this gives him reason to value it more than in the second, even though, *ex hypothesi*, it is better in the second. Making comparisons of this kind provides a good heuristic device to determine when we have reason to value actions as free expressions of our agency.

Now contrast assault. The values that he will set back if he harms the other person not only supply him with a decisive reason against performing the act, they undermine the value of his action as an expression of his agency. The values that the assault sets back, then, not only provide him with a decisive reason against action, they make it inappropriate for him to value the free performance of that action. Again, we can use our heuristic device to see this. Compare his performing the assault freely with the victim being harmed by his muscle spasm. He has no good reason to prefer the former to the latter. Indeed, he should prefer the latter to the former.

This explains the idea that wrongdoing constrains—these constraints naturally follow from a recognition that it would be inappropriate to value the free performance of an action as an expression of one's agency. We see the values that our actions would fail to respect as sufficiently important that any free performance of the relevant action would lack value. It would then be inappropriate for us to value our freedom to act in the relevant way, and hence we find ourselves constrained.

ii) A refinement

Having the freedom to act can be valuable in a range of ways. *Respecting Value* is concerned with one specific way. One reason why it is valuable to be free to act has to do with the value of the act. The freedom to act can also be valuable independently of its performance. Options can have 'selection-independent value'. Consider:

> *Crime and Tennis*: Jane knows that she will lead a life of crime unless she commits herself to fostering her ability to play tennis. Without the opportunity of a life of crime, she would never have succeeded as a tennis player.

Her option of living a life of crime is instrumentally valuable. It is not inappropriate for her to value this option in this way. She does not value *exercising* her ability to live a life of crime. She values having the ability.

A person may also value wrongdoing because of its effects. Consider:

> *Reform*: Dave commits a series of petty thefts when young. He realizes the error of his ways, and devotes himself to charity, saving many lives. Had he not committed these thefts, he would have been a selfish lawyer.

It is instrumentally valuable that Dave committed petty thefts. It is not inappropriate for Dave to value having committed these thefts for this reason.

The option of acting can also be valued because it improves the quality of the actions performed in a less instrumental way—unselected options affect the value of the options one chooses. For this reason, people value a choice of careers independently of the value of the career they choose. A lack of options can undermine the sense that one's career is one's own.

But wrongful alternatives do not normally enhance the value of one's choices in this way. Consider:

> *Dealer and Football*: Harry plays for a lower league football team. He had very few career options due to lack of education and social circumstances. He could have had an equally lucrative career dealing dangerous drugs to kids.

Harry's option to be a dealer might lead him to value being a footballer more than he would have were he to lack this option. But this seems inappropriate. Treating his decision to become a footballer rather than a drug dealer as an expression of his autonomous agency shows an inappropriate attitude to being a dealer.

This might suggest the following: an act is wrong if the option to perform it lacks non-instrumental value. But we can immediately see that this view is false. Many permissible acts lack non-instrumental value. Completely pointless acts, such as grass counting, lack non-instrumental value, but they are not wrong.

What distinguishes wrongful acts, such as assault, from permissible but pointless acts, such as grass counting? In both cases it is inappropriate to value the option of performing such acts, and the free performance of those acts lacks value as an expression of autonomous agency. The answer is in the way that the values that give people decisive reasons not to perform the actions explain why their autonomous performance lacks value.

Consider the reasons why it is inappropriate non-instrumentally to value one's ability to commit assault. The importance of the harm that the victim will suffer provides a decisive reason against committing the assault. That is because of the value of the victim's welfare. And this value also explains why the autonomous performance of the action lacks value. Proper respect for the victim makes it inappropriate to value the free performance of an assault. There is no such failure of respect in the case of pointless acts. Such acts cannot be valued as expressions of autonomous agency, but not because performing them sets back some value that the agent fails to respect in their performance.

This suggests:

> *Respecting Value*: An act is wrong because the values that provide decisive reasons against acting explain why the act is not a valuable expression of autonomous agency. Where this is so, respecting the value that provides a decisive reason against performing the action makes it inappropriate to value the action as an expression of autonomous agency.

To understand *Respecting Value*, consider some act, *v*, that I have a decisive reason against performing. Here is how to determine whether that act is wrong. Consider the value that gives me a decisive reason not to *v*. Does the value that supplies this reason undermine the value of *v*ing as an expression of autonomous agency? If so, it is inappropriate to value *v*ing as such an expression. And when this is so, one ought to see that reason as grounding a constraint on one not to *v*. Where one ought to see things in this way, it is wrong to *v*.

VI. Defending the Respecting Value View

Respecting Value explains the distinction between wrongful acts and merely irrational acts by appealing to the way in which we should disvalue our ability to act in the former case when compared with the latter. Why should we accept this view?

First, it naturally explains the intuitive idea that we are not free to act wrongly, but free to act in a way that is merely irrational. Morality is constraining. These constraints are appropriate because judging oneself to be free to act wrongly would involve a failure adequately to value the fact that gives one a decisive reason against acting.

Furthermore, *Respecting Value* provides a natural account of our deliberations in determining whether an act is wrong. We have seen that decisive reasons against acting do not always found wrongdoing. In deliberating about whether it is wrong, a person reflects on the significance of the value that supplies the decisive reason not to act and justifies a constraint on acting.

In making this decision, we consider the value of freedom itself. Consider supererogation. A person may have a decisive reason to perform a supererogatory act. In such cases, the value that gives the person a decisive reason is insufficient to constrain the person's freedom, given the importance of her shaping her own life.

Second, *Respecting Value* provides a unified account of moral motivation. Earlier I suggested that wrongness plays a similar role in practical reasoning whether the value that explains why the conduct is wrong concerns another person, a non-human animal, or is impersonal. We are now in a position to explain this. Just as respect for the value of persons can make it inappropriate to value harming them as an expression of autonomous agency, so does respect for the value of non-human animals and for impersonal value.

But *Respecting Value* can also make room for the special value of persons, and the more particular idea that persons have special claims on us because of their ability to make judgements of their own. We value others in a distinctive way because they can shape their own life in the light of the judgements that they make. This determines the content of the duties we owe to them. And violating complying with these duties is especially important. This is in part because respect for others is a condition of sharing moral community with them. *Respecting Value* can thus make room for the plausible ideal that underpins Scanlon's contractualism.

Respecting Value also provides us with a more natural understanding of conflicts between personal and impersonal value that arise in morality. It is sometimes wrong to respond to a legitimate demand that another person makes on me because compliance destroys impersonal value—I am required to break a promise in order to ensure that the rainforests are not destroyed simply because of the value they have. This is so because the value of the rainforests is greater than the value underpinning the promise, and respecting this value makes it inappropriate to value keeping the promise as an expression of autonomous agency where doing so destroys the rainforests. Unlike *Respecting Value*, interpersonal views struggle to explain this.

Third, *Respecting Value* naturally explains why distinctive responses are appropriate to wrongdoing without reversing the natural order of explanation between wrongness and response. As I noted in the previous chapter, both wrongdoing and mere irrational action can make a person the subject of appropriate criticism. But our responses to wrongdoing are distinctive—blame is normally appropriate only for wrongdoing; or at least the kind of blame that is reserved for wrongdoing is distinct. As with moral motivation, a good account of wrongdoing ought to explain both differences in kinds of blame for different kinds of wrongdoing, but also the basic unity of our reactions to wrongdoing of different kinds.

Blame is a somewhat elusive idea. As moral philosophers increasingly recognize, it potentially captures a wide range of responses that we make to wrongdoing.[26] Different

[26] See, for example, M Fricker 'What's the Point of Blame?' (2016) 50 *Noûs* 165; T M Scanlon 'Forms and Conditions of Responsibility' and D Pereboom 'A Notion of Moral Responsibility

accounts of blame treat different responses as central to the practice of blaming. A good account of what blaming is should accommodate the full range of responses. A good normative account of blame should explain which of these responses is warranted. A good normative account of blame might be quite revisionist, in the sense that some things that are central to how blame is normally understood, such as resentment, might be rejected.[27]

Some kind of blame is commonly regarded as an appropriate response to all wrongful acts, if further conditions, such as responsibility, are met. And some kind of blame does seem warranted for all kinds of wrongdoing. But there are also important differences between the kinds of blame that are warranted in cases of interpersonal wrongdoing when compared with wrongdoing of other kinds. The most obvious is that in cases of interpersonal wrongdoing, the person who has been wronged has special standing to blame the person who has wronged her, and to forgive her and thus to withhold blame.

Respecting Value naturally explains both what unifies blame, and differences in kinds of blame. The unity of blame is explained by the fact that in all cases of wrongdoing, the person who has acted wrongly has failed to recognize a constraint that applies to her in virtue of the value that her action sets back. Blame is a warranted response to this lack of respect.

It can also explain the special standing victims of wrongdoing have to blame perpetrators. In wronging the victim, the perpetrator fails to conform to a constraint that applies to him. The constraint is explained by some valuable fact about the victim, such as her well-being. As the victim is the source of the constraint that applied to the wrongdoer, she has special reason to care about the lack of respect shown, and thus has special standing to blame him.

Fourth, *Respecting Value* helps to explain a fact I noted earlier: that it is sometimes appropriate to value the outcome of an act that it would be wrong to perform. Recall that in *Sinking Ship*, the Captain rightly refrains from saving his child rather than giving each child a fair chance, but appropriately values the fact that his child is saved by the First Officer's wrongdoing.

Here is how this conjunction of attitudes can be explained. Each child on the ship has an equal claim to a place on the lifeboat. The Captain is in a special position to ensure that his child is saved, which would achieve something that he appropriately values a great deal. But his role is to ensure that each person's claim is properly respected. To regard himself as free to save his child would involve a failure to respect the equal claim that each person has to a place on the lifeboat. He thus sets aside the fact that he is able to achieve something that he greatly values in determining who has a place on the lifeboat. In doing this, he recognizes that the value of the equal claim that each person has constrains the considerations that he can bring to bear in the case. This explains why something that he values a great deal, the life of his child, is excluded from his deliberations about whom to save.

The important aspect of this case that *Respecting Value* captures is that the Captain's decision to conduct the lottery fairly is not best understood as a conflict of value between conforming to the demands of morality and the value to him of his child being saved. His role makes it inappropriate for him to consider the value of saving of his child in his deliberations about how to conduct the lottery at all. It is thus appropriate for him to set aside his ability to achieve the result that he most values. He cannot value the saving of his child as an expression of his autonomous agency, for the equal

Immune to the Threat of Causal Determination', both in R Clarke, M McKenna, and A M Smith *The Nature of Moral Responsibility: New Essays* (Oxford: OUP, 2015).

[27] See, further, Chapter 5.

claims that each person has on being saved ensure that expressing his free agency is, in this case, inappropriate. His role is simply to ensure that each person's claim has the appropriate weight in the decision whom to save.

VII. Conclusion

To summarize, *Respecting Value* explains the special role that respect for other people has in our deliberations about what is wrong, and the motivating force of that respect. It can also explain the distinctive responses that are appropriate in the case of wrongdoing, that are not appropriate in cases of mere irrational action. And it can do so without reversing the natural order of explanation between wrongdoing and the responses that are appropriate to it. It can make room for the special value of interpersonal relationships, but it is sufficiently broad and unified accurately to reflect the role that wrongdoing plays in practical reasoning in both cases involving interpersonal demands and those involving impersonal value.

4

The Punitive Response

At least in central cases, the criminal law responds to wrongdoing. Wrongful conduct is criminalized, and those who violate the law are punished for their wrongdoing. Our question concerns when these responses are justified.

The account of wrongdoing offered in the previous chapter helps us understand one objection to the criminalization of permissible conduct that does not apply in the case of wrongdoing. By making threats, and by warranting preventive measures, the criminal law restricts freedom. Where conduct is permissible, a person is free in the moral sense to act. How can legal restriction on freedom be justified where there are no moral restrictions?

But if there is a moral restriction on acting, as indicated where the act is wrong, the person lacks one kind of complaint about criminalization: the law restricts her freedom to act, but she was not free in the moral sense to do so anyway. Criminalizing wrongdoing thus does not show disrespect for autonomy in the way that criminalizing permissible conduct does. Of course, there is a range of objections to criminalization, and this is only one. But it is an important one, and it helps to explain the powerful relationship between wrongs and crimes.

This chapter is concerned with another issue, and one that is perhaps even more important in understanding the proper contours of the criminal law. By criminalizing conduct, the state threatens wrongdoers with punishment. When people violate the law, it executes these threats. As most criminal laws will be violated, criminalization is normally justified only if it is permissible to punish those who breach it. Central to the explanation of the permissibility of doing this is the idea that wrongdoers lose their rights against punishment. This chapter aims to explain how those rights can be lost by wrongdoing.

I. Punishment and Respecting Wrongdoers

The central aim of this chapter is to show how punishing some wrongdoers is consistent with respecting them as autonomous agents by exploring the deep relationship between wrongdoing and liability to punishment.

i) Two kinds of respect

We should respect wrongdoers in one sense, but not in another. In one sense, the respect that we owe to others depends on particular characteristics that they have, or actions that they have performed. I might respect you for your integrity, or for the important work that you have done. This kind of respect is what Stephen Darwall calls 'appraisal respect'—it involves the appraisal that a person is, or has done something, admirable.[1] Wrongdoers lose respect of this kind by acting wrongly, and by having the

[1] 'Two Kinds of Respect' (1977) 88 *Ethics* 36; *The Second-Person Standpoint: Morality, Respect and Accountability* (Cambridge, Mass: Harvard UP, 2006).

attitudes that explain their wrongdoing. Of course, this is consistent with their being owed respect for other admirable things they have done.

Although wrongdoers lose appraisal respect, they are owed another kind of respect. Wrongdoers, like all other persons, are non-derivatively valuable. Their wrongdoing does not diminish the moral importance of their lives. Respecting their value in this more basic way involves responding appropriately to their personhood. Darwall calls this 'recognition respect'. My aim is to explore what recognition respect requires of us, given the loss of appraisal respect. I do so by drawing on and developing the duty view of punishment that I defended in *The Ends of Harm*.[2] I deepen the general account of punishment offered there and explore more carefully the relationship between duties that wrongdoers incur and the justification of punishment.

ii) Valuing wrongdoers

The fact that a person has acted wrongly often demands a response, but it does not permit victims, other people, or the state to do just anything to wrongdoers. That is so because they are owed recognition respect.

Although this is more controversial, recognition respect demands that we continue fully to value the welfare of wrongdoers. This makes it inappropriate to value the suffering of wrongdoers, or diminutions in their welfare. Harsh treatment of wrongdoers may be warranted, but such treatment is not valuable, or less disvaluable, because they have acted wrongly. Such treatment is justified only if it secures some further good, such as harm prevention, or recognition by the wrongdoer that she has acted wrongly.

But the respect that we owe to wrongdoers is not restricted to concern for their welfare. Wrongdoers have their own lives to lead, their own point of view, and their own values and aims. They have good reason to be concerned about their own lives, the lives of their families and friends, and the particular things that they have come to value. And they have good reason to value their freedom. As a result wrongdoers, like others, do not have a general obligation to bring about the impersonally best outcome, or to do what they have a decisive reason to do. We have good reason, where we can, to ensure that wrongdoers are treated in a way that is consistent with these distinctive plans, values, and attitudes.

But their wrongdoing makes a difference to how they may be treated. A person's actual aims are not always decisive in restricting our right to treat her in a certain way. This is as a result of a more general limit on what is owed to others in virtue of their capacities as autonomous agents. As I noted earlier, at least one central objection to having one's freedom restricted does not apply where one is prevented from acting wrongly. A person is not morally free to act in the relevant way, so she cannot appeal to the idea that she is free to live her life according to her own values in objecting to such restrictions.

This idea helps to explain why punishing wrongdoers may be justified. They may reject the ends that we serve by punishing them, but their rejection is not decisive where they have duties to serve these ends. Wrongdoing makes a difference to the way wrongdoers can be treated in part because they incur duties to respond to their wrongdoing.

[2] (Oxford: OUP, 2011).

iii) The use of punishment

Let us investigate the way in which state punishment involves offenders in securing the aims that a political community may legitimately have. From that we can explore how the duties that wrongdoers incur help to justify the infliction of punishment.

The central legitimate aim of state punishment is to protect people from serious wrongdoing; or more accurately from the facts that make acts seriously wrong.[3] This aim is supported by a range of social institutions, but the criminal justice system is perhaps the most controversial and difficult to defend. The importance of this aim cannot be underestimated: it is necessary to support all other social institutions that depend on compliance with the criminal law. This provides the central justification for the creation, development, maintenance, and operation of the criminal justice system.[4]

The criminal justice system is justified only if it is effective in securing this aim. It is made effective, when it is, by making and executing threats that wrongdoers will be punished. The threat of punishment gives people a prudential reason not to act wrongly. It also gives a prudential and moral reason to people to help others to shape their plans in a way that does not involve serious wrongdoing. The threat of punishment is effective in part, for example, because it motivates parents to ensure that their children are educated not to act wrongly.

Wrongdoers are involved in the pursuit of security, typically against their will. Few wrongdoers consent to be punished. And as these wrongdoers will be harmed in order to influence other people to conform to the demands of the criminal law, they are harmfully used. For this reason, to justify state punishment we must justify harmfully using those who breach the criminal law with the aim of security.

In the light of this, one very general question for a theory of punishment to answer is: how can we justify intentionally inflicting harm on wrongdoers in service of the aim of crime prevention without their consent? And a very general question for a theory of criminalization to answer is: which wrongs justify such an intentional infliction of harm on wrongdoers?

II. The Wrongness of Using

I defended the distinct and stringent prohibition on using others without their consent elsewhere.[5] Here I summarize that account in order to sharpen our focus on an exception—that which applies to those with enforceable duties to secure certain ends. I explore the justification of this exception and its limits. I then explore some extensions beyond the exception.

Here is a more careful statement of a principle prohibiting use:

> *The Using View*: If D executes an intention to use V to serve an end without V's consent, and D knows or believes that using V in this way will cause V to be harmed, D's act or omission is more difficult to justify than if V had not featured in D's intention in this way.

If this is correct, it is part of a more complete account of the significance of intentions to permissibility. For example, it is concerned only with a subset of intentions to affect others, rather than the full range of intentions that might affect the permissibility of

[3] For an explanation why this is more accurate, see Chapter 9.
[4] See, further, V Tadros *The Ends of Harm*, especially Part I.
[5] See, especially, *The Ends of Harm*, chs 6 and 7 and 'Wrongful Intentions Without Closeness' (2015) 43 *Philosophy and Public Affairs* 52.

harming others.[6] And it is silent on the important question of whether a good outcome can justify a harmful action only if the person performing the harmful action intended the good outcome. We need not resolve these difficult issues here.

The *Using View* attractively explains the wrongness of a range of acts that many intuitively find wrong, at least when they are inflicted on innocent people, even if the conduct is effective in preventing a great deal more harm than it causes. These include punishment of the innocent, torture, terrorism, and forcible reallocation of body parts for health reasons.

It also explains our intuitions about cleaner pairs of hypothetical cases. The most famous is:

> *Bridge*: Dorabella is on a bridge with Fiordiligi. A trolley is heading on a track under the bridge towards five people who will be killed if Dorabella does nothing. Dorabella can save the five only by throwing Fiordiligi from the bridge onto the tracks. Fiordiligi's body will stop the trolley, saving the five, but Fiordiligi will be killed.
>
> *Trolley*: A trolley is heading on a track towards five people. If Dorabella, a bystander, does nothing the five will be killed. Dorabella can save the five only by pulling a lever diverting the trolley to another track where Fiordiligi is situated. Fiordiligi will then be killed.

The problem is to explain why it seems wrong for Dorabella to kill Fiordiligi in *Bridge*, but not in *Trolley*. Whilst there are many competing explanations, one attractive explanation is that if Dorabella kills Fiordiligi in *Bridge*, Dorabella uses Fiordiligi to save the five. This is not true in *Trolley*.

Here is an argument to support the *Using View*. It rests on the following premise: people are entitled to determine for themselves which ends to pursue, even if their ends are not the most valuable ends considered impartially. A person has her own life to lead, everyone will agree. But what does this mean? One idea is that the person has her aims and plans that are adopted and formed in the light of the things that she values. A significant extent to which her life is a success depends on whether these aims and plans succeed, and succeed in responding to what she values.

A central element of a valuable independent life involves action in the pursuit of what one values. In such a life a person comes to value some things amongst the wide range of valuable things; she sets herself aims in the light of the things that she values; she forms plans to secure those aims; and she executes those plans. This is a dynamic activity: over time a person revises her judgements of value and in the light of those revisions she alters her plans. As she begins to execute her plans, she finds new things to value, or rejects certain things that she had valued. She adopts new aims and rejects old ones, and revises or abandons her prior plans. This is all appropriate behaviour for people who have the capacities to shape distinctive lives in the light of what they come to value by setting themselves aims and forming plans.

This behaviour is appropriate only if the person's aims and plans are pursued within the constraints that morality sets for her. In Chapter 3, we saw that morality can constrain a person from pursuing goals that she rightly values. A person who values correctly recognizes the values that constrain her from bringing about outcomes that she values—not only do they provide her with decisive reasons for action, they constrain her by making it inappropriate to value the autonomous pursuit of her goals.

In the light of this, we can outline one non-consequentialist idea. There are some ends that must not be pursued, and there are circumstances in which the only thing to do is also impartially best. But the fact that some end is impartially best does not

[6] I explore such cases in 'Wrongful Intentions Without Closeness'.

in and of itself give rise to a duty to pursue it. Whilst this non-consequentialist idea is controversial it is much less controversial than the *Using View* itself.

This idea has implications for interpersonal duties. One person, D, is not always entitled to compel another person, V, to serve D's ends, even if this achieves the impersonally best end. This is so because it is normally wrong to compel a person to serve an end that the person lacks a duty to serve. More precisely, if the value of V's performing an act does not ground a duty on V to perform it, that value is normally insufficient to permit D to compel V to perform it. Together, these ideas imply that it is sometimes wrong to compel a person to serve the impersonally best end.

To illustrate the argument so far, consider the following variation on *Bridge*. Fiordiligi is standing on the bridge with Dorabella. Dorabella wishes to save the five and asks Fiordiligi to throw herself in front of the trolley. It is, let us suppose, impersonally best for Fiordiligi to save the five. Yet she seems permitted not to do so. She would have been required to save five were she able to do so at no cost to herself, but not at the cost of her life. She is free to pursue other ends.

If saving the five is insufficient to support a duty on Fiordiligi to save them, it is normally insufficient to permit Dorabella to coerce Fiordiligi to do so; otherwise Dorabella would be permitted to coerce Fiordiligi to serve an end that Fiordiligi is not required to serve. The close relationship between Dorabella's permission to coerce Fiordiligi and Fiordiligi's duties flows naturally from the idea that our moral obligations determine the scope of our freedom that I defended in Chapter 3. If it is not wrong for a person to act in a certain way, that person is free to do so in the moral sense. If the value of Dorabella's goal is insufficiently important to constrain Fiordiligi's moral freedom, it is normally also insufficiently important to justify Dorabella restricting Fiordiligi's freedom through coercion.

Given that Fiordiligi is free not to jump off the bridge in *Bridge*, if Dorabella coerces her to jump off the bridge in order to save the five, Dorabella imposes her end of saving the five on Fiordiligi. The end of saving the five is also the impersonally best end. But that fact is insufficient to ground a duty on Fiordiligi to pursue the end of saving the five. As Fiordiligi lacks a duty to serve that end, when Dorabella coerces her, Dorabella wrongfully imposes her ends on Fiordiligi. This captures the distinctive wrongness of compelling a person to act in the service of one's ends, even when one's ends are impersonally best.

There is a further difference between *Bridge* itself and the case of coercion. When a person is coerced, they are forced to act. In *Bridge*, in contrast, Fiordiligi's body is used, but she is not coerced to act. Some might accept that it is normally wrong to compel a person to do something that she is not required to do but deny that Dorabella acts wrongly in *Bridge*. Coercing a person to act exploits their agency whereas using their body bypasses their agency.

Perhaps the distinction between exploiting a person's agency and bypassing a person's agency to use her body against her will is morally important. A person's agency might demand special respect, and interfering with it might be especially difficult to justify. This is especially so where the person's agency is exploited in a way that results in her being harmed. But even if the distinction between exploiting and bypassing agency is morally important, it is normally wrong to bypass a person's agency to use her body to secure an end if she lacks a duty to serve that end, especially if this will result in her being harmed.

To illustrate, suppose that Dorabella tries to persuade Fiordiligi to jump from the bridge. Fiordiligi refuses. Dorabella, recognizing her moral obligations, refrains from threatening Fiordiligi. Fiordiligi then immediately falls unconscious. Surely Dorabella must refrain from throwing Fiordiligi's body from the bridge because of her refusal to jump. Normally, Fiordiligi alone may determine which ends to use her body to serve, especially if the use will result in her being harmed.

We are now well placed to explain the contrast between *Bridge* and *Trolley*. The explanation offered for the wrongness of Dorabella killing Fiordiligi to save five in *Bridge* relied on the close relationship between forcing a person to act in service of a certain end and using that person's body against her will to serve that end. In *Trolley*, like *Bridge*, Fiordiligi is harmed in the course of Dorabella's pursuit of his end of saving five. The question is whether harming a person as a side effect in pursuit of one's ends is also akin to compelling her to act in service of that end. I think that it is not, for the following reason.

The question to be asked about using another person's body is whether it is permissible to co-opt her physical resources to help me advance my goals when she would not be required to do this. I suggested that it is normally wrong to do this in virtue of the fact that a person is entitled not only to determine which ends to pursue but also which ends to use her body in service of.

In contrast, the question to be asked about the permissibility of harming others as a side effect is whether the fact that they will be harmed should prevent me from pursuing my goals; goals that I can pursue without relying on the other person's agency or her body. In order to justify this I am not normally required to show that the person would have an enforceable duty to serve the end that I am pursuing at the relevant cost. As long as the costs that I impose are proportionate to the importance of my goal, I need not establish that the person who bears the costs either does, or must, share my goal. Fiordiligi would not be required to turn the trolley away from the five toward herself in *Trolley*, for example. But as she is not used to turn the trolley, this fact may not decisively restrict Dorabella's pursuit of the saving of the five.

III. Respect and Duty

Respect for other agents requires us to consider their point of view, and adjust our actions in the light of the implications of those actions for them. To respect autonomous agents we must take account of the fact that these agents come to value some things over others, and set their aims and plans in the light of what they value. When we take into consideration the implications of our actions for autonomous agents, we must take into consideration the particular things that the agent values, and her aims and plans.

In the previous section, we saw that this idea has implications for the permission to use others to serve our ends. Respect for others typically requires that we do not do this if those people do not consent, at least if they will be harmed. We will explore why consent is important in this way in more depth in Chapter 11. Our focus here is on another important exception to the principle that it is wrong to impose our ends on others. I first consider a central case of the exception—one considering those who have duties to serve the ends that the person is used to serve—before considering its scope.

The central instance of the exception has four dimensions. First, the person is used to serve an end that the person has a duty to serve. Second, it is necessary to harm the person to some degree in order to serve the relevant end. Third, the harm that is inflicted on the person is no greater than the harm that she would be required to bear herself were she to pursue the relevant end. Fourth, certain further conditions that make the duty enforceable are satisfied.

I have defended this view in outline elsewhere.[7] My aim here is to provide a deeper and more general defence of it. I then consider whether we can extend the permission to use a person beyond this central case.

i) Use and duty

Suppose that X uses Y to serve some end without Y's consent. Y may object that he rejects X's end. Y may not think that X's end is valuable. Or Y may recognize that X's end is valuable, but not value it. Or Y may value X's end, but value other things that he would be able to do were X not to have used Y more. Y, in that case, may object to X imposing his end on Y. But this objection has force only if Y is free not to pursue X's end.

The kind of freedom that is involved in this last claim is moral—the kind explored in Chapter 3. If Y is required to pursue an end, and X compels her to serve it, or uses her in service of it, Y cannot object that X failed to respect her entitlement to shape her life according to her own values, judgements, decisions, or choices. She was not free to shape her life in the relevant way, so there is nothing of the relevant kind for X to respect. Thus, one objection to X compelling her to serve an end, or X using Y to serve it, can be met.

ii) The preference for autonomy

But this is not the only objection that Y could make. Even if a person is required to pursue an end, she may have a reason to prefer the autonomous pursuit of that end to being controlled by others. Consider:

> *Forced Save*: Susanna is required to save a drowning child. Figaro compels her to save the child and as a result she does so. Had Figaro not compelled Susanna to do this she would voluntarily have saved the child.

Susanna may object to being compelled to save the child. If she autonomously executes her duty, her act is her own in a way that is not true if Figaro compels her to do so. By compelling her to save the child, Figaro fails adequately to respect Susanna in the appraisal sense of respect—he fails adequately to acknowledge her disposition to respond to the child's circumstances. The fact that we have an interest in autonomously doing our duty provides one reason against enforcing duties, or at least enforcing them by the direct use of force.

But this idea also has limited importance. This reason obviously does not exist in cases where Susanna would not have done her duty without Figaro's involvement, for in that case the person cannot appeal to the value that she places on doing her duty herself. And it does not provide a general objection to coercion.[8] Where moral obligations are backed up by coercion, a person can respond only to the moral requirement and not to the coercion. This is typically true of the criminal law: most people wouldn't dream of murdering others regardless of the threat of punishment. But it is a reason

[7] See, especially, *The Ends of Harm*, especially ch 6.

[8] For a contrary view, see M S Moore *Placing Blame: A Theory of Criminal Law* (Oxford: OUP, 1997) 747–8; 'Liberty's Constraints on What Should Be Made Criminal' in R A Duff, L Farmer, S E Marshall, M Renzo, and V Tadros *Criminalization: The Political Morality of the Criminal Law* (Oxford: OUP, 2015). For a more developed response to Moore, see V Tadros 'The Wrong and the Free' in K K Ferzan and S J Morse *Legal, Moral, and Metaphysical Truths: The Philosophy of Michael S Moore* (Oxford: OUP, 2016).

against punishing a person who would otherwise have responded appropriately to their wrongdoing. The justification of punishment that I offer thus relies on the fact that most wrongdoers will not respond to their wrongdoing appropriately if they are not punished; but, of course, this is plausible in most cases.

iii) Unenforceable duties

Here is a further objection to being used. Y may have a duty to serve an end, and yet Y's duty may be unenforceable. If so, Y has a right that no one interfere with her to ensure that she does not act wrongly.

There may be either instrumental or inherent reasons why a duty is unenforceable. Many duties are unenforceable for instrumental reasons—enforcing them, or attempting to enforce them, has bad effects. Enforcing a duty may harm others as a side effect or it might violate some other right of the duty-holder.

Furthermore, some duties are inherently unenforceable. The nature of the content of some duties ensures that they can only be fulfilled voluntarily. For example, in certain circumstances I have a duty of reciprocity to give gifts. But forcing a person to give a gift is typically impossible—it conflicts with what a gift is. If I am forced to 'give a gift' I have not fulfilled my gift-giving duty. Similarly, I may have a duty sincerely to apologize for my wrongdoing. I can be forced to say the words that an apology contains, but my duty to apologize remains unfulfilled.

Even in these cases, people can be influenced to fulfil their duties. For example, I could create the circumstances in which people are more likely to give gifts or to apologize. There is a question whether this behaviour is problematic if it is not done with the duty holder's consent. That question is related to the next issue that we will consider—some duties may be inherently unenforceable in a deeper sense. They may be unenforceable simply because of the interest that people have in not being controlled by others.

It may seem puzzling that a person has an interest in not being controlled by others to ensure that they do what they are required to do. If a person is not morally free to perform a certain action, what is objectionable about forcing her to not to do so? Yet people do have such a reason in some cases—we reject being controlled by others, even where this ensures that we do what we are required to do.

This suggests that two different kinds of freedom are valuable. The first idea is the freedom that a person has to shape her own life, according to what she values. I call this the value of authenticity. This is distinct from a second idea: the idea that a person is free from being controlled by others. I call this the value of independence.

These values come apart—suppose that some action, when it is autonomously performed, cannot contribute to a valuable life. This person has no reason to perform the action, and no reason to value the free performance of it. But she may nevertheless have good reason not to want to be controlled by others. This distinction will occupy us again when we consider political liberalism in Chapter 8 and consent in Chapter 11.

But even if independence is distinctively valuable there are limits to a person's interest in not being controlled by others. If the duty that a person has is very important, there is no value in independence. Nothing valuable is lost when murder is prevented. The importance of not killing the innocent not only outweighs the value of independence, it negates it.[9]

[9] See, further, Chapter 8, and also V Tadros 'The Wrong and the Free'.

Here is why. We have powerful reasons to prefer that we conform with very important duties, such as the duty not to kill the innocent. We do so if we do not kill the innocent. It is less important that we comply with that duty—something we do only if we respond to the reasons that underpin the duty.[10] We are grateful to those who ensure conformity with our duties, especially if, without their interference, we would not have complied.

This intuition applies powerfully in the case of the criminal law. Obviously criminalizing very serious wrongdoing, such as torture, murder, and rape, does not violate people's right to be free to perform these acts. But more, it does not even infringe their rights. There is no *pro tanto* right to be free to torture, murder, or rape that needs to be overridden.

This also applies to our duties to respond to our serious wrongdoing by protecting others. Because wrongdoers have important and stringent enforceable duties to respond to their wrongdoing, they lack a right not to be harmed in service of the ends of punishment.

iv) The costs of enforcement

A further objection to being used is in the harm that the person used suffers. Suppose that X uses Y to serve an end that Y has a duty to serve, harming Y. Y may object that even though she had a duty to serve the relevant end, the harm inflicted on her was too great. That depends on the stringency of Y's duty.

The relevant sense of stringency is a function of the costs to Y that are sufficient to vitiate the duty. We can call this the self-focused stringency of the duty, to distinguish it from the costs to others that relieve Y of the duty. To illustrate, the self-focused stringency of the duty that Y has to rescue V from lethal harm depends on the costs to Y that are sufficient to vitiate the duty that she has to rescue V.

If the harm that X inflicts on Y in the course of using her to achieve the relevant end is no greater than the self-focused stringency of her duty to serve that end, her objection that X has harmed her lacks force. X only inflicts costs on Y that she would have been required to bear in the course of serving the relevant end.

Even if the harm that X inflicts on Y is less than the self-focused stringency of her duty to pursue the relevant end, Y may nevertheless object to X harming her if the harm that X inflicts on her was greater than was necessary to achieve the relevant aim. Furthermore, Y may object to being used if there was a morally better way to achieve the relevant aim. For example, other things bring equal, if X could achieve the aim by using either Y or Z and the harm that X would inflict on Z is less than the harm that X would inflict on Y, X must use Z rather than Y. Fully spelling out what alternatives count as morally superior is a complicated task that I leave aside.[11] But this idea is central to explaining why it is often wrong to criminalize conduct where the harm that the conduct causes can be met by less intrusive or harmful means.

In some cases, though, the conditions that make duties enforceable may be met. In such cases, where the person would not fulfil her duty herself, she lacks an objection

[10] This distinction between conformity and compliance is drawn from J Raz 'Postscript to the Second Edition: Rethinking Exclusionary Reasons' in J Raz *Practical Reasons and Norms* (Oxford: OUP, 1999).

[11] For relevant work in the philosophy of self-defence, see especially S Lazar 'Necessity in Self-Defense and War' (2012) 40 *Philosophy and Public Affairs* 3.

to being forced to do it. Where her duty is positive—a duty to secure a goal—she also lacks an objection to being used to secure that goal.

IV. Responding to the Victims of Wrongdoing

To justify punishment, we need to justify using offenders to serve the end of protection. In the central case, justifying this involves demonstrating that offenders have enforceable duties to protect other people in a society, and that the costs that are inflicted on them through punishment are no greater than their duty is stringent, in the self-focused sense.

Difficult questions must be answered to establish that wrongdoers incur the relevant duties.[12] Why should wrongdoers respond to their wrongdoing at all? How do we explain the idea that responding to one's own wrongdoing is a moral duty? And what does the duty involve? I leave one difficult issue until the next chapter—some might claim that as wrongdoers lack free will, or are not responsible for their actions in general, they lack a duty to respond to their wrongdoing. Assuming that this challenge can be met, what can be said for the idea that wrongdoers are required to respond to their wrongdoing?

i) Attitudes to wrongdoing

We have powerful reasons to respond to the fact that we have acted wrongly, especially if our wrongdoing is serious. One question concerns the attitudinal and emotional responses that are inherently appropriate for wrongdoing. We have powerful reasons to recognize that we have acted wrongly. Some also claim that it is apt to feel bad about our wrongdoing. My own view is that recognition is very important, and this will inevitably cause a psychologically normal person to feel bad. But we do not aim at the bad feelings themselves.[13] I do not press that point here.

Another way in which guilt is distinct has to do with its motivational qualities. People who recognize that they have acted wrongly are impelled to act. One aspect of this impulse to act is backward looking, and the action cannot be executed. Where one regrets what one has done, one imagines oneself in the circumstances that one was in, and feels impelled to make a different choice. Of course, one cannot now make that choice.

But there is also an appropriate forward-looking response. When a person acts wrongly, she fails appropriately to respond to the values that she sets back by her action by recognizing or responding to the moral constraint that applies to her. She thus fails to acknowledge that she was unfree. A natural response is to recognize a new constraint that applies to her: one that arises from her failure to respond adequately to the values that supported the original constraint that she was under.

What supports this new constraint? In part, it is the very facts that made her original action wrong. For example, if her wrongful action results in another person being threatened with harm, she must now prevent that harm from occurring. And if the harm has occurred, she must negate it, compensate the other person for it, or ameliorate it. This idea is relatively uncontroversial. If some fact makes it wrong for X to *v*,

[12] See, especially, *The Ends of Harm*, chs 12 and 13, and 'Punishment and the Appropriate Response to Wrongdoing' *Criminal Law and Philosophy*, forthcoming.

[13] See, further, *The Ends of Harm*, 44–51 and 'Responses' (2013) 32 *Law and Philosophy* 267–74.

and X *vs*, and X can still respond to that fact, X must do so, other things equal. If she can only secure part of the value that she would have secured by refraining from acting wrongly, for example by ameliorating the bad consequences of her conduct, or compensating a person for those consequences, she must do that.[14]

But the fact that we have breached a primary obligation also shapes our secondary obligations more directly. A person responds not only to facts that supported her original duty, and that persist. She responds to the fact that she failed to recognize that her previous actions demonstrated a failure on her part to respond appropriately to these values by constraining her conduct. This alters the character of the duties that she now has.

One way to illuminate this focuses on our special reasons to respond to the particular people that we have wronged, rather than responding to others, who have also been wronged, but not by us. Consider:

> *Non-Swimmer*: In a fit of anger, Mary throws Billy into a lake, knowing that Billy can't swim. Coincidentally, in a fit of anger, Nora, who is standing next to Mary, throws Clive into a lake knowing that Clive can't swim. Nora runs off. Mary recognizes that what she did was wrong. She can now save either Billy or Clive but not both.

Mary should rescue Billy. One simple argument in favour of this view is that if she rescues Clive, she will have murdered Billy whereas if she rescues Billy she will have murdered no one.

It might be thought that this argument is underpinned by the moral significance of causation. It is worse to cause a death than it is to fail to prevent a death. If Mary saves Clive, she has caused Billy's death. If she saves Billy, she has failed to prevent Clive's death. As it is worse to cause a death than it is to fail to prevent a death, Mary ought to save Billy.

But the idea that we have a more stringent obligation to save a person from harm if the harm comes about as a result of wrongdoing does not depend on the distinction between causing and failing to prevent harm. The intuition that we have stronger reasons to save those who we have wronged persists where the wrongdoing is an omission rather than an action. Consider:

> *Non Swimmer 2*: Billy is drowning in a river. Mary could easily pull him out at no cost to herself, but as she finds him annoying, she refrains from doing so. He is being swept away by the river, and she follows him down the river. She comes to her senses, and decides that it was wrong not to pull him out. However, Mary now sees Clive, who has also been swept away by the river. Someone else has failed to rescue Clive. Mary can either rescue Billy or Clive but not both.

Mary ought to rescue Billy rather than Clive. Obviously, this is not because if she does not do so she will have caused a death rather than failing to prevent one. Whatever she does she will have failed to prevent a death. It is better explained by the fact that she has an obligation to respond to her earlier wrongful conduct of failing to save Billy. As a result of her wrong, Billy is now in peril. She must respond to that wrong by negating the harm that her wrongdoing gave rise to. She can do so by saving Billy.

Perhaps it might be argued that Clive has an equal right to be saved, for otherwise Mary's initial wrongdoing will have denied him a chance of being rescued. I agree that there is something to this idea, but I think that it is insufficiently powerful to require

[14] See J Gardner 'What is Tort Law for? Part 1: The Place of Corrective Justice' (2011) 30 *Law and Philosophy* 1.

Mary to give Billy and Clive equal chances of survival. For Mary's initial wrongdoing affects Billy in a much more direct way than Clive if she does not rescue him.

We can reinforce our confidence in this result by noting the following. Generally, the duty that one innocent person has to rescue another from harm is not very stringent. However, the duty to rescue can become much more stringent if the person who needs to be saved is in peril as a result of wrongdoing, even if that wrongdoing is an inaction. Consider:

> *Non-Swimmer 3*: Billy is drowning in a river. Mary could easily pull him out at no cost to herself, but as she finds him annoying, she refrains from doing so. He is being swept away by the river, and she follows him down the river. She comes to her senses, and decides that it was wrong not to pull him out. However, Mary realizes that in order to pull Billy out now, she must put herself at grave risk.

Had Mary not acted wrongly in the first place, she would not have been required to put herself at grave risk to rescue Billy. But as Billy is in peril as a result of her prior wrongdoing, she must now put herself at grave risk in order to rescue him.[15]

The following explanation underpins our intuitions in all three *Non-Swimmer* cases. Mary's initial conduct was wrong because of the importance of Billy's life. But the proper way to value that life responds to its value for Billy. Mary must respond to Billy by considering the demands that he can legitimately make on her in virtue of the implications of her conduct for him. Billy values his life and the things that he can do with it more than he values Clive's life, and he is not mistaken in valuing his life in this way. She must respond to this fact about Billy, and the constraint that it places on her. Preventing Clive from being killed would be an inadequate response to her wrongdoing because the importance of a life is not reducible to its impersonal value—the value that it has for anyone regardless of the connection they have with it.

This holds even if Mary did not appreciate that it would be Billy in particular whom she would wrong. Consider:

> *Non-Swimmer 4*: A person is drowning in a river. Mary is unsure whether this person is Billy or Clive. It is Billy. She could easily pull the person out at no cost to herself, but as she finds both Billy and Clive annoying, she refrains from doing so. Billy is being swept away by the river, and she follows him down the river. She comes to her senses, and decides that it was wrong not to pull him out. Mary now sees Clive, who has also been swept away by the river. She can either rescue Billy or Clive but not both.

In deciding not to rescue the person who is drowning, Mary has not failed to give weight to the particular value that Billy places on his life when compared with the particular weight that Clive places on his life. There is a person who is drowning, and she has failed to give weight to the particular value that that person places on his life, but she is unsure whether that person is Billy or Clive.

Some might conclude that Mary has no more reason to rescue Billy than Clive. As she has failed to value the particular importance that Billy and Clive each gives to his own life to an equal degree, her response to her wrongdoing ought to give equal weight to the life of each of them.

The fact that Mary's act expresses an equally bad attitude to Billy and Clive does seem important in determining how Mary should respond to her wrongdoing. Billy's

[15] See, further, V Tadros 'Resource Wars' (2014) 33 *Law and Philosophy* 361, 364–7; C Barry and G Øverland 'The Implications of Failing to Assist' (2014) 40 *Social Theory and Practice* 570.

claim that he should have priority over Clive to be rescued seems weaker in *Non-Swimmer 4* than *Non-Swimmer 2*. But other facts about the case may nevertheless provide Billy with a stronger claim to be assisted by Mary than Clive has. Mary did not know that she was wronging Billy rather than Clive when she failed to pull him out of the river at an earlier time. But she was in fact wronging him, and she is required to respond to this fact. So although it is less clear that Mary ought to rescue Billy rather than Clive in *Non-Swimmer 4*, she still seems required to do so.

ii) Responding to the person one has wrongfully harmed

The *Non-Swimmer* cases are concerned with threats resulting from a person's wrongdoing, and that she can now avert. In central cases of criminal wrongdoing, in contrast, the question is what duties wrongdoers owe where the bad consequences of wrongdoing have already occurred.

If a person has a duty to avert a threat that she poses to another, she also has a duty to negate, compensate, or ameliorate a harm that she has caused. One important way to do this is to protect the person who has been harmed from further threats that they might face. If I have harmed a person to a certain degree, I can make the person as well off as she would have been by preventing a similar harm being inflicted on her that she would otherwise have suffered. This is why it is less controversial to harm a person in order to deter others from attacking the victim of one's crime in particular, rather than to protect others from similar attacks.

It might be thought that all that a wrongdoer need do in response to wrongfully threatening others or wrongfully harming others is to make his conduct 'cost neutral' in this sense, either by compensating the victims of wrongdoing, or negating the effects of his wrongdoing. They might believe:

> *The Internalization Principle*: If a wrongdoer fully compensates the victim of his wrongdoing, the duty of protection he owes to that victim and others is no more stringent than the duty that an innocent bystander owes to the victim and others.[16]

This principle might be supported partly on the grounds that if a person has internalized the costs of her wrongful action she has at least come close to negating the harm that she is responsible for. And, it might be thought, this is just as good as not having acted wrongly in the first place. An idea of this kind explains why many people believe that wrongful attackers are liable to be harmed in self-defence only to avert threats that they are responsible for creating.[17]

But *The Internalization Principle* is not even close to the truth. There are many cases where wrongdoers owe duties to victims even where their wrongdoing does not make the victim worse off than she would have been had the wrongdoing not occurred. One set of examples involves simultaneous overdetermination. Consider:

> *Fire*: Ivan and Andrei independently, and without knowledge of each other's actions, maliciously light fires in order to burn Marjana's house down. Each fire would have been sufficient to burn Marjana's house down. The fires merge and Marjana's house is burned down.

[16] In ch 12, V of *The Ends of Harm* I outlined some reasons to doubt this idea, but they were underdeveloped. The arguments here extend what I say there.

[17] See, for example, J McMahan 'The Basis of Moral Liability to Defensive Killing' (2005) 15 *Philosophical Issues* 386; J McMahan *Killing in War* (Oxford: OUP, 2009).

Ivan's action makes Marjana no worse off than she would have been had he not acted and the same thing is true of Andrei's action. *The Internalization Principle* has the implausible implication that neither Ivan nor Andrei owes Marjana compensation.

Second, *The Internalization Principle* implausibly implies that one can create permissions to act in ways that would otherwise be wrong by benefiting the victims in advance. Consider:

> *Protection in Advance*: Nadine desperately wants to hit Pascal, who will not consent. Nadine protects Pascal from being hit by Christine and then Yvonne, which she had no duty to do. She then punches Pascal.

Nadine's group of acts makes Pascal better off than he would have been had she performed none of them. And she would not have acted wrongly had she performed none of them. But Nadine obviously acts wrongly in performing this group of acts. She owes stringent duties to Pascal even though she has made him better off overall. Her obligation not to punch Pascal is no less stringent because of the supererogatory protective acts that she has performed. Internalizing the costs of a set of actions does not make that set of actions permissible, and does not vitiate the duties that the wrongdoer incurs as a result of individual wrongful actions within the set.

Third, *The Internalization Principle* implausibly implies that we do not owe duties to those whom we create if these people are not harmed overall, even if they are created simply for the benefit of others. Consider:

> *Slave Child*: Cornelius wants a slave and is willing to pay Sylvia £1000 to create one for him. Sylvia does not wish to have children for herself. She creates Angela to be Cornelius's slave, pocketing the £1000. Cornelius is a benevolent slave master, so Angela has a reasonably happy life in his service.[18]

No one is worse off than they would have been had Sylvia not acted. How we should describe Angela's circumstances is a controversial matter (is she benefited by her creation?). But the judgement that her creation does not make her worse off than she would have been had she not been created is clear. Yet Sylvia has a stringent duty to free Angela from her life of slavery and to protect her from being enslaved in the future. These judgements, though, conflict with *The Internalization Principle*.[19]

These cases illustrate the falsity of *The Internalization Principle*. What deeper explanation can we offer to doubt it? Different cases may call for different analyses, and I lack the space to investigate all of these cases here. Nevertheless, we can see that *The Internalization Principle* does not limit the duties we owe to others. It is often insufficient in responding to the value of others that we ensure that we do not make them worse off as a result of our actions.

Given that wronging a person does not depend on harming that person overall, it is also plausible that the duties that we incur to those that we wrong are not always satisfied by counterbalancing the harm that we cause. We can be expected to respond to the fact that we have wronged a person by committing ourselves to benefiting that person. The view that fully counterbalancing the harm that we have caused

[18] This case is drawn from G Kavka 'The Paradox of Future Individuals' (1982) 11 *Philosophy and Public Affairs* 93, 100.

[19] We will explore some related issues in Chapter 12.

through our wrongdoing satisfies the duties that we owe her is in conflict with that commitment.

V. Responses Beyond the Victim

The aims of punishment and compensation are often thought to be different. Compensation is owed only to the victim of wrongdoing, and not to other people. Punishment, in contrast, can be carried out not only for the sake of the victim but also for the sake of others. The question is how to extend the duty view of punishment to justify protection of others. There are many different paths to explore. I will not aim to develop anything like a complete account here.[20]

i) The victim's aims

One possibility is that other-regarding protective aims of the victim can help to justify extending the duties of offenders to the protection of non-victims. A parent's ambition to protect her children provides the most powerful and obvious example. Consider:

> *Child Protection*: Jones has broken Smith's arm. Robson now threatens Smith's child, Little Smith, with a broken arm. If Smith harms Jones, Robson will be deterred from harming Little Smith.

The argument in the previous section can be extended to this case, permitting Smith to harm Jones.

One reason why this might be thought true is that if Jones has a duty to benefit Smith at some cost to himself, it is for Smith to choose how Jones benefits her. As long as Smith imposes no more cost on Jones than Jones is liable to bear, Smith may harm Jones for any purpose that she chooses. On this view, Smith could harm Jones to some serious degree to serve any of Smith's projects, such as washing her car, as long as the harm that Smith imposes on Jones does not exceed the maximum harm that Jones is liable to suffer in virtue of his wrongdoing.[21]

But this is not plausible. The fact that Jones has wronged Smith does not give Smith a right to harm Jones for the sake of any trivial ends that Smith happens to have. She may harm Jones only if doing so is proportionate in two senses. First, the harm she inflicts must be no greater than the maximum harm that he is liable to suffer (*the maximum harm threshold*). Second, each unit of harm imposed on the offender must be justified by the magnitude of the benefit that it brings about (*the internal justification principle*).[22] These ideas draw on and develop an idea that is familiar from the

[20] I say more about this in *The Ends of Harm*, ch 13.

[21] For this objection, see K Ferzan 'Rethinking *The Ends of Harm*' (2013) 32 *Law and Philosophy* 177, and for an initial response, see V Tadros 'Responses'. Kit Wellman is tempted by the view that if a wrongdoer forfeits her right against being harmed, she may be harmed for any reason at all. See 'The Rights Forfeiture Theory of Punishment' (2012) 122 *Ethics* 371.

[22] This is one dimension of what Jeff McMahan calls 'narrow proportionality'. Narrow proportionality is concerned with whether harming a liable person to secure certain ends is proportionate (see *Killing in War* (Oxford: OUP, 2009), 20–32. This is contrasted with wide proportionality, which is concerned with harm to non-liable people. McMahan is primarily concerned with the *maximum harm threshold*. The *internal justification principle* provides one way of responding to aggregation problems that McMahan identifies. See *Killing in War*, 23–4.

philosophy of self-defence. The fact that a liable attacker has forfeited her right against being harmed does not imply that she may be harmed for *any* reason, and she retains a right against being harmed where the relevant goal is not secured, or the harm inflicted on her is not necessary for securing it.[23]

The *maximum harm threshold* and the *internal justification principle* are sensitive to qualitative as well as quantitative considerations, such as the identity of the beneficiary, and the quality of the value advanced. One reason why this might be true draws on the argument that I offered for the idea that offenders can incur protective duties in virtue of their wrongdoing. In that discussion I appealed to the idea that in responding to their wrongdoing, it is appropriate for wrongdoers to take as their end the protection of the person they have harmed. The wrongdoer has failed to recognize the importance of a particular set of values. It is primarily these values to which he must attend in responding to his wrongdoing. Aiming to promote other valuable things is a second-best substitute.

This also suggests a reason why the victim must be a central focus of his concern. The central appropriate response to wrongfully harming the victim is to commit himself to advancing the interests of the victim. But it is also appropriate for the offender to commit himself to advancing the particular moral property of the victim that grounded the right that he violated. For example, if the right that the offender violated was grounded in the offender's interest in having control of her property, he has a special reason to set the protection of her property as his end. If the right that the offender violated was grounded in the offender's interest in sexual autonomy, he has a special reason to set the protection of the victim's sexual autonomy as his end. This may also constrain, to some degree at least, the way that the offender can be harmed. It may be easier to justify harming him in order to protect the moral property of the victim that he has failed to attend to than it is to protect other moral properties that she has.

I doubt that this feature of the offender's duties always provides a decisive restriction on the way that he can be harmed. For example, although it may be easier to justify harming a rapist in order to protect the victim against being raped, the offender may sometimes be harmed to protect her against having her house destroyed. If he cannot set the particular moral property that grounds the right which he has violated as his end, he must set the victim's well-being as a whole as his end.

Furthermore, if there is something more valuable about the victim that he can protect, he typically ought to do that. Other things equal, and assuming that this is what the victim prefers, if a rapist could either protect the victim against being raped now or protect her against being murdered later, he ought to protect her against being murdered. Although the fact that he has raped her provides a reason to protect her against rape in particular, this reason is outweighed by the importance of protecting her life.

ii) The victim's duties

So far, I have advanced a version of general deterrence that is limited to protecting the victim and those who she wishes to protect and who are intimately related to her.

[23] See McMahan *Killing in War*, ch 1. Not everyone in the philosophy of self-defence agrees with this view. For different dissents, see, for example, J Quong and J Firth 'Necessity, Moral Liability and Defensive Harm' (2012) 31 *Law and Philosophy* 673 and H Frowe *Defensive Killing* (Oxford: OUP, 2014) ch 4.

General deterrence can be grounded in the idea that the offender owes something to the victim in virtue of wronging her. In advancing her aims, he responds appropriately to the wrong that he has perpetrated against her.

Not all victims have the aim of protecting others. If so, protecting another person, even a person to whom the victim is intimately related, does not advance the aims of the victim. If the offender incurs a duty only to advance the aims of the victim, the argument that I have provided for general deterrence cannot be extended to other people.

A further extension of the account builds not on the aims that the victim has, but on her duties. The idea is that the offender can sometimes be harmed to serve certain ends if doing so furthers an end that the victim has a duty to serve. This can be done even if the victim does not recognize that she has the relevant duty. Offenders and victims can be expected to endorse this practice, even if they don't in fact do so.

Consider:

> *Transfer*: Drucilla has seriously assaulted Vera. Xavier threatens seriously to assault Yolanda. If Vera harms Drucilla, which she can do at little cost to herself, Xavier will be deterred from seriously assaulting Yolanda. There is no other benefit that Drucilla can provide to Vera.

My question is not whether it is permissible for Vera to harm Drucilla to promote an end that Vera actually has. My interest is in whether it is permissible for a third party to punish Drucilla in order to deter Xavier from assaulting Yolanda if Vera does not care about Yolanda.

Here is one possibility. Suppose that Vera would be uninterested in saving Yolanda, even were she able to do so at no cost to herself. Were she able to save Yolanda at no cost to herself she ought to do so, but Vera would not be inclined to do her duty. By assaulting Vera, Drucilla incurs an obligation to Vera. Vera owes an obligation to protect Yolanda if she can do so at no cost to herself. It follows that Vera has a duty to ensure that Drucilla is punished for the sake of Yolanda. If that is right, it is permissible to punish Drucilla for the sake of Yolanda. Doing so can be justified to Vera in virtue of her obligation to Yolanda, and to Drucilla in virtue of her obligation to Vera. There is a chain of obligation from Drucilla to Vera and Vera to Yolanda that supports Drucilla's obligation to Yolanda.

Chains of obligation like this clearly arise in other contexts. Consider:

> *Car*: Paul destroys Quentin's car and Quentin destroys Rudolf's car.

Paul owes Quentin a car and Quentin owes Rudolf a car. If the only way that Quentin can provide a car to Rudolf is to receive a car from Paul, Quentin has a duty to receive a car from Paul to give to Rudolf. Quentin is not permitted to waive his right to a car because receiving the car is the only way in which he can satisfy his duty to provide a car to Rudolf. Furthermore, if Paul cannot provide a car to Quentin, he has a duty to provide the car directly to Rudolf. Paul cannot complain about being required to do this because he owes a duty to provide a car to Quentin. Quentin cannot complain about it because he owes a duty to provide a car to Rudolf.

It might be objected that the analysis in *Car* cannot be applied to *Transfer* for the following reason. In *Car*, Quentin has a special duty to Rudolf to supply Rudolf with a car. In *Transfer*, in contrast, we rely on the general duty of rescue. But the scope of a person's duty to rescue depends on the resources available to her. Thus, in *Transfer*, it is artificial to rely on the duty that Vera owes Yolanda, for any duty that Vera owes to Yolanda is owed only because Drucilla has incurred an obligation to her through harming her.

Compare:

> *Resources*: Jeri steals £1000 from Avery. Milton is impoverished. Return of the £1000 cannot benefit Avery or anyone else.

Now consider the following argument. Jeri has a duty to return £1000 to Avery if Avery demands it. Avery has a duty to demand it, for if she demands it she can provide £1000 to Milton. She can do this at no cost to herself. Therefore, £1000 can be taken from Jeri to give to Milton. This argument might be thought redundant. It might be argued that even if it is permissible to take £1000 from Jeri to give it to Milton, this is not because of any duties that Avery owes to Milton. It arises simply because Jeri is not entitled to the money.

However, we cannot simply rely on the idea that Jeri is not entitled to the money. The way the money ought to be spent depends on Avery's obligations. Suppose that libertarians are right that there are no positive obligations to benefit those in need, even if this can be done at little or no cost. Then it would be difficult to justify taking the money from Jeri to give to Milton, even though Avery is uninterested in the money. If the money is owed to Avery in particular, and Avery chooses to give it to Jeri, we would not be permitted to take it from Jeri for the sake of Milton. Avery is not entitled to give up the money: she has duties to help those in need, including Milton. It is thus because Milton has a duty to protect Avery that the money may be taken from Jeri to benefit Milton.

We can further support the idea that the obligations of protection are not restricted by the desires of victims, but may be extended via the victim's duties, by considering the following:

> *Preferred Child*: Amina seriously assaults Idris. Idris has three children, Apple, Bear, and Cupcake. Amina can rescue either Apple or (Bear and Cupcake) at some high cost to herself. Amina can do nothing else to benefit Idris. As Apple is Idris's preferred child, Idris would rather see Apple rescued than (Bear and Cupcake).

Because of the protective obligation that Amina owes to Idris, Amina ought to rescue either Apple or (Bear and Cupcake). Idris has a preference in favour of Apple being rescued, but a duty to ensure that (Bear and Cupcake) rather than Apple is rescued (I assume that we have an obligation to save the greatest number, and that this applies to our children as well as to strangers). Assuming that Idris's duty to ensure that (Bear and Cupcake) rather than Apple are rescued is enforceable, which is uncontroversial, Amina ought to rescue (Bear and Cupcake). The fact that Idris prefers not to fulfil his enforceable duty does not affect the decision that Amina ought to make.

Perhaps it might be argued that *Transfer* can be contrasted with both *Car* and *Preferred Child*. In *Transfer*, Drucilla's obligation to Vera is much more stringent than Vera's obligation to Yolanda. Perhaps this does reduce the costs that it is permissible to impose on Drucilla. She owes a stringent obligation to Vera if she is acting for Vera's sake. But she owes a less stringent obligation to Vera if she is acting to ensure that Vera's obligation to Yolanda is fulfilled, it might be argued. This may be true, but if it is true it has implications only for proportionality. It is reasonably plausible, for example, that the *maximum harm threshold* is lower, and the *internal justification principle* more difficult to satisfy, if non-victims rather than victims are the beneficiaries of punishment in cases such as *Transfer*.

We can also extend our analysis to see the special role that the victim plays in the duties of protection that offenders incur. This helps to vindicate the victim-focused argument that I have provided for general deterrence. Consider:

Kids or Strangers: Dennis has seriously assaulted Valentin, and owes a stringent obligation to Valentin as a result. Dennis can rescue, at some significant cost to himself, either Acorn, who is Valentin's child, or Bean and Crow—children who are strangers both to Dennis and Valentin.

As Acorn and Dennis are strangers, were it not for the assault that he perpetrated against Valentin, Dennis would not be permitted to rescue Acorn rather than (Bean and Crow). If Dennis chose to bear a cost for the sake of rescuing either Acorn or (Bean and Crow), he must rescue both Bean and Crow.[24] Yet it is not intuitive that Dennis ought to rescue (Bean and Crow) in *Kids or Strangers*. The fact that Dennis has seriously assaulted Valentin places an obligation on Dennis to Valentin. As Valentin has a duty to rescue Acorn rather than (Bean and Crow) (plausibly assuming that a person must rescue one of his children rather than two strangers), Dennis has a duty to rescue Acorn. This seems true even if Valentin does not care about Acorn.

Kids and Strangers helps to support the view that the criminal law should not be thought of as 'public' in the strong sense that some criminal justice scholars assume. Some criminal justice scholars suggest that criminal law and private law are to be contrasted as follows. Private law is concerned with duties that wrongdoers incur to particular individuals. Criminal law is focused on duties they incur to the citizenry more generally. *Kids and Strangers* suggests that this view is misleading. Whilst it may be true that offenders can be harmed for the sake of public protection, as *Transfer* suggests, even in criminal law we ought to prioritize the protection of the victim and those that the victim has a stringent duty to protect.

iii) Protection and the value of persons

Here I consider a further way of defending the idea that the obligations of offenders can be extended beyond protection of the victim. The idea to be explored is that offenders, through their wrongdoing, incur obligations to protect people against wrongdoing of a similar kind, regardless of whom that wrongdoing is perpetrated against, and without relying on the rights and duties of victims.

One way to explore this possibility is to consider the case of death, as in:

Death: Leonora wrongfully kills Ines, an innocent person. Leonora could protect Ruiz, another innocent person, from being killed by Conte at some cost to Leonora.

The question we are concerned with is the source and stringency of Leonora's obligation to protect Ruiz from Conte. Let us suppose that there are no special relationships between the characters in the example (other than the fact that Leonora is Ines's murderer). Nevertheless, it might be argued that Leonora has a more stringent duty to protect Ruiz than other people have. An argument for this view need not depend on the idea that Leonora has a stringent duty to fulfil Ines's duty to protect Leonora from Conte.

Consider how Leonora should respond to wrongfully ending Ines's life. She has violated a duty that she owes to Ines in particular. But that duty is an instance of a more general duty not to kill. Her most central secondary duty concerns Ines—she should aim to benefit her if she can. However, as Ines is dead, there may be a limited amount, perhaps nothing, that she can now do for her. It is not plausible that if Leonora cannot

[24] For this feature of ordinary morality, see S Kagan *The Limits of Morality* (Oxford: OUP, 1989) 16.

benefit Ines, she lacks any duties that she would not have had but for killing Ines. Killers ought to redeem themselves insofar as they can. They may not be able to redeem themselves by benefiting the victim. If they cannot, they must find other ways to do so.

One way to redeem oneself is to secure and advance the value that one has set back through one's wrongdoing. Leonora ought to refrain from killing in the future, and to revise her attitudes to killing. But the obligation to refrain from killing, and the obligation to adopt the appropriate attitudes to killing, do not depend on Leonora having killed. She had these obligations anyway.

If Leonora seeks redemption, then, she must aim at something else. Perhaps she might in part redeem herself by treating the prevention of wrongful killing as her end. Showing such a commitment to preventing wrongful killing is a way of committing herself more thoroughly to protecting the value that she failed to acknowledge and respond to in performing her earlier wrongful act.

To explore this possibility, imagine that Leonora has now revised her judgements, and recognized the wrongfulness of her murderous act. Reflecting back, she realizes that she has wrongly treated Ines as lacking the moral importance that she had. She would like to wind the clock back and undo the wrong she has done to Ines. Of course, this is impossible. She cannot even negate or compensate for the harm she has caused her. The fact that these things are impossible will be a deep source of regret for Leonora.

How should she respond in the light of this regret? She should do so by deepening her commitment to the value and importance of human life. She should commit herself to protecting the lives of others. More particularly, she should commit herself to the struggle against the kind of wrongdoing that she herself once perpetrated. Her commitment to this end will be demonstrated by her willingness to accept significant burdens in pursuit of this aim.

In this way, punishing a person to protect other people can be justified to the offender. In punishing her, we aim at protecting other people against wrongdoing of the kinds that she perpetrated. This is an end that, were she well motivated, she would also intend to pursue. Were she well motivated she would share our ends. This helps to demonstrate that using her in a way that harms her is consistent with respect for her as an autonomous agent. We harm her to pursue an end that she is required to pursue.

VI. Conclusion

I have argued that the practical responses that those who commit serious wrongs ought to make to their wrongdoing are not plausibly restricted to providing the victim with full compensation. This is why it is permissible to harmfully use serious wrongdoers for a wider range of ends than the provision of full compensation.

When we consider the scope of the criminal law later in the book, we will consider which wrongs give rise to the duties to serve the ends that criminal punishment serves. This determines what wrongs render a person liable to punishment, and that will play a role in answering the larger question of what wrongs can be criminalized.

5

Personal Practical Responsibility

In the previous chapter we saw that it is intuitively plausible that some wrongdoers have powerful duties to respond to their serious wrongdoing. We began to explore the scope of those duties, and to see the role that they play in the justification of punishment. But I left aside a difficult issue: it might be argued that we should not rely on our moral intuitions about the duties of wrongdoers in this way because these intuitions are caused by a mistaken everyday view about responsibility.

A familiar kind of responsibility scepticism is that blame cannot be vindicated because it relies on a kind of free will that we lack. The same thing might be said of the account of punishment that I have offered. If we are not responsible for our wrongdoing, we lack stringent duties to respond to it. And hence, no such duties can justify punishing wrongdoers. So if we are to justify criminal justice institutions, which publicly blame and punish wrongdoers for what they have done, we must address sceptical arguments against the idea that we incur duties as a result of acting wrongly.

As we have already begun to see, intuitively plausible moral norms that govern interpersonal relationships are sensitive to responsibility for wrongdoing. As common-sense morality has it, if X is responsible for wronging Y, it is apt for Y to resent X and to blame X for his wrongdoing. Y might justly demand of X that X apologize for his wrongdoing and compensate Y for the harm that his wrongdoing has caused. And, at least in the case of serious wrongdoing, it is apt for Y or others to punish X for his wrongful conduct, either through social sanctions or, in some cases, state sanctions. Let us call these norms 'social responsibility norms'.

Investigations into free will and responsibility typically aim to investigate whether these norms, or some subset of them, are compatible with the kind of free will (if any) that we have by answering two questions. First, in what way, if at all, are any of our actions free? Second, to what extent can common-sense norms of social morality be vindicated in the light of the kind of freedom we have?

The norms that have typically been the target of these investigations are sometimes thought to depend on what is called 'basic desert'.[1] For example, it is asked whether wrongdoers can basically deserve blame, resentment, or punishment for their wrongdoing given the kind of freedom they have. It is not always clear, in these debates, what interlocutors mean by basic desert.[2]

Here is a minimal account of desert: if X deserves some outcome, O, it is non-instrumentally valuable that X gets, or is given, O. Given this idea of desert, the aim of investigations into free will and responsibility is to discover whether blaming,

[1] For some examples, see D K Nelkin *Making Sense of Freedom and Responsibility* (Oxford: OUP, 2011) 2–3; D Pereboom *Free Will, Agency, and Meaning in Life* (Oxford: OUP, 2014) 2; C Sartorio *Causation and Free Will* (Oxford: OUP, 2016) 7.

[2] This complaint is also made in M McKenna *Conversation and Responsibility* (Oxford: OUP, 2012) 120. Some progress has been made, though, by drawing distinctions between attribution and the imposition of costs. See, for example, G Watson 'Two Faces of Responsibility' in G Watson *Agency and Answerability: Selected Essays* (Oxford: OUP, 2004); Nelkin *Making Sense of Freedom and Responsibility*, ch 2.

resenting, and punishing wrongdoers for their wrongdoing can be non-instrumentally valuable, given the kind of freedom that we have.

Though the question whether we have basic desert is important, the broad set of social responsibility norms, and the most important social institutions that affect people's life chances, including the criminal justice system, need not depend on desert. They might be supported by the fact, if it is a fact, that responsibility makes a difference to how people who are otherwise equally placed are treated. Responsibility for wrongdoing might affect the rights that people have, and that might affect how they may treat each other, without relying on the idea that it is non-instrumentally valuable that they are treated in these ways.

For example, if a person has lost certain rights as a result of being responsible for her wrongdoing, she may be liable to be harmed for the sake of a certain goal, even if it is intrinsically bad that she is harmed. Doubts about free will would have much more profound implications if wrongdoers could not lose rights, or victims and others gain rights, as a result of responsibility for wrongdoing.

The duty view of punishment is a member of a family of views about social institutions that depends on our rights, and not on desert. In the previous chapter, we saw that one way in which a person can lose a right against being harmed in service of an end has to do with that person's duties. If the person has a duty to serve a certain end at a certain cost, and certain conditions of enforceability are fulfilled, inflicting the cost on her in service of the end does not wrong her.

Showing that wrongdoers can lose rights in this way relies on the idea that they incur obligations to further the relevant goals through wrongdoing. Thus, a central aim of a theory of responsibility that has implications for central social institutions, such as the criminal justice system, is to show that people can be responsible for wrongdoing in a way that gives rise to the relevant duties.

We might call the general set of norms that govern the conduct of wrongdoers in response to their wrongdoing 'personal practical responsibility norms'. These norms are personal in that they govern the way wrongdoers ought to respond to their own conduct because of their responsibility for it. They are practical in that they are concerned with action or the disposition to act.

Those interested in free will and responsibility have paid relatively little attention to these norms.[3] Discussions of free will and responsibility typically consider social responsibility norms directly—for example, norms governing blame, or resentment, or practices that hold them responsible as part of a conversational process—without directing their attention first to the responses that it is appropriate for responsible wrongdoers to make to their own wrongdoing.[4]

I aim to show that personal practical responsibility norms are compatible with determinism. That is, I aim to show that when compatibilist conditions of responsibility are met, wrongdoers have distinctive reasons to respond to their wrongdoing. That will

[3] That is not to say that they have been ignored altogether. For an important contribution to our understanding of them, see L Radzik *Making Amends: Atonement in Morality, Law, and Politics* (Oxford: OUP, 2009).

[4] In the philosophy of punishment, Antony Duff has long emphasized the importance of holding others responsible in a communicative process to the idea of being responsible. See, most importantly, *Punishment, Communication, and Community* (Oxford: OUP, 2001), but also *Answering for Crime: Responsibility and Liability in the Criminal Law* (Oxford: Hart, 2007). More recently, Michael McKenna has developed a conversational account of moral responsibility in *Conversation and Responsibility*.

provide a general reason to doubt the challenge that responsibility sceptics might make to the argument for criminal punishment outlined in the previous chapter.

There are many different sceptical arguments. I restrict myself to showing that one argument that has been mounted against compatibilism does not undermine these norms—Derk Pereboom's four-case manipulation argument.[5] However, this argument is widely regarded as one of the most powerful arguments against compatibilism.[6] Furthermore, given that this argument goes to the heart of what many people find troubling about compatibilism, responding to it will also do a great deal to vindicate the compatibility of personal practical responsibility norms with determinism. I also show how my response to this argument helps to vindicate the permissibility of harming wrongdoers to serve certain protective ends in virtue of their wrongdoing.

I proceed as follows. Section I outlines Pereboom's four-case manipulation argument. In Sections II and III, I question the force of Pereboom's argument. Section II tentatively offers a soft-line response to Pereboom. In Section III, I argue that even if this soft-line response fails, it paves the way for a hard-line response. In Section IV, I show that even if Pereboom's argument is successful in undermining basic desert, it is not successful in undermining personal practical responsibility. In Section V, I offer reasons to think that personal practical responsibility helps to vindicate the case for deterrent punishment that I have offered in the previous chapter and elsewhere.

I. Pereboom's Four-Case Manipulation Argument

Roughly, if determinism is true, the state of the world prior to our existence, in conjunction with the causal laws that govern it, makes inevitable everything that subsequently occurs, including all of our actions. Compatibilists claim that responsibility is compatible with determinism. They claim that people are responsible for their actions if they fulfil certain conditions that we can call 'compatibilist conditions of responsibility'.

Compatibilists disagree about what these conditions are—for example, whether responsibility depends on control over our actions, or the ability to do otherwise in a compatibilist sense, or on endorsing or valuing the desires that cause the action, or on an action being reflective of the agent's character. We need not decide which proposal is best. Pereboom aims to show that responsibility cannot be vindicated when a very wide range of conditions that compatibilists deem sufficient for responsibility are mutually satisfied. Let me simply stipulate that by 'compatibilist conditions of responsibility' I refer to the best compatibilist proposal without making progress on what proposal is best.

Here is Pereboom's argument in a nutshell. A person can fulfil all plausible compatibilist conditions of responsibility and yet be manipulated by external agents to act wrongly, where the manipulation makes it certain that the person will act wrongly. Intuitively, such a person is not responsible for her wrongdoing. There is no important moral difference between such manipulation cases and cases where a similar set of causal influences determine the person's wrongful action but the person is not

[5] The argument was originally developed in D Pereboom 'Determinism *al Dente*' (1995) 29 *Noûs* 21. It is best known from D Pereboom *Living Without Free Will* (Cambridge: CUP, 2001), but it has been importantly refined and updated in various papers, culminating in *Free Will, Agency, and Meaning in Life*, ch 4. I will consider the presentation in this latter book.

[6] For example, in his excellent book *Free Will and Luck* (Oxford: OUP, 2006), 193–4, Alfred Mele suggests that a related manipulation argument is all that prevents him from fully endorsing compatibilism.

manipulated. If determinism is true, all wrongful action is determined by such causal influences. Hence, there is no difference between manipulation cases and all standard cases of wrongful conduct. Hence, if determinism is true no one is responsible for her wrongful conduct.[7]

Pereboom develops this argument by beginning with the most powerful manipulation case. He then moves through a series of cases where, he suggests, each case is shown to be relevantly similar to the previous case, until we arrive at ordinary everyday cases of wrongdoing. If there are no relevant moral differences across this series of cases, and he is right that the person is not responsible in the first case, no one is responsible for wrongdoing.

Here is the first case:

> *Case 1*: A team of neuroscientists has the ability to manipulate Plum's neural states at any time by radio-like technology. In this particular case, they do so by pressing a button just before he begins to reason about his situation, which they know will deterministically result in his decision to kill White. Plum would not have killed White had the neuroscientists not intervened, since his reasoning would then not have been sufficiently egoistic to produce this decision. But at the same time, Plum's effective first-order desire to kill White conforms to his second-order desires. In addition, his process of deliberation from which the decision results is reason-responsive; in particular, this type of process would have resulted in Plum's refraining from deciding to kill White in certain situations in which his reasons were different. His reasoning is consistent with his character because it is frequently egoistic and sometimes strongly so. Still, it is not in general exclusively egoistic, because he sometimes regulates his behaviour by moral reasons, especially when the egoistic reasons are relatively weak. Plum is also not constrained to act as he does, for he does not act because of an irresistible desire—the neuroscientists do not induce a desire of this sort.[8]

Case 1 is intentionally designed so that Plum satisfies familiar compatibilist conditions of responsibility proposed by David Hume (it is in character), Harry Frankfurt[9] (conformity of first-order desires to second-order desires), John Martin Fisher and Mark Ravizza[10] (Plum is reason-responsive), R Jay Wallace (he has the general capacity to conform to moral reasons), and Alfred Mele[11] and Ishtiyaque Haji[12] (he has the capacity reflectively to revise and develop his moral character and commitments over time). Presumably, we could add others.

Furthermore, this version of *Case 1* is designed to avoid a powerful compatibilist reply that was offered to an earlier version of the case in which the neuroscientists '"locally" manipulate Plum to undertake the process of reasoning by which his desires are brought about and modified, directly producing his every state from moment to moment'.[13] The neuroscientists, in the earlier version, seem to undermine Plum's agency altogether. Compatibilists have rightly objected that a person is responsible for her actions only if her agency is not undermined in this way.[14]

[7] For a related argument, see Mele *Free Will and Luck* 189–94. Mele finds this argument against compatibilism less decisive than Pereboom.

[8] *Free Will, Agency, and Meaning in Life*, 76–7.

[9] Frankfurt's most important essays are in *The Importance of What We Care About* (Cambridge: CUP, 1988).

[10] *Responsibility and Control: A Theory of Moral Responsibility* (Cambridge: CUP, 1998).

[11] Mele's position is subtle, and not adequately captured here. See *Autonomous Agents: From Self-Control to Autonomy* (Oxford: OUP, 2001); *Free Will and Luck*.

[12] See *Moral Appraisability* (Oxford: OUP, 1998).

[13] *Living Without Free Will*, 112–3.

[14] For somewhat related criticisms, see L R Baker 'Moral Responsibility without Libertarianism' (2006) 40 *Noûs* 307; K Demetriou 'The Soft-Line Solution to Pereboom's Four-Case Argument' (2010) 88 *Australasian Journal of Philosophy* 595; J M Fischer 'Responsibility and Manipulation' in

In the new *Case 1*, the interventions of the neuroscientists do not undermine Plum's agency in this way. Pereboom supports this by noting that whether we act egoistically or not may depend on a range of influences. For example, we may be more inclined to behave egoistically if our team has lost a game, or less inclined if we have won a prize.[15] Agency is not undermined by these facts. Pereboom's neuroscientists intervene in a comparable way, and hence do not undermine agency.

Although the intuition that Plum is not responsible in *Case 1* is weaker than that we have about his original *Case 1*, it is reasonably powerful. Pereboom concludes that compatibilist conditions of responsibility are insufficient for moral responsibility, and that causal determination of Plum's action explains why Plum's responsibility is undermined.

Pereboom then compares:

> *Case 2*: Plum is just like an ordinary human being, except that a team of neuroscientists programmed him at the beginning of his life so that his reasoning is often but not always egoistic (as in *Case 1*), and at times strongly so, with the intended consequence that in his current circumstances he is causally determined to engage in the egoistic reasons-responsive process of deliberation and to have the set of first and second-order desires that result in his decision to kill White. Plum has the general ability to regulate his actions by moral reasons, but in his circumstances, due to the strongly egoistic nature of his deliberative reasoning, he is causally determined to make his decision to kill. Yet he does not decide as he does because of an irresistible desire. The neural realization of his reasoning process and of his decision is exactly the same as it is in *Case 1* (although their causal histories are different).

Pereboom claims that Plum does not seem morally responsible for his decision. He also plausibly argues that it would be unprincipled to claim that *Case 1* and *Case 2* are different because of the difference in the time between the neuroscientists' intervention and Plum's homicidal decision.

Pereboom then claims that there is no important responsibility-relevant difference between *Case 2* and:

> *Case 3*: Plum is an ordinary human being, except that the training practices of his community causally determined the nature of his deliberative reasoning processes so that they are frequently but not exclusively rationally egoistic (the resulting nature of his deliberative reasoning processes are exactly as they are in *Cases 1* and *2*). This training was completed before he developed the ability to prevent or alter these practices. Due to the aspect of his character produced by this training, in his present circumstances he is causally determined to engage in the strongly egoistic reasons-responsive process of deliberation and to have the first and second-order desires that issue in his decision to kill White. While Plum does have the general ability to regulate his behaviour by moral reasons, in virtue of this aspect of his character and his circumstances he is causally determined to make his immoral decision, although he does not decide as he does due to an irresistible desire. The neural realization of his deliberative reasoning process and of the decision is just as it is in *Cases 1* and *2*.

Pereboom suggests that the fact that others causally determine Plum's actions in both *Cases 2* and *3* explains the verdict that *Plum* is not responsible in either case.

Case 3 is much more like our ordinary circumstances. In *Case 3*, like *Cases 1* and *2*, intentional human action causes Plum to act egoistically. But it is worth emphasizing a difference between *Cases 2* and *3*. In *Case 2*, the neuroscientists intend Plum to kill

J M Fischer *My Way: Essays on Moral Responsibility* (Oxford: OUP, 2006); A Mele *Free Will and Luck* 138–44.

[15] *Free Will, Agency, and Meaning in Life*, 76.

White. In *Case 3*, those whose training causes Plum to kill White do not intend Plum to kill White.

He then suggests that there is no responsibility-relevant difference between *Case 3* and:

Case 4: Everything that happens in our universe is causally determined by virtue of its past states together with the laws of nature. Plum is an ordinary human being, raised in normal circumstances, and again his reasoning processes are frequently but not exclusively egoistic, and sometimes strongly so (as in *Cases 1–3*). His decision to kill White issues from his strongly egoistic but reasons-responsive process of deliberation, and he has the specified first and second-order desires. The neural realization of Plum's reasoning process and decision is exactly as it is in *Cases 1–3*; he has the general ability to grasp, apply, and regulate his actions by moral reasons, and it is not because of an irresistible desire that he decides to kill.

If causal determinism is true, *Case 4* is relevantly similar to any wrongful action we perform. Pereboom argues that as there is no responsibility-relevant difference between *Cases 1* and *2*, *Cases 2* and *3*, and *Cases 3* and *4*, there is no responsibility-relevant difference between *Cases 1* and *4*. As Plum is not morally responsible in *Case 1*, he is not morally responsible in *Case 4*. *Case 4* is like everyday cases where we seem to be responsible for wrongdoing. He concludes that the compatibilist case for moral responsibility fails.

II. Does Manipulation Matter?

To distinguish different responses to Pereboom's argument, consider this schematic presentation:

1) Suppose that X manipulates D to perform some wrongful action, *v*, by introducing some external event, *e*, in order that D *v*s where otherwise D would not have *v*ed, and that determines D's *v*ing. Then D is not responsible for *v*ing even if compatibilist conditions of responsibility are satisfied.
2) It makes no difference to whether D is responsible for *v*ing whether X causes *e* with the intention that D *v*s or no person causes *e*.
3) If determinism is true, for all actions, there is some *e*-like event that causes D to act where otherwise D would not have acted.
4) Therefore we are not responsible for any of our actions.

Both hard-line and soft-line responses have been mounted to this argument. A soft-line response accepts premise 1) and thus accepts Pereboom's diagnosis that Plum is not responsible for killing White in *Case 1*. Soft-liners challenge the implications of this judgement by exploring differences between manipulation cases and standard cases of responsibility. A hard-line response challenges premise 1). A hard-liner thus claims that Plum is responsible for killing White in *Case 1*. This section offers a soft-line response; the next offers a hard-line response. These responses are general—they are available to compatibilists who defend the relevance of responsibility across the board, whether or not they are friends of desert.

Before mounting this soft-line response, a forewarning. In Section IV, I will offer my overall diagnosis of the best response to Pereboom. The soft-line response offered here, I there argue, should lead us to conclude that there are important responsibility-relevant differences between *Case 1* and *Case 4*. However, these differences are insufficient completely to undermine Plum's responsibility in *Case 1*. Hard-liners are thus right to conclude that if compatibilist conditions of responsibility are fulfilled, agents have personal practical responsibility for their wrongdoing even if they are manipulated. Manipulation weakens, rather than destroys, responsibility.

At first blush, premise 2) seems secure. Whether a person is responsible for her wrongdoing depends on there being a proper relationship between the wrongful conduct and the person. At least in the central case, the relationship is between the wrongdoing and the facts that are central to autonomous agency (if, indeed, we are autonomous agents). These include our capacities to make choices, evaluate our actions, develop our plans, and so on.

But whether this relationship is sufficiently strong to make a person responsible for her conduct cannot depend on whether events that are external to her, and that influence her actions, are produced by other people or occur naturally. Otherwise, whether an act is attributable to a person *qua* agent can depend on facts that are external to the relationship between the act and the person. This may be why Pereboom believes there to be no difference between *Case 1* and a case where all else is equal, but the event that the neuroscientists produce in *Case 1* is produced by a machine or a force field rather than by neuroscientists.[16] Call such a case *Case 1**.

Admittedly, whether an action can be attributed to a person *qua* agent cannot depend on whether she was caused to act by other people or by other events. But there may be more to responsibility than attribution. Suppose that a person is responsible for acting in a certain way only if certain responses to her wrongful conduct are apt. If there is such a thing as basic desert, these responses might include the wrongdoer feeling guilty. If not, such responses might be forward looking—for example, being disposed to apologize or to correct the harm that she has caused. Whether such responses are apt might depend on facts that are independent of attribution. The aptness of certain responses to one's conduct might depend on the implications of those responses being apt. The aptness of such responses might be undermined if certain facts make their aptness objectionable.

Why might manipulation undermine the aptness of responding to one's wrongdoing? Let us say that it is apt to respond to an act if that act is 'response-worthy'. To claim that an act is response-worthy does not imply that such responses ought always to be made all things considered. It does imply that there is a reason to respond.

Now suppose that my manipulated wrongdoing is response-worthy as long as I fulfil compatibilist conditions of responsibility for that wrongdoing. This implies that I ought to be disposed to respond to manipulated wrongdoing in some of the ways outlined above. Having such a disposition objectionably places my practical reasoning under the control of those who are capable of manipulating me. This provides a reason against the aptness of me responding to my manipulated wrongdoing.

Let me describe the kind of control that others have over me if my manipulated wrongdoing is response-worthy. Manipulators control our conduct. If manipulated wrongdoing is response-worthy, manipulators also control our dispositions to respond to our conduct. Being disposed to respond to my manipulated wrongdoing

[16] See *Free Will, Agency, and Meaning in Life*, 79. Alfred Mele agrees. See *Free Will and Luck* 141–2 and also *Autonomous Agents: From Self-Control to Autonomy*, 168–9. Neither Pereboom nor Mele supply any argument why there is no difference between cases involving intentional manipulation and otherwise identical cases involving non-intentional events, so in attributing the argument of the previous paragraph to them I am only speculating about their reasoning.

allows manipulators to determine not only what I do but also my response to what I have done.

I have good reason to avoid manipulation. If I am not disposed to respond to my manipulated wrongdoing, I avoid others manipulating those dispositions. If I ought not to be so disposed, manipulated wrongdoing is not response-worthy. And if manipulated wrongdoing is not response-worthy, I am not responsible for it. Hence, there is a responsibility-relevant difference between *Case 1* and *Case 1**.

Ideally, at this point, the analysis should be extended to a wider range of cases. In *Case 1* the neuroscientists intend Plum to kill White. We might consider cases where the neuroscientists know that Plum will, or might, kill White but do not intend him to do so, as well as cases where the neuroscientists have no reason to suspect that their actions will cause Plum to kill White. I lack the space to evaluate such cases. I simply report that the objection to being under the control of others seems weaker in the case where the neuroscientists know but do not intend Plum to kill White, and much weaker still if the neuroscientists have no reason to believe that Plum will kill White.

Here is an objection: this argument confuses whether a person is responsible for her wrongdoing with the aptness of her holding herself responsible for it. To support this objection, note that the aptness of another person holding me responsible for my wrongdoing can be undermined without casting doubt on my responsibility.

This is true in cases of a lack of standing. For example, if you are complicit in my wrongdoing it is not apt for you to hold me responsible for my wrongdoing, at least if you do not hold yourself responsible at the same time. Similarly, hypocrisy can make holding another responsible inapt.[17] But lack of standing has no implications for my responsibility. Your lack of standing to hold me responsible does not imply that I am not responsible. Whether I am responsible and whether it is apt for you to hold me responsible thus come apart. Similarly, it might be argued that even if Plum's manipulation undermines the aptness of holding him responsible for what he has done, it has no bearing on his responsibility. To claim otherwise confuses holding responsible with being responsible.

In reply, in cases of loss of standing, the unwarranted response is local to the particular person who has lost standing. It is apt for others, including the wrongdoer herself, to hold the wrongdoer responsible. In cases of manipulation, though, it is inapt for anyone to hold the wrongdoer responsible, for to do so would compound the ways in which the wrongdoer is a victim of manipulation.

Another response: some might argue that this soft-line response, even if it is successful, shows only that it is inapt for Plum to respond to his wrongful conduct. It does not show that it is inapt for others to respond to his wrongful conduct, for example, by blaming him.

In reply, interpersonal responsibility norms plausibly depend on personal responsibility norms. Here is why. Interpersonal responsibility norms are typically addressed to agents; blaming, for example, addresses wrongdoers. And even where they are not, they are apt only if the relevant address would have been warranted—I can blame a person after they are dead, but this means that addressing the person in a certain way would be warranted were they around. If it is inapt for wrongdoers to hold themselves responsible for their wrongdoing, addressing wrongdoers in this way is inapt. Hence,

[17] See, further, V Tadros 'Poverty and Criminal Responsibility' (2009) 43 *Journal of Value Inquiry* 391.

if personal responsibility norms do not apply in manipulation cases, neither do interpersonal responsibility norms.

A final response: even if a person's responsibility can turn on whether he is manipulated, manipulation cannot affect whether a person acts freely, or exercises free will.[18] In reply, I have acknowledged that attribution cannot depend on manipulation. Freedom, though, does not have a single meaning. There are senses of freedom where manipulation makes no difference to how free a person is and others where it does make such a difference. Perhaps free will, in one core sense, is not sensitive to whether the person acting has been manipulated. If Plum cannot claim that he did not choose freely in *Case 1**, on this view, he cannot claim that he did not choose freely in *Case 1* either.

We are interested in whether Plum has the kind of freedom required for responsibility. If we have a special interest in not being under the control of others, there is a sense of freedom that depends on whether we are under such control. Indeed, it is common to claim that the extent of my freedom depends on whether others interfere with me. It is plausible, then, that the kind of freedom required for responsibility is eroded in *Case 1* but not in *Case 1**.

To conclude, it is plausible that responsibility is a response-dependent idea: a person's responsibility is explained by the aptness of making certain responses to her conduct. As manipulation can undermine the aptness of these responses quite generally, there is a responsibility-relevant difference between *Case 1* and *Case 1**. It follows that Pereboom's argument fails.

III. Hard-Lines for the Manipulated

Suppose that the soft-line response just offered fails because responsibility is not a response-dependent notion. On this view, the aptness of holding people responsible depends on their being responsible rather than the other way around. Hard-liners accept that there is no responsibility-relevant difference between *Case 1* and *Case 4*. They claim that Plum is responsible in *Case 1*.

If soft-line responses fail, we must endorse a counterintuitive conclusion about either *Case 1* or *Case 4*. The question is whether Pereboom is right that we should endorse the counterintuitive conclusion about *Case 4* rather than *Case 1*. Hard-liners have noted that Pereboom's four-case manipulation argument can be run backwards. We have a powerful intuition that Plum is responsible in *Case 4*. If Pereboom is right that there is no responsibility-relevant difference between *Case 4* and *Case 1*, and this intuition is right, Plum is responsible in *Case 1*.[19]

We can make progress in assessing the hard-line response by distinguishing two features of intuitions that might determine their force in philosophical argument: their initial power and their reliability. The initial power of an intuition about a case measures how compelled we are to endorse a certain verdict about it prior to investigating causes of that intuition that cast doubt on its reliability. I call this the *initial* power of our intuition, for the power of an intuition may alter when it is explained. The

[18] Carolina Sartorio, for example, thinks it clear that manipulation cannot make this kind of difference in the relevant cases. See *Causation and Free Will*, 161.

[19] See M McKenna 'A Hard-line Reply to Pereboom's Four-case Argument' (2008) 77 *Philosophy and Phenomenological Research* 142; 'Resisting the Manipulation Argument: A Hard-Liner Takes It on the Chin' (2014) 89 *Philosophy and Phenomenological Research* 467; D Nelkin *Making Sense of Freedom and Responsibility* 54–8.

reliability of an intuition measures the extent to which our initial intuitions are trustworthy by examining explanations for those intuitions. If our initial intuitions are explained by facts that ought not to increase our confidence that the initially intuitive verdict is true, we have reason to reject those intuitions.

My initial intuition that Plum is responsible in *Case 4* is significantly more powerful than my initial intuition that Plum is not responsible in *Case 1*. Some people's intuitions might be shaken by noticing that it is a matter of chance whether some event causes Plum to act on his egoistic or his moral reasons. This fact alone does not shake my confidence in Plum's responsibility in *Case 4*. I take it that others share this intuition, although some may initially be more inclined than I am to judge that Plum is not responsible in *Case 1*. Later, I will support the judgement that Plum is responsible in both cases, though to different degrees.

Now focus on the reliability of our intuitions. Pereboom argues that the intuitive judgement that Plum is responsible in *Case 4*, even if it is powerful, is unreliable. Pereboom follows Benedict de Spinoza's diagnosis of the intuition that we are free. In everyday life we assume responsibility in the basic desert sense, Pereboom suggests, because we are unable fully to grasp causal determinism. The process of consciously deliberating and deciding makes our place in the causal universe less apparent to us.[20]

This idea supports Pereboom's argument that we ought to begin with *Case 1*, and assess our intuitions about *Case 4* in the light of it. *Case 1* brightly illuminates the compatibilist proposal that we are responsible for our actions if we fulfil compatibilist conditions of responsibility even if our actions are fully causally determined. Reflecting on *Case 1* helps us to grasp the way in which our agency, on the compatibilist proposal, is fully causally determined by events that we cannot be responsible for.

I agree that the ordinary experience of deliberating and deciding makes our place in the causal universe difficult to grasp, and that the reliability of our intuitions about *Case 4* to some degree.[21] But Pereboom's argument relies on the claim that our initial intuitions about *Case 4* are less reliable than our initial intuitions about *Case 1*.

There are also reasons to think that our intuitions about *Case 1* are unreliable that have their source in the considerations we explored in the context of the soft-line response offered in Section II. Even if that response fails, it has a bearing on the reliability of our initial intuition about *Case 1*.

Even if the inaptness of holding a person responsible does not undermine responsibility, we recoil from the idea that manipulation by evil scientists affects the burdens of responsibility. This plausibly explains why we are inclined to think Plum is not responsible in *Case 1*.

And there is a further reason to doubt our initial intuition about *Case 1*. We judge Plum not to be responsible in part because we hold the neuroscientists primarily responsible for his conduct. If Pereboom's Spinozist argument is valid our intuitions about their responsibility are confounded, as the causes of their decision to manipulate Plum are obscured. *Case 1* thus confounds our grasp of the idea that in a deterministic world *everyone's* actions are fully causally determined. We contrast Plum's responsibility with the neuroscientists' responsibility, and find the former comparatively weak.[22]

[20] Pereboom *Free Will, Agency, and Meaning in Life*, 90 and 92, drawing on B Spinoza *Ethics* (London: Penguin, 1996).

[21] See also V Tadros *The Ends of Harm: The Moral Foundations of Criminal Law* (Oxford: OUP, 2011) 63–6; K Lippert-Rasmussen 'To Serve and Protect: *The Ends of Harm* by Victor Tadros' (2015) 9 *Criminal Law and Philosophy* 49; V Tadros 'Answers' (2015) 9 *Criminal Law and Philosophy* 73.

[22] For a related argument, see Sartorio *Causation and Free Will*, 167–70.

It is tempting to add further neuroscientists to ensure that our intuitions about these neuroscientists are not confounded in this way. But, of course, that would only push the problem back further.

Suppose that we are presented with two alternatives: either both the neuroscientists and Plum are responsible for White's death or no one is responsible for White's death. Many will conclude that the neuroscientists and Plum are responsible for White's death. The idea that no one is responsible for White's death is hard to swallow. Our initial intuition about *Case 1* might result from us being distracted by a third alternative: that the neuroscientists and not Plum are responsible for White's death. This alternative, though, is irrelevant to the debate and ought to be excluded.

In order to evaluate whether Plum is responsible in *Case 1*, then, we are best to begin with *Case 1**, in which Plum's act is not caused by intentional human intervention. But our initial intuition that Plum is not responsible in *Case 1**, considered without *Case 1*, is much less powerful than our initial intuition about *Case 1*. Pereboom's response to hard-liners thus fails.

IV. What is it Apt to Respond to?

I have found general reasons to doubt Pereboom's manipulation argument. Either a soft-line response succeeds, or if it fails it helps to support a hard-line response. In this section I argue that Plum is responsible in all four cases, even if his responsibility comes in varying degrees. I focus on personal practical responsibility rather than desert, for that is central to the argument for punishment offered in the previous chapter.

Personal practical responsibility is concerned with the responses that we ought to make to our wrongdoing when we are responsible for it. A compatibilist view of personal practical responsibility is that such responses are apt if compatibilist conditions of responsibility are fulfilled.

My argument begins with a more general claim about the reasons we have to respond to certain events regardless of responsibility. These reasons, I claim, depend in part on our involvement in those events independently of responsibility. In the light of this, I explain why compatibilist conditions of responsibility make a difference to the strength and quality of such reasons.

i) Responding without responsibility

We typically have powerful reasons to respond to the harm we cause even when we are not responsible for it. These reasons are distinct in strength and quality when compared with bystanders.

Consider:

> *Lorry*: Dave is sitting in a stationary lorry. As a result of a completely involuntary and unforeseeable muscle spasm, he presses the accelerator when Veronica, a little girl, is in front of the lorry. She is badly injured. Xavier, a stranger to Dave and Veronica, sees this occur.

One question is whether Dave has a stronger reason than Xavier to assist Veronica. I suggest that he does. Xavier has a duty to assist Veronica if he could do so at little cost to himself, and no one else would help her. Dave's reason is more powerful. To see this, suppose that many other injured little girls are in the vicinity. Xavier has no more reason to assist Veronica than any of these other little girls. This is not true of Dave.

It is also intuitive that Dave has a more stringent duty than Xavier to compensate Veronica for the injury that she has suffered. To support this view, notice that a person's duty to avert a threat intuitively depends on whether she is causally involved in the threat, whether or not she is responsible for posing it. For example, a person who is about to fall on another, intuition tells us, has a more stringent duty than a stranger to ensure that the threat is not realized.[23] There is a close relationship between our duties not to cause harm and our duties to compensate others. It follows that our duties to compensate depend on whether we have caused harm.

The aptness of these personal practical responses to causal involvement in harming or threatening others is related to our response to the unforeseen harmful consequences of our actions. Bernard Williams called that response 'agent-regret'. In Williams's example, unlike *Lorry*, the little girl is killed as a result of the driver's action, but the consequence of this action is simply bad luck and not a result of fault on his part (*Lorry 2*). The driver in *Lorry 2*, Williams claimed, responds to the fact that the result would not have occurred had he acted differently.[24] There is a question whether the characteristic emotional response to such actions is best characterized as a form of regret, or rather dismay.[25] Whatever the right view, neither agent-regret or agent-dismay is apt in *Lorry*, for D was not acting.

Intuition, then, tells us that mere causal involvement in harm to others supplies us with distinctive reasons to respond to that harm. But this intuitive view faces an objection. Whether we are causally involved in the misfortune of others is simply a matter of luck. Isn't it unfair that those who are so involved have more powerful reasons to respond to the harm than those who are not?[26]

The answer relies on a more general claim about our reasons: they depend not simply on the impersonal importance of certain facts, but on the relationship we have to those facts. Whether a certain fact supplies me with a reason depends on the connection between that fact and me. Certain facts demand a response in virtue of their deep connection to me. Other facts are less connected to me, and thus do not demand such a response.

Dave has a reason to respond to the harm that he has caused Veronica that bystanders lack because Veronica's harm is importantly connected to Dave in a way that is not true of strangers. This relies on the idea that there is an ethically significant sense of 'Dave's life' that is independent of Dave's acts. Unlike Xavier, Dave cannot claim that Veronica's injury is nothing to do with him. He is involved. The question is how to respond to his involvement.

Now recall the objection that if Dave has reasons to respond to Veronica's injuries that Xavier lacks, whether Dave has such reasons is a matter of luck. If Dave is worse off because he has such reasons, Dave might be considered unlucky to have them. Dave is pressed to bear the burdens of responding that Xavier lacks. However, excluding such luck-dependent inequalities comes at a price. All things considered, we should

[23] For somewhat related views, see F M Kamm *Creation and Abortion: A Study in Moral and Legal Philosophy* (Oxford: OUP, 1992) 47–50; V Tadros *The Ends of Harm*, ch 11.

[24] 'Moral Luck' in B Williams *Moral Luck* (Cambridge: CUP, 1981) 27–9.

[25] For the latter view, see D Jacobson 'Regret, Agency, and Error' in D Shoemaker *Oxford Studies in Agency and Responsibility* vol. 1 (Oxford: OUP, 2013).

[26] The view that luck undermines moral responsibility is defended most fully in N Levy *Hard Luck: How Luck Undermines Free Will & Moral Responsibility* (Oxford: OUP, 2011). Compare, also, Samuel Scheffler's discussion of responsibilities that can arise through special relationships in 'Relationships and Responsibilities' in S Scheffler *Boundaries and Allegiances: Problems of Justice and Responsibility in Liberal Thought* (Oxford: OUP, 2001).

not regret the fact that we have different reasons for action depending on our circumstances. We should value the fact that our lives are distinctive in this way. One way in which our lives are distinctive is in virtue of the special reasons that we have to respond to certain facts—those that are important in shaping our lives and the context within which those lives are lived. A life in which only our choices supply us with distinctive reasons is less rich and meaningful than one in which we respond to a broader range of facts that are connected to us.

Does Dave have a reason to prefer it that someone else harmed Veronica, so that the other person rather than him would face the burden that he faces? Perhaps he does. But his distinctive reasons persist in the face of this complaint. Mere causal involvement in Veronica's misfortune connects him to Veronica. He may regret this fact, but he ought not to regret the overall idea that we do not control all of our obligations. To do so would undermine the many ways in which our lives are ethically distinct. And it is valuable that our lives are ethically distinct.

To support this view further, consider a broader range of events that we are not responsible for, but that demand a response in virtue of the connection that they have to us. First, suppose that my sperm is secretly taken from me and is used to create a child. The child makes contact with me, claiming that I am her father. The child demands more than that I acknowledge the biological connection between us. She demands that I acknowledge that a certain kind of relationship with me is possible—a father–child relationship. It is apt to foster this relationship, even if I am not required to do so. Compare a child who is completely unrelated to me. If this second child demands that I acknowledge the aptness of a father–child relationship between her and me, I will meet her only with confusion.

Second, suppose that my father, now dead, tortured a person. These events occurred before I was born. It seems apt for me to apologize for my father's behaviour. Children of wrongdoers sometimes feel responsible or guilty for the wrongdoing of their parents. This response seems to many confused, and I agree. But it is not confused to think that one has distinctive reasons to respond to the wrongful acts of one's parents, even if they occurred before one was born. These distinctive reasons arise simply because of the relationship that one has to one's parents. The confusion that there is in children of wrongdoers' feelings of guilt for the acts of their parents is a confusion between being responsible for their parents' wrongdoing and having distinctive reasons to respond to that wrongdoing.

Even if we are unlucky to have these reasons we should not aim to eliminate this kind of bad luck by rejecting the special reasons that we have to respond to such facts. To do so would be to reduce the things that have special significance to us to those that we are responsible for. A life that is distinctive only in that way is an attenuated life.

ii) The difference that responsibility makes

This idea illuminates how we should assess compatibilism when we focus on the personal responses we ought to make to our wrongdoing. The right question to ask is whether the strength and quality of our reasons to respond to bad events that we are causally involved in depends on whether we have fulfilled compatibilist conditions of responsibility. In assessing this, we should consider whether determinism undermines any intuitive differences that we find.

First, consider whether our reasons to respond to harm if we are causally involved are distinct and more powerful if we fulfil compatibilist conditions of responsibility than if we are causally involved in harming others, but do not fulfil compatibilist conditions of responsibility. I believe that these conditions make a difference in the quality and strength of such reasons.

Before I defend the view that this is so, let me emphasize a central feature of my approach to responsibility. The kind of compatibilism that I defend is comparative—it investigates whether fulfilling compatibilist conditions of responsibility makes a difference rather than supporting an all things considered assessment whether the person is responsible or not.

This comparative approach is attractive, given that responsibility is a scalar notion. Furthermore, it allows us to take into consideration facts that erode our confidence in responsibility without implying complete scepticism. For example, I noted that Pereboom's Spinozist challenge to the reliability of our intuitions about responsibility in standard non-manipulation cases is convincing. This challenge is insufficient to support general responsibility scepticism, but it may have implications for the strength and importance of all claims about responsibility. Furthermore, it may support the kind of desert scepticism that Pereboom defends.[27]

To investigate whether compatibilist conditions of responsibility are difference-making, compare pairs of cases where other things are equal, but compatibilist conditions of responsibility are fulfilled in one case but not in the other. We should aim to bring to light as clearly as possible the fact that the acts in these cases are fully determined. And, for reasons outlined in the previous two sections, our cases should not involve manipulation.

First, let me fully describe a case considered earlier:

*Case 1**: A series of naturally produced imperceptible electromagnetic flashes deterministically result in Plum's decision to kill White. Plum would not have killed White had these shocks not occurred, since his reasoning would then not have been sufficiently egoistic to produce this decision. But at the same time, Plum's effective first-order desire to kill White conforms to his second-order desires. In addition, his process of deliberation from which the decision results is reason-responsive; in particular, this type of process would have resulted in Plum's refraining from deciding to kill White in certain situations in which his reasons were different. His reasoning is consistent with his character because it is frequently egoistic and sometimes strongly so. Still, it is not in general exclusively egoistic, because he sometimes regulates his behaviour by moral reasons, especially when the egoistic reasons are relatively weak. Plum is also not constrained to act as he does, for he does not act because of an irresistible desire—the shocks do not induce a desire of this sort.

One important feature of *Case 1** is that Plum kills White because the imperceptible electromagnetic flashes determine which reasons Plum brings to bear on his decision whether to kill White. In a nearby world where these flashes do not occur, Plum brings different reasons to bear on his decision, and he does not kill White.

Now compare:

Case 5: A series of naturally produced imperceptible electromagnetic flashes deterministically result in Plum killing White. Plum would not have killed White had these shocks not occurred. The killing of White does not result from his reasoning at all. The shocks cause Plum to have muscle spasms that are completely outside Plum's control that result in White being killed.

Plum is causally involved in White's death, but he does not fulfil compatibilist conditions of responsibility.

Our discussion in the previous subsection implies that Plum has more powerful reasons to respond to White's death than do strangers in both *Case 1** and *Case 5*. Our

[27] For my own part, I reject desert in part for this reason, but mainly for independent reasons.

question here is whether Plum has reasons of different strength and quality to respond to White's death in these cases. In Section V I consider the implications of the aptness of such responses for the responses of others.

I suggested earlier that our reasons to respond to facts depend on the connection between our lives and those facts. Different connections make different responses apt. When we act wrongly, and fulfil compatibilist conditions of responsibility, our wrongdoing is central to our lives. And this affects the quality and strength of our responsive reasons.

Compare the reasons that Plum has to respond to White's death in *Case 1** and *Case 5*. The much deeper connection between Plum's life and White's death in *Case 1** gives Plum a much more powerful reason to respond to White's death than in *Case 5*. In *Case 5*, Plum's causal involvement in White's death supplies him with a reason to express to White's family his sorrow at the death. Plum's reasons to respond in *Case 1** though are much more powerful because the death is attributable to Plum as a person. It would be quite inapt in *Case 1** for Plum to send flowers to White's family. Such a gesture trivializes the kind of involvement that he has in the death. The fact that he decided to kill White explains this. He must acknowledge the fact that the death is deeply connected to his failings as a person.

Suppose that Plum in *Case 1** were to claim that the response he owes is no different to that owed in *Case 5* because both actions were produced by electromagnetic flashes that were beyond his control. He would treat the fact that he chose to bring about the death, and his choice reflected his egoism, as unimportant in shaping the response he owes. This is hard to accept. The powerful and distinctive reason that Plum has to respond to White's death in *Case 1**, then, does not evaporate once determinism is brought fully to light. Furthermore, the fact that he would not have acted in this way had the electromagnetic flashes not occurred does not undermine the difference in the response that is owed in *Case 1** and *Case 5*.

Now recall the familiar concern that in a deterministic world Plum is simply unlucky given that his act was determined by the state of the world prior to his existence in conjunction with the full set of causal laws. There is a sense in which this is true. We have good reason, I think, to see wrongdoers as unfortunate in this way.[28] But, as I have already suggested, the fact that we might be lucky or unlucky in having distinctive reasons to respond to certain facts is insufficient to undermine our having those reasons.

This idea seems even more powerful here. Plum may be unlucky in being the kind of person who is inclined to kill in these circumstances. But this does not plausibly threaten his powerful reasons to respond to his deep personal connection to White's death. Reflecting back on one's conduct, and treating it as a special object of concern in one's practical reasoning, is central to an integrated and distinctive life. Noticing that there is a sense in which what we do is a matter of luck does not undermine the importance of this idea.

What, then, should we say about manipulation? Recall *Case 1*. I noted in Section II that there are reasons why it is inapt for Plum to respond in certain ways to his action. Any disposition that he has to respond to his wrongdoing makes him the victim of the control that the neuroscientists exercise over his conduct. But whilst this difference between *Case 1* and *Case 1** is important, and weakens the reasons that Plum has to respond to his conduct, it does not make *Case 1* comparable to *Case 5*. In *Case 1*,

28 See Tadros *The Ends of Harm*, 63–4 for a brief discussion of how we might respond to this kind of misfortune.

Plum's act is attributable to him as a person. In responding to White's family, for example, Plum surely could not deny his deep involvement in White's death. The fact that he was manipulated is insufficiently important for him completely to distance himself from the death he chose to bring about.

Here, then, is my overall diagnosis of the best response to manipulation arguments against liability. Soft-liners are right to reject the claim that there are no important responsibility-relevant differences between *Case 1* and *Case 4*. There is such a difference, and it is important. Nevertheless, hard-liners are right that Plum is, in an important sense, responsible in *Case 1*. Manipulation weakens rather than undermines responsibility when compatibilist conditions of responsibility are fulfilled.

V. Blame

Now let us explore the implications of this argument for criminal justice. The criminal justice system responds to wrongdoing by publicly blaming wrongdoers and punishing them. Can wrongdoers be responsible in a way that vindicates these responses?

In common-sense morality, we make demands of wrongdoers. These demands almost always have a forward-looking dimension. Some of these demands are warranted simply for forward-looking reasons; others have an irreducibly backward-looking dimension. For example, we might demand that a wrongdoer refrain from acting wrongly. We point to her past wrongdoing in expressing this demand, but the reference to the past is not essential to what it is apt to demand. It just provides evidence that making the demand is necessary. The demand appropriately has this content simply because acting in the relevant way is wrong, and the person is likely to act wrongly unless the demand is made.

Other demands have an irreducible backward-looking dimension. I noted earlier that a person who has acted wrongly had a duty to respond in certain ways to her victim—for example, by expressing a deep personal apology or by aiming to rectify the harm that her wrongful conduct has caused. These demands are warranted because wrongdoers incur duties by acting wrongly.

Demanding of wrongdoers that they respond to their wrongdoing is closely related to blame; it might even be thought a kind of blame.[29] Our blaming practices involve many aspects and only some of these can be justified. In order to understand the role of demands in blame, contrast two other familiar accounts. One is that blame expresses resentment.[30] However, blame without resentment is possible. Recall the case where one wrongdoer criticizes another for wrongdoing. This, I suggested, is inapt if the wrongdoer does not criticize herself at the same time—to do so would be hypocritical. If it is conjoined with self-criticism, it can be apt for wrongdoers to blame each other. But even if one believes that resentment is sometimes apt, it is certainly not apt for one wrongdoer to resent another in the course of criticizing her. To resent the wrongdoer for her wrongdoing would be hypocritical even if the blamer acknowledges her own wrongdoing. At best, throwing the stones of resentment is apt only if one is not in a glasshouse.

[29] For the idea that demands are closely related to blame, see also G Watson 'Two Faces of Responsibility'; D K Nelkin 'Accountability and Desert' *Journal of Ethics*, forthcoming.

[30] See, for example, S Wolf 'Blame, Italian Style' and R Jay Wallace 'Dispassionate Opprobrium: On Blame and the Reactive Sentiments', both in R Jay Wallace, R Kumar, and S Freeman *Reasons and Recognition: Essays on the Philosophy of T M Scanlon* (Oxford: OUP, 2011).

Now focus on whether it is apt for one wrongdoer to blame another for her wrongdoing, whilst at the same time blaming herself. This seems apt. If I am right that wrongdoers might aptly blame each other but not aptly resent each other, resentment is not necessary for blame. I think that blame is apt because it is apt for wrongdoers to make responsive demands on each other, on condition that the wrongdoer accepts these demands herself.

Some claim that reactive sentiments such as resentment are inevitable if a person has the distinctive kind of care and concern for moral values.[31] The example of one wrongdoer blaming another suggests otherwise. Although it is inappropriate for the first wrongdoer to resent the second, the first wrongdoer may come to have a deep commitment to moral values that he expresses by acknowledging that both he and the other wrongdoer have acted wrongly.

Another view of blame, that T M Scanlon defends, is that blaming involves an erosion of certain relationships that we have with others.[32] Scanlon thinks that there is sufficient reason for a person to distance herself from a person who has wronged her simply because of the wrongful conduct. This distancing involves a range of attitudes towards the other, including withdrawal of trust, decreased readiness to enter into special relationships with the person, decreased willingness to help the person, and an erosion of the disposition to value the other's welfare. These attitudes need not involve resentment.[33]

If Scanlon intends to imply that there is a *pro tanto* non-instrumental reason to distance oneself from wrongdoers in these ways, and that this reason will sometimes be sufficient in itself to justify the distancing, I doubt that his view is right. A person who refrains from distancing herself in these ways from a person who has wronged her is, I think, especially admirable, whereas on Scanlon's account she fails to adopt the dispositions she has a sufficient reason to adopt. Unlike Scanlon, then, I doubt that this kind of distancing is deserved. The wrongdoer may lack a complaint if her victim distances herself from her. But this implies only that the wrongdoer is liable to be treated in this way, and not that she deserves it.[34]

Furthermore, blaming a person does not always involve the kind of distancing that Scanlon refers to. Blame often takes place within intimate relationships where there is typically no such distancing.[35] Similarly, where one wrongdoer blames another, I doubt that it is apt for the one to distance herself from the other in the ways Scanlon indicates. Repentant wrongdoers do not have a reason to distance themselves from wrongdoers who are yet to repent.

To support the view that issuing demands is a kind of blame we need to characterize the demands involved more carefully. After all, we can demand of a person that she fulfils her duties even where those duties have not been incurred through wrongdoing. If the truck driver has a duty to assist the person that he has accidentally injured, others can demand that he offer assistance, at least if he appears inclined not to do so. Blaming the driver for the injury, though, would be inappropriate.

31 See Wallace 'Dispassionate Opprobrium' 368–9.

32 See *Moral Dimensions: Permissibility, Meaning, Blame* (Cambridge, Mass.: Harvard UP, 2008) ch 4; 'Interpreting Blame' in D J Coates and N A Tognazzini *Blame: Its Nature and Norms* (Oxford: OUP, 2013); 'Giving Desert Its Due' (2013) 16 *Philosophical Explorations* 1.

33 See, especially, Scanlon 'Giving Desert Its Due', 105–9.

34 I think that Scanlon is inclined to accept this. For discussion, see the exchange between Scanlon and myself on PEA Soup: <http://peasoup.typepad.com/peasoup/2013/05/featured-philosopher-tm-scanlon.html>.

35 See, also, Wolf 'Blame, Italian Style'.

At least in central cases, the demand that is distinctive of blame is a demand to respond to the defect in one's practical reasoning that led to the wrongdoing. In blaming the wrongdoer, the blamer demands that the wrongdoer acknowledges this defect and responds to it appropriately. Blaming a person does not simply express the demand that the wrongdoer recognize a duty that she has. It expresses the demand that the person recognizes that her defective practical reasoning led her to act wrongly, and that she has incurred duties as a result. If I am right that wrongdoers have deep and distinctive reasons to respond to their wrongdoing if they are responsible for it, it is not difficult to understand the distinctiveness, urgency, and power that blame for serious wrongdoing typically has.

Furthermore, we have a simple explanation why blaming wrongdoers is apt if and only if the person is responsible for the wrongdoing. Blaming a person implies responsibility in that it refers to the distinctive, urgent, and powerful reason that only responsible wrongdoers have to respond to their wrongdoing. This distinguishes blame from other kinds of demands that people make of each other.

It is, of course, a further step to show that public blame is warranted for serious wrongdoing. That depends on the state having a role in blaming people for certain kinds of wrong. I leave an assessment of this role for Chapters 7 and 8.

VI. Responsibility and Deterrence

Even if compatibilist blame can be justified, can compatibilist punishment equally be justified? Using wrongdoers for deterrence is especially difficult to justify. Pereboom doubts that it can be justified.[36] His concerns with deterrence are mostly independent of his free-will scepticism. I show how those concerns can be met elsewhere.[37]

The challenge addressed here is to show that wrongdoers are differently placed from non-wrongdoers with respect to being used to avert threats because of their responsibility for wrongdoing. If they are, this would help to justify a criminal justice system that focuses on wrongdoers for non-derivative reasons.

The wrongness of harmfully using a person for the sake of a greater good has a great deal of intuitive support. Recall:

> *Bridge*: Dorabella is on a bridge with Fiordiligi. A trolley is heading on a track under the bridge towards five people who will be killed if Dorabella does nothing. Dorabella can save the five only by throwing Fiordiligi from the bridge onto the tracks. Fiordiligi's body will stop the trolley, saving the five, but Fiordiligi will be killed.

It is intuitively wrong for Dorabella to kill Fiordiligi.

But whilst harmful using is often intuitively wrong, it is not always intuitively wrong. Consider:

> *Wrongdoer on the Bridge*: As *Bridge* except Fiordiligi has wrongly started the trolley in order to kill the five, simply because she will enjoy seeing them die.

It is intuitively permissible to use Fiordiligi to save the five. Many will think that this is permissible on similar grounds to the permission to harm others in self-defence. Given that Pereboom explains the wrongness of using a person by appeal to intuition, perhaps he should also accept intuitive limits to the idea.

36 See *Free Will, Agency, and Meaning in Life*, ch 7.
37 See 'Doing Without Desert' *Criminal Law and Philosophy*, forthcoming.

However, he might claim that the intuition that Dorabella may kill Fiordiligi in *Wrongdoer on the Bridge* is explained by the significance of responsibility, and his arguments for free-will scepticism undermine the credibility of this intuition. This, though, is too swift. Pereboom mainly directs his fire against the idea that we have the kind of responsibility that could vindicate what he calls 'basic desert'. But to justify self-defence, or deterrent punishment, we need not appeal to basic desert. A person may lack a right against being harmed, even if she does not deserve to be harmed. Many think that responsibility is important in determining which rights we have. The fact that I am responsible for posing a threat to you, for example, plausibly explains why I have lost my right not to be harmed in self-defence, regardless of whether I deserve to be harmed.[38]

Our question is whether Pereboom's arguments against desert also apply to the loss of rights. To answer this question, consider a variation on Pereboom's manipulation argument against the claim that basic desert is compatible with determinism.[39] It is not plausible that those who are manipulated by evil scientists to pose threats to others lack rights against being harmed to avert the threat that they pose, even if they fulfil all compatibilist conditions of responsibility. There is no moral difference in the rights of a person who has been manipulated in this way by evil scientists and a person who has been subject to otherwise similar casual influences without the intervention of the evil scientists. All of our actions are subject to causal influences that are relevantly similar. Therefore, we are not liable to be harmed because we fulfil compatibilist conditions of responsibility in acting wrongly.

Against this, even those who are convinced by Pereboom's views about desert might give responsibility and wrongdoing a greater role in determining whether a person is liable to be harmed. Suppose that Pereboom is right that there is no important difference in desert or liability between those who are manipulated by evil scientists and those who are subject to otherwise similar causal influences. How does this argument apply to *Wrongdoer on the Bridge*? That depends on what we should think about a variation on that case where evil scientists have manipulated the wrongdoer on the bridge, but the wrongdoer fulfils compatibilist conditions of responsibility.

Consider:

> *Manipulated Wrongdoer on the Bridge*: As *Wrongdoer on the Bridge*, except that scientists have manipulated Fiordiligi's brain to ensure that she acts wrongly. However, Fiordiligi fulfils all plausible compatibilist conditions of responsibility—her effective first-order desire to kill the five conforms to her second-order desires; her process of deliberation from which the decision results is reason-responsive, in that it would have resulted in her refraining from posing this threat were her reasons different; her reasoning is consistent with her character, because she is egoistic; but she sometimes regulates her behaviour by moral reasons; she is not constrained to act as she does and she does not act out of an irresistible desire.

Pereboom's arguments imply that Fiordiligi is not responsible for the threat that she poses to the five, in the sense that Fiordiligi does not deserve blame or suffering in virtue of this act. Our question is different—whether it is permissible to use Fiordiligi to save the five. It may be permissible to use Fiordiligi even if she is not responsible in Pereboom's sense.

Pereboom will surely conclude that there is no difference with respect to responsibility between *Manipulated Wrongdoer on the Bridge* and *Wrongdoer on the Bridge*. If we

[38] See, also, J McMahan *Killing in War* (Oxford: OUP, 2009) 8–9.
[39] *Free Will, Agency, and Meaning in Life*, ch 4.

doubt that it is permissible to use Fiordiligi in *Manipulated Wrongdoer on the Bridge*, and there is no important difference in Fiordiligi's responsibility for the threat posed to the five between this case and *Wrongdoer on the Bridge*, we might reasonably doubt that it is permissible for Dorabella to use Fiordiligi to save the five in *Wrongdoer on the Bridge* as well. We might draw that conclusion even though it is initially intuitive that Dorabella would permissibly use Fiordiligi in the latter case—our intuitions may have been corrupted by a false conception of responsibility.

But we need not draw this conclusion. I find it intuitively plausible that it is permissible to use Fiordiligi to save the five in *Manipulated Wrongdoer on the Bridge*, regardless of whether Fiordiligi is responsible in Pereboom's sense. If this intuition is sound, wrongdoing seems to make a difference to a person's liability to be used, even when the wrongdoing is secured through manipulation. Even if there is no important moral difference between *Wrongdoer on the Bridge* and *Manipulated Wrongdoer on the Bridge*, and even if Fiordiligi deserves neither blame nor suffering in either case, it may be permissible for Dorabella to use Fiordiligi to save the five in both cases. That is consistent with accepting a stringent prohibition on using—a prohibition sufficiently stringent to imply that it is wrong for Dorabella to use Fiordiligi to save the five in *Bridge*.

Drawing on the idea that I defended earlier—that even manipulated wrongdoers incur duties to respond to their wrongdoing—can help us defend this view. The manipulated wrongdoer on the bridge is deeply involved in the threat that the five face. She has a powerful reason to ensure that she is not the author of their deaths; much more powerful than the reason that innocent bystanders have to do so. If she could save their lives at some moderate cost to herself, she is required to do so.[40] If she is thrown from the bridge to save the five, the cost that is inflicted on her is no greater than the cost that she would be required to bear in service of the end that she is used to serve. In that case, her complaint against being used in this way seems weak.

If this is right, we should doubt Pereboom's objection to general deterrence. Although those punished would be used, they would permissibly be used. The fact that they wrongly lead us to be vulnerable to attack by others by undermining the credibility of our threats may be sufficient to render it permissible to use them. This may be so even if these wrongdoers deserve neither blame nor suffering.

Perhaps not everyone shares my intuition that it is permissible to use Fiordiligi in *Manipulated Wrongdoer on the Bridge*. But even if this intuition is unsound, it does not follow that wrongdoing makes no difference to the permissibility of using a person. Even those who reject the permissibility of Dorabella using Fiordiligi in this case might accept that there is an important moral difference between Fiordiligi's circumstances in this case and her circumstances in *Bridge*. Suppose that we gradually lower the costs that Fiordiligi must bear if she is used to save the five in both cases. There may be some cost at which it is permissible for Dorabella to use Fiordiligi in a relevant variation on *Manipulated Wrongdoer on the Bridge*, but not the equivalent variation on *Bridge*.

Finally, we should not draw conclusions too quickly from any strong initial intuition that Fiordiligi may not be used in *Manipulated Wrongdoer on the Bridge*. Soft-line responses to Pereboom's manipulation argument apply to this argument as well. There

[40] Pereboom rejects the idea that we have duties in the conventional sense, on the grounds that ought implies can do otherwise, and we lack the free will necessary to be able to do otherwise. But these reasons for rejecting duties do not rule out the idea that the reasons that people have to avert harm depends on their involvement in the threat of harm. Even if they do not have duties in the conventional sense, they may have powerful reasons to avert harm that could figure in an equivalent of the argument that I offer here. For the sake of brevity, I will not spell the equivalent argument out in detail.

might be reasons not to impose costs on Fiordiligi in *Manipulated Wrongdoer on the Bridge* that do not apply in *Wrongdoer on the Bridge* that depend on our reasons not to have costs inflicted on us as a result of manipulation.

And even if we reject these soft-line responses, hard-line responses may succeed. We saw reasons to think that our intuitions about *Case 1* are not very reliable, given that the causal history of the decision of the neuroscientists to manipulate Plum are not brightly illuminated. The same thing is true here. This sceptical argument against using, then, does not give us powerful reasons to reject the permissibility of using wrongdoers.

Responsibility for wrongdoing makes an important difference to the permissibility of using a person to avert threats that they pose. And that may be sufficient to justify a system of punishment that is focused on wrongdoers rather than on innocent people. Perhaps this argument only justifies a system of punishment that is much milder than our current punitive practices. But as our current punitive practices already seem abhorrently harsh (especially in the US), this is a welcome result.

VII. Conclusion

Pereboom's manipulation argument poses a challenge to the widespread belief that we are responsible for our actions. This challenge can be met. Furthermore, the norms of blaming are not threatened by Pereboom's argument, at least if the demands that we make of each other are central to blame in the way that I have suggested. And I doubt that it undermines the permissibility of harming wrongdoers for the purposes of deterrence.

Perhaps there is a sense in which basic desert, as Pereboom understands it, is incompatible with the kind of freedom that we have. I find this idea less troubling, though, in that practices grounded in basic desert, such as resenting wrongdoers and punishing them on retributivist grounds, seem unappealing independently of questions about free will. If we can vindicate personal practical responsibility, and I think that we can, we have all of the responsibility that we should want.

PART B

CRIMINALIZATION IN PRINCIPLE

6

How Not to Think About Criminalization I: Restrictive Principles

What should, and what should not, be criminalized? To answer that question it would help us to know what criminalization is. It is tempting to look for the necessary and sufficient conditions of something being a criminal law. We should resist this temptation. One reason is that the task seems hopeless. Core cases of criminal laws have many features: for example, they authoritatively declare that some conduct is not to be done; they give rise to certain procedures and standards of proof for those who are accused of violating the law; they warrant public blame and punishment for those who violate the law; and so on. In peripheral cases, some features are missing. Which peripheral cases are still criminal laws? It is difficult to make progress in answering this question. We should try to get by without answering it.

More importantly, the constitutive features of criminal laws may or may not have the greatest normative significance. For example, criminal laws might be distinguished from other laws because the state, rather than the complainant, decides whether to bring a legal action against an individual for violating the law. But this fact may not be at all important, let alone the most important fact, to determine what we should criminalize.

For the purposes of this chapter let some conduct, C, be criminalized if state officials with the relevant powers create a law authoritatively declaring that C must not to be done, they warrant public blame and punishment for those who are shown to have Ced by a public trial with a high standard of proof, and they sincerely and credibly threaten state punishment for those who C. As I said 'if' and not 'if and only if', this account allows peripheral cases where some of these features are not present—for example, it allows that conduct may be criminalized without the threat of punishment; and that conduct may be criminalized without warranting public blame.

If this is how we should understand criminalization, what should be criminalized? The most influential discussion concerns restrictive principles that mandate limits to the scope of the criminal law. Given the troubling expansion in the inept use of the criminal law to address a wide range of social problems (and non-problems), this discussion seems attractive. Although I share many of the moral commitments and political ambitions of these defenders of restrictive principles, I doubt that focusing on them makes for good philosophy. We make more progress by thinking about criminalization in a more structured way that I sketch in Chapter 9. My main aim here is to explain why the more familiar approach of finding restrictive principles should be abandoned.

Section I outlines two kinds of restrictive principle: content-focused and effect-focused principles. Section II provides a general argument to show that content-focused principles fail. Section III shows that any simple effect-focused principle either fails or fails to illuminate. However, discussion of both sets of principles helps us to see something important that should feature in a good theory of criminalization.

I. Two Kinds of Restrictive Principle

Restrictive principles come in two kinds. Content-focused principles claim that it is only permissible to criminalize certain kinds of thing. Normally, criminal law prohibits conduct—by which I mean to include both acts and omissions. A content-focused restrictive principle claims that only conduct of a certain kind—harmful conduct, for example—is permissibly criminalized. Effect-focused principles claim that it is only permissible to criminalize some conduct if criminalizing that conduct has certain effects. The most familiar is the (for now vaguely stated) principle that it is permissible to criminalize conduct only if doing so prevents harm.

The relationship between these types of principle is contingent. Consider content-focused and effect-focused restrictive principles that are concerned with harm. Criminalizing harmful conduct does not necessarily prevent harm. And criminalizing non-harmful conduct might prevent harm. So a principle that permits only the criminalization of harmful conduct might permit criminalization even if criminalization does not prevent harm, and it may rule out the criminalization of conduct where doing so would prevent harm. Similarly, a principle that permits criminalizing conduct only if doing so prevents harm might permit the criminalization of some non-harmful conduct, and rule out the criminalization of some harmful conduct.

I will argue that restrictive principles do not have an important role to play in a theory of criminalization. Familiar content-focused principles are overly restrictive. If the effects are good enough, conduct should normally be criminalized regardless of its inherent features. This is especially so where people can easily avoid punishment if the conduct is criminalized.

Effect-focused principles either fail or fail to illuminate. They fail in one of these two ways because they do not capture the complex questions of proportionality that govern the scope of the criminal law. Different goods contribute to a case for criminalization, including prevention of wrongdoing and harm prevention. Any one type of good is in principle sufficient on its own to justify criminalization if a sufficient magnitude of that good is brought about and if the costs of criminalization to both wrongdoers and non-wrongdoers are sufficiently low. It is an empirical question whether proportionality is satisfied in any particular case. Although the empirical questions are difficult, we have no reason to accept simple effect-focused restrictive principles. Doing so relies on empirical conjecture that philosophers are poorly placed to make.

Furthermore, there are difficult questions about how non-consequentialist principles apply to criminalization. Simple restrictive principles of criminalization focus our attention away from the complex questions of proportionality that arise. Hence, although this chapter seems mainly destructive, it has a constructive aim: although familiar content-focused and effect-focused principles fail, thinking about these principles helps us to structure our thinking about criminalization.

It helps us to distinguish two kinds of consideration that we must attend to when thinking about what to criminalize. One consideration concerns liability to punishment. The concerns of those who defend content-focused restrictive principles are better understood as concerns about liability. A second consideration concerns proportionality. Consider the principle that it is permissible to criminalize conduct only if doing so reduces harm. This is best understood as a claim about proportionality—the claim that criminalization will always be disproportionate, given the harm that it causes, if doing so does not reduce harm. Seeing why simple effect-focused principles fail encourages us to develop a better account of proportionality.

II. Rejecting Content-Focused Restrictive Principles

Content-focused restrictive principles aim to restrict the scope of the criminal law by specifying the conduct that can permissibly be criminalized.

i) Clarifying the principles

Here are some familiar examples:

> *Harm Constraint 1 (HC1)*: It is wrong to criminalize conduct that is not harmful.
>
> *Wrongness Constraint 1 (WC1)*: It is wrong to criminalize conduct that is not wrongful.[1]
>
> *Sovereignty Constraint 1 (SC1)*: It is wrong to criminalize conduct that does not interfere with another person's sovereignty.

These principles are not very clear. One reason has to do with the interpretation of 'wrong'. Ambitious principles claim that criminalizing the relevant conduct is wrong all things considered. Modest versions claim that doing so is *pro tanto* wrong. Defenders of the *pro tanto* version of *HC1*, for example, claim that it is *pro tanto* wrong to criminalize harmless conduct, but doing so may be permissible if it is necessary to save many lives.

A second way in which they are unclear is that they rely on an account of their key terms: harm; wrongness; and sovereignty respectively. Because these terms are vague and contested, even if one of these principles is true, it needs a great deal of work to be made illuminating.

They are also unclear in a third way: where are they intended to apply? For example, after 'wrong' in such principles, we could insert 'in the UK now'; or 'anywhere now'; or 'in any liberal democracy'; or 'in all circumstances that are likely ever to occur anywhere', or 'in all possible worlds'. Let us say that differences of this kind are differences of 'domain'. Defenders of content-focused restrictive principles are often unclear about the intended domain of their principles.

The broadest variations—those that are intended to apply in all possible worlds—are most amenable to armchair defence. They do not rely on empirical claims. The standard reason to narrow principles is empirical. For example, some might claim that although non-harmful conduct could permissibly be criminalized in some possible world, it could not be criminalized in the UK now. This claim depends on features of the UK now that are not features of the possible world in which the harmless conduct can be criminalized. And it is presumably an empirical question whether the UK has these features.

The fact that some principle is based on empirical claims does not necessarily rule out armchair defence: some empirical claims are obviously true. For example, it might be argued that only harmful conduct may be criminalized in the UK now because criminalizing conduct in the UK now is inevitably costly—it results in some people being harmed, or altering their behaviour in disadvantageous ways, for example.[2] The costs of criminalization need not be significant. Each year, hundreds of criminal offences are created in the UK. I don't find armchair defence of the claim that each of these criminal offences inflicted significant costs on people compelling. Still, the

[1] This principle is ambiguous—it does not specify whether the conduct must be wrong independently of it being criminalized, or wrong once criminalized, or both. See, further, Chapter 17.

[2] Not that this argument would support *HC1*, as we will soon see.

claim that criminalization inevitably imposes some costs in the UK now is amenable to armchair defence.

These principles are unclear in a fourth way, though clarity is more difficult to achieve here. Consider the general question: which moral principles apply to me? I could aim to establish the fundamental moral facts that determine what my duties are. Principles that rely only on such facts are independent of my judgemental failures. But, common sense suggests, people also govern their conduct by adopting policies, or rules of thumb, that do not respond directly to the fundamental reasons that apply to them. Such policies, or rules of thumb, may be aimed at ensuring conformity with moral reasons or requirements.

Here is a familiar illustration of the common-sense idea: during a war, the fundamental moral facts may require combatants sometimes to shoot civilians. But combatants may comply best with their duties overall by adopting a policy of refraining from shooting civilians. If they adopt such a policy, they will sometimes act wrongly. But, given that they are fallible, they will act wrongly less often and less egregiously than they would were they to attempt to consider the fundamental moral facts directly. In such a case, some people might claim that combatants are required to adopt the relevant policy or rule of thumb.

Similarly, some might argue that principles such as the harm principle are best thought of as policies or rules of thumb that state officials ought to adopt when considering what to criminalize. Although the fundamental moral facts would warrant, or perhaps mandate, criminalization of non-harmful conduct, they may claim, adopting the harm principle, as a policy or rule of thumb, will lead the state to comply better with the duties or reasons that apply to it.[3]

Roughly speaking, then, we can distinguish between fundamental principles of criminalization, and policies or rules of thumb. This book is about fundamental principles of criminalization, and not policies or rules of thumb. Before moving on, here are a few remarks about policies or rules of thumb.

As I suggested, there is a common-sense idea that we sometimes ought to employ policies or rules of thumb in order to increase conformity with the reasons or duties that apply to us. But these policies or rules raise a range of difficult philosophical and empirical questions. To illustrate, consider the following. We can distinguish what the state ideally ought to criminalize, the second best, and the third best. Suppose that the second best is much better than the third best. Suppose also that the state ideally ought to criminalize some non-harmful wrongdoing but if it aims to criminalize the harmful and non-harmful wrongdoing that it ideally ought to criminalize, it will make egregious errors. This will produce the third best result. If it aims to criminalize only harmful wrongdoing, it will produce the second best result. Those who defend some kind of harm principle might claim that such a principle is valid on this basis—abiding by such a principle will produce second best results where otherwise the state would produce third best results.

One question about this view concerns the moral status of the harm principle if this defence succeeds. It seems that the view leads to a troubling 'conflict of oughts'. The state, at once, ought to criminalize some non-harmful wrongdoing, and yet ought to abide by a principle that rules out criminalizing that conduct. Some might claim that the second 'ought' takes priority because of what will in fact occur if the state attempts

[3] Roughly this idea is suggested in L Green 'The Nature of Limited Government' in J Keown and R P George *Reason, Morality, and Law: The Philosophy of John Finnis* (Oxford: OUP, 2013). See, also, J Edwards 'Master Principles of Criminalisation' *Jurisprudence*, forthcoming.

to abide by the first ought. Hence, it ought not to criminalize any harmless wrongdoing. But this has the troubling implication that the fallibility of state officials deprives them of an obligation that they would otherwise have. And the greater their fallibility, the fewer obligations they have. I think that this problem counts decisively against the idea that rules of thumb have moral priority.

We are better to understand the rule of thumb as conditional—*given that it will not do what it ought to do*, the state ought to abide by the rule of thumb. But that does not imply that it ought to abide by the rule of thumb. The rule of thumb is, as the example suggests, a rule of the second best.[4]

A second question is how to establish that a rule of thumb is valid. To do this, proponents need to rank three options—what the state ideally ought to do; what it will do if it follows the proposed rule of thumb; and what it will do if it attempts to do what it ideally ought to do. Ranking these options obviously relies on the difficult moral questions that this book is concerned with, about the nature, sources, and importance of wrongdoing, its relationship with harm, and so on. Proponents then need to show that what the state will do if it follows the proposed rule of thumb is what it ought to do when compared with what it will do if it attempts to do what it ideally ought to do.

For example, suppose that some non-harmful wrongdoing ideally ought to be criminalized. However, if the state attempts to criminalize the non-harmful wrongdoing that ideally ought to be criminalized, it will criminalize some conduct that ought not to be criminalized. If it abided by *HC1*, in contrast, it would fail to criminalize some harmless wrongdoing that ideally ought to be criminalized, but it would also refrain from criminalizing conduct that ought not to be criminalized.

Some might argue that the state ought always to err on the side of non-criminalization when such conflicts arise in virtue of the fact that it should do everything that it can to avoid punishing the innocent. But this view is subject to an obvious response: any criminal justice system punishes some innocent people, so on this view, the state ought not to criminalize anything. This is not intended as a *reductio*—abolitionism is not completely absurd—but it does show that friends of this argument ought to defend abolitionism rather than *HC1*.

Alternatively, some might argue that whilst it is very important to criminalize harmful wrongdoing, it is not very important to criminalize harmless wrongdoing. So in the case of harmless wrongdoing, the concern about punishing the innocent is always decisive, but not in the case of harmful wrongdoing.

This position has some plausibility, but it depends on the idea that criminalizing non-harmful wrongdoing is not very important. I doubt that this is right. As I will argue later in the book, many of the most serious wrongs are not wrong in virtue of the harm that they will cause. In the light of this, it would be surprising if harm had such an important role in guiding criminalization policy.

Furthermore, the empirical claims that proponents of any rule of thumb implicitly rely on are difficult to assess. These include both claims about the effect of abiding by the policy, and claims about the effect of being guided by the ideal. But they also include claims about other potential policies that could guide the state. The empirical claims that underpin the defence of the harm principle, or any other general principle of criminalization, as a policy or rule of thumb seem contestable.

[4] I say more about this in 'Anarchic War' unpublished ms. For a similar response to a related question about what we ought to do given predictions about what we will do in the future, see Chapter 16.

Armchair defence of particular rules of thumb or policies is no easy matter, and as far as I am aware, no one has successfully defended any general principle of criminalization on this basis.

I make no claims about what rules of thumb or policies ought to guide state decisions. My interest is in the ideal principles of criminalization. In the light of these, those who have a better grasp of the empirical questions than I do can fashion rules of thumb or policies.

ii) Blame and liability

Let us return to the idea that there are fundamental principles that restrict the scope of the criminal law, rather than policies or rules of thumb. Content-focused restrictive principles of this kind are vulnerable to single counterexamples. For example, *HC1* is false if it is permissible to criminalize any harmless conduct. Consequently, such principles are more plausible if they are vague. Because harm is a broad and vague idea, and because there are many ways in which conduct can cause harm, defenders of *HC1* can meet many objections to it.

To illustrate, many attacks launched at *HC1* identify harmless wrongs that, everyone will agree, ought to be criminalized. Defenders of *HC1* have plenty of resources to respond to these attacks—by showing that the conduct causes harm. But defences of this kind come at a cost—they buy plausibility at the cost of illumination. *HC1* was supposed to guide decisions about criminalization, but it tends to be interpreted in the light of pre-existing judgements about what should be criminalized. Furthermore, when the principle is interpreted to respond to objections from harmless wrongdoing it rules out very little.[5]

Even when interpreted broadly, though, content-focused restrictive principles are vulnerable to a different kind of objection, and it is decisive. To see the objection, focus on the most plausible content-focused principle: *WC1*. One way to defend this principle relies on the communicative or expressive functions of the criminal law, such as public blame. Only wrongdoers can be blamed, so only wrongdoing can be criminalized.

Here is the argument:

Blame

1) Criminalizing conduct authorizes state officials publicly to blame those who violate the criminal law.
2) It is wrong to authorize public officials publicly to blame those who do not merit blame.
3) Therefore, it is permissible to criminalize conduct only if those who violate the criminal law warrant public blame.
4) Only wrongdoers warrant public blame.
5) Therefore, it is wrong to criminalizing conduct unless that conduct is wrong.

Blame is at first blush attractive. Public blame is a central function of the criminal law. And, as we saw in Chapter 2, the idea that only wrongdoers merit blame is roughly right. However, *Blame* either fails, or if it succeeds it does so by conceptual fiat, and does not get to the heart of the matter.

The blaming function of the criminal law is not its most troubling function. Unwarranted public blame is very bad. But the aspect of criminal law that is most

[5] See, also, R A Duff *Answering for Crime: Responsibility and Liability in the Criminal Law* (Oxford: Hart, 2007) 126–35.

difficult to defend is the intentional infliction of harm on wrongdoers (especially for reasons of deterrence). *Blame* tells us nothing about laws that warrant the infliction of harm on those who violate it simply for reasons of deterrence without warranting public blame. But such laws seem to be criminal laws, and even if they are not, they have the feature of criminal laws that troubles us most.

Consider a criminal law framed as follows: 'those who *v* are liable to state punishment'. Many criminal laws are framed roughly like this. The state enforces this law by imprisoning those who *v* simply in order to deter people from *v*ing. The state does not warrant anyone publicly to blame those who *v*, and no one is in fact blamed. *Blame* leaves such laws untouched. For all it says, the state has done nothing wrong.

Friends of *Blame* might respond that such laws do not warrant punishment because punishment is inherently a blaming practice. They might also claim that such laws are not criminal laws because criminal laws inherently warrant punishment.

This is a poor response. To my ears, it would not be wrong to describe the laws I have just described as criminal, and to describe the sanctions they impose as punitive. But more importantly, we should hope that principles of criminalization tell us something about the most morally important facts about criminal law, not simply those facts that are necessary for a criminal law to exist. Even if my ears mislead, *Blame* cannot show that *WC1* has anything to say about the features of the criminal law that make it most difficult to justify—namely the intentional infliction of harm, sometimes grave harm, on others.

Suppose that the laws I describe are not criminal laws, and the sanctions they inflict not punitive. The state could abolish its system of criminal law and punishment and replace them with a system of deterrent sanctions. *Blame* would tell us nothing about this practice. But this practice shares the features of criminal law and punishment that are most difficult to defend. Even if *Blame* successfully defends *WC1*, its implications are modest, and it does not go to the heart of what troubles us about the criminal law.

For this reason, friends of *WC1* ought to seek an argument for it that is more directly connected to the intentional infliction of harm on those who violate the law. Here is one such argument:

Liability

1) Criminalizing *v*ing authorizes state punishment of those who *v*.
2) It is permissible to authorize state punishment of those who *v* only if it is permissible for the state to punish those who *v*.
3) Therefore criminalizing some conduct, *v*, is justified only if it is permissible for the state to punish those who *v*.
4) Punishment involves the intentional infliction of harm.
5) It is permissible intentionally to inflict harm on a person only if they are liable to be treated thus.
6) Therefore, it is permissible to criminalize *v* only if those who *v* are liable to the intentional infliction of harm.
7) Only wrongdoing makes a person liable to the intentional infliction of harm.
8) Therefore, it is wrong to criminalize *v*ing unless *v*ing is wrong.

As this argument is directly concerned with intentional harm infliction, it has a better focus than *Blame*. Furthermore, in Chapters 4 and 5 I have supported the idea that wrongdoing can make a person liable to punishment if that person is responsible (in the compatibilist sense) for the wrongdoing because of the duties incurred through wrongdoing. And we can see why non-wrongdoers are not normally liable to punishment: a person does not incur enforceable protective duties by acting in a way that is merely irrational.

iii) The benefits of criminalization

Liability fails. It is sometimes permissible to criminalize non-wrongful conduct because doing so prevents a great deal of harm. That is true even if premise 7) is true. Sometimes our rights against intentional harm-infliction are overridden. Thus premise 5) is too strong.

Here is the argument. Generally, acting in a certain way is permissible if acting in that way prevents a great deal of harm, and does not cause much harm, even if those who are harmed retain rights not to be harmed. This is no less true of criminalization. Now consider any principle that takes the following form: 'in all possible worlds, it is all things considered wrong to criminalize any C that is not *f*'. Now suppose that failing to criminalize some conduct that is not *f* will have extremely bad consequences, and criminalizing it will be nowhere near as bad. Furthermore, suppose that it is easy for people to avoid punishment if Cing is criminalized, simply by refraining from Cing. It is normally permissible, in fact required, to criminalize C.

Consider:

> *Total World Destruction*: If the UK government fails to criminalize hopping, the world will be destroyed.

Obviously, the UK government ought to criminalize hopping, even though hopping is not harmful, not wrong, and does not interfere with sovereignty.

This simple example demonstrates the falsity of these principles:

HC1 (APW): In all possible worlds, it is wrong all things considered to criminalize any conduct that is not harmful.
WC1 (APW): In all possible worlds, it is wrong all things considered to criminalize any conduct that is not wrongful.
SC1 (APW): In all possible worlds, it is wrong all things considered to criminalize any conduct that does not interfere with another person's sovereignty.

These principles implausibly imply that it is wrong for the UK government to criminalize hopping in *Total World Destruction*.

The fact that these principles fail does not show that versions that apply to a narrower domain fail. The argument would be more interesting if it applied in more realistic cases. I believe that there are such examples. In Chapter 17, I will suggest that possession of firearms is one such example—there I will argue that it is sometimes permissible to criminalize possession of firearms even in circumstances where possession of firearms, in contravention of the law, is often permissible.

As the argument in Chapter 17 is complex, consider a simpler example:

> *US Threat*: Possession of a certain recreational drug, Happy Pill, does not violate any plausible content-focused restrictive principle—for example, it is not wrongful, not harmful, and does not interfere with anyone else's sovereignty. A poor country is deciding whether to criminalize possession of this drug. US subsidies, that are necessary for the provision of essential medicines to a very large number of people who will otherwise suffer severely, will not be provided if possession of Happy Pill is not criminalized, or the prohibition is not adequately enforced.

This case is not far from the real world. Though the empirical questions are difficult, something like it has probably occurred. Criminalizing possession of the drug is justified in order to ensure that citizens receive essential medicines. Doing so prevents a great deal of human suffering. But the prevention of harm has nothing to do with the content of the criminal law. Content-focused restrictive principles are vulnerable to counterexamples like this even if they have a relatively narrow domain.

Perhaps it might be argued that these content-focused restrictive principles are valid when the domain is narrowed still further, for example, to Western democracies. The answer to this question is empirical: do Western democracies face difficulties like those identified in *US Threat* that permit the criminalization of some non-harmful, non-wrongful, non-sovereignty-interfering conduct? It would be a brave, or foolish, philosopher who argues that they do not—empirically proving this large negative is a difficult task.

Some might respond that if criminalizing conduct prevents harm, the conduct must be harmful. For example, if failure to criminalize possession of Happy Pill prevents US subsidies being provided, harming citizens, possessing Happy Pill is harmful. But we have already seen that the relationship between content-focused and effect-focused principles is contingent, so we know this is false. The provision of the subsidies might have a causal relationship with the decision to, or not to, criminalize, and not with the conduct criminalized. In *US Threat*, for example, the US might refuse to subsidize a country that is insufficiently vigorous in its approach to the war on drugs. This depends on the attitude and actions of the government of this country, and not on whether its citizens possess drugs.

Some might argue that although possession of Happy Pill is non-harmful, non-wrongful, and non-sovereignty interfering prior to it being criminalized, once possession is criminalized, the conduct becomes harmful, or wrongful, or sovereignty interfering. The question of how the moral status of conduct is altered by criminalization is a difficult one that I consider in more detail in Chapter 17. Here I just state the conclusion that prohibition need not, and often does not, change the moral status of the conduct in the relevant way. Indeed, this conclusion is initially attractive—possession of Happy Pill for private use does not seem wrong given that it does nothing to set back the purposes of the law: to ensure that subsidies continue.

Some might argue that it is wrong for the state to criminalize possession of Happy Pill because it warrants punishment of the innocent. If possessing Happy Pill is not wrong, those who are punished have their rights infringed. But suppose that US subsidies depend not only on possession being prohibited by the law, but also on punishment of those who violate it. The state might justify punishing violators on the grounds that if it does not do so it will not be able to provide essential medicines to those whose lives depend on them.

Can't those who are punished complain, though, that they are used to benefit those who need essential medicines? Consider this attractive principle that I discussed in Chapter 4:

> *The Using View*: If D executes an intention to use V to serve an end, and D knows or believes that using V in this way will cause V to be harmed, D's act or omission is more difficult to justify than if V had not featured in D's intention in this way.

Perhaps those who are punished in *Happy Pill* are used. That depends on how we spell out the idea of 'using', which is controversial. But even if they are used, and *The Using View* is valid, using a person to benefit others without her consent is not always wrong.

If the good achieved is sufficiently great, and the harm done sufficiently small, *The Using View* does not prohibit the conduct. One reason is that innocent people who possess the drugs might have an enforceable duty to ensure that the essential medicines that the US provides continue to be provided at the relevant cost. If they do, they cannot complain about being used for this end.

Furthermore, if the state prohibits possession of Happy Pill and no one violates the law, those in need of the subsidies receive essential medicines without anyone being used. Those who violate the law thus put the state in a dilemma. Either it must use the people who have violated the law to ensure the survival of those who need the essential medicines, or they must leave those who need the medicines to die. Those who possess Happy Pill could have avoided putting the state in this dilemma by refraining from possessing the drugs. As the drugs are only recreational, this comes at little cost. Hence, their complaint that they should not be used to protect those who need the essential medicines is weak.

In other words, although possessing the drugs is not harmful, those who possess the drugs will have harmed others if the state abides by a principle where they are not punished—their possession, coupled with such a policy, makes those who need the essential medicines worse off. This also is a powerful reason to reject principles such as *HC1, WC1*, and *SC1*. If the state abides by these principles, it renders it possible for some citizens to harm others by possessing drugs in *US Threat*.

Although content-focused restrictive principles are generally vulnerable to this argument, the argument also indicates what those friendly to such principles should be focused on. They should aim to identify considerations that typically make a person liable to punishment. For example, friends of *HC1* might argue that only harmful conduct typically makes a person liable to state punishment. They might argue for this on the grounds that people lose rights not to be harmed only by harming others. I doubt that this is true, but it is not vulnerable to the argument that I have offered here.

Cast as a general principle of criminalization, *HC1* has implausible implications. Cast as a principle that aims to identify the sole basis of a person's liability to be punished, it is more plausible (though, as I will argue later in this book, still false).

iv) *Pro tanto* wrongdoing

My argument is consistent with a more modest version of *WC1*: one concerned with the *pro tanto* wrongness of criminalization. Here are variations with wider or narrower domains:

> *WC1* (*Pro Tanto* APW): In all possible worlds, it is *pro tanto* wrong to criminalize any conduct that is not wrongful.
>
> *WC1* (*Pro Tanto* current Western democracies): In all current Western democracies, it is *pro tanto* wrong to criminalize any conduct that is not wrongful.

These principles survive my argument against *Liability*. I am not sure whether to endorse them, though, as I am not sure how to understand *pro tanto* wrongness.

Recall *US Threat*. Is the criminalization of possession of Happy Pill wrong *pro tanto*? I'm not sure. Certainly, citizens of the poor country have a reason to want to be free to possess Happy Pill, and the state curtails this freedom. Furthermore, punishment is threatened, and sometimes carried out, for non-wrongful conduct. But I am not sure whether these facts decisively support the claim that criminalization is *pro tanto* wrong.

Many regulatory criminal prohibitions, such as those imposing speed limits, licensing schemes for possession of weapons, and health and safety requirements, restrict the liberty of some in order to benefit others. But if citizens are given plenty of notice, so they can avoid violating these prohibitions, they also seem relatively unobjectionable. Do government officials wrong citizens, even *pro tanto*, when creating these prohibitions? I have some doubts.

To answer the question more completely we need a general theory of *pro tanto* wrongdoing—not a conceptual theory, but a theory that distinguishes the set of *pro tanto* wrongful acts from the larger pool of permissible acts with downsides. Such a theory could tell us whether the downsides of doing some justified action are sufficient to make that action a case of justified wrongdoing, or whether the action is not wrongful at all. Unfortunately, I have no such theory, and as far as I know, no one else does either. As it is difficult to make progress with such a theory, it is hard to know whether *pro tanto* versions of content-focused restrictive principles are true.

Fortunately, it is not very important to develop such a theory. Any theory would not tell us very much about the most important questions of criminalization that we face. It would only help us answer the question whether a particular law is *pro tanto* wrong, or rather has downsides that do not make it *pro tanto* wrong. This question is not very interesting.

III. Effect-Focused Restrictive Principles

This discussion might lead some to eschew content-focused restrictive principles in favour of effect-focused restrictive principles such as:

HC2: It is wrong to criminalize conduct unless criminalizing that conduct prevents harm.
WC2: It is wrong to criminalize conduct unless criminalizing that conduct prevents wrongdoing.
SC2: It is wrong to criminalize conduct unless criminalizing that conduct prevents interferences with sovereignty.

These principles are not vulnerable to the challenge offered to content-focused restrictive principles in the previous section. *WC2* and *SC2* are vulnerable to the same counterexamples, though.

For example, suppose that in *Total World Destruction*, the destruction would not come about as a result of wrongdoing. If *WC2* is given the broadest domain, it implausibly implies that prohibiting hopping is wrong. Similarly, criminalizing the possession of Happy Pill may not prevent wrongdoing in *US Threat*. Whether it does depends on whether the US is required to provide subsidies to the poor country.

But provision of the subsidies may not be required—the US may have discretion to provide them either to this country or to another as it wishes. If so, *WC2* fails even if its domain is narrowed significantly. *SC2* fails for the same reasons. Perhaps it might be argued that it could not be permissible for the US to make criminalization of permissible conduct a condition of the provision of subsidies. This raises difficult questions that I cannot fully address, but it seems possible to fashion an example where this is permissible: where the provision of the subsidies is a supererogatory act, and criminalizing permissible conduct has benefits to the country providing the subsidies. At any rate, as *HC2* is not vulnerable to these counterexamples, let us focus on that.

i) Clarifying HC2

Effect-focused restrictive principles can be clarified by specifying more carefully the relevant effect. Some who endorse something like *HC2* fail to do this. For example, John Gardner and Stephen Shute write:

> It is no objection under the harm principle that a harmless action was criminalized, or even that an action with no tendency to cause harm was criminalized. It is enough to meet the demands of the harm principle that, if the action were not criminalized, *that* would be harmful.

This passage is confusing—it is not clear how failing to criminalize something would be harmful. Rather, failing to criminalize would fail to prevent harm. I take it, then, that Gardner and Shute mean to endorse something like *HC2*. More importantly, they do not clarify how much harm needs to be prevented in order to satisfy their version of the harm principle.

To understand different solutions to this problem, and to see problems with a wide range of solutions, let us explore more carefully why they favour *HC2* over *HC1*: because they believe that there are harmless wrongs that should be criminalized.[6] As we have rights against certain kinds of interference where that interference does not set back well-being, there are harmless wrongs. Some of these wrongs are serious, and criminalization seems permissible.

Although this feature of their view is controversial, for reasons offered in Chapter 11, I support it. For now, I rely on Gardner and Shute's own example:

> *Unconscious Rape*: Mirella is in a coma from which she never wakes up. Giuseppe, a stranger, has intercourse with her. Mirella suffers no physical effects from the intercourse.[7]

Giuseppe's conduct is seriously wrongful, and he would have no complaint against being punished for his conduct. But, Gardner and Shute claim, his conduct is not harmful. If they are right that his conduct is harmless, liability to punishment does not depend on harmful wrongdoing. It follows that *HC1* should be rejected.

But friends of the harm principle, they then argue, need not worry. For the harm principle, best understood, is effect-focused, not content-focused: it is concerned with whether criminalizing conduct prevents harm. Criminalization of harmless wrongdoing is permitted as long as doing so prevents harm.

Beyond these remarks, Gardner and Shute offer little defence of *HC2*. Here is a familiar argument that is said to support it. Because the criminal law is a clumsy tool, criminalizing conduct inevitably harms the innocent. It inevitably results in some innocent people being convicted of criminal offences; it costs money; it harms the families and friends of wrongdoers; it causes crime as well as preventing it; it causes

[6] Examples of harmless wrongdoing are now widely discussed. See, for example, 'The Wrongness of Rape' in J Gardner *Offences and Defences: Selected Essays in the Philosophy of Criminal Law* (Oxford: OUP, 2007); A P Simester and G R Sullivan 'On the Nature and Rationale of Property Offences' in R A Duff and S P Green *Defining Crimes: Essays on the Special Part* (Oxford: OUP, 2005); A Ripstein 'Beyond the Harm Principle' (2006) 34 *Philosophy and Public Affairs* 215; V Tadros 'Harm, Sovereignty and Prohibition' (2011) 17 *Legal Theory* 35; D Owens *Shaping the Normative Landscape* (Oxford: OUP, 2012).

[7] Their own description of the example has a few more bells and whistles. See 'The Wrongness of Rape', 5.

people not to do desirable things to avoid the possibility of wrongful conviction and punishment; and so on.[8] It is normally wrong to harm others in these ways. The only justification for doing so is that harm would be prevented.

ii) A trivial version of the harm principle

In the light of this argument, let us consider some different versions of *HC2*. One reasonably natural way to read Gardner and Shute's account of *HC2* is:

> *HC2* (Some Harm): It is wrong to criminalize conduct unless criminalizing that conduct prevents some harm.

This version of *HC2* is permissive—it only requires some harm reduction. It certainly does not require that more harm will be prevented than is caused by the criminalization.

Even specified in this very weak way, though, *HC2* is false if the domain is broad. Consider:

> *HC2* (Some Harm APW): In all possible worlds, it is wrong to criminalize conduct unless criminalizing that conduct prevents some harm.

Surely Gardner and Shute would accept that this principle is false, at least if they intend to rely on the 'clumsy tool' argument outlined above. That argument depended on the idea that criminalization *inevitably* causes harm. But even if it is inevitable in the real world that criminalization causes harm, it is possible to criminalize without causing harm. We can easily imagine worlds where criminalization is not harmful.

Consider:

> *Sharp Tool*: Were some country to criminalize wrongful sex with unconscious people, only those people who did this would be convicted of the relevant offence. This would prevent a great deal of sex with unconscious people, and would cause no harm to anyone else.

Sharp Tool may be unrealistic, in the sense that it could occur only in worlds unlike ours, but it is easy enough to imagine.[9] Surely Gardner and Shute would agree that criminalization of wrongful sex with unconscious people is permitted in *Sharp Tool*. We have powerful reasons to prevent sex with unconscious people even if doing so does not prevent harm. Given this, *HC2* (Some Harm APW) fails. This leaves open the possibility that some version of *HC2* (Some Harm) with a narrower domain succeeds.[10]

But we need not consider the empirical questions that must be answered to determine whether it does. For *HC2* (Some Harm) faces a more serious problem: it is so permissive as to be uninteresting. Almost any criminal prohibition could meet this standard because criminalizing almost any conduct prevents some harm. For example, the harm principle is often thought to rule out criminalization of conduct that some think is wrong, but which does not cause harm to others—gay sex is an obvious example.

[8] This argument is developed most completely and clearly in J Edwards 'Harm Principles' (2014) 20 *Legal Theory* 253. Something similar is suggested in J Raz *The Morality of Freedom* (Oxford: OUP, 1986) ch 15.

[9] Though Raz seems to think that this world is so far from our own that we cannot evaluate it! See *The Morality of Freedom*, 419.

[10] Raz, for example, is explicit that his defence of the harm principle is contingent on the effects of criminalization. See *The Morality of Freedom*, 419.

But *HC2* (Some Harm) does not rule out criminalization of gay sex. Criminalizing gay sex may prevent a few people getting into harmful relationships. If all that is needed to satisfy *HC2* is that some harm is prevented, *HC2* does not prohibit criminalizing gay sex. Even were *HC2* true, it would not be an important part of a theory of the criminal law.

iii) Consequentialism and harm

A more ambitious version of *HC2* claims that the criminal prohibition must prevent harm overall, or on balance:

> *HC2* (Lesser Evil): It is wrong to criminalize conduct unless criminalizing that conduct prevents more harm than it causes.

Criminalizing conduct typically causes harm. *HC2* (Lesser Evil) is satisfied only if the harm caused is outweighed by harm prevented, for example, through deterrence.

HC2 (Lesser Evil) is not attractive, though. Those who endorse widely divergent moral views can converge on its falsity. At first blush it might seem attractive to consequentialists. And this has good historical pedigree. John Stuart Mill was famous for proposing an effect-focused version of the harm principle—on his view, the only reason to criminalize conduct (or coercively interfere with liberty in any other way) is to prevent harm[11]—but Mill was also a consequentialist.

But these two views that Mill held are in tension. Good consequentialists should reject *HC2* (Lesser Evil); indeed they should reject all versions of the harm principle. Consequentialists claim that the only thing that makes an act right or wrong is the consequences of that act. But no sensible consequentialist thinks that harm prevention is the only consequence of an act that can make it right or wrong; indeed Mill did not think this. If consequentialism is true, other good consequences of criminalization can contribute to its justification. For example, some of the harm that criminalization causes might be outweighed by increased employment opportunities for police officers and prison guards that it creates. Non-consequentialists might argue that these good consequences of criminalization are irrelevant to its justification; consequentialists will be unmoved.

Mill's enthusiasm for the harm principle can be attributed to an empirical belief—that abiding by the harm principle would promote good consequences overall. He thought it would do so by allowing people to experiment with different ways of life to achieve human flourishing. His main reason for believing this was that those with conservative moral views restricted human creativity in different ways of life by imposing those views on others.

It is hard to believe that sex with unconscious people should be legally permitted on this basis, though, even if criminalization did not prevent more harm than it caused. This conduct diminishes sexual autonomy. It prevents people from developing a sex life according to their own judgements. So those who are sympathetic to Mill's concerns should reject *HC2* in favour of the protection of a broader set of rights that help to support autonomous pursuit of one's own conception of a good life. Mill's defence of the harm principle, I think, is explained by the fact that he did not have a very clear grasp of the idea that interference with autonomous pursuit of one's legitimate goals need

[11] J Gray (ed), *On Liberty and Other Essays* (Oxford: OUP, 1991) 14.

not be harmful. Once we see this, Mill's consequentialist defence of the harm principle is vulnerable to the charge that it does too little to protect people against non-harmful interference.[12]

iv) Instrumentalism and the significance of harm

HC2 (Lesser Evil) is not very attractive for non-consequentialists either. One problem is that it treats harm done to wrongdoers and non-wrongdoers equally. The harm that is inflicted on wrongdoers is justified only if a greater amount of harm to innocent people is prevented. Many non-consequentialists reject this. Many who believe in desert reject this because they think that the harm inflicted on wrongdoers is good. For them, only harms that the criminal justice system causes to the innocent need to be outweighed.[13]

But many instrumentalists who (like me) reject desert will also reject this implication of *HC2* (Lesser Evil). Instrumentalists believe that the harm that punishment inflicts is intrinsically bad. The state is justified in inflicting this harm, when it is so justified, because of its good effects—most importantly, the reduction of harmful wrongdoing that is secured through deterrence. But instrumentalists need not be consequentialists. They need not believe that punishment is justified if and only if it achieves the best consequences.[14]

One way in which instrumentalism might depart from consequentialism is to do with liability. Instrumentalists might argue that the harm that is inflicted on wrongdoers when they are punished does not count as heavily against criminalizing wrongdoing as it would were the harm inflicted on innocent people because the wrongdoers are liable to be harmed. For similar reasons, instrumentalists need not believe that it is wrong to harm wrongdoers if it prevents less harm than it causes.

Compare self-defence. Many non-consequentialists offer instrumentalist justifications of self-defence—they believe that a person is permitted to harm wrongful attackers only if doing so is necessary to secure some independently valuable goal—typically protecting oneself from the attack. But many non-consequentialists also believe that self-defence is sometimes justified even if the harm that is inflicted on the attacker is greater than the harm that the attacker will otherwise wrongfully inflict. They believe, for example, that it is permissible to kill a wrongful attacker to prevent him from causing severe long-term disability, even if death is worse than suffering the disability.

Now return to punishment. Suppose that punishing a person who has committed a serious assault to some degree, *n*, will result in one innocent person being protected from an assault, which would otherwise result in her being harmed to some degree slightly less than *n*. As the person who has committed the assault is liable to be punished, punishment might be justified. But if the wrongdoer is punished, the punishment causes more harm than it prevents.

Instrumentalists may also believe that it would be permissible to harm more wrongdoers to some degree to prevent the same amount of harm to fewer innocent people.

[12] See, further, V Tadros 'Harm, Sovereignty, and Prohibition'.

[13] For discussion, see, for example, D N Husak 'Retribution in Criminal Theory' (2000) 37 *San Diego Law Review* 959; M Berman 'Punishment and Justification' (2008) 118 *Ethics* 258.

[14] See, generally, V Tadros *The Ends of Harm: the Moral Foundations of Criminal Law* (Oxford: OUP, 2011) ch 2.

For example, suppose that punishing twenty people for an unusual kind of assault to degree *n* will prevent nineteen people from being assaulted in this way, where they will otherwise be harmed to degree *n*. Instrumentalists may favour punishment because the wrongdoers are liable to be punished.

Of course, I have not shown here that the punishment can be justified in some cases even when it does more harm than good. But the view that it can is highly plausible. When we justify harming others we take into account not only how much harm we will do, but also the ability that people have to avoid being harmed, and any duties they have incurred to suffer harm in service of certain ends.

HC2 (Lesser Evil) also runs into trouble because of standard non-consequentialist constraints on harming, such as *The Using View*. It is often wrong harmfully to use one person to prevent a similar harm to a larger number of people. Consider:

> *Child Torture*: Brad is a member of a terrorist organization who has been captured by Larry's government. Brad has information about terrorist acts but will not give in to torture. If Larry tortures Brad's child, though, Larry will reveal the information. Doing this will prevent more harm to innocent people than Larry will inflict.

The Using View implies that it would be wrong for Larry to torture Brad's child, even though doing so prevents more harm than it causes.

Now suppose that criminalizing torture would prevent a great deal of torture occurring, and would not prevent other harms. Preventing the torture would prevent harm to those who would be tortured, but would result in even more harm being inflicted—the harm that the torture would have prevented. *HC2* (Lesser Evil) implausibly implies that it would be wrong to criminalize this conduct. This would be so because criminalizing it fails to prevent more harm than it causes.

It may be objected that as *Child Torture* is stylized, I have not shown that *HC2* (Lesser Evil) is false in the domain of Western in the real world. But non-consequentialist arguments have played an important role in defending the stringent right against torture. Many believe that the torture of innocent people (and also of guilty people) ought to be prohibited even if relaxing the prohibition would prevent more harm than it causes. It would be surprising if these arguments fell foul of the best version of the harm principle. So although the example is stylized, the general problem is real.

Of course, a complete argument against *HC2* (Lesser Evil) relies on a more complete defence of the non-consequentialist principles that I have relied on here, as well as a range of empirical questions. But we can already see that we have little reason to accept *HC2* (Lesser Evil).

v) Proportionality and goods

Criminalization typically harms some and prevents harm to others. Principles governing harming and preventing harm are complex. This explains why there is no simple way to specify effect-focused restrictive principles that renders them both true and illuminating.

This might be thought to favour a version of *HC2* that allows us to consider more complexity in the relationship between harm caused and harm prevented:

> *HC2* (Proportionality): It is wrong to criminalize conduct unless doing so is proportionate. It is proportionate only if the harm that criminalization causes is outweighed by the harm that it prevents.

This principle is sufficiently vague that it allows us to appeal to non-consequentialist principles to determine the significance of harm caused and harm prevented. It allows us to discount the significance of harm inflicted on wrongdoers. And it allows us to discount the significance of harm prevented if harm prevention is wrong, as in the case of harm preventions secured by torture. But it is still distinctively a harm principle, in that it suggests that only harm figures in the proportionality calculation.

But *HC2* (Proportionality) is also vulnerable because of this limitation—non-consequentialists, like consequentialists, should not restrict their attention to harm reduction when assessing whether their acts are permissible or required. A range of goods is relevant to determining whether it is proportionate to inflict harm on others. Our legitimate aims are not restricted to harm prevention. Criminalization is surely easier to justify if doing so prevents some harmless wrongdoing, for example. It follows that prevention of harmless wrongdoing can figure in the proportionality calculation, contrary to *HC2* (Proportionality).

We will consider this in more depth in Chapter 9, but for now recall Gardner and Shute's discussion of harmless rape. Suppose that they are right that the rapes they describe are harmless. Surely it would be a very good reason to criminalize such rapes that the state would prevent these rapes from occurring. And surely the fact that the state would prevent these rapes from occurring would help to justify any harm that the prohibition causes, either through punishment of the rapists, or to others.

More strongly, Gardner and Shute provide no argument why prevention of these wrongs could not be sufficient *on its own* to justify the harm that results from criminalizing them. They suggest that a prohibition on harmless rape could not be justified, given the costs of the prohibition, unless the prohibition also prevented harmful rapes. But is this really true? Suppose that we discovered that a narrower prohibition, one that included an exception for harmless rapes, was equally effective in preventing harmful rapes, but would result in many harmless rapes that a broader provision would prevent. It is hard to believe that the broader prohibition could not be justified in this case, even if the broader prohibition resulted in some liable and some non-liable people being harmed.

If so, *HC2* (Proportionality) must go. When we determine whether criminalizing some conduct is proportionate, we consider a range of good effects that the criminal law would have. This includes preventing harm, but it is not restricted to preventing harm. The harm that the criminal law causes can be outweighed by harm prevention, but also by the prevention of harmless wrongdoing. And it is at least plausible that the prevention of harmless wrongdoing could be sufficient on its own to justify the criminalization of the relevant conduct. In that case, to justify the extension of the criminal law, it is unnecessary to show that criminalization prevents harm. This suggests that all interesting versions of *HC2* fail.

IV. Conclusion

Whilst there are good reasons to reject familiar content-focused and effect-focused restrictive principles, considering them points us in a better direction. Friends of content-focused restrictive principles have led us to one important set of questions: questions about what renders a person liable to punishment. Friends of effect-focused restrictive principles have led us to another important set of questions: when criminalization is justified all things considered, because of its good and bad effects. Distinguishing these questions, and understanding the relationship between them, helps us properly to structure our thinking about criminalization.

7

How Not to Think About Criminalization II: Justificatory Principles

In the previous chapter, I argued against restrictive principles of criminalization. Here, we consider a different kind of principle that might seem more promising: justificatory principles. Justificatory principles identify reasons or duties that uniformly support criminalization.

Like restrictive principles, justificatory principles come in several flavours. The strongest principles are concerned with duties:

Abstract Duty: The state is always required to criminalize conduct if *x*.

This principle is ambiguous, for duties can be either all things considered or *pro tanto*. As we saw in the previous chapter, a person need not be all things considered required to do what she has a *pro tanto* duty to do. And she may be all things considered required not to do what she has a *pro tanto* duty to do. Weaker duty principles put *pro tanto* in front of 'required'; stronger principles put 'all things considered' there. Given the wide range of conditions that need to be met to justify criminalization all things considered, all things considered duty principles will either be vague and unilluminating or very complex. *Pro tanto* versions may be simpler.

Weaker principles make claims about reasons for criminalization:

Abstract Reason: The state always has reason to criminalize conduct if *x*.

We can see that this principle is weaker from the fact that we always have a reason to do what we have a duty (either *pro tanto* or all things considered) to do, but not the converse.

Like restrictive principles, justificatory principles can also be either content-focused or effect-focused.[1] Contrast:

Abstract Reason (Content): The state always has reason to criminalize conduct if that conduct is *x*.

Abstract Reason (Effect): The state always has reason to criminalize conduct if criminalizing that conduct will *x*.

We saw in the previous chapter that content and effect-focused restrictive principles are only contingently related, and the same is true of content and effect-focused justificatory principles. Thus, compare these different versions of the justificatory harm principle:

Harm Reason (Content) (HR Content): The state always has reason to criminalize conduct if that conduct is harmful.

[1] Below, we will also see that more attractive justificatory principles are neither content-focused nor effect-focused.

Harm Reason (Effect) (HR Effect): The state always has reason to criminalize conduct if criminalizing that conduct will prevent harm.

As should be clear from the previous chapter, these principles have different implications. Criminalizing non-harmful conduct might prevent harm and criminalizing harmful conduct might not prevent harm.

Section I rejects effect-focused justificatory principles. Sections II and III reject two arguments in favour of the idea that we always have a reason or a duty to criminalize wrongdoing, and shows how that rejection can be extended to other content-focused justificatory principles. Section IV is concerned with the idea of public wrongdoing. It rejects a familiar version of the idea of public wrongdoing as a platform for considering a more plausible version in the next chapter.

I. Rejecting Effects

A difficulty in assessing justificatory principles is that they rely on more general, but deeply contested, claims about reasons and duties. Consequently, it is often hard to know what these principles mean and what their implications are. Once we make progress with our understanding of reasons and duties, we find that no content-focused or effect-focused principles are both illuminating and true. However, I will suggest one principle that is neither content-focused nor effect-focused, and that is both illuminating and plausible.

i) Consequences, *pro tanto* duties, and complex duties

Most familiar *pro tanto* duty effect-focused principles are either false or unilluminating. Here is why most familiar principles of this kind fail. Take some good effect. Now notice that criminalizing highly admirable conduct can in principle achieve this effect. *Pro tanto* duty versions of effect-focused principles imply a *pro tanto* duty to criminalize desirable, or even admirable, conduct when this is true.

Consider this principle:

Serious Harm Duty (Effect): The state always has a *pro tanto* duty to criminalize conduct if criminalizing that conduct will prevent serious harm to others.

Criminalizing desirable conduct can have the relevant effect, so the principle has implausible implications. For example, criminalizing all procreation would prevent serious harm to others because some children will cause serious harm to others. Criminalizing procreation will prevent some of these children from existing. *Serious Harm Duty (Effect)* implausibly implies that the state has a *pro tanto* duty to criminalize all procreation.

Pro tanto duty effect-focused principles might be valid if they focus on effects that are extraordinarily good: the prevention of nuclear war, for example. But, obviously enough, these principles make a relatively unimportant contribution to our theory of criminalization.

It might be argued that such principles can be valid if they guarantee restrictions on how the effects will be achieved. Consider:

Accountability Duty (Effect): The state always has a *pro tanto* duty to criminalize conduct if criminalizing that conduct will result in those who commit public wrongs being held to account through a legitimate process of trials and punishments.

This principle might seem more plausible, given that a legitimate process of trials and punishments relies on criminalization. But this principle also fails, because the effect of criminalizing some legitimate conduct might have the relevant effect through a circuitous causal route that would involve criminalizing desirable or admirable conduct.

Consider:

> *Homophobic Cops*: Homophobic cops regularly discriminate against gay people with impunity. If all sexual contact between gay people is criminalized, homophobia will receive a great deal of public attention. This will lead to some of these homophobic cops being held to account for their conduct.

Accountability Duty (Effect) implausibly implies that the state has a *pro tanto* duty to criminalize all sexual contact between gay people.

We could amend the principle to avoid this objection by referring to the direct effects of criminalization, where criminalization has direct effects if the relevant criminal offence describes the wrong that the wrongdoers are publicly held accountable for. Thus:

> *Accountability Duty (Direct Effect)*: The state always has a *pro tanto* duty to criminalize conduct if criminalizing that conduct will directly result in the state fulfilling its duty to hold wrongdoers publicly to account for their wrongdoing, and to punish them.

Whether this principle is true depends in part on an account of *pro tanto* duties. I noted how hard it is to make progress with such an account in the previous chapter. To see the problem here, suppose that criminalization of some conduct is costly. If it happens, though, the state will fulfil its duty to hold some wrongdoers to account for their wrongdoing. Does the state have a *pro tanto* duty to criminalize the conduct given the costs? That depends on an account of *pro tanto* duties that I lack.

If this problem can be solved, the principle may seem both true and illuminating. It illuminates the connection between the central functions of criminal justice, such as public accountability and punishment, and criminalization. But even this principle is not illuminating. The reason is that the focus on the actual effects of criminalization is unwarranted. What matters is not the actual effects of criminalization, but the broader normative context in which criminalization operates.

To see the difference, recall that criminalizing wrongdoing is a necessary condition of the just performance of the general functions of the criminal justice system. The state has a duty to perform these general functions: it has a duty to call serious wrongdoers to account for their wrongdoing and to punish them. Its duty to criminalize conduct does not arise from the fact that it will in fact perform these functions if the conduct is criminalized, but rather from the duty that it has to perform these functions.

Its duty to criminalize the conduct does not depend on what it will do if it criminalizes the conduct, but rather on what it ought to do if it does so. For example, suppose that the state has an all things considered duty to hold marital rapists to account for rape, and to punish them. This generates a duty to criminalize marital rape. Now suppose that if marital rape is criminalized, the state will not in fact fulfil its duty to hold marital rapists to account, and to punish them, because the sexist government will not put any resources into investigating and prosecuting marital rape. This does not vitiate its duty to criminalize marital rape. It has a duty to criminalize marital rape, and then to punish rapists for marital rape. This explains why the duty to criminalize marital rape does not depend on the actual effects of criminalization: the duty to criminalize is part of a larger complex duty to criminalize, prosecute, convict, publicly condemn, and punish rapists. The existence of the duties that are parts of the whole do not depend on whether other duties that are parts of the whole will be fulfilled.[2]

So there is a principle of criminalization that is close to an effect-based principle that seems both true and illuminating. It is this:

> *Responsive Duty*: The state always has a *pro tanto* duty to criminalize conduct if criminalizing that conduct is necessary for the state to fulfil its all things considered duty to hold wrongdoers publicly to account for their wrongdoing, and to punish them.

This principle is neither a content-based, nor an effect-based principle. It is a principle that explains the role of criminalization in the context of the broader range of duties that the criminal justice system fulfils. Even this principle needs clarification for the reason noted above: we lack a good account of *pro tanto* duties. But it is plausible, and it does pick out something important and illuminating. We will return to different versions of it below.

ii) Reasons for criminalization

As the principle just outlined is narrow, let us focus on broader reason-based versions of effect-focused justificatory principles. A great deal of work needs to be done to clarify such principles. Here is one important problem. The idea that an agent has a reason to *v* is unclear in various ways. One way arises from the fact that the claim that D has a reason to *v* suggests that we assess a contrast between D *v*ing and D doing something else. But what is the relevant contrast? Is it: 'doing nothing'; or 'the best alternative'; or 'the worst alternative'; or 'the worst permissible alternative'; or 'the thing that the person would do if he does not do this'; or are reason claims incomplete without specifying what the contrast is?

The last proposal seems attractive.[3] To see why, suppose that a person, D, can perform one of two actions, *x* and *y*, or do nothing. There is only one value that can be achieved by performing these actions—harm prevention. Each comes at a cost. These actions have identical effects in securing this value, and each is better in this respect than doing nothing. All other things are equal, except that *x* requires more effort than *y*. Does D have a reason to *x*? It depends on the question. Contrast *x* with doing nothing and he has a reason to do it. Contrast *x* with *y* and he has no reason to do it. When it is asked whether D has a reason to do *x*, then, we should specify the contrast: D has a reason to do *x* rather than do nothing, but no reason to do *x* rather than do *y*. There is no simple answer to the question whether D has a reason to do *x*.

In the light of this, consider the implications of *HR Effect*, for example, for criminalization, where some other method is available for tackling the problem that criminalization aims at:

> *Two Options*: Criminalizing some conduct, *v*, will prevent some harm at a price. Some of the resources required for criminalization to achieve this effect could also be used for public education, and this would be equally effective in preventing the harm at less cost. No other facts favour criminalization.

[2] For a fuller defence of this idea, see Chapter 16, Section III(ii).

[3] See, for a good critical overview, J Snedegar 'Contrastivism about Reasons and Ought' (2015) 10 *Philosophy Compass* 379.

Other things equal, does the state have reason to criminalize the conduct? In one sense it does, in another it does not.

To see this, note first that if the state criminalizes the conduct it does prevent harm. Like reasons, claims about harm involve making contrasts. It is a complex matter what the relevant contrast is.[4] But the relevant contrast in determining whether harm is prevented in *Two Options* is not what will occur if it puts the resources into public education.

Whether it has a reason to criminalize the conduct, though, may depend on this contrast. The answer to the question 'does the state have reason to criminalize *v* rather than providing public education' is that it does not. Hence, if this is the question being asked, the state has no reason to prevent harm. Thus *HR (Effect)* is shown to be false.

But friends of *HR (Effect)* might respond that they do not mean to compare criminalization with other things that might be done, but rather with something else. *HR Effect* might seem more plausible if 'doing nothing' is taken as the comparison:

> *HR (Effect 2)*: The state always has a reason to criminalize conduct rather than doing nothing if criminalizing that conduct will prevent harm to others.

HR (Effect 2) is also unclear, though, because it is not very clear what 'doing nothing' means. Suppose that the state is already providing public education to prevent the relevant harm in *Two Options*. Does it have a reason to criminalize *v* according to *HR (Effect 2)*? The state can either continue to provide the public education, or it can stop. Which of these amounts to its doing nothing for the purposes of *HR (Effect 2)*?

If it is the former, *HR (Effect 2)* implies that the state has a reason to criminalize the conduct rather than continuing with public education, and that seems false. *HR (Effect 2)* is plausible only if 'doing nothing' involves refraining from continuing with the public education programme in this case. But it is difficult to make the case that this amounts to the state doing nothing—cancelling the programme, instructing public officials not to provide education, and so on, are all actions. Still, perhaps there is a way of rescuing *HR (Effect 2)* by providing a more complete account of what it means for the state to do nothing that has plausible implications for criminalization. That seems very hard to provide.

Given how hard it is to clarify these principles, we should try to do so only if they will turn out to be important. I doubt they will, and my doubts are reinforced by the fact that in trying to make progress with *HR (Effect)*, we don't seem to be learning much that is very interesting about criminalization. We are in a discussion of whether some version of *HR (Effect)* is true that has taken us deeply into difficult questions about the nature of reasons and the metaphysics of doing nothing without making important progress with the central moral and political questions that ought to be at the heart of a theory of criminalization.

For this reason, philosophers of the criminal law do better not to explore any principles that make claims about what we have reason to do. These principles are typically stated in a way that is unclear. Clarifying them in a way that makes them plausible is extremely difficult. And in doing so, we take ourselves into difficult normative and metaphysical questions that are a long way away from the moral and political issues that are more directly at stake in thinking about the criminal law.

[4] See, further, Chapter 10, drawing on V Tadros 'What Might Have Been' in J Oberdiek *Philosophical Foundations of the Law of Torts* (Oxford: OUP, 2014).

Compare the principles governing the use of lethal force. A great deal of progress has been made in our understanding of the use of lethal force by thinking about the principles that constrain its use, such as principles concerning liability to be harmed and principles of proportionality. But no one, in that context, would think it important to evaluate a principle like:

> *Lethal Force (Reason)*: It is always a reason to use lethal force that it will prevent some harm to others.

Consider the implications of this principle for:

> *Killing Children*: Mikey, who is five, is about to pinch Bella, his three year old sister. Margo, his mum, can prevent him from doing this either by shooting Mikey with her sawn-off shotgun or by telling him to stop.

Lethal Force (Reason) implies that Margo has a reason to shoot Mikey. There may be a way of spelling out *Lethal Force (Reason)* that makes this true. But we really don't have a reason to make progress with *Lethal Force (Reason)* to see if it can be spelled out in a way that makes it true. A principle that implies that Margo has a reason to shoot Mikey is unimportant in a theory of the use of lethal force. *HR (Reason)* seems to me no better as a principle of criminalization.

To reinforce this point, notice that harm prevention is only one good thing amongst the range of good things that we have reason to bring about. Principles like *HR Effect* are just more specific versions of a more general principle like:

> *Good Reason (Effect)*: The state always has a reason to criminalize some conduct if criminalizing that conduct will do some good.

This is a more specific version of an even more general principle like:

> *General Good Reason (Effect)*: Anyone always has a reason to act if acting will do some good.

These principles are plausible enough. They can be spelled out in a way that makes them true, with some work.

But they are also not good principles of criminalization, just like *Lethal Force (Reason)* is not a good principle to illuminate the morality of the use of lethal force, even if it is true. We can confirm the conclusion that principles like this are not very good by noticing that they warrant the criminalization of everything. Here is the argument for that conclusion:

1) All acts of criminalization have very many effects.
2) At least one of the effects of criminalizing anything at all will be good.
3) We have a reason to perform an act if performing that act will do some good.
4) Therefore we have a reason to criminalize anything at all.

This argument seems quite plausible. Take an obviously silly act of criminalization: the criminalization of ear-scratching. Doing this will have some good effects: it will make someone laugh; it will give someone something to write home about; it will expose the idiocy of some government official; and so on. If *General Good Reason (Effect)* is true, the state has a reason to criminalize ear-scratching. But no one who is interested in thinking about the scope of the criminal law should be interested in this fact.

This problem infects all effect-based justificatory principles. They are most plausible when they make claims about the reasons that states have. These versions can be made true with careful work. But that work also makes them uninteresting.

II. Retributivism and Criminalization

These criticisms of effect-focused justificatory principles might lead some to prefer content-focused principles. We have already seen that reason-based versions of these principles will be true but uninteresting, because criminalizing anything will have some good effects, and the state has good reasons to bring these good effects about. Better to focus, then, on duty-based versions.

Michael Moore defends one such principle:

> *Wrongness* Pro Tanto *Duty* (*Content*) *(WDC)*: All moral wrongs should be criminally prohibited.[5]

We have already seen one way in which this principle is unclear. But it is easily clarified. By 'should' Moore must mean to refer to *pro tanto* duties. This is clear, as he thinks that reasons of liberty can make it wrong all things considered to criminalize some wrongdoing.[6] But as we don't know how to identify *pro tanto* duties, it is still not very clear.

i) Retributivism and criminalization

Let us, though, consider Moore's argument for this principle, which might be illuminating even if the principle is not. This argument draws on his retributivist view of punishment. Moore's retributivism is the view that punishment is justified because it ensures that wrongdoers get what they deserve. He believes that this supports *WDC*.

Here is the argument I think he intends:

Retributivist Criminalization:
1) All wrongdoers who are morally responsible for their wrongdoing deserve punishment.
2) The state ought to ensure that all of those who deserve punishment get what they deserve.
3) Therefore the state ought to punish all wrongdoers.
4) The state ought to punish a person for wrongdoing only if it has criminalized the wrongdoing.
5) Therefore, the state ought to criminalize all wrongful conduct.

One objection to *Retributivist Criminalization*—in my view a decisive objection—is that premise 1) is false because no wrongdoers deserve punishment. As many criminal justice scholars are retributivists, let us explore other aspects of the argument.

Here is a further doubt. Moore moves quickly from the claim that wrongdoers deserve to suffer the burdens of punishment to the claim that *all* wrongdoers deserve to suffer the burdens of state punishment without much argument. Retributivists need not believe this. Some retributivists defend their views by pointing to the intuition that it is intrinsically good that very serious wrongdoers live sad lives.[7] Even if they

[5] *Placing Blame: A Theory of the Criminal Law* (Oxford: OUP, 1997) 662.

[6] See *Placing Blame*, ch 18 and 'Liberty's Constraints on What Should Be Made Criminal' in R A Duff, L Farmer, S E Marshall, M Renzo, and V Tadros *Criminalization: The Political Morality of the Criminal Law* (Oxford: OUP, 2014). For some doubts about Moore's approach to liberty, see V Tadros 'The Wrong and the Free' in K K Ferzan and S J Morse *Legal, Moral, and Metaphysical Truths: The Philosophy of Michael S Moore* (Oxford: OUP, 2016).

[7] See, for example, Moore *Placing Blame*, 145 and 163; L Zaibert 'Instruments of Abolition, or Why Retributivism is the Only Real Justification of Punishment' (2013) 32 *Law and Philosophy* 33. For a response, see V Tadros 'Responses' (2013) 32 *Law and Philosophy* 241, 256–74.

are right, the same thing need not be true of less serious wrongdoers. They might not deserve to suffer at all.

Perhaps Moore might argue that as wrongdoers deserve to suffer in proportion to their wrongdoing, trivial wrongdoers ought to suffer a trivial amount. But not all retributivists need accept this. Even if we ought to feel very bad about our serious wrongdoing, it does not follow that we ought to feel a little bit bad about our trivial wrongdoing. Compare pride. Suppose that a person ought to feel very proud of her great achievements. It does not follow that she ought to feel a little bit proud of her tiny achievements. Pride might be appropriate only once some threshold is met. Desert might also have a threshold.

More importantly, even if Moore's wide-scope view of desert is right, his legal moralism does not follow. Even if all wrongdoers deserve something bad, they may not all deserve the bad things that punishment inflicts. And even if they deserve the bad things that punishment inflicts, they need not deserve the bad things that state punishment inflicts. It doesn't seem very plausible that trivial wrongdoers deserve to suffer the burdens of state punishment. State punishment is a sledgehammer. Trivial wrongdoing is a nut. We lack a duty, even a defeasible duty, to use this sledgehammer to crack this nut.

For example, some friends of wide-scope desert might believe trivial wrongdoers deserve only to feel weak pangs of guilt. State punishment inevitably inflicts suffering and deprivation that is different in kind and degree from weak pangs of guilt. Trivial wrongdoers who are punished by the state inevitably suffer the wrong kind of thing, and suffer disproportionately. Even tiny fines would be disproportionate. Hence, even friends of Moore's wide-scope desert should acknowledge that the state ought not to criminalize trivial wrongdoing.

Moore might respond that even if a trivial wrongdoer only deserves pangs of guilt, there would always be a duty to punish the wrongdoer—the duty to bring about these pangs of guilt. Given that it will inevitably do much more than this, the state ought not to perform this duty, but it has the duty nevertheless.

Here are two doubts about this response. First, there would be a duty to punish wrongdoers only if the state can cause trivial wrongdoers to feel pangs of guilt—ought implies can (at least in this case). It may not be able to do this because using the state's machinery will inevitably cause such resentment that wrongdoers will not suffer weak pangs of guilt. Whether these things are true, of course, is an empirical matter. But as Moore claims that the state ought to punish all wrongdoing, his argument will fail if they are ever true, and it would be hard to show that they are not.

A second worry takes a little longer to flesh out. Moore's analysis implies that the state has a duty to punish trivial wrongdoing even though, given that it will inevitably punish the wrongdoing disproportionately, it ought not to punish such wrongdoers in any circumstances. To support this view, Moore might reasonably argue that we sometimes have duties that we ought not to fulfil, because fulfilling them would be disproportionate.

However, punishing wrongdoers will *inevitably* harm them disproportionately. If the state harms them at all, it will harm them too much. To vindicate his view Moore needs to show that the state is required to punish trivial wrongdoers even though it ought *never* to fulfil such duties because it couldn't do so without inflicting disproportionate harm. We might doubt that we have duties that we ought never to fulfil in any circumstances that are likely to arise. Or, more modestly, we might doubt that the state has such duties in this case.

To investigate further, suppose that the following three things are true of some agent, D:

a) D would have a duty to *x* if D could *x* and not *y*.
b) In all actual cases, and all nearby possible worlds, where D can *x*, D can either 1) not *x* or 2) both *x* and *y*. D cannot *x* without *y*ing.
c) It is all things considered wrong for D to *x* and *y*.

The question is whether, in these circumstances, D has a duty to *x*. Moore might claim that although, given that he will inevitably *y*, D ought not to *x* all things considered, nevertheless D has a duty to *x*. When D refrains from *x*ing, he violates a *pro tanto* duty to *x*. He ought to violate this duty in virtue of the fact that if he *x*s he will also certainly *y*.

This view is coherent: a person can have a *pro tanto* duty that she ought not to fulfil all things considered. There are three possible views that one might take for the set of circumstances where a), b) and c) are true:

1) In all cases, D has a *pro tanto* duty to *x*.
2) In all cases, D lacks a *pro tanto* duty to *x*.
3) In some cases D has a *pro tanto* duty to *x*, but in others he does not.

Which view is correct? Moore moves quickly from the view that wrongdoers deserve to suffer, and that this can ground a duty to give them what they deserve, to the view that there is always a *pro tanto* duty to do this, even where this duty is defeated. As he offers no further argument for this move, perhaps he believes 1).

Here is a *reductio* of 1). Suppose that if I devoted all of my time and resources to rescuing others, causing me to suffer a great deal over the course of my life, I could rescue several people from serious disease. If I could rescue this same group of people at no cost to myself I would have a duty to do so, on the relatively uncontroversial assumption that there is a duty of easy rescue. 1) implies that I have a *pro tanto* duty to rescue several people from serious disease, even though I could only do so by devoting all of my time and resources to rescuing these others. But this seems false. In pursuing other projects, I do not infringe a *pro tanto* duty to rescue these people; I lack that duty altogether. Hence, 1) is false.

To reinforce this view, notice that 1) implies that my range of *pro tanto* duties is vast. There are many significant goods that I lack all things considered duties to bring about because bringing them about is too costly. 1) implausibly implies that I have *pro tanto* duties to bring about all of these goods.

If 2) is true, Moore is wrong to think that the state has a *pro tanto* duty to punish trivial wrongdoing. For if 2) is true, the fact that state punishment for some kinds of wrong is inevitably disproportionate vitiates any *pro tanto* duty to give trivial wrongdoers what they deserve. Moore might claim, though, that my arguments against 1) do not demonstrate that 2) rather than 3) is true. 3) leaves open the possibility that the state has a *pro tanto* duty to punish trivial wrongdoing, even though doing so would be all things considered wrong in every case.

However, even if 3) is true, I doubt that the state has a duty to punish trivial wrongdoing. It seems more plausible that the fact that the state cannot punish trivial wrongdoing without doing so excessively vitiates any duty that it would otherwise have to punish trivial wrongdoing.

Compare defence of others. I have a duty to defend others against wrongful attacks when I can do so at no cost to myself, and when the harm that I inflict on the attacker is both necessary and proportionate. Now suppose that the only way that I can avert the wrongdoer's attack is gravely disproportionate. I then lack a *pro tanto* duty to save the victim in the disproportionate way. To see this, consider:

Driver Defence: As I am driving along in my monster truck, I see a schoolyard bully on the pavement about to twist the arm of his weakling victim. I can prevent this only by running the bully over with my monster truck.

It is not very plausible that I have a *pro tanto* duty to run the bully over, but doing so is all things considered wrong. It is much more plausible that I lack any *pro tanto* duty to run him over.

By analogy, it is not very plausible that the state has a *pro tanto* duty to punish trivial wrongdoers, but doing so is all things considered wrong. As inflicting state punishment on trivial wrongdoers is inevitably disproportionate, the state lacks either a *pro tanto* or an all things considered duty to do so. Hence, even if wide-scope desert is true, *Retributivist Criminalization* is false.

III. The Rough Ride from Criminal Justice to Criminalization

Here is another objection to *Retributivist Criminalization*, and it is an objection that applies to a wider range of justificatory principles. The objection also helps us to understand the relationship between the responsive functions of the criminal justice system and criminalization.

The criminal justice system has certain responsive functions: functions that it is valuable to perform in response to wrongdoing, involving wrongdoers. For retributivists, one function is giving wrongdoers what they deserve. For communicative theorists it is public blame. For duty theorists, it is the ensuring that the secondary duties that arise through wrongdoing are performed, or the aims of those duties secured. There is room for disagreement about whether these functions apply to all wrongdoers, or only to a subclass of wrongdoers—those who have committed public wrongs, understood in one way or another.

The state normally ought to publicly blame and punish wrongdoers only if it has first criminalized their wrongdoing. And even if criminalization is not always required for punishment to be permissible, the state is typically required to criminalize conduct as part of its more general duty to respond to serious wrongdoing. This is so for familiar reasons: for example, to ensure that people are given notice that their conduct will result in punishment, to ensure that criminal trials have a clear focus, and to ensure that public condemnation and punishment is properly supported by a political process.

These reasons to criminalize conduct might seem to provide a general reason in favour of criminalizing all wrongs, or certain classes of wrongs. The criminal justice system can provide a valuable response to some or all wrongs. Such responses are permitted, or are closer to being just, if the conduct is criminalized. Therefore, there is a general reason in favour of the criminalization of these wrongs.

Here is why this argument generally fails: reasons or duties in favour of responding to wrongdoing do not imply reasons or duties to create the conditions where responding will be permissible if the reasons in favour of responding will be defeated. If the reasons in favour of responding to wrongdoing will be defeated, there are no reasons to create the conditions that would improve the deontic status, or the value, of that response. I first spell out this objection by focusing on Moore's view, and then extend it to other views.

Moore defends a content-focused principle on the basis of an effect. The effect is wrongdoers getting what they deserve. Wrongdoing is criminalized in order to achieve this effect. But we have already seen that the relationship between content and effect is contingent. The criminalization of wrongdoing may not have the effect of any wrongdoers getting what they deserve. That is so even if criminal justice officials behave well. The reason is that any reasons in favour of giving wrongdoers what they deserve will be systematically defeated. Moore himself believes this. He claims that there is a set of wrongs that the state has a *pro tanto* duty to punish, but an all things considered duty never to do so. Reasons of liberty, he suggests, will often defeat the *pro tanto* duty to punish wrongdoing.

He nevertheless seems to believe that the state has a *pro tanto* duty to criminalize these wrongs in order to enhance the value or deontic status of punishment. But this is puzzling. It is hard to see what reason, let alone *pro tanto* duty, the state has to perform an act that would alter the value or deontic status of an act that it has a duty not to perform.

To put this another way, Moore's argument depends on the idea that our *pro tanto* duty to perform an act generates a *pro tanto* duty to create a condition necessary for the legitimate performance of that *pro tanto* duty, even when, as we well know, we have an all things considered duty not to fulfil that *pro tanto* duty, and we will never do so. That is hard to believe. We have no reason at all, let alone a duty, to satisfy a necessary condition of permissible punishment if the remaining conditions that would be needed to make it permissible will, we know, never be fulfilled, and we will therefore never perform the relevant action.

To exemplify and illustrate, I begin with cases outside the context of criminalization:

> *Non-Arrest*: Mary, a police officer, has discovered that Bill has probably committed a serious crime. However, Bill is very elderly, and if she arrests him he will die of a heart attack. As a result she decides not to arrest him.

Mary, it seems, has a *pro tanto* duty to arrest Bill, but an all things considered duty not to do so. Now suppose that it is wrong to arrest a person without first informing that person of his right to silence. It is wrong all things considered for Mary to arrest Bill. Given this, it doesn't seem at all plausible that she has a *pro tanto* duty to inform Bill of his right to silence. Her *pro tanto* duty to arrest him cannot generate a reason, let alone a *pro tanto* duty, to do this, given that Mary has decisive reasons not to arrest him, and as a result will not do so.

Or consider:

> *Warning*: The local council promises the local community to build a new youth centre on a site near a town. After it has made this promise, it is discovered that building the youth centre there will have a devastating effect on an endangered species.

Suppose that the council has a *pro tanto* duty to build the youth centre on the proposed site, but doing so is all things considered wrong. It is permissible for the council to build the youth centre only if signs are put up warning people not to enter the building site. But as it would be wrong all things considered for the council to build the youth centre on the site, it lacks a *pro tanto* duty to put up the warning signs. It even lacks any reason to do so.

Now compare criminalization. Suppose that as adultery is wrong, there is a *pro tanto* duty on the state to punish people for adultery, but for reasons of liberty it would always be wrong for the state to actually punish adulterers. Under these conditions, the fact that it is permissible to punish adulterers only if adultery has been criminalized cannot generate a *pro tanto* duty on the state to criminalize adultery. It cannot even generate a reason to do it. What would be the point, given that the remaining conditions to make punishment permitted all things considered will never obtain?

Now let us explore further the more general idea that this argument illuminates. One reason to criminalize conduct is that criminalization alters the value or deontic status of the performance of central functions of the criminal justice system. These functions include holding wrongdoers to account, publicly blaming them, and punishment. But the state's reasons to do these things to wrongdoers supply reasons to criminalize on this basis only if it will sometimes have sufficient reason to act on its reasons to perform these functions. If its reasons to perform these functions will always be defeated, the value of their performance cannot supply a reason in favour of criminalization.

To be clear, the idea is not that it is wrong to criminalize the conduct because of what the state will do if it does so. I have already suggested that our duties depend not on what we will do, but on what we ought to do, if we fulfil them. The objection is that a *pro tanto* duty to *v* cannot give rise to a *pro tanto* duty to do the things that are necessary to facilitate *v*ing, or to do the things that are necessary to make *v*ing permissible, if it will be all things considered wrong to *v*.

> This argument suggests that the value of performing central functions of the criminal justice system cannot support a wide range of principles that it has been thought to support. For example, some might think that Moore's argument cannot support *WDC*, but that it does support a weaker cousin: *Wrongness* Pro Tanto *Reason* (*Content*) *(WRC)*: There is a reason to criminalize all moral wrongs.

But Moore's argument supports this principle no more than it supports *WDC*. If our reason to punish certain kinds of wrong will inevitably be morally defeated, our reasons to punish the wrongdoing do not support any reason to criminalize the conduct. There would be no point at all in criminalizing the conduct. The fact that criminalization is a necessary condition of just punishment does not give rise to a reason in favour of criminalization if it will never form part of a set of sufficient conditions to do so.

Similarly, some think that Moore's argument does not apply to all wrongs, for there are wrongs that are not the state's business, but that a similar argument applies to a narrower range of wrongs: public wrongs. Sandra Marshall and Antony Duff, for example, think that there is always a reason to criminalize public wrongs on the basis that there is a reason to hold wrongdoers to account for public wrongdoing.[8] They thus endorse:

> *Public Wrongness Reason (PWR)*: There is a reason to criminalize all public wrongs.

But Marshall and Duff acknowledge that there are some public wrongs where the reasons for the state to hold certain public wrongdoers to account for them will always be defeated. For example, they argue that there are some public wrongs that are too trivial to merit any kind of formal legal response, such as minor acts of public rudeness and incivility.[9] If so, the state's reasons to hold the wrongdoers to account cannot supply a reason in favour of criminalization.

[8] See 'Public and Private Wrongs' in J Chalmers, F Leverick, and L Farmer *Essays in Criminal Law in Honour of Sir Gerald Gordon* (Edinburgh: EUP, 2010) 75; R A Duff 'Towards a Modest Legal Moralism' (2014) 8 *Criminal Law and Philosophy* 217, 230.

[9] 'Public and Private Wrongs', 77.

IV. Public Wrongness

Some argue that principles of criminalization should attend more closely to the fact that the criminal justice system is an arm of the state, and is therefore subject to political considerations that shape its appropriate use. We have seen that the principle that Duff and Marshall think flows from this view fails. Nevertheless, the idea of public wrongdoing might still have an important role to play in a theory of criminalization.

Recall this principle that I thought plausible:

> *Responsive Duty*: The state always has a *pro tanto* duty to criminalize conduct if criminalizing that conduct is necessary for the state to fulfil its all things considered duty to hold wrongdoers publicly to account for their wrongdoing, and to punish them.

Duff and Marshall think that the responsive functions of the state are aptly used only for those who have committed a subclass of wrongs: public wrongs. Here is a principle that captures this view that does not have the problematic implications identified in the previous section:

> *Responsive Duty* (*RPW*): The state always has a *pro tanto* duty to criminalize public wrongdoing because, and when, criminalizing that conduct is necessary for the state to fulfil its all things considered duty to hold wrongdoers publicly to account for their wrongdoing, and to punish them.

This principle also seems plausible and illuminating. But it relies on the vague idea of public wrongdoing. Duff and Marshall offer a distinct conception of public wrongdoing. I examine and reject their view in this section. In the next section I explore an alternative based on the duty view of punishment. In the next chapter, I explore a further alternative based on political liberalism.

i) Public wrongs, reasons, and deliberation

The view that there are distinctively public wrongs suggests that there is a principled divide between private morality and political morality. An extreme and implausible version of that view is that there is no connection between moral and criminal wrongdoing at all. The reasons to criminalize murder, rape, torture, and so on, on this view, are completely independent of the fact that these things are wrong, or the considerations that make these things wrong.

Duff and Marshall more plausibly argue that public wrongs are a subclass of wrongs: those wrongs that are the proper business of the polity. This idea is best explicated as the idea that the public take a proper interest in condemning and punishing wrongdoers for their conduct, rather than the idea that the public are the victims of the wrongdoing.[10]

One interpretative complication that I will mostly leave aside involves a further dispute about the nature of reasons. There is a dispute between Moore, Michelle Dempsey, and John Gardner on the one hand and Duff and Marshall and Massimo

[10] See S E Marshall and R A Duff 'Criminalization and Sharing Wrongs' (1998) 11 *Canadian Journal of Law and Jurisprudence* 7; R A Duff *Answering for Crime: Responsibility and Liability in the Criminal Law* (Oxford: Hart, 2007); R A Duff and S E Marshall 'Public and Private Wrongs'; R A Duff 'Towards a Modest Legal Moralism'; R A Duff 'Legal Moralism and Public Wrongs' in Ferzan and Morse *Legal, Moral, and Metaphysical Truths*. See, also, D N Husak *Overcriminalization: The Limits of the Criminal Law* (Oxford: OUP, 2008) 136–7.

Renzo on the other about whether there is a reason to criminalize all moral wrongdoing.[11] Duff, Marshall, and Renzo claim that there is no reason for public officials to be concerned with certain kinds of wrong. Moore and Gardner think there is a reason to be concerned with all wrongs. Gardner, though, thinks that this reason is consistent with the view that public officials have no reason to consider whether to criminalize the relevant act: they have a reason to respond to the wrongdoing, but lack a right or a duty to do so.

One way to reduce the tension between these positions is to clarify different things that might be meant by the question whether the state has a reason to criminalize some conduct. Duff and Marshall are focused on the way that lawmakers should reason when determining what to criminalize. For example, Duff's question is: 'what lines of deliberation about how to deal with or respond to some state of affairs could properly lead us to see criminalization as an, at least in principle, appropriate option?'[12] In claiming that there is no reason to criminalize certain wrongs, he might rely on the view that some fact, *r*, is a reason for X to *v* only if *r* should feature in X's practical reasoning about whether to *v*. As certain wrongs are 'off the table' from the start, no value that would be brought about by criminalizing these wrongs count as reasons in favour of doing so.

Dempsey, Gardner, and Moore, in contrast, may think that one can have a reason to act where one also has a reason against that reason figuring in one's practical reasoning. They can agree that certain values ought not to feature in the practical reasoning of lawmakers, whilst believing that these values count as reasons in favour of criminalizing the conduct. They might claim, for example, that the facts that make certain wrongs not the state's business exclude reasons in favour of criminalizing the conduct. But excluded reasons persist even when they are excluded from practical reasoning.[13] On this view, something can be a reason for someone even if that thing cannot play a proper role in a person's deliberations: it is a reason that the person can conform to, but not comply with.[14]

This dispute should not be resolved by thinking about criminalization directly but by thinking about how best to understand reasons for action. I don't take a side.

ii) Pragmatic and comparative reasons against criminalization

Duff and Marshall do not mean simply to rely on the idea that certain values ought not to play a role in the practical reasoning of state officials, though. Their main idea is that there are principled reasons why certain wrongs are beyond the attention of criminal justice officials. It would be wrong for state officials publicly to blame wrongdoers for some wrongs because of principled limits to the use of state instruments.

[11] M M Dempsey 'Public Wrongs and the "Criminal Law's Business": When Victims Won't Share' and J Gardner 'Relations of Responsibility', both in R Cruft, M H Kramer, and M R Reiff *Crime, Punishment, and Responsibility: The Jurisprudence of Antony Duff* (Oxford: OUP, 2011); M Renzo 'Responsibility and Answerability in Criminal Law' in R A Duff, L Farmer, S E Marshall, and V Tadros *The Constitution of the Criminal Law* (Oxford: OUP, 2013).

[12] For a clear indication from Duff, see 'Towards a Modest Legal Moralism', 226.

[13] See J Raz 'Postscript to the Second Edition: Rethinking Exclusionary Reasons' in J Raz *Practical Reasons and Norms* (Oxford: OUP, 1999). The possible implications of this idea are explored in L Green 'The Nature of Limited Government' in J Keown and R P George *Reason, Morality, and Law: The Philosophy of John Finnis* (Oxford: OUP, 2013) and J Edwards 'Master Principles of Criminalisation' *Jurisprudence*, forthcoming. See, further, Chapter 6.

[14] See Raz 'Postscript to the Second Edition'.

It is not controversial that some wrongs are not the state's business in two senses. Here is one: were state officials to make addressing these wrongs their business, things would go very badly, so these wrongs are not their business. For example, cheating in a relationship where there is an expectation of fidelity is often wrong. A very powerful reason against criminalizing this conduct is that any attempt by the state to investigate, prosecute, and punish people for cheating would involve investigating the intricacies of intimate relationships and making judgements about whether cheating has occurred and whether it is wrong in particular cases. The state will then invade privacy, and it will make these judgements badly. Let us call these 'pragmatic' considerations for short. We don't have a definition of what considerations are pragmatic, but the example offered gives us a rough grasp of the idea.

Another set of reasons why the state ought not to respond to wrongdoing is also uncontroversial: reasons to do with a division of labour between institutions. It is important that wrongdoing is appropriately addressed. The criminal justice system is one amongst many institutions and social practices that do this. Other branches of the law and other social institutions play this role: private law, educational institutions, families, friendships, and so on.

Whether conduct ought to be criminalized depends on the potential of other institutions to respond adequately to the wrongdoing. A range of factors relating to effectiveness and proportionality determine which institution is best placed. But whatever the right way to measure 'best', the idea that the decision to criminalize involves comparing different institutions is obviously right and practically important. Let us call these 'comparative' considerations for short.

Many of the examples that Duff and Marshall rely on to make intuitive the significance of public wrongdoing seem reasonably well explained by the pragmatic and comparative considerations I have just sketched. Insofar as we mean by a public wrong a wrong that is the state's business because of pragmatic and comparative considerations, everyone should sign up. It is not always clear whether Duff and Marshall think that these factors contribute to making a wrong a public wrong, or whether a wrong is public only in virtue of more principled considerations.[15]

Consider Duff's idea that we understand public wrongdoing by thinking about the appropriate purposes of the state: we first understand the point of a certain institutional arrangement, including its practices of responsibility, and determine what might be an appropriate subject for that institution to address in the light of that.[16] For example, medical professionals might come together to address certain bad practices by doctors. They would not, Duff rightly notes, consider whether to respond to marital infidelity, even if marital infidelity is wrong.

But now consider a prior question: which institutions ought we to develop, with what aims? The answer seems to depend on pragmatic and comparative considerations. If some institution is addressing some kind of wrongdoing well, there is normally no reason to create a new institution, or a new role for an institution, to address it. If there is a wrong that is not adequately addressed at present, we have reason to create an institution to do so, or to give an institution a role in doing it. Which institution

[15] Duff and Marshall make clear that the idea of public wrongs is independent of these considerations, as well as exploring some of them, in 'Public and Private Wrongs', 75–9. However, Duff seems to rely on these reasons in arguing that adultery is not a public wrong in *Answering for Crime*, 144, where he writes that adultery is a public wrong only if 'it is a wrong that cannot be left to the individuals concerned to deal with (or to ignore), but that it *must* be publicly condemned and sanctioned'.

[16] 'Legal Moralism and Public Wrongs'.

depends at least partly on pragmatic and comparative considerations just outlined: can it be done without disproportionate bad effects, and which institution will do it best? In many cases, the answer will not be the criminal law, coercive and clumsy tool that it is. But this only shows that we have pragmatic and comparative reasons against criminalizing some wrongs, and everyone accepts that.

To be clear, the concern is not that Duff is wrong to think that those governing particular social institutions have reason to respond only to those wrongs that concern the particular domain that they are concerned with. It is rather that the reasons for the division of labour that underpins the relevant institutions' structure might simply be pragmatic and comparative. If these considerations explain why certain wrongs are public, the idea of public wrongs is uncontroversial. If not, a case remains to be made for a more principled division of labour.

iii) Intrinsic appropriateness

One of Duff's suggestions is that comparative and pragmatic reasons cannot capture the idea of public wrongs because they imply that institutions serve ends that are independent of those institutions. When we refer to comparative and pragmatic reasons, we treat an end that is external to the criminal justice system as fixed, Duff claims, and identify the best way to satisfy the end. For example, we might have harm prevention as an end, and identify the best institution to serve that end.

When it comes to certain kinds of wrongdoing, though, the responsive functions of criminal law are intrinsically rather than instrumentally appropriate. And this, he suggests, shows that we cannot rely on pragmatic or comparative considerations in determining what to criminalize. In deciding what to criminalize, we should rather begin with intrinsic features of criminal justice.[17]

Duff's conclusion does not follow from the idea that the criminal law provides an intrinsically appropriate response to wrongdoing, for two reasons. First, the fact that a response to some conduct is intrinsically appropriate does not imply the irrelevance of comparative reasons. We can see this from ordinary interpersonal responses to wrongdoing. Suppose that I have acted wrongly. It may be intrinsically appropriate for John to blame me and intrinsically appropriate for Jane to do so. And it may be intrinsically inappropriate for John to blame me if Jane has done so, and vice versa. In this case, subject to certain further conditions, either John or Jane should blame me.

We might nevertheless compare whose response is most valuable. This involves comparing both the intrinsic and the instrumental value of their responses. For example, blaming may have greater intrinsic value if a person closely related to the victim does it; it may have greater instrumental value if it is more effective in ensuring that I will recognize that I have acted wrongly. These facts determine whether John or Jane should blame me. But if either does, and the other does not, the response is intrinsically appropriate.

Thus, even if certain responses that the criminal law makes to wrongdoing are intrinsically appropriate we can set goals independently of the criminal law: the goal of ensuring that intrinsically appropriate responses are made to wrongdoing and the goal of ensuring that wrongdoing is prevented by holding wrongdoers to account. We can then ask whether the best institutional response to the wrongdoing overall involves the criminal law.

17 See, for example, 'Towards a Modest Legal Moralism'.

It might be responded that the responsive functions of the criminal justice system and criminal law are not only intrinsically appropriate, but also unique. The criminal justice system might be the only institution that appropriately blames wrongdoers with a public voice. And this might have distinctive intrinsic value. This seems plausible. When we determine what to criminalize, Duff might then argue, we should primarily focus on its unique intrinsic value.

But even if we have good reason to focus primarily on the unique capabilities of the criminal justice system, why do we have good reason to focus primarily on its unique intrinsically valuable capabilities? The criminal justice system may also be uniquely instrumentally valuable: it may uniquely have the capability of reducing instances of serious wrongdoing in a just way by responding to wrongdoing. If so, why should this not be our main focus? Whether it is does not depend not on whether its functions are intrinsic or instrumental, but rather on the importance of those functions. And it is much more important that serious wrongdoing is prevented than that it is responded to.[18]

Perhaps Duff might argue that the uniquely valuable responses that the criminal law makes to wrongdoing nevertheless limit the application of the criminal law. Because the criminal law is uniquely capable of realizing the intrinsic values associated with public blame, conduct ought not to be criminalized where there is no such value to realize. Thus, if public blame is not warranted for some conduct, that conduct ought not to be criminalized.

But this argument cannot succeed. The fact that the criminal law *can* realize the value of publicly blaming wrongdoers for their conduct does not imply that it must do so in every case. The criminal law has many functions. Not all criminal laws must involve every function that it has, including those functions that it uniquely performs. Suppose that some conduct does not warrant public blame, because it is not wrongful, or not wrongful in the right way. There are very powerful reasons against publicly blaming the person for that conduct. But the criminal law has many other functions. It could refrain from issuing public blame, and carry out its other functions.

We might *define* criminal laws as laws concerned with public blame, and in that case laws that do not warrant public blame are not criminal laws. But we saw problems with that approach in the previous chapter. Those interested in the scope of the criminal law should not narrow their focus to exclude laws that make people liable to be harmed for deterrent reasons without publicly blaming violators.

iv) The values of the political community

In their earlier work Marshall and Duff suggest another argument for the distinctive qualities of public wrongdoing.[19] What should be criminalized, they argue, depends on contingent facts about the political community under consideration. Whether a wrong is public depends on whether the wrongdoing attacks values that bind the political community as a community. This makes the wrong a violation not only of the rights of the individual victim, but a wrong against the community more generally. And it is only if it is a wrong against the community more generally that a public response is warranted.

[18] See, further, V Tadros *The Ends of Harm: The Moral Foundations of Criminal Law* (Oxford: OUP, 2011) ch 5.

[19] 'Criminalization and Sharing Wrongs'.

They ask us to consider, by analogy, how a group of women respond to a sexual attack against one of them:

> They may see it as a collective, not merely an individual, wrong (as an attack on *them*), insofar as they associate and identify themselves with the individual victim. For they define themselves as a group, in terms of a shared identity, shared values, mutual concern—and shared dangers which threaten them: an attack on a member of the group is thus an attack on the group—on their shared values.[20]

They then extend from this smaller scale case to political communities, to whom a response is owed insofar as the 'individual goods which are attacked are goods in terms of which the community identifies and understands itself'.[21]

The argument suggested is this:

1) A public wrong is a wrong that a political community aptly responds to as a community.
2) A political community is a group of individuals bound together by shared values.
3) A political community aptly responds to a wrong against an individual only if it is a collective wrong.
4) A collective wrong is a wrong that attacks values that define the group, giving them their shared identity.
5) A state ought to criminalize conduct because, and only if, it is apt for the political community to respond to the wrongdoing as a political community.
6) Therefore the only wrongs that ought to be criminalized are those that attack values that give the political community its shared identity.

We have already seen, in Chapter 6, that claims like premise 5) need to be weakened to be plausible.

But even qualified in this way, the argument is problematic. The relativism implied by premises 3) and 4) together is troubling. The trouble goes in two directions. First, suppose that a political community in fact defines itself according to certain shared values, but it ought not to do so. The argument seems to imply that the state has a reason to criminalize the conduct.

The objection, here, is not that the political community might define itself according to values that are not real, and therefore that do not make conduct wrong.[22] Marshall and Duff can respond that public wrongdoing is a particular kind of wrongdoing. The problem, rather, is that a political community could, in principle, define itself according to any value that underpinned any wrong. If so, any wrong is a public wrong, on condition that the community has in fact bound itself according to the value underpinning it, even if it ought not to have done so.[23] If the ambition of the argument from public wrongdoing is to explain the intuition that there are some wrongs that are none of the state's business in principle, this version of public wrongdoing cannot do the job. For any wrongdoing could become the state's business by the public binding itself together by the values that underpin the wrong.

The more serious problem is that this argument rules out the use of the criminal law to respond to very serious wrongs that are underpinned by values that the community fails to accept. One of the great problems that the criminal law ought to address, though, is that of serious wrongdoing that the broader community supports

[20] 'Criminalization and Sharing Wrongs', 19.
[21] 'Criminalization and Sharing Wrongs', 20.
[22] See M S Moore 'Liberty's Constraint on What Should be Made Criminal', 199.
[23] See L Farmer *Making the Modern Criminal Law: Criminalization and Civil Order* (Oxford: OUP, 2016) 18–19. Duff recognizes the problem in 'Legal Moralism and Public Wrongs', 102.

because they don't recognize the values that underpin the wrongdoing. The most obvious examples are wrongs against women in very sexist societies: the wrongs of domestic abuse, female genital mutilation, sexual harassment, exploitation, and rape are not recognized as wrongs in many societies, or they recognize some of these wrongs only to a limited extent. This is often because they don't adequately recognize the values of female personal and sexual autonomy that underpin these wrongs. A powerful reason in favour of criminalizing this conduct is that criminalization challenges problematic attitudes in these societies about the wrongs in question.

Of course, there are many practical problems with criminalizing conduct that is not widely seen as wrong. There are difficult empirical questions to address, but I find it plausible that the criminal law is part of a package of government measures to tackle systematic wrongdoing that is not widely recognized as such in practice as well. But whatever the answers to the relevant empirical questions, these wrongs are appropriate targets for the criminal law, even though they don't attack the self-understanding of the political community.

Understanding why helps us distinguish different kinds of public response that officials might appropriately make to wrongdoing through the criminal justice system. Suppose that a group is not bound together by a certain value, but it ought to bind itself together by that value. I doubt that it would then be inapt for the group to blame a person who acts wrongly by attacking that value. For example, suppose that a group of women don't define themselves as a group by the values that underpin the wrongness of domestic abuse. Suppose that this is because some members of the group have internalized sexist norms, and thus think that a certain degree of violence by husbands against wives is legitimate. There is a sense in which it is apt for a member of the group who does see the conduct as wrong to condemn a domestic abuser as a representative of the group.

The official condemning the wrongdoing, of course, cannot claim that all members of the group authorize her condemnation, and that her words convey the intentions and sentiments of those members. They do not. But she can claim to speak on behalf of these women in another sense. Women with adequate self-regard will believe that their autonomy and well-being underpin the wrong of domestic abuse. The wrongdoer fails to recognize this about his particular victim, but this is also a part of a larger phenomenon, where domestic abuse is treated as legitimate. Thus, the abuser reflects and reinforces the sexist culture. The woman who condemns the wrongdoers as a representative of the group might convey the way in which the abuser's attack is also a contribution to this culture, which victimizes the group. This does not depend on members of the group recognizing the values underpinning the wrong of domestic abuse; indeed their failure to recognize it is a symptom of the more general social problem with domestic abuse.

But I think that we can go further. Suppose that public officials charged with decisions about criminalization rightly find some conduct seriously wrong. The political community does not share the values that are attacked by the wrongdoing. These values do not identify them as a political community. However, the political community ought to endorse the values that make the conduct wrong. It ought, also, to come together to protect people from those wrongs.

If the public officials criminalize the wrongdoing, they warrant judges in condemning conduct publicly. But, it might be objected, this would be inapt, because the condemnation could not be done in the name of the political community. It could then not be public, in the appropriate sense. That does not follow, though. For the act of public debate and criminalization might result in the political community coming to recognize the relevant values. Decisions about the scope of the criminal law are one way in which communities develop a sense of the values that come to bind them together. Domestic abuse seems a good example of this: decisions about criminalization and the use of the criminal law helped to provide one focus for public engagement, where a wider range of people came to share the values that underpin the view that domestic abuse is seriously wrong.

But now suppose that this does not occur, and often it will not, at least in the short term. It still seems as though public blame is warranted in a sense. Public blame may imply simply that the conduct is sufficiently important that a political community ought to take a stand against it by blaming perpetrators, by indicating to victims that they can expect protection from it by state institutions, and by helping to foster a sense in the political community that it is wrong.

Finally, even were Marshall and Duff right that public blame for wrongdoing is warranted only if a community is in fact bound together by the values that underpin the wrong, the legitimacy of other functions of the criminal justice system surely does not depend on community values in this way. Our reasons to use public resources to protect people from serious wrongdoing do not depend on the values that we actually hold. People have good reasons to support public institutions that protect people from wrongdoing simply in virtue of their duties of protection, and these duties are not plausibly dependent on the values we accept.

v) A modest relativism?

This argument leaves open the possibility of a more modest relativism. Massimo Renzo develops one view of this kind.[24] Renzo distinguishes two kinds of wrong. The existence of some wrongs is not contingent on the establishment of any institutional arrangements. Other wrongs exist only because certain institutional arrangements come into existence. Call the first kind of wrong non-contingent, and the second contingent. For example, he argues that rape is a non-contingent wrong, because it exists regardless of any political arrangements that we might have. Theft is a contingent wrong, in contrast, because it depends on the establishment of a property regime, and thus on the development of institutions.[25] He then suggests that anyone may call a person to answer for non-contingent wrongs, as these wrongs are owed to us simply in virtue of our humanity, but only those who share a political community with us may call us to account for contingent wrongs.

It is doubtful that this sense of contingency matters. First, people in the political community may have a natural duty of justice, owed to people simply in virtue of their moral importance, to develop and sustain certain political arrangements. This duty can also explain why certain wrongs come into existence when those arrangements occur, even though the relevant wrongs are contingent on the actual development of those arrangements.

Even those who think that there are no fully fledged property rights in the state of nature endorse a non-contingent duty to develop the political arrangements that create those property rights, and then not to violate them. And this should not be surprising: given how important property rights are to a meaningful autonomous life, if there are

[24] See 'Crimes Against Humanity and the Limits of International Criminal Law' (2012) 31 *Law and Philosophy* 443; 'Responsibility and Answerability in the Criminal Law'.

[25] I doubt that this is true about theft. See V Tadros 'Independence Without Interests?' (2011) 31 *Oxford Journal of Legal Studies* 193. Disenfranchisement, which I consider below, seems a clearer case.

no property rights in the state of nature, we have powerful duties to escape the state of nature by creating a legal regime which creates and enforces those rights. In roughly Kantian language, there is a natural duty to create, maintain, and improve a rightful condition.[26] Given this, it is difficult to see why the contingency of a wrong on the existence of a state determines accountability for wrongdoing. Although the wrongs exist only once certain political decisions are taken, there is an underlying universal natural duty to take the decisions that gives rise to the wrongs.

Consider disenfranchisement. Disenfranchisement is often wrong. But the wrong of disenfranchisement depends on the existence of democratic institutions. But now suppose, as is plausible, that people in a political community have a natural duty of justice to develop democratic institutions, given the instrumental and inherent value of democratic institutions. With this duty goes the duty not to disenfranchise. But this is a duty that is owed simply in virtue of the properties that make us people. It is hard to see, in that case, why we do not all have standing to hold each other to account for the wrongs of disenfranchisement. And it seems very plausible that we do have such standing: it is appropriate to hold states that disenfranchise ethnic minorities accountable in the international arena for their wrongdoing. Although the wrong of disenfranchisement is contingent on political decisions, then, its source is universal.

Second, it is more generally difficult to see why the standing of a person to address wrongdoing depends on whether they are part of the group that creates the conditions for that wrong to exist. That seems doubtful independently of whether there is a natural duty to create the relevant conditions. Suppose that I am permitted either to *v* or not to *v*. If I *v*, acting in a certain way will be wrong, and a wrong of that kind will not exist if I do not *v*. Why does it follow from my permission not to *v* that others lack the standing to hold me to account for my wrongdoing?

In general, it does not seem true that this kind of contingency determines the conditions of accountability. Here is an example: I am permitted to have a child or not to do so. The wrong of parental neglect exists only because I have chosen to have the child. But the fact that this wrong is contingent on my having a child implies nothing about whether the moral status of the child underpins the wrong of parental neglect. Indeed her moral status surely does underpin that wrong. This makes the wrongdoing apt for interpersonal accountability, as indeed it is.

Perhaps Renzo might argue that the contingency in this case is not of the right kind. The wrong is contingent on certain facts rather than on normative relations of the kind that we develop in a state. But it is hard to see why this difference should matter. The basic point holds that the connection between the contingency of wrongdoing on some relationship we have with each other and practices of accountability is not tight.

Return to the case of political arrangements. Suppose that it is permissible to create some institutional arrangement, or not. The existence of these institutions may change normative and non-normative facts, giving rise to kinds of wrong that did not previously exist. But relevant duties, when they exist, might be owed to others simply in virtue of the moral importance of those people to whom they are owed. If so, it is hard to see why those who are not involved in creating the relevant political arrangements lack the standing to hold people accountable for these wrongs.

This response to Renzo, though, leaves open an even more modest relativism. The view that there is something special about our standing to hold each other to account on the basis of the values involved in a shared relationship does seem

[26] See, for example, A Ripstein *Force and Freedom: Kant's Legal and Political Philosophy* (Cambridge, Mass: Harvard UP, 2009) 223.

plausible in certain interpersonal contexts. For example, a view of this kind nicely explains the intuitive idea that it is wrong for strangers to call friends to account for certain wrongs that depend on the existence of the friendship. It may be wrong for one friend to let another down in virtue of the fact that they are bound together by norms of their friendship, and the values that underpin those norms. People need not bind themselves together in this way. When we bind ourselves in this way, we become accountable only to those who are bound together by these values. And this might help to explain why it is wrong for strangers to call these people to account for these wrongs.

An analogous case might be made for certain state wrongs. A political community, it might be argued, is permitted but not required to bind itself together according to certain values. If it does, certain duties between citizens of that community arise. And the community is uniquely placed to publicly condemn those who violate the duties, and to enforce both the primary and secondary duties through the threat and execution of punishment.

On this more modest view, the rights of a political community to address certain wrongs are limited by a different kind of contingency. A political community ought to commit itself publicly to some values, and if these ground wrongs, everyone has standing to hold the wrongdoers to account (subject to pragmatic and comparative reasons of the kind outlined earlier). A political community ought not to commit itself publicly to other values. The state lacks standing to call wrongdoers to account for their wrongdoing regardless of whether it does so. But there are also values that may bind a political community together. Whether wrongs grounded in these values ought to be criminalized, it might be argued, depends on whether it is bound together by these values.

I have some doubts about this picture too. The case of friendship seems plausible because friends quite naturally value aspects of their friendship, and value the fact that these aspects are valued. The idea that they are bound by the distinctive values underpinning the friendship then seems plausible. This seems much less plausible in the case of large political communities, where there is inevitably a great deal of disagreement about what to value, as well as a wide range of different things that are in fact valued.

The doubt is powerful especially in societies that abide by basic liberal principles, such as those protecting free speech—a theme of John Rawls's political liberalism that we will consider in the next chapter. It is also powerful in the light of international migration, which results in communities that draw their attitudes and values from a wide range of cultures and practices. In such circumstances, the suggestion under consideration seems unlikely to arise.

Indeed, it is arguable that the rise in importance of procedural, distinctively legal, and democratic values in the criminal law, such as the rule of law, precision, and codification by elected officials after public debate, results from the diminishing prospects of a criminal law that is underpinned by shared values in a community.[27] In the light of this, the idea that shared values in a community can determine which wrongs are public seems anachronistic. The right question to ask is not how the criminal law should respond to different values that bind political communities together, but rather how it should respond to the fact that political communities are no longer bound together in this way.

[27] See N Lacey *In Search of Criminal Responsibility: Ideas, Interests, and Institutions* (Oxford: OUP, 2016) 125–7.

V. The Duty View of Punishment and the Limits of the Criminal Law

Recall:

> *Wrongness* Pro Tanto *Duty* (*Content*) (*WDC*): All moral wrongs should be criminally prohibited.[28]

I have shown that a retributivist justification of this principle fails even if retributivism is true. In this section I show that my objections to *WDC* extend to the duty view of punishment I favour, and that I outlined in Chapter 4. This allows us further to examine the relationship between the responsive functions of criminal justice and criminalization.

To be clear, we are here focused only on a certain kind of argument for criminalization: one that justifies criminalization by the value of the responsive functions of criminal justice. This leaves open the possibility that criminalization can be justified or limited on other grounds: for example, the effects of criminalization.

The duty view, recall, is that it is permissible, and sometimes required, to punish wrongdoers to deter crime because of the protective duties wrongdoers incur by acting wrongly. If a wrongdoer incurs a duty to serve some end that punishment serves, and that duty is enforceable, punishing him does not infringe his rights. It is normally permissible to punish wrongdoers, I claim, only if the harm that is inflicted on them by the punishment is no greater than the harm that they would themselves be required to bear in order to serve the ends that their punishment serves.

This suggests three limits on the right to punish wrongdoers. First, punishing some wrongdoers might not serve any valuable goal at all. Second, some wrongdoers might not incur duties to serve a valuable goal that punishment can secure. Third, state punishment might inevitably inflict costs on wrongdoers that they would not be required to bear to serve any such goal. All three limits have implications for the relationship between the responsive functions of criminal law and criminalization.

The first limit is obvious, and I will spend little time on it. The duty view is instrumentalist—it justifies punishment on the basis of goods that it can achieve rather than on any inherent value of harming wrongdoers. When punishing a wrongdoer lacks instrumental value, it violates her rights. Through wrongdoing she loses her right against being harmed, but only on condition that she is harmed for good reason, and the only good reasons are extrinsic to the infliction of harm itself. The duty view thus supports the criminalization of wrongs only where punishing wrongdoers achieves the aims of punishment, such as deterrence and recognition.

The other two limits on punishment that the duty view recommends raise more complex issues, and we will consider some of them in more depth later in the book. All wrongdoers incur duties to respond to their wrongdoing; at least the duty to recognize that they have acted wrongly. But not all wrongdoing gives rise to a duty to further the protective aims of punishment.

Furthermore, some of the duties that wrongdoers incur may not be legitimately enforced by the state. Duties that arise through the less serious wrongs committed in families are an obvious example. Family life (or at least my family life) is full of wrongdoing. Members of my family, including me (... especially me), can be rude, thoughtless, forgetful, self-centred, insensitive, boorish, lazy, destructive, disrespectful,

[28] Moore *Placing Blame*, 662.

and dishonest. But much of this conduct, though wrong, is not very seriously wrong. And very little is required of us to respond to this wrongdoing—an apology is often enough (or at least I hope so!). Punishing these wrongs would be unwarranted not only because punishment could not plausibly lead to these wrongdoers satisfying the duties they have, but also because these duties are unenforceable due to the interest that people have of being free from interference from others, and especially from state interference.

Second, even if all wrongdoers incur enforceable duties to serve the ends of punishment, many wrongdoers need not serve these ends in a way that harms them. The duties that trivial wrongdoers incur are not duties to bear significant financial costs, or the costs associated with deprivations of liberty. As state punishment involves the infliction of these costs, punishing these wrongdoers would infringe their rights. Even the costs inflicted by publicly blaming others through an institution like the criminal justice system would be more than the wrongdoer would be required to bear.

Consider insults. It is often wrong publicly to insult another person. Now suppose that those who do so ought not only to apologize, but also to prevent others from wrongly insulting people publicly. The aim of punishment is to prevent further instances of wrongdoing, and it might be argued that the person who acts wrongly incurs a duty to serve this end.

But those who publicly insult others are not liable to state punishment for this reason: even if the person incurs a duty to prevent other public insults if she can, the burdens that she would be liable to suffer for this end are so small that the use of the criminal law would inevitably be disproportionate. The 'sledgehammer' argument that I offered against Moore would apply equally to this case. On the duty view, then, trivial wrongdoing does not render a person liable to state punishment.

Even some serious wrongdoing may not render the wrongdoer liable to state punishment. For example, it is sometimes argued that it is wrong for pregnant women to abort their foetuses early in pregnancy because of the impersonal value of human life that would be destroyed by the abortion. I doubt that this is typically true, but let us suppose for the sake of argument that it is. On the view described, the wrongness of early abortion does not rest in the fact that these foetuses have rights. It rests in the fact that human life is worthy of respect, and that ending a human life is disrespectful, even if the living being that is killed does not yet have the agential, evaluative, emotional, and cognitive properties that most importantly explain the special value that human beings typically have.

Those who hold this view might believe that the wrongdoing committed by women who have early abortions is serious—they may think that the impersonal value is deep and important. Even if they are right, it does not follow that those who act wrongly for these reasons are liable to state punishment. If the duty view is right, in order to investigate this we need to investigate the duties that these women incur as a result of their early abortions. If they incur general duties to prevent other early abortions occurring, at some significant cost to themselves, it might be permissible to punish them for reasons of general deterrence.

But this seems doubtful. If early abortion is wrong, the appropriate response to that wrongdoing may simply be deep personal reflection on what has been done. In support of this view, first focus on the grounds offered for the claim that early abortion is wrong. A pregnant woman brings a foetus into existence. It does not yet have its own life to live, in the sense that a person has his or her own life to live. And the foetus is still deeply embedded, and intimately connected, to the pregnant woman's body. The view under consideration is that it is nevertheless wrong for the woman to destroy the foetus because of its great impersonal value.

Now focus on the duties that a woman might incur for aborting her own foetus, if this is true. The duty arises because of the impersonal value of the foetus. But the fact that the mother has created this thing of value, and it is still deeply embedded within her, may shape the duties that she incurs when she destroys it. A wrong that is so intimate and personal might warrant only an intimate and personal response. And the duty to make that response may be unenforceable.

In order to justify punishment on the duty view, the duties that the woman incurs must be of a more 'public' kind in a different sense than that intended by Marshall and Duff. Those who wish to inflict punishment on these women must show that they have duties to serve plausible goals of punishment, the most important being deterrence. They must thus show that women who have had early abortions have a stringent duty to prevent other women having early abortions. Even if we grant that early abortion could be wrong, even seriously wrong, this view does not seem attractive. If this is right, the responsive functions of criminal justice cannot support the criminalization of early abortion, even if early abortion is seriously wrong.

To be clear, I doubt that early abortion is wrong at all, and I doubt that women who do this incur any duties by having early abortions. My argument is only that if this is seriously wrong because of the impersonal value of the foetus, as some people claim, criminalization might not be the right response, simply because the wrongdoing does not merit the kind of response that justifies punishment.[29]

Later in the book, I will explore the implications of the duty view for criminalization further. My aim here is only to highlight the ways in which the duty view places principled limits on the kind of wrong that are appropriate subjects for criminalization.

VI. Conclusion

There is a powerful relationship between our reasons to respond to wrongdoing and our reasons to criminalize conduct. The fact that wrongdoing demands a response, and the fact that public institutions aptly make that response, can provide a powerful case for criminalizing wrongdoing.

But there are limits to this argument. This case for criminalizing wrongdoing only has force if the state will sometimes have sufficient reason to make the relevant response. There are some wrongs that merit such a state response, but there are decisive reasons against the state making it. And there are others that don't merit a state response at all.

[29] Compare R Dworkin *Life's Dominion: An Argument About Abortion, Euthanasia, and Individual Freedom* (New York: Vintage Books, 1993), but see further Chapters 14 and 15.

8

Political Liberalism and Criminalization

In the previous two chapters, we began to consider the limits of the criminal law and the relationship between wrongs and crimes. We did so both by thinking about principled restrictions on the criminal law and the appropriate use of the responsive functions of the criminal law. Even if we cannot justify the most familiar restrictive principles that claim limits to the scope of the criminal law, we saw that state responses of public blame and punishment are unwarranted for some wrongs, both on pragmatic grounds and on principled grounds. We also began to explore the idea of public wrongdoing, which suggests that there are limits to the criminal law that arise from the fact that the criminal justice system is a state institution.

It is trivially true that the philosophy of the criminal law is part of political philosophy in that it is concerned with the proper exercise of state power. The question is what implications this has for the relationship between wrongs and crimes. Much of the philosophy of the criminal law rests on the assumption that there is a close relationship between moral wrongdoing and criminalization. Criminal law has an irreducibly backward-looking element, and in central cases it looks back at wrongdoing.

The assumption, though, has also been questioned. For example, it has been argued that the primary function of the criminal law is not to respond to wrongdoing, but rather to stabilize public institutions with the ambition of developing and maintaining cooperation in complex modern societies. Criminal law, it is argued, is thus not an extension of our interpersonal practices of responsibility.[1]

The duty view suggests that this view relies on a false contrast. Punishment is inflicted in order to deter wrongdoing. Doing this not only helps to prevent the wrongs that destabilize public institutions, it also provides participants in those institutions with the confidence that they can form plans together without the prospect of those plans being undermined by wrongdoing.

A whole range of criminal laws contribute to this project, including crimes of dishonesty and other financial crimes, but also standard interpersonal wrongs, such as assault, coercion, and sexual offences. Responding to these wrongs is appropriate in part because they threaten and undermine the possibility of secure cooperation in modern institutional and social settings.

There are limits on the pursuit of these aims. As threatening and executing punishment interferes with liberty and inflicts harm, it must be shown that securing these ends does not violate the rights of those who are punished. The duty view of punishment makes a contribution to this project: it shows that people's rights against being punished for these ends are not violated, or even infringed, if they have duties to serve the relevant ends. If certain wrongs will undermine the stability of public institutions, or threaten to do so, people who commit those wrongs have a duty to support

[1] See, for example, M Thorburn 'Criminal Law as Public Law' in R A Duff and S P Green *Philosophical Foundations of Criminal Law* (Oxford: OUP, 2011); V Chiao 'What is the Criminal Law For?' (2016) 35 *Law and Philosophy* 137.

the stability of these institutions. Thus, securing the aim of responding adequately to wrongdoing complements the aim of stability.

There is another argument that implies a division between interpersonal morality and public life: the political liberal idea that political institutions must not draw on the whole truth of morality, including a comprehensive resolution of disputes that we find between competing moral views in a liberal society. Surprisingly, although political liberalism is popular and influential, little work has been done to assess its implications for one of the most deeply coercive and important branches of the state—the criminal justice system.[2]

In the previous chapter, I criticized one view of public wrongdoing—the view that public wrongs are wrongs that are connected to values shared by a political community—on the grounds that in modern societies, we cannot expect people to be bound together in the way that this vision of the criminal law suggests. Political liberalism, in contrast, suggests that political institutions in liberal societies must be governed by distinctively political values precisely because we cannot expect a political community to be bound together by a comprehensive moral vision. This might give rise to a distinct idea of public wrongdoing.

I will argue that a modest version of political liberalism is plausible, but it has modest implications for criminalization: those who accept this version of political liberalism and those who do not largely converge on decisions about what to criminalize. Despite this, philosophers of the criminal law ought not to ignore political liberalism. Political liberalism does have some implications for the criminal law. More importantly, understanding it helps us to understand why the deep connection between wrongs and crimes survives the disagreements that inevitably, and quite reasonably, arise in liberal states.

Section I explores different claims that political liberals make, and begins to develop one version of the view. Section II outlines the values of authenticity and independence that are best thought of as underpinning political liberalism. It also responds to an alternative idea: that political liberalism arises from moral uncertainty that arises from peer disagreement. Section III provides an argument for the view that laws should be acceptable to those who disagree morally, against a challenge that all that matters is that these laws are accepted. Sections IV indicates one way in which this version of political liberalism is modest: it provides only a *pro tanto* reason not to rely on disputed moral ideals, and that reason does not apply to all laws and political institutions. Section V outlines another way that it is modest: the values that underpin it are not engaged by every political or legal dispute. In particular, the values of political liberalism are irrelevant to disputes about core crimes that rest on serious wrongdoing. Section VI shows that this version of political liberalism nevertheless has implications for the scope of the criminal law.

I. Disagreement and Power

The general idea of political liberalism is that, given widespread reasonable moral disagreement in modern liberal societies, there is a reason to ensure that state institutions, laws, and acts do not depend for their justification on controversial moral views.

[2] I raised and briefly discussed the possibility that political liberalism may have implications for the criminal law in 'Wrongness and Criminalization' in A Marmor *The Routledge Companion to Philosophy of Law* (London: Routledge, 2012). For a more developed discussion, though one that is not closely related to the one I develop here, see M Matravers 'Political Neutrality and Punishment' (2013) 7 *Criminal Law and Philosophy* 217.

Rather, they should be justified by reference to political values that all must accept. If this succeeds, everyone can be expected to endorse these views without revising their basic moral ideas.

I am unsure whether political liberalism is true. I sketch the most plausible version of it, and consider the implications of that version for questions of criminalization. This version is in the spirit of John Rawls's *Political Liberalism*.[3] I make no claims about how close it is to Rawls's view. It might even be disputed whether this is really a version of political liberalism at all. As it is not clear what qualifies a view as a version of political liberalism, I also leave this question aside.

i) A state that we can endorse

Political liberalism is best understood as an answer to a problem that arises in societies that abide by more basic liberal principles.[4] Certain fundamental freedoms, such as freedom of thought, freedom of speech, occupational freedom, freedom of movement and association, and so on, occupy a central place in all liberal views. Call these the basic liberal freedoms. Assume that these freedoms can be justified, which is relatively uncontroversial. The question is whether we should accept some further principle—roughly, a principle that we abstain, in political disputes, from drawing on our comprehensive moral ideas.

Here is an argument for this. Given our different life experiences, different traditions, and the difficulty of establishing which moral views are correct, we cannot expect convergence on any particular comprehensive moral conception, let alone the correct one, at least if the basic liberal freedoms are protected. This must be tolerated, and may be welcomed, even when education about morality and justice is ideal.[5]

It is valuable for reasonable citizens to be able to endorse the set of institutions that govern their lives, and that give rise to the difference of views that exist in a classically liberal society, without abandoning their fundamental moral views. If they can endorse these institutions, they share a certain kind of valuable political community with each other despite their disagreements. A political community of this kind is a community in which members with different views are able to integrate their social plans together in a way that is structured and advanced by the political and legal institutions that govern them, and where disagreements between them do not result in political conflicts about the use of state power.

To further understand political liberalism, and to assess its plausibility and scope, it helps to focus on the following challenge. A person has reason to endorse a set of institutions, it might be argued, when those institutions are governed by morality. When there is disagreement about morality, some people have the right moral view and some the wrong moral view. Those with the right moral view can endorse institutions governed by the right moral view. But so can those who have the wrong moral view. This is because a person's moral mistakes cannot give them reasons to reject a set of institutions that reflect the true view. The fact that I make a mistake about what morality requires, for example, cannot supply a reason against me endorsing institutions that

[3] *Political Liberalism: Expanded Edition* (New York: Columbia University Press, 2005).

[4] See, especially, J Quong *Liberalism Without Perfection* (Oxford: OUP, 2011) and also C Larmore 'Political Liberalism: Its Motivations and Goals' in D Sobel, P Vallentyne, and S Wall *Oxford Studies in Political Philosophy* (Oxford: OUP, 2015).

[5] This is what Rawls calls 'the burdens of judgement'. See *Political Liberalism*, 54–8.

compel me to do what morality requires. I have a moral reason to endorse such institutions regardless of my mistakes. That is so even if the mistake was inevitable given my circumstances.

We do not owe it to each other to ensure that those with mistaken moral views find, or could find, our institutions acceptable without abandoning those moral views. Insofar as they satisfy genuinely valuable goals there is no further requirement to make them acceptable to everyone. They already *are* acceptable to everyone in the relevant sense—everyone has a reason to accept a set of institutions that reflects their moral obligations, even when they disagree.

Suppose that the criminal law prohibits conduct that is in fact morally wrong, but many reasonable people do not believe that the conduct is morally wrong, given their other moral commitments. The fact that these people are mistaken, the objector suggests, gives them no less reason to endorse the law prohibiting the conduct. Answering this challenge will both deepen our understanding of the most plausible version of political liberalism, and help us to understand its implications.

ii) Wrongdoing and imposing one's will

The most familiar idea that might be thought responsive to this objection is that, in political morality, we are subject to a principle of reciprocity where each person refrains from imposing her comprehensive moral views on others on condition that they do the same. On this view, when deciding what ought to be criminalized, we must reason only using political principles, and not the facts that actually make conduct wrong, or not. For were we to do the latter, those whose arguments are successful in the political realm, and thus converted into policy, would be imposing their comprehensive moral conception on others.

For example, although Rawls did not think that a decision for or against the criminalization of abortion inevitably followed directly from political liberalism, he argued that political liberalism does constrain the kinds of reasons that could be offered for or against the criminalization of abortion in the public sphere, and he thought that arguments could be found for abortion rights in the public sphere. Citizens could not, he thought, appeal to their comprehensive moral views to establish that abortion is seriously wrong or not, but could only appeal to political values. If a standoff occurs, the issue should be subject to a vote, where citizens determine how to vote only by considering the ordering of political principles that they think is correct.[6]

The idea of public reasoning is somewhat obscure. Some doubt Rawls's view because they find it difficult to see how a person could possibly reason about some of the most important political decisions without appealing to their comprehensive moral views. For example, it seems impossible to debate whether abortion ought to be criminalized without considering the reasons that might or might not make it wrong: in particular whether any status and significance of the lives that will be ended through abortion is sufficiently important to restrict the choices of pregnant women. Furthermore, it

[6] *Political Liberalism*, lii–lv; *Collected Papers* (Cambridge, Mass: Harvard UP, 2001) 605. It is not completely clear why voting is the appropriate response in cases of a standoff, or how votes would be cast without people being guided in how to vote, without appealing to comprehensive moral views. For some further discussion, see A Williams 'The Alleged Incompleteness of Public Reason' (2000) 6 *Res Publica* 199, 209–11.

seems wrong to constrain those on either side of the debate to appeal to those reasons in an attempt to persuade others that their view ought to be reflected in the law.[7]

But this objection to the idea of public reason, and the restrictions on political debate that it calls for, as Rawls understands them, is difficult to make convincing. Consider again the right of women to have first trimester abortions. All those who think that foetuses have no moral importance can endorse this right, as well as those who think that any moral importance that they have is insufficient to constrain the procreative choices of women. These people can all support the law without referring to their fundamental moral views about the moral significance of foetuses. There are those who disagree, and think that their moral importance is sufficient to restrict such procreative choices. But any such view may be thought unreasonable. If so, the fact that these views are not reflected in public discourse is not an objection. Rawls is only aiming at an overlapping consensus between reasonable views.

This leaves open two difficult questions. Rawls's political liberalism aims at a middle ground between the right moral view and the full range of moral views that people have in a liberal society. It aims for political institutions that are acceptable to those with reasonable views, even if these views are not true, but only to those with reasonable views. Why should this be? Rawls relies on a principled distinction between reasonable and unreasonable views. Without an account of this, political liberals might be accused of securing the plausibility of their views by excluding objections that some people might have to certain public policies on an ad hoc basis. But whilst there are challenges to be met, the mere existence of people whose moral views are in conflict with political rights does not undermine Rawls's project in itself.[8]

The more important objection is that it is not clear what argument Rawls intended for the general idea that it is wrong for some people to impose comprehensive moral views on others, when those comprehensive moral views are the right views. Or to put it more simply, what is wrong simply with imposing the right moral view on others through legislation, simply in virtue of the fact that this is the right view? Rawls did not provide a fully satisfactory account of the value of reciprocity that is supposed to explain the wrongness of doing this.

The objection that one has acted in a partisan way if one imposes a moral view on others hardly seems powerful when truth is on one's side—it is the truth rather than the fact that the truth is 'on one's side' that justifies the decision. For example, suppose that the sanctity of life makes abortion wrong. Legislators judge that this is why abortion is wrong, and criminalize it in order better to protect human life. Citizens who think that abortion is permitted object that these legislators have imposed their own moral views on them.[9] Why should the legislators not respond: 'We didn't impose our moral views on you. We required you not to do what you are morally required not to do. It is, of course, our belief that you are morally required not to do it. But we did not require you to do it because it is our belief; we did it because you are morally required not to do it.'

[7] Compare Ronald Dworkin's discussion of religion in *Is Democracy Possible Here? Principles for a New Political Debate* (Princeton: Princeton University Press, 2006) 63–6. Rawls makes some concessions about the permissibility of admitting comprehensive moral views into political debate in 'The Idea of Public Reason Revisited' in *Collected Papers* (Cambridge, Mass: Harvard UP, 1999). I leave the details aside.

[8] See, further, Williams 'The Alleged Incompleteness of Public Reason', 208.

[9] Rawls implies that this is the relevant objection in *Political Liberalism*, lv.

The idea that it is generally wrong to compel a person to do what they are required to do, because this would impose one's beliefs on another, is hard to believe. The claim that the compulsion involves 'imposing one's beliefs on others' is misleading. When one person imposes the correct moral view on another, this imposition does not amount simply to an imposition of one person's beliefs on another in any morally important sense. It is an imposition of the right view on the other person, and must be assessed as such. Adding that it is also the person's belief is simply a distraction.[10]

Rawls's response is that all people with reasonable beliefs could equally claim that they are imposing the right view on others. He concludes:

> When we make such claims others, who are themselves reasonable, must count us unreasonable. And indeed we are, as we want to use state power, the collective power of equal citizens, to prevent the rest from affirming their not unreasonable views.[11]

This response is no good. First, nothing prevents others affirming their reasonable moral views. Indeed, classic liberal principles protect their right to do this, and classical liberals are hardly short of arguments for these principles. The question is whether we must go further and ensure that mistaken but reasonable moral views are somehow realized through state institutions, or at least that those institutions are compatible with these views.

More importantly, although all may be equally placed with respect to reasonableness, all are not equally placed with respect to truth. The argument seems to be that the epistemic equality between those with reasonable views is morally significant, even given a further inequality between them; inequality with respect to the truth. But it is not clear why the former equality matters in the light of the latter inequality. Rawls's defence begs the question.

iii) Stability: The conclusion, not the argument

A further idea draws on the political value that motivated Rawls's development of political liberalism in the first place: the value of stability. Here is one way to understand Rawls's problem. Classically liberal political institutions, including those that abide by Rawls's basic principles of justice, might seem inevitably unstable because they give rise to a diversity of views. Members of such a society will thus fail to endorse the institutions that give rise to them. And the citizens that exist within them therefore cannot endorse such institutions. This undermines the idea that a liberal political society can cooperate autonomously within political structures that each accepts. It is therefore inevitably unstable.

Rawls's initial solution to this problem, in *A Theory of Justice*, aimed to show that acceptability was inevitable given the nature, conditions, and intrinsic good of human agents.[12] He later came to regard this solution as inadequate given the depth of disagreement about the human good that would be generated in a liberal society. So his later solution is to ensure that political legal institutions are capable of being affirmed by a range of people with reasonable views.[13]

It is, of course, better that political institutions that are otherwise just are stable over time. But two points are worth noting about the argument for stability. First,

[10] See, also, D Enoch 'The Disorder of Public Reason' (2013) 124 *Ethics* 141, 159–60.
[11] *Political Liberalism*, 61.
[12] See *A Theory of Justice*, revised edn (Oxford: OUP, 1999) Part III.
[13] See Quong *Liberalism Without Perfection*, 143.

whether a set of institutions is stable depends not on the degree to which citizens could affirm them, but on the degree to which they do so, and will continue to do so. Rawls acknowledges, as of course he must, that classical liberal principles give rise not only to reasonable comprehensive moral views, but also to unreasonable ones. And not everyone who has a reasonable comprehensive moral view recognizes the implications of their view for political institutions.

Ensuring that reasonable citizens can affirm political institutions without abandoning their comprehensive moral view only makes stability possible without people having to go through moral conversion; it may not promote actual stability at all. But it is not clear why the mere possibility of stability is morally important given that the degree of actual stability does not correspond to its possibility.

Perhaps political liberalism improves the actual prospects of stability of a set of liberal institutions over time. But this is an empirical question; much depends on the views of the range of people who will in fact exist in a society, and that depends as much on their local circumstances and prevalent traditions as it does on the institutions that govern them.

Furthermore, as Rawls accepted, stability is a scalar property and it must be traded off against other legitimate goals.[14] A state can increase stability by ensuring that a larger number of the citizens that exist within that state actually endorse it. It has reason to do this. But this should not come at too high a price. Sometimes, the state should ensure that justice is done, according to the best moral view, even if this erodes stability to some degree. This is true whether stability is undermined because reasonable people do not have the right moral view, or because unreasonable people do not have the right moral view.

Finally, Rawls is interested not in stability, but stability *for the right reasons*. Stability for the right reasons is especially valuable, it might be argued, because a set of institutions that satisfy this demand are ones in which citizens with different comprehensive conceptions of the good can jointly and freely participate, without dominating each other, secure in their ambitions to realize their long-term plans and goals.[15]

But if this is right, the idea of stability for the right reasons only has derivative importance as the upshot of something else that we have reason to value: for example, the value of some not dominating others, or the value of autonomy. To vindicate political liberalism, then, we must show respect for our fellow citizens, which requires us to shape our institutions according to politically liberal criteria. And that requires a deeper analysis of the facts about mistaken fellow citizens in virtue of which they are owed respect, and the implications of such respect.

II. Authenticity, Independence, and the Value of Political Liberalism

Political liberalism is the view that citizens have rights to a set of political and legal institutions that they can stably endorse consistent with their comprehensive moral views, even if those views are mistaken. Those with the correct moral view obviously have reason to value a set of institutions that they can endorse in the light of their view.

[14] For more on the modesty of political liberalism, see Section IV.

[15] Something like this is also suggested in Quong *Liberalism Without Perfection*, 167–8.

The challenge is to explain the value of such a set of institutions to people who have mistaken but reasonable views.

i) The values of political liberalism

The explanation points to a negative value and a positive value. Both values relate to the way in which states allow citizens to cooperate together through state institutions to achieve valuable goals. By cooperating, citizens can together realize valuable goals: they can instantiate a just society by creating opportunities for the advancement of personal goals and plans of life, the production of goods, and so on, as well as providing their citizens with security and protecting their well-being. This is done by the cooperative provision of a system of education, an advanced legal system that enforces obligations in private law and secures stability through criminal justice, a set of social services and health services, and so on. When this is achieved, each person is part of a complex cooperative enterprise in which these valuable ends are secured. Increasingly, of course, these ends are secured not only nationally, but also internationally. I leave aside the complexities that this raises for the scope of political liberal ideas.

In the light of this, we can understand both the positive value that one can instantiate if a person endorses public institutions of this kind, and the negative value where a person finds herself unable to do this. A person who does this is able fully to participate in the cooperative enterprise. She can advance her plans of life as a part of a more general cooperative enterprise where together citizens secure the goals just identified. She thus secures her own valuable goals in the context of a cooperative enterprise where each citizen ensures that other citizens are able to do the same.

As a result, she can secure the value of authenticity for herself—she can carry out her own plans of life in the light of what she values. But not only that, she can do so in coordination and cooperation with others through a set of political structures, where she helps to realize the potential of each person to secure that value.

If she finds herself unable to participate, because she cannot endorse the institutions that govern her, in contrast, she is alienated from public life. Her inability to mesh her own plans with the larger cooperative enterprise detaches her from her fellow citizens. The complex achievements of the political community are not achievements that she shares in, or fully shares in, because the institutional structures that make cooperation possible are ones that she rejects, given the conflict between these structures and her basic moral convictions.

Furthermore, state institutions will secure compliance with the law through threats, rather than by appealing to her moral judgement. It will force her to do what she is required to do to secure justice. Not only will she be unable autonomously to participate in public life, she will be interfered with by the state to prevent her from acting in accordance with her judgement to secure justice. When she is free from this kind of interference, she is independent.

To summarize, the right political institutions realize two distinct ideals. First, the ideal of authenticity, which is secured when a person lives her life according to her own judgements, values, and goals through the autonomous exercise of her capacities. Second, the ideal of independence, which is secured when others do not interfere with her against her will, but only do so on a cooperative basis. In the right kind of political institutions these ideals are jointly realized through cooperation, and so a certain kind of valuable political community where each person participates in the realization of these ideals for others is secured.

The wrong kind of political community, in contrast, realizes the disvalue of alienation. A person whose moral conception is inconsistent with state institutions only responds to the incentives that state institutions give her. She thus does not realize the values of authenticity and independence. And as she does not see herself as part of the cooperative enterprise, she does not participate in the collective goal of securing these values for all members of the polity.

Given how pervasively political institutions govern our lives, there are weighty reasons to realize the values that politically liberal institutions can secure, and to avoid alienating people from those institutions.

ii) A modest non-epistemic political liberalism

It is often thought that political liberalism arises, or is best supported by, epistemic claims, such as uncertainty, or peer disagreement, about morality. However, the version of political liberalism that I defend relies on values of authenticity and independence that are themselves controversial. It might thus be seen as in conflict with the aims of political liberalism. Epistemic considerations, though, are not central to political liberalism, as it is best understood.

Our confidence in at least some moral ideas is not very high, and that confidence can be in part eroded by the fact that others, who seem reasonable, have a different view. Furthermore, this disagreement seems to arise even though the kinds of consideration that lead us to favour one moral view over another are widely available: we can all consider the implications of different moral views, for example, by imagining scenarios where they would apply. Experience of these scenarios may help us to judge the significance of these implications. But this often does not seem required: we have powerful moral intuitions without experience. And yet we often disagree about these scenarios, and about the intuitive plausibility of principles themselves.

These facts might be thought to support public institutions that do not depend on judgements about controversial moral ideas as some political liberals claim. But this is hard to support. The problem is that the proper response to controversies of this kind is itself controversial. There is widespread disagreement between those who are competent to judge the matter, and who have thought carefully about it, about whether to endorse political liberalism. We should have no more confidence that political liberalism is acceptable to all epistemically reasonable people than any other substantive moral or political view. Politically liberal institutions will thus be imposed on reasonable people who reject those institutions.

The aim to defend neutral institutions without relying on controversial moral claims in the light of epistemic uncertainty about morality is thus self-defeating. If we are to endorse political liberalism, we must do so because of substantive moral arguments that can be given for it. These arguments must be shown to count decisively against imposing comprehensive moral views on others when there is just as much evidence for those comprehensive views as there is for political liberalism.

For this reason, I will often consider the implications that certain political and legal norms have for those with true moral views and for those with false moral views, as though we know which view is right. This is not because everyone can be expected to endorse the right moral view, or because any of us can be certain about what morality requires, but to avoid being distracted by questions of uncertainty that are irrelevant to the best case for political liberalism.[16]

[16] A small caveat: below, I will suggest one way in which difficulties of coming to the right moral answers might have implications for political liberalism.

III. The Value of Acceptability

Now that we have understood the values underpinning political liberalism, let us focus on the appropriate way of securing these values. It may seem that the extent to which a society is politically liberal depends on the extent to which citizens live authentic and independent lives free from alienation. This outcome-oriented view can be contrasted with another: one that rests with the provision of adequate opportunities for authenticity and independence, and not to be alienated.

The second view is preferable. Whether a person has a complaint about her alienation from public life depends not only on whether she is in fact alienated, but also on the quality of the protection that she is given against alienation. Protection is given both by helping citizens to see that they can shape their lives authentically and independently in cooperation with others through state institutions, but also by creating the conditions where a person can, through the exercise of judgement, ensure that she is not alienated. If sufficient opportunities for this are created, actual alienation is much less objectionable.[17]

This idea helps us to understand an otherwise puzzling feature of political liberalism: it aims at a set of political institutions and laws that are capable of being accepted by people with a range of different moral views. Here is a familiar objection. What matters is not that laws are acceptable, but that they are actually accepted. For a person who is governed by an acceptable law that she does not accept will have been governed against her will. But we cannot hope that all reasonable citizens will in fact accept the laws that we create. Mere acceptability, it might be argued, adds nothing. Either we are permitted to govern because citizens consent to our doing so, or we must justify doing so by force. The middle position, where acceptability but not acceptance is achieved, is no better than governing by force without acceptability.[18]

I agree that actual acceptance is the gold standard that acceptability aims at. To help to achieve this standard, in developing its laws, the state should engage in wide-ranging public debate before legislators come to a view about what the law should be, and they should aim to persuade citizens to accept those laws after coming to a decision about what they should be.

As many people will not revise their most basic moral commitments, it should aim to do so by showing that its laws are compatible with a range of views. Rational engagement between citizens in shaping laws is essential to the project of ensuring that people endorse the laws that they are governed by for this reason—those who are involved in making the law, and whose arguments for or against acceptability from their point of view, are more likely in fact to accept laws rather than seeing them simply as imposed on them.

But it is equally obvious, as the objection notes, that this project will not be universally successful. Some people will fail to see the justice of just laws or political institutions, even if those laws and political institutions are not in conflict with their moral conception. Where this is so, laws and political institutions are imposed on them, even if they had the opportunity to participate in shaping them, and even if a proper explanation

[17] Compare T M Scanlon's views about the protective value of choice in other contexts in *What We Owe to Each Other* (Cambridge, Mass: Harvard UP, 1998) ch 6.

[18] See, for example, J Raz 'Facing Diversity: The Case of Epistemic Abstinence' in *Ethics in the Public Domain: Essays in the Morality of Law and Politics* (Oxford: OUP, 1994); D Enoch 'The Disorder of Public Reason', 165–7 and 'Against Public Reason' in D Sobel, P Vallentyne, and S Wall *Oxford Studies in Political Philosophy* (Oxford: OUP, 2015) 126–30.

for the justice of these institutions and laws has been offered to them. Our question is whether it makes a difference to the justification of such laws and institutions that they could be accepted without the person abandoning her moral conception.

Consider the following pair of cases. Fundamental aspects of the lives of two people are governed by a set of political institutions. In both cases, the person does not endorse aspects of those institutions. In the first case, the person could see the law as just without abandoning her more basic and general moral outlook. She is mistaken about the implications of this outlook for the institution in question. In the second case, she could accept the law only by abandoning this outlook.

One question is whether the values of authenticity and independence are equally set back in these cases. I doubt that they are. Our lives lack authenticity to the extent that forces beyond our control shape them. They lack independence to the extent that they are shaped by the will of others. But the strength of our objection to having our lives shaped by the will of others depends on how deeply they interfere with what we value, and how deeply we value what they interfere with. A person who is forced to act in a way that conflicts with her deepest moral commitments has a much more powerful reason to regret the interference—this aspect of her life is more fundamentally at odds with the central values that govern her life, and in the light of which she has reason to value her life as authentic and independent. This suggests that where actual consent or acceptance cannot be achieved, the extent to which an act conflicts with the deeply held convictions of a person makes a difference to whether it is permissible to proceed without consent or acceptance.

But there is another reason why acceptability is valuable in the absence of acceptance. If a law is acceptable, the fact that a person is alienated will often be her own responsibility. If a law is not acceptable, it will not. This makes a difference to the justification of imposing the law on that person. If a person rejects a set of laws that appropriately reflects the right moral view, the person does not accept the law due to a mistake she has made. She is alienated from her political and legal institutions as a result of that mistake. And she thus will not fully secure the values of authenticity and independence within the cooperative enterprise. The extent to which the state ought to ensure that alienation does not occur as a result of such mistakes depends on the expectations that it ought to have of its citizens not to make them. The state, I will argue, typically has better reasons to expect the person to accept the law if she can endorse it without revising her fundamental moral views than if she cannot.

First, what might we mean when we claim that the state can *expect* the person to accept the law? There is a purely predictive sense of expectation, but it is the normative sense that is relevant here.[19] To expect someone to do something, in this sense, does not imply merely that the person is predicted to do the relevant thing. Furthermore, it does not merely imply that the person ought to do it: that she would not be in error for failing to do it. It implies not only that the person ought to do it, but also that doing it is not especially demanding for her, and she is not constrained by any special impediments.

Our expectations depend on the degree of difficulty for a person to do what she ought.[20] We do not expect a person to do some things that she ought to do, given the

[19] On these senses of expectation, and the relationship with excuses, see further V Tadros *Criminal Responsibility* (Oxford: OUP, 2005) ch 13.

[20] The idea that there are degrees of difficulty in conforming to moral requirements is intuitive, but requires more careful thought than I can give it here. For an illuminating discussion, see D K Nelkin 'Difficulty and Degrees of Moral Praiseworthy and Blameworthiness' (2016) 50 *Noûs* 356.

difficulty of acting. For example, sometimes a person is morally required to sacrifice her own life rather than killing another person. She ought to do so. But in circumstances of stress and fear where there is little time for reflection, and given the natural inclination to prefer one's own survival, it is wrong to expect her to do so. That is why we excuse her.

With this in mind, consider whether the state can expect its citizens to endorse a law that conflicts with their deepest moral commitments. Suppose that the law is just, but the person doesn't see that it is just because it conflicts with her deepest moral commitments. This person ought to endorse the law. She ought to do so because her most basic moral views are wrong. But the state cannot expect her to endorse the law—to do so would involve revising her deepest moral commitments. Giving up the moral principles that one is most fundamentally committed to, even when they are demonstrably mistaken, is psychologically and practically difficult.

And there is a further reason why revising one's basic moral beliefs cannot be expected. Rawls plausibly claims that if certain basic principles of liberal societies, such as freedom of thought and expression, are respected, disagreement about fundamental moral questions is a pervasive feature of a society—they give rise to what Rawls calls 'the burdens of judgement'.[21] All liberals, not only political liberals, accept these principles. But the value they provide to members of a society comes at a cost—they leave citizens vulnerable to alienation. A politically liberal society ameliorates this cost by creating opportunities for its citizens to avoid alienation. They do so by making it possible for them to accept these institutions without revising their basic moral beliefs. Beneficiaries of basic liberal principles arguably have a duty to ensure that the cost I identified is ameliorated in this way, even if this hampers to some degree their ability to secure valuable goals.

In contrast, if it is demonstrated to a person that her own deep moral commitments should lead her to endorse the law, she can normally be expected to do so. That is not to say, of course, that she will do so. But if she fails, the responsibility will often be hers. Although she feels alienated from political institutions her complaint against alienation is relatively weak given that state officials could expect her to resolve the conflict for herself.

Perhaps it might be argued that it is a pervasive feature of liberal societies that people disagree about the implications of basic moral ideas as well as what those ideas are. This is true, but liberal societies already take significant steps to ameliorate this concern. By investing resources in liberal systems of education, they provide citizens with the critical tools to evaluate the implications of their views. And, insofar as is possible, they publicly justify the creation of laws by showing that they are consistent with a wide range of moral views. This is often enough to satisfy any legitimate demand that people have to ensure that they are not alienated from their political and legal system.

IV. The Strength of Liberal Claims

My case for political liberalism relies on comparative claims about the strength of different objections that might be made to political institutions and laws being one way or another. I divided legal and political institutions into three categories—those that are accepted, those that are acceptable, and those that are unacceptable. The idea that a

[21] See *Political Liberalism*, 54–8.

political institution can govern only reasonable people who actually accept them is very demanding. Many institutions can surely be justified without reaching this standard.

There is nevertheless value in them meeting a lower standard—the standard of acceptability—where the alternative is an institution that is neither accepted nor acceptable. People thus have a legitimate claim that their institutions are shaped in a way that they can accept given the different reasonable moral conceptions that arise under classically liberal conditions.

What is the strength of this claim? Political liberals often seem to believe that conformity with the demand that political and legal institutions be acceptable to reasonable people is required, all things considered. This then gives rise to a constraint on the reasons that can be offered in the public arena—only reasons connected to very basic liberal ideas, such as freedom and equality, can be offered in public discourse to justify a set of laws.

For example, Jonathan Quong argues that, on the best political liberal view, it is insufficient that reasonable people give weight to liberal demands. A reasonable person must not aim to shape the content of political justice in the light of her comprehensive moral views. He gives the example of a person who gives weight to an anti-discrimination principle in employment decisions, but who thinks it outweighed by the prohibition on hiring Catholics. Such an unjust person, Quong claims, is not granted the normative authority to shape the content of political justice.[22]

The better view is that there is a *pro tanto* obligation to secure such institutions rather than creating institutions that these people cannot endorse.[23] The crucial distinguishing feature of Quong's case of religious discrimination is that the person's moral ideal is false, and even were it true it is unimportant. For this reason, it is difficult to grasp the idea, in this example, that political liberal demands are outweighed by other demands or values.

But now recall the example of abortion. Suppose that the sanctity of life makes early abortion gravely morally wrong, even though reasonable people believe otherwise. Those who wish to prevent these wrongs would not be wrong to do so because others could not accept their views. The importance of ensuring that everyone can endorse the law that they live under is surely insufficiently important to justify a restriction on people from preventing a large number of very serious wrongs. Indeed, I will argue later that the values that underpin political liberalism may not even apply in cases of this kind.

If so, it is also permissible to argue for restrictions on abortion on this basis in the public sphere. To do so would be to argue for a set of laws that other reasonable people will not be able to endorse consistent with their basic moral commitments. But, *ex hypothesi*, the wrong of abortion is very serious. The complaint that people have against having the law 'inflicted' on them is comparatively weak, or does not exist.

This suggests that arguments for a more liberal view of abortion must engage with the moral case that people provide for its wrongness. I believe that the liberal view is right: either abortion is not wrong, or the wrong is of a nature or a degree that objections to criminalizing it are decisive.[24] But the moral arguments cannot be bypassed. If it is wrong for anti-abortion campaigners to offer arguments in the public sphere based on the moral wrongness of abortion, this is because of

22 See *Liberalism Without Perfection*, 169–70.

23 Rawls' own considered view is modest in roughly this way. See, especially, his 'Reply to Habermas' in *Political Liberalism*, for example at 386 and 392.

24 See, further, chapter 7.

the substantive mistakes they make, and not because they would be imposing their views on others.

V. Acceptable to Whom?

Political liberals often claim that the state ought to be acceptable to the range of people with reasonable moral conceptions. To be reasonable, they claim, a moral conception need not be true. A range of citizens can cooperate with each other on fair terms, it is suggested, despite disagreeing between each other about the answers to some basic moral questions.[25]

In the light of this, another familiar objection to political liberalism arises. The objection takes the form of a dilemma. Either reasonable disagreement implausibly constrains state power, or the reasonable/unreasonable distinction is made on an ad hoc basis to preserve plausible implications of political liberalism.

In the context of criminal law, the problem is as follows. Any set of laws with a plausibly wide scope, including criminal laws, is objectionable in the light of some moral conception or other. And as it is very difficult to know what moral view to endorse, some reasonable people have grounds to object to any set of criminal laws beyond a very narrow core.

One response is that the state ought not to criminalize conduct unless everyone with a reasonable moral view could conclude that the conduct ought to be criminalized without revising their basic moral views. This view faces three objections that together seem decisive. First, it implies an implausibly narrow criminal law. For example, reasonable people disagree sharply about when consent to medical treatment, sex, or the transfer of property is seriously wrong. Some reasonable moral views warrant criminalization in a narrower range of cases than others. The view under consideration narrows the scope of the law to the most minimal common denominator.

Second, it is unclear why the default position should be to refrain from criminalization. Just as there are objections by those with different moral views to some conduct being criminalized, so there are objections by those with different moral views about conduct not being criminalized. Victims, and potential victims, of serious wrongdoing would surely have an objection to the law being narrowed in this way simply because those with mistaken but reasonable moral views cannot see that the conduct in question is seriously wrongful.

The third objection is a little more complex. It relies on the fact that determining what we might call the primary scope of the criminal law has knock-on implications for secondary laws. Typically, for example, if it is not criminally wrongful for a person to do something, it is a criminal offence for others to prevent the person from doing that thing. There is a defence in the criminal law for those who prevent crime, but not a wider defence for those who prevent serious wrongdoing that is not criminal.

It follows that narrowing the criminal law in one respect normally expands it in another. When *v*ing is decriminalized, preventing people from *v*ing is criminalized. Some may object to the criminalization of *v*ing. When the law is narrowed, these people are satisfied. But those who believe that *v*ing is seriously wrongful are dissatisfied. They are dissatisfied not only because more people will *v*, and those who do will get

[25] See, for example, Rawls *Political Liberalism* 48–54.

away with it. They are also dissatisfied because they are not legally permitted to prevent others from *v*ing.

For example, suppose that some serious sexual wrongdoing is not criminalized. Not only are people permitted to engage in that conduct, people are also prevented from using force to prevent the conduct. To use force against a person to prevent them from doing something that is permitted by the criminal law is itself normally criminally wrong. So decriminalizing some serious sexual wrongdoing simply 'moves a bump in the carpet'.

Perhaps it might be responded that the state could both decriminalize some conduct, and also acts that prevent people from acting in the relevant way. That way, it would do more to ensure that people have the liberty to pursue their goals in the light of their moral views. But this is only a compromise, and it is not normally the right compromise.

Suppose that there is a dispute about whether some act, *v*, is seriously wrong. In response to this dispute, *v*ing is not criminalized, but nor are acts that prevent people from *v*ing. The police and citizens are thus permitted to prevent people from *v*ing, but not to deter *v*ing through prosecution, conviction, and punishment. This package of laws is unacceptable both to those who think that *v*ing is seriously wrong, and to those who think it permissible. Those who think it is seriously wrongful object that they are prevented from taking steps necessary to prevent *v*ing by punishing those who *v*. Those who think that it is not seriously wrongful will object that they are prevented from *v*ing by police officers and citizens who interfere with them to prevent them from doing this.

Perhaps it might be argued that the limit on freedom that occurs by criminalizing conduct is more important than the limit on freedom that occurs if the conduct is not criminalized. But this is not so. Recall the dispute about whether certain sexual acts are seriously wrong. To be clearer, take cases where sex is secured by making certain threats or offers, where there is a genuine and reasonable dispute about the wrongness of the conduct. Anyone who doubts that such a disagreement could be reasonable is invited to turn to Chapter 12, where we will see just how difficult the questions are. If those who think it not wrong are right, they have their freedom seriously constrained by not being allowed to make these threats or offers. But if the conduct is wrong, the freedom from being subject to such threats or offers is also seriously constrained.

A tempting response to this objection, but the wrong response, is to develop an intuitively attractive independent account of what makes a moral view reasonable, even if it is mistaken, and show that views defined as reasonable in this way converge on core questions in criminal law. Such an account aims to distinguish between those people whose views seem reasonable even if we disagree about them, and those whose views show a lack of basic concern for others.

For example, some might argue that a view is reasonable if it acknowledges the basic fundamental rights of all people, or if it has an adequate conception of basic freedom and equality of all citizens, or if it concerns foundational moral issues that cannot be established through argument. This leaves plenty of room for reasonable disagreement about morality. The way to respond to the remaining moral questions is to develop a political solution, such as voting, that all reasonable citizens can accept as a way of resolving intractable disputes between them.

This response, though tempting, is inadequate. First, it does not adequately resolve the issue under consideration. Suppose that after political deliberation, some serious wrongdoing is not criminalized. As a result, some people are vulnerable to that wrongdoing. And they face criminal sanctions if they aim to prevent it. It is not very plausible that they should accept such a law simply because it has both democratic provenance and it is consistent with a plausible conception of freedom and equality. If they are attacked, they are surely permitted to defend themselves from being wronged, even though they would violate the law in doing so.

This view does not depend on the controversial view that there is no general obligation to obey the law. I am sympathetic to the view that there is no such obligation. But even those who argue for a general obligation do not think it very powerful—surely insufficiently powerful that it cannot be defeated by the importance of protecting oneself against serious wrongdoing. It follows that the police would also be permitted to defend them. This is so even if one accepts that the police have promissory or other institutional obligations to uphold the law—any such obligations are overridden by the importance of preventing sexual wrongdoing. Furthermore, given that the person would not act wrongly in defending herself, she ought not to be prosecuted for doing so, despite the fact that her acts violate the law.

More importantly, this response fails to relate the idea of what is reasonable directly to the underlying values that are supposed to explain political liberalism. The better approach considers the values of authenticity and independence that, I have suggested, underpin political liberalism. If we continue to use the word 'reasonable', in this context, it should be understood as a technical term. The aim is to pick out the moral ideas that can support the values of independence and authenticity and those that cannot. Some mistaken moral conceptions may be able to support these values, and others not. If they cannot, there is no unfairness in the law being imposed on the person, because there is nothing valuable that imposing the law on the person interferes with. This need not depend on whether the moral conception under consideration is one that could reasonably be held in the ordinary sense of that word—that a person holding the view is a reasonable person, and does not have abhorrent moral ideas.

Here is a good heuristic device for determining whether a person has reason to value acts, or to disvalue constraints on her acts, where she wrongly believes that her acts are permitted, valuable, or required: consider how she would appropriately respond to the relevant facts later in life, when she revises her moral views so that she is no longer mistaken.

For example, suppose that a person has a mistaken set of religious beliefs. She devotes her life to certain ideals that are not valuable. Later in life, she discovers the mistake. She will regret devoting her life to these ideals. But nevertheless, she may value these aspects of her life as authentic. And if no one interfered with her ability to pursue this life, she may value it as independent.

Of course, it is a matter of dispute whether she should value these aspects of her life, given her mistakes. This dispute is at the heart of the debate about whether we should accept political liberalism. I find it at least plausible that she should. If so, the state has good reason to ensure that its political institutions and laws do not conflict with her moral conception, for if they do, her aim to live an authentic and independent life will be in conflict with the demands of the state.

We can also see from this why abhorrent moral conceptions do not count as reasonable for the purposes of political liberalism. Consider a person who has lived her life according to an abhorrent set of moral views, but who, later in life, recognizes her mistake. She cannot plausibly value these aspects of her life as part of an authentic and independent life. It is terrible to have lived one's life according to abhorrent moral views, and the fact that one has done so autonomously, without the interference of others, does nothing to improve the situation. The reason why these people's views are excluded from the political conception, then, is because there is nothing of value that would be advanced by ensuring that political institutions can be endorsed without correcting these mistakes.

But this limit on the moral conceptions that are relevant to political liberalism extends well beyond abhorrent views. Some moral disagreements may seem reasonable, but the values that are at stake are not relevant to the values of authenticity and independence that underpin political liberalism. Consider:

> *Involuntary Attack*: X has an epileptic seizure and attacks Y, threatening Y with lethal force. Y defends herself, killing X. There was no other way for Y to save her life.

It is disputed whether Y has acted wrongly, because X is not responsible for the threat that she poses. Some people think that non-responsible attackers are not liable to be harmed to avert the threat they pose, and thus where the harm inflicted is no less than the harm to be prevented, it is wrong to defend oneself.[26] But arguments have also been mounted for the permissibility of self-defence in such cases.[27] There are reasonable people on either side of this debate.

Let us suppose that the right view is that non-responsible attackers are not liable to be harmed, and that therefore this person is not permitted to inflict the force that would be necessary to avert the attack. However, this person believes that the non-responsible attacker is liable. She wishes to defend herself, and believes that she is permitted to do so. It may seem that this person has a reasonable moral view, and that the law should therefore seek to accommodate that view. It is certainly difficult to criticize the person for holding this view as unreasonable. Smart moral philosophers hold this view, others hold the opposing view, and the dispute between them shows no sign of easy resolution.

In that case, should the state refrain from criminalizing her conduct, even if she would act wrongly, on the grounds that she could not accept the law as applied to her? It should not. Although her view is reasonable, as that term is normally understood, this has no implications for the use of force. The explanation is that defending oneself against an attacker in a way that is morally impermissible cannot plausibly be valued as part of an authentic and independent life. Consider the person who recognizes her mistake later in life. She cannot reasonably value the fact that she has wrongly defended herself in this way as part of an authentic or independent life.

This is not because her values do not underpin her decision to defend herself, nor that her values are abhorrent. It is for two reasons: first, because moral ideas of this kind are not central to the person's self-conception, and so are less central to an authentic and independent life; second, and more importantly, because she commits a serious and harmful wrong against the person suffering the seizure. The fact that doing this was in accordance with her mistaken conception of the good does not render doing it valuable in the relevant sense.

Of course, she may value the outcome of her wrongful conduct: the fact that she acted wrongly also resulted in her saving her own life, and she has every reason to prefer this outcome to one where she dies and the attacker survives. But, as I noted in Chapter 3, this is consistent with her recognizing that she had no reason to value

[26] See, for example, M Otsuka 'Killing the Innocent in Self-Defense' (1994) 23 *Philosophy and Public Affairs* 74 and J McMahan 'Self-Defense and the Problem of the Innocent Attacker' (1994) 104 *Ethics* 252.

[27] See, for example, J J Thomson 'Self-Defense' (1991) 20 *Philosophy and Public Affairs* 283, J Quong 'Killing in Self-Defense' (2009) 119 *Ethics* 507 and V Tadros *The Ends of Harm: The Moral Foundations of Criminal Law* (Oxford: OUP, 2011) ch.11.

her freedom to do this. There is thus nothing objectionable in a state that prevents her doing what she believes she is morally permitted to do.

This suggests that the fact that it is difficult for citizens in a liberal society to develop the correct moral conception, and that we cannot expect citizens to do so, does not necessarily have implications for what we should criminalize. In some cases a person cannot be expected to form the correct moral view, and yet there would be nothing wrong, even *pro tanto*, with coercing the person to comply with what morality requires. The reason is that the values of authenticity and independence are not engaged in these cases. Indeed, as we will see in the next section, the value of authenticity cannot be secured in *any* case of wrongdoing.

A person who reasonably forms mistaken views of this kind cannot be expected to endorse the law in the sense outlined above—she has an excuse for not doing so. But this has no implications for the use of coercion. She has a reason to prefer coercion, in that case, in order that she better conforms to the reasons that apply to her, even if she cannot see what these reasons are. The fact that she cannot see that the law is right is neither here nor there—she has reason to prefer others, with the right view, to prevent her from acting wrongly rather than acting on her own mistaken view. For this reason, imposing the law on her does not breach fair terms of cooperation.

VI. Authenticity, Independence, and Criminalization

With a sketched defence of political liberalism in hand, we are better placed to assess the implications of political liberalism for criminalization. There are obvious and powerful objections to the idea that political liberal values can provide a justification for criminalizing non-wrongful conduct. The infliction of punishment on those who are not morally liable to suffer it cannot be justified by the fact that some people wrongly believe their conduct to be wrong. The question, then, is whether by refraining from criminalizing some wrongdoing the state can secure the values of authenticity and independence.

Suppose that the state refrains from criminalizing some wrongful conduct on the basis that some citizens do not believe that the conduct is wrong. These citizens wish to act in a way that is in fact wrong, but that they believe is permissible or required. Our question is whether the performance of the action, or perhaps just the legal permission to do so, can contribute to an authentic or independent life, and whether people have a claim against being alienated from state institutions by being forced to do what they are required to do. Public officials may also have an objection to being forced to cooperate in coercing these people, and taxpayers may object to the use of their resources to secure coercion. If these objections are sound, there are political liberal grounds to decriminalize the conduct. This conduct might be thought wrong, but not publicly wrong—it is not a wrong that the state can permissibly condemn and because were it to do so it would alienate its citizens.

In assessing this case, recall that decriminalization also expands the criminal law—by restricting the ability people have to prevent wrongdoing, or to prevent the bad things that wrongdoing involves or causes.[28] We must evaluate the importance of this fact by considering the extent to which individuals are hampered from pursuing their

[28] In the next chapter, we will see that we do not have reasons to prevent wrongdoing as such, but to prevent the facts that make acts wrong from occurring.

own moral conception by preventing the wrongdoing. So a political liberal case for decriminalization must also rest on a case to restrict private citizens and the police from preventing the wrongdoing. In other words, it rests on a case for a general right to do wrong in the following sense: a right of citizens not to be prevented by anyone, state official or private citizen, to act wrongly.[29]

i) Authenticity

In the previous section, I suggested that whether a person has reason to object to the imposition of a law on her which she does not, and cannot reasonably be expected to, accept depends on whether the law sets back the values of authenticity and independence. But the argument about nature of wrongdoing that I advanced in Chapter 3 immediately narrows our focus—it is only the value of independence, and not the value of authenticity, that can be set back in the case of wrongdoing.

A crude summary of the argument in Chapter 3 is that the distinction between all things considered wrongful conduct and the broader class of conduct that we have decisive reasons not to perform is that the autonomous performance of wrongful conduct is not valuable. Wrongdoing is thus not a valuable part of an authentic life. A person may appropriately value her life as her own—as conducted by her own will and judgement—even if it involves mistakes of value. The contribution of an action to an authentic life, this suggests, does not depend on it being rational to perform the action. What makes wrongdoing special is that it is inappropriate for the person to value these aspects of her life as her own. Hence, even if the person autonomously pursues goals that she deeply values, it is inappropriate for the person to value them as authentic. She has no grounds for rejecting coercion on that basis.

It follows that the state cannot respect or protect the value of authenticity by decriminalizing wrongdoing. For even if the mistaken person values the act that she performs as authentic, her act does not advance the value of authenticity.

To illustrate, recall the question whether early abortion ought not to be criminalized even if it is wrong. Suppose that pregnant women who abort their foetuses in the first trimester act wrongly. If they do, it is inappropriate for them to value their decision to do so as a contribution to an autonomous life. The facts that make early abortion wrong also undermine the idea that doing this contributes to an authentic life. Hence, the value of authenticity is not a consideration in favour of decriminalizing early abortion.

ii) Independence

Even if the value of authenticity has no implications for the scope of the criminal law, the same cannot be said for the value of independence. The value of independence is primarily negative—a person lives an independent life if others do not intentionally control her actions.

The idea that the values of authenticity and independence are distinct draws on the following idea. If it is wrong for a person to act in a certain way, the values that make the act wrong render it inappropriate for the person to value the performance of the

[29] For this meaning of the right to do wrong, see, for example, D Enoch 'A Right to Violate One's Duty' (2002) 21 *Law and Philosophy* 367; O Herstein 'Defending the Right to Do Wrong' (2012) 31 *Law and Philosophy* 343.

action as part of an authentic life. But they need not make it inappropriate for the person to value being free from being controlled by others to ensure that the wrongful actions are not performed. The relevant contrast is between valuing the fact that one lives one's life according to values that one endorses and valuing the fact that others do not shape one's life against one's will.

The facts that make an act wrong may be sufficiently important to render it inappropriate for the person to value the performance of the act as part of an autonomous life, but they may be insufficiently important to render it inappropriate for the person to value being free from the control of others.

To reinforce this contrast between independence and authenticity, consider the following. Psychological experiments have shown that finding a small amount of money increases the likelihood that a person will perform a virtuous action. Now compare:

> *Lucky Help*: Karl finds a small amount of money that has been dropped by chance. Soon afterwards he helps a little old lady across the road. Had he not found the money, he would not have helped the little old lady.
>
> *Manipulated Help*: Karl finds a small amount of money that has intentionally been left there by Nicola, who wants Karl to perform a generous act. Soon afterwards he helps a little old lady across the road. Had he not found the money, he would not have helped the little old lady.

In both *Help* cases, Karl's act may be authentic. Karl decides to do this, let us suppose, in the light of the things that he values. We may be troubled by the fact that whether Karl helps the little old lady or not depends on whether he finds the money—his disposition to help the old lady is not very robust. Some may conclude from this that Karl's act is not truly free, or that Karl does not deserve praise, or a reward, for doing so. We have explored views of this kind in Chapter 5.

Here, we are interested in a further question that was raised in that chapter. Even though Karl's act is equally authentic in the two cases, it is not equally independent. In the second case Nicola manipulates Karl into performing the action. She does not bypass Karl's will. Rather, she intentionally creates the conditions in which Karl will exercise his will in a certain way. Karl has good reason to regret being controlled in this way. In both cases, he should be glad that he has performed a generous act, and glad that this is an expression of his values. But it is doubtful that he should value performing this act identically. In the first case, his act is both authentic and independent; in the second, it is authentic but not independent.

When a person is forced not to act wrongly, she is not manipulated in the subversive way that is true in *Manipulated Help*. One distinct objection to Nicola's behaviour in *Manipulated Help* does not apply in this case. If the state criminalizes wrongful conduct, the state attempts to engage the rational agency of its citizens rather than bypassing their rational agency. It outlines that the conduct is wrong, and may also outline reasons why it is wrong. Citizens are then able to assess for themselves the reasons against acting in the relevant way.

But the state also backs up criminal laws with threats of punishment. In doing so, it provides its citizens with a prudential reason to comply with the law, in case they are not motivated by the moral content of the law. Those who fail to comply for moral reasons, but do so only for prudential reasons, are controlled by the state. They are forced to act in a way that they do not wish to act, or alternatively forced not to act in a way that they wish to act. A person who believes an act to be permissible, but complies with a law because of the prudential reason that the state supplies to do so, does not act independently.

Our question is when any objection that a person has to being controlled in this way can make a difference to the scope of the criminal law. It is not plausible that the disvalue of independence makes such a difference in the case of core wrongs. Consider a person who thinks it permissible to inflict serious harm on others, but who does not do so because she is subject to a threat. There is nothing objectionable in her being controlled in this way. She should be grateful to be controlled because this prevents her from wrongly inflicting serious harm on others. To see this, recall our heuristic device for testing the value of independence: suppose that later in life she comes to realize that she would have acted wrongly were it not for the threat of punishment. There is no room for her to regret having been controlled. Had she inflicted serious harm on others, her act would have been independent. But given the kind of wrongdoing involved, she ought not to value that fact. She does not have grounds to object to other people preventing her life from being blighted by her own serious wrongdoing.[30]

When it comes to more trivial wrongdoing, though, independence is plausibly valuable. Consider:

> *Painter*: Della worships a false God. She believes that she is duty-bound not to work on Wednesdays. She is contracted to paint Gerry's house by the end of Wednesday, and intends to do so on Tuesday. Unfortunately, her child falls sick and she is unable to complete the job. If she does not paint the house on Wednesday, she can complete the job on Thursday. Gerry will be inconvenienced if the job is not completed on time.

It is wrong for Della not to paint Gerry's house on Wednesday. She will breach her contract if she does so, and will wrongly inconvenience Gerry. And she will do these things for no good reason—she is not in fact duty bound to worship her false God; she lacks any reason to do so at all.

Now consider whether it is objectionable to force Della to paint the house. There may be many instrumental reasons not to do so—she will be upset by being threatened, and by the belief that she has acted in conflict with her duty. The threat may be ineffective, and she will be harmed if it is carried out, and so on. But the objection is deeper than that. The very fact of forcing Della to act in conflict with her beliefs seems objectionable in this case. The fact that she is duty bound to act in this way seems an insufficient response to this objection.

To evaluate this objection further, suppose that Della comes to realize that her God is false. And suppose that any value she got from this is insufficient to render her act permissible all things considered. She had a *pro tanto* duty to do so, and she was mistaken in thinking that she was permitted to infringe this *pro tanto* duty—the duty that she thought she had, which explained why she thought she was so permitted, was no duty at all.

In the light of this it would be inappropriate for her to value the fact that she worshiped her God rather than fulfilling her duty to Gerry. She should regret, all things considered, her choice to violate that duty—she cannot value this decision in the light of the fact that it expressed her values, because to do so would show inappropriate regard for the values that give rise to her duty.

Nevertheless, she may value her independence from control by others. She may value not being forced to act in a way that conflicted with her beliefs, even when those beliefs are false, and acting in accordance with them resulted in her acting

[30] The idea that the lives of wrongdoers are blighted by their serious wrongdoing is further defended in Chapter 1.

wrongly. Her objection is not that acting in accordance with her judgement was in itself valuable, but rather that she does not wish her life to be under the control of others.

Political liberalism thus has implications for the scope of the criminal law. Certain wrongful acts cannot be criminalized because to do so would fail to respect the value of independence. The state should refrain from shaping the lives of its citizens in some respects even if in doing so it refrains from preventing them from acting wrongly. This provides a decisive reason against criminalizing some kinds of wrong, even though the wrongdoer has no reason to perform the wrongful act.

This also helps to respond to an objection we considered earlier. If some conduct is not criminalized, interference with a person to prevent them acting in the relevant way is criminalized. But interference with a person to prevent them acting in the relevant way may be wrong, and even seriously wrong, because it fails to respect the value of independence. So citizens do not necessarily have an objection to the expansion in the scope of the criminal law that decriminalizing some wrongful conduct involves.

If Della's act is decriminalized, neither police officers nor private citizens are permitted to force Della to fulfil the contract she owes to Gerry. They cannot do something that they may value—ensure that Gerry's contract is completed on time by enforcing Della's duty. But forcing Della to do her duty may wrong her, for it may violate her right of independence. Furthermore, the restriction on others to secure independence does not seem powerfully eroded by the criminalization of their interference with Della. In that case, not only is there an objection to criminalizing Della's wrongful conduct, there is also no objection to criminalizing conduct which interferes with her to prevent her from acting wrongly.

Respect for Della, as an independent person, undermines the value of criminalizing her wrongful conduct. This suggests that the basic idea of political liberalism has some implications for the scope of the criminal law. Respect for others, as independent agents, requires that they are not prevented from pursuing their reasonable conception of what is good or right, and that restricts the scope of the criminal law.

VII. Conclusion

Political liberalism, outlined above, gives further content to the idea of public wrongdoing. There are wrongs that are beyond the realm of state control because people who mistakenly believe that the wrongful conduct is permitted have reason to value being free from state control to perform these actions.

But this argument does not have implications for the scope and content of core crimes, which are concerned with seriously harmful wrongs. The value of independence is not engaged in the case of such wrongs. Their content and scope is, for that reason, not determined by the ambition to ensure that the law is acceptable to those with different basic moral views. Those who reject the scope of the law because of their mistaken views, in such cases, have no objection to state interference to prevent them from acting wrongly. They may feel alienated from their state, but any disvalue in their alienation is outweighed or negated by the importance of ensuring that serious wrongdoing does not occur.

It may well follow that political liberalism has few implications for the scope of the criminal law in practice, when we acknowledge other reasons to restrict the scope of the criminal law, such as those considered in the previous chapter. Because state punishment inevitably inflicts serious harm on wrongdoers, the scope of the criminal law is already limited. State punishment would not be warranted for trivial wrongdoing independently of any arguments from political liberalism. At most, political liberalism provides an additional set of arguments why some non-serious wrongs ought not to be criminalized. The fact that people in liberal societies reasonably disagree about what is wrong is thus not very important in understanding core cases of criminalization. If it has a role, it is at the margins where the value of independence more plausibly bites.

9

The Core Case of Criminalization

In the previous three chapters, most of the progress that we have made is negative. I have suggested that a range of restrictive and justificatory principles either fail or fail to illuminate. And I have suggested that the idea of public wrongdoing, properly interpreted, only has modest implications for the scope of the criminal law.

A starting point to develop a more positive view focuses on core cases of criminalization. Only abolitionists doubt that seriously harmful wrongful conduct, such as murder, rape, and serious assault, may be criminalized. Although abolitionists need to be answered, our main question is not whether these things should be criminalized, but why. A good account should deepen our understanding of the aims of the criminal law; show how they are related and how criminalizing seriously wrongful conduct can help to secure them; and make their pursuit legitimate.

Section I offers an account of the central functions of the criminal law. Section II considers the preventive aims of the criminal law in more depth. Section III shows how criminalization pursues these ends in the case of core crimes, and responds to objections that might be made to the use of the criminal law. Section IV outlines different kinds of proportionality judgement that determine whether the pursuit of these aims is permissible all things considered.

I. The Functions of the Criminal Law

The criminal law has many proper functions. It is relatively uncontroversial that it ought to be used to prevent at least some kinds of wrongdoing and to hold wrongdoers responsible for their wrongdoing. It is also relatively uncontroversial that it ought to be used to prevent wrongdoing by prohibiting it, or at least declaring that it is prohibited, and by enforcing those prohibitions through both policing and the threat of punishment. And it ought to be used to hold wrongdoers responsible by trying and convicting wrongdoers, and punishing them for their wrongs. In doing so, public officials communicate with the wrongdoer, the victims, and people more generally. There is some dispute over what is communicated. To use a not very precise term, let us say that the state publicly blames wrongdoers for what they have done. This leaves open what blame involves, and so is less controversial.

In suggesting that these are central functions of the criminal law, I don't mean to suggest that they are either necessary or sufficient for a law to be a criminal law. I have already suggested that the necessary and sufficient conditions of criminal law, even if they could be found, do not necessarily pick out its most important features. What I intend, then, is a normative account of the central features of core criminal laws.

i) Enforceable prohibitions

The criminal law expresses to citizens that they are under obligations. In core cases at least, it expresses the demands that the state has of its citizens. Typically, these demands are negative—it demands that citizens must not perform the acts prohibited by the criminal law because those acts are seriously wrongful. The criminal law thus communicates moral duties to citizens. I leave aside the difficult question whether the criminal law adds the authority of the state to the moral demand that citizens already have not to act wrongly in core cases.

The criminal law is not unique in expressing demands. Private laws also do so: not to defame or trespass, for example. There may be conditional permissions in private law. They take the form: you may *v* as long as you pay compensation for any harm you cause. But these laws are the exception rather than the rule.[1] However, although the criminal law is not unique in expressing moral demands, expressing such demands is a central feature of the criminal law.

Furthermore, the state threatens to enforce these demands. One way this is done is through direct police and private action. The criminal prohibition of *v*ing, in core cases at least, triggers a legal permission on the police and private citizens to interfere with liberty and prevent people from *v*ing by using or threatening force.

This feature of the criminal law distinguishes it from many other laws. For example, contract law prohibits breach of contract, but there is no legal permission on either the police or private citizens to use or threaten force to compel citizens to fulfil their contracts (though legal action for breach can, of course, be threatened). Similarly, tort law prohibits defamation, but there is no legal permission on either the police or private citizens to use force to prevent defamation.

The permission on the state to enforce the law is neither a necessary nor a sufficient condition of criminal law. There are some private laws that are enforceable: it is permissible for police officers to use force to prevent negligent harming, even where negligent harming is not criminal. Furthermore, not all criminal laws are coupled with a legal permission to enforce. Withdrawing the permission to enforce a criminal law does not amount to decriminalization. To see this, suppose that because the police are corrupt, they will misuse their power to enforce a certain law, so they are instructed not to enforce that law. The state does not thereby decriminalize the conduct that the law prohibits.

But enforceability may nevertheless have a central role to play in the criminal law. Even the law just described may be enforceable in a sense. In one sense, whether a law is enforceable does not depend on whether there should be a permission to enforce it all things considered but rather on whether people who would otherwise commit the wrong in question would have a complaint against the use of force to prevent them from doing this by those properly motivated. Even in the previous example, the decision to withdraw the permission to enforce need not imply that the law is unenforceable in this sense. Core criminal laws are enforceable in this sense.

ii) Responsibility, public blame, and punishment

The criminal justice system is also a responsibility institution: one of its purposes is to determine whether those accused of criminal wrongdoing have acted wrongly, and whether they are responsible for doing so. At least at its best, it offers those it accuses opportunities to respond to accusations made against them, and it convicts them of

[1] A familiar complaint about some work in legal realism and law and economics is that it fails adequately to explain this familiar feature of private law. See D A Nance 'Guidance Rules and Enforcement Rules: A Better View of the Cathedral' (1997) 83 *Virginia Law Review* 837; J Goldberg and B Zipursky 'Accidents of the Great Society' (2005) 64 *Maryland Law Review* 364.

criminal wrongdoing after proving, to a stringent evidential standard, both that the defendant acted wrongly, and that he was responsible for his wrongdoing. It holds them responsible for wrongdoing, and publicly blames them for it, because of their responsibility for wrongdoing. And it inflicts appropriate sanctions on them.[2]

State communication about wrongdoing is important for many reasons. It helps victims recognize that they were wronged, to understand that the broader community recognizes this, and through that to recognize that they are valued. It can help to foster a stronger commitment to justice amongst citizens and to prevent wrongdoing by getting people to recognize what behaviour is, and is deemed, unacceptable in a society. It can also serve preventive ends by deterring wrongful conduct: being publicly blamed is unpleasant, and people will be motivated to avoid it even if they are not morally motivated. Finally, communication, either through punishment or independently, can encourage wrongdoers to recognize the wrongs that they have committed. This can be important both for them and for others, especially for victims who may have a right that the wrongdoer recognizes the wrong they have done.

The communicative functions of the criminal law thus often complement the aim to prevent crime. Whilst I believe that the most important aim of criminal justice is preventive, I don't doubt that there are independent communicative aims of punishment, and that these play an important role in a complete theory of the criminal law.[3]

Here is one way of understanding the relationship between this feature of the criminal justice system and criminalization. When the state criminalizes conduct it warrants certain state responses to that conduct. To criminalize *v* is to warrant accusing people of *v*ing (if there is sufficient evidence to do so), calling those who have *v*ed to account for having done so, publicly blaming those who have been demonstrated to have *v*ed (if they lack a justification or excuse for having *v*ed), and inflicting sanctions on them. Criminalizing *v*ing is normally justified, then, only if doing these things is warranted.

One part of this process—public blame—has provided an important focus for scholarship on criminalization.[4] As public blame is a kind of blame, to understand it we need to know more about blame. There is no uniform understanding of blame. It clearly involves expressing disapproval to, or about, wrongdoers for their wrongdoing. But blame involves more than that—even if blame *itself* does not involve more than that, it is at least an expression that more than that is warranted. As T M Scanlon notes, otherwise blaming might be reduced to the 'pointless assignment of moral "grades"'.[5]

As Scanlon also notes, blame is forceful, but it is controversial how the force of blame should best be understood. For some, blame involves resentment;[6] for others—Scanlon himself—it involves a kind of normative distancing from the person blamed.[7] As I argued in Chapter 5, I doubt either of these things is necessary for blame—blame

[2] For a fuller account of this element of the criminal law that still seems to me roughly right, see R A Duff, L Farmer, S E Marshall, and V Tadros *The Trial on Trial* vol 3 (Oxford: Hart, 2007).

[3] See, further, V Tadros *The Ends of Harm: The Moral Foundations of Criminal Law* (Oxford: OUP, 2011) ch 5.

[4] I mean to include those who focus on things closely related to blame, such as public condemnation and public censure. For well-known examples, see R A Duff *Answering for Crime: Responsibility and Liability in the Criminal Law* (Oxford: Hart, 2007); A P Simester and A von Hirsch *Crimes, Harms, and Wrongs: On the Principles of Criminalisation* (Oxford: Hart, 2011).

[5] *Moral Dimensions: Permissibility, Meaning, Blame* (Cambridge, Mass: Harvard UP, 2008) 127.

[6] See, for example, S Wolf 'Blame, Italian Style' in R Jay Wallace, R Kumar, and S Freeman *Reasons and Recognition: Essays on the Philosophy of T M Scanlon* (Oxford: OUP, 2011).

[7] *Moral Dimensions*, ch 4.

could also involve expressing disapproval of the conduct with a forceful demand for appropriate responses. Public blame, on this view, might then involve a public demand for a response from a wrongdoer for his wrongdoing.

Now focus on the public aspect of public blame. There is some sense in which serious criminal wrongdoing wrongs the public. People cooperate in a state to protect each other from serious wrongdoing. Parents, schools, the police, and a wide range of other people in a state, and between states, contribute to this cooperative aim. Criminal wrongdoing sets back their ambitions to do this, and thus may wrong these people.

But the main target of serious criminal wrongdoing is the direct victim, and public blame is warranted primarily for the wrong that is done to her.[8] As I noted in Chapter 7, given the duties that people have to each other to ensure that people are protected from serious wrongdoing, it is not hard to explain why state officials are warranted in publicly blaming serious wrongdoers for their wrongful conduct, even if the wider community does not believe the conduct to be wrong. As people have a general duty to support institutions in pursuing the ends that are pursued, such as the duty to communicate with the offender, the victim, and others, as well as the duties of protection, public officials are not only permitted, but also required, to treat the violation of the relevant wrongs as a public matter.[9] Even though there are some wrongs that are not the state's business, and perhaps there are serious wrongs like this, it is not plausible that serious harmful wrongdoing, such as murder, rape, mutilation, and other serious assaults, is private.

II. What Preventive Aims?

The criminal law, I have already suggested, has both communicative and preventive functions, and these functions are complementary. We saw in Chapter 2 that wrongdoing is the standard target of blame. So insofar as the criminal law blames, it ought to be concerned with wrongdoing.

The criminal law also has a more important preventive function. Insofar as these things come apart, we have more reason to prevent murders, rapes, and serious assaults than we do to ensure that our communicative response to them is adequate once they have occurred. In this section I explore this preventive aim. Although the state clearly has good reason to prevent murders, rapes, serious assaults, and so on, it is less obvious why this is so.

One view is that the state has good reason to prevent these things because they are harmful, and it has good reason to prevent harm. A second view is that these things are serious wrongs, and the state has good reason to prevent serious wrongdoing because it is wrong. A third view is that the state has good reason to prevent a range of bad things occurring. Harm is only one of these things. These things can make acts wrong, but the state does not have a powerful reason to prevent wrongful acts because they are wrong.

[8] See, also, R A Duff *Answering for Crime*, 51–3; R A Duff and S E Marshall 'Public and Private Wrongs' in J Chalmers, F Leverick, and L Farmer *Essays in Criminal Law in Honour of Sir Gerald Gordon* (Edinburgh: EUP, 2010)

[9] See, also, S E Marshall and R A Duff 'Criminalization and Sharing Wrongs' 11 *Canadian Journal of Law and Jurisprudence*, 19–20, though they make the sharing contingent on sharing identity, values, and mutual concern, where I do not think the obligation of mutual concern as contingent in this way.

I argue that the state sometimes owes it to wrongdoers to prevent them from acting wrongly, but subject to that qualification the third view is true.

This first view has influential defenders—recall that John Stuart Mill thought that the *only* reason to interfere with the liberty of others is to prevent harm. Furthermore, there are some reasons to doubt that there are powerful reasons to prevent wrongdoing as such. There is no reason to prevent at least some wrongs: inchoate wrongs. And it is plausible that the explanation is that doing so does not prevent harm.

Consider:

> *Attempt*: Markus is pointing a gun at Florian, and is about to pull the trigger. He thinks that the gun is loaded. Florian is completely unaware that this is happening. Jon can prevent Markus from doing this by wrestling Markus to the floor. However, Jon knows that Markus's gun is unloaded.

It seems wrong for Markus to pull the trigger.[10] Yet Jon seems to have no reason to wrestle Markus to the floor. This supports the conclusion that there is no reason to prevent Markus from doing what it is wrong for him to do. Furthermore, that seems true, at least at first sight, because preventing the wrong would not prevent Florian from being harmed: he will not be harmed regardless of what Jon does. Some might then argue as follows. An attempt is a complete wrong minus the harm that the wrong would normally do. We don't have reasons to prevent wrongs when we remove the harm. Therefore we only have a reason to prevent harm and not wrongdoing.

Furthermore, when we hold other things equal, it seems that our reasons to prevent harmful wrongdoing are no greater, or not significantly greater, than our reasons to prevent naturally occurring harm. Consider:

> *Two Boulders*: Maria has recklessly caused a boulder to roll towards Claudio. If nothing is done, this boulder will crush Claudio's leg. Another boulder has been blown towards Ralph. If nothing is done, this boulder will crush Ralph's leg. Sylvie can prevent either the first or the second boulder from reaching its target, but not both.

Intuitions differ about this case, but one plausible reaction is that Sylvie has no stronger reason to prevent Claudio's leg being crushed than Ralph's, or if her reason to do the first thing is stronger, it is not significantly stronger.[11] This again suggests that our preventive aims are properly focused not on wrongdoing as such, but on harm. Any interest we have in preventing wrongdoing, it might be argued, is derivative of our interest in preventing harm.

This view is consistent with the view that we ought to prevent one person harming another only if that person will act wrongly in harming the other. If it is permissible for X to harm Y, X typically ought not to be prevented from harming Y.[12] This provides a reason to deter harmful conduct only on condition that the harm will wrongfully be inflicted (subject to certain exceptions). But the idea that wrongdoing provides a constraint on harm prevention is consistent with the idea that there is no non-derivative reason to prevent wrongdoing—wrongdoing might provide a constraint on harm prevention without providing an aim.

[10] I defend the idea that it is in Chapter 16.

[11] See, for example, J McMahan 'Humanitarian Intervention, Consent, and Proportionality' and P Singer 'Bystanders to Poverty', both in N A Davis, R Keshen, and J McMahan *Ethics and Humanity: Themes from the Philosophy of Jonathan Glover* (Oxford: OUP, 2010); V Tadros *The Ends of Harm*, 105–8.

[12] Everyone agrees that there are exceptions. Some think there are more exceptions than others. See *The Ends of Harm*, ch 9 for discussion.

Here is one challenge to these examples. Even if we have no inherent reason to prevent wrongdoing for the sake of victims, we do have inherent reasons to prevent wrongdoing for the sake of would-be wrongdoers. In the introduction to the book I suggested that wrongdoing blights the lives of wrongdoers. A person has an interest in not being a wrongdoer. Not only do people have an interest in not being wrongdoers, we owe it to others to ensure that they are not wrongdoers. For example, we owe it to people to educate them, when they are children, to prevent them from becoming wrongdoers, not only for the sake of victims, but also for their sake. And we owe it to people to remove the temptation to become wrongdoers. This is a reason against entrapment. The criminal justice system has a role to play in the ambition to prevent people from being wrongdoers: it helps to support other institutions in ensuring that people are guided to develop more positive plans rather than being steered into lives of crime.

Does our concern to prevent people being wrongdoers extend to cases like *Attempt*, though? I doubt it. It is wrong for Markus to attempt to kill Florian. He should prefer that he does not do this. But, I am inclined to think that this provides others with a reason to prevent him from committing his attempt only in certain ways. Jon has a reason to persuade Markus not to pull the trigger, but not a reason to use pure coercion to do so. If Markus does not pull the trigger after being persuaded not to do so, the difference between his attempting and not attempting is a result of his judgement, and he has an interest in not acting wrongly through the exercise of his judgement. He can value the fact that he came to think better of his decision to try to kill Florian. And Florian also has a reason to prefer it that Markus thinks better of his decision to kill him. But I doubt that either Markus or Florian have an interest in Markus not attempting to kill Florian where simple physical interference prevents the attempt.

It might be argued that things are different in the case of completed crimes. I should prefer it that others prevent me from completing a murder, even if this is done simply through the use of physical force. Of course, they would have a reason to prevent me doing this for the sake of the victim. But they also have a reason to prevent me doing it for my sake. And this seems true: I have a powerful reason not to be involved in the loss of another person's life, especially when this results from my decision to act wrongly.

This might incline some people to distinguish *Attempt* and *Two Boulders*. If Sylvie prevents Claudio's leg from being crushed, she prevents Maria wrongly causing Claudio's injury, and Maria has a powerful interest in not being involved in this way. This, it might be argued, suggests that Sylvie ought to save Claudio rather than Ralph. I doubt that this is right. This view implies that Ralph loses his right to an equal chance of being saved in order to prevent Sylvie becoming a wrongdoer. This seems hard to support. So I am inclined to think that although Maria has an interest in Sylvie saving Claudio over Ralph, this interest makes no difference to what Sylvie has reason to do.

Still, even with these qualifications, people may still owe it to potential wrongdoers to prevent them from acting wrongly by using the criminal law. The criminal law does not affect behaviour only in the way that Jon would affect Markus in *Attempt*. It not only offers threats, it expresses to people the reasons that they have not to perform certain acts. And the threats that it offers may have a more indirect role in shaping people's decisions, encouraging them not to act wrongly. When it operates in these ways, it is valued partly because it prevents people from acting wrongly.

Now focus again on the idea that we do not owe it to victims of wrongdoing to prevent wrongdoing as such. Even if examples like *Attempt* and *Two Boulders* support this view, they do not show that we owe it to victims only to prevent them from suffering harm. The evils that explain why some acts are wrong are not all harm-related, and victims may have interests in these other evils not occurring.

We already saw in Chapter 6 that some wrongs are not harm-based. Some of these non-harmful rights violations include interferences with a person's body or property. But we often have powerful reasons to prevent these violations from occurring. For example, paternalistic interference with a person often seems wrong. But paternalistic interference is done for the person's own good, and it may be good for her. The wrongness of paternalistic interference is not dependent on whether it is harmful, and the fact that it might be harmful does not provide an exhaustive explanation of its wrongness. It is wrong in part because one person takes control of the other. We have reason not only to condemn such interference when it occurs, but also to prevent it from occurring. We have these reasons even when the wrongful interference is not harmful; even when it is beneficial. Similarly, in Chapter 6 we briefly explored the idea that sex with an unconscious person can be wrong, even when doing this has no psychological or physical effects on the person interfered with. We have reason not only to condemn such conduct when it occurs, but also to prevent it from occurring.

These examples may seem to support the view that we owe it to potential victims to prevent wrongdoing because it is wrong. But this does not follow. An alternative is that we owe it to potential victims to prevent the facts that make the conduct wrong from occurring. For example, the fact that one person will control the life of another explains why we have a reason to prevent paternalistic interference, and also a reason why paternalistic interference is often wrong. The fact that that one person will control the body of another both explains why we have reason to prevent interference with another person's unconscious body, and also why such interference is wrong. On this view, we owe it to victims to prevent certain kinds of conduct because of the facts that make that conduct wrong, and not because it is wrong.

In the light of this, how can we explain the intuitive view that wrongdoing did not seem to make a difference to our preventive aims in *Attempt* and *Two Boulders*? Markus's conduct in *Attempt* is wrong because of the harm that it is intended to cause. Although Markus's conduct is not harmful, harm has a central role to play in explaining its wrongness. But as Markus's conduct will not cause the harm that makes it wrong, such harm cannot supply Jon with a reason to prevent the wrongness. Hence, Jon does not owe it to Florian to prevent the wrongdoing.

Similarly, the harm that Maria will do to Claudio in *Two Boulders* is the most important fact that makes her conduct wrong. But Ralph will suffer the same harm if Sylvie does not rescue him. This explains the intuition that many people have: that Sylvie has little reason to save Claudio over Ralph. If there is a reason for Sylvie to save Claudio over Ralph, this is explained by other facts that make Maria's act wrong—for example, that her act will manifest her ill will to Sylvie. As I noted earlier, there is some divergence in our reactions to *Two Boulders*, and therefore some disagreement about whether Sylvie has a reason to save Claudio over Ralph, and the strength of that reason. But we can accommodate the idea that Sylvie has a reason to save Claudio over Ralph without relying on the idea that we owe it to victims to prevent wrongdoing as such.

In conclusion, we may owe it to potential wrongdoers to prevent them acting wrongly. Where we are concerned with conduct that is wrong only because of the harm that it causes, our reasons to prevent the wrongdoing are derivative of our reasons to prevent harm. Victims of wrongdoing have no interest in us preventing the occurrence of some wrongs, such as inchoate wrongs, because the fact that explains the wrongness of the act will not occur regardless of whether we prevent the wrong. But we do have reason to prevent some non-harmful rights violations. We have good reason to prevent these acts from occurring, even though they are not harmful, and our reasons have to do with the facts that make them wrong.

In Chapter 6, I argued against the following principle:

> *HP2 (Proportionality)*: It is wrong to criminalize conduct unless doing so is proportionate. It is proportionate only if the harm that criminalization causes is outweighed by the harm that it prevents.

I did so on the grounds that it excludes the prevention of harmless wrongdoing from the proportionality calculation. We can now see why some harmless wrongdoing should be included in that calculation. The criminal justice system can contribute to preventing wrongdoing by helping people to make better judgements. Potential wrongdoers have an interest in being helped in this way, and this can help to outweigh the harms that criminal justice may cause. Furthermore, the prevention of harmless wrongdoing can contribute to the proportionality calculation, outweighing some of the harm that criminalization causes.

III. Freedom and Liability

Given the argument in the previous section, the central explanation why criminal law is normally concerned with wrongdoing is not to do with its aims but because of the way in which it pursues these aims. The powerful relationship between wrongs and crimes has to do with the conditions that make the pursuit of the aims of the criminal justice system permissible.

i) Freedom

I noted earlier that the criminal law prevents wrongdoing both through the use of direct force, and by issuing and executing threats of punishment. It thus restricts freedom in two distinct ways. First, it restricts people's freedom to do what the criminal law prohibits. It does this both through the use of preventive force and by threatening people with punishment for violating the law. Second, it uses wrongdoers for the sake of its preventive goals. This restricts freedom in a distinct way: wrongdoers are involved in the plans of state officials, who use them to ensure that their aims of protecting other people are fulfilled. Thus, they are not only restricted from pursuing their own goals, but others impose their goals on them.

Restricting freedom in these ways often seems objectionable. It is often wrong to prevent a person doing what they want to do, either through the use of force or the threat of force. Furthermore, it is often distinctively, and even more powerfully, wrong to use a person to serve our ends, especially when doing so harms them. The idea that there is a powerful relationship between wrongs and crimes is explained by showing that restrictions on freedom of the two kinds outlined are not objectionable in the case of serious wrongdoers.

First, consider the objection to the use of coercion, including state coercion: that it restricts freedom. Some think that freedom provides a general reason against criminalization.[13] But in the case of serious wrongdoing, the fact that a person's freedom is restricted is either completely unproblematic, or is at least much less problematic.

In central cases, the objection to the use of force to restrict a person's freedom rests on the two independent values that I considered in the previous chapter: the value of authenticity and the value of independence. The value of autonomy is the value of living one's life by pursuing goals that one values. The value of independence is the value of being free from control by others.

When a person's freedom to act in a seriously wrongful way is restricted, neither value is engaged. The value of autonomy is not engaged because there is no autonomy-related value in acting wrongly. If my argument about the nature of wrongdoing in Chapter 3 is right, this *must* be true, for the distinction between wrongness and permissibility is just the distinction between acts whose performance can directly contribute to a valuable autonomous life and those that cannot.

The value of independence retains force in some cases of wrongdoing, or so I argued in Chapter 8: we have an interest in not being controlled by others, even when we lack an autonomy-related interest in performing the acts that others prevent us from performing. But this value is not plausibly engaged in the case of serious wrongdoing. If another person prevents me from committing a serious wrong, I should be glad of the prevention. The interference is not something that I have reason to regret.

Now consider a second objection—that a person who violates the law will be punished. Such a person will be used to advance the goal of protecting others from wrongdoing. The response to this objection is that by acting in a seriously wrongful way, we incur duties to serve these protective ends. As this is so, wrongdoers are only controlled to use ends that they have duties to serve, and that at least plays an important role in meeting the objection against being used. As I have discussed this second idea at length in Chapter 4 and elsewhere, I do not develop it further here.

The central aim of the criminal law, then, is to prevent the occurrence of facts that make acts wrong. It does not primarily take aim at wrongdoing itself. But the two main objections that people otherwise have to having their liberty restricted by criminalization do not apply to serious wrongdoers. They have little or no reason to want an option to behave wrongly, given that their conduct is already morally constrained. And they have no objection to being used to serve the ends of the criminal justice system if they act wrongly, given that they incur duties to serve these ends.

ii) Liability

These arguments also support two intuitive ideas about the rights that people have against criminalization and punishment: the idea that people are liable to the use of force to prevent their serious wrongdoing, and the idea that serious wrongdoers are liable to punishment.

The idea that a person is liable to be treated in a certain way that I am focused on is the idea that the person lacks a right against being treated in that way without their

[13] See, for example, M S Moore *Placing Blame: A Theory of Criminal Law* (Oxford: OUP, 1997) ch 18 and 'Liberty's Constraints on What Should Be Made Criminal' in R A Duff, L Farmer, S E Marshall, M Renzo, and V Tadros *Criminalization: The Political Morality of the Criminal Law* (Oxford: OUP, 2014); G Gaus *The Order of Public Reason: A Theory of Freedom and Morality in a Diverse and Bounded World* (Cambridge: CUP, 2011) ch 23. I offer a more complete response to Moore than the one I offer here in 'The Wrong and the Free' in K K Ferzan and S Morse *Legal, Moral, and Metaphysical Truths: The Philosophy of Michael S Moore* (Oxford: OUP, 2016).

consent. This has become a familiar idea in the philosophy of self-defence.[14] Suppose that Harry wrongly attacks Jane. Not only is it permissible for Jane to use force to defend herself against Harry, she does not wrong him if she does so. This is because by attacking her, he loses his right against having force used against him, if the force used is necessary to avert the threat he poses and proportionate to the harm that she will suffer if she does not defend herself.

Liability claims typically take the form: X is liable to *v* for *g*. X is a person, *v* is something burdensome that, subject to some conditions, may be imposed on X, and *g* is a goal for the sake of which *v* may be imposed on X. If X is liable to *v* for *g*, some agent, Y, has standing to impose *v* on X for *g* under some conditions. Y may be anyone, but may be restricted to particular agents—the state, for example.

Although liability is importantly connected to permissibility, liability does not imply permissibility; nor does permissibility imply liability. Liability does not imply permissibility because facts that do not relate to the liability of the person affected can make the conduct wrong. For example, if making me pay compensation for negligently harming another person will harm other people, it is wrong to make me pay it, even if I am liable to do so. Compelling me to pay the compensation may not wrong me, but it may wrong those who are harmed by making me pay it.

Permissibility does not imply liability in that a non-liable person's rights against being harmed may be overridden. For example, in war it may be permissible to harm non-combatants as a side effect of the pursuit of a just cause even if they are not liable to be harmed: they retain their rights against being harmed, but their rights may be overridden by the importance of the goal that is achieved by harming them.

Here is a serviceable account of liability:

> *Liability*: X is liable to *v* by Y in order to *g* if Y does not wrong X by imposing *v* on X for *g* without X's consent.

Liability captures standard usage of the term 'liability' in legal and moral contexts. For example, X's liability to pay taxes implies that the state (Y) does not wrong X by taking X's taxes without X's consent. X's liability to be conscripted implies that the state does not wrong X by conscripting X without X's consent.

I noted that rights can be overridden by the good consequences that are achieved if the right is infringed. A person may have a right not to be harmed, but her right may be overridden if harming her is necessary to prevent a much greater harm. Doug Husak relies on this idea in the context of criminalization.[15] He argues that offenders have a fundamental right not to be punished. When criminalization is justified, the state warrants the infringement of this right. As it is difficult to justify infringing a fundamental right, the state needs a compelling interest to justify criminalization.[16]

But although there are good reasons to regret inflicting harm on wrongdoers, and those reasons have to do with the importance of the wrongdoer, it does not seem true that the rights of wrongdoers are infringed when they are punished. The intuitive view

[14] The literature on liability is now enormous. The most influential account is J McMahan *Killing in War* (Oxford: OUP, 2009) ch 1. My own account is influenced by McMahan's. It comes apart in various ways that I won't detail here. See V Tadros 'Orwell's Battle with Brittain: Vicarious Liability for Unjust Aggression' (2014) 42 *Philosophy and Public Affairs* 42 and 'Causation, Culpability, and Liability' in C Coons and M Weber *The Ethics of Self-Defense* (Oxford: OUP, 2016).

[15] D N Husak *Overcriminalization: The Limits of the Criminal Law* (Oxford: OUP, 2008) ch 2.III.

[16] *Overcriminalization*, ch 3.I. For a similar view, see G Gaus *The Order of Public Reason*, 481–4.

is that they have forfeited these rights.[17] Furthermore, people more generally don't seem to have certain kinds of right against the criminalization of serious wrongdoing. A state that criminalizes murder, torture, and rape does not infringe the rights of its citizens to murder, torture, and rape. And people who will otherwise carry out these wrongs lack a right against the threat and use of force to prevent them doing this.

We should then explain why people don't have a right to be free from coercion to commit serious wrongs, and why serious wrongdoing results in the wrongdoer losing a right not to have harm intentionally inflicted on her in pursuit of the legitimate aims of punishment. Such an explanation rests on a more general account of how rights against the infliction of harm can be lost. But again, whilst this is plausible, it needs explaining.

The freedom-based arguments offered in the previous subsection provide the explanation. Those arguments not only show that restrictions on freedom are permissible in the case of serious wrongdoing, they show that the central interests that people have in being free from interference are not engaged in the case of serious wrongdoing. As these interests are not engaged, people lack a right against coercion in these cases. Hence, criminalization of serious wrongdoing does not infringe the rights that people have to commit serious wrongs, nor does it infringe their rights against being punished if they violate the law.

This leaves open the possibility that there are cases outside the core where people's rights are infringed. In some cases, people may retain a right against certain conduct being criminalized, and yet the right is overridden by the goals of criminalization.

iii) Legal Moralism

In the light of this, we can understand the relationship between the view outlined here and legal moralism. Very roughly, legal moralism is the view that there is an important connection between moral wrongdoing and criminal wrongdoing. A contrast is drawn between two versions of this view: a positive and a negative version. The positive version claims that the fact that conduct is wrong (or a wrong of a certain kind) is a reason in favour of criminalizing it. The negative version claims that morally wrongful conduct ought not to be criminalized.[18]

If negative legal moralism is the view that it is always all things considered wrong to criminalize non-wrongful conduct, I reject it. As I noted in Chapter 6, this leaves open the possibility that some weaker negative legal moralist principle is true, such as:

> *WP1 (Pro Tanto APW)*: In all possible worlds, it is *pro tanto* wrong to criminalize any conduct that is not wrongful.

This principle is vague, given its reliance on the inherently unclear idea of *pro tanto* wrongdoing. But I have not shown it to be false.

However, although I reject stronger versions of negative legal moralism, the view outlined here is related to negative legal moralism: in core cases of wrongdoing, at least, certain constraints that would otherwise apply to action that interferes with the

[17] For responses to doubts about rights forfeiture in this context, see C Wellman 'The Rights Forfeiture Theory of Punishment' (2012) 122 *Ethics* 371. Wellman, I should note, has a much broader conception of forfeiture than I do. He thinks that wrongdoers forfeit their rights against harm independently of any good aim being served by harming them. Wellman does not argue for this aspect of his view, and I find it troubling.

[18] For these different versions, see R A Duff 'Towards a Modest Legal Moralism (2014) 8 *Criminal Law and Philosophy* 217 and 'Legal Moralism and Public Wrongs' in K Ferzan and S J Morse *Legal, Moral, and Metaphysical Truths: The Philosophy of Michael S Moore.*

liberty of others do not apply. The fact that conduct is wrong therefore plays a negative role in judgements about criminalization: certain reasons that sometimes count against criminalization do not count against it in the case of serious wrongdoing.

Furthermore, although the fact that criminalizing wrongful conduct can prevent it from occurring provides a reason in favour of criminalizing it, the central reason is not that the conduct is wrong. The central reasons to prevent the conduct have to do with the facts that make it wrong: facts that we have independent reasons not to want to occur.

There is, nevertheless, some truth in the positive legal moralist idea. The criminal law has a blaming function. There are positive reasons to communicate about wrongdoing. And this provides a reason in favour of criminalizing it. A society that fails to condemn the serious wrongs that are at the heart of the criminal law fails in its moral duty to respond to these wrongs by engaging with offenders, victims, and the public at large. This reason extends to potential wrongdoers: we owe it to them to help to ensure that they do not become wrongdoers, and the criminal law has a role to play in achieving this, by outlining the reasons they have not to act wrongly.

IV. Two Kinds of Proportionality

Serious wrongdoers are liable to punishment, and potential serious wrongdoers are liable to the use of preventive force. If I am right that the central explanation of a wrongdoer's liability to punishment is the duties that she incurs through wrongdoing, it follows that the limits of a person's liability to punishment are normally set by the stringency of the duties that she incurs through wrongdoing. There is a proportionality relationship between the gravity of a person's wrong and the stringency of the duties that she incurs through her wrongdoing. This explains why there is also a proportionality limit on the punishment that an offender is liable to.[19] Following Jeff McMahan, we can call this the 'narrow proportionality' limit on punishment.

From the narrow proportionality limit on punishment, we can infer a narrow proportionality limit on criminalization: conduct should normally be criminalized only if the punishment that criminalization warrants is proportionate to the crimes that have been committed. As state punishment is inevitably non-trivial, this also provides one kind of limit on the criminal law. As we saw in Chapter 7, certain wrongs ought not to be criminalized because the punishment that the state inflicts will inevitably be disproportionate.

McMahan contrasts narrow proportionality with wide proportionality. Wide proportionality is concerned with the bad consequences that our conduct causes, excluding consequences inflicted on the liable. There are wide proportionality constraints on both punishment and criminalization.

A wide range of bad consequences of criminalization is relevant here. They include the side-effect harms that will be caused by punishing offenders. They also include the harms that will be done to the innocent, some of whom will inevitably be convicted

[19] This helps to respond to Larry Alexander's concern about theories of punishment, like mine, that draw on the relationship between defensive and punitive harm—that they cannot explain intuitive proportionality judgements. See L Alexander 'The Doomsday Machine: Proportionality, Punishment and Prevention' (1980) 63 *The Monist* 199; 'Self-Defense, Punishment, and Proportionality' (1991) 10 *Law and Philosophy* 323. In response, see *The Ends of Harm*, 333.

and punished, and a range of effects that criminalization can have on behaviour—criminalizing some wrongful conduct, for example, will inevitably result in some people not acting permissibly for fear that they will be thought wrongdoers. One powerful reason against criminalizing wrongful speech, for example, is that people will be afraid of saying things that they have an interest in saying, and that are not wrongful, because of a fear that they will be thought to be wrongdoers. Criminalization is widely proportionate if the aims secured by it are sufficiently important to outweigh these bad consequences.

It is worth emphasizing the fact that although I reject desert, the justificatory structure that I outline is available to retributivists.[20] I appeal to the idea that wrongdoers make themselves liable to be punished by acting wrongly, and this explains why punishment does not infringe their rights. Retributivists can similarly argue that wrongdoers deserve punishment, and rely on this to explain the intuition that punishment of serious wrongdoers is not rights-infringing.

The important difference between the instrumentalist view that I defend and retributivism is in how the harm that is inflicted on the wrongdoer is assessed. I think that this has only negative value that needs to be outweighed by the goods of punishment. In contrast, many retributivists think that this has positive value.[21] For them, the instrumental goods of punishment are not needed to outweigh the harm that it causes.

There is, though, a kind of proportionality that plays a role that is similar to the role that narrow proportionality played in the argument offered above: punishment can be proportionate in the sense that it is fitting. Where it is fitting, nothing is needed to outweigh the suffering it causes.

This leaves open the possibility that it is sometimes permissible to criminalize non-wrongful conduct on both retributive and non-retributive views. Recall this case from Chapter 6:

> *US Threat*: Possession of a certain recreational drug, Happy Pill, does not violate any plausible content-focused restrictive principle—for example, it is not wrongful, not harmful, and does not interfere with anyone else's sovereignty. A poor country is deciding whether to criminalize possession of this drug. US subsidies, that are necessary for the provision of essential medicines to a very large number of people who will otherwise suffer severely, will not be provided if possession of Happy Pill is not criminalized, or the prohibition is not adequately enforced.

People who possess Happy Pill have a right against being punished that is infringed by the poor country. But even if they do, their right is overridden by the importance of ensuring the continuing provision of essential medicines. The argument for this is available to retributivists and non-retributivists alike.

This lessens, to some degree, the importance of the distinction between the duty view of punishment, that I defend, and retributivism for the question of what we should criminalize. Retributivists will typically see stronger reasons in favour of criminalization than I do, in that they think that the suffering that punishment inflicts on

[20] The view of criminalization for retributivists outlined in what follows bears a relationship with Mitch Berman's retributivist view, defended in 'Punishment and Justification' (2008) 118 *Ethics* 258. See, also, his 'Two Kinds of Retributivism' in R A Duff and S P Green *Philosophical Foundations of Criminal Law* (Oxford: OUP, 2011).

[21] Some people think that their suffering is good in one way and bad in another. See, for example, J Gardner and F Tanguay-Renaud 'Desert and Avoidability in Self-Defense' (2011) 12 *Ethics* 111. I leave this more complicated view aside, though it is easy enough to see how the arguments here apply to it.

wrongdoers is an additional reason in favour of criminalization, rather than a bad to be outweighed.

But this difference will have implications only in some cases. In some cases, the goods achieved through criminalization would be insufficient to outweigh both the bad effects caused to non-wrongdoers and those inflicted on wrongdoers through punishment were the duty view true. But these goods would be sufficient to outweigh the bad effects that criminalization has for non-liable people alone, especially if the harm inflicted on wrongdoers can itself contribute to outweighing these effects.

The more important difference between these views, though, is in the explanation they offer for criminalization, and especially for the idea that wrongdoers lose their rights against punishment.

V. Conclusion

In the light of our discussion, we can see how an explanation of the criminalization of seriously wrongful conduct should go. Take some serious wrong, such as a grave assault. First, we need to explain why this conduct is wrong. This involves both understanding the nature of wrongdoing and the source of this wrongdoing in particular. Second, as criminal laws are typically enforceable prohibitions, we need to explain why the state would be warranted in creating an enforceable prohibition on this conduct.

Third, as those who violate the criminal law will be punished, we need to show that punishing these wrongdoers is permissible. This normally involves showing that those who violate the prohibition are liable to punishment. As liability to punishment is grounded in the duties of offenders, we need to show that the wrongdoer has a duty to respond to her wrongdoing, and that this duty is related to the ends of the criminal law. As the ends of the criminal law are primarily protective, this will normally involve showing that those who commit grave assaults incur protective duties.

Finally, we need to show that criminalizing the conduct is proportionate in the two senses articulated above. It is proportionate in the narrow sense if the punishment that the criminal law warrants inflicting on offenders is appropriately related to the stringency of the (primarily protective) duties that these wrongdoers incur through their wrongdoing. It is proportionate in the wide sense if its bad effects are outweighed by the good that criminalization will achieve. The relevant goods include not only harm prevention, but also protection from a range of other bad effects, including those involved in some instances of non-harmful wrongdoing. And they may include preventing people from becoming wrongdoers, at least if this is done in the right way.

Though this claim relies on some empirical considerations, there are good reasons to believe that these conditions can be met in core crimes such as murder, rape, and assault, though there are, of course, difficult questions about the scope of these crimes. Later in the book, we will consider a range of questions about criminalization beyond this core. In considering those questions, it will be helpful to bear in mind the structure of argument necessary to justify criminalization offered here.

PART C

WRONGS, HARMS, AND CONSENT

10

Harm: Its Currency and Its Measure

As we have seen, it is often claimed that the criminal law is especially concerned with harm. Some claim that it is always a reason to criminalize some conduct that it is harmful, or that it is a wrongful harm. Some claim that only harmful conduct may be criminalized. Some claim that conduct may be criminalized only if doing so prevents harm, or prevents more harm than it causes. And many people who are unsympathetic to all of these views, as I am, will agree that the state often has powerful reasons to criminalize harmful wrongdoing, and has powerful reasons to criminalize such conduct in order to prevent harm.

We have already seen two ways in which harm might figure in the theory of criminalization that I advocate. First, the fact that one person has wrongly harmed another might make her liable to punishment. She may have especially powerful reasons to respond to harmful wrongdoing in a way that grounds her liability to punishment. Second, harm prevention is one central aim of criminalization.

In order to understand the relationships between harm, wrongdoing, and criminalization, we need a firmer grasp of harm. Harm is a more complex notion than at first meets the eye. I aim to show both the importance of harm, and also its limits, in a complete account of wrongdoing. Many wrongful acts are wrong in part because of the harm that they cause. But harm is not central to the explanation of all wrongdoing, even some very serious wrongdoing. Furthermore, even where it is relevant, the harm that wrongdoing causes is often not the only fact that explains the wrongdoing, and the degree of harm inflicted often does not determine the gravity of the wrongdoing. Harm, properly understood, has a more limited role in an account of serious wrongdoing than many people who work on criminalization believe, and not only because there are harmless wrongs.

The fact that this conclusion is not often noticed is explained in part by divergent interpretations of harm. For example, one suggestion is that a person is harmed whenever an interest that she has is set back. This idea is only attractive if one is aiming to vindicate the claim that all wrongdoing is connected with harm, or that only harmful wrongdoing may be criminalized. Attempts to rescue the harm principle, especially, have led scholars to an extensive notion of harm.

Extending the notion of harm in this way comes at a high price. It fails to illuminate different reasons why we care about different things. More importantly, it implies that the reason why we care about many of the things that we have rights over has to do with our own well-being, rather than because of the value that we put on the things in themselves. This last point will be explored at length in the next chapter. This chapter explores harm itself.

I. The Currency and the Measure of Harm

There are two dimensions of harm: the currency of harm and the measure of harm. The currency of harm is a subset of the bad things that might happen to a person.

Wrongs and Crimes. First Edition. Victor Tadros. © Victor Tadros 2016. Published 2016 by Oxford University Press.

In Section II, I will explore that subset. I canvass three views about the currency of harm:

> *The Preference View*: Whether E harms V depends on whether the state that E causes V to be in is preferred by her.
>
> *The Alienation View*: Whether E harms V depends on the relationship(s) between the state that a person is in and her will.
>
> *The Well-Being View*: Whether E harms V depends on the affect of E on V's well-being, where a person's well-being is not reducible to preference satisfaction.

The goodness or badness of a state is a function of its quality and duration.[1] I will briefly defend *The Well-Being View* against its rivals. As we will see in the next chapter, the precise contours of the currency of harm are less important in a theory of wrongdoing.

A second question concerns measure of harm. Harm comes in degrees. What is the form of the scale on which these measures are marked? Let well-being be the currency of harm. How do we determine how much E harms V? Is it simply the non-comparative level of well-being that E causes V to be in? Or is the magnitude of harm a comparative matter?

I canvass three views of the measure of harm:

> *The Non-Comparative View*: the magnitude of harm that some event, E, causes the victim, V, depends on the non-comparative badness of the state of affairs that E causes V to be in.
>
> *The Temporal View*: the magnitude of harm that E causes V depends on the difference between the state that V was in prior to E and the state that E causes V to be in.
>
> *The Counterfactual View*: the magnitude of harm that E causes V depends on the difference between the state of affairs that E causes V to be in and some other state of affairs that V could have been in.

I defend a version of *The Counterfactual View* over its rivals.

Let me briefly explain. Whilst counterfactual accounts of harm are intuitive in standard cases, they appear to be threatened by the problem of overdetermination. The problem is as follows. A simple counterfactual view holds:

> *The Simple Counterfactual View*: E harms X only if X is worse off than he would have been had it not been for E.

The problem of overdetermination demonstrates the falsity of this view.

For example:

> *Finger*: D chops off one of V's fingers, pre-empting that finger and another being chopped off by X.

E harms V even though V would have been harmed to an even greater degree were it not for E. Hence, E does not render V worse off than he would have been had it not been for E. In some cases, where E pre-empts E2, E harms V even though E also prevents V from suffering a worse harm.

[1] Matthew Hanser, in 'The Metaphysics of Harm' (2008) 77 *Philosophy and Phenomenological Research* 432, defends an interesting event-based view of harm against a state-based view. I do not consider that here. For criticisms, see J J Thomson 'More on the Metaphysics of Harm' (2011) 82 *Philosophy and Phenomenological Research* 436. For Hanser's response, see M Hanser 'Still More on the Metaphysics of Harm' (2011) 82 *Philosophy and Phenomenological Research* 459. Further important criticisms of Hanser's view are developed in A Slavny 'How Eventful is the Event-Based Theory of Harm?' (2014) 48 *Journal of Value Inquiry* 559.

Many people think that the overdetermination problem threatens counterfactual views.[2] On the contrary, I argue. Overdetermination cases provide powerful support for a more complex counterfactual view—one that allows more than one contrast to be drawn between the actual world and other worlds in which the relevant event did not occur:

> *The Complex Counterfactual View*: E harms X only if X is worse off than he would have been in a relevant possible world where E did not occur. Comparison with more than one possible world may be warranted in a single case, yielding different verdicts about harm and benefit.

To find out why, read on.

II. Preferences and Alienation

Well-being is the currency of harm. I support and clarify this view as follows. First, in this section I consider two rival views, and offer reasons to reject them. In the next, I provide a sketch of well-being.

i) Rejecting the preference view

One rival to *The Well-Being View* is *The Preference View*. On this view, whether a person is harmed and to what degree depends on the satisfaction of her preferences. Consider Robert Nozick's account of compensation:

> Something fully compensates a person for a loss if and only if it makes him no worse off than he otherwise would have been; it compensates person X for person Y's action A if X is no worse off receiving it, Y having done A, than X would have been without receiving it if Y had not done A. (In the terminology of economists, something compensates X for Y's act if receiving it leaves X on at least as high an indifference curve as he would have been on, without it, had Y not so acted).[3]

Like me, Nozick defends a version of *The Counterfactual View* about the measure of harm. My interest, though, is in another feature of his view. In the passage in brackets, Nozick implies an idea familiar from economics—that X's preferences are the currency of harm and compensation. Whether a person is indifferent between two states of affairs depends only on her preferences about these states of affairs.

The Preference View is both too broad and too narrow. One problem is that a person may have preferences about being harmed or benefited. She may prefer to be harmed or prefer not to be benefited. She may also prefer to avert a smaller harm rather than receiving a greater benefit or prefer a greater harm to a smaller benefit. Consider:

> *Expiator.* Y wrongly chops X's finger off. Because X believes that he deserves to suffer for his sins, he prefers to have lost a finger to not having lost it.

The Preference View implies that Y does not harm X. But even X agrees that he has been harmed—he just thinks he deserves it.

Another problem is that *The Preference View* cannot explain the familiar intuition that people can make fundamental mistakes about what is good for them and bad for

[2] See, for example, J J Thomson *The Realm of Rights* (Cambridge, Mass: Harvard UP, 1990) 261–2; S Shiffrin 'Harm and Its Moral Significance' (2012) 18 *Legal Theory* 357, 367–8.

[3] *Anarchy, State, and Utopia* (Oxford: Blackwell, 1974) 57.

them. A person might think that her life is going very badly when in fact it is going very well, and vice versa. And that may simply be a matter of her failure to appreciate the good or bad facts about her life.

Mistakes about well-being pose further problems. Consider:

> *Amnesia*: X is in an accident and suffers partial amnesia for one year. She forgets many of the things that were important to her. She thus does not think that she has been very severely harmed.

X has been harmed to a much greater degree than she realizes. She has forgotten the facts that explain how much she has been harmed. *The Preference View* struggles to explain this.

Defenders of *The Preference View* may respond that the time after she has suffered is not the appropriate time to assess her preferences. But it is difficult to see how to set the appropriate time without referring to the objectively correct assessment of well-being. To see this, consider two other times at which we might assess her preferences: *t1* (just before the accident) and *t3* (when she has had time to think about it). The challenge for *The Preference View* is to pick a time with plausible implications without referring to objective criteria.

A person may make mistakes that render her preferences an unreliable guide to how much she has been harmed at any of these times. For example, before she has been harmed she may not realize how important a good memory is. She may be the kind of person who is willing to enter Nozick's famous Experience Machine[4]—a machine that makes a person happy but makes her forget all of her actual commitments. Now suppose that at *t3* she realizes that she was wrong about this. The accident nevertheless harms her a great deal.

Perhaps her *considered* preferences provide a better measure. But the mere fact that she has considered things for longer or more carefully at *t3* than at *t1* seems relevant only because there is something else that the person's preferences better reflects when she considers her preferences: the things that she has reason to prefer. What else is a person trying to do when considering her preferences? She is surely not trying to work out what preferences she actually has! If preference satisfaction is good for a person in itself, why worry about whether the preferences are considered or not? The move to considered preferences may have more plausible implications than a simple preference-satisfaction view, but that is only because it smuggles in a more objective currency of well-being.

Perhaps *The Preference View* can be revised to meet these concerns. For example, we might consider a person's ideal preferences—the preferences that she would have were she fully rational with full information. This version of the preference-based view is an improvement. As preferences change over time, though, it would still face the problem of identifying the appropriate moment at which to idealize a person's preferences.

And there are further problems. Many of the things that we have preferences about have no connection to how well our lives are going. For example, I may prefer it that you are not made worse off. But it hardly counts as harmful to me that you are made worse off, simply in virtue of this fact, when I have no further connection to you. I may prefer you not to have certain attitudes about me—I want you not to

[4] *Anarchy, State, and Utopia*, 42–5.

dislike me, for example. But your disliking me does not harm me simply in virtue of this fact.

Finally, there seems no reason to favour ideal preferences as the currency of harm compared either with bare preferences, or with the more objective criteria. A person may not have her ideal preferences at all. If so, preference satisfaction seems to have fallen out of the picture, as something to value, altogether. So the core idea that seemed initially attractive about the preference-satisfaction view—that a person gets what she wants—has fallen out of the picture altogether. Ideal preferences just track other facts that are more fundamentally important. Overall, I doubt that preferences are very important in determining whether a person has been harmed.

ii) Rejecting The Alienation View

Seana Shiffrin tentatively defends *The Alienation View*.[5] This is a complex view. Her account is confused in one way that needs addressing before assessing *The Alienation View*. Shiffrin presents *The Alienation View* as a non-comparative account of harm. But her defence of *The Alienation View* is independent of her defence of non-comparativism. *The Alienation View* is compatible with all three accounts of the measure of harm described above. *The Alienation View* is better understood as a view about the currency of harm.

To see this, notice that counterfactualists and temporalists may endorse *The Alienation View*. A counterfactualist might claim that E harms V if E causes V to be in a state where she is more severely alienated from her will than she would have been in some other possible world. A temporalist might claim that E harms V if E causes V to be more seriously alienated from her will than she was. I leave assessment of Shiffrin's defence of non-comparativism (or rather, her attack on comparativism) to Sections V and VI.

Much of Shiffrin's discussion of alienation of the will is otherwise attractive. Whether some state of affairs is harmful to a person, and the degree to which it is harmful, depends at least in part on the relationship between the state that the person is in and the person's will. This idea is well captured by *The Well-Being View* as well. As Joseph Raz[6] and T M Scanlon[7] emphasize, successful pursuit of valuable projects is plausibly an important component of well-being. The importance of the will is thus naturally involved on *The Well-Being View*. The question is whether alienation of the will is either necessary or sufficient for harm. I have some doubts about both ideas.

Alienation of the will does not seem necessary for harm. Causing pain to newborn babies or non-human animals harms them. That is not because of the relationship between their will and the pain caused. Furthermore, a person can wilfully harm herself. She may will herself to be harmed, either as an end in itself, for example if she believes that she deserves it, or as a means to some further end. In that case, the harm that she suffers does not conflict with her will, and this suggests that a person can be harmed even when she is not alienated from what happens to her.

This objection extends to some other theories of the currency of harm. For example, Andrew Simester and Andreas von Hirsch claim that E harms V only if V's opportunities to engage in valued activities and relationships, and to pursue self-chosen goals, is

[5] She outlines this view in 'Harm and Its Moral Significance', 385–97.
[6] *The Morality of Freedom* (Oxford: OUP, 1986) ch 12.
[7] *What We Owe to Each Other* (Cambridge, Mass: Harvard UP, 1998) ch 3.

impaired.[8] This view of harm is implausibly narrow. A simple way in which a person's life may go well or badly is that they suffer physical pleasure or pain. Sinking into a warm bath may enhance well-being simply because of the positive sensation. Sinking into a scalding bath diminishes well-being simply because of the pain experienced. This aspect of well-being is obviously available not only to humans but to many non-humans as well.

The lives of many animals can go well or badly because of the physical sensations they experience, but many of them lack the capacities to have the opportunities Simester and von Hirsch refer to. Surely causing them pain harms them, though. In this respect, many non-human animals share something with humans that flowers do not—they share the capacity for physical pleasure and pain. And this is at least one respect in which things can be good or bad for non-human animals.[9]

Alienation of the will is also insufficient for harm. Wrongful interference with autonomy is not always, or even typically, harmful. A person may be wronged when others interfere with her autonomy even when she is not harmed—even when she is benefited. As I will explore this latter idea in greater depth later in the book (especially in Chapters 11 and 12), I will leave it aside here, other than to emphasize again that we should not morally overburden the concept of harm. One reason why Shiffrin is driven to her account of harm is that she wishes to capture the central role that harm has in morality. It is true that harm is central to morality, but not every wrong, nor every value, relates to harm. Shiffrin, I think, tends to give harm a more prominent role in morality than it has.

The reason why wrongfully alienating a person from her will is not always harmful is that autonomy is often to be respected even when a person chooses what is not good for her. Consider Shiffrin's claim that fraud is necessarily harmful in that it is 'inconsistent with respect for one's status as an independent autonomous agent'.[10] I agree that fraud is typically wrong for this reason, but that does not show that fraud harms the person in virtue of this fact. Fraud can be wrong even if the victim of the fraud is benefited. For example, fraudulently inducing a person to end a bad relationship is wrong even if the person is benefited. This idea seems difficult to capture on Shiffrin's view.

III. Well-Being

The better view is that some event, E, harms some agent, V, if E sets back V's well-being.

i) Well-being or opportunity for well-being?

Before outlining an account of well-being, let me consider one objection to this view. It might be thought that harm does not involve diminishing well-being itself, but rather diminishing a person's opportunities or capacities for well-being. For example, it might be thought that imprisonment harms a person not because of the diminution in well-being that it causes, but rather because it makes certain levels of well-being impossible to achieve, or reduces the person's opportunities to achieve a certain level of well-being. This view might be thought attractive because imprisonment might seem to harm a

[8] *Crimes, Harms, and Wrongs: On the Principles of Criminalization* (Oxford: Hart Publishing, 2011) 36–8.

[9] Their view of harm, coupled with their restrictive view of what can permissibly be criminalized, also has troubling implications for the criminalization of conduct that causes animal suffering.

[10] 'Harm and Its Moral Significance', 385.

person even if the person imprisoned would have made very bad choices had they not been imprisoned.

I doubt this view is right, though. One problem is that it does not naturally explain many simple cases of harm. Consider self-harming. A person who cuts her own arm self-harms simply because of the pain this causes her. But this is not very plausibly explained by the fact that she has denied herself the opportunity or capacity not to suffer pain. Furthermore, depriving a person of an opportunity for welfare often does not seem harmful where the person would not have taken that opportunity. Consider people who will never watch football, because they mistakenly believe that it is a complete waste of time. Their welfare would be greatly increased were they do to so. I don't harm these people by cancelling a football match, even though doing so deprives the person of an important opportunity for welfare. The fact that cancelling the match does not affect their well-being explains this.

The same thing seems true in the imprisonment case. Suppose that a person will sit in a prison cell regardless of whether I lock the door. Locking the door will make no difference at all to her well-being. If I lock the door I don't harm the person. It is worth remembering that this judgement does not imply that depriving people of opportunities that they will not take is permitted. I may wrong the person by locking the door—I deprive her of an opportunity that she has reason to value, even if she does not value it, and some may find this wrong. But this conclusion does not rely on the idea that locking the door harms her.

ii) Rights and interests

The idea that harm sets back well-being requires us to explore what well-being is and what it means to set it back. Both things are controversial. In this section I focus on what well-being is. The concept of well-being is largely a philosopher's term of art. I use it in a fairly conventional way—to denote how well a person's life is going. This leaves open the possibility of different dimensions of well-being, some of which are to do with the happiness that a person has at objective features of her life, and others that have to do with those objective features themselves.[11]

Fortunately, we can do without an understanding of the precise boundary between well-being and other facts about persons that are morally significant. If we are willing to accept that people have interests that are independent of whether they are harmed, and that these interests can also support rights, we don't have a strong reason to outline a precise boundary to the concept of well-being or of harm. And we can therefore do without a precise account of well-being as well. Nevertheless, it is helpful to have a grasp of some of the main features of well-being, as this will structure our understanding of harm and its limits in a full account of wrongdoing. The general approach to harm that I recommend can be grasped by the contrast with some further alternatives.

One alternative provides an understanding of harm that is directly related to the role that harm has in structuring our moral life. For example, it might be claimed, as Joel Feinberg does, that harm must be understood with reference to rights. He claims: E harms V only if E sets back V's interests by violating his rights.[12]

Here are two reasons to reject this view. First, it is highly revisionist. There are all sorts of non-human causes of harm: tsunamis, wild animals, rivers, viruses, and so on.

[11] Others use well-being only to refer to the former, or some subset of the former. See, for example, S Kagan 'Well-Being as Enjoying the Good' (2009) 23 *Philosophical Perspectives* 253.

[12] *Harm to Others* (Oxford: OUP, 1984) 36.

These things can neither infringe nor violate rights. People have reasons not to harm me, and also to protect me from harm. They can do the latter by protecting me from tsunamis, wild animals, rivers, viruses, and so on. These reasons explain why harm can ground certain rights. Our ordinary idea of harm is detached from wrongdoing, and helps to explain certain kinds of wrongdoing.

The second reason is more closely related to the purposes of our endeavour. Feinberg argues that we ought to restrict our use of harm to cases where rights are interfered with because no proper rendition of the harm principle would be concerned with harms that are not also rights violations.[13] It turns out that Feinberg is wrong about that: as we saw in Chapter 6, some versions of the harm principle are concerned with harm prevention, and the relevant harm prevention might not be restricted to rights-violating harm prevention. It would count in favour of the criminalization of some conduct that doing so would prevent some naturally occurring harm. This is so, even though it would be unusual for criminalization to do this in practice.

More importantly, Feinberg defends a version of the harm principle by gerrymandering the concept of harm to make the harm principle more attractive. We have no reason to do this unless we set at the outset the bizarre goal of defending the harm principle, as though it were an old friend who we would betray by showing it to be false, rather than the goal of finding out whether it is true. It is better to distinguish between harms and rights violations to see how these different things feature in a normative theory of the criminal law.

I should also indicate why well-being rather than interests is the right idea here. Our interests are much broader than the things that make a difference to how our lives go. This is not only true about our interests in things other than ourselves, such as the well-being of strangers, or the existence of life on other planets; it includes some interests that we have because of our own normatively significant properties. The idea that all setbacks to self-regarding interests are harmful is implausibly broad for this reason. For example, I have a self-regarding interest in other people thinking well of me. But other people failing to think well of me does not, or at least not typically, harm me. They cannot affect how well my life goes simply by thinking badly of me. This intuitive idea is captured by the fact that how other people think of me does not, in and of itself, affect how well my life goes. Harm is more plausibly connected to how well my life goes—ie to well-being.

iii) Consciousness

Here is another way in which the idea of well-being that I focus on is narrow. A broad idea of well-being might apply to beings that can flourish but that lack interests. For example, a flower can flourish, and we might say that a flourishing flower has a high level of well-being. When we deprive a flower of water we diminish its well-being.

But even if there is an idea of well-being that applies to flowers this idea is distinct from the narrower idea that I am interested in, and that applies exclusively to conscious beings. A creature with consciousness can experience aspects of their lives, and it is in connection to the creature as a conscious being that we use the term 'well-being' in the narrower and more restricted sense that I intend here.

[13] *Harm to Others*, 36.

We might wonder why consciousness should be so important in a conception of well-being. The reason is that only a conscious being, or at least a being with the capacity for consciousness or which has had consciousness, has a perspective of its own which we can imaginatively adopt, perhaps at most partially, in determining how well or badly its life is going for it. Although it may require a stretch of the imagination, we can imagine what it is like to be a dog (or, at least, we can imagine what it is like to have some dog-like experiences from our own perspective), and hence imagine what pain is like for a dog. When we do so we imaginatively adopt the perspective of the dog. Obviously, this is impossible with respect to creatures that lack consciousness. There is no perspective that we can adopt in determining how well the life of a flower is going from its perspective because it has no such perspective. And hence there is no sense in saying that a flower's life is going badly or well for it independently of the idea that it is doing badly or well *simpliciter*.

This is not to say that the only things that make a difference to well-being are those things the being is conscious of. Whether a person's life goes well or badly might depend on things that she is not conscious of, such as whether her relationships are authentic. That she has reasons to care about these things draws on the fact that she has a perspective of her own, which determines how well her life is going for her.

Because there is something distinctive and important about a being's life going well from its perspective, I will restrict talk of well-being to those beings that have such a perspective. This narrower idea of well-being picks out something morally important—the idea that there are perspectives from which to consider how well things are going, or the effects of our actions, or the implications of our principles.[14] I will call facts that are significant in virtue of a being's perspective facts that have 'perspectival significance'. I will call facts about the being whose perspective it is 'first-personal perspectival significance'.

For example, the well-being of a stranger has perspectival significance for me—it is significant from my perspective how well off they are. But their well-being lacks first-personal perspectival significance for me. In that sense, I have an interest in the suffering of strangers in that I have a reason to care about how their lives go. My own pain, in contrast, has first-personal perspectival significance, including any pain that I might feel at the suffering of others.

Close personal relationships are a more complex case. Consider the impact on a parent of harm to her children. Parents clearly have a reason to care a great deal about the welfare of their children. But is that interest purely third personal, as in the case of the welfare of strangers, or does it have a first-personal dimension? Obviously, harm to children has first-personal effects on parents—it causes them to suffer pain, and that is bad for the parents. But does harm to a child have an inherent first-personal dimension? I think it may: parents set their children's welfare as an end. When children are harmed, these aims are frustrated. And that makes harm to children have a direct first-personal effect on parents. Because of this, I think it right to say that harming children directly as well as indirectly harms the parents.

The fact that flowers lack a perspective does not show that damaging or destroying flowers is normatively inert. But any normative significance that these things have is not in virtue of the flower's perspective. Hence, I will not say that the flower's

[14] As we saw in Chapter 3, contractualism is one in a range of moral theories that view the different perspectives that beings have as having irreducible moral importance.

well-being is diminished or that they are harmed. If it is wrong to damage them, it is wrong in virtue of some other fact about flowers—for example, their value as beautiful things. And that may have either perspectival significance for people, or may be non-perspectivally significant. We will take up these issues in more detail in Chapter 15.

When we focus on the first-personal perspectival significance of facts about conscious beings we also grasp the possibility that these facts may not be the only facts about conscious beings that we have reason to value. Our reasons not to affect conscious beings in certain ways are not exhausted by the facts that make a difference from their perspective. We have a reason not to harm children, for example, because their lives have significance for their parents. Some may also think that we can act wrongly by ending a person's life even though her life now has no value *to her*. We may act wrongly because her life is sacred, some might argue.[15] Similarly, it may be wrong to kill a tiger both because it has an interest in continued life, but also because it is beautiful, where its beauty is not something that makes a difference from its own perspective. If any of these things are true, well-being is not the only thing to value.

iv) Pain, pleasure, and happiness

Understanding harm involves understanding the range of things that have first-personal perspectival significance. Different theories of harm might claim that all things that have negative significance of this kind are harmful. Other views, including the one I favour, are narrower—we have first-personal perspectival reasons that are not to do with well-being. Nevertheless, well-being encompasses several different kinds of thing that have the relevant kind of value.[16] Rather than aiming at a general definition of well-being, I provide some components of it.

We have seen that positive and negative sensations are a component of well-being. But positive and negative sensations are only one way in which well-being can be advanced or set back. Central emotions and attitudes that are obviously connected with well-being, such as happiness, are not best understood as reducible to positive sensations, even if they have a sensational aspect.[17] They also have a judgemental dimension.

We can see this from the fact that happiness, along with other emotions such as pride and satisfaction, is typically directed at something. Perhaps there is non-directed happiness—a person may feel happy without being happy at anything, this view suggests—but even if so, this is a deviant case. I am typically happy at something, such as the fact that my child has a good friend, or the fact that my joke made someone laugh. Any sensation of happiness, if that is essential to it, could be replicated in me, but that sensation would not be valuable to me in the same way as my happiness at these things. Happiness, we can conclude, is important to well-being, and not simply because of the sensations that partly constitute it.

For this reason, even if non-human animals can be happy or sad (and I am not sure whether these terms are appropriately used in a non-metaphorical way about non-human animals) they can only be happy or sad in a diminished way, for they lack the

[15] This need not be a religious idea. See R Dworkin *Life's Dominion: An Argument About Abortion, Euthanasia, and Individual Freedom* (New York: Vintage Books, 1993). See, further, Chapter 14..

[16] Here I have been especially influenced by T M Scanlon *What We Owe to Each Other* (Cambridge, Mass: Harvard UP, 1998) ch 3.

[17] See, for a good discussion, F Feldman *What Is This Thing Called Happiness?* (Oxford: OUP, 2010). I don't comment on whether there is a sense of happiness that is purely sensational.

capacity for the complex judgemental dimension that accompanies sensation in cases of great happiness or sadness.

v) Achievement and knowledge

A person's life goes better if she is happy. But many believe that there is more to well-being than happiness. One thing that is commonly thought part of well-being is achievement. Achievements do seem to contribute to a good life. When she evaluates how well her life has gone, a person will often focus on what she has done, and not merely on how she feels about what she has done.

Even if we include achievement as part of a conception of well-being, there is a further question whether it should be included conditionally or unconditionally. A conditional view is that achievement makes a contribution to well-being only if the achievement is connected to the person in the appropriate way. The relevant connection might be subjective: that the person takes pleasure at the achievement, or values it, or values it because of the contribution that it makes to her own life. Or it might be counterfactual: that the person would take pleasure in it, or value it, were she to know about it.

Consider a person who finds a cure for cancer, but does not know that others will discover her work, and so does not realize that she in fact prevents illness and suffering in the lives of many people. Does her achievement in preventing illness and suffering, which is obviously a great achievement, make her better off? I don't think that there is a determinate answer to this question because well-being is a somewhat technical term. We can distinguish well-being in a narrower sense and a broader sense to capture these different ideas, and we can do the same with harm.

Extending well-being to include achievements, either unconditionally or conditionally, is unproblematic as long as it is remembered that the reasons why people value their achievements is not limited to the contribution that those achievements make to their own lives. A person might value her achievements not, or not simply, because they make her life go better, but because she values what is achieved.

Even taking pride in one's achievements does not depend on the achievement having made one's life go better. To see this, note that a person may take pride in having sacrificed her well-being for the sake of a certain goal. If success in pursuit of the goal contributed to her well-being to a greater degree than she has lost, she would not be able to take this stance towards her sacrifice. She would have sacrificed her well-being in one dimension for the sake of advancing it in another. But this is not how we understand self-sacrifice.[18] This point does not count against achievements contributing to well-being—it counts only against the idea that the full first-personal perspectival value of a person's achievements is captured by the contribution they make to well-being.

The same remarks go for knowledge. A person has good reason to value knowledge, especially knowledge of things that are important, and are importantly connected to her own life. It is a contested question whether knowledge contributes to well-being. A person clearly has reason to value having more knowledge of the relevant things, and she has a reason to value it for her own sake (even if this is not the main reason why she values it). There is no problem in extending well-being to this case along with achievements subject to similar caveats to those explored in relation to achievements above.

[18] See, also, S Darwall *Welfare and Rational Care* (Princeton: Princeton University Press, 2002) 52–3.

IV. Psychological Connectedness

Well-being is the main currency of harm. But harm does have a further dimension: it concerns the relationship between the person and her future self. In a moment, I will defend a counterfactual account of harm—an account that holds that whether some event E harms a person V depends on a comparison between V's circumstances given E, and his circumstances in some possible world. Let us suppose, for the moment, that this view is right.

The issue that I focus on here is one most completely explored by Jeff McMahan.[19] When E occurs, V might lack the psychological capacities to have an important connection to her future. This will be true, for example, if V is a very small infant. We develop our psychological capacities that connect ourselves with our future selves over time, and these capacities are not fully developed when a person is very young.

Because very young infants lack these capacities, it is also plausible that the harm that they suffer when their future is negatively affected is equally diminished. This has the plausible implication that killing a very young infant harms her less than killing her when she is somewhat older. The reason why is that the connection between her in infancy and the future that she would have had if she had lived is quite weak due to her more limited psychological capacities.

This view may seem implausible because acting in a way that alters her future, but does not kill her, can very seriously harm a person, even if the act occurs whilst she is a very small infant. For example, it would very seriously harm a person to make her suffer very serious pain for the rest of her life, even if the act that caused this occurred whilst she was an infant. But the causal effects of the action on the person at a later time can explain this judgement. For example, infecting a child with a disease when she is very young can cause her great harm because the disease will have an effect on the child when she is older, and we can compare how her life proceeds from that point with how it would have proceeded from that point had she not been infected. This case, then, might be understood as a case where an event that occurs early in life harms her very gravely at some point in the future, but does not harm her very gravely now.

Perhaps even McMahan's sophisticated view about the relationship between harm and continuing psychological connectedness is incomplete. A person might be very powerfully connected to her future self, and yet she may lack other features that make deprivation of well-being significant to her. One such feature may be her history: if a person lacks a history, altering her circumstances may not harm her.

To see this, consider:

> *Frank*: Frank builds Monster. Monster is identical to Frank, except that Monster's consciousness has not yet been turned on. Frank can flip a switch to turn Monster's consciousness on. When he does this, Monster will have identical brain states to Frank. Hence, Monster's conscious experiences will be almost identical, at the moment that he is turned on, to Frank's. Betty sneaks into Frank's lab. She wants to see if Monster works, so she turns him on at time *t*, and after a millisecond turns him off again.

Before evaluating *Frank*, it is worth noticing that although Monster has identical brain states to Frank, Monster does not have identical mental states to Frank. There are mental states that Frank has that Monster lacks (and vice versa). For example, a person has a memory of something only if they have actually experienced that thing.

[19] Especially in *The Ethics of Killing: Problems at the Margins of Life* (Oxford: OUP, 2002).

A phenomenologically identical mental state to a memory is not a memory if it has been implanted—false memories are not memories. Frank has memories that Monster lacks. Monster has false memories in their place.

Nevertheless, if Betty had not immediately turned Monster off just after *t*, Monster's psychological state at *t* would have been strongly connected to the future psychological states that he would have had. It is plausible that Monster's psychological state at *t* is not significantly less connected to the future psychological states that he would have had if Betty had not switched him off than Frank's psychological state at *t* is connected to the future psychological states that he actually has.

Does Betty harm Monster, and if so how much? The view that this depends only on the magnitude of well-being and on the psychological connectedness of a person to his future self would seem to suggest that she harms him a great deal. For my own part, I do not find it intuitive that Betty harms Monster at all by switching him on and off again very quickly like this. But even if some doubt this, and think that Monster has been harmed, the view that the harm that Monster suffers is at all comparable to the harm that Frank would suffer were Frank killed is implausible.

Perhaps it might be argued that this intuition can be explained by the fact that there is a big difference in the contribution of future events to Frank's well-being when compared with Monster. For example, Frank gets a great deal of well-being from the continuation of the actual projects that he has. Monster has no such projects to continue, only false beliefs in projects. And so their 'continuation' cannot contribute much to his well-being.

True, Frank has greater capacity for future well-being than Monster because of his past. But yet, Monster still has a great deal of capacity for future well-being. Turning him off takes away all of the future goods that he would otherwise have had in his life, and these future goods may be great. Differences in their capacity for well-being, for this reason, cannot explain the judgement that there is a vast difference in harm caused by killing Frank and killing Monster.

This suggests that there is more to harm than well-being and psychological connectedness. I think that the reason why it does not seem as though Betty harms Monster, or at least that she does not harm Monster very gravely, is that at the moment that she switches him off, Monster has not invested anything in his life. The badness of death depends on the extent to which death frustrates the investment that a person has made in her life. This depends not only on the level of psychological connectedness between the person when she is killed and her future psychological states, but also on the relationship between features of her history, including her plans, her self-development, her relationships, and so on, and the future that she would have had. Because Monster has not lived a life at all when he is switched on, there is no 'invested' person who is harmed by switching him off.

V. Incomparable Problems

Now that we have a better, even if incomplete, grasp of the currency of harm, let us consider the measure of harm. Recall these three views:

> *The Non-Comparative View*: the magnitude of harm that some event, E, causes the victim, V, depends on the non-comparative badness of the state of affairs that E causes V to be in.

> *The Temporal View*: the magnitude of harm that E causes V depends on the difference between the state that V was in prior to E and the state that E causes V to be in.

The Counterfactual View: the magnitude of harm that E causes V depends on the difference between the state of affairs that E causes V to be in and some other state of affairs that V could have been in.

This section is concerned with *The Non-Comparative View*. To simplify our discussion, let us leave aside difficulties to do with psychological connectedness considered in the previous section, and suppose that well-being is the sole currency of harm. If well-being is the currency of harm and non-comparativism is true, to be harmed is to be caused to have a low level of well-being. This view is contrasted with various comparative views that harm depends on comparing a person's level of well-being with an alternative.

The contrast between comparative and non-comparative views can also be clarified by distinguishing a different contrast: between relative and non-relative views. A relative view of harm is that the level of harm that a person suffers depends on the other properties that set our expectations for well-being. Non-comparativists need not be anti-relativists about harm. They may believe that whether having some property puts a person in a harmed state is relative to other properties of that agent. As Judith Jarvis Thomson notes, having the mental capacity of a two year old may be a harmed state for an adult, but not for a two year old.[20] Non-comparativists need not deny this. They deny that being harmed is relative to some other state that the person was or could have been in.

Shiffrin has given the most sustained defence of non-comparativism to date.[21] She defends it mainly by attacking comparativism.[22] Here I outline some familiar and some new problems for non-comparativism. I then meet Shiffrin's complaints about comparativism.

One problem is that non-comparativists cannot explain why making a well-off person slightly worse off harms her.[23] Consider:

Novelist: You are writing a brilliant novel. Out of jealousy, I mildly poison you. This slightly diminishes your talents. The novel you write, though brilliant, is worse than it would have been.

Surely I have harmed you even though you are non-comparatively well off.

Shiffrin thinks that it is a threat to counterfactual accounts of harm that small losses to the very well off are harmful. Billionaires are not harmed by losing one thousand dollars, she claims, even 'assuming that the billionaire has a stake in his stockpile, as many billionaires do'.[24] But this seems intuitive only because the loss of one thousand dollars has no impact on the billionaire's well-being. At most this case demonstrates that losing something that one has a stake in is insufficient for harm. That is better understood as a claim about the currency of harm than about the measure of harm.

Here is an even worse problem for non-comparativists. We have powerful reasons to benefit those who are very badly off, even if those benefits are very small, and hence do not lift the person out of a non-comparatively bad state. For example, providing food to the starving is required even if the person remains sickly. It is difficult for the non-comparativist to explain the idea that this person is benefited, as she is caused to be in

[20] 'More on the Metaphysics of Harm', 438.

[21] Originally, in 'Wrongful Life, Procreative Responsibility, and the Significance of Harm' (1999) 5 *Legal Theory* 117, but more recently and in a more sustained way in 'Harm and Its Moral Significance'.

[22] As I suggest above, her positive proposal is not best understood as an alternative to comparative accounts of harm.

[23] See, also, Hanser 'The Metaphysics of Harm'.

[24] 'Harm and Its Moral Significance', 371.

a bad state—her state is bad but better than it was and would have been. But 'better' is a comparative judgement.[25]

The basic problem with non-comparativism is this. Events cause harm. Whether some event causes harm depends not simply on the state in which the event leaves the person affected by the event. It depends on whether the event improves or erodes the person's quality of life. Shiffrin thinks that it is unclear why comparisons ought to be central to assessments of harm.[26] The answer is that without comparisons, we have not described harm but something else. We distinguish between whether a person is well off or badly off, which is a non-comparative matter, and whether a person is harmed or benefited, which is a comparative matter. As we need both comparative and non-comparative ideas in descriptive and normative work, we are better retaining a comparative account of harm, and using other words such as 'badly off' in making non-comparative assessments.

VI. Meeting Comparative Complaints

Here I address the four main challenges that Shiffrin mounts to comparativism. First, comparativism implies that it is possible that A is harmed and B is benefited by some event, and yet A is left better off than B.[27] Shiffrin wrongly finds this counterintuitive. If a very poor person steals my wallet she harms me and benefits herself. That is so even though she remains worse off than me, and even if the stealing is permissible.

Or consider:

> *Transplant*: A has two arms and two legs. B has no limbs. If I flip a switch an arm will be transplanted from A to B. No other harms or benefits will be caused.

Shiffrin implies that it is a weakness of comparative accounts of harm that they imply that flipping the switch harms A and benefits B. This verdict seems intuitive though.

Perhaps Shiffrin would explain this verdict by appealing to the legitimate expectations and the investments that A and B have in their long-term projects. But whilst it is true that legitimate expectations and investments may make a difference to how harmful some event is, that does not fully explain *Transplant*. Whether A is harmed does not depend on his legitimate expectations and projects. Suppose that A and B are newborn babies or monkeys. They have no projects or expectations. The transplant still harms A and benefits B.

Second, Shiffrin claims that comparative accounts of harm cannot adequately capture the idea that a person who has severe disabilities at birth is harmed if those disabilities, or their cause, alter the personal identity of the person. Non-identity cases are complex, and they warrant more attention than I give them.

Here are three possible responses. First, we do not need the idea of harm accurately to characterize non-identity cases where the person is very badly off. A person who is born with very severe disabilities is born in a very bad state. It adds nothing to this to say that the person is harmed. That the person is not harmed does not imply that the person causing her to come into existence owes her no duties. She may be owed duties simply because she is badly off. If we can make adequate evaluative and normative

[25] See, also, Thomson 'More on the Metaphysics of Harm', 441.

[26] 'Harm and Its Moral Significance', 369.

[27] 'Harm and Its Moral Significance', 372–3.

judgements about non-identity cases without referring to harm, what is objectionable about the view that these people are not harmed?

A second response is that a comparative account of harm can be supplemented by non-comparativism for this case. For reasons given above, a non-comparative account would seem *only* adequate for this special case.[28] Otherwise, it is difficult to avoid the implication that B is harmed in Transplant.

A third response is that there are relevant counterfactual claims that can be made to yield the verdict that the person born in a very bad state is harmed because she is worse off than she would have been in some relevant possible world. True, *The Simple Counterfactual View* implies that people who are badly off are not harmed in non-identity cases. More complex counterfactual views need not imply this.[29] Overall, comparativists have plenty of resources to respond to this complaint.

Shiffrin's third complaint is that comparativism cannot explain why causing pain is harmful. As I suggest above, I agree with her that short sharp shocks are intrinsically harmful. But here again Shiffrin confuses an issue about the currency of harm with an issue about the measure of harm.[30] If E causes V to suffer pain, comparativists may claim, E harms V in virtue of the fact that E causes V to be in pain rather than to be free from pain.

Furthermore, comparative accounts of harm seem better placed than non-comparative accounts to handle the case of pain. If E slightly relieves V's pain E benefits V, even if she remains in great pain. It is not clear how non-comparativism can explain this. Overall, the problems with non-comparativism extend to the problem of pain, and pain provides no problem for comparativism.

Shiffrin's fourth complaint is that comparativism, especially *The Simple Counterfactual Account*, cannot adequately explain the moral asymmetry between harming and failing to benefit. Shiffrin writes that 'on these accounts, enduring harm and not being benefited, for example, suffering an opportunity cost, are identical'.[31] This complaint is unclear to me. Perhaps Shiffrin worries that counterfactualists cannot explain the moral difference between harming a person and failing to provide her with a benefit because they can offer no reason to pick out any particular possible state of affairs with which to compare the person's current state. If this is her complaint, she might be clearer about why she thinks this.

I doubt the force of this complaint. Consider:

Leg 1: X cuts V's leg off, leaving V with one. He could easily have cut two legs off.

Leg 2: V has no legs. Y could easily provide V with two prosthetic legs but provides him only with one.

Perhaps Shiffrin worries that comparativists must treat these cases as morally identical. In both *Leg 1* and *Leg 2*, we compare the one-legged V with the two-legged V.

But comparativists need not treat these cases alike. For example, the standard comparison that counterfactualists make is between V's state and the state that V would have been in had E not occurred. X harms V even though he could easily have harmed

[28] This is more or less the conclusion reached in J McMahan 'Causing People to Exist and Saving People's Lives' (2013) 17 *Journal of Ethics* 5, and see Thomson *The Realm of Rights*, 262, fn 7.

[29] For a brief discussion of this possibility, see Thomson 'More on the Metaphysics of Harm', 450–3. Thomson plausibly thinks that only some of these cases, cases where the child's disabilities are genetic, are non-harming cases. If she is right, the first response is sometimes the right one. See, further, Chapter 15.

[30] The failure to distinguish these questions hampers her discussion throughout.

[31] 'Harm and Its Moral Significance', 372.

him more. Y benefits V even though he could have benefited him more. This helps to explain why X's wrong is more serious than Y's. Perhaps Shiffrin thinks that the decision to set the baseline that this view relies on is arbitrary—why not compare V's circumstances with the circumstances that he would have been in had X cut off both legs? It is true that counterfactualists need to answer that question, and it is difficult to answer. But until we are shown that it cannot be answered, we lack a decisive reason to reject the counterfactual view.

Furthermore, as I noted above, we should not morally overburden harm. Here is another difference between *Leg 1* and *Leg 2*: in *Leg 1* X interferes with V in a way that he would not consent to. That is not true in *Leg 2*. This fact seems at least as important as the difference between the harm and benefit done. But its significance does not depend on harm.

In general, as I have already suggested, the wrongness of interfering with a person's autonomy does not depend powerfully on the magnitude of harm caused. For example, the wrongness of killing a person does not depend in a very significant way on the magnitude of harm that death causes the person. It is typically much more harmful to die when one is twenty than it is to die when one is fifty. Yet the wrongness of killing a fifty year old is almost as grave as the wrongness of killing a twenty year old.[32] The fact that this verdict is not yielded by an account of harm does not count against that account of harm. Harm simply has a more limited role in morality than Shiffrin thinks. And finally, given that D is left with a single leg in both *Leg 1* and *Leg 2*, it seems that it is non-comparativism rather than comparativism that fails adequately to capture the moral difference between harming and benefiting.

Shiffrin's attacks on comparativism do not seem decisive. Her non-comparativism faces insurmountable difficulties. I conclude that the best account of harm is comparative.

VII. Why Time is Not of the Essence

If comparativism is right, 'E harms X' implies that E causes X to be worse off than some other state. Two comparativist possibilities present themselves—temporalism and counterfactualism. Temporalism, which I focus on here, is the view that E harms V (if and)[33] only if E causes V to be worse off after E than she was before E.

Temporalism has the virtue that it seems plausibly to explain the verdict that harm is caused in standard pre-emption and overdetermination cases. Recall:

> *Finger*: D chops off one of V's fingers, pre-empting that finger and another being chopped off by X.

In determining whether E harms V, we determine whether E caused V to be in a state that is worse than the state that he was in prior to E. This seems to give the appropriate verdict in *Finger*—V is worse off than he was in virtue of D's chopping. Furthermore, at first blush it seems to have plausible implications for the magnitude of harm done in this case. It asks: how much worse off is V without a finger than he was? Finally, the

[32] See, further, J McMahan *The Ethics of Killing*, 189–203.

[33] This part of temporalism is bracketed for the reason that Thomson, in *The Realm of Rights*, endorses temporalism but rejects the bracketed element. In *The Realm of Rights* she offers no defence of temporalism other than a swift rejection of counterfactualism. In 'More on the Metaphysics of Harm' she indicates that she now prefers counterfactualism to temporalism.

temporal view appears to avoid pre-emption problems. V is worse off than he was, but not worse off than he would have been but for the finger chopping. Hence, temporalism seems preferable to counterfactualism.

i) Duration, recovery, and decline

Nevertheless, *The Temporal View* faces significant problems. One problem arises from the fact that the extent to which E harms V depends on the duration of its effects. It is difficult to find an appropriate comparison to make about duration without appealing to counterfactuals. For example, suppose D negligently causes my mobility to be restricted for two months. The duration of my immobility is obviously relevant to how much harm I suffer. How harmful is this? Temporalism invites a comparison between the immobility that I now have for the duration of two months and the mobility that I had. To make a comparison, though, we need some duration of the mobility that I had to compare my prospective two months of immobility with.

The answer cannot be the moment prior to being harmed, for well-being without duration is inconceivable. The most natural answer for temporalists compares the two months after the harm-causing event with the two months prior to the harm-causing event. But this answer has unappealing implications. Suppose that I was in a coma for the two months prior to being harmed and had just woken up. I was not at all mobile for the two months prior to being harmed. Temporalism implausibly seems to imply that I have not been harmed. Counterfactual comparison seems necessary to explain the right result: what matters is how mobile I would have been over the two months following the harm-causing event.

Relatedly, temporalism seems unable to capture one important way to harm people: by diminishing their good prospects.[34] Similarly, it struggles to explain how ameliorating a person's bad prospects benefits them. Consider:

> *Recovery*: A is recovering from a serious illness. His recovery is assisted by the use of a drug. B tampers with the drug. The drug is less effective in assisting A's recovery than it would have been had B not tampered with it.

Intuitively, B harms A. But as A is better off after taking the tampered drug than he was before taking it temporalists reach the opposite conclusion.

Now consider:

> *Decline*: A has a degenerative disease. He is declining quickly. B gives him a drug to ameliorate his decline.

Intuitively, B benefits A. But as A is worse off than he was before being given the drug temporalists reach the opposite conclusion.

ii) Nature and options

The recovery problem has not led all scholars to abandon the temporal view. Stephen Perry notices the problem but thinks it non-fatal. He tentatively offers two responses. He considers the problem of a person whose recovery from injury is interfered with by another person, and agrees that the person is harmed. His first suggestion is this person is harmed because a natural process of healing is interfered with.[35] This suggestion is

[34] See, also, M Hanser 'The Metaphysics of Harm'.

[35] S Perry 'Harm, History, and Counterfactuals' (2003) 40 *San Diego Law Review* 1283, 1297–8.

insufficiently broad to meet the concern. In *Recovery*, B does not interfere with a natural process, but rather with a drug-assisted process, yet B harms A.

Perry's second response is as follows: if a person is denied a benefit that she would otherwise have received, she is harmed because her options are restricted. To evaluate this response we need to characterize it more carefully. It is, of course, true that A was denied the option of recovering. But it is not clear how referring to A's options makes a difference here. After all, it is the recovery that A cares about, not the option of recovering. If B harms A, this is not in virtue of denying A an option, it is in virtue of interfering with A's recovery.

I think that Perry means to rely on the idea that a person's options are valuable to a person in a 'selection-independent' way. That is, the value of a person having an option is not reducible to the benefits to him if he selects the option. A person may be better off having an option even if he does not select it. I think that Perry means this, because it would allow him to point to a pre-event advantage that is removed in cases such as *Recovery*. If the option of recovering is valuable to A independently of whether he actually recovers, B harms A by removing that option.

I agree that options can have selection-independent value.[36] Perhaps the most important reason is that options improve autonomy independently of their selection. But this explanation why B harms A in *Recovery* is unappealing. To see this, notice that A is harmed even if A is unconscious, a newborn baby, or a non-human animal in *Recovery*. But options lack selection-independent value to unconscious people, newborn babies, and non-human animals.

Moreover, the magnitude of harm that A suffers in *Recovery* is not determined by the value of the option of recovering independently of whether A selects that option. We could consider the selection-independent value of the option by imagining that A would not have selected the option. The harm that B does to A is more plausibly calculated, though, by comparing A's state with his circumstances where he selects the option. What is most important in recovery is not that A had the option of recovering; it is that A would have recovered.

iii) Prospects

David Velleman develops the temporal view in a way that has more general application, and thus might be preferred.[37] Velleman thinks that how well off a person is depends on his prospects. In *Recovery*, B harms A, Velleman might suggest, by diminishing A's prospects. Similarly, B benefits A in *Decline* by improving A's prospects. As the unconscious, newborn babies, and non-human animals have prospects, the challenge outlined to Perry's proposal can be evaded.

Here is a problem with Velleman's proposal: when it is adjusted for prospects, *The Temporal View* is not obviously distinct from *The Counterfactual View*, for a person's prospects are understood counterfactually. It follows from this that the apparent advantage that temporalists claim over counterfactualists—that temporalism can respond more adequately to pre-emption cases—is lost. To see this, recall *Finger*. Had D not chopped off V's finger, X would have chopped off two. If X's chopping is part of V's

[36] See V Tadros *Criminal Responsibility* (Oxford: OUP, 2005) 200–7 for further discussion.

[37] J D Velleman 'Persons in Prospect' (2008) 36 *Philosophy and Public Affairs* 221, 242–3. See, also, Thomson's suggestion that the temporal view might be rescued from this objection by referring to a person's chances. See 'More on the Metaphysics of Harm', 445. I suspect, though I will not demonstrate it here, that my objections to Velleman extend to Thomson.

prospects, *Finger* is like *Decline*. As D has improved V's prospects, does temporalism not imply implausibly that D has not harmed V? But, intuitively, D harms V in finger whereas B does not harm A in *Decline*. There is no obvious way to distinguish *Finger* from *Decline* without relying on counterfactual comparison.

To illuminate this problem even more brightly consider:

> *Recovery 2*. A is recovering from a serious illness using a drug. B tampers with the drug. The drug is less effective in assisting A's recovery than it would have been had B not tampered with it. Had B not tampered with the drug, C would have tampered with the drug more severely, rendering it even less effective.

B harms A. If C's potential action is part of A's prospects, though, the temporalist cannot explain this result. The judgement that B harms A relies on us excluding what C would have done from the picture. We must compare A's state with his state had neither B nor C acted. The temporalist can deliver the right result—that B harms A—only by including the effects of the unaffected drug as part of A's prospects but excluding C's potential act. Prospect-adjusted temporalism thus provides no improvement over counterfactualism in explaining the case. Once prospects are built into *The Temporal View, The Temporal View* seems a confusing restatement of *The Counterfactual View*, inheriting all of its strengths and weaknesses.

iv) Regret

Velleman offers a further argument in support of the temporal view. He claims that judgements about harm and benefit are judgements about which we sensibly feel regretful or gratified. The counterfactual view of harm and benefit, Velleman thinks, cannot make sense of these emotions. It suggests that we compare the person as he is and the person as he might have been. But as the people that he might have been are not objects of self-concern they do not appropriately figure in judgements of regret or gratification.[38]

This argument is mysterious. For one thing, non-human animals can be harmed even though they are incapable of feeling regret or gratification. This suggests that these emotions are less central to the idea of harming than Velleman suggests. More importantly, the idea of regret depends on us imagining how things might have been. For example, suppose I go to a restaurant with my partner. She chooses steak and I choose fish. Our dishes come. The fish looks rubbish and the steak delicious. I regret choosing the fish.

How is regret explained? Here's how. I compare 'me with steak' to 'me with fish' and find that I would have been better off being 'me with steak'. Velleman implies that this natural way of seeing the decision is inappropriate. 'Me with steak' cannot be an object of self-concern, and hence can play no role in feeling regret. But I don't need to be concerned with the person that I would have been to experience regret. I can be concerned with the person that I am, but wish that my circumstances had been different. And that involves imagining what it would have been like to have steak.

Seeing how Velleman's own account of regret is misplaced bolsters this simple idea further. The temporal account understands regret by comparing how I am with how I was. But when I regret ordering fish I don't compare 'me with fish' with 'me prior to ordering, with the option of fish or steak'. We can see this because prior to ordering,

[38] 'Persons in Prospect', 242.

although I had options, I may also have been grouchy and hungry. Insofar as we can compare my circumstances with my circumstances prior to ordering, my choosing of fish improved my circumstances, though not by as much as they would have been improved had I ordered steak.

Perhaps it might be argued that I was better off prior to ordering because I have the option of choosing the steak and that option is preferable. But the value of that option depends on how well off I would be were I to receive the steak. The value of an option depends on the value of its content. And the value of its content depends on how things would be were I to select it. Regret is filled with counterfactual imagining.[39] This reinforces the idea that prospect-adjusted temporalism is simply a confusing restatement of counterfactualism.

VIII. In Defence of Counterfactualism

I offer a further argument in support of *The Counterfactual View*. The argument depends on the following idea. In cases of overdetermination various judgements about harm and benefit are relevant to normative enquiry. These judgements draw on various comparisons. These comparisons are made by imagining different ways the world might have been. Hence, various counterfactual comparisons are involved in assessing these cases. This provides a compelling reason to believe a version of *The Complex Counterfactual View*. This argument also has a nice irony about it—pre-emption cases are normally thought to be a weakness in counterfactual accounts of harming. On the contrary, I argue, they reveal their strength.

i) Harm, liability, and pre-emption

Recall again:

> *Finger*: D chops off one of V's fingers, pre-empting that finger and another being chopped off by X.

Here are three judgements about *Finger* that are relevant to normative enquiry. First, D harms V by chopping off his finger. Second, D benefits V by pre-empting V being harmed by X. Third, D benefits V overall, because the harm that he causes is less serious than the harm that he pre-empts.

Not all counterfactualists think these judgements are warranted. Derek Parfit accepts that it is intuitive that D harms V. He claims that we should revise the concept of harm and adopt *The Simple Counterfactual View*.[40] This view implies that D does not harm V in *Finger* because V is better off than he would have been had D not acted. As his view makes it more difficult clearly to ask the range of morally salient questions that we wish to ask about *Finger* we should reject Parfit's view.

For example, we wish to ask:

1) Does D owe V compensation for the chopping even though the chopping pre-empted an even worse chopping? And

[39] This is also the standard view in the psychology of regret. See, for example, M Zeelenberg and E van Dijk 'On the Comparative Nature of Regret' in D R Mandel and D J Hilton *The Psychology of Counterfactual Thinking* (London: Routledge, 2005)

[40] See *Reasons and Persons* (Oxford: OUP, 1984) 69–70.

2) Does D's obligation to pay compensation to V depend on whether D was aware of the chopping that he pre-empted? And
3) Does D's obligation to pay compensation to V depend on the reasons why D chopped?

Our questions can naturally be stated in a more general way:

1) Does one person owe compensation to another for harming him even though he pre-empts a greater harm?
2) Where the harm caused is overdetermined, does the obligation of the person causing the harm to compensate the victim depend on whether she knew that the harm was overdetermined?
3) Where the harm caused is overdetermined, does the obligation of the person causing the harm to compensate the victim depend on the reasons for which she acted?

At least the last of these questions is difficult to answer. Our account of harm should make them easy to ask.

The answer to 1) is surely: at least sometimes. This is because the answer to 2) is clearly yes. If D is unaware that he has pre-empted X's more harmful action, D owes V compensation. X's potential action cannot vitiate D's liability. If X does nothing and has no influence over D's action, X owes V nothing. We do not owe compensation for the harm we might have caused, only for the harm that we have caused. If D owes no compensation, V is not entitled to compensation. That is hard to believe.

Here is a brief defence of the idea that D is liable to compensate V. Consider a world in which D is not liable to compensate V because he pre-empted X's action. X's plan to harm V vitiates D's liability to V. In such a world, how ought we to respond to the harm that V has suffered? We could let the harm remain with V. If so, V remains very badly off as a result of the combination of D's action and X's plan. We have strong reasons not to let V remain in this state.

Alternatively, other citizens could compensate V. They will then bear the costs for the harm caused by the combination of D's action and X's plan. There would seem little more reason to require these citizens to compensate V than to provide funds for other citizens that are badly off. There is more to say about this possibility, but I believe that it should be rejected.

There are strong reasons, in this world, to hold X liable to compensate V. Here is why. If X is not liable to compensate V, X will have made V much worse off than he would have been had X not formed a plan to harm V, for in that case V would have been able to secure compensation from D for the harm that he has suffered. Hence, in this world, X would have rendered D worse off than he would have been had he not formed his plan.

The fact that X would have harmed V supports X's liability to compensate V. It may not support it decisively—perhaps fault is also required. A good reason to make fault a condition of compensatory liability is that this allows people to avoid becoming liable to pay compensation.[41] They can do so by refraining from acting in a faulty

[41] For more on avoidability, see Scanlon *What We Owe to Each Other*, ch 6. I develop Scanlon's account of the significance of choice in V Tadros *The Ends of Harm: The Moral Foundations of the Criminal Law* (Oxford: OUP, 2011) especially chs 3 and 8.

way. Suppose, then, that it is wrong for X to plan to chop V's fingers off. X's objection to being held liable is weak because he could have avoided being held liable simply by refraining from forming a plan to chop V's fingers off. The two most important components of liability—causation and avoidability—are both present.

To summarize, in the world that we are considering, we have three reasons to hold X liable to pay compensation—1) were we not to do this, X would have made V worse off than he would have been had X not formed his plan; 2) even if liability is imposed, it could easily have been avoided by X; 3) if X does not compensate V, innocent people will have to bear the cost.

Now return to the actual world of *Finger*. From our discussion, we can see that someone, either D or X, ought to be liable to compensate V. If D is not liable to compensate V, X is. Who should we hold liable, then, D or X? The main reason in favour of holding D liable is that D has actually affected V. It is only if we refrain from holding D and X liable for the harm done to V that X will have rendered V worse off than he would have been had he not formed his plan. If D is liable to pay compensation to V, X has not affected V. The idea that we are especially responsible for the outcomes that we actually cause is, of course, somewhat controversial. It is also highly intuitive. I will not attempt to defend it here. I only claim that *if* this plausible idea is true, it follows that D rather than X is liable to compensate V.

This view relies on the idea that D has harmed V and hence rejection of *The Simple Counterfactual View*. We thus have two reasons to reject Parfit's revisionist account of harm. First, it makes the relevant questions difficult to ask. Second, in *Finger* it is highly plausible that if D is unaware of X's potential action, D is liable to compensate V for the harm that he has caused. Parfit's revision makes this description unavailable.

ii) Multiple Comparisons

Some may think that the analysis of *Finger* above provides a reason to favour non-comparativism or temporalism. It doesn't. It provides a reason to reject *The Simple Counterfactual View*, but only in favour of *The Complex Counterfactual View*. Recall:

> *Recovery 2*: A is recovering from a serious illness using a drug. B tampers with the drug. The drug is less effective in assisting A's recovery than it would have been had B not tampered with it. Had B not tampered with the drug, C would have tampered with the drug more severely, rendering it even less effective.

The intuitive idea that B harms A relies on a comparison between the recovery that A actually has with the recovery that he would have had if neither B nor C had tampered with his drugs. This comparison also provides an intuitive account of the magnitude of harm that A suffers. The amount that A has been harmed is the difference between his actual state and the state that he would have been in had no one tampered with his pill.

This judgement is only one of a range of morally significant judgements to make about the case. As well as harming A, B has benefited A. It is only because of B's act that C did not harm A. There are two different judgements to make here. First, we can consider the magnitude of the threat that B's act averts. This is the difference between the state that A would have been in had B not acted and the state that he would have been in had C but not B acted. Second, we can consider how much better off A is than he would have been had B not acted. This is the difference between the state that A would have been in had B not acted and A's actual state.

Here is a more complete account. The numbers at the end of the descriptions are illustrative of the magnitude of the difference in well-being between the first state and the second:

1) *The Harm B Causes*. The difference in A's well-being between the world where B tampers with the drug and the world where no one tampers with the drug (5);
2) *The Magnitude of C's Threat*. The difference in A's well-being between the world where C severely tampers with the drug and no one tampers with the drug (12);
3) *The Overall Benefit that B Provides*. The difference in A's well-being between the world where C severely tampers with the drug and the world where B tampers with the drug (7).

We use all three judgements in this simple and natural characterization of B's act: B harms A (judgement 1), but he also benefits A by pre-empting a greater harm (judgement 2), benefiting A overall (judgement 3). Thus, B has harmed A by five units of well-being, he has pre-empted a harm to A of twelve units of well-being, and hence he has benefited A overall by seven units of well-being.

A strength of *The Counterfactual View* is that it makes possible a range of judgements in pre-emption cases. These judgements describe pre-emption cases more fully than *The Non-Comparative View* or *The Temporal View* (insofar as it is distinct from *The Counterfactual View*). Neither *The Non-Comparative View* nor *The Temporal View* pick out the idea that B both harms A but also benefits him.

This is because only single verdicts are available on the alternative views. On *The Absolute View* A is harmed only if he remains badly off. If he does remain badly off, though, it cannot pick out the idea that B benefits A. On *The Temporal View* A is harmed if he is worse off than he was prior to B's act. But without counterfactual comparison, there is no way to represent the idea that B is also made better off by A. Hence, the ability to handle pre-emption cases such as *Recovery 2* is a comparative strength of counterfactualism.

Some might doubt that we need both the idea that B harms A and the verdict that B benefits A. To see why both ideas are useful, consider whether B is required to compensate A. Earlier I supported the conventional view that the person who causes harm pre-empting a greater wrongful harm owes full compensation for the harm that he causes if he was unaware of the benefit that he provides. Similarly, in *Recovery 2*, if B was completely unaware that he was pre-empting C's action B owes A compensation for five units of harm.

Now suppose that B acts only in order to benefit B by pre-empting C's action. There is no way for B to benefit A other than by tampering with the drug. Furthermore, B cannot seek A's consent. In that case, intuitively, B does not owe A compensation. Doing this noble deed for the sake of A cannot make B liable to any cost. If anything, A owes B a debt of gratitude. If anyone owes A compensation in that case, it is C. C may owe A compensation because he wrongly creates the conditions in which B justifiably harms A. I conclude that B does not owe compensation to A only if he was aware that he was pre-empting C's act. Only if he was aware that he was pre-empting C's act can he point to the benefit that he has provided to vitiate A's claim to compensation.

I do not claim that B's awareness of C's potential action is sufficient for him to avoid liability to pay compensation to A. B's liability may also depend on whether B was motivated to assist A. If B was aware of C's action, but hated A so much that he wanted to be the one who harmed A, it is plausible that B owes A compensation. On this view, awareness of a normative reason that would justify one's action is insufficient to avert a person's liability to pay compensation for causing harm. To avert liability, one's harm-causing action must not only be justifiable, it must be justified.[42] Another way to put this is that in assessing B's liability it is relevant to compare A's current state with the state that he would have been in had C harmed A only if B was aware of C's potential action, and perhaps also only if he was motivated to avert it.

So far I have established that there is good reason to refer both to the harm that B causes and the benefit that B provides overall. Depending on further facts in the case, these judgements will determine whether B is liable to pay compensation, deserves gratitude, or ought to be compensated for any losses that he suffered in benefiting A overall.

Do we also need to use our second judgement—the magnitude of the threat that C posed to A? There are a number of reasons why we may wish to determine not only the magnitude of harm that B averted overall, but also the magnitude of the threat that C posed. First, there is an important sense in which B has not only benefited A, but has also benefited C. He has benefited C by preventing C from harming A. This benefits C not least because C would have been liable to compensate A for a loss of twelve units of well-being had B not intervened. Though it is even more unlikely than the cases that I have described, we could imagine a variation of the case where the tampering that C would have done had A not intervened would have been negligent rather than intentional. C would then be grateful to B for intervening.

Second, referring to the harm that C would have caused had B not intervened is important in guiding C's conduct in the future. It has attractively been argued that appealing to the role that causation has in practical reasoning can vindicate a counterfactual analysis of causation.[43] We develop causal concepts, it has been suggested, in order to learn how to intervene to bring about certain results. It is for this reason that we distinguish between causation and correlation. The fact that one event, E, correlates with another, E2, helps us in predicting whether E2 will occur—it will occur whenever E occurs. It does little to help us bring E2 about. The fact that changes in a barometer reading correlate with a storm does not allow us to control the weather. If we discover that E is a cause of E2, in contrast, we learn how to bring E2 about. That depends on it at least typically being the case that bringing E about will bring E2 about.

Whatever the right account of causation, the idea that our account of harming has the practical function of securing our level of well-being by guiding us to manipulate the world is attractive. C has good reason to learn how not to cause harm. He can find that out by investigating how much harm he would have caused had B not intervened. C should make that judgement given that he cannot normally rely on B to intervene.

Finally, if C plans to act out of bad motives, he may be liable to be harmed even though he does not pose a threat. C attempted to cause twelve units of harm. In Chapters 16 and 17 we will explore whether and why attempters are liable to punishment. Here I note that it is plausible that the magnitude of harm that attempters are liable to suffer in punishment is determined in part by the magnitude of the harm that they attempted to cause. If so, this judgement about C is relevant to the criminal law.

[42] For a parallel view in the context of criminal law, see J Gardner 'Justifications and Reasons' in J Gardner *Offences and Defences: Selected Essays in the Philosophy of Criminal Law* (Oxford: OUP, 2007) and V Tadros *Criminal Responsibility*, ch 10. The problem of overdetermination also helps to establish that intentions are relevant to permissibility. For further discussion, see V Tadros *The Ends of Harm*, ch 7 and 'Overdetermination and Obligation' unpublished ms.

[43] See, especially, J Woodward *Making Things Happen* (Oxford: OUP, 2003).

IX. Conclusion

Perhaps some may doubt the importance of the defence that I have provided for *The Counterfactual View*. They may believe that my cases are so unusual that our conception of harm ought not to be driven by them. These cases are, of course, unusual. Unusual cases help us to clarify the implications of different theories. But overdetermination itself is extremely common. It is very often true that the harm that one person causes to another is overdetermined, and it is thus very important that our theory of harm is adequate to handle these cases.

Furthermore, the problem of overdetermination has provided a key reason why counterfactual views of both harm and compensation have been rejected. Were it not for odd overdetermination cases, almost everyone would be a counterfactualist. If this apparent weakness of counterfactual views turns out to be a significant strength, a great deal of support has been provided to counterfactualism more generally.

This is a welcome and significant result. Counterfactualism is highly attractive in cases where harm is not overdetermined. In these cases, *The Simple Counterfactual View* is ideal in determining the magnitude of harm suffered and the magnitude of compensation owed. That test is inadequate in more complex cases. But as we have seen, *The Complex Counterfactual View* performs excellently in these cases. Our theory of compensation and harm is thus nicely unified.

Of course, large problems remain. As there are many counterfactuals that we could refer to, how are we to pick out those that are salient for the purposes of compensation?[44] *The Counterfactual View* itself does not provide us with a solution to this complex problem. We need principles within that view to develop solutions. But even if *The Counterfactual View* does not provide us with all of the answers, it does help us to get clear about the best way to ask the questions.

[44] Context will clearly be important in picking out the relevant counterfactuals. For discussion in the context of causation, see, for example, C Hitchcock 'Counterfactual Availability and Causal Judgment' and P Menzies 'The Role of Counterfactual Dependence in Causal Judgements' both in C Hoerl, T McCormack, and S R Beck *Understanding Counterfactuals, Understanding Causation: Issues in Philosophy and Psychology* (Oxford: OUP, 2011).

11

The Value of Consent

Wrongdoing is often harmful and the harm that it causes often partly explains why the conduct is wrong. Nevertheless, most wrongdoing is not fully explained solely by the harm that it causes. One reason is that some considerations that count against performing an action, and that can make it wrong, lack perspectival significance—they are bad, but not bad for anyone in the sense outlined in Section III(*iii*) of the previous chapter. These considerations are sometimes called 'impersonal', and they will occupy us in Chapter 15.

This chapter is concerned with interpersonal wrongdoing. If one person wrongs another, she violates a directed duty: a duty she owes to another. When this is true, the wrongdoing has perspectival significance for the victim. The question is what considerations are significant in this way—only those relating to harm, or a broader range of considerations? I will argue for the latter view, and this will provide the foundations for thinking about the importance of consent.

Section I is concerned with cases of harmless wrongdoing. Section II investigates consent-sensitive duties—duties that a person can be released from by consent. It also considers what it takes to give consent. Section III argues against the idea that consent-sensitive duties are fully explained by our interests in well-being. Section IV argues that an alternative view—that we have non-derivative interests in having normative powers—partly explains consent-sensitive duties. Section V argues that the more important foundation of such duties is the control they give us over important features of our lives.

I. Harmless Wrongs

One reason that has been offered to doubt the centrality of harm to wrongdoing, and especially to criminal wrongdoing, is that it is intuitive that a person can be wronged without harming them. Examples of harmless theft, harmless trespass, harmless rape, and so on have become familiar in criminal law theory. In such cases, an attempt is made to describe an instance of the wrong with the harm stripped away. This is typically done by making it the case that the person wronged is not, and cannot become, aware of the wrong, and the wrong has no other effect on anything that the person is, or will become, aware of.

John Gardner and Stephen Shute offer perhaps the most discussed example. We briefly explored it in Chapter 6 (I have simplified it):

> *Unconscious Rape*: Mirella is in a coma from which she never wakes up. Giuseppe, a stranger, has intercourse with her. Mirella suffers no physical effects from the intercourse.[1]

[1] 'The Wrongness of Rape' in J Gardner *Offences and Defences: Selected Essays in the Philosophy of Criminal Law* (Oxford: OUP, 2007) 5.

Here is a similar example of 'harmless trespass':

> *Secret Trespass*: Ulrica sneaks into Florence's house and sleeps in Florence's bed leaving no trace. Florence never discovers, and there is no chance she will.[2]

And here is a real case of harmless theft:

> *Coffin Lids*: Gustavo works in a crematorium. After a coffin passes through the curtain to be burned, he takes off the coffin lid to sell it. Amelia, the owner, never finds out.[3]

These examples have primarily been used to explore the harm principle, and have led people to a range of views.

One response is that the victims are harmed in these cases.[4] Whether this is so depends on the best understanding of harm. In the previous chapter I argued that harm is a setback to well-being. But well-being is something of a term of art. On the best version, is the victim's well-being set back in the above cases? One reason to think it might be is that there are non-experiential dimensions of well-being. Consider Robert Nozick's famous experience machine: entering the machine gives a person excellent 'experiences', such as a happy family, a great job, and so on, but none of these 'experiences' are real. Nozick plausibly thought that many people would not permanently enter such a machine.[5] Authentic experiences are preferable to inauthentic 'experiences' even when the latter seem much better from the inside. It is also plausible that entering such a machine reduces a person's well-being. Although the person feels much better than they would have done had they not entered the machine, they are deprived of the objectively valuable features of a life that make it go well.

Now consider:

> *Wrongful Experience Machine*: Leo secretly plugs Herbert into an experience machine at night. Herbert believes that he can act. The rest of his life seems to him identical to the way that it would have seemed to him had he not been plugged in.

It is plausible that Leo has harmed Herbert.

Those who think that the wrongs in the above examples are harmless might respond as follows. Even if there are non-experiential dimensions of well-being, some experience is necessary for a diminution in well-being. In *Wrongful Experience Machine*, Herbert only has inauthentic 'experiences'—they are not experiences of anything real. As it is better for a person to have authentic rather than inauthentic experiences, Leo harms Herbert. Those who think this might nevertheless believe the victims in the 'harmless wrongdoing' cases are not harmed because they have no experiences, authentic or otherwise, about the events in question.

These cases seem at best marginal cases of harm. In *Unconscious Rape*, for example, Mirella clearly has a powerful first-person perspectival interest in Giuseppe not having sex with her whilst she is unconscious. I am not sure that there is a determinate answer to the question whether she is harmed. We don't have strong reasons to give a determinate answer to this question—we are very confident that the conduct is wrong,

[2] See A Ripstein 'Beyond the Harm Principle' (2006) 34 *Philosophy and Public Affairs* 215, 218.

[3] *Dewar v HMA* 1945 SLT 114.

[4] See, for example, J Stanton-Ife 'Horrific Crime' in R A Duff, Lindsay Farmer, S E Marshall, M Renzo, and V Tadros *The Boundaries of the Criminal Law* (Oxford: OUP, 2010). Stanton-Ife thinks that the victim suffers 'dignitary harm'. Given what I say below, I doubt that harm should be extended in this way.

[5] *Anarchy, State, and Utopia* (Oxford: Blackwell, 1974) 42–5.

that it makes the perpetrator liable to punishment, and that we have good reason to prevent it occurring.

Whatever answer one gives, there are some clear cases of harmless wronging. One clear case involves self-sacrifice, an idea we began to explore in the previous chapter. The basic idea is this. In cases of true self-sacrifice, a person harms herself for the sake of some goal. Self-sacrifice can be noble. One person can wrong another by preventing her from sacrificing herself for the sake of the goal. But as self-sacrifice involves harming oneself for the sake of that goal, preventing self-sacrifice prevents the person suffering harm rather than harming her.

It might be objected that preventing self-sacrifice harms the person in one respect. A person who sacrifices herself for the sake of a valuable goal might be thought to enhance her well-being in one sense: she has achieved something, and she values the achievement. If achievement contributes to well-being, preventing the person from sacrificing herself harms her in this respect. But as self-sacrifice involves harming oneself overall for the sake of an end that one cares about, preventing self-sacrifice prevents a person from harming herself overall for the sake of that end. Given this, it is not plausible that the harm that the person suffers properly explains the wrong.

Another clear case is paternalistic interference. It is often wrong to interfere with a person for her own good. This is not only because such interference tends to do more harm than good. Even if the interference was predictably good for the person, interfering with her is often wrong. This is explained by the interest that we have in not being controlled by others. But our interest in this is not reducible to the fact that the interference makes our lives go worse. These examples further support the arguments I offered to reject various versions of the harm principle in Chapter 6.

Our reason to investigate non-harmful wrongdoing is not limited to determining whether there is such a thing. In order to assess the role of harm in a theory of criminalization, we need to investigate how important harm is to understanding wrongdoing. Even if most wrongdoing is harmful, and even if most cases where criminalization is warranted involve harm prevention, it does not follow that harm plays an important role in explaining criminalization. Compare the following. Suppose there is no smoke without fire and no fire without smoke. We could then endorse the smoke principle for arson: a person should be convicted of arson only if he causes smoke. This principle does just as good a job in criminalizing the right people as a fire principle: a person should be convicted of arson only if he causes fire. Yet it does not follow that smoke and fire equally explain why we criminalize arson (though, of course, people in fires often die of smoke inhalation, so perhaps they do!).

Similarly, certain wrongs, such as torture, might always cause the victims to suffer distress. The distress may provide a reason to criminalize the wrongdoing. But that may not be the most important explanation why the wrongdoing is criminalized—our main reason to criminalize it might be the facts about torture that give rise to the distress rather than the distress itself. Or both things might be important. Even if we could find harms in cases of so-called harmless wrongdoing, they help us understand wrongdoing in a way that focusing simply on harm does not.

One thing they plausibly point us to is the importance of consent. It seems plausible that the wrongs in cases we explored above demonstrate that lack of consent determines what is wrong, and that this is not so only because requiring consent protects a person from harm. Exploring the way in which consent relates to wrongdoing illuminates harmless wrongdoing, but it also illuminates a much wider range of harmful wrongs. I begin by spelling out how consent seems to work in ordinary morality, before exploring its moral underpinnings. This will set the stage for an investigation, in the following three chapters, of different limits to the normative power of consent.

II. Consent-Sensitive Duties

Typically, when X owes a consent-sensitive duty to Y not to *v*:

1) X owes a duty to Y not to *v*;
2) Y can release X from this duty by consenting to X *v*ing.
3) If X *v*s without Y's consent, X wrongs Y; but not if Y consents.

There are exceptions. Sometimes, the person whose consent can release X from the duty is not the person to whom the duty is owed—for example, a doctor may owe it to his patient not to perform an operation without the consent of his superior. The duty not to operate, in this case, is not owed to the superior. In standard cases, though, the person whose consent can release X from a duty is the person to whom the duty is owed.

i) Consent and validity

Many duties are consent-sensitive. We owe people duties not to use their property, not to perform surgery on them, not to enter their homes, not to have sex with them, and so on. Consent can make all of these things permissible. Consent-sensitive duties are also of fundamental importance in understanding the criminal law. Whilst consent is not always treated as decisive in the criminal law, it often is. Consent makes the difference between permissible taking and theft, permissible sex and rape, permissible touching and battery, and so on.

The idea that the duties we owe to others are consent-sensitive is at least as important in explaining the scope of the criminal law as harm. It is often legally permissible to harm a person if she consents to being harmed. It is often criminally wrong to do things to a person who doesn't consent without harming the person. It is, for this reason, surprising that harm has had such prominence in criminalization theory, and consent a relatively minor role. Even if the duty not to harm others is independently important, and I think it is, consent-sensitive duties are at the heart of the criminal law.

Here is how I understand standard cases of valid consent. If Y consents to X *v*ing, X is under a consent-sensitive duty to Y not to *v*; Y intends to release X from this duty; and Y does so by granting permission to X that he may *v*. Part of the debate about the nature of consent involves a debate about whether consent involves 'granting permission' and what 'granting permission' involves if it does.

Before getting to this, let me briefly address a concern: some reject the idea that consent is reducible to granting a permission because they think that this leaves out the context in which the permission is given.[6] Those who favour the idea that consent involves granting permission, though, need not be insensitive to these contextual factors in the overall investigation as to whether X is required not to *v*. This is because

[6] See, for example, S Cowan 'Choosing Freely: Theoretically Reframing the Concept of Consent' in S Cowan and R Hunter *Choice and Consent: Feminist Engagements With Law and Subjectivity* (London: Routledge, 2007) 93.

whether Y consents to X *v*ing does not determine whether X is permitted to *v*, even if X owes Y a consent-sensitive duty not to *v*. Whether X is permitted to *v* depends on a wider range of factors, but most importantly it depends on whether Y's consent is valid.

Y's consent is typically invalid either if X does not owe a consent-sensitive duty to Y not to *v*; or if Y does not have the normative power to release X from this duty; or if Y does not have the power to release X from this duty in these circumstances, or by acting in this way. The conditions of validity are at least as important as understanding consent itself. I explore validity in depth in the next three chapters.

If X is under a consent-sensitive duty to Y not to *v*, Y has the normative power to release X from the duty not to *v*. In order to explain this, we need to consider both why X has a duty not to *v* if Y does not release X from this duty, and why Y has the normative power to release X from this duty. An explanation of the second fact relies on an understanding of what a normative power is.

Y has a normative power over X when Y can directly intentionally alter X's rights and duties. The validity of consent illustrates this idea. At least in standard cases, where X owes a consent-sensitive duty to Y not to *v*, X's rights are subject to Y's intentional control in the following sense: Y has the power directly to release X from an obligation simply by her decision (or, perhaps, her announcement of her decision) that this is the case. By granting X consent to *v*, Y intends directly to affect X's obligations, and her execution of this intention is directly effective.

ii) How to consent

There are three features of this idea of a normative power worth highlighting. The first feature is that consenting is an intentional action—the intentional action of releasing a person from a duty. This requires some clarification. Some argue about whether consent is a mental state or whether it is reducible to outward behaviour. In this debate, it is sometimes assumed that the question is whether consent is an attitude, such as desiring, or whether it involves outward expression.

This question assumes a simple contrast between mental states on the one hand and outward behaviour on the other that doesn't capture the range of options. Some mental phenomena are states of mind: intentions, beliefs, desires, and so on. But we also perform mental actions—forming intentions and beliefs, deciding, choosing, and so on. Those who think that consent can be given without outward behaviour thus need not hold the implausible view that consenting is reducible to certain desires or intentions. They may believe that it is a mental action, similar to the action of deciding or choosing.

Similarly, actions normally have both a physical and a mental dimension. Performative acts are an example. They include signalling, commanding, inviting, and so on. They are intentional actions—actions that execute intentions through communication. A plausible view is that consenting is a performative act. But these other performative acts cannot be completed without a public manifestation. One cannot invite someone to dinner in one's own head. Nevertheless, saying the words 'please come to dinner' need not involve inviting you to dinner: I might be joking. So those who think that outward behaviour is required for consent need not hold the implausible view that consenting simply involves the saying of certain words, regardless of the intention with which they are said.

If consent is a performative act, there is a range of views that we might hold about how the act is performed. At one end of the spectrum, consenting might involve successful communication. On this view, not only is a publicly expressed attempt to communicate required, consent does not occur without uptake. Uptake occurs when the person to whom consent is given understands that consent is given—he understands that the person giving consent intends to release him from the duty he owes her.

But those who believe that consent is communicative might think that consent is complete with something less: an attempt to communicate, whether or not it is successful, may be sufficient. Those who hold this view might differ about what is required for an attempt. In particular, they might disagree about whether consent occurs where there is an attempt, but the attempt does not result in public expression, for example in the case where a person tries to speak but fails.

So we have three views:

1) Consent is an act that can be performed purely mentally, without any attempt to communicate;
2) Consent is an act that requires an attempt to communicate;
3) Consent is an act that requires both an attempt to communicate and uptake.

The last of these views does not track our intuitions about when consent is given. To see this, suppose that X owes Y a consent-sensitive duty not to *v*. Y attempts to communicate her consent to X to *v*, but mumbles. X is not quite sure what Y has said, but thinks that she has indicated that she has consented to X *v*ing. X thinks that Y has consented, but is unsure. But if X is unsure about whether Y has consented, it must be true or false that Y has consented—there is something, Y's consent, about which X is unsure. Hence, Y's consent must be independent of whether X knows that Y has consented. Successful communication of consent is not required for consent. At most, consent requires an attempt to express something to someone else—one need not communicate successfully to consent.

Furthermore, it seems that consent is given at the moment when the person giving consent expresses her permission. If there is a delay between expression and uptake, consent is given at the moment of expression and not at the moment of uptake. Consider:

> *Delay*: On Monday, Bill asks Sally if he can borrow her car on Wednesday. On Tuesday Sally writes an email to Bill that he can. Bill does not read the email until Thursday.

The view that consent requires uptake counterintuitively implies that Sally did not consent to Bill borrowing her car until Thursday when it was too late. The better view is that Sally consented on Tuesday, but Bill did not find out until Thursday.[7]

Consent, then, is unilateral. It need not involve a transaction, a negotiation, or an agreement.[8] One person can give consent to another without the other person being aware of consent having been given, and without meeting minds. This is not to say that

[7] Tom Dougherty supports his view that uptake is required for consent by the relationship between promising and consent. See 'Yes Means Yes: Consent and Communication' (2015) 43 *Philosophy & Public Affairs* 224. He thinks that as promising requires uptake, so does consent. But delays seem to have a similar effect in promising. Sally could promise that Bill could use her car on Tuesday, even if Bill only finds out on Wednesday. Dougherty seems to imply that the promise is only complete on Wednesday, which is not the intuitive view. That is when he finds out that Sally promised on Tuesday.

[8] The idea that consent is a transaction is suggested in E Sherwin 'Infelicitous Sex' (1996) 2 *Legal Theory* 209. Negotiation is centre stage in M Anderson 'Negotiating Sex' (2005) 78 *Southern California Law Review* 1401, though she sees negotiation as replacing consent.

consent is valid, in such circumstances, or that the person who is unaware that consent has been given acts permissibly, only that consent has in fact been given. It is a complex moral question what implications there are for a person who acts with consent, but who does not know it.

And there is a reason why consent does not require the recipient to understand that he has been released from a consent-sensitive duty. One explanation why X owes Y a consent-sensitive duty not to *v* is that it is valuable to Y that she has control over the duties that X owes her. She may have an interest in determining whether X wrongs her by *v*ing. But she will not be well placed to do this if consent requires uptake. Whether X wrongs her would then depend not only on Y's conduct, but also on X's understanding of it. And thus with all the will in the world, Y may not be able to determine whether X wrongs her by *v*ing.

Consider:

> *Capacity Mistake*: Pistola believes that Nanetta lacks mental capacities that Nanetta possesses. When Nanetta communicates to Pistola that he is released from a consent-sensitive duty that he owes her not to borrow her car, he does not believe her. He thus refrains from borrowing the car.

If Nanetta's consent is not valid, she cannot achieve something that she has reason to value—releasing Pistola from the duty not to use the car—due to Pistola's mistaken assessment about her capacities. As we will see below, Nanetta's interest in this is not reducible to Pistola's actually taking the car. She may have an irreducible interest in controlling the duties that Pistola owes her. Nanetta's interest in this is better protected if consent does not require uptake.

I do not take a strong stance between whether consenting is a mental act or whether it necessarily involves at least an attempt to express something to someone else. There is something in favour of the first view. It gives Y even more control over the duties that X is under: she can release X from his duties without outward behaviour. That might be thought important for those who are unable to communicate.

However, there is also something to be said for the second view, and I tend to favour this view. One idea is that Y must communicate to X in order to consent to X *v*ing because only then can consent play the role that it has in supporting the interests that X and Y have in the power of consent. If Y is not required to communicate with X, she can release X from his duty not to *v* without him having any reason to believe that he has been released from this duty. He will thus lack a duty that he has no reason to believe he lacks. X and Y have an interest in knowing what duties he is under, and so Y lacks this power.

This argument, though, seems to favour more than mere public expression. After all, 2) does not give X a good opportunity to find out what duties he is under. X might not have any evidence that Y's public expression was a public expression of her intention to release X from the duty he is under. Perhaps, then, we should favour:

4) Consent is an act which requires public expression that gives the person to whom consent is given sufficient evidence of the intention to release him from a consent-sensitive duty he is under.

This view would make Nanetta's consent effective in releasing Pistola from his duty in *Capacity Mistake*.

However, this view still seems problematic. Consider:

> *Foreign Lovers*: Brenda consents to sex with Ahmed in a language that Brenda thinks Ahmed understands, but he does not.

4) implies that Brenda has not consented to sex with Ahmed, which is powerfully counterintuitive. It is more plausible that Brenda has consented even if Ahmed does not realize that she has. Furthermore, Brenda and Ahmed might have a powerful interest in Brenda having consented. By consenting, Brenda grants Ahmed permission to have sex with her. The value of this might be partly to do with the relationship that she forms with Ahmed by doing this.[9] Now suppose that Ahmed does not understand that she has consented, and so does not have sex with her. When she later tells him that she consented in a language that he understands, they might value her having done this, and not merely having tried to do it.

Here is a reason that might seem to have less moral force, but that might have more power to explain the intuitions that support 2). When Y consents to X, Y releases X from a duty that he is under. Our question is how Y can achieve this. In order to understand what makes this possible, we need a grasp of what duties are.

For example, on the response-dependent view of duties, we need to understand when consent can determine whether certain responses, such as blame, are warranted. It might then be argued that consent must be public, because only then can it play its appropriate role in accountability practices.[10] This is not so, though. Suppose that Y decides to release X from the duty that he owes her not to *v*, but cannot even attempt to communicate this to X prior to his *v*ing. X *v*s. As long as Y can communicate with X after he has *v*ed, she can indicate to him that certain responses that otherwise would be appropriate are inappropriate in virtue of her decision. The view that duties are response-dependent, then, does not count against the idea that a mental act is sufficient for consent.

Furthermore, the view that consent does not require uptake, or even evidence of consent, allows for more complex judgements about wrongdoing, and these judgements seem warranted. As Y has released X from the duty he owes her not to *v*, he does not violate that duty even if he believes that she has not consented. But that does not imply that he has not acted wrongly in another sense—he had good reason to believe that he was under a duty not to *v* and he did believe it. What he did was thus wrong in the evidence-relative and in the belief-relative senses.

And there is a sense in which he wrongs Y—in acting without believing that Y has consented, he fails to recognize that Y is in control of his duties, and thus normatively constrains his conduct. He can be held accountable for his wrongdoing, and Y has special standing to do so given the attitudes about her that his conduct demonstrates. Thus, the response-dependent view of wrongdoing does not count against 1); if anything it supports 1).

The view of duties I argued for in Chapter 3, though, does count against 1). The primary function of X's duties is to constrain X's practical reasoning. Hence, on this view, when Y consents to X *v*ing, she must execute an intention to affect X's practical reasoning: she releases X from a constraint that he would otherwise have not to *v* because of what he owes to her. But she cannot execute such an intention without intending to communicate with X. This is because it would be impossible for her to alter the role that *v*ing has in X's practical reasoning without communicating with X. She cannot intend to do something that she believes is impossible to do. Hence, Y consents only if she intends to communicate to X that he has the option to *v*. This is why it seems incoherent of Y to claim to consent to X *v*ing, but intend to keep this a secret from X—she can desire that X *v*s without attempting

[9] I discuss this idea further below.

[10] See, further, Dougherty 'Yes means Yes'.

to communicate this to X, but she cannot consent to X *v*ing without attempting to communicate this to X.

But she can execute an intention to release X from a duty without actually affecting X's practical reasoning. By attempting to communicate to X that she permits him to *v* she alters the facts that X has a reason to respond to. If he fails to recognize that she has done this, he fails to respond to something that he has reason to respond to. So by attempting to communicate her permission to X, she already succeeds in releasing him from his duty. After she has done so, he may or may not realize that something relevant to his practical reasoning has changed.

This is unfortunate for those who cannot communicate—they cannot release people from the consent-sensitive duties that others owe them because they cannot even try to affect the practical reasoning of those who owe them consent-sensitive duties. Perhaps those in such a situation do something that is morally close to consenting without attempting to communicate—as they cannot consent, we give their desires more force in determining whether others have wronged them.[11] This might also affect whether it is warranted to blame those who violate such duties. But the concern that we have for those who cannot communicate may not alter the more general way in which consent is given—by attempting to communicate with the person to whom consent is given.

Overall, then, I favour the idea that consent requires an attempt to communicate. Public expression is not required for consent. A person who tries and fails publicly to express her consent may nevertheless consent. Consider a person who thinks that she can communicate telepathically. She can consent without any public expression of consent. Her attempt to communicate telepathically is sufficient. But if a person knows that she cannot communicate with another person, she cannot consent.

iii) The target of consent

The second feature of the view is that Y has the power to release X from a consent-sensitive duty by executing an intention to release X from that duty. The object of Y's intention is X's duty, not X's action. It is sometimes suggested that Y's consent to X *v*ing is necessarily related to Y's intention that X *v*, or Y's intention to cause or enable X's *v*ing.[12] Similarly, it is sometimes suggested that if Y authorizes X's *v*ing, Y desires X to *v*.[13] But Y may consent to X *v*ing whilst lacking any such intention or desire. Y may consent to X *v*ing whilst intending and desiring that X choose not to *v*. In such cases, Y releases X from a duty owed to Y not to *v*. But his reason for doing this may be that he prefers X to be free from the duty not to *v*, not that he prefers that X *v*.

Consider:

> *Borrow*: Jess wants to skip class to go to a party, and asks to borrow Betty's car. If Betty does not consent, Jess will go to class. Betty thinks it Jess's decision whether to skip class, but wants Jess to go to class. Betty says to Jess: 'take my car if you want to, but I really want you to go to class.'

[11] Compare the discussion of those who do not understand they are owed consent-sensitive duties, below.

[12] See, for example, H Hurd 'The Moral Magic of Consent' (1996) 2 *Legal Theory* 121, 129–32.

[13] See P Westen *The Logic of Consent* (Aldershot: Ashgate, 2004) 32–3. Similarly, it is sometimes suggested that consent involves a resolution for an action to occur. See A Pundik 'Coercion and Deception in Sexual Relations' (2015) 28 *Canadian Journal of Law and Jurisprudence* 97, 103.

Jess owes Betty a consent-sensitive duty not to take Betty's car. Betty consents to Jess taking her car, and by doing this releases Jess from her duty. Jess thus does not wrong Betty if she takes Betty's car. But Betty does not intend Jess to take her car, nor does she desire this. She intends to release Jess from a duty not to take her car, but not with the intention of Jess taking her car. Betty, in this case, may not want Jess to stay in class *because she is under a duty to Betty*. She may nevertheless want Jess to go to class.[14]

It also follows that we should reject another familiar idea about consent—the idea that if Y consents to X *v*ing, Y complies with X's desire to *v*, or that Y acquiesces to X *v*ing.[15] A person who consents releases the other from a duty that he owes her, but, as *Borrow* shows, this does not depend on her complying with his desires, or acquiescing in what he does. All that is required is that she releases X from a consent-sensitive duty that he is under. There may be a whole range of reasons why one person releases another from the duties that he is under, and not all of them imply compliance or acquiescence in what the person does.

Similarly, Y might want X to *v* without Y's consent. This is familiar in entrapment cases: in such cases, one person wants another person to act wrongly in order that the wrongdoer suffers the implications of having acted wrongly. One way for me to entrap a person is to get that person to do something to me without my consent where consent is required. If I do, this person does what I want them to do, and yet violates the consent-sensitive duty that she owes to me.

Consider:

> *The High Ground*: Sean always claims the moral high ground in conversation with Vincent. Vincent would thus prefer it if Sean were sometimes to act wrongly, so that he could claim the moral high ground. He leaves his fancy pen lying about, hoping that Sean will take it so that he can take the moral high ground.

Vincent wants Sean to take the pen, but does not consent to the taking. He wants Sean to take the pen without his consent, for only then will Sean act wrongly. In cases where consent-sensitive duties are owed, we can conclude that Y might desire that X *v*s, intend that X *v*s, and will that X *v*s, without consenting to X *v*ing.

Finally, Y's consent to X *v*ing might be given because X wants to *v* and is willing to offer something in return. Consider:

> *Exchange*: Polly offers Wendy £100 if Wendy will let Polly use Wendy's car. Wendy agrees.

Wendy consents to Polly using her car, but not because Wendy wants Polly to use her car. She may prefer it if she gets to keep the £100 without Polly using her car. This is one way in which the ability to consent to X *v*ing can be valuable independently of whether Y wants X to *v*. Y's power to withhold or offer consent gives her something that X may value.

iv) Direct and indirect ways of affecting duties

The third feature of the view is that Y has the power to release X from this duty directly.[16] To understand the difference between direct and indirect ways of releasing a person from a duty, notice that the duties that a person is under depend on her

[14] See, also, D Owens *Shaping the Normative Landscape* (Oxford: OUP, 2012) 172–6.

[15] For this view of consent, see Anderson 'Negotiating Sex', 1408.

[16] For roughly the same idea in the context of authority, see D Enoch 'Authority and Reason-Giving' (2014) 89 *Philosophy and Phenomenological Research* 296.

circumstances. Y can intentionally alter X's duties by altering her circumstances. If she can, X's duties are under Y's control, but they are not directly under Y's control. Y must alter other facts in order to alter X's duties. X's duties are under Y's direct control only if Y can intentionally alter X's duties simply by making decisions about X's duties.

To illustrate the contrast between direct and indirect ways of controlling another person's duties, notice that we can alter another person's duties by altering facts or evidence that give rise to duties on others. Consider:

> *Drown*: Zubin is drowning next to Xavier. Xavier can rescue Zubin at little cost to himself. Yoshi can rescue Zubin, but only at greater cost to himself. Yoshi prefers Xavier not to be under a duty to rescue Zubin, so Yoshi bears the greater cost and rescues Zubin before Xavier has the chance.

Were Yoshi not to bear the cost of rescuing the child, Xavier would have a duty to rescue the child. By rescuing the child Yoshi, in a sense, 'releases' Xavier from this duty. Yoshi does so with the intention of affecting Xavier's duties. Yet Yoshi does not exercise a normative power. He simply alters the facts that gave rise to Xavier's duty to rescue Zubin—the fact that Zubin was in peril.

Similarly, consider:

> *Drown 2*: Xavier reasonably believes that Zubin is drowning in a lake nearby, and that he can rescue her. Yoshi wishes Xavier not to be under this duty, so tells Xavier that Zubin is not drowning. Xavier has good reason to believe what Yoshi says.

Suppose there are evidence-relative duties: duties that we have to respond to evidence that we have that certain acts are valuable. Xavier had an evidence-relative duty to rescue Zubin until Yoshi altered his evidence, 'releasing' him from this duty. But Yoshi does not release Xavier from his duty directly; he does so by altering the evidence that gave rise to the duty.

In contrast, suppose that Zubin has the normative power to release Xavier from his duty of rescue. Zubin can then release Xavier from his duty directly, simply by announcing to Xavier that he is no longer under this duty. Zubin's consent does not alter the facts that gave rise to Xavier's duty: that Zubin is in peril. It directly alters the normative relationship between Xavier and Zubin.

v) Consent without recognizing duties?

Now let us consider an objection to the idea that consent involves the exercise of a normative power. In order for Y to exercise a normative power, Y must know the relevant normative facts, or at least have a true belief about them. The reason is that a normative power involves the execution of an intention directly to affect normative facts. A person can intend this only if she believes that these facts obtain. And her intention is effective only if they actually obtain. In this context, in order for Y to release X from a duty by consenting, Y must know (or at least truly believe) that X owes her a consent-sensitive duty. If she does not, she cannot intend directly to release X from this duty by consenting.

In the light of this consider:

> *Internalized Slave*: Terri consents to be Sandra's slave. Both Terri and Sandra believe that Terri is thus Sandra's slave. Both believe that Sandra is permitted to do with Terri what she wishes, irrespective of consent. Terri loves Sandra. Sandra needs a kidney transplant to save her life. Terri wishes Sandra to take her kidney—she says, truly, that she cannot bear to see Sandra die. As she loves Terri, Sandra takes Terri's kidney only because Terri wills it.

Assume that a person cannot consent to be a slave. On the view that consenting involves the exercise of a normative power, Terri does not consent to Sandra taking her kidney. As she does not believe that Sandra owes her a consent-sensitive duty not to take her kidney, Terri cannot directly intentionally release Sandra from any such duty. But, it might be argued, it is intuitive that Terri consents to the taking of the kidney.[17]

One possibility is that consent operates in different ways in different circumstances. We have seen powerful reasons to support the idea that desiring or willing that a person *v*s and consent to *v* come apart. I can consent to you *v*ing without willing that you *v*, and desiring that you do not *v*. As *Borrow* shows, a person can have reasons to release another person from a duty to *v* that are independent of that person's interest in the other *v*ing. As consent clearly has this role, we should doubt the general identification of willing and consenting: neither willing nor desiring is necessary for consent. Furthermore, one person can will another person to do *v* without the first person's consent. One person can want another to wrong her. This suggests that neither willing nor desiring is sufficient for consent.

Nevertheless, it might be argued that Y willing that X *v*s is sufficient for Y to consent to X *v*ing in the absence of Y's belief that X owes a consent-sensitive duty to Y where X does in fact owe such a duty to Y. We noticed earlier that willing is insufficient for consent. But that is because Y can will herself to be wronged by X *v*ing. This possibility, though, depends on the person believing that she will be wronged if X *v*s. In *Internalized Slave* there is no such possibility. In those circumstances, then, it might be argued that Terri's willing Sandra to act amounts to consent.

The better view, I think, is that Terri does not consent to Sandra taking the kidney. In the absence of the possibility of consent, there may be good reason for Sandra to do what Terri wills even if she cannot offer consent. We might also reasonably conclude that Terri would consent to the taking of the kidney were she able—were she to know that Sandra owes her a consent-sensitive duty not to do so. Hypothetical consent sometimes renders it permissible for one person to interfere with another when a person is incapable of consenting. As Terri does not believe that Sandra owes her a consent-sensitive duty, she is incapable of consenting. These facts may be sufficient to render Sandra's conduct permissible—it is plausible that Sandra does not assault Terri even though she takes her kidney without her consent.

However, whilst Sandra may act permissibly, this case is morally deficient when compared with standard cases of consensual organ transplant. The idea that Terri does not consent picks out the deficiency. The deficiency is that in willing Sandra to act, Terri does not act in recognition that she has control over Sandra's normative situation. Furthermore, when Sandra acts she does not act in recognition that she is governed by a duty owed to Terri.

One way to illuminate this deficiency is to compare the complaint that we have against a person who treats their duties as favours—for example, those who think that paying their taxes is an act of charity. Such a person may act from altruistic motives. They may do as much or more than the person who has a strong sense of justice. Yet there is something defective about the person's conduct. Even though the person does not act wrongly, criticism is warranted. The fact that her giving is an act of 'charity'

[17] For a somewhat related objection, see Westen *The Logic of Consent*, 31–2.

alters the meaning of the action. It indicates that her action does not express the relationship between her and those who her action is intended to help—the relationship of being bound by duties of justice.[18] There is some similarity in the way that Terri's act is morally defective, even if it is permissible.

To summarize: when X is under a consent-sensitive duty to Y, X is under a duty that Y can release X from directly—simply by declaring that X is no longer under this duty. That is what consent amounts to—when Y consents to X *v*ing, Y intentionally and directly releases X from his obligation not to *v*. There may be special circumstances where other things, such as willing, perform a similar moral role to consent. But in standard contexts, where X and Y recognize the consent-sensitive duties that they are under, consent is required to release a person from a duty they would otherwise be under, and consent is the exercise of a normative power.

III. Interests and Consent

A directed duty is a duty that one person owes to another. In standard cases, there is some fact about the person to whom the duty is owed, which is valuable in itself, and that plays a central role in explaining why the other person is subject to the duty. In this sense, there is some truth in the interest theory of rights: the theory that X's right that Y *v* is explained by X's interests.

One simple explanation of consent-sensitive duties appeals to the following idea. Sometimes, Y is permitted to *v* only if X has an interest in Y *v*ing. X will often be the best judge of whether he has such an interest. Y, in that case, ought to *v* only if X consents because only if he does so can he ensure that he complies with his duty only to *v* if X has an interest in Y *v*ing. Let us call this *the independent interest view*.

John Stuart Mill advocated this view. He wrote:

> The reason for not interfering unless for the sake of others, with a person's voluntary acts, is consideration for his liberty. His voluntary choice is evidence that what he so chooses is desirable, or at the least endurable, to him, and his good is on the whole best provided for by allowing him to take his own means of pursuing it.[19]

Mill went on to argue that this explains the limited significance of consent in the case of slavery. A person cannot sell herself into slavery, for to do so would make her unable to ensure, through consent, that the interference by others would be for her own good. Whilst this partly explains consent-sensitive duties, it fails as a complete account of such duties. Whilst the view is obviously not very plausible, it is worth considering different ways in which it fails in order to guide us to a better account.

i) The moral magic of consent

One problem is that this view does not explain what Heidi Hurd calls the 'moral magic' of consent.[20] In at least some cases, consent alters the character of the action

[18] For more on the way intentions alter the meaning of actions, and its relationship with permissibility and blame, see Chapter 2.

[19] *On Liberty and Other Essays* (Oxford: OUP, 1991) 114.

[20] 'The Moral Magic of Consent', 121.

consented to, and through altering its character alters its value. Hurd illustrates this magic by example:

Consent turns a trespass into a dinner party; a battery into a handshake; a theft into a gift; an invasion of privacy into an intimate moment; a commercial appropriation of name and likeness into a biography.[21]

Whilst Hurd is right that consent is transformative, none of her transformative claims is quite true. For one thing, consent is not required to turn commercial appropriation of name and likeness into a biography. I can write a biography of you without your consent. An unauthorized biography is a biography nevertheless. And its value as a biography does not completely depend on whether it is authorized. Consent may nevertheless seem important to the permissibility of the writing of a biography; this does not establish that the value of biographies *qua* biographies depends on whether they are consented to, let alone whether they are biographies at all.

More importantly, consent is not sufficient for the first four transformations.[22] Mere consent doesn't turn a trespass into a dinner party. What is needed is cooperation in a complex joint activity involving eating and conversation. Similarly, consenting to a person taking my property does not amount to giving a gift—I must intend to transfer the property to the other person for free. Even this is normally insufficient for valuable gift-giving—valuable gift-giving depends on the good will of the gift-giver. And an intimate moment is more than an invasion of privacy plus consent—an emotional connection is required.[23]

This illuminates an important question. Consent is often insufficient to secure the value of certain autonomous activities. More is required: voluntary participation in pursuit of a certain aim, for example. A person may consent to another person *v*ing for a range of reasons, or for little reason. Y may consent to X *v*ing without sharing X's end of *v*ing, and even without wishing X to *v*. Where X owes a consent-sensitive duty to Y not to *v*, Y's consent is typically sufficient to render X's *v*ing permissible. But if consent alone cannot make the difference between valuable and disvaluable instances of X *v*ing, why is consent typically sufficient to render it permissible for X to *v*? Why is more not required?

A more plausible view about the transformative effect of consent is that its lack can alter the character of an activity in a negative direction. For example, consent makes the difference between wronging a person and not doing so. This is so independently of what the owner wants. Your taking my property wrongs me even if I want you to have it. Consent must be secured before the taking is permissible. To see this, notice that I can indicate to you that I want you to have something of mine and yet withhold consent. If I do, you wrong me by taking it.

Some might doubt that there could be any reason to do this. But there can be. For example, I might want you to have the property but think it wrong for me to give it to you. Withholding consent does not, in this case, indicate that I do not want you to have the property; it indicates that I am unwilling to do what I want to do given the conflict between what I want and what I believe is required of me. If you take my property without my consent, you wrong me. This is so even if I would be glad that you had taken it.

21 'The Moral Magic of Consent', 123.

22 See, also, R West 'A Comment on Consent, Sex, and Rape' (1996) 2 *Legal Theory* 233, 249–50.

23 A similar thing can be said about the transformative claims in Westen *The Logic of Consent*, 15. For example, Westen wrongly thinks that consent transforms kidnapping into vacation.

The independent interest view, then, wrongly gives consent, or its lack, only a derivative role in explaining wrongness. The importance of consent is not merely that consenting people tend to get things that they want independently of whether they have consented.

ii) The scope of consent

A second problem is that the validity of consent often does not depend on whether the interests of the consenting person, or anyone else, are served. Consent-sensitive duties, and hence the power to consent, have value independently of whether the consenting person will act wisely.[24]

This objection has two strands. One is that it can be wrong to interfere with a person without her consent even if that person is benefited. The familiar problem of paternalism exemplifies this. For example, cosmetic surgery may be in my interests. It is wrong, though, to force cosmetic surgery on me. This cannot be explained by appealing to the fact that I will get less pleasure out of my better looks if cosmetic surgery is forced on me. Forcing cosmetic surgery on a person is wrong even when this is not true.

Furthermore, lack of consent often decisively makes acting in certain ways wrong even if the person who refrains from consenting will be benefited by the relevant actions. Y's consent can release X from a duty owed to Y not to *v* even when *v*ing does not advance anyone's interests. Perhaps consent is not valid if the person's interests are set back to a sufficient degree, for example, if Y is gravely harmed by X *v*ing with Y's consent. But the fact that *v*ing is not in Y's interests is insufficient to establish that it is wrong for X to *v* with Y's consent. For example, if I consent to you giving me a silly haircut, you don't wrong me by giving me the haircut. This is true even if it is completely against my interests, and in no one else's interests, that I have the silly haircut.

The independent interest view, then, has counterintuitive implications for the scope of consent-sensitive duties. Perhaps, though, defenders of the view might respond that interests will best be advanced if consent is treated as decisive, even in cases where a person's decisions are not in her, or anyone else's, interests. This response is unsatisfactory: even if the effects of consent could adequately be explained in this way, the force of consent could not. Intuitively, consent plays a non-derivative role in explaining the cases just discussed.

iii) Consent and advice

A third problem: *the independent interest view* cannot adequately explain the difference between the duty not to *v* unless consent has been obtained and the duty to defer to the judgement of others in determining when to *v*. Suppose that X ought to *v* when it is in Y's interests that X *v*s. The fact that Y is better able to assess her interests than X is a good reason for X to defer to Y's judgement regarding when to *v*. But a duty to defer to Y's judgement whether to *v* need not be a consent-sensitive duty. The distinct qualities of consent-sensitive duties are not well explained by *the independent interest view*.

Our account of the character of consent-sensitive duties helps us to grasp the difference between X's duty not to *v* unless he seeks and follows Y's advice and X's duty not to *v* unless he seeks and secures Y's consent. If X is under a duty to operate

[24] For a contrasting view, see J Raz *Value, Respect, and Attachment* (Cambridge: CUP, 2001) 115.

on Y only when this is in Y's interests, X has a duty to determine what Y's interests are. He thus has a duty to find out what Y's interests are from any available sources, including Y. Suppose that Z knows a great deal about Y's interests. X should seek Z's advice. When Z provides advice, though, he does not provide consent. He indirectly rather than directly alters X's duties: he does so by altering the evidence available to X.

In principle, the same thing could be true of Y: Y might give X advice about her interests without consenting to the operation. So the duty to defer to Y's judgement does not amount to a duty to act only if consent has been secured. The fact that Y knows her interests best might contribute to the explanation why Y's consent must be sought. But as it does not explain why consent rather than advice must be sought, the explanation is incomplete.

IV. Relationships and Normative Powers

To explain consent-sensitive duties we need to explain why one person should have direct control over the rights and duties of others. *The relationship view* explains this as follows: if we are under consent-sensitive duties, others can form special relationships with us by consenting. If Y consents to X that X may *v*, Y signals a certain relationship with X—X is marked out from others as the one who may *v*. This relationship can be valuable. Its value depends on everyone being under a duty not to *v* unless Y consents to them *v*ing. This idea has something in common with David Owens's view that we have irreducible normative interests.[25]

Whilst the value of such relationships can contribute to a full account of consent-sensitive duties, *the relationship view* is not plausible as a complete account of such duties.

i) Relationships and bare wronging

Owens thinks it a virtue of his account, perhaps its central virtue, that it can explain bare wronging, in the sense that he understands it:

> *Bare Wronging*: X barely wrongs Y by *v*ing if X wrongs Y by *v*ing but Y lacks an interest in X not *v*ing.

The relationship view promises to explain bare wronging by explaining how X can have a duty to Y independently of any interest that Y might have in X not breaching that duty. Such duties can exist, it is claimed, because of the relationships they make possible. Neither the possibility, nor the instantiation, of such relationships depends on the duty being complied with.[26]

This idea might initially seem puzzling. The following case helps to illustrate its plausibility:

> *Records*: Dino has a collection of vintage jazz records that he keeps in an outbuilding. As he and Felix are friends, Dino consents to Felix entering the outbuilding to listen to records whenever Felix wants to. When he is sure that Dino and Felix are not there, Nicolas, who

[25] See Owens *Shaping the Normative Landscape*, Part II.
[26] See Owens *Shaping the Normative Landscape*, 147, in the context of promising.

Dino dislikes, sneaks into the outbuilding to listen to the records. Nicolas is very careful not to damage anything. Dino never finds out what Nicolas has done.

It is plausible that Nicolas wrongs Dino. It is also plausible that Nicolas does not set back Dino's interests by listening to the records.

Here is an explanation. One way in which Dino expresses and develops his friendship with Felix is by granting him permission to listen to his records. In doing this, he distinguishes Felix from others. But doing this is possible only if others are under a duty not to listen to the records without Dino's consent. Were there no consent-sensitive duty on everyone not to listen to the records without Dino's consent, Dino would not be able to distinguish Felix from others by releasing him from this duty. As it is valuable for Dino to be able to express and develop his friendship in this way, it is valuable that there is a consent-sensitive duty on everyone not to listen to Dino's records without Dino's consent. The value of there being such a duty is sufficient to justify its existence. Therefore, everyone owes a consent-sensitive duty to Dino not to listen to Dino's records without his consent.

However, although this duty is owed to Dino, Dino's interests may not be set back by the violation of the duty by Nicolas. Here is why. When Nicolas violates the duty, he does not set back Dino's ability to express and develop his friendship with Felix. He does not even erode Dino's opportunities to do this. As he has not consented to Nicolas listening to the records, the distinction that Dino makes between Felix and Nicolas is unaffected by what Nicolas does. It is still only Felix that Dino permits to listen to his records—his special relationship with Dino thus persists. This helps to explain why although Nicolas violates a duty that he owes to Dino, he does not set back Nicolas's interests in doing so.

Before assessing this view, let us characterize the nature of the duty that Nicolas is under more carefully, assuming that there is such a duty and *the relationship view* best explains it.

ii) Reasons and values

The relationship view provides a plausible explanation of bare wronging in at least some cases. One doubt about it is revealed by our discussion in the previous section, about our reasons to abide by prohibitions that are explained by *the relationship view*. When we reflect on whether we have a duty to *v*, we normally reflect on the significance of our *v*ing—normally on the significance of *v*ing for others, or for things that have value. This is because value has a grip on us.

The relationship view, however, suggests that our focus should not be limited in this way. We should focus not on the significance of *v*ing for things of value, but on the signficance of a prohibition on *v*ing for things of value. If a duty not to *v* is valuable, it is wrong to *v*, even if *v*ing itself has no effect on the value that explains the duty not to *v*. But it is more difficult to see how such a duty can get a grip on us. It may be valuable that there is a duty of a certain kind, but such a duty exists only if we could have a reason to comply with it. *The relationship view* cannot explain why we have such a reason, and hence there is no such duty.

This objection has a similar flavour to some objections to some rule-consequentialist and contractualist accounts of duties—those that identify the rules that would be best, or best justified, to groups of people given the implications of adopting such rules. These accounts, it might be claimed, wrongly focus on the value of our being subject to certain rules or prohibitions rather than focusing on the significance of the actions that these rules or prohibitions refer to.

For example, a generally accepted rule prohibiting *v*ing might be best at promoting certain consequences, or it might be easiest to justify to a group of people given the consequences of them abiding by those rules for each of them. But we have no reason to be motivated by such a rule simply on this basis where a particular act has no effect on the good that purportedly justified the rule, or on the facts that made the rule capable of being justified to those subject to it. And if our act has no such implications, we have no reason against performing the act, regardless of the good effects of the rule. If we have no reason against performing the act, we lack an obligation not to perform it.

There is admittedly something unusual in the idea that a person can have a duty to act in a way because it is valuable that he is under the duty, even if violating the duty has no implications for the value that explains the existence of the duty. Yet I think that the challenge to *the relationship view* can be met.

Owens accepts that the value of the relationships that are made possible by Nicolas's duty cannot supply Nicolas with a reason. He denies that this vitiates the duty that Nicolas is under—he has a duty, but lacks a reason to do what he is required to do. In cases like *Records*, he claims not only that Dino lacks an interest in Nicolas refraining from listening to his records, but also that Nicolas lacks a reason not to do so. This is because, for Owens, any reasons for action that Nicolas has are grounded in Dino's interests. As Nicolas does not set back Dino's interests, he does not act wrongly. It makes sense for us not to commit a bare wrong, Owens believes, but this is not because we have a reason not to do so.[27]

The claim that underpins this view is that reasons for action are necessarily directly connected to promoting or protecting value. X having a reason not to *v*, Owens thinks, implies that some value will be set back by X *v*ing, or some value will be advanced if X does not *v*. As cases of bare wronging are cases of where wronging does not set back value, he suggests, we lack a reason not to perform these wrongs.

I doubt that Owens offers the best characterization of *the relationship view* in this respect. If Owens's explanation of bare wronging is right, it can be wrong for X to *v*, and yet no value is set back by X *v*ing. But there are two ways of accommodating this idea. We can sever the link between *v*ing being wrong and X having a decisive reason against *v*ing, as Owens does. However, as the fact that *v*ing is wrong can clearly motivate X not to *v*, we are then required to supply an alternative characterization of the role that *v*ing has in X's practical reasoning. In Owens's account, this is done by the idea that it can make sense for X not to *v*. The 'making sense' characterization, though, is elusive. Owens offers examples, but he does not tell us much about what making sense is, and how it is distinguished from having a reason. And it is not clear how to make progress.

Furthermore, the idea that it can be wrong for X to *v* implies that X is under a constraint against *v*ing. X, if he reasons correctly about *v*ing, will conclude that he is not free to *v*—he is free from external coercion, but he is not morally free, to *v*. It is difficult to see such moral constraints as implying merely that it makes sense for X not to *v*. When we are under a moral constraint, we do not merely think that it makes sense to abide by the constraint.

The second way of making room for *the relationship view* is to sever the link between X having a reason not to *v* and X promoting or protecting value by not *v*ing. This seems the preferable way to understand bare wronging, on Owens's account of it. It

[27] For Owens's account of the contrast between *v*ing for a reason and *v*ing because *v*ing makes sense, see *Shaping the Normative Landscape*, 14–15.

is independently plausible that we can have a reason to *v* without implying that *v*ing promotes or protects value. The fact that things have value provides us with reason to respond to those things in certain ways. But promoting or preventing the setting back of these things may not exhaust the appropriate way to respond to values.[28]

For example, certain valuable properties of persons or things give rise to reasons of respect. When we respect something in virtue of its value, we do not promote that value. For example, it may show a lack of respect to mock a person behind her back. We have a reason not to mock, even though mockery need not set back value.

This also makes room to respond to the challenge mounted earlier—that any putative duties grounded in interests that we do not set back by violating the duties could not get a grip on us. We could respect the fact that it is valuable that we are under a consent-sensitive duty not to *v* by refraining from *v*ing. We respect our duty not to *v* by treating ourselves as constrained from *v*ing even when the value of the constraint that we are under not to *v* is not set back by our *v*ing. This idea is familiar from the idea that respect for the law requires us not to violate it even when doing so does not set back the value that justified the creation of the law. I am not completely confident that this view is right. I find it at least plausible. If it is right, we have good reason to accept *the relationship view* as at least part of the explanation of consent-sensitive duties.

V. Control and Consent

We have already seen that we can value consenting to the actions of others for a range of reasons. For example, in *Borrow*, Betty's consent is given not with the intention of altering which actions Jess performs, but to alter the reasons with which those acts will be performed. A natural explanation is that Betty does not wish to constrain Jess's freedom in order that she gets Jess to do what she wants her to do. In other words, Betty wishes to avoid controlling Jess. In *Records*, Dino gives consent to Felix not because he wishes Felix to listen to his records (though he may wish this), but in order to express his friendship to Felix. These ideas partly explain consent-sensitive duties. They are nicely captured by *the relationship view*.

Although *the relationship view* plausibly captures some ways in which consent-sensitive duties are valuable, it does not plausibly fully explain them. For example, Owens thinks that *the relationship view* can explain the wrongness of rape. Recall *Unconscious Rape*. I noted that it is controversial whether this is a case of harmless wrongdoing. But even if it is not, it is not very plausible that rape is wrong simply because of the harm it causes. We can see this from the fact that the wrong done in *Unconscious Rape* is grave, whereas it is not very plausible that the harm done is equally grave.

And it is more generally true that the gravity of wrongdoing does not track harm. We can see this, for example, from the wrongness of killing. It is much worse for me to die at twenty than to die at fifty—I am deprived of an extra thirty years of good life in the former case when compared with the latter. But the difference in the gravity of the wrongdoing of those who murder twenty year olds when compared with murdering fifty year olds is quite small.[29]

[28] See, generally, T M Scanlon *What We Owe to Each Other* (Cambridge, Mass: Harvard UP, 1998) ch 2.

[29] See, also, J McMahan *The Ethics of Killing: Problems at the Margins of Life* (Oxford: OUP, 2002) ch 3.

This is plausibly because interfering with a person's life in this way without her consent is gravely wrong in itself, independently of the harm it causes. We can see this by noticing the following. It is plausibly wrong to kill a person who has plenty of good life left to live even with her consent.[30] Suppose that this intuitive view is correct. It also seems much more gravely wrong to kill a consenting twenty year old with plenty of good life left to live than a consenting fifty year old. When we remove the fact that the interference is against the person's will, the degree of harm caused is much more significant. This reinforces the importance of the person's will in explaining the gravity of wrongdoing.

X's duty not to interfere with Y's body without Y's consent is not best explained by the fact that such a duty allows Y to form special relationships with others by consenting to such interference by them and only by them either, though. Y is able to form special relationships with others by consenting to bodily interference by them and only by them. But this fact does not plausibly exhaust the significance of the duty not to interfere with a person's body without her consent.

A more centrally important idea is that consent-sensitive duties, if they are conformed with, provide the right-holder with control. We value shaping our own lives, and this is so both in our relationships with others and independently of those relationships. One crucial way in which we can enhance our ability to shape our own lives is to give people control over the important things in them. And one way to achieve this is to regulate interpersonal interference.

There is more than one way in which control explains the wrongness of violating such duties. Suppose that Y interferes with X by *v*ing without X's consent. Y may not want X's *v*ing to occur, with or without consent. She may wish to take her life in a different direction. Suppose that Y scars X without X's consent. X may not have wanted the scars. If he didn't, Y has shaped X's appearance, where X values a different appearance. X wishes to be in control of his appearance.

At root, the explanation of the wrongness of Y's conduct, in this case, may not be interpersonal. X may value being in control of his physical appearance independently of whether anyone else alters it. He may not have wanted the scarring, regardless of whether it came about as a result of Y's act or through an attack by a wild animal.

But there is also an interpersonal dimension to control. X may wish Y to *v* with X's consent, but not without X's consent. Suppose that X did want the scars, and would have consented to Y scarring him. X may nevertheless object to Y scarring him if Y scarred him without his consent. One reason that might be offered is that consent may alter the nature of the action—a version of the 'moral magic' of consent. However, as we have seen, the difference in the nature of the actions involved in consensual and non-consensual interference *just is* the difference between interference that wrongs the person and interference that does not.

To illustrate the problem, recall the falsity of Hurd's claim that consent transforms a theft into a gift. We saw that this is not so in virtue of the fact that I could consent to you taking my property, or to a transfer of ownership, without giving you a gift. Gift-giving involves more than consenting to transfer. Nevertheless, if I consent to you taking my property, you do not wrong me in doing so, gift or not. The value of gift-giving, then, could not explain the moral magic of consent in the property case, it might be argued, for consent weaves its magic even where morally important features of gift-giving are absent.

[30] I will say more about why in Chapter 14.

In response, it might be argued that even if consent to taking is not sufficient for gift-giving, it is necessary for gift-giving. The value of giving and receiving could not be realized without consent. Furthermore, it could not be realized without consent-sensitive duties. We can realize the value of gift-giving only because we are owed consent-sensitive duties regarding property.

Furthermore, a wide range of valuable activities is made possible by consent-sensitive duties. It is only because others owe me consent-sensitive duties regarding property that I am capable of gift-giving, exchanging, selling, lending, sharing, and so on. Consent is necessary for any of these distinctively valuable activities. Consent-sensitive duties constrain us because without them people do not have the option of shaping their lives and relationships by performing the wide range of distinctively valuable activities that depend on the exercise of a person's will.

Whilst there is a great deal of truth in this, it wouldn't explain the difference between the most basic pair of cases where X consents to Y's interference and X does not consent, all other things equal. Consent seems important even when all other things are held equal. The fact that consent makes possible acts that are valuable in virtue of their other morally salient properties would not explain this highly intuitive idea.

The same thing is true of the distinctively disvaluable features of typical acts of interference that are done without consent. A person's lack of consent is necessary for, or at least exacerbates, many different wrong-making features of different kinds of interference. For example, certain kinds of treatment may be humiliating, degrading, exploitative, or dehumanizing. Whether they are, and the extent to which they are, depends in part on whether the treatment is consented to. But mere consent seems sufficient to make interference wrong independently of these further facts.

The wrong of rape illustrates the problem. Consider the argument by Gardner and Shute that the wrong of rape is the sheer use of a person that rape involves.[31] Some might then argue that Y is a victim of sheer use only if Y does not consent. If Y consents, she is not a victim of sheer use.

Gardner and Shute do not believe this—they believe that X can be subject to sheer use by Y even if Y consents. In such cases, they think, Y's consent is sufficient to 'license' the behaviour. But it only licenses the behaviour in law. If Y consents to sheer use by X, they claim, Y wrongly disrespects herself, and X shares in Y's wrong by disrespecting her.[32] Others, though, might claim that if a person consents to be used, this is not sheer use in the relevant sense.

However, even if lack of consent is necessary for sheer use, the wrong of rape does not plausibly depend on sheer use. If X has intercourse with Y without Y's consent, Y is raped regardless of whether she is used. It is not completely clear what Gardner and Shute mean by 'sheer use'. But sheer use implies, at least, that the person raped is used. However, whilst rapists use their victim in many cases of rape, and this fact helps to explain what is distinctively wrong about those rapes, the wrong of rape does not plausibly depend on use more generally. In general, X's wrongful interference with Y without Y's consent does not depend on X using Y. This also seems true of rape.

For example, X might have intercourse with Y without her consent simply because he thinks she deserves to be treated in this way—this sometimes occurs in the context of domestic abuse. It is not clear that X uses Y by punishing her. In general, inflicting harm on a person with the intent to give them what they deserve does not amount to using the person—that is why some retributivists think that punishment on the

[31] See 'The Wrongness of Rape', 16. [32] 'The Wrongness of Rape', 18–20.

grounds of desert is superior to punishment for reasons of deterrence. But even if X does not use Y, X surely rapes Y.

Even if this is not a counterexample, even if there are no counterexamples, the fact that Y did not consent to sexual intercourse seems sufficient to explain why Y is raped without appealing to the further idea that X uses Y. X should not have intercourse with Y without Y's consent regardless of whether he uses her. If he does, he rapes her. Even if he uses her, her lack of consent is sufficient to explain why he rapes her independently of whether she is used.

I conclude from this that the control that Y has if X owes her, and abides by, a consent-sensitive duty not to interfere with her body cannot be explained in a deeper way. We value having this control, and other people respecting our control, simply in itself. When we are subject to consent-sensitive duties, and we respect those duties, we are independent of each other, just in the sense that we can restrict bodily interference by others. This kind of independence is no deeper than the respecting of the consent-sensitive duties that characterize it.

VI. Conclusion

Consent plays a fundamental role in the criminal law. Most of the wrongs that the criminal law is concerned with are consent-sensitive—if the person to whom the duty is owed consents, that person is not wronged. This fact needs explaining. I doubt there is a single explanation available—there is more than one source of consent-sensitive wrongs. But the idea that we value having control over our lives, including, importantly, control over the actions of others who would interfere with us, is central to explaining these wrongs.

12

Coercion and Consent

Coercion and deception can undermine valid consent. When do they do so? Why do they do so? What affects the gravity of the resultant wrongdoing? And when should the conduct that the victim does not consent to be criminalized as a result? Although these questions are general I will explore them in the important and difficult realm of wrongful penetrative sex. The reason is that whilst there are some issues that apply generally across contexts, there are other context-specific issues. A focus on sex helps us to see how complex the issues are in a way that a general account cannot. This chapter is concerned with threats, the next with deception.

There is sharp disagreement about sexual wrongdoing, not only about what we should think, but also about how we should think about it. Some are hostile to the use of my standard philosophical method in this context, especially the use of unusual hypothetical cases. Using this method, some think, trivializes sexual wrongdoing, or fails to show respect to victims of wrongdoing.

In employing this method, I aim at a clearer and deeper grasp of sexual wrongdoing. As we will see, the nature and scope of sexual wrongdoing is by no means obvious. We owe it to victims and potential victims of sexual wrongdoing to use the tools that are best suited to develop a clear and deep grasp of that wrongdoing. The use of examples and arguments, which has helped many of us make progress across moral, political, and legal philosophy, can assist us.

My aim in using examples is the opposite of trivialization—it is to explore not only what makes sexual conduct wrong, but also the facts that can make it gravely wrong. It is regrettable that there has been little systematic work on the gravity of sexual wrongdoing in particular. The criminal law cannot plausibly be used to control all sexual wrongdoing. This is because some sexual wrongdoing is insufficiently serious to warrant state punishment, but also because there are other social and legal mechanisms for regulating and controlling sexual wrongdoing. Criminalization should normally be reserved for the most serious sexual wrongdoing. And the criminal law ought appropriately to distinguish between more and less serious instances of sexual wrongdoing, both by distinguishing offence categories and at the sentencing stage. Understanding what makes sexual wrongdoing more or less serious, then, has great practical importance.

I do not make direct policy suggestions in this chapter. I aim only to explore the limits and gravity of sexual wrongdoing. As we saw in Chapters 6 and 9, decisions about criminalization turn on a range of facts beyond the wrongness of the conduct—especially the effects of criminalizing conduct. Investigating the scope and gravity of wrongdoing helps us to answer a more limited question: the question whether wrongdoers are liable to state punishment if punishing them would be effective. An investigation into the scope and gravity of sexual wrongdoing is an important starting point for a more complete investigation into criminalization.

Section I explores how threats and coercive offers work, and provide an account of when they are effective. Section II responds to a narrow view of which threats undermine consent: when what is threatened is wrong. It shows three ways in which the narrow view is mistaken. Section III is concerned with offers. It explains why offers can be coercive even when it would have been permissible not to make the offer, and the offer improves the situation of the victim compared with its not being made. I leave questions of the gravity of coercive sexual wrongdoing until the end of the next chapter, where I compare coercion and deception cases.

I. Effective Threats

It is uncontroversial that sex secured by threats of death or serious bodily injury ought to be criminalized. Almost everyone agrees that it ought to be criminalized as rape. Historically, the law has been quite restrictive about which other threats render sex criminally wrongful. Typically, legislatures explicitly restrict the relevant threats to threats of violence, or are vague about which threats count. Economic threats, threats of loss of employment, threats to reputation, and threats of prosecution have often been used to secure sex; victims are often traumatized when sex is secured through these threats; and the relevant conduct is often clearly and seriously wrong. Yet the law has often failed to criminalize seriously wrongful conduct of this kind.[1]

One explanation is that it is difficult to draw the line between serious and trivial cases. Line-drawing in this area is undoubtedly difficult, but we should not abandon the task at the outset. Difficult line-drawing problems arise in many areas of the criminal law. These problems do not generally lead lawmakers to abandon the criminalization of seriously wrongful conduct.

The criminal law could expand the range of threats that undermine consent by type—include threats to employment, or to reputation, or of prosecution—and the law may then seem more acceptable. But even if this is the right response it is a compromise that is made for reasons of clarity and certainty. There will be threats that do not fall within these categories that are equally grave and that the law will not capture. At least at first, we should aim to grasp the deeper reasons why certain threats undermine valid consent, and the gravity of the wrongdoing that results. We can then determine what practical measures will best track these deeper considerations whilst preserving a reasonable degree of clarity and certainty.

Threats are normally made either to cause the person threatened to do something, or to cause the person threatened not to prevent the threatener, or another person, from doing something. For example, a threat of violence may induce the victim of the threat to perform a sex act or it may induce the victim not to prevent the threatener from performing a sex act—for example, by escaping or calling for help. Is it morally worse for X to force Y to perform the sex act than to force Y not to prevent X from performing the sex act? Perhaps, but I leave that question aside. For brevity, when I say that X forces Y to have sex with him, I mean to capture both kinds of case.

We are concerned with threats that undermine valid consent to sex. Here is how these threats work: X owes Y a duty not have sex with Y without her consent; X expresses to Y that if Y does not have sex with him, X will execute this threat; X does this in order that Y has sex with him; and in order to avoid him executing the threat, Y has sex with him.

Offers are structurally similar. X owes Y a duty not to have sex with Y without Y's consent; X expresses to Y that if Y does not have sex with him, X will not do something

[1] See, also, S Schulhofer *Unwanted Sex: The Culture of Intimidation and the Failure of Law* (Cambridge, Mass: Harvard UP, 1998) ch 7.

that he has offered to do in return for sex; X does this in order that Y has sex with him; and in order to ensure that he does what he offers to do, she has sex with him.

The question of wrongful coercion is often approached through the unnecessary detour of distinguishing threats from offers. As we will see, it can be wrong to secure sex either through threats or coercive offers, and the wrongness is similar in either case. Given this, we can safely avoid the question how to distinguish threats from offers and concentrate directly on wrongful sex. I will continue to use the language of threats and offers where they seem most appropriate without aiming to make progress on how the distinction is best drawn.

A threat or offer makes sex wrongful only if it is effective in undermining valid consent to sex. In order to establish this, we should investigate what makes a threat effective—what makes it true that Y had sex with X in response to the threat, so that if certain further conditions of wrongdoing are fulfilled, the threat undermines valid consent?

It is obviously insufficient for effectiveness that X threatens Y and X has sex with Y. Y's performance of the sex act may have nothing to do with X's threat. The threat and the sex act must have some relationship with each other. Here is a better view:

> *The Counterfactual View*: A threat or offer is effective if and only if Y would not have had sex with X but for X making the threat.

Counterfactual thinking in the area of sexual wrongdoing is tempting. But we should be wary.[2] A threat can be effective, and can render sexual wrongdoing grave, even when the victim would have had sex with the wrongdoer without the threat, and the sex would not have been wrongful. Consider:

> *Pre-emptive Threat*: Nina goes on a date with Dick, intending to have consensual sex with him. Thinking that she will not consent, Dick threatens Nina with violence. Terrified, Nina responds to the threat by having sex with Dick.

Dick's threat is effective, and it makes sex with Nina wrongful, even though it did not make a difference to whether Nina would have consented.

Perhaps it might be argued that Nina would not have had sex at exactly this time and exactly this way if Dick had not threatened Nina. Nina has a right not only to determine whether she has sex with Dick, but also the time and way in which they have sex.[3] But this does not best explain why the threat is effective and undermines consent in *Pre-emptive Threat*. Where Dick's threat is a dominant and direct explanation of Nina's decision, what Nina would have decided had the threat not been made seems irrelevant.

Here is an explanation. One reason why people owe consent-sensitive duties to each other is to protect welfare. But *Pre-emptive Threat* shows that consent would not do this job well were the *Counterfactual View* true. Even though Nina would have consented to sex with Dick had she not been threatened, the sex she has harms her. We see this when we compare either with the consensual sex that she would have had were she not to have been threatened, or not having sex with Dick at all. In the next chapter, we will see that this is not the only reason to reject counterfactual views of the validity of consent.

[2] In the next chapter, we will see further problems with counterfactual thinking in this area in the context of sex secured by deception.

[3] This idea has affinities with David Lewis's attempt to rescue a counterfactual theory of causation. See 'Causation as Influence' (2000) 97 *Journal of Philosophy* 182. Deficiencies in this view are nicely exposed in J Schaffer 'Causation, Influence, and Effluence' (2001) 61 *Analysis* 11.

The *Counterfactual View* also wrongly identifies the sufficient conditions for a threat to be effective. A decision can counterfactually depend on whether a threat is made in a range of ways. Counterfactual dependence is sometimes insufficient to make a threat effective in the right way to undermine valid consent because the threat is superseded by facts that make consent valid. Consider:

> *Sex Life*: Mike and Jo are in a long-term relationship, and their sex-life has declined. Mike threatens Jo that if she does not have sex with him he will have sex with Jo's sister, who has always been attracted to Mike. They argue, and then reconcile. Because they have argued, Jo sees how bad their sex life has become. They talk through why their sex life has declined. They commit to turning things around, and their sex life improves.

Let us suppose, plausibly enough, that Mike's initial threat is wrongful. Jo's decision to have sex with him counterfactually depends on this threat. But Mike's threat may not be effective in undermining valid consent because it is not the dominant and direct explanation why Jo consents. Rather, it may cause Jo to consent for reasons that make consent valid.

Of course, in cases like *Sex-Life*, consent may be invalid for other reasons—for example, because Jo is in other ways dominated by Mike. I suggest only that consent could be valid in a case like this because the threat has been superseded by the more proximate reasons why Jo decides to have sex with Mike.

When we assess the effectiveness of a threat, then, we should identify its actual role in explaining Y's decision rather than considering what Y would have agreed to had she not been threatened. If Y's decision is a direct response to X's threat, X's threat is effective.

II. Wrongful Threats Without Threatening What is Wrong

Suppose that X owes Y a consent-sensitive duty not to do something and Y does not prevent X doing that thing because of a threat or offer that X has made. Whether X's threat or offer to Y undermines Y's valid consent depends on two things. First, the opportunity that Y has to secure things she has reason to value. And second, the importance to X that he can use his resources to secure performance of the action. These reasons, I will argue, help to explain why threats and offers undermine valid consent to sex in a range of cases where they would not undermine valid consent to other kinds of act.

i) The permissible baseline view

To illuminate and defend this view, I consider a range of ways in which it departs from a familiar narrow view. It might be argued it is wrong for X to secure his ability to act by making an effective threat if and only if X threatens to do something that would be wrongful, or offers to do something that he is required to do. Call this the *Permissible Baseline View*.[4]

[4] Something like this view is suggested in H Hurd 'The Moral Magic of Consent' (1996) 2 *Legal Theory* 121, 144–5. It is also somewhat close to the view in A Wertheimer *Consent to Sexual Relations* (Cambridge: CUP, 2003) ch 8 and L Alexander 'The Moral Magic of Consent II' (1996) 2 *Legal Theory* 165.

Here is the rough idea. If Y is permitted not to do something, and X threatens her that if she does not do that thing he will do something that it is wrong for him to do, X wrongly constrains Y's choices. His decision not to act wrongly should not depend on what she does. Threats undermine consent by depriving their victims of options that they are entitled to have—in this case, the option of X refraining from acting wrongly without Y acting. However, when a person threatens another with doing something that he is permitted to do, he improves her choice situation over simply doing that thing. She cannot complain about him performing the threatened act, as doing so is not wrong. If performing that act is not wrong, it is not wrong to do something that is at least as good for her. By making a threat that he will perform a permissible act if she does not act in a certain way, she has the option that he performs the permissible act. And she has another option—she can avoid him performing the permissible act by complying with the threat. He cannot wrong Y by providing her with an additional option over his acting permissibly, for she can always ensure that he does the permissible act by refraining from complying with the threat. Therefore he does not wrong her by securing her action by threatening her with a permissible act.

Here is the argument more precisely. Suppose that X sincerely and credibly expresses to Y that if Y does not *v*, X will *w*. X thus gives Y two options: either she *v*s or X *w*s. In that case, Y is at least as well off as she would be were X simply to *w*; for Y is in a position to ensure that X *w*s. If X *w*ing is wrong, X wrongly constrains Y's choices. He denies her an option that she is entitled to: the option of X refraining from *w*ing without Y *v*ing.

However, if the effect of X *w*ing is insufficiently bad for Y to make it wrong for X to *w*, it cannot be wrong for X to give Y a broader range of options than he will give her if he simply *w*s. By threatening Y that if she does not *v* he will *w*, X gives Y a broader range of options than she would have were he simply to *w*. She can secure X *w*ing by refraining from complying with the threat, and that would leave her no worse off than she would be were X simply to *w*. She just has an extra option: the option of avoiding X *w*ing by her *v*ing. Her having this option cannot make her worse off. X thus improves her situation relative to the baseline of what it is permissible for him to do by making the threat. Improving her situation relative to that baseline is not wrong.

Two features of this view make it seem attractive. First, it seems generally true that having extra options does not make us worse off. The main value of an option is the value of its content. If the value of the content of an extra option is greater than that of the other options that we have, selecting it makes us better off than we could have been without the option. Thus, having the option makes us better off. If the value of the content of that option is less than that of the other options that we have, we need not select it. So the extra option does not make us worse off. Hence, having an extra option normally leaves us as well off or better than we would be without the option.

Second, if a person is free to perform an act that makes me badly off, I often have reason to prefer it that he has the option to perform a second act that makes me better off than that act. That is so, it might be thought, at least if he would perform the act that makes me badly off were he to lack the option. This seems to support the idea that my interests cannot support a duty on him not to perform the second act. For that is against my interests. Therefore, by performing the second act he does not wrong me.

I argue that neither idea supports the *Permissible Baseline View*.

ii) The disvalue of options

Although options can make us better off, they do not always do so.[5] We know this from:

> *Sophie's Choice*: A Nazi sincerely and credibly tells Sophie that he will kill both of her children, Jan and Eva, if she does not select one to be killed. Sophie chooses Eva to be killed.

The conduct of the Nazi in *Sophie's Choice* seems clearly worse than that of the many Nazis who killed Jewish children. But does he not give Sophie an option that other Nazis failed to provide to mothers? And in that way, does he not do more than other Nazis to ensure that her preferences are satisfied?

But Sophie surely is worse off for having the choice whether the Nazi kills Jan or Eva than she would be were the Nazi simply to have killed Eva (or, for that matter, Jan). And even if she is not worse off, she has good reason not to want to have the choice she is given. The Nazi acts especially wrongly in inflicting this choice on her rather than simply killing one of her children.

Here are three reasons why. First, having the choice is itself distressing—making it involves vividly imagining the death of each of her children in turn, and evaluating how bad that will be. She may attempt to avoid thinking about the choice in this way but this will be very difficult. Making the choice is itself harrowing, then.

Second, in making the choice, she will likely express greater love for one of her children over the other. Even if she does not intend to express this—if she attempts randomly to select one child over the other—she will appear to express greater love for one than the other. This will be both painful, and will harm the child who is chosen to die.

Third, and I think most importantly, through her choice she is involved in Eva's death. It is awful to be involved in one's own child's death in this way. Even when one makes a forced choice, one is still haunted by that choice. Perhaps it might be argued that it is irrational for her to regret being involved where she is not responsible for that involvement. I doubt that this is irrational—as I argued in Chapter 5, our reasons to respond to our involvement in some event do not depend only on our responsibility for that involvement. But even if it is irrational, it is inevitable that she will be haunted by her involvement.

Now compare:

> *Cop Threat*: Bobby, a police officer, has discovered compelling evidence that Han, Yolanda's husband, has committed armed robbery, for which he will serve several years in prison if he is convicted. Bobby tells Yolanda that he will bury the evidence if she has sex with him. To avoid him doing this, she has sex with him.

Bobby is permitted, or even required, to do what he implicitly threatens Yolanda that he will do if she does not have sex with him—to give the evidence to the prosecuting authorities. His doing this will make Yolanda very badly off. He gives her an option to avoid this outcome by having sex with him, and her having this option may seem to improve her situation. How, then, does he wrong her by giving her this option?

The badness of giving her a choice partly explains this. First, as in *Sophie's Choice*, it is distressing for Yolanda to have this choice. She can save her husband from a terrible

[5] See, more generally, G Dworkin 'Is More Choice Better than Less?' (1982) 7 *Midwest Studies in Philosophy* 47.

fate, but only by doing something that she may well be disgusted by. Second, suppose that she does not have sex with Bobby in order to secure her sexual integrity, but in doing so seals her husband's fate. She may well find this distressing and difficult to live with. Third, if she decides not to have sex with Bobby, she will be involved in the trial and punishment of her husband, at least in the sense that she had an opportunity to avoid his suffering this fate.

Now suppose that she chooses sex with Bobby, and she makes her choice according to what she most values. This suggests that she values *her choosing* sex with Bobby more than *her choosing* Han's trial and punishment. But it does not follow that she values sex with Bobby more than Han's trial and punishment, where her choice is not involved, or that she prefers *her choosing* sex over Han's trial and punishment when that is not chosen by her. She may prefer Han being tried and punished where she lacks a choice over whether this occurs to sex with Bobby. The fact that she has a choice makes a difference to the value of what is chosen. For this reason, Bobby may make Yolanda worse off by giving her a choice, and this partly explains why Bobby's threat undermines the validity of Yolanda's consent.

Perhaps it might be argued that our intuitions in *Cop Threat* depend on the fact that Bobby is required to give the evidence to the prosecuting authorities independently of the effect on Yolanda. But extra options can also be regrettable, and can be wrongly provided, in cases where the person creates the option and where there are no independent reasons that make giving the person the option wrong. Consider:

> *Rescue Choice*: Two of Barry's children are drowning in the sea. Barry can't swim. Martha can rescue either of his children, but not both. She asks Barry which child he would prefer to be rescued.

The disvalue of options seems to make it wrong for Martha to ask Barry which child to rescue. She should just rescue one or other of the children. The reasons why having a choice is disvaluable in *Sophie's Choice* also explain why Martha acts wrongly in *Rescue Choice*. This supports the idea that the wrongness of giving Yolanda options in part explains why Bobby acts wrongly in *Cop Threat*.

iii) Acting without justification

The argument from the disvalue of choice shows that the *Permissible Baseline View* is wrong even if we accept the following premise:

> *No Wrong Without Comparative Harm*: if it is permissible for X to put Y in a certain state, X does not wrong her by giving her the choice of being either in that state, or in a better state.

Here I show that we should reject this premise, and this provides a more powerful objection to the *Permissible Baseline View*. Here is the rough idea. Suppose that X makes Y better off than he could permissibly make her by giving her the option of avoiding some bad outcome if she does what he wants. Suppose, also, that X could permissibly make Y worse off than he makes her because doing so serves a certain valuable goal: for example, making Y worse off might protect other people from being even worse off. X's permission to make Y worse off, in such cases, is conditional. He may do so only if he fulfils the goal that justifies making Y worse off—that he protects other people against being even worse off. It would be wrong for him to make Y worse off if he does not achieve this goal. Furthermore, if X makes Y worse off without achieving his goal, he wrongs Y.

To illustrate this view, begin with a different kind of case where one person can make another person worse off only if he achieves a valuable goal:

> *Birth and Joyride*: Sally is about to give birth. Dave can get her to the hospital on time only if he takes Chris's car. Dave take's Chris's car, but does not take Sally to the hospital with it; rather he goes for a fun ride around the city.

Let us suppose that Dave is permitted to take Chris's car to take Sally to the hospital. By taking his car for a fun ride around the city, Dave renders Chris no worse off than he would be had Dave acted permissibly. Some may conclude that Dave does not wrong Chris. These people may still believe that Dave wrongs Sally. But Chris has no right against Dave taking his car for a fun ride around the city.

But this view cannot be right. Chris has a right that Dave does not use his car without his consent. The importance of Sally being taken to the hospital explains why there is a narrow exception to this right. But this does not imply a more general exception that permits Dave to take Chris's car for any other reason. The limit on Chris's right depends not only on *there being* a goal that is sufficiently valuable to justify performing the action; it depends on this goal being achieved. Dave may wrong Chris even if Chris is better off than he would have been had Dave used his car to take Sally to the hospital—say because the joyride is shorter than the ride to the hospital.

It is insufficient to justify harming a person that the person could have been harmed for the sake of some justifying goal where the justifying goal is not secured. The justifying goal cannot do its justifying work if the person acts in a way that does not achieve that goal (at least if the person knows the goal will not be achieved). In that case, the rights infringement has not been justified, and consequently the right-holder is wronged all things considered.

Things are a little bit more complicated in *Cop Threat*, but a similar argument applies. Bobby is permitted to render Yolanda worse off by giving evidence of Han's crime to the prosecuting authorities. Yolanda's interest against Bobby harming her in this way is outweighed by the importance of bringing Han to justice. It does not follow that Bobby may act in any way that harms Yolanda, where he does not bring Han to justice. That is so even if the harm that he inflicts on Yolanda is less than the harm that he could permissibly inflict on her were he to bring Han to Justice. In other words, *if* Bobby is going to bring Han to justice, he may render Yolanda worse off. But Yolanda retains a right against him rendering her worse off if he does not bring Han to justice.

When he threatens Yolanda, he uses the fact that he can make Yolanda worse off than she is to secure unwanted sex with her. Suppose that when he has sex with her, he makes her worse off than she would be were he neither to have sex with her nor to bring Han to justice, but better off than she would be were he not to have sex with her but to bring Han to justice. He cannot justify making her worse off than she would be were he neither to have sex with her nor bring Han to justice by appealing to the value that would be secured by bringing Han to justice. He has not achieved this goal, so he cannot use it to justify making her worse off. Just as in *Birth and Joyride*, when Bobby makes Yolanda worse off without achieving the relevant justifying goal, he violates her rights—specifically, her right that he makes her worse off only if he does so with justification. This explains why Bobby not only violates his professional duty, but also wrongs Yolanda.[6]

[6] It seems that Wertheimer believes that X does not wrong Y in cases like this. See his brief analysis of a somewhat similar case, *IRS*, in *Consent to Sexual Relations*, 182.

Against this, it might be argued that we should not draw conclusions about *Cop Threat* from *Birth and Joyride*. In *Birth and Joyride*, Chris cannot make Dave take Sally to the hospital. When considered from his perspective, the harm that is inflicted on him necessarily comes without the good that could have justified it. In contrast, in *Cop Threat*, Yolanda can ensure that Bobby gives the evidence to the police—she can do so by resisting Bobby's threat. When considered from her perspective, the harm that is inflicted on her does not necessarily come without the good that could have justified it.

But this difference is not decisive, and may be irrelevant. Bobby intends Yolanda to have sex with him. He thus intends to harm Yolanda without doing the thing that would justify harming her in this way. Suppose that Bobby is sincere. After Yolanda has sex with him, he refrains from giving evidence about Han's crime to the prosecuting authorities. He cannot appeal to the value of bringing Han to justice in helping to justify making Yolanda worse off in this way because he intends not to bring Han to justice.

Perhaps it might be argued that this wrongly implies that Bobby would not wrong Yolanda were he to have sex with her and then give the information to the prosecuting authorities. But there is an obvious response to this concern: if Bobby does this, he harms her both by having sex with her that she does not want, and by ensuring that Han is prosecuted. The first harm cannot be justified by the value of Han being prosecuted, for inflicting that harm on Yolanda is unnecessary for securing the goal of bringing Han to justice.

Perhaps, in response, it might be argued that as Yolanda could have avoided Bobby harming her without justification, he has not wronged her. However, the fact that Bobby left it open to Yolanda to bring about the justificatory good that would have permitted him to harm her to a greater degree hardly exonerates him when she, as he intends, does not bring about this good. Again, compare *Birth and Joyride*. Suppose that Chris could have caused Dave to take Sally to the hospital, but he was not required to do this. The fact that Chris could have ensured that Dave secured the benefit that would have justified the harm inflicted on him hardly shows that Dave did not violate his rights.

To reinforce this idea, note that Bobby may be permitted to bring some outcome about that harms Yolanda, but Yolanda may be permitted not to cause Bobby to do so. The fact that Yolanda could do so is, at least in that case, irrelevant. In *Cop Threat*, Bobby has an institutionally grounded duty to bring Han to justice. Yolanda lacks this duty. And given Yolanda's relationship with Han, she has powerful reasons not to harm him. Furthermore, Yolanda has powerful reasons not to harm herself by causing Bobby to bring Han to justice. Bobby may have a decisive reason not to give Yolanda the option of having sex with him where he could otherwise bring Han to justice. Yolanda, in contrast, may have strong reasons to take the option that he gives her. The fact that she could have ensured that Han is brought to justice is, in that case, irrelevant.

Here is another way to put the point. Yolanda has a right that Bobby harms her only if he brings about a justificatory benefit. He harms her without the justificatory benefit. The fact that she could have caused herself to be harmed with the justificatory benefit by refusing to succumb to his threat cannot exonerate him. For she need not have caused herself to be harmed, realizing the justificatory benefit, and she may have good reason not to do so. If Bobby chooses not to bring about the justificatory benefit, he is required not to harm her, and he has violated her right that he not do so.

What if Yolanda *is* required to cause Bobby to bring Han to justice? Has he not violated her rights by having sex with her in that case? The case for this might seem somewhat weaker, but I think that he has still violated her rights. By threatening her, he has given her an opportunity to act wrongly that he hopes that she will take, and if she takes that opportunity he has made her worse off without justification. He ought not to give her this opportunity to act wrongly, especially if he does so with the intention that she takes it. Given this, he can hardly appeal to the fact that it was wrong for her to succumb to the threat in claiming that her rights have not been violated.

The explanation that I have offered for the intuitive view that Bobby wrongfully has sex with Yolanda in *Cop Threat* extends to a wide range of threats to perform permissible acts. Many threats to act permissibly are effective because executing the threat harms the person threatened.

For example, it may be permissible for one person to give embarrassing information about another to the newspapers even though doing so will ruin the other person's reputation. If the first person secures sex from the second by threatening to do this, the first threatens to do something that he is permitted to do. But he is permitted to do this, even though it harms the second, because doing so serves some further valuable goal.[7] If the first person secures sex with the second by threatening this, he harms the second without the justification that he would have were he to give the information to the newspapers, and hence this is a case of wrongful sex.

Similarly, it may be permissible for one person to sack another given her poor performance at work. It would be wrong for him to secure sex with the second by threatening to do this, because the justification that he has for harming her by sacking her cannot justify his having sex with her where this makes her worse off.

The argument also provides at least part of the solution to the more general thorny problem of blackmail.[8] The cases that I have been discussing are just like standard blackmail cases, except that it is sex rather than money that is provided by the victim. Unlike many familiar explanations of the permissibility of criminalizing blackmail, the explanation offered has the merit of explaining in a direct and straightforward way the relationship between the moral wrongness of blackmail and the reasons the state has to criminalize it.[9] A person may be permitted (morally, legally, or both) to perform some harmful act because of the value of that person performing the act, or the value in being permitted to do so. But this does not imply a more general right to use one's permission to perform the act to achieve certain other ends, such as sex or financial transfers, where the value that explains the permission to perform those acts is not secured.

iv) Exploiting weakness

So far, we have seen that X's threats may make sex wrongful even when he threatens to do something that he is permitted or required to do. In such cases, X exploits Y's circumstances—in particular, the circumstances where harming her is permissible for the sake of certain ends—to secure sex with her.

[7] Things get more complicated when the reason why the person has the permission to act is the value of the permission rather than the value of the act permitted. I leave these complications aside.

[8] For an excellent critical overview of existing theories of blackmail, see M Berman 'Blackmail' in J Deigh and D Dolinko *Oxford Handbook of Philosophy of Criminal Law* (Oxford: OUP 2011). I lack the space to consider Berman's solution, which aims to show that the token act threatened is in fact wrongful in virtue of the motivations with which the blackmailer would act.

[9] Berman argues, rightly in my view, that familiar solutions to the problem of blackmail that explain why the law prohibits it, but do not explain why it is morally wrong, are unsatisfying—surely some of the central reasons to criminalize blackmail are the reasons that make blackmail wrong.

In evaluating the significance of a threat, though, we must bear in mind not only the actual costs that a person will bear if the threat is executed, but also her perception of those costs. A person might be vulnerable to threats not because it is possible to harm her, but because it is possible to do something that she believes will harm her, or something that she has a strong aversion to.

Phobias are the clearest example,[10] though the issue extends well beyond this narrow case. Suppose that Y is phobic about X *v*ing. X threatens to *v*. X's threat is likely to be effective. Yet if X executes his threat, he does not do something that Y actually has a reason not to want. A person who is phobic about being in confined spaces does not have a reason to disvalue being in a confined space, for example.

It might be responded that when Y's phobia makes X *v*ing disvaluable, she will suffer if X *v*s. But whilst that is often true, it need not be true. Phobias motivate people because of their perception that they will suffer were the relevant thing to happen. Their motivational effectiveness does not depend on the accuracy of this perception. Confronting the thing that she is phobic about might lead the phobia immediately to evaporate; nevertheless her phobia may have a powerful hold on her.

Similarly, the gravity of the threat in *Cop Threat* depends not only on what Y should rationally prefer. It also depends on her perception of the execution of the threat. Let us suppose that Y acts wrongly in having sex with X—she wrongly participates in his obstruction of justice, and his subversion of his role as a police officer. Y may nevertheless be excused from taking this option, given the consequences for her and those she loves if she takes it, and given the pressure that she is under. If X achieves his goal of having sex with Y, he harms her without justification. The fact that she could have done what she felt compelled not to do is irrelevant.

This is one reason why tests for rape that ask whether a reasonable person would have responded to the threat by having sex with the defendant are underinclusive—they leave people vulnerable to having their weaknesses exploited.

III. Coercive Offers

The argument offered in the previous section does not extend to offers that seem coercive. For example, a hotshot lawyer offers legal advice to a desperate person who is seeking asylum only if she has sex with him. Or a man offers to pay the debt that a woman owes to a gangland boss who is threatening her family only if she has sex with him. Can we extend our analysis to explain these cases?

I'll focus on the following case developed by Joel Feinberg,[11] but the analysis can be extended to the above cases:

> *Expensive Treatment*: Betty's son needs very expensive treatment to save his life that she cannot afford. Don, who is wealthy, offers to pay for the treatment if she has sex with him.

Suppose that Don is permitted not to pay for the treatment. Is it permissible for him to offer to pay for it in exchange for sex? It seems not; but some argue that appearances are deceiving.[12]

One immediately troubling feature of the case is that Betty seems to have no real choice but to accept this exchange. Losing her son is such a bad alternative that sex

[10] On which, see also Wertheimer *Consent to Sexual Relations*, 185.
[11] *Harm to Self* (Oxford: OUP, 1986) 229–30.
[12] See Wertheimer *Consent to Sexual Relations* 175.

with Don does not seem optional. It may seem that what Don does is no different from forcing Betty to have sex with him. Furthermore, Don seems wrongly to exploit the terrible circumstances that Betty is in to secure what he wants from her.

But this does not fully explain the case. Compare:

> *Expensive Treatment 2*: As *Expensive Treatment*, but Don does not ask Betty for sex. Rather, he says: I will pay for your son's treatment; all I ask in return is that you paint my house.

Betty has no real option but to paint Don's house. Yet it does not seem wrong for Don to ask for the house to be painted in return for funding the treatment. What Don does is not morally akin to forcing Betty to paint his house.

It is sometimes thought that the scope of sexual wrongdoing is narrower than the scope of exploitation for property and services.[13] Comparing *Expensive Treatment* and *Expensive Treatment 2* suggests otherwise, at least in some cases. It seems that Don is entitled to seek something in return for paying for Betty's son's treatment, but not sex. But why should it be much worse to leave a person without the option not to have sex than to leave the person without the option not to paint a house?

The answer has to do with the role that sex plays in our lives. I can provide only a partial view of this. We have powerful reasons to protect options regarding sex because it is intimate, and because of the psychological distress that unwanted sex might cause.[14] But this is not the only reason. People value sexual integrity. What I mean by this is not simply that they choose when to have sex and with whom. I mean that their sex lives, as a whole, are governed by certain values and commitments that they endorse. Sexual integrity can be realized in many ways. A person might value a sex life in which she only has sex that she values for its intrinsically valuable properties. Or she might value a monogamous sex life. Or she may value a wild sex life—one in which she has sex with whoever she wants whenever she wants it. As people value, and value deeply, shaping their sex lives according to their values, we have powerful reasons to provide them with adequate opportunities to do so.

House painting integrity is much less important to people. People do not typically value a life of house painting that they value only for its intrinsically valuable properties, or that is exclusive to a particular house, or a wild house painting life—one in which the person paints whichever house she wants whenever she wants. In *Expensive Treatment*, Don leaves Betty without an adequate opportunity to have something she has powerful reasons to value—sexual integrity. This is not true in *Expensive Treatment 2*.

Still, a puzzle remains. Don provides Betty with an opportunity that he could permissibly deprive her of—the opportunity to save her son's life. If he has sex with her, he makes her worse off than she would be were he to pay for her son's treatment with nothing in return. But he makes her much better off than she would be were he to do nothing, as he is permitted to do.

Furthermore, *Expensive Treatment* and *Cop Threat* differ in the following respect. In *Cop Threat*, Bobby threatens Yolanda with harm—by securing her husband's conviction. In contrast, in *Expensive Treatment*, if Don does nothing, he does not harm Betty. We generally require a justification for harming others. We do not generally require a justification for failing to help others; indeed, I stipulated that Betty is not entitled to help from Don. This helps to explain why we are inclined to see Bobby as making a threat in *Cop Threat*, but we see Don as making an offer in *Expensive Treatment*.

[13] Schulhofer thinks there are reasons on both sides. See *Unwanted Sex*, 116.

[14] See Schulhofer *Unwanted Sex*, 117–18.

Nevertheless, Don's conduct is wrong. Here is why. He is permitted to use his resources either to save Betty's son, or for some other goal. However, *if* he chooses to save Betty's son, it is wrong for him to demand sex in return. This is true even though Betty is better off with the conditional offer than she would be without it.

Although this may seem puzzling, conditional requirements of this kind are not uncommon. Compare:

> *Racist's Three Options.* The lives of fifty white people and fifty black people are in peril. Derek, a racist, is the only person capable of saving anyone. He has three options:
> 1) rescue no one;
> 2) rescue only the whites, causing Derek to lose his foot;
> 3) rescue everyone, causing Derek to lose his foot.

Derek, let us suppose, is not required to rescue anyone given the cost to him of doing so. Nevertheless, it would be wrong for him to rescue only the whites. If Derek saves the whites he must save the blacks as well.

This is because if he chooses to save the whites, he can also save the blacks at no extra cost to himself. If Derek is willing to bear the cost of losing a foot for the sake of rescuing the whites, he must also rescue the blacks. This is so simply because if he can rescue fifty people at no extra cost to himself, he must do so.[15] But if Derek is required to rescue the fifty blacks, he makes them better off than they would be were he to take some other permissible option—the option of rescuing no one. The same conclusion is warranted even if Derek must bear some extra cost by rescuing everyone, as long as the extra cost is small.

Derek is free to shape his life in the light of what he values. This explains why he is not required to sacrifice his foot for the sake of rescuing others. Now suppose that he values the lives of the whites more than his foot, and so plans to rescue them. *Given that decision*, he cannot offer the value of his foot as a reason not to rescue the blacks. He must point to something else that justifies his failure to do so. But if doing so is cost-free, or is low-cost, he cannot justify this failure. Therefore, if he decides to rescue the whites, he must rescue the blacks as well.

A somewhat similar idea explains *Expensive Treatment*. Don need not sacrifice his money for the sake of Betty's child. Now suppose that he is willing to do this. He can either rescue Betty's child without demanding sex with Betty, or he can do so and demand sex with Betty. He may keep his money, but if he decides to pay the money in a way that rescues the child, he must do so in a way that protects Betty's control over her sex life.

Here is another way to see this. Suppose that Don forms the conditional intention to give Betty his money to save her child if she will have sex with him. He is then required to drop the condition, pay for the treatment, and receive nothing in return rather than execute his conditional intention. For it is not at all important that he secures sex with Betty—sex that Betty does not want—and it is very important that Betty's opportunity for sexual integrity is protected. Of course, he need not form the intention to pay for the treatment. And it is permissible for him to revise his intention to pay for the treatment. What it is wrong for him to do is to retain the intention to pay for the treatment with the relevant condition.

We can articulate this in the same way as we did in *Racist's Three Options*, though doing so is crude. The 'extra cost' to Don of simply rescuing Betty's child rather than

[15] For a similar analysis of a closely related case, see D Parfit 'Future Generations: Further Problems' (1982) 11 *Philosophy and Public Affairs* 113, 131.

rescuing Betty's child and securing sex is small. The difference in cost to Betty, in contrast, is very large. Imposing this high extra cost on Betty for the sake of the benefit he will secure cannot be justified.

This way of expressing things is crude because it treats Don's inability to secure sex with Betty, sex that she does not want, as a cost to Don. But this way of putting things misleadingly implies that Don suffers a loss when he does not secure sex with Betty under these conditions. Don may want sex with Betty, and may find it frustrating that he cannot secure sex with her. There may even be a sense in which his life would go better if he had sex with her in these conditions. But his failure to be able to secure sex with her in these conditions cannot plausibly support a permission to choose saving her child with the condition of sex over simply saving her child. Either there is no value to Don in securing sex with Betty in these conditions, or if this is valuable to Don, the value is irrelevant in assessing which options are open to him.

Some may doubt the argument offered so far for the following reason. It is often permissible to put conditions on the provision of great benefits others, even when those conditions are of little value to the person offering the benefit, and fulfilling them is very burdensome to the beneficiary. Indeed, this might seem true in the sexual realm.

Consider:

> *Cash for Sex*: Ben wants to have sex with Kath. He offers her £1,000,000 in return. Kath is already well off, but would be much better off with £1,000,000.

It may seem permissible for Ben to have sex with Kath. Even if it is not, this does not seem a case of *coercive* sex in any way that is comparable with *Expensive Treatment*. The main difference between *Expensive Treatment* and *Cash for Sex* is that Betty is left with no real opportunity for sexual integrity. This is not true of Kath. Hence, either Ben acts permissibly, or if he acts wrongly his wrongdoing is nowhere near as grave as Don's. I think he acts permissibly.

The argument in this section also helps to resolve a disagreement about the philosophical foundations of sexual offences. Nicola Lacey suggests that the criminal law should aim to protect sexual integrity.[16] John Gardner and Stephen Shute disagree.[17] They claim that whilst sexual integrity is valuable, a person does not act wrongly as long as they respect sexual autonomy. This is so even if the person exercising her autonomy compromises her sexual integrity.

There is an element of truth in both views. A person need not act wrongly by inducing another person to compromise her sexual integrity for some reward, even if the inducement is certain to be sufficient to lead to the compromise. *Cash for Sex* suggests this. In this sense, Gardner and Shute are right that the law need not protect sexual integrity—it is sufficient that sexual autonomy is protected.

But the value of sexual integrity nevertheless underpins sexual wrongdoing, and helps to explain the role of the law, as Lacey suggests. The value of sexual integrity explains why it is coercive to make certain offers in return for sex, and why sexual wrongdoing occurs when these offers are accepted. Such coercive offers violate sexual autonomy, it might be argued. But the importance of sexual integrity explains why this is true.

[16] 'Unspeakable Subjects, Impossible Rights; Sexuality, Integrity and Criminal Law' in N Lacey, *Unspeakable Subjects: Feminist Essays in Legal and Social Theory* (Oxford: Hart, 1998) 117–124.

[17] 'The Wrongness of Rape' in J Gardner *Offences and Defences: Essays in the Philosophy of Criminal Law* (Oxford: OUP, 2007) 21—see especially fn 27.

Let me summarize the view that has been defended. Suppose that X offers Y that he will *v* if she *w*s. Whether such an offer is coercive depends on two things. First, there is the difference that it makes to Y whether she *w*s or not. This is not simply a matter of the costs that this imposes on Y, but on whether she is left with an adequate opportunity to pursue things that she, for good reason, values, or may value. Second, there is the difference that it makes to X whether Y *w*s or not. Again, this difference is not simply to be understood as a matter of costs. X's reasons to value Y *w*ing do not depend, or do not only depend, on whether Y *w*ing makes X better off. There may be some things that Y could do that make X better off, but, at least in this context, he has no reason to value Y doing these things. Let us call this the *Exploitation View*, because it explains sexual wrongdoing by identifying different ways in which one person may exploit his power over another, or by exploiting another's circumstances.

v) Why the bad effects of moral principles don't falsify them

Perhaps it will be objected that the bad effects of the *Exploitation View* undermine it. Suppose that morality does not give those in Don's position the option of offering their money in return for sex. And suppose that Don is keen to comply with the moral demands that apply to him, but will do what he prefers within the constraints of morality. Now suppose that Don ranks his options as follows:

1) Save Betty's child and have sex with Betty.
2) Keep his money.
3) Save Betty's child without having sex with Betty.

Don will comply with the moral demands that apply to him if he does either 2) or 3). He ranks 2) over 3). So he will choose 2). But 2) makes Betty worse off than 1). A moral obligation that aims at protecting Betty leaves Betty worse off in these circumstances.[18] To put this idea in contractualist language: Betty has a reason to reject a principle that restricts Don from making this offer to her.

This objection seems more important than it is. First note that if it is valid, it also applies in a problematic way to *Racist's Three Options*. Suppose, as I have suggested, that morality requires Derek to rescue the blacks if he chooses to rescue the whites. Suppose also that Derek is keen to comply with the moral obligations that apply to him, but will do whatever he prefers within the range of morally permissible acts. Now suppose that Derek's racist tendencies are very powerful. He would rather rescue only the whites than rescue no one, but he would rather rescue no one than rescue the whites and the blacks. If it is wrong for Derek to rescue only the whites, he will rescue no one. But it is much better that Derek rescues the whites than that he rescues no one. Yet it is not at all plausible that Derek acts permissibly if he rescues only the whites.

More generally, our moral obligations do not depend on the effects of our having those obligations given the actual dispositions that people have. The fact that people who are motivationally deficient will make things worse if certain moral principles

[18] See, for example, Wertheimer *Consent to Sexual Relations*, 180–1 and T Christiano 'What is Wrongful Exploitation?' in D Sobel, P Vallentyne, and S Wall *Oxford Studies in Political Philosophy* (Oxford: OUP, 2015) for views that shape the scope of valid agreements by considering the effects of principles governing those agreements on those they are designed to protect.

apply does not falsify those moral principles. The fact that some racists will rescue fewer people if it is wrong for those in Derek's position to rescue only the whites does not vitiate the moral requirement to rescue both the whites and the blacks.

We can see how implausible it is that moral requirements are sensitive to motivational deficiencies by considering:

> *Cool*: In some world, it is considered very cool to act wrongly. People strongly want to be cool. If it is morally wrong to save people from the dire consequences of extreme poverty, many people will do so, in order to appear cool. If it is not morally wrong to do so, they will not.

It being morally wrong to save people from extreme poverty has excellent consequences. Indeed, there may be very few downsides to this being morally wrong. Those in extreme poverty, it might be argued, have a reason to reject a principle that permits people to rescue those in extreme poverty. Yet it is not at all plausible that this makes it morally wrong to save people from extreme poverty.[19]

It may be that because there are unscrupulous people, the *Permissible Baseline View* would have better consequences than the *Exploitation View*. This does not make the *Permissible Baseline View* true.

vi) Motivation, morality, and the law

The fact that Betty has an interest in Don making the exploitative offer to her, when compared with doing nothing, may provide a reason for the state not to criminalize Don's conduct. Criminalization may make those in Betty's position worse off. Those in Don's position will have an incentive not to make exploitative offers, and this may make those in Betty's position worse off. A law that seems designed to protect Betty thus may end up harming her.

This concern does not extend to all cases. If those like Don are not permitted to secure sex with those like Betty, they will likely fritter away their money on useless projects. A similar concern may be less powerful in the case of hotshot asylum lawyers—those who cannot secure sex with clients may nevertheless go on to represent clients without aiming to secure sex. True, there may be a disincentive to the sexually voracious to become hotshot lawyers. But I doubt that this concern is sufficient to justify a legal permission on hotshot asylum lawyers to secure sex with their clients.

Even if there is a decisive reason against criminalizing Don's behaviour, as some might believe,[20] his conduct may nevertheless be criminally wrong, in the sense that his conduct makes him liable to public blame and punishment. But there may not be such a reason. It is difficult to predict the effects of criminalizing Don's behaviour. Criminalization may incentivize those in Don's position to keep their money rather than making coercive offers to those in Betty's position, and that counts against it. But criminalization may also have countervailing indirect positive effects. Uniform public condemnation and punishment for serious sexual wrongdoing may foster respect for sexual integrity, helping to protect people from sexual wrongdoing. It is difficult to know how great these benefits are, and whether they are sufficient to outweigh disadvantages to those in Betty's position.

[19] This also follows from, and helps to support, the first-personal account of wrongdoing defended in Chapter 3.

[20] Larry Alexander draws a conclusion like this in 'The Moral Magic of Consent II', 170–1.

One of the main ways in which the criminal law is effective in changing behaviour is through fostering and reinforcing attitudes about wrongdoing that directly shape interpersonal relations. This role is at least as important as the provision of direct incentives to people not to act wrongly when they are tempted to do so.

IV. Conclusion

Threats undermine consent because they undermine the value of being owed consent-sensitive duties. The value of such duties to the person to whom they are owed is primarily in being in control over whether others are free to do what the duty conditionally prohibits. The reason why this is valuable is mainly to do with the value of being in control over the non-performance of the relevant acts. The person to whom the duty is owed can prevent its performance by refusing consent, assuming that the person who owes the duty does what he is required to do. She can also make others free to perform those acts, often in the hope that they will be performed. If the person who owes her the duty can secure her consent by making threats, he controls whether she consents, and her control over his conduct is thereby negated, diminished, or made less valuable.

13

Error and Consent

One of the main reasons why threats undermine valid consent is that they undermine the control that the person has over her sex life. Sex secured by error seems in some respects similar. If a person is in error about facts that are relevant to her decision to give consent, her control over the conduct of those who owe her consent-sensitive duties is also negated, diminished, or made less valuable. This is because the value of conduct prohibited by a consent-sensitive duty often depends on facts about the conduct, or about the circumstances in which it is performed. If the person is in error about these facts, she cannot assess their value for herself, and she thus loses control over whether an act that she values is performed. This supports the view that error sometimes undermines the validity of consent.

Yet it is commonly thought that threats have a much more powerful role in undermining the validity of consent than error. And securing the performance of the conduct prohibited by a consent-sensitive duty by threats is generally thought much more gravely wrong than securing that conduct by inducing or relying on error. This is especially true in the context of sexual wrongdoing—many people find it permissible, and certainly not criminally wrong, to rely on error to secure consent to sex in a wide range of cases.

In this chapter I partially support this commonly held view: sex secured by threats is often more gravely wrong than sex secured by error. Yet sex secured by error can be gravely wrong. The familiar restrictive view about when error undermines the validity of consent, both in morality and in law, cannot be sustained. Furthermore, I offer an account of the facts that affect the gravity of wrongdoing in cases of wrongful sex secured by consent and error. Some of the considerations that make sex secured by threat gravely wrong can also make sex secured by error gravely wrong. But these facts are not present in all cases where error has a causal role to play in the decision to consent.

Section I is concerned with different sources of errors, and their relationship to consent. Section II rejects the common supposition that whether an error undermines consent depends on whether that error makes a difference to whether the person consents. Section III explores the view that errors undermine the validity of consent whenever they make a difference to consent. This view is shown to be powerfully counterintuitive. Section IV clarifies an argument that might be offered to defend the counterintuitive view explored in Section III. Sections V and VI explain the interest that people have in being in control over information. Section VII offers an explanation why cases of threat and error that seem otherwise similar are morally different. Section VIII comparatively explores the gravity of wrongdoing in cases of threat and cases of error in a more complete way.

I. The Source of Error

Suppose that X owes Y a consent-sensitive duty not to *v*, and there is some fact, *f*, that is material to Y's consent. Roughly, a material fact is a fact that plays a role in the decision to consent, or would play such a role were the consenting person to be aware of it. Y is in error about *f*. What difference does the cause of Y's error make to the validity of consent? This might seem to depend on X's involvement in the error. At one end of the spectrum, X has no involvement in Y's error at all. X is unaware of *f*, or is unaware of Y's error about *f*. At the other end of the spectrum, X induces Y's error by lying to her about *f*.

Let us focus on cases where the error about the material fact is very important in explaining consent. To explore the first end of the spectrum, consider:

Twins 1: Harry consents to sex with Beth thinking that Beth is her identical twin sister, Elsa. Beth has no evidence at all that she has a twin sister, and is completely unaware that Harry has made a mistake about her identity.

Clearly Beth is not criminally responsible for her conduct. Our question, though, is whether Harry's consent is valid. The answer determines whether Beth non-culpably wrongs Harry, or whether, alternatively, Beth does not wrong Harry at all.

I find the view that Beth wrongs Harry intuitive. His consent is not valid, although Beth reasonably believes that it is. If this is right, Beth wrongs Harry in the fact-relative sense. This view gains support from the following heuristic—if Beth were to know about Harry's mistake, she would not be free (in the sense outlined in Chapter 3) to perform the act. Beth acts permissibly in the evidence-relative sense because she has good reason to believe that Harry has given valid consent.

Perhaps it might be argued that we should distinguish evidence-relative validity and fact-relative validity of consent. On this view, Harry's consent is valid in the evidence-relative sense but invalid in the fact-relative sense. I doubt this is right. To see this, consider whose evidence is relevant to whether Harry has given valid consent. It cannot be Beth's evidence. As we saw in Chapter 11, Section II, whether Harry consented does not depend on Beth's beliefs.[1] But it also cannot be Harry's evidence, for otherwise there would be a sense in which Harry's consent is valid even where he has intentionally been deceived into consenting. So I think that the idea of 'evidence-relative consent' is a bad one.

Those who accept this might conclude that whether consent is valid does not depend on the source of the error. The source of errors, on this view, only makes a difference to culpability and not to fact-relative permissibility. Some might doubt this, though, because we can validly consent to others imposing risks on us. At least in some cases, when we do so, consent seems to extend to the bad results that occur. Consider:

Risky Operation: Elaine has symptoms of a cancerous tumour, but the tumour may be benign. Dr Martha can perform an operation to remove the tumour. There is no way of discovering whether the tumour is cancerous or benign without removing it. If it is cancerous this will save Elaine's life. If it is benign, Elaine will be harmed for little benefit. Elaine consents to the operation. Dr Martha removes the tumour, which is benign.

Had Dr Martha known that the tumour was benign, it would have been wrong for her to perform the operation, and Elaine's consent would have been invalid. But some may find it counterintuitive that Dr Martha wrongs Elaine by removing a benign tumour. Her consent to the operation seems valid.

It seems that if Y consents to X *v*ing where *v*ing involves a risk of harm, and the harm eventuates, the validity of consent to the risk extends to the harm, at least in

[1] See, further, Chapter 11.

this case. Elaine consents to the risk that the operation that Dr Martha performs will harm her with little benefit. If the harm eventuates, Dr Martha does not wrong her in inflicting the harm.

Although this is intuitive, there is a sense in which Dr Martha wrongs Elaine. Relative to the facts, it is wrong for her to perform the operation. We can see this from the standard heuristic for fact-relative wrongdoing—it would have been wrong for her to perform the operation were she to have known all the facts even though Elaine consented to the risk. Elaine's interests explain that fact-relative wrong, so the fact-relative duty that Dr Martha violates is owed to Elaine. So there is a sense in which errors about material facts undermine the validity of consent even in risk cases.

Our inclination to say otherwise is explained by the fact that Elaine has no complaint against Dr Martha if things turn out badly, given that she was fully aware of all of the evidence that Dr Martha had, and consented to her act on that evidence. This is not an 'evidence-relative' sense of consent. We can see this from the fact that Elaine could have consented to Dr Martha acting on the evidence that Dr Martha has, but Dr Martha might have no evidence that Elaine has consented to this—for example, where Elaine has written Dr Martha an email issuing consent, but the email has not yet been picked up.

Furthermore, this is consistent with the view that Dr Martha acted wrongly in the fact-relative sense—Dr Martha owes nothing in response to her fact-relative wrongdoing, but her act may nevertheless be wrong in this sense. Elaine's consent to Dr Martha acting on the evidence that she has does not undermine this judgement.

What this case points to is that consent and validity can attach to different things. Y can consent to X *ving on the evidence that X has about* v. When this is true, X does not normally wrong Y by acting on this evidence. But this does not imply that Y's consent is valid in the fact-relative sense.

These cases suggest that the validity of consent is a fact-relative matter, even if consent can be given to a person acting on evidence that she has. Nevertheless, there are cases where the source of the error affects permissibility. Consider the difference between failing to inform a person about a material fact and lying about it. Sometimes, this can make the difference in wrongdoing. This is commonly thought true, and it is surely sometimes true, in commercial transactions, for example. This should not be surprising, as lying seems distinctly and more powerfully wrong than failing to inform more generally.

Where this is true, though, the person who secures the transaction in the light of an error does not act in a way that is wrong in the fact-relative sense if she is in ignorance of the error. We can see this from the standard heuristic: were the person to know all of the facts, she would be permitted to act.

This suggests that consent is invalid in all cases where the person acts in a way that would be fact-relative wrong were the person unaware of the error. But the source of the error can make a difference to permissibility in cases where the act would be fact-relative permissible were the person unaware of the error.

I will mostly leave aside questions regarding the source of a person's error, not because these questions are unimportant, or that the answers to them are obvious, but only because my attention is elsewhere. I will focus primarily on cases where Y is in error about some material fact; X knows that fact; X could, but does not, inform Y of that fact; and Y consents. I will mention differences that lying might make only in passing.

II. Counterfactual Views

As in the case of threats, there is a tempting view that the moral significance of error to consent depends on whether consent counterfactually depended on the error. And as in the case of threats, this temptation should be resisted.

Consider this simple view:

The Counterfactual View:

Suppose:

1) X owes Y a consent-sensitive duty not to *v*.
2) Y consents to X *v*ing.
3) Y is in error about some fact *f*.
4) X has the relevant state of mind about *f* and about Y's error, and could inform Y of *f*.
5) Y would not have consented to X *v*ing if Y had known *f*.
6) X *v*s.

Then, and only then, is Y's consent to X *v*ing invalid because of Y's error about *f*. If so, X wrongs Y by *v*ing.

This view has some attractions that draw on the significance of errors outlined in the introduction to the chapter. The fact that X owes Y a consent-sensitive duty suggests that it is valuable that Y is in control over whether X is under a duty to *v*. This suggests that she has an interest in it being wrong for him to *v* without her consent, and it being permissible for him to *v* with her consent. The primary interest that she has in this is in controlling whether he is free to *v*. Her interest in having control over his duties, though, plausibly depends on the level of information that she has about his *v*ing. But that is so only where that information made a difference to whether she consented. If she would have consented even with the information, she does not disvalue the performance of the relevant action, and hence her consent is valid.

Furthermore, this version of *The Counterfactual View* has some plausible implications. It picks out the difference between completely irrelevant errors and some errors that seem to undermine valid consent in a seemingly plausible way—by considering whether those errors made a difference to the person's decision to consent. It might thus be claimed that it offers Y all the control she could want over her decisions.

It is commonly objected that *The Counterfactual View* fails because it is overinclusive.[2] This objection might be thought forceful because it offers Y a great deal of control at X's expense. But what interest of X is threatened by the view? It might be thought that it insufficiently protects X's interests in keeping information about *f* private. But here is an initial response: this view does not require X to disclose any information at all. It only requires him to refrain from *v*ing. It might then be objected that the view is insufficient in protecting X's opportunity to *v*. But the fact that X owes Y a consent-sensitive duty to *v* already implies that X's interest in *v*ing is insufficiently important to deny Y control over whether X *v*s. So if the objection is to succeed, it needs careful defence.

Later, I will suggest some ways in which these responses are inadequate. But many who think that *The Counterfactual View* is too expansive typically think that counterfactual dependence of consent on the error is necessary for error to undermine the

[2] See, for example, A Wertheimer *Consent to Sexual Relations* (Cambridge: CUP, 2003) ch 9. Something quite close to *The Counterfactual View* is defended in T Dougherty 'Sex, Lies, and Consent' (2013) 123 *Ethics* 717.

validity of consent.[3] As in the case of threats, this is not so, and for similar reasons. Whether an error undermines the validity of consent depends on its actual role in the person's decision to consent, not on what the person would have done were she to have known the fact.

Consider:

Twins 2: Harry consents to sex with Beth thinking that Beth is her identical twin sister, Elsa, to whom Harry is married. Beth knows that Harry thinks that she is Elsa, but chooses not to inform him because she thinks it fun to pretend to be her sister. Harry has always fantasized about having sex with Beth, and would have consented had he known who she was.

The Counterfactual View implies that Harry's consent is valid, and thus Beth does not wrong Harry. This seems false. Harry's error alters the meaning that the sex act has for him. He thinks that the act is part of his ongoing sexual relationship with his wife when it is not. The fact that he would have had sex with Beth is irrelevant because the sex he would have had with her would have had a profoundly different meaning for him had he known Elsa's identity.

Here is an objection. In the previous chapter, we saw that the comparable *Counterfactual View* about threats is objectionable because it does not secure the role that consent has in protecting people from harm. But, it might be argued, Harry is not harmed in *Twins 2*, and so *The Counterfactual View* has not been shown to be objectionable in deception cases.

Here are two replies. First, it is not completely clear whether Harry is harmed. I suggested in Chapter 10 that an event can harm a person even if that event does not affect that person's experiences. Harry, then, is plausibly harmed in *Twins 2* even if he does not discover the mistake that he has made. Second, and more importantly, we saw in Chapter 11 that wrongdoing does not always involve harm. A person is entitled to control her own life. Even if Beth has made Harry no worse off than he would have been in the relevant world where she did not deceive him, she wrongly interferes with the control that he has over his own life. So even if *The Counterfactual View* is not inadequate in securing one role that consent has, it is inadequate in securing another role that it has.

Another response to *Twins 2* expands *The Counterfactual View* by amending the test in the light of the following observation: although Harry would have consented to sex with Beth were he to have known who she was, he would not have consented to sex with a person where he was unsure whether the person was Beth or Elsa. It might be thought that this counterfactual explains why Harry's consent is invalid in *Twins 2*.

This amendment may have the right implication in *Twins 2*. But whilst this is an improvement, it does not get to the root of the problem. The problem in *Twins 2* is that Harry is deceived about a fact that makes a significant difference to the meaning that the sex act has for him. Sex with Beth and sex with Elsa have completely different meanings for Harry, even though he would happily consent to sex with either.

We can bring this insight to bear to show that the amended test also has the wrong implications in some cases: cases where a person would consent to sex even in the case of uncertainty. Consider:

Swingers' Deception: Yolanda and Terry are in a relationship with each other. They have intimate sex with each other, and this is central to their relationship. They also attend parties

[3] See, for example, D Archard *Sexual Consent* (Oxford: Westview, 1998) 46.

together where people have sex whilst wearing masks. Sometimes they end up having sex with each other by chance. Xavier pretends to be Terry, and Yolanda has sex with him believing this to be an intimate encounter.

Yolanda is willing to have sex with a person where she is unsure whether that person is Terry or someone else. Yolanda would consent to sex with Terry on this basis. But Xavier clearly wrongs Yolanda. Sex with Terry has a special meaning to Yolanda. The value of the sexual encounter to her depends on its being with Terry. Xavier denies Yolanda control over the meaning of her sex life.

The Counterfactual View wrongly reduces the importance of consent to control over whether one has sex or not regardless of whether one is in error about facts about the sex one has. But it also matters that one is in control of the meaning of one's sex life. And that depends on one not making certain errors about the sex one actually has. Later, we will see that this helps to explain why *The Counterfactual View* seems too broad.

III. The Conventional View

Even if I am right that *The Counterfactual View* does not describe necessary conditions for wrongful sex by error, it might describe sufficient conditions for wrongful sex by error.

i) Intuitions

It is not intuitive that error undermines consent in all of the cases where *The Counterfactual View* is satisfied, and this is true in sexual and non-sexual contexts.

Consider these examples:

Sex with Married: Yolanda believes that Xavier is single. She consents to sex with him. She would not have consented to sex with him had she known that he was married.

Sex with Poor: Yolanda believes that Xavier is rich. She consents to sex with him. She would not have consented to sex with him had she known that he is poor.

Racist Sex: Yolanda, who is anti-Semitic, believes that Xavier has no Jewish heritage. She consents to sex with him. She would not have consented to sex with him had she known that he has a Jewish mother.

Many people believe that Xavier does not wrong Yolanda even if he lies about the relevant facts in some or all of these cases. And many of those who believe that he does act wrongly also believe that Xavier's conduct ought not to be criminalized.

Intuitions are similar in comparable property cases. Consider:

Married Visit: Yolanda believes that Xavier is single. She consents to him spending time with her in her beach hut. She would not have consented to him doing so had she known that he was married.

Poor Golfer: Yolanda believes Xavier is rich. She consents to Xavier using her private golf course. She would not have consented to Xavier doing this had she known that Xavier is poor.

Racist Sale: Yolanda, who is anti-Semitic, believes that Xavier has no Jewish heritage. She sells Xavier her house. She would not have consented to the sale had she known that he has a Jewish mother.

Again, many will find Xavier's conduct permissible in some or all of these cases, and very few people will believe that this conduct is sufficiently serious to fall within the scope of the criminal law.

In the realm of sexual wrongdoing, criminalization is common, and commonly endorsed, in two kinds of case. One is the case of mistaken identity that we have already considered. Here is a simple abstract version:

> *Identity*: Yolanda consents to sex with a person believing that person to be Zac, when really the person is Xavier.

Legal systems typically criminalize some cases of these kinds. The criminal laws often have further restrictions—for example, Yolanda's conduct is criminal only if Yolanda is sexually intimate with Zac, or knows Zac personally.

The other involves deception about the sexual nature of the conduct, such as:

> *Bogus Treatment*: Yolanda believes that Xavier is giving her medical treatment. Xavier is performing a sex act.

These cases are sometimes called cases of fraud in the *factum*, and this is contrasted with fraud in the inducement, where criminalization is generally rejected.

ii) Are the legal cases special?

It is tempting to explain why consent is invalid in *Identity* and *Bogus Treatment* in a 'technical' way. The contrast between error about identity or about the nature of the act on the one hand and error that is not about these things might be explained as follows. The identity of a person or nature of an act is robust, in the sense that changes in the properties of that person or act do not alter the identity of the person or nature of the act. I am the same person whether or not I am wearing a hat, for example. Similarly, sex has the same nature whether done in the day or at night.

Y gives consent to a particular person and to do a particular thing. Her consenting to one person doing something cannot be transferred to others. Her consenting to one thing being done cannot be extended to other things. In contrast, if Y consents to X *v*ing, and Y was in error about properties of X or properties of *v*, or circumstances in which *v*ing would occur, Y has still consented to X *v*ing. In consequence, Yolanda's consent is not valid in cases like *Identity* and *Bogus Treatment*, but is valid in cases like *Sex with Married, Sex with Poor*, and *Racist Sale.*

But whilst the metaphysical claims that this view rests on may be valid, this idea does not adequately explain why there is a moral difference between errors about the identity of a person or the nature of the act on the one hand and properties of the person or the act on the other. What is required is a deeper analysis of the reasons why errors of the former kind are particularly important whereas errors of the latter kind are not, given the function of consent.

There are differences in the properties of people and acts in *Sex with Married, Sex with Poor*, and *Racist Sex*. In these cases, Yolanda does not consent to exactly what she gets. For example, in *Sex with Married*, Yolanda consents to sex with a single man and gets sex with a married man. Why should her consent to sex with a person with one set of properties be valid when the person has another set of properties? Any good answer is not metaphysical, but moral.[4]

[4] See, also, Wertheimer *Consent to Sexual Relations*, 206–9.

This conclusion can be reinforced: the contrast between the nature of an act and its properties often does not make a significant moral difference. Compare these two variations on *Bogus Treatment*:

Bogus Treatment (Object): Xavier deceives Yolanda that she needs to be penetrated with a surgical device in order to cure her from a fatal disease. He puts a curtain over her and penetrates her with his penis. She thinks she is being penetrated with the surgical device.

Bogus Treatment (Motive): Xavier deceives Yolanda that penetration with his penis is necessary to cure Yolanda from a fatal disease. She consents to being penetrated with his penis for this reason.[5]

Perhaps Xavier's conduct is not quite as bad in *Bogus Treatment (Motive)* as *Bogus Treatment (Object)*. But the difference between these cases is not profound. Criminalization seems warranted in both cases. Yet in *Bogus Treatment (Motive)*, Yolanda is not deceived about the nature of the act, but only about its properties—Xavier's motive for doing it.[6]

Similar judgements are plausible in cases outside the sexual realm, even if sex has some special moral significance. Consider the following variation:

Bogus Treatment (Collection): Xavier deceives Yolanda that she needs a medical procedure which involves inserting a small camera in her ear to cure her from a serious illness. Inserting the camera is harmless. Xavier is collecting photographs of the inside of people's ears for fun.

The conduct in *Bogus Treatment (Collection)* does not seem anywhere near as bad as the conduct in the other variations on *Bogus Treatment* that we have considered. Yet it does still seem seriously wrong, and it is plausible that the conduct ought to be criminalized.

To summarize, one common view is that *The Counterfactual View* is implausibly broad, both as an account of when error renders consent invalid for moral purposes, and even more so as an account of when the resulting wrongdoing is sufficiently serious to warrant criminalization. Nevertheless, some kinds of deception are sufficiently grave to undermine valid consent—many people who reject *The Counterfactual View* endorse criminalization in at least some variations on *Bogus Treatment* and *Identity*. Many also endorse criminalization in variations on *Bogus Treatment* where the error does not make a difference to the nature of the act. And whilst error may render conduct more gravely wrong in cases involving sex, error seems to undermine the validity of consent in non-sexual cases as well.

All we really have here is a set of intuitions about some cases, though. We do not have an explanation why some cases seem wrongful and warrant criminalization, why others seem wrongful but do not warrant criminalization, and why a further set of cases do not seem wrongful at all. *The Counterfactual View* has implications that many find implausible. Yet this may not be decisive. In order to know whether it is, we need a deeper investigation why error need not undermine valid consent.

IV. Comparing Errors and Threats

Before getting to the explanation, let us clarify and strengthen an argument offered earlier for *The Counterfactual View*. This argument suggests that we should reject our

[5] This is a simplified version of what happened in *Boro v Superior Court*.

[6] See, also, J Feinberg *Harm to Self* (Oxford: OUP, 1986) 300. At the time of *Boro*, California did not criminalize cases of fraud in the inducement, and hence the defendant was acquitted. California amended its criminal code soon after to criminalize the conduct in *Bogus Treatment (Motive)*.

intuitions that sex is not wrongful, or not seriously wrongful, in cases such as *Sex with Married*, *Sex with Poor*, and *Racist Sex*.

The argument has four elements. First, consent to sex is normally required to give people control over their sex lives. Second, threats and error equally undermine this control. Third, if consent would be required were the person to know the information she is in error about, the interest in control is sufficient to defeat the interests that others have in performing the relevant act without consent. Fourth, the interest that people have in not providing information to each other is adequately protected because they can avoid providing this information by refraining from having sex.

To understand the third element, note that if Y knows all of the relevant facts, and Y does not in fact consent only because of the information we are concerned with, X is required not to *v*. X's duty not to *v* does not depend on Y's reasons for not consenting, even if they are bad or obnoxious.

Recall:

> *Racist Sex*: Yolanda, who is anti-Semitic, believes that Xavier has no Jewish heritage. She consents to sex with him. She would not have consented to sex with him had she known that he has a Jewish mother.

Some think that Yolanda's consent is valid, because the reasons for that error that she makes would only give her an obnoxious reason for not consenting. But now compare:

> *Racist Sex II*: Yolanda, who is anti-Semitic, believes that Xavier has no Jewish heritage. She consents to sex with him. Before having sex with her, he reveals that he has a Jewish mother. She immediately withdraws her consent only for this reason.

Yolanda refuses to consent simply due to her anti-Semitism. Yet in the absence of actual consent, Xavier is required not to have sex with her. Her withdrawal of consent is decisive even though she withdraws it for an obnoxious reason. If Xavier has sex with Yolanda, by threat or use of force, he surely rapes her. And this is true even if the threat or use of force does not inflict any further harm on her.

In the light of this, here is the defence of the idea that counterfactual dependence of consent on an error is sufficient for consent to be invalid that we are considering. The fact that Xavier owes Yolanda a duty not to have sex with her in *Racist Sex II* is best explained by the importance of Yolanda having control over her sex life. The importance of sexual autonomy is decisive, even when Yolanda's exercise of autonomy is governed by obnoxious reasons. Yolanda's sexual autonomy defeats any reason that Xavier has to override Yolanda's decision, including any interest that Xavier has in sex with Yolanda and any interest in Yolanda not having the power to determine whether Xavier has sex on obnoxious grounds.

But, the argument suggests, Yolanda's sexual autonomy is just as seriously undermined in *Racist Sex*. She is not given the opportunity to control her sex life according to her own values and judgements by being deprived of information that would make all the difference to her decision whether to have sex with Xavier. Thus, if Xavier acts in a seriously wrongful way by having sex with Yolanda in *Racist Sex II*, he also acts in a seriously wrongful way by having sex with her in *Racist Sex*.

This analysis can be extended to all of the cases that we have considered so far. In all of these cases, we can imagine comparison cases where Yolanda is not in error and thus does not consent. In all such cases, Xavier is not released from his duty. If autonomy considerations are central to explaining why consent is required in the cases where Yolanda does not make an error, why does the same value not support the wrongness of the relevant error case?

V. Autonomy and Information

Even if this argument succeeds in showing that there is no moral difference between *Racist Sex* and *Racist Sex II*, nothing like *The Counterfactual View* follows. Here is one reason why: not only do people have an interest in having control over the duties of action that others owe them, they have an interest in having control over the duties others owe them to provide them with information. *The Counterfactual View* satisfies the first interest, but at the expense of the second.

Y can control the information that others are required to provide her with by having the power to waive her right to information. Because of this Y's waiving of the right to information makes her consent valid, even though her error would otherwise have made her consent invalid.

Consider:

> *Rebound*: Yolanda doesn't have sex with people who have just ended a long relationship. As Yolanda is a friend of Xavier's friend, Xavier knows this about her. She meets Xavier in a bar and asks him not to tell her anything about himself. Xavier and Yolanda have consensual sex. Yolanda would not have consented had she known that Xavier had just ended a long relationship.

Yolanda's consent is valid even though she would not have consented had she known of a fact that Xavier could have informed her about, for she has waived her right to the information.

A person can waive his right to information actively or tacitly. We expect to be informed of certain facts in certain contexts and not in others. This depends in part on conventions. There are contexts in which we expect to be informed of all of the facts; in others we expect to be told only those things that we ask about. A person may tacitly waive a right to be informed of certain pieces of information that would be important to her because of these conventions. She can avoid waiving the right tacitly by asking for the information.

As with consent to an action, however, the waiving of the right to information may be valid or invalid. This depends on the value of the relevant convention. Conventions where people waive information can be valuable, or they can lead to destructive exploitation. Y might waive her right to be informed of *f* by X, and consent to sex with X, and yet X may wrong Y if he has sex with her without informing her of *f*.

A second reason why the argument does not support *The Counterfactual View* has to do with different ways in which facts might affect consent: they might do so by giving the person a normative reason not to consent, or by giving the person a motivating reason not to consent, or by having a causal effect on a person's decision without supplying a reason of either kind. Error in the last kind of case does not have the same effect on autonomy as it does in the first two. The explanation is that both autonomy and well-being are sometimes enhanced if we are deprived of information that would cause us to act in a way that is insensitive to our values and plans.

Consider:

> *Headache*: Xavier and Yolanda are in a loving relationship and have consensual sex. Yolanda suffers from acute irrational anxiety about Xavier's health. Xavier has a very mild headache. Before sex, he tells Yolanda that he feels great. He knows that had he told Yolanda about his headache she would not have enjoyed sex, and would not have consented as a result.

Yolanda's consent to sex is not plausibly invalidated by Xavier's lie. A natural explanation is that although Xavier's headache would have had a psychological effect on

Yolanda, causing her not to consent to sex with Xavier, she would not have regarded Xavier's headache as a reason against having sex with him. For this reason, Xavier's lie does not undermine Yolanda's autonomous choice to have sex with Xavier: her response to his headache would not have been autonomous. Yolanda's consent is valid even though if Xavier had told Yolanda about his headache and Yolanda then refused to consent to sex, Xavier would have wronged by having sex with her.

The same idea is true in non-sexual contexts. Consider:

> *Flying*: Xavier flies a light aircraft. He offers to take Yolanda up in his plane. The plane was recently infested with rats. Yolanda has a great fear of rats. If Xavier told Yolanda about the rats, she would not be able to enjoy the flight, and so would not consent to be taken up. Xavier does not tell Yolanda, and they have a fun flight together.

Yolanda's consent to be taken up in the plane is valid.

Again, Xavier not telling Yolanda about the rats does not seem to interfere with her autonomy; it helps to protect it. The fact that the plane was rat infested is not a reason for her not to fly, and she would not regard it as a reason. Were she to know about the rats, her knowledge would interfere with her autonomy, in that it would interfere with her ability to do something that she values.

VI. Privacy

Even if these arguments are right, a close cousin of *The Counterfactual View* survives.

> *The Counterfactual View II*: If X owes Y a consent-sensitive duty not to *v*, and Y is in error about a fact, *f*, and Y would have regarded *f* as a decisive reason not to *v* were she to have known about it, and Y has not validly waived her right to be informed of *f*, Y's consent to X *v*ing is not valid.

This view does not make the counterfactual dependence of consent on error a necessary condition of valid consent, so it is not vulnerable to the objection in Section II. It has an exception for the valid waiving of the right to information. And it is concerned only with motivating reasons and not causes.

This view still seems broad, though, for it implies that sex in cases like *Racist Sex* is wrongful. One element of the defence of *The Counterfactual View* we have been exploring concerns the interest that people have in not providing information. Earlier, I suggested a quick argument that might be offered why *The Counterfactual View* is not vulnerable to challenges from privacy: no one is required to provide the relevant information, only to refrain from sex with those who would otherwise act on it. Let us explore this argument more carefully.

One reason why many duties are consent-sensitive is that it is not typically costly for people to refrain from violating those duties. If X owes Y a consent-sensitive duty not to *v*, Y has a great deal of control over whether X *v*s. The scope of these duties depends both on the value to Y of having control over whether X *v*s, and also by any interests that X might have in not being subject to such a duty. X's interest in not being subject to such a duty is typically his interest in doing what the duty would proscribe.

For example, the duty not to have sex with a person without consent is explained both by the importance of Y having control over her sex life and the fact that X's interest in having sex with Y where she does not choose to have sex with X is (at the most) much weaker. Sex with unwilling partners is not typically valuable to either person, even if one person may think that it is!

We have already seen some reasons why Y may lack an interest in having information that would make a difference to her decision to consent to sex. Now consider X. If consent is undermined by every error that would determine whether the other person consents to the activity, the only way for X to engage in the conduct that the duty prohibits, *v*, is to find a partner who will consent to X *v*ing despite the relevant facts. There may be few or no people who are willing to consent to X *v*ing because of these facts. Thus X will be unable ever to *v*.

There are facts about almost any person that would put almost any other person off from having sex with him or her. If errors always undermined the validity of consent, consent is almost never valid. People may not have a powerful interest in having sex with anyone in particular, on any particular occasion. But they do have a powerful interest in having adequate opportunities to develop a sex life. This includes the ability to form relationships with others where a person gradually reveals things that at first are kept private.

The concern with privacy is especially powerful for those who will be victims of discrimination if they are required to reveal all of the facts about themselves. Consider:

> *Racists*: Hasan, an Arab, lives in a very racist society, where non-Arabs assume that all Arabs are swindlers, and Arabs are a very small minority. No one will trade with Arabs. Hasan conceals that he is an Arab, and Jonathan trades with him. Jonathan would not have traded with him had he known that Hasan is an Arab.

Jonathan's consent to the transfer of his property is not plausibly undermined by Hasan's deception. Jonathan has no interest in not trading with Arabs, despite the fact that he is unwilling to do so; prejudices are not reasons. It is very costly to Hasan to be under a duty only to trade with those who are willing to do so knowing that Hasan is an Arab—he will be able to trade only with other Arabs, and that will severely restrict his autonomy and welfare.

A similar thing can be true in the case of consent to sex. It is sometimes very costly for a person to refrain from all sex that would not have been consented to if the person had revealed certain information. For example, in many very sexist societies, rape victims are ostracized from their communities. A rape victim has a very powerful interest in keeping secret her victimization. Her ability to marry and to have children will be severely hampered if others know that she has been raped. *The Counterfactual View II* condemns her to a life in which she has little prospect of future sexual relationships, marriage, and children in virtue of the pervasive sexual norms in that society. This is surely a clear exception to *The Counterfactual View II*.

To take a less extreme case, note the pervasive difference in attitudes to men and women who have had many sexual partners. This sexist norm already hampers the sexual autonomy of women. Women are less sexually free, in the light of this norm, because sex comes with a reputational price. *The Counterfactual View II* significantly raises this price. Thus, in sexist societies, *The Counterfactual View II* severely restricts the sexual autonomy of women—if they choose to have sex earlier in life, they will be hampered in finding sexual partners later in life simply because of obnoxious pervasive attitudes about women and sex. Their sexual autonomy is significantly increased if they are permitted to have sex earlier in life and then lie about it later.

VII. Error and Meaning

Now consider an objection to this argument that might seem to support *The Counterfactual View II*. There are some people who lack adequate opportunities to have consensual sex in prejudiced societies, because others are aware of the relevant facts about them. Consider those people who are victims of rape in sexist societies where the information about them is publicly available. They may lack adequate opportunities for a sex life unless they are permitted to threaten others to have sex with them. But it is not at all plausible that they are permitted to threaten others to have sex with them.

This suggests that the interest in a meaningful sex life cannot defeat *The Counterfactual View II* on its own. It must be shown that there is an important difference between typical cases of sex secured by threats and sex secured by error. To understand why there is such a difference in typical cases, we need a better grasp of the reason why sex by error is sometimes seriously wrong. That will allow us to see why sex secured by error is sometimes not wrong or not seriously wrong. We will then see how this idea extends to sex secured by threats.

Compare two cases, one where the validity of consent seems not to have been undermined and another where it seems clear that it has. Here is a case where the error seems trivial:

> *Sex and Telly*: Herbert is in a long-term sexual relationship with Enrico. He consents to sex with Enrico, not realizing that he will miss his favourite television show. He would not have consented had he realized this. Enrico knew that Herbert would not have consented had he so realized.

Here is a case where it seems much more serious:

> *Undercover Cop*: Bill, a police officer, infiltrates a patently non-dangerous group of eco-warriors in order to discover whether they are up to no good. In order deeply to embed himself in the group, he starts a sexual relationship with Mike. When the operation ends, after it is discovered that the group have no violent motives, he disappears.

Obviously, one could imagine circumstances where a police investigation is sufficiently important that it might justify conduct like this. This is not such a case (and the real-world case on which it is based seems not to be such a case either).[7] Though not everyone agrees, it seems clear to me that Mike's consent to sex is not valid in this case, and that Bill seriously wrongs him.

The fact that there is a big intuitive difference in the gravity of the wrongdoing in these cases should lead us to doubt *The Counterfactual View II*. That view implies that consent is not valid in either of these cases. But even were this true, we should doubt that *The Counterfactual View II* properly explains them. There is normally some relationship between the facts that determine whether conduct is permissible and how gravely wrong it is when it is not. *The Counterfactual View II*, though, tells us nothing about the gravity of wrongdoing in these cases. And so we should doubt that it explains why they are wrong even if they are.

The explanation of the difference between the cases is not to do with what these people would have chosen were they to have known the facts, but rather with how deeply the error they make undermines the meaning that the act has for them as part of their sex life. In *Sex and Telly* Herbert's error does not undermine the meaning that the sex act has for him. He is not deceived about any of the facts that motivate him to have sex with Enrico. So the meaning of the act as part of his sex life is not

[7] In the real case, which was widely reported, officers of the Metropolitan police deceived several women in a left-wing environmental organization into long-term sexual relationships in order to infiltrate the organization. As part of an out of court settlement, the Met issued a statement apologizing unreservedly, and acknowledged that the relationships were 'wrong and a gross violation of personal dignity and integrity'. See the report in *The Guardian*, Friday 20 November 2015 available here: <https://www.theguardian.com/uk-news/2015/nov/20/met-police-apologise-women-had-relationships-with-undercover-officers>.

undermined. He simply fails to get something else that he might want more at that time: to watch his favourite television programme. In contrast, Mike values the sex he has as part of an authentic relationship between people who are committed to the same ideals. But he values something that is not valuable in this way, given that he is simply being used for ends he is opposed to. The actual reasons that Bill has for sex with Mike are in conflict with the reasons that he thinks he acts on, and this gives rise to a stark divergence between the meaning that he assigns to the act and centrally important facts about it.

This analysis also helps to explain the puzzle that I introduced above. We need an explanation why it is normally wrong to use threats to secure sex in cases where it is permissible to rely on error. A solution to that puzzle involves considering the meaning that the act will have in the different cases. Compare *Sex and Telly* with:

> *Sex and Telly II*: Herbert is in a long-term sexual relationship with Enrico. He consents to sex with Enrico, not realizing that he will miss his favourite television programme. He then discovers that the programme is on, and withdraws his consent. Enrico then threatens Herbert with violence to secure sex with him.

Sex and Telly II involves serious wrongdoing, where *Sex and Telly* involves at most very trivial wrongdoing. Here is why. In *Sex and Telly II*, if Herbert has sex with Enrico only because he is threatened, the value of the sex act is completely undermined. The threat transforms the quality of the act—he will value it only insofar as it avoids Enrico carrying out his threat, and he will not see it as having any value as a part of his relationship.

Later, we will see that even threats need not have this effect on the meaning and value of a sex act, and this explains why sex secured by threats is sometimes not seriously wrong. But at least in typical cases, trivial errors do not undermine the value and meaning of a sex act for a person, even where the person would not have consented were she not to have been in error, whereas effective threats often do undermine the value and meaning of that act.

VIII. The Gravity of Sexual Wrongdoing

Suppose that X has wrongful sex with Y because X has made an effective wrongful threat or offer to Y, or because Y is in error about some fact that undermines the validity of consent. What considerations affect the gravity of X's wrongdoing?

Answering this question is extremely important, for at least three reasons. First, the strength of our reasons to criminalize wrongdoing depends at least in part on the gravity of the wrongdoing. Some sexual wrongdoing may be insufficiently grave to warrant criminalization at all. Second, the demands of fair labelling require us to decide not only whether some sexual wrongdoing ought to be criminalized, but also whether it ought to be criminalized as rape. And this depends on gravity. Third, the magnitude of punishment that a person renders herself liable to also depends at least in part on the gravity of wrongdoing.

A complete account of all of the facts that affect the gravity of sexual wrongdoing is well beyond the scope of this chapter. I leave a range of important questions aside; most importantly, those concerned with the *mens rea* of the offender. But I will investigate some issues that are central to cases involving coercion and error, both because they are independently important, and in order to assist us in comparing such cases.

i) The effects on victims

It might be argued that the gravity of sexual wrongdoing depends on the effect of the wrongdoing on the victim, or on the effects that the wrongdoer could reasonably have predicted his wrongdoing to have. Many people think that rape is wrong in virtue of the fact that rape blights the lives of victims, leading to severe psychological trauma, depression, and suicidal tendencies. They might argue that the gravity of an instance of sexual wrongdoing depends either on its actual effects, or on the effects that the wrongdoer could reasonably have predicted it to have, or on both.

These facts do make a contribution to the gravity of sexual wrongdoing. The psychological impact of the sex will often depend, at least in part, on the prospect of the threat being carried out—sex with a knife to one's throat, for example, is especially terrifying because of the vivid prospect of being killed, and terrifying attacks may well typically have worse effects on their victims.

Sex in error often seems less bad, simply because the act itself is not typically traumatic at the time; any trauma comes about later, when the person discovers her error. In some cases, this trauma can also be severe. Some of the women who later discovered that they had been used by undercover police officers to infiltrate environmental organizations in the real-world version of *Undercover Cop* reported profound feelings of violation and trauma. But in those cases, the wrong seems more severe in part for this reason.

The psychological effects of sexual wrongdoing, and hence its effects on the well-being and autonomy of victims, depend on psychological differences between victims and differences in their support networks. If the gravity of sexual wrongdoing depends primarily on its effects, these differences are important in determining the gravity of the wrongdoing.

It is plausible that these things do make a difference to the gravity of wrongdoing—it is worse to have wrongful sex with a person who is psychologically more fragile because of the expected effects that the wrongdoing will have. The view that gravity is solely determined by the effects of the wrongdoing is less attractive. There are inherent qualities of wrongful sex that affect the gravity of wrongdoing independently of its effects. This should not be surprising given that well-being and harm are themselves not reducible to experience, wrongdoing is not concerned only with harm, and the importance of consent is not reducible to its role in protecting people from suffering and promoting happiness.[8]

There are several ways to illustrate that this is also the intuitive view. Here are three. First, the view that the gravity of a rape depends only on its effects has the implausible implication that it is *much* less bad to have wrongful sex with a person who will not suffer grave psychological effects than a person who will. But even if there is a difference in gravity between these cases, the difference does not seem profound. Consider the rape of a person who has been involuntarily intoxicated, and who does not remember the rape occurring as a result. It is hard to believe that this rape is not very grave because the rape has less serious effects on the victim. Similarly, even if the victim in *Undercover Cop* did not discover that she was duped, and there was no likelihood that she would discover this, the wrongdoing is serious.

Second, consider a victim who is raped several times by several men who threaten her with violence if she attempts to resist, as is the case, for example, in the most serious cases of trafficking. The acts of the last perpetrator might have less additional effect

[8] See Chapters 10 and 11.

on the victim than the earlier rapes. Suppose that they do. It is not very plausible that the acts of the last perpetrator are significantly less wrongful as a result. It might be thought that this conclusion is warranted only because the rapists act together, and are thus jointly responsible for all of the rapes. But the same conclusion would equally be warranted in cases where the last rapist arrives late on the scene, without his having participated in the earlier rapes.[9]

Third, many sexual assaults have effects on a person for the remainder of their lives. The view that the gravity of the wrongdoing depends on its effects implies that it would be much less bad to rape a person later in life than earlier in life because the negative psychological effects of the latter rape would not last as long as the psychological effects of the former. Again, this is hard to believe. Compare killing: it is much more harmful to kill a person who would otherwise have lived for many happy years than to kill a person who would otherwise have lived for fewer less happy years. The difference in the gravity of these wrongs is much less pronounced.[10] The same thing is true of rape.

Some might doubt that the gravity of sexual wrongdoing depends in any way on its effects. Here is why they might draw this conclusion.[11] Sexual wrongdoing does not merely cause victims to react negatively; the negative reactions of victims to rape are warranted. They are warranted in virtue of the wrongness of the conduct. And the gravity of these reactions ought to be proportionate to the gravity of the wrongdoing. So the gravity of the wrongdoing does not depend on the gravity of its effects—on the contrary, the gravity of the *warranted* effects of sexual wrongdoing depend on the gravity of the wrongdoing. As unwarranted effects of sexual wrongdoing cannot affect its gravity, the gravity of sexual wrongdoing does not depend on its effects.

This argument is not persuasive for two reasons. First, the gravity of wrongdoing depends in part on its warranted effects independently of the facts that make these reactions warranted. The fact that rape victims are warranted in feeling violated by their assailants does not make this effect of rape irrelevant to the gravity of wrongdoing. Warranted reactions can still be regrettable, and can exacerbate the gravity of the wrongdoing. Compare grief. The grief of the parents at the killing of a very small child is warranted, but it also helps to make the killing of very small children especially grave.

More importantly, the gravity of sexual wrongdoing depends in part on its unwarranted effects. For example, victims of rape often experience deep but unwarranted feelings of shame and guilt for the attack they have suffered. These feelings can be debilitating. The fact that the feelings are unwarranted does not make them irrelevant to the gravity of wrongdoing—the fact that rape has this effect on victims provides a reason against committing rape, and helps to explain the gravity of the wrongdoing.

Overall, the effect of sexual wrongdoing makes a difference to the gravity of the wrongdoing, but it is not the only thing that matters.

ii) A doubt about the gravity of the threat

One thing that might seem to matter to the gravity of wrongdoing secured by threats is the gravity of the threat. An analogous idea seems plausible in the case of coercive offers: the gravity of the wrongdoing depends on the gravity of the situation that the

[9] As may have been the case in *Johnson v State*, 94 SW3d 344 (Ark App 2002).

[10] See, also, J McMahan *The Ethics of Killing: Problems at the Margins of Life* (Oxford: OUP, 2002) ch 3.

[11] For related discussion, see J Gardner and S Shute 'The Wrongness of Rape' in J Gardner *Offences and Defences: Selected Essays in the Philosophy of Criminal Law* (Oxford: OUP, 2007).

person will be left in if the offer is not fulfilled. For ease of expression, I will focus on the gravity of threats, but what I say can be extended to coercive offers. If the gravity of a threat makes a difference to the gravity of sexual wrongdoing, we can also see why sex secured by threats is often more gravely wrong than sex secured by error.

It seems obvious that the gravity of the threat makes a difference to the gravity of sexual wrongdoing secured by that threat—sex secured by a threat of death seems worse than sex secured by a threat of loss of employment. But is this true independently of the effects that these different threats typically have on their victims?

Let us begin with a doubt. Suppose that X threatens Y that he will *v* if Y does not have sex with him, intending that she responds to the threat by having sex with him. If his threat is effective, and Y has sex with him, he does not execute his threat. As X intends Y to respond to the threat, he does not intend to *v*. And as his threat is effective, he does not in fact *v*. How can the gravity of his wrongdoing then depend on the gravity of *v*ing, given that he neither *v*s, nor intends to do so?

To illustrate this concern, consider:

> *Two Rapes*: Harry threatens Jane with a broken arm if she does not have sex with him. Ivan threatens Kate with two broken arms if she does not have sex with him. Harry and Ivan are equally confident that their threats will be effective. Both threats are in fact effective. Harry and Ivan thus rape Jane and Kate respectively. Jane and Kate are identical in all salient respects. They are equally terrified by the encounters, and equally traumatized afterwards. The encounters thus have equal effects on their lives afterwards.

Obviously, it is worse to break both of a person's arms than it is to break one of their arms. But can this make a difference to the gravity of the rapes?

The argument offered above might lead us to think not. The wrongdoing that Ivan threatens is graver than the wrongdoing that Harry threatens. But Ivan does not intend to break two arms, and he does not in fact break two arms, just as Harry does not intend to break an arm, and he does not in fact break an arm. Their threats are made in order to secure sex with their victims. What they threaten does not occur, and they do not intend it to occur. What, then, is the difference between them?

iii) Offender and victim dispositions

Some people argue that the gravity of sexual wrongdoing depends on the degree of involuntariness or unwillingness of the victim.[12] This might be thought to support the view that the gravity of the threat affects the gravity of the wrongdoing. If X wrongly secures sex with Y, the gravity of his wrongdoing depends on how unwilling Y was to have sex with X. If X secures sex with Y using a less serious threat, Y was less unwilling to have sex with X than if X secures sex with Y by issuing a more serious threat. Therefore, those who issue graver threats commit more serious wrongs than those who issue less grave threats.[13]

This argument fails. One reason is that Y's degree of voluntariness does not depend on the gravity of X's threat. We are not entitled to conclude from the fact that Y responded to a grave threat that she was powerfully unwilling to have sex with X. That depends on her disposition to respond to a range of threats. If X secured sex with Y by issuing a grave threat, but Y would have responded in the same way to a trivial threat, Y was not powerfully unwilling to have sex with X. For example, in *Two Rapes* we are

[12] See Feinberg *Harm to Self*, 300. [13] See Archard *Sexual Consent*, 52.

not entitled to conclude that Kate is less willing to have sex with Ivan than Jane is with Harry. That depends on whether Kate would have had sex with Ivan were she threatened with a broken arm. Her response to Ivan cannot tell us that.

Perhaps it might be argued that the gravity of the threat is a good rough proxy for how unwilling the victim was to have sex with the person who threatened her. But this argument in favour of the view that the gravity of wrongdoing is sensitive to the gravity of the threat is doubtful for two reasons. First, it seems intuitive that the gravity of X's threat makes a difference to the gravity of his wrongdoing independently of how willing the victim was—Ivan's wrongdoing seems worse than Harry's even if Kate would have responded to the threat of a broken arm in the same way.

Second, the view that the gravity of wrongdoing depends on willingness runs up against a problem with the idea that sexual wrongdoing depends on how a person would have decided were she not threatened. Recall this case from Chapter 12:

> *Pre-emptive Threat*: Nina goes on a date with Dick, intending to have consensual sex with him. Thinking that she will not consent, Dick threatens Nina with violence. Terrified, Nina responds to the threat by having sex with Dick.

Dick wrongs Nina even though Nina would willingly have had sex with Dick without being threatened. The qualities of the actual encounter, and not what Nina would have done were other things to have occurred, determines the wrongness of the conduct. The same thing seems true of the gravity of sexual wrongdoing. If the defendant secures sex by threatening violence, the fact that the victim would have had sex with him were he to have threatened much less, or nothing at all, seems irrelevant.

Here is an alternative view. It might be argued that if X issues a grave threat to Y, he demonstrates that he is willing to have sex with Y even if she is very powerfully unwilling to do so. This is not true if he issues a much less grave threat. But this idea also runs into difficulties. First, a person who makes a less grave threat does not demonstrate that he is unwilling to secure sex with a victim who is powerfully disposed not to have sex with him. That depends not on the actual threat that he uses, but on the threats that he would have been willing to use were Y to have refused. Suppose that X secures sex with Y by making a less grave threat. Had this threat failed, he would have made a much graver threat. X's attitude to Y's willingness to have sex with him seems no better in this case than it is in the case where he makes the graver threat in the first place.

Second, cases like *Pre-emptive Threat* not only show that the gravity of sexual wrongdoing does not depend on what the victim would have done, they also show that it does not depend on whether the wrongdoer conditions his conduct on what the victim would have done. Consider the odd variation where Dick threatens Nina in *Pre-emptive Threat* only on condition that she would have sex with him without being threatened. His conduct is nevertheless wrong.

Finally, whilst a person's dispositions can make a difference to some kinds of moral judgement, they do not normally make a difference either to whether an act is wrong, or to the gravity of wrongdoing. We can see the first thing clearly from Derek Parfit's case:

> *Coffee*: D, a violent person, forms an intention to get a coffee at his local coffee shop. V is the barista. D asks for his coffee and V serves him. If V had not served him, D would have killed V and served himself.[14]

X has terrible dispositions. But these dispositions do not make his act of buying coffee wrong. More generally, it seems doubtful that dispositions can affect either whether

[14] *On What Matters* vol 1 (Oxford: OUP, 2011) 216.

an act is wrong, or the gravity of the wrongdoing.[15] Dispositions typically make a difference to the way we judge people, but not their acts. When bad dispositions do not result in actions, they cannot make acts wrongful, or affect the gravity of wrongdoing. The fact that X would threaten Y with a graver wrong to secure sex cannot affect the gravity of his sexual wrongdoing when he threatens less. The gravity of his wrongdoing more plausibly depends on what he actually threatens than on what he would threaten were these threats ineffective.

Earlier, I rejected the view that the victim's willingness to have sex with the wrongdoer determines the gravity of the wrongdoing. But there is a closely related view that seems true. My central reason for rejecting the significance of the victim's willingness to have sex with the wrongdoer is that this willingness might play no role in the victim's decision to succumb to the threat. The threat might render the victim's willingness causally irrelevant. *Pre-emptive Threat* exemplifies that possibility. But the fact that a threat is causally effective in explaining a person's decision to have sex does not imply that facts that would have rendered her willing to have sex with the wrongdoer are causally ineffective.

We have already seen that causally effective errors need not undermine the value of a sexual encounter, as exemplified by *Sex and Telly*. This is so where other facts about the encounter that are more valuable are also causally effective in the right way. We now see that the same thing can be true in the case of threats. Consider:

> *Mockery*: Paul and Mary are seventeen years old. They are have been dating for a while. Paul wants to have sex with Mary, but Mary feels she is not ready. Paul tells Mary that if she does not have sex with him he will tell her friends, who will mock her. Paul has sex with Mary.

There are different explanations why Mary might decide to have sex with Paul. On one variation, the threat plays no causal role, or only an indirect causal role, in explaining Mary's decision. Alternatively, it may completely dominate other explanations of Mary's decision—she has sex with Paul only to avoid mockery and for no other reason.

In another variation of the case, Mary decides in part because of the threat, but in part in virtue of the fact that she is sexually attracted to Paul, and wants to develop their relationship in this way. If the threat is causally significant in Mary's decision, Paul's sex with Mary may be wrongful. But the wrongdoing is less grave because of Mary's other causally effective motivations. A similar thing might be true in cases where Mary responds to Paul's threat simply because she is not strongly disinclined to have sex with Paul.

This helps to explain why many people are not inclined to see all wrongful sex secured by threats as rape, and to see some sex secured by threats as insufficiently serious to fall within the scope of the criminal law. A victim may have been disposed to have sex with the wrongdoer, or only weakly disposed not to do so, and these dispositions may play an important role in explaining her decision to have sex with the wrongdoer. This can be true even if she is threatened, and the threat is causally effective. Her dispositions, in that case, make a difference to the gravity of the wrongdoing, not simply because she has those dispositions, but because those dispositions play an important role in shaping her decision to have sex with the wrongdoer.

[15] Not everyone agrees. In 'The Doctrine of Illicit Intentions' (2006) 34 *Philosophy and Public Affairs* 39, Alec Walen argues that dispositions can make a difference to wrongdoing. For further doubts, see V Tadros 'Responses' (2013) 32 *Law and Philosophy* 241, 287–8.

This helps us better to understand the relationship between the role of threats and error in undermining consent. Causally effective threats and causally effective errors need not undermine the validity of consent, and if they do the wrongdoing may not be grave, because they need not undermine the meaning and value of the sexual encounter. They do not do so if the person also acts on more positive values that shape the sexual encounter. This helps to show why the comparison between error and threats that was used to support *The Counterfactual View* fails: it relies on the implicit assumption that when other things are held equal between cases of threat and cases of error, we will retain the intuition that sex secured by threats is seriously wrongful. That is not so where we hold constant the fact that the sexual encounter is also shaped by more positive values of the person who responds to the threat.

iv) Options

Recall *Two Rapes*. Perhaps it might be argued that Ivan's wrongdoing is graver than Harry's because of the options that they leave their respective victims with. Jane has these options: either have sex with Harry or suffer a broken arm. Kate has these options: either have sex with Ivan or suffer two broken arms. Kate's options are worse than Jane's. Ivan causes a person to have a worse set of options than Harry. Therefore Ivan's wrongdoing is graver than Harry's.

In response, some might argue that it is valuable for a person to have extra options, or better options, only if she will select the extra option, or the better option. On this view, Kate's options are worse than Jane's only if Kate would select the option that Jane has, but that she lacks, were she to have it—in this case the option of a broken arm. If Kate would not select a broken arm were she to have had Jane's options, Jane's options are no better for Kate than her current options. If that is right, Ivan's wrongdoing is graver than Harry's only if Kate would have selected a broken arm had Ivan threatened only that. As it is stipulated that Jane and Kate are identical in all salient respects, Kate would not have selected a broken arm had she had Jane's options. Therefore Ivan's wrongdoing is no graver than Harry's.

This response seems to rely on the mistaken idea that one's only reason to have an option is that one will select the option. A person might prefer having more options on a menu to fewer, for example, because then the choice that she makes will be an expression of her autonomy. The act of selecting between options may, in itself, enhance the value of the option selected. We see the selection-independent value of options even more clearly in big life choices. It is better to live in a society where I choose to be an academic rather than one where I am assigned the job of being an academic. In the former society, the decision to be an academic is an expression of autonomy. This is not true, or much less likely true, in the latter society.

However, the fact that options have selection-independent value has limited importance in cases of sexual wrongdoing. In order for an unselected option to contribute to the expression of my autonomy, my unselected option must have sufficient value. The value of choosing to be an academic is not enhanced by the provision of extra valueless options, such as the option of breaking my arm with a hammer.

In the case of serious threats, the alternative options are typically valueless. Kate has little reason to value Jane's better option of suffering only a broken arm if she would not choose this option. This extra option could hardly improve the value of her choice to have sex with Ivan. Furthermore, the fact that Jane may be torn between her options, where Kate is not, hardly makes things better for Jane. In fact, it may make things worse. As we saw when considering *Cop Threat* in the previous chapter, when one is presented with awful options, deliberation is painful, and one may prefer it that one's fate is not the product of one's deliberations.

The selection-independent value of options may make a more significant difference in cases where the threat is much less grave. A person who has sex to prevent a much more trivial threat being executed might be more inclined to see the sex that she has as an expression of her autonomy than one who has sex to prevent a much more serious threat being executed. But this would only explain why the gravity of the threat affects the gravity of wrongdoing in cases where threats are less serious. Beyond a certain level of threats, it would lack explanatory power.

Overall, I find it hard to believe that Ivan's wrongdoing is worse than Harry's because of the options they make available to their victims. Where sex is secured through a threat of serious harm, the value of a set of options to the victim does not seem inherently morally important.

v) Exploiting one's ability to act wrongly (and related ideas)

Here is another idea. Suppose that Harry and Ivan sincerely threaten their victims. The earlier suggestion that they did not intend to harm their victims is, then, false. They conditionally intend to harm their victims—if Jane and Kate do not respond to their threats. As Ivan conditionally intends to do something worse than what Harry conditionally intends to do, his subsequent wrongdoing is graver.

One doubt about this idea is that it implies that the gravity of a threat can affect the gravity of wrongdoing when the threat is sincere, but not when it is insincere. The effectiveness of their threats depends not on sincerity but on credibility. But, it might be argued, the gravity of sexual wrongdoing does not depend on whether the threat that a person makes is sincere. If one person rapes another by putting a gun to her head, the gravity of the wrongful sex may depend on whether he intends to pull the trigger, but the difference does not seem profound.

Here is a second doubt. Suppose that Harry and Ivan make sincere threats—they conditionally intend to inflict the harm threatened on their victims. It is no doubt worse for Ivan to form his conditional intention than it is for Harry to form his, simply in virtue of what he conditionally intends. But it is not clear how this difference can affect the gravity of the sexual wrongdoing when the threat is effective, and the relevant condition is not fulfilled.

Compare:

> *Two Robberies*: Larry and Mike are both desperate for money. Larry intends to rob a bank. He also intends that if the robbery is unsuccessful, he will kill his rich uncle to secure his inheritance. Mike also intends to rob a bank. He also intends that if the robbery is unsuccessful, he will kill his rich uncle and his rich aunt to secure his inheritance. Larry and Mike each successfully rob their respective banks, and kill no one.

As it is more seriously wrongful to kill two people than one, Mike's conditional intention is worse than Larry's, and forming this intention is morally worse. But this does not plausibly affect the gravity of the bank robbery. It might similarly be argued that although it is worse for Ivan to form his conditional intention than it is for Harry to form his conditional intention, this does not impact on the gravity of their sexual wrongdoing.

Still, there seems to be a difference in the two cases. The rough difference is that the conditional intentions in *Two Rapes* are more closely related to the conduct than the conditional intentions in *Two Robberies*. How can this difference be characterized more precisely in a way that is morally compelling?

Here is how: people have the power to form future plans, conditionally or unconditionally, to act wrongly. Having this power can help us to get what we want. But it is normally wrong to use this power to get what we want. When we do so, we treat acting wrongly as optional, and this is in itself wrong. When we secure an end by the wrongful use of this power, our action of securing the end is wrong, and the gravity of the wrongdoing depends on the gravity of the wrong threatened.

To see the force of this idea, note that it can be wrong to force others to act in a certain way by threatening to act wrongly, even when it would be permissible to use force to achieve the relevant end. For example, suppose that you wrongly take my car keys. It may be permissible for me to use some degree of force to get them back. But suppose that I sincerely and credibly threaten you that if you do not give them back I will shoot your children. Not only is it wrong to threaten you in this way, it seems wrong to secure my car keys in that way. The gravity of the wrongdoing seems a function of the gravity of the wrong I threaten.

Given this, it should not surprise us that the gravity of the wrongdoing that a person threatens affects the gravity of sexual wrongdoing. When X wrongly threatens Y that X will wrong Y if Y does not have sex with him, X uses his ability to act wrongly to secure sex with Y. It is wrong for him to use his ability to act wrongly in this way. The gravity of the wrong that he perpetrates when he uses this ability in this way depends on the wrongness of using this ability to secure sex. And the gravity of the wrongdoing of using this ability to secure sex depends on the gravity of the wrongdoing threatened.

Recall *Two Rapes*. Harry and Ivan both secure sex by threatening wrongdoing. They use their ability to act wrongly to secure sex. The gravity of the wrong of securing sex with their victims in this way depends on the wrongness of using this ability. And that depends on the gravity of the wrong that the person threatens to perform. Harry uses his ability to break an arm to secure sex. Ivan uses his ability to break two arms to secure sex. It is worse to use the latter ability than the former, because it would be worse to perform the latter act than the former. Therefore Ivan's wrongdoing is worse than Harry's.

Here are two objections to this view. First, earlier we saw that it can be wrong for X to secure sex with Y by threatening to do something that it is permissible for him to do. Doesn't the account of gravity offered here imply that such acts would not be grave at all? It wouldn't. One simple reason is that I only claim that the gravity of the wrongdoing threatened makes a difference to the gravity of the wrongdoing that results from the threat. I don't claim that this is the only thing that affects gravity.

More importantly, though, the account offered can easily be extended to threats to act permissibly. Recall *Cop Threat* that we discussed in Chapter 12. I argued that Bobby has wrongful sex with Yolanda even though he threatens to do something that he is morally required to do. Here is why. Bobby threatens to do something that will harm Yolanda. He would be justified in harming Yolanda in this way. But in making the threat to harm Yolanda to secure sex, he cannot appeal to this justification, for he intends to harm Yolanda without bringing about the result that would justify doing so.

A similar idea helps to explain why the police officer's wrongdoing is grave. When we consider why it is wrong for him to make the threat, we consider the harm that the act threatened will inflict on Yolanda, but not the justification that he would have for inflicting that harm—he cannot appeal to this justification in explaining why his threat lacks gravity because he does not intend to bring the relevant justificatory fact about. He wrongly uses the harm that his justified act would cause to Yolanda to secure sex with her. Because the harm that he threatens to inflict on her would be grave, it is also gravely wrong for the police officer to secure sex by making that threat.

A second objection: this view cannot explain the wrongness of securing sex through insincere threats. If X makes an insincere threat to Y, it might be argued, he does not use his ability to act wrongly to secure sex with Y. This seems clear from the fact that one person may secure sex from another by making a credible threat that he knows he cannot execute.

Consider:

> *False Hostage*: Ron takes Maddy's child hostage and locks him in a remote cabin. He threatens Maddy that he will kill the child if she does not have sex with him. He knows, but she does not, that the police have already taken the child to safety. She complies with his demand.

Ron's threat is credible but insincere. Not only does he fail to form an intention to harm the child if she does not comply, he could not do so. His threat, and the sexual wrongdoing that results, seems gravely wrong nevertheless in virtue of the gravity of what he has threatened.

Ron does not exploit his ability to act wrongly—he lacks that ability. But a closely related explanation can be offered why his conduct is gravely wrong. He creates in Maddy's mind the prospect of his acting wrongly. He cannot bring this prospect about. But he creates in Maddy the belief that he can, and he uses this prospect to secure sex with her.

The fact that he will not, and cannot, execute this act may make a difference to the gravity of the wrongdoing. I am sympathetic to the idea that it does. But the gravity of sexual wrongdoing plausibly depends on the gravity of what the wrongdoer threatens even when these threats are insincere, for even in this case the prospect of serious wrongdoing is exploited to achieve Ron's sexual aims.

If it is right that there is something inherently wrong in exploiting one's ability to act wrongly to secure what one wants, or exploiting the appearance that one will do so, we have another reason to think that sex secured by threats is often worse than sex secured by error. In sex secured by error a person does not exploit their ability to act wrongly to secure what they want.

But there is also a way in which sex secured by error can be seriously wrong in a way that sex secured by threat is not—an error can be induced, as in the case of lying. And it may be wrong, perhaps even seriously wrong, to lie. The wrongness of lying is too complex for a full assessment here. Some of the lies that are used to secure sex can be seriously wrongful—for example, lies in relationships that depend on trust, such as doctor–patient relationships, seem especially bad, and that helps to explain why the conduct in cases such as *Bogus Treatment* seem especially bad.

In these cases, sex is wrong in part because it is secured by doing something that is independently gravely wrong—it is gravely wrong for a doctor to lie to a patient about whether she is suffering from a serious illness, or to lie about what effective treatment for the illness might be. To secure sex through exploiting a person's vulnerability to illness, and the fear that this causes, seems at least comparable to exploiting one's ability to act in other wrongful ways. Again, this suggests that there are similar factors that can make sex secured by error as bad as sex secured by threats.

IX. Conclusion

A complete account of all of the facts that affect the wrongness of wrongful sex is beyond the ambition of these chapters. By comparing the source and gravity of wrongness in threat and error cases, though, we come to a better understanding of what should be criminalized. The gravity of sexual wrongdoing affects a person's liability to be punished, and the strength of our reasons to prevent sexual wrongdoing plausibly depends on facts that make it grave. So our reasons to criminalize sexual wrongdoing normally depend on facts that affect gravity. Similar facts affect gravity in both threat cases and error cases, even if typical threat cases are graver than typical error cases. Our reason to focus the attention of the criminal law on the former set of cases rather than the latter is more empirical than fundamental: the facts that make threat cases grave may tend to arise more often than the facts that tend to make error cases grave.

14

Consent to Harm

Consent can sometimes make harm to others permissible because the person inflicting the harm is released from a consent-sensitive duty she owes to the person harmed. Consent can be invalid because of the way it is obtained, as we saw in the previous two chapters. It can also be invalid simply because of what the person consents to.

Here are some examples where this has been thought true. In *R v Brown*,[1] a group of sado-masochists were convicted of a range of offences against the person. The fact that all members of the group consented did not vitiate criminal liability. In Germany Armin Meiwes, a self-confessed cannibal, ate Bernd-Juergen Brandes, whom he had met on the internet. Brandes was a willing victim, and actively participated in his own killing. Meiwes was initially convicted of manslaughter, but a murder conviction was substituted carrying a sentence of life imprisonment. And many people think that duelling, bare-knuckle fighting, and gladiatorial combat ought to be criminalized regardless of consent. Some people also think that voluntary euthanasia and assisted suicide are, in most cases, appropriately criminalized.

Some who defend the criminalization of some of this conduct might do so on the basis of the effects of criminalization, or the effects the conduct might have on third parties, and not because they think consent is invalid. For example, some think that assisted suicide ought to be criminalized, even though a person can validly consent to being killed in some cases, because vulnerable people will agree to be killed without valid consent. But some think that the conduct is wrong simply because a person cannot validly consent to some things being done to them.

Some of these cases are more controversial than others. *R v Brown* has received a great deal of criticism in part because the decision is seen as moralistic and homophobic, especially considering the care that the participants took not to cause long-term serious injuries to each other and to reduce the risk of disease. Many people also argue that voluntary euthanasia and assisted suicide are sometimes permissible, especially to relieve a terminally ill person suffering from a slow and painful death. Those who endorse these views may accept that consent to harm does not vitiate liability in other cases. Some go further and argue that consent ought to vitiate criminal liability even in Meiwes's case, and in duelling or gladiatorial combat, but many others view this as mistaken.

My aim in this chapter is not to pass final judgement on how these cases should be decided in law, or even whether the relevant conduct is morally wrong. I do wish to make progress with both questions. Whether consent to harm is morally valid, I argue, depends in part on whether the person consenting violates a self-regarding duty in giving it. And that depends on whether she would violate a self-regarding duty in harming herself for the sake of the goal that harming her aims at. I then support the existence of such duties. Finally, I explore reasons why harming others who consent may render a person criminally liable even if the person giving consent is not liable.

Section I clarifies the questions. Section II explores and rejects the idea that the validity of consent depends simply on the magnitude of harm that will be inflicted

[1] [1994] 1 AC 212.

on the consenting person. Section III defends the existence of self-regarding duties on the basis of the importance of well-being and autonomy. Section IV explores the question whether the sanctity of life makes a difference to self-regarding duties. Section V investigates some complexities in the relationships between self-regarding and other-regarding duties. Section VI considers the question whether the relevant duties are enforceable, drawing tentative conclusions concerning criminalization.

I. Clearing the Territory

Suppose that Y consents to X harming her: she attempts to release X from a consent-sensitive duty that he owes her not to harm her. Suppose also that Y is a fully responsible agent—she is not a child and she has normal mental functioning; she is fully aware of all of the relevant information; and there are no particular circumstances that might interfere with Y's agency, such as intoxication, fear, confusion, or threats. We then exclude factors that are often relied on by those who argue for criminalization of harm inflicted with consent.[2] We have explored some of these in the previous two chapters.

Now suppose that consent to harm does not release a person from his duty not to inflict it, at least in some cases. For example, suppose that even if I consent to you killing me you are not permitted to kill me. If that is true, consent to being killed cannot amount to valid consent. We can call the thing consented to the *content* of the consent. The supposition here is that the validity of consent can depend on the content of consent in the following sense—there are certain things, such as death, that cannot validly be consented to. Where this is true, any consent given is invalid—the person who gives consent does not release the other person from her duty not to inflict harm.

Finally, it is one thing to claim that Y's consent to *v* cannot release X from his moral duty not to *v*. It is another thing to claim that this makes a difference to X's liability to punishment, let alone to the justification, all things considered, of criminalizing the relevant conduct. My interest is in both issues, but I focus mainly on the first.

II. Magnitude of Harm

A familiar view from the criminal law is that there is a limit to the magnitude of harm that a person can validly consent to. My consent cannot release you from a duty not to harm me if the harm that you inflict is too great. If consent is ever invalid because of the content, the magnitude of harm will play a role. However, there is no upper limit to the magnitude of harm that a person may validly consent to.

One argument against an upper limit fails, but it fails instructively: were there an upper limit that limit would rule out surgery. Surgery sometimes harms people very severely, and consent to surgery is valid if the benefit to the consenting person is sufficiently great. For example, consent to an amputated leg is valid if doing so is necessary to prevent even greater harm.

Those who claim that there is an upper limit to harm can respond that the limit is not to harm, but to harm *overall*. As I explained in Chapter 10, whether an event harms a person overall depends on whether that person is worse off than she would have been had the event not occurred. If amputation does more good than harm, the

[2] See, especially, J Feinberg *Harm to Self* (Oxford: OUP, 1986).

view that there is an upper limit to the harm that a consenting person may be caused to suffer overall does not condemn it.

Still, the view fails even when qualified in this way. It implies that consent may be valid if harm to the person who gives consent can be valid because a greater harm to that person will be prevented, but not because a greater harm to others will be prevented. But a person is permitted to sacrifice her well-being for the sake of others. It is not wrong to help her to do this if she consents. That can be so even if grave harm is inflicted on the consenting person.

Consider:

> *Rescue*: A child is trapped in a burning building. The child will die unless Mary pulls him from the flames. Mary is willing to do this even though doing so will result in her losing an arm.

Mary's act of saving the child would be heroic. She harms herself a great deal to prevent a greater harm to the child. Most people do not believe that Mary is required to save the child: doing so is supererogatory. But supererogatory acts are not wrong.

Now consider:

> *Assisted Rescue*: As *Rescue*, but Mary cannot rescue the child unless Jean assists her by pushing her into the building on a shopping trolley. If Jean does this, Mary will directly lose an arm in the flames. Mary asks Jean for help.

Given that it would be supererogatory for Mary to save the child at the cost of an arm, it would be wrong for Jean to *force* Mary to save the child. But Mary's consent can release Jean from her duty not to cause her harm.

In *Assisted Rescue*, the person who agrees to be harmed for the sake of the child agrees to do something that does more good than harm. It is often wrong to harm a person as a means to the greater good without that person's consent. If the person consents, however, it is permissible to harm the person as a means to the greater good. Here's why that should be so. Were we to use the person without her consent we would fail to respect her right to determine which ends to serve, or to use her personal resources to serve.[3] But if we act with her consent, we respect that right—she has decided to allow herself to be used for the relevant end.

This suggests that one way to think about the limits of valid consent is to think about the limits to a person's freedom to determine her own ends. We have already seen that there are limits to this: these limits determine what a person is required to do.[4] Drawing on this idea, consent to harm normally seems invalid if the person giving consent is required not to harm herself in service of some end.

Consider:

> *Parental Sacrifice*: My child has an ailment that causes her short-term discomfort. Transfusing blood from me to her will prevent the discomfort but will shorten my life by twenty years. I consent to a doctor performing the transfusion.

My consent to the transfusion seems invalid. Why might this be so? The answer I will explore suggests that it is wrong for the doctor to perform the transfusion because it is wrong for me to give up twenty years of my life to save my child from discomfort.

This answer implies that the validity, or otherwise, of consent to harm depends on whether the person consenting acts wrongly in giving consent in virtue of the harm that she will suffer. And this depends on whether her giving consent violates a self-regarding duty.

[3] See, further, Chapter 4. [4] See Chapter 3.

III. Self-Harm and Self-Regarding Duties

The idea that it may be wrong for a person to harm herself is controversial. Some may contest it on the basis that all moral duties have correlative rights. But the right-holder of any self-regarding duties that I have must be me. That suggests that I have a right against my self not to self-harm. I am both the right-holder and the duty-holder, and that seems odd.

There is something in the idea that I can 'owe it to myself' not to harm myself, so the idea of a self-directed duty might not be as odd as it at first seems. But we need not posit the existence of self-directed duties to explain the wrongness of self-harm. Even if we lack self-directed duties, we may have self-regarding duties: duties that a person has because of her own value.

Of course, there is a sense in which all duties are grounded in morally salient features of the duty-holder—it is the duty-holder's capacity to value, her relationships and other circumstances, that determine whether she has duties, and which duties she is under. We are interested in a different idea—the idea that a person has certain duties because the value of her own life, or her well-being, or her agency, constrain her actions.

The idea of self-regarding duties might be thought to derive simply from the fact that a duty-holder has the same features as other people to whom duties are owed, and that explain these duties. For example, suppose that we have a duty to ensure that all living things survive. If this is true, this duty picks out some characteristic—life—that we share with other living things, and that can constrain our actions. If life itself is sufficiently important to ground a duty, and I am alive, why should I not have a duty to protect *my* life? The duty applies to me, a member of the class that the duty requires us to protect. I am a living thing. Hence, I have a duty to ensure that I survive.

This justification of self-regarding duties encourages us to see ourselves, as duty-holders, as members of the class that duties protect. This view would also seem to imply that our self-regarding duties have central importance. Duties are typically held, perhaps exclusively held, by persons. And the characteristics of personhood explain many of the duties that we are under. If personhood grounds our most important and stringent duties, and we are persons, we should expect that our self-regarding duties are important and stringent.

Against this, it might be argued that the most important duties that we owe to other persons are owed because of their autonomous agency. We owe these duties to others because they are entitled to control their own lives by determining what to value, forming plans, making decisions, and executing intentions. Indeed, I have argued that many of our most important duties are explained in this way, and this explains why people can release others from duties they owe them by consenting. Those who reject self-regarding duties might then argue that if I harm myself I shape my own life in the light of what I value. Hence, the facts that explain other-regarding duties cannot explain self-regarding duties.

Joel Feinberg suggests that considerations of autonomy are decisive in this way.[5] Feinberg is more concerned with the legal question of whether interference with autonomy by the state is permitted. But he draws on the idea that autonomy explains why we lack in self-regarding duties. However, his argument is not convincing. His conception of autonomy relies on the parallel between a person's rights over her own body and a state's rights over its territory. But there are limits to the significance of

[5] *Harm to Self*, especially ch 19.

state sovereignty—states may interfere with each other to prevent violations of human rights, for example. And sovereign states owe duties to their citizens—or, rather, the citizens of sovereign states owe duties to each other, as well as to outsiders, and sovereign power must be exercised with this constraint. So if the analogy holds, we should expect there to be self-regarding duties.

That is not to say that this explanation helps to support self-regarding duties either—sovereign states are unlike persons, in that people are members of sovereign states, and they owe duties to each other. People, in contrast, are not composed of parts to which duties can be directed. So the analogy with sovereign states should not be taken seriously either for or against the existence of self-regarding duties.

Here is a further argument in support of self-regarding duties. Through the exercise of my autonomous agency, I can erode or destroy my autonomous agency—I can do so by killing myself, by taking autonomy-eroding drugs, or by seriously diminishing my will power or my intelligence. When I do these things, I don't act against my will in the sense that we typically act against another person's will when we wrong them. I nevertheless show the same lack of respect for my own will that I show to the will of others by acting against their will.

A second response draws on the fact that some acts are wrong simply because of the harm they cause and without autonomy being interfered with. For example, it is wrong to cause pain to sentient beings, even if they lack the abilities necessary for autonomous agency.[6] If it can be wrong to harm non-autonomous beings, why can't it be wrong to harm myself regardless of whether my moral autonomy has been engaged?

Similarly, as Derek Parfit's compelling arguments show, it can be wrong to create a group of people with a very low level of well-being when I could create a different group of people with a much higher level of well-being instead.[7] When I do so, I do not interfere with autonomy. If it can be wrong for me to create a person with a low level of well-being rather than a different person with a high level of well-being, why can I not have the same kind of duty with respect to myself—to cause a version of myself to exist with a higher level of well-being rather than a lower level of well-being?

These arguments suggest that well-being can be a source of duty independently of autonomy. But it might be responded that the exercise of autonomy cancels the significance that well-being would otherwise have as a source of duty. Why should autonomous agency have this cancelling effect? The most obvious answer is that this will ensure that a person has maximal freedom over her life. If I have no duties to protect my well-being I am free to determine for myself how my life goes. Respect for my own autonomous agency, it might be argued, makes it inappropriate for my freedom to be constrained by my well-being.

But even if I should value my autonomous agency in this way, I should also value my capacity for well-being. Respecting these different capacities is appropriate given the central importance that each has to the value of my life. It is difficult to see why respect for my autonomous agency should always cancel the respect that I owe for my capacity to live well.

In the light of this, recall:

Parental Sacrifice: My child has an ailment that causes her short-term discomfort. Transfusing blood from me to her will prevent the discomfort but will shorten my life by twenty years. I consent to a doctor performing the transfusion.

[6] See, further, Chapter 10.

[7] In *Reasons and Persons* (Oxford: OUP, 1984) Part IV. See, further, Chapter 15.

We can now explain why it seems wrong for me to sacrifice twenty years of my life for the sake of curing my child's ailment.

I should value myself both because of my capacities as an autonomous agent, and because of my capacity to live well. Given that I am an autonomous agent, I should respect myself as free, and this implies that I have a certain degree of latitude to determine how my life goes. This supports the permissibility of my sacrifice. But both respect for autonomous agency and respect for my capacity for well-being counts against this being permissible. I respect my autonomous agency by not destroying it, and I respect my capacity for well-being by not self-harming. Shortening my life by twenty years for a trivial end fails to show the appropriate degree of respect for the facts that are valuable about me. Hence, it is wrong for me to consent to give up twenty years of life for the sake of my child.

IV. Sanctity and Self

Well-being and autonomy are important sources of self-regarding duties, but they may not be the only sources of these duties. In the context of assisted suicide and voluntary euthanasia, some think that it may be wrong to kill a person even with her consent because life is sacred, where the sanctity of life has moral significance independently of well-being or autonomous agency.

Sanctity is a difficult idea to capture, especially if it is understood non-theistically, as I intend. Here is an example that may help. A grave is sacred ground because of the close relationship that it has with the person whose remains are contained within it. We respect the person's importance even after they are dead. The grave has a certain relationship to the person that makes it inappropriate to perform certain acts on or around the grave. The grave does not merely represent the person whose remains are contained within it. The remains of the person were once a central part of that person, and it because of this that they demand respect.

A similar idea explains the sanctity of life. Consider a human being who has lived a good life through the exercise of her autonomy. This human being is now in considerable pain, and completely lacks autonomous agency. The life, which persists, was a central component of her autonomous agency and her well-being. Her life no longer has value to her, given that all that it will contain is pain. Nevertheless, the life in itself demands a response in just the same way that a person's grave demands a response. One reason why is that the life can provide a focus for us to regret the loss of the capacities that gave the person's life value. An even more difficult question concerns lives that have not yet been filled with autonomy and well-being. Are these lives also sacred? Perhaps. In that case, our focus is on the potential of those lives, or on the lives that they could become, rather than on how they were and could still be.

If these lives are sacred, how should we respond to them? The central question is whether the sanctity of life gives us a reason to preserve it or not to end it, as some assume. For example, Ronald Dworkin[8] and Robert Merrihew Adams[9] both suggest that it is in the nature of the sacred that it not be violated, and that destroying or causing lasting damage to the sacred thing count as violations of it.

[8] *Life's Dominion: An Argument About Abortion, Euthanasia, and Individual Freedom* (New York: Vintage Books, 1993) 74.

[9] *Finite and Infinite Goods* (Oxford: OUP, 1999) 107–8.

But it is not true that destruction of a thing violates its sanctity. Consider cremation. The corpse of a person is a sacred thing. It demands respect, and hence it would be wrong merely to throw the body of a person in a wheelie bin once they are dead. A great deal of the horror that we experience in seeing or hearing about mass graves is in the destruction of human lives that were flourishing or had the potential to flourish that the graves remind us of. But part of that horror is in the fact that the dead bodies in the graves were simply dumped *en masse*—their relationships with the particular persons that they once partly constituted were unrecognized by those who disposed of the bodies.

But although the body is sacred, its destruction need not violate its sanctity. The body of a person need not be preserved and may be destroyed through cremation, as long as this is done with the due solemnity and dignity. Dignified cremation is an acceptable way to respect the sanctity of the corpse. Through cremation, we acknowledge in a respectful way the relationship we had to the person, and the fact that the body, although it was constitutive of the person, is no longer capable of sustaining the things that gave their life value.

Providing a dignified end to a person's life may also be a proper way to respond to the sanctity of their life. Because the person's life is sacred, it would be wrong to end the person's life simply in a mechanical way, like turning the lights off at the end of the day. But ending the person's life, where the life no longer retains value nor supports the interests of the person who lives it, need not violate the sanctity of life if it is done in the appropriate way.

Similarly, an autonomous person need not show disrespect for the sanctity of her own life by deciding to end it, if that life is no longer capable of sustaining the things that gave it value. A person whose future contains only suffering and the gradual erosion of her autonomous agency need not show disrespect for the sanctity of her own life by ending it.

Some might continue to find the sanctity of corpses and of life mysterious. Why should the fact that something that once sustained great value be a source of moral demands when it is no longer capable of sustaining that value? And how do we distinguish things that are sacred from those which are not? I don't have a complete view.

One possibility is to offer a derivative explanation of sanctity.[10] We have an obligation to show respect to others. We can do so by treating their lives as important and by refraining from interfering with their autonomy. This obligation is related to another: the obligation to *foster* respect for others. We can do so by adopting and supporting the social practices which help to generate respect. Practices such as showing respect for a person's life or body irrespective of whether the person continues to exist or live a flourishing life can create conditions under which the respect that we ought to have for each other tends to develop.

Consider the way in which we treat a person's corpse. There is nothing *good* about a corpse in itself. We can see this from the fact that there is nothing wrong with cremating a person. But a person's corpse also provides a focus which helps us to remember a person who is dead and to show respect for her. Were we not to treat corpses with respect, we may fail to foster proper respect for a person after she is dead.

Fostering respect for the dead is important because a person's importance does not end with their death. It is, of course, controversial that we owe duties to people after

[10] In 'Consent to Harm' (2011) 64 *Current Legal Problems* 23, on which this chapter is roughly based, I was tempted by this idea. I am now less confident in it.

they are dead. I believe that we do in part because the projects of a person's life may still be completed, for example by using her estate in certain ways, or by publicizing the things that she did with her life. And we can wrong a person who is dead by denigrating or defaming her, or by treating her life as though it was unimportant. Treating a person's corpse with respect helps to promote the appropriate attitudes to the dead—attitudes that we owe to them. We should treat a person's body and life as sacred, even though they lack intrinsic value, then, because we owe obligations to a person after they are dead, and we will tend to fulfil those obligations in a more satisfactory way if we treat the person's life and body with respect.

This account of the obligation to show respect for the sanctity of life and the sanctity of the body is instrumental. We must participate in the social practice of showing such respect in order to foster and support the respect that we must show towards persons both when they are alive and when they are dead. This idea is compatible with a range of different social practices through which respect can be shown. There are many ways to specify the obligation to generate and support the practices that amount to showing due respect for a life or for a corpse. Cremation and burial are two ways of showing respect for a corpse, but there may be many others. The value of a particular practice depends on its effectiveness in fostering respect for persons.

But whilst there are many different practices that may adequately achieve this aim, there are some ways in which lives and bodies can be treated that are insufficient in generating the proper degree of respect. Hence, the idea of the sanctity of life and the sanctity of the body does provide a standard against which we can judge societies. A society that has a practice of dumping human corpses in a field without anyone giving it a second thought may be criticized for failing adequately to foster respect for persons even if no one is upset by this treatment of corpses.

If a person's life or body can be treated with a lack of respect in a way that fails to respond appropriately to the sanctity of life or the body, can a person treat her own life or body with a similar lack of respect? Here I follow the same strategy as the previous section. In the previous section I showed that one source of the obligation not to cause harm to oneself is the fact that one has the features that are the source of the obligation not to harm others: those concerned with autonomy and well-being.

The same thing should be said in the case of the sanctity of life and the body. We are required to foster and support respect for the lives of persons. That requires us to treat as sacred the lives and bodies of human beings. Furthermore, it requires that we treat the lives and bodies of *all* human beings in this way. And that includes the life and body of the person herself. She can treat her own life or body with a lack of respect—in a way that violates a practice that tends to foster and support respect for all human beings.

This argument depends on the idea that the practices that foster and sustain mutual respect between human beings will be set back if people treat their own bodies and lives in certain ways. But this seems true. When a person treats her own life or body as worthless, she may contribute to a culture in which lives and bodies are more generally regarded as worthless. And she may contribute to a culture that undermines the tendency that other people have to develop attitudes of self-respect. For this reason, a person must treat her own life and body as sacred.

Some might be tempted by arguments that are less instrumental than this. On the non-instrumental view, the life and body that once sustained a person has non-derivative moral importance even once personhood has ended, and once it can no longer be a site of well-being. Non-instrumental claims about the continuing value of the life and the body are still more controversial. Perhaps we value the life and the body because of what it could have been. But this view requires a robust and restrictive account of the 'could' in question. Once personhood has ended, there is a sense in which a body could have sustained a person. But then isn't there the same sense in which a nettle could sustain a person? The distance between our world and a world in which the body sustains a person might be shorter than the difference between our world and a world in which a nettle sustains a person. But this is only a difference in degree rather than a difference in kind.

In response to this last concern, moral and evaluative thinking is deeply infused with counterfactual thinking. Consider regret. I have reason to regret that a body no longer sustains the person that it once sustained after personhood has ended. I lack a reason to regret that a nettle does not sustain a person. As I argued in Chapter 10, regret is also counterfactual: it relies on differences between our world and worlds in which some alternative occurs that are a matter of degree. The conclusion that we should abandon regret in the light of this observation seems implausible. The same thing is true about counterfactual accounts of harm and benefit, and counterfactual accounts of causation.

I am at least tempted by the idea that there is a non-derivative account of the moral importance of lives and corpses. Such an account seems closely related to the comparisons that make regret appropriate and inappropriate. The properties that make it appropriate to regret the fact that a human body, now a corpse, no longer sustains a person with a certain level of well-being may also contribute to our reasons to treat corpses with respect. This may be true as a non-derivative matter.

Spelling out a complete view of this kind is no easy matter, and I am not sure how to do it. Yet I am reluctant to rely solely on a derivative account of the moral importance of lives and corpses. I find it more plausible that these things have moral significance in themselves, independently of the attitudes that they help to foster.

V. Oneself and Others

If there are self-regarding duties, what implications do they have for the validity of consent to harm? Here is one possibility. Suppose that Y consents to X harming her in service of a goal that Y has set herself. If it would be wrong for Y to harm herself to the relevant degree in service of that goal, her consent that X does so is normally invalid.

Recall:

> *Parental Sacrifice*: My child has an ailment that causes her discomfort. Transfusing blood from me to her will prevent the discomfort but will shorten my life by twenty years. I consent to a doctor performing the transfusion.

Here is a natural explanation why my consent is invalid. Sacrificing twenty years of life to cure my child is wrong because of the disrespect it shows for my own life. Because it is wrong for me to sacrifice twenty years of my life for this end, it is wrong for the doctor to assist me. Hence, my consent to harm is invalid.

i) The nature of the wrong

In a moment, we will explore the limits of this argument. Before that, let us consider its implications when it applies. One important implication is that even though the doctor has not been released from his duty not to harm me, the nature of his wrongdoing is altered given that I have consented to his act. We can see the intuitive force of this view by noticing that the wrong that he does is different in gravity and kind from the wrong that he would have done had he performed the transfusion without my consent.

One possible characterization of this difference is that whilst the doctor acts wrongly, he does not wrong me. As he does not wrong me, I have no special standing to complain about what he has done. There is certainly something intuitive about the idea that I cannot complain about what the doctor has done. But there is more than one way to explain this intuition. I might lack standing to complain because no right of mine has been violated. But alternatively I might lack that standing because complaining would be hypocritical. It is hypocritical because just like the doctor, I failed adequately to value my life. Thus I cannot demand a response from the doctor even if he has violated my rights. It would not be hypocritical of me to criticize his conduct if I criticize my decision to consent at the same time.[11] The question is the form that this criticism should take were I to self-criticize.

Whilst there is something intuitive about the idea that the doctor has not violated my rights if he acts without my consent, there is also a sense in which it is intuitive that he has violated them. The doctor's duty is explained by the importance of my life. But the importance of my life cannot be divorced from its importance for me. It may be objected that a human life has impersonal as well as personal value. But even the impersonal value of my life is derivative of its importance for me. The fact that I have my own life to lead gives it value for everyone.

Overall, I think we gain nothing by deciding whether the doctor has violated my rights. We can agree the following. The doctor has acted wrongly. He has acted wrongly because of the value of my life. The value of my life cannot be divorced from its importance to me. But he has not acted against my will and he has not failed to respect the choices that I make for myself, or the control that I have over the things that I have most reason to care about. It may be hypocritical for me to complain about what he does, at least if I do not at the same time criticize myself for consenting. But there is a sense in which I have special standing to complain if I do not do so hypocritically, given that the value that the doctor has failed to respect in his actions is especially connected to me. Whether this constitutes a rights violation depends on how we understand rights. I don't have a complete theory of rights, and I doubt that it would be fruitful to develop one.

ii) Different duties

As I noted in Chapter 11, valid consent only releases a person from the particular consent-sensitive duty that the consenting party is owed. If I validly consent to be harmed by you, you do not wrong me by harming me. But that does not imply that you do not act wrongly all things considered. That depends on whether your act violates other duties that you have.

Consider:

> *You and I*: Paul's child is drowning. Paul is willing to bear some great harm to save him. But he can do so only with Millie's help. If Millie helps Paul, she will not be able to save her child, who is also drowning.

Millie does not wrong Paul if she helps him. But she does act wrongly—by violating the duty to save her own child.

[11] For this limit to the charge of hypocrisy, see V Tadros 'Poverty and Criminal Responsibility' (2009) 43 *Journal of Value Inquiry* 391.

It is also sometimes permissible for you to harm me if I consent, even if it is wrong for me to harm myself, and hence wrong for me to give my consent. Consider:

> *Leg Art*: Mona wants to amputate her leg to turn it into a piece of art. Logan is a surgeon, who can amputate it cleanly. Mona consents to Logan doing this. If Logan does not do this, Mona will amputate it herself, but she will be harmed much more seriously. There is no way for Logan to prevent Mona from doing this.

Logan may be permitted to amputate Mona's leg, even if it is wrong for Mona to amputate her own leg, and wrong for her to consent to Logan doing this.

Here is why. Mona has the option of refraining from amputating her leg. Because of this, it is wrong for her either to get Logan to amputate it, or to amputate it herself. It is wrong because she has an option which she must take because of the value of her autonomy and well-being. Logan lacks this option. He cannot bring it about that Mona's leg is not amputated. For him, there are only two choices: either Logan amputates it or Mona does so. Because Mona has an option that Logan does not have, it may be wrong for Mona to consent to the amputation, and yet permissible for Logan to carry it out.[12]

Here is another way to see this, which draws on the complex counterfactual analysis of harm that I offered in Chapter 10. If Mona consents to the amputation, she makes herself much worse off than she could have made herself by not consenting. If Logan amputates, in contrast, he makes her as well off as he could, given that he could not have prevented the amputation from occurring. For this reason, if Mona consents to the amputation and Logan carries it out, Mona causes herself to be harmed overall by consenting, whereas Logan does not.

This also explains why consensual harm should sometimes be permitted in law, even when the act of the person who gives consent is wrong—if we do not do so, people may harm themselves to an even greater degree. This has significant implications for the criminalization of assisted suicide.[13] I believe that there are clear cases where assisted suicide is permitted in that the person who kills herself does not harm herself and does not violate the sanctity of her life. But that is not my focus now. There are some cases where a person who kills herself would violate a self-regarding duty. Nevertheless, there may be a justification for permitting assisted suicide even in some of these cases. For in permitting assisted suicide we create the conditions where people who want to kill themselves can do so without causing themselves unnecessary suffering.

iii) Intrapersonal and interpersonal issues

It might be argued that there are more fundamental disanalogies between the intrapersonal and the interpersonal case. The duties that I have because of the value of my life or my body might be different from the duties that you have because of these values. The argument that there are such disanalogies might go in two directions.

The first view claims that I have greater freedom with respect to my life and my body than you. On this view, the value of my life and my body may not constrain my own actions, but it may nevertheless constrain yours, even when I consent. My freedom to set back certain self-regarding values, on this view, does not extend to a freedom to secure your assistance in setting back these values, even if you are willing to assist me.

[12] Compare the discussion of coercive offers in Chapter 11, Section III.

[13] A similar idea is briefly explored in J McMahan *The Ethics of Killing: Problems at the Margins of Life* (Oxford: OUP, 2002) 457.

For example, some might claim that because I am free, I am permitted to kill myself in certain circumstances. But it may nevertheless be wrong for you to assist me to do so. This is because the value of my life constrains you in a way that it does not constrain me. So if I can kill myself on my own, I am permitted to do so. But it would be wrong for you to help me, and thus it would be wrong for me to seek your assistance.

The second view claims that I have less freedom with respect to my life and my body than you. On this view, the value of my life and my body may constrain my actions, but it may nevertheless not constrain yours, as long as I consent. This view might be defended on the grounds that I have a special responsibility to ensure that my life is well lived. As you lack this special responsibility, you are permitted to act where I am not.

For example, some might claim that it is wrong for me to kill myself in certain circumstances, given the special responsibility that I have to ensure that my life is well lived. The value of my life constrains my decision, though, in a way that it does not constrain yours. If I consent to you killing me, you do not act wrongly, on this view, even though I act wrongly in giving consent.

I am not sure how to make further progress with these arguments. I am fairly sceptical of both. With respect to the first, we have already seen that you may have certain duties that prevent you from helping me to do things with my body or my life that I am permitted to do. Beyond these arguments, what further reason is there to suppose that I am not free to secure your assistance to do with my body what I wish to do with it? If the value of my body or my life is insufficiently important to restrict my freedom to do a certain act, why should we think it sufficient to prevent us doing the same thing together?

With respect to the second, I acknowledge that I do have a greater responsibility than you to ensure that my life is well lived. But if performing a certain act demonstrates a failure in this respect, and is wrong as a result, you assist me in acting wrongly. It is at least normally true, subject to the exception noted just now, that it is wrong to assist a person to act wrongly. It is not clear what founds a further exception based on the different relationships that a person has to her own well-being compared with third parties.

VI. Enforceability and Criminalization

It is sometimes wrong to harm a person even if that person consents. A central explanation is that a person has self-regarding duties, and hence she is not free to do with her life or her body as she wishes. This can make it wrong for her to consent to harm, and thus her consent is not valid—it does not release the person to whom she has consented from his duty not to harm her. We should not draw conclusions about criminalization too quickly from this argument. The moral relationship between self-regarding duties against self-harm and other-regarding duties not to harm a consenting person that I have defended may not translate into a similar legal relationship.

One way to understand the law of England and Wales on assisted suicide relies on this distinction. There is now no crime of suicide in England and Wales, and yet assisted suicide is a crime.[14] Some find this puzzling. How can it be legally wrong to assist someone to do something that they are legally permitted to do? One answer is

[14] See the Suicide Act 1961.

that although both suicide and assisting it are morally wrong, only assisting it can be criminalized. Of course, it is not very plausible that suicide is *always* morally wrong, and this calls into question whether assisting suicide should *generally* be a crime. But even where suicide is morally wrong, it does not follow that it should be criminalized. And if it should not, it does not follow that assisting it should not be criminalized.

There are two questions to ask about criminalization. The first concerns enforcement. The second is concerned with the justification of punishment for violation of these duties.

i) Enforcement

Some self-regarding duties may be unenforceable, but the related other-regarding duties may nevertheless be enforceable. We are here concerned primarily with preventive enforcement. For example, suppose that it is wrong for me to kill myself, and thus you have a duty not to assist me, or to do so with my consent. My duty may be unenforceable, but your duty may be enforceable. What this means is that it would be wrong to force me not to violate my duty, but it would be permissible to force you not to assist me in violating it.

This may be true for contingent rather than fundamental reasons. For example, an enforceable duty against suicide would typically be intrusive in a way that enforceable duties on others not to assist would not be. And enforcing self-regarding duties against suicide will typically harm a person who is already in distress. It would thus typically make a person who is very badly off even worse off.[15] The enforcement of the duty not to harm a person who has consented may not have these effects, or not to the same degree.

Some might argue that the divergence in enforceability arises for more fundamental reasons. Suppose that I wrongly wish to inflict harm on myself. This may be unenforceable for this reason. If another person prevents me from inflicting harm on myself, he directly controls me through physical interference. As we have seen, being subject to this kind of control may be objectionable even with respect to some wrongful actions. In contrast, if the police officer prevents you from assisting me, he does not control me in this direct way. He does so only by making the option of assistance unavailable. Some might argue that this way of controlling me is less direct because it merely deprives me of the assistance of others. Given this, my objection to it is less profound.

This argument fails to attend to different methods by which a duty can be enforced. What matters is not whether I am controlled directly or indirectly in this sense. What matters is whether the method of control involves depriving me of an option, or interfering with me in a more direct way. It may be wrong for a police officer to physically restrain me to prevent me from self-harming in some circumstances. But it may not be wrong for him to deprive me of the tools that I would need to do the self-harming. If a police officer could deprive me of assistance from others, she could also deprive me of tools that I need to self-harm. What matters is whether enforcement involves direct interference or rather simply the removal of an option. It does not matter whether the removal of an option arises due to the control of others or not.

Nevertheless, even thus understood, the argument has important implications for the criminal law. The fact that I have a self-regarding duty not to self-harm may justify

[15] Some of these issues are similar to those we find in the enforcement of paternalistic laws. For a good discussion, see D Husak 'Paternalism and Consent' in F G Miller and A Wertheimer *The Ethics of Consent: Theory and Practice* (Oxford: OUP, 2010).

the criminal prohibition of assistance, and it may also justify restricting the availability of tools for self-harm. It does not follow that self-harming should be criminalized in itself, at least if criminalization legally warrants police officers to prevent the relevant behaviour by direct physical interference.

ii) Punishment

A more fundamental contrast can be drawn with respect to the justification of punishment. In Chapter 4, I further supported the duty view of punishment: that it is central to the justification of punishing a person in pursuit of a certain end that the person has a duty to serve that end, and that duty is enforceable. As we saw in Chapter 7, this idea has implications for criminalization. We should normally criminalize conduct only if the conduct makes people liable to be punished by giving rise to duties that can serve the ends of punishment, the most important of which is deterrence.

In the light of that, consider:

> *Leg Art 2*: Mona wants to amputate her leg to turn it into a piece of art. Logan is a surgeon who can amputate it cleanly. She consents to his doing this. If he does not do this, Mona will not amputate her leg.

My arguments so far suggest that if it is wrong for Mona to amputate her leg to turn it into a piece of art, it is wrong for Logan to assist her. This is because in *Leg Art 2*, unlike *Leg Art*, both parties have the option of ensuring that Mona's leg is not amputated. They each have a duty to select this option.

Now suppose that Logan amputates Mona's leg and she turns it into a piece of art. The question is what duties these people incur by doing this, and can they support punishment? The value that they have set back through the amputation concerns the value of Mona's autonomy and well-being. The central end that they ought to pursue because of this would be to protect and advance the value of her autonomy and welfare. They could do this, for example, by aiming to develop her other physical capacities, and by protecting her from having harm inflicted on her, either by herself or by others.

Punishing Mona herself will normally be pointless in advancing these aims. Doing so will inflict further harm on her. More importantly, even if it was effective, punishing her for the sake of this end seems difficult to defend. Although she has a duty to ensure that she does not throw her life away by harming herself further, her relationship with her own life is deeply personal. It is difficult to believe that other people are permitted to interfere with her in ways that intrude profoundly into her personal life to ensure that she succeeds in responding appropriately to her wrongdoing.[16]

Perhaps it might be argued that the appropriate response to her failure to value her own life is to ensure that other people value theirs. If punishing Mona would prevent other people from turning their body parts into works of art, doing so, it might be argued, is permissible. I am not sure whether she has such duties. But even if she does, it is difficult to move from these duties to a justification of general deterrence. Those who have self-harmed might have duties to educate others not to self-harm. But these duties are more plausibly duties of persuasion. Threatening people not to self-harm seems unwarranted.

Things seem different with respect to Logan. Threatening doctors not to perform amputations on those who will wrongfully self-harm does not seem at all

[16] Compare my discussion of abortion in Chapter 7.

intrusive—their acts are not at all personal in the relevant sense. It is also quite plausible that doctors who do this could be forced to prevent others doctors from carrying out such practices. And it is plausible that these duties can be extended beyond protection of the particular victim to protection of others.

A policy of punishing doctors to prevent other doctors wrongly from amputating the limbs of those who wrongly wish to self-harm seems quite attractive—much more attractive than a policy of punishing self-harmers to prevent other people from self-harming. This is a powerful reason in favour of the criminalization of harming others without consent, and against the criminalization of self-harm.

VII. Conclusion

I have focused on the moral question of when it is permissible for one person to do harm to another with the consent of the other. In the light of that discussion I hope that we have a clearer way to make progress in thinking about some of the problematic cases with which I began. For example, when considering *R v Brown*, we can consider whether it is permissible for a person to harm herself for the sake of the goals that the defendants had in that case. These goals obviously include sexual gratification, but they may also include further goals such as the development of certain kinds of relationship, of exploring the limits of human sensation, and so on. Those rejecting the judgement in that case, as I do, may do so on the basis that these goals are sufficiently important, or at least may be sufficiently important, to justify the relatively modest harms that were done to the participants. Those affirming the decision may claim that their goals were unacceptable, or that they were insufficiently important to justify permitting the harm that was done to them.

Another possibility is that the defendants in *R v Brown* violated the sanctity of their bodies. Those defending the decision in *R v Brown* may claim that they treated their bodies as lacking the kind of significance that the human body has, undermining practices which foster and sustain respect for people's bodies. Again, I doubt that this is true. I suspect that quite extreme alterations in people's bodies for aesthetic or sexual reasons are perfectly compatible with an acceptable set of practices that support and sustain respect for the body, and may even positively contribute to the best set of practices that we could endorse. The idea that some set of practices ought to be sustained to ensure that attitudes of respect are fostered and sustained should not lead us to be conservative about which set of practices ought to be developed. The defendants in *R v Brown* may have been violating a particular set of conventions held by some members of the community, but it does not follow that their actions undermine mutual respect more generally, and the converse may be true.[17]

Finally, even these people did act wrongly, an argument needs to be made that the duties they incur through their wrongdoing are to prevent other people from acting in a similar way. Given the fact that the harm was inflicted in the context of intimate personal relationships, where consent was secured, such an argument seems hard to support.

It is much more plausible that both the defendant and the victim acted wrongly in the Meiwes's case. The victim failed to respect the value of his own life by sacrificing

[17] This second approach to *R v Brown* is similar to that advocated in R A Duff *Answering for Crime: Responsibility and Liability in the Criminal Law* (Oxford: Hart, 2007) 130–2.

it in this way. Although the victim consented, his consent was not valid. By treating his consent as decisive, Meiwes also failed to respond appropriately to the value of the victim's life. I also find it quite plausible that Meiwes is liable to be punished, if doing so prevents other people from engaging in practices like this.

These views, of course, rely on judgements about the kinds of duties that arise through wrongdoing in these cases. I doubt that there is a general theory which establishes what these duties are. I only have my own intuitive judgements about what kinds of duties arise in which cases. But even in the absence of a more complete theory of this kind, we can at least see the kinds of argument that are needed to support criminalization.

PART D

FURTHER REACHES OF THE CRIMINAL LAW

15

Further Beyond Harm

Central wrongs that the criminal law is concerned with, such as murder, rape, assault, and theft, are harmful rights violations. Many who are sympathetic to the view that the criminal law is primarily concerned with such wrongs, though, recognize that there are wrongs that can be criminalized that are not harmful. In Chapter 11, we explored one kind of case of harmless wrongdoing—the case where the wrongdoer violates a consent-sensitive duty owed to another. That kind of harmless wrongdoing is primarily grounded in the interest that people have in controlling what happens to them.

These cases are not the most familiar cases of harmless wrongdoing, though. More familiar cases are often discussed under the label 'offensive conduct'. A familiar view is that a content-focused harm principle, such as the principle that only harmful conduct may be criminalized, is too restrictive. Room must be made for the criminalization of offensive conduct.[1]

The topics discussed under this umbrella, such as the criminalization of the treatment of corpses and graves, offensive speech, public sex, and pornography, raise large issues that I will not be able to give full justice to here. My aims are more general. First, I show that offensiveness is not itself a reason in favour of criminalization. Either offensive conduct is harmful, or the reasons to criminalize it have to do with facts that make the conduct offensive, rather than the fact that the conduct is offensive.

A further set of wrongs has nothing to do with offence at all. Such wrongs have their source in 'impersonal value'. Again, I will only make a dent in this large topic. Impersonal value is value that does not make things better or worse from any perspective. Some deny that there is such value. I follow familiar arguments to show that this is not plausible. I then argue that impersonal value can be a source of wrongdoing, and that this wrongdoing can be criminalized.

Section I is concerned with so-called offensive conduct and its effects. Section II shows that offensiveness does not make conduct wrong. It rather rests on independent judgements about wrongness. Section III offers a brief account of two kinds of impersonal value. Section IV begins to explore the criminalization of wrongdoing grounded in impersonal value. Section V considers questions of enforcement.

I. The Effects of Offence

One criticism that is often levelled at the harm principle is that it implausibly restricts the criminalization of offensive conduct. One kind of example that is useful in testing this claim is public sexual conduct. It is difficult to believe that it is wrong ever to criminalize sex in public. But, it may be argued, sex in public causes no harm. Perhaps it might be argued that sex in public can be criminalized because it would harm children to see it. But that doesn't seem the only reason why sex in public may be criminalized.

[1] For a classic defence, see J Feinberg *Offense to Others* (Oxford: OUP, 1985).

In response to this argument, we might doubt that sex in public is non-harmful. Let us specify the example a little bit more. Suppose that Bob and Jane will have sex on a bus that Margaret wishes to take. Margaret now has two options: either take the bus and be exposed to Bob and Jane having sex, or don't take the bus. I assume that *removing* the option of going by bus harms Margaret if the option of going by bus is valuable to her. But the option of going by bus has not been removed. Now suppose that if Margaret goes by bus seeing Bob and Jane having sex will distress her. This diminishes the value of her option of going by bus. Better to go by bus without distress. Hence, if Bob and Jane have sex on the bus, Margaret is worse off. Diminishing the value of a valuable option is not as harmful as removing it. But it is harmful nevertheless.

One response to this argument is to suggest that the distress that Margaret will feel if she goes by bus and sees Bob and Jane having sex on it is not harmful.[2] This is hard to believe. Suppose that Margaret feels an anxious churning in her stomach when she sees Bob and Jane having sex. This feeling is unpleasant. Surely experiencing this unpleasant feeling is harmful.

It is sometimes doubted that this is so. It is claimed that feelings like this are too transient to count as the kinds of harm that the criminal law should protect us against, or at least that are engaged by the harm principle. This is sometimes argued for on the basis that it is only restrictions of autonomy, or personal projects, or opportunities that count as harms for the purposes of the harm principle.[3]

In Chapter 10, I rejected this view of harm—pain is harmful independently of whether it restricts the autonomous pursuit of personal projects. But we can also see that the resulting version of the harm principle is not very plausible. To see this, imagine that Bob could cause the same anxious churning by interfering with Margaret's body by using an electronic device that interferes with her brain. No sensible rendition of the harm principle would restrict criminalization of that. Surely this counts as a legitimate kind of harm for the purposes of the harm principle, regardless of whether a person's projects or goals are frustrated. If harm is to be understood as a set-back to one's interests or to one's well-being, there is no good reason to exclude unpleasant feelings from the idea of harm. For unpleasant feelings erode well-being, and one has an interest in not experiencing them.

An alternative idea is that the harm principle is not concerned with protecting people from the feelings that they experience on judging that another person's conduct is wrong. Perhaps Margaret feels an anxious churning in her stomach only because she judges Bob and Jane's conduct to be wrong. Her distress is mediated by her judgement. It is not the conduct which is harmful, it might be argued, but her judgement of it.

We can unpack this argument in the following way. Margaret is responsible for the judgements that she makes. If her judgements cause her to feel a certain way, she is responsible for feeling that way. Margaret's responsibility for her judgement breaks the chain of causation from Bob and Jane's conduct to the anxious churning in her stomach. Therefore, Bob and Jane's conduct does not cause Margaret's distress. It follows that Bob and Jane's conduct is not harmful.

Here are three responses. First, Margaret's anxious churning in her stomach may not be mediated through her *judgement*. The conduct may cause her to feel anxious

[2] See J J Thomson *The Realm of Rights* (Cambridge, Mass: Harvard UP, 1990) ch 10. Thomson's discussion is, I believe, flawed in that it is not restricted to distress caused by the perception of wrongdoing. For a step in the right direction, see A Ellis 'Thomson on Distress' (1995) 106 *Ethics* 112.

[3] See, for example, A P Simester and A von Hirsch 'Rethinking the Offense Principle' (2002) 8 *Legal Theory* 269, 280–1.

independently of any assessment she makes of the conduct.[4] Second, the fact that she is responsible for her judgements does not imply that the chain of causation is broken. It is not plausible that *all* conduct that a person is responsible for breaks the chain of causation. For example, suppose that I threaten you that if you don't stamp on Eric's foot I'll kill Eric. You stamp on Eric's foot. In this case, you are responsible for stamping on Eric's foot. But I nevertheless caused Eric to be harmed. That is so because I created conditions under which you were justified in stamping on Eric's foot.[5]

A similar thing might be argued about Margaret's case. If Margaret is justified in judging Bob and Jane's conduct as being wrong, her judgement that Bob and Jane's conduct is wrong is caused by Bob and Jane's conduct. And the consequences that unavoidably occur from that judgement are also caused by their conduct. Hence, their conduct is harmful in just the same way as it was harmful for me to threaten you to stamp on Eric's foot.

Let us support this argument a little further. Suppose that Margaret gets on the bus and that the anxious churning in her stomach arises due to the judgement that Bob and Jane's conduct is wrong. How could she avoid the anxious churning in her stomach? Only by making the judgement that Bob and Jane's conduct is not wrong. But we cannot expect her to make that judgement if Bob and Jane's conduct is wrong. That would require her to adopt the wrong moral view, or to corrupt herself, to avoid the anxious churning in her stomach. Hence, Bob and Jane put Margaret in a position where she must choose one of three options: not to take the bus, or to feel an anxious churning in her stomach, or to corrupt herself. She is worse off having these options than she would be were she to be able to get on the bus without watching Bob and Jane having sex. We can conclude that Bob and Jane having sex on the bus results in Margaret being harmed.

Here is a third argument. The spirit of the harm principle is that we are motivated to protect people from harm through the criminal law, and in this spirit, no sensible rendition of the harm principle would exclude all harms that are mediated by judgement. To see this, suppose that the judgement that Bob and Jane's conduct is wrong did not only cause Margaret to suffer an anxious churning in her stomach, it also caused her leg to fall off. The loss of her leg is mediated by her judgement. But it does not follow that it is wrong to criminalize their conduct to protect her from suffering the loss of a leg. No sensible rendition of the harm principle would regard Bob and Jane's conduct as being harmless in that case.

And that is so even if Margaret makes the wrong judgement about their conduct. It is sometimes supposed that conduct which is not objectively offensive, but which nevertheless causes offence, cannot be a legitimate object of the criminal law. But this is not, as is often supposed,[6] simply because the harmful effects of such conduct are mediated through wrongful judgement. To see this, suppose that there is nothing wrong in itself about Bob and Jane having sex on the bus. However, they know that if they do this and Margaret is on the bus she will form the wrong judgement about their conduct and will lose her leg. They surely have a strong reason not to have sex on the

[4] See, also, J Tasioulas 'Crimes of Offence' in A von Hirsch and A P Simester *Incivilities: Regulating Offensive Behaviour* (Oxford: Hart, 2006) 152–3.

[5] This is also the view of the criminal law. See, for example, *R v Pagett* (1983) 76 Cr App R 279.

[6] Feinberg, in *Offense to Others*, argued against an objective criterion for offensiveness. His view has been widely criticized. See, for example, J Tasioulas 'Crimes of Offense' and R A Duff and S E Marshall 'How Offensive Can You Get?' in von Hirsch and Simester *Incivilities: Regulating Offensive Behaviour* and A von Hirsch and A P Simester 'Rethinking the Offense Principle'.

bus—the reason is that Margaret will suffer serious harm as a result of their conduct, albeit harm that is mediated through her wrong judgement. But Bob and Jane don't have strong reasons to have sex on the bus. On this basis, we may prohibit Bob and Jane from having sex on the bus. And if we do prohibit them from doing that, we do so in order to prevent Margaret suffering the harm of the loss of a leg.

But the difference between this case and the more realistic case where Margaret feels an anxious churning in her stomach is only in the gravity of the consequences for Margaret. And we have already seen that the anxious churning that she feels can amount to the kind of harm that the criminal law can protect us from suffering. It follows that the harm principle does not rule out criminalizing sex on the bus.

Of course, whether criminalizing this conduct is permissible all things considered is another matter. That depends on all of the reasons against criminalizing the conduct, such as protecting the liberty of Bob and Jane, the costs of criminalization, the availability of alternative methods of protecting Margaret, and so on. A proper understanding of the restrictions on criminalizing offensiveness should draw on these ideas to show that the harm caused by offensive behaviour is often insufficient to warrant criminalizing it. This may well motivate a general principle against criminalizing offensive behaviour, as well as explaining some familiar exceptions to that principle. But denying that offensiveness is harmful is mistaken.[7]

It might be suggested that this argument, if it is valid, implausibly allows the criminal law to be used to enforce 'conventional morality'—it allows the prohibition of things that people find offensive simply on the grounds that the conduct will have bad effects on them.

But I only argued that if the distress is serious enough and the liberty to be protected insufficiently important, it may be permissible to criminalize some conduct that people find offensive even if that conduct is not wrong independently of the distress it causes. This will normally not be the case. What we need to protect people against the criminalization of permissible conduct, even if it causes distress, is not something like the harm principle, but rather an adequate account of the interest that people have in pursuing their goals, even when others reject these goals, and even if the pursuit of these goals comes at some cost to others. The importance of this idea to morality and the criminal law runs through the earlier part of this book.

Furthermore, the reason given to criminalize the conduct concerned is not that people find the conduct wrongful or offensive. It is rather the effects of that conduct on others. There may be wrongful conduct that does not tend to cause judgement-mediated distress. The mere judgement that there is wrongful conduct going on does not typically cause the relevant distress, or cause it only to a trivial degree. On the contrary, 'the righteous' often feel a great deal of pleasure at condemning permissible conduct that they find wrongful. Such conduct would not be capable of being criminalized on the basis that it was wrong, but only on the basis that it causes distress, and hence the harm-based argument would not justify criminalizing the conduct.

Consider gay sex. Whilst knowledge that some people are having gay sex may cause some people to suffer distress, this would hardly provide a powerful reason to restrict people's liberty to have gay sex. The harm done is a trivial reason to restrict liberty to this degree. Even those who think that gay sex is wrong would find it difficult to justify criminalizing it on this basis.

[7] For an extended defence of this view in the context of freedom of expression, see J Cohen 'Freedom of Expression' (1993) 22 *Philosophy and Public Affairs* 207.

II. The Relationship between Wrongdoing and Offensiveness

The fact that some offensive conduct causes distress might not seem the most important reason to criminalize it. Some might argue that conduct can be wrong because it is offensive, and this provides a reason to criminalize it. They might argue as follows. Whether conduct is distressing to others depends on whether the conduct actually offends others. But the reason to criminalize offensive conduct is not the offence it causes. Offensiveness is an objective property of the conduct, and it is this property that justifies criminalizing it. People rightly feel offended at offensive conduct because it has this property. But whether anyone is actually offended is neither here nor there.

It is true that when we are offended by conduct, we find the conduct offensive. And that suggests that offensiveness is understood independently of our being offended. But even so, I doubt that offensiveness itself provides a reason in favour of criminalization. The judgement that conduct is offensive derives from other moral properties that might provide reasons in favour of criminalization. Offensiveness is not itself a reason in favour of criminalization.

Here is what I mean. Certain moral properties of conduct make certain negative reactions to that conduct appropriate. These reactions include distancing ourselves from it, being repulsed by it, and so on. These moral properties are independent of any judgement about the appropriate response. Because the relevant reactions are appropriate, the conduct is offensive—it is conduct about which it is apt to respond in the various ways that constitute taking offence at it. But the morally salient characteristics of the conduct that give us reasons to criminalize it are the grounds that make the conduct offensive. The fact that it is offensive is not a reason to criminalize it; the facts that make it offensive are.

Consider the public burning of effigies of black people in a racist society. It is controversial whether this may be criminalized. Let us suppose that it is. It might be argued that it is permissible to criminalize it because the conduct is offensive. But there are facts that explain why the reactions that constitute taking offence are warranted—the gross disrespect that the conduct shows for black people, for example. These facts make the conduct offensive. And they are also reasons why the conduct is wrong. These facts are both grounds for criminalizing the conduct, and explain why it is appropriate to take offence at it.

Perhaps it might be argued that conduct should sometimes be criminalized because it is offensive even where there are no objective properties that make it so. Consider the destruction of objects that are not important in any other way, but are regarded as sacred by religious people. Assume that these religious people have unreasonable and false beliefs. Such conduct might be thought offensive, even though there are no facts about it that make it offensive. It is offensive simply because these religious people have good reason to be offended by it.

Such conduct might be thought offensive because it shows disrespect for the beliefs of these religious people. If it does, the reason is to do with the way in which the relevant religious people are treated by the conduct, and not because they in fact take offence at it, or would be warranted at taking offence at it. If the way they are treated gives them reason to take offence at the conduct, the conduct is offensive. If not, the fact that they feel offended does not make the conduct offensive.

We should not criminalize conduct simply on the basis that people are offended by it. Even the fact that the conduct is disrespectful is not normally sufficient reason for criminalization. There are (over)familiar concerns that if we criminalize disrespectful conduct we will restrict freedom of expression and freedom of speech—a bad thing for all of the reasons that are too well known to be worth recounting here.

Another view is that offensive conduct should be criminalized only if it both has certain normative properties that make it offensive, and people are actually affronted by it.[8] But why should it be a condition of criminalizing the conduct that people are actually affronted by it? The fact that they are not seems a reason in favour of criminalizing it. Return to the burning of effigies of black people in public. The fewer people who are offended at this conduct, the more reason there is to criminalize it. This is because one reason to criminalize the conduct is to ensure that a proper response is made to the conduct. Black people have a right that the conduct is appropriately condemned. Where the conduct is roundly condemned without state intervention, their grounds for demanding a state response is weaker. In societies where this does not occur, there is a powerful role for the state to condemn the conduct—it should do so in part to encourage the appropriate social response.[9]

Perhaps it might be argued that this conduct may be criminalized only if some people are actually offended by it. In the example just considered, the case for criminalization might be thought to rest on the demand that black people make that this is done. Not so. If (as is very unlikely) they were so cowed that they did not find the conduct offensive, there would be even stronger reasons to criminalize it.

To see this sharply, imagine that the Nazis were successful in eradicating the Jews in Nazi Germany. The bodies of Jews were dumped in mass graves. Nazi citizens then further desecrated these graves by marking them with swastikas. The Nazi state ought to have prohibited this even if no one was offended by the desecration. Of course, they will not do what they ought to do: if no one is offended by the conduct, no one will lobby for its criminalization. But the fact that no one will do what they are required to do does not tell against the existence of the requirement.

To conclude: the fact that conduct is offensive is not a reason to criminalize it. The effects of the offensive conduct on the lives of those who are offended might provide reasons to criminalize the conduct, though these reasons will typically be weak. The facts that make conduct offensive might provide more powerful reasons to criminalize the conduct. Where these facts provide reasons in favour of criminalization, the fact that people are not offended does not count against criminalization, and may provide a reason in favour of it.

III. Impersonal Value

Those who supplement the harm principle only with the offence principle may limit the scope of the criminal law to wrongs that are deeply connected to actual conscious beings. Conduct that wrongly harms them, or that wrongly interferes with their autonomy, or that wrongly treats them with contempt or disrespect, may be criminalized. All of these wrongs are grounded in interests that these beings have in not being treated in the relevant ways. Not all value, though, is grounded in interests in this way. That which is not is often called 'impersonal value'. I will stick with this term, even though, for reasons we will explore later, it is not ideal.

[8] See A P Simester and A von Hirsch *Crimes, Harms, and Wrongs: On the Principles of Criminalisation* (Oxford: Hart, 2011) 96.

[9] See, further, the discussion of public wrongdoing in Chapter 7.

i) Personal and impersonal value

To make progress with our understanding of impersonal value, begin with some platitudes about value and valuing. To value something is to have some kind of positive attitude towards that thing. There are various kinds of positive attitudes, including interest, enjoyment, pleasure, respect, reverence, and awe. Something is valuable if such attitudes are appropriate. For example, something may be valuable because it is interesting. If it is interesting, it is worth taking an interest in. Or something may be valuable because it is awe-inspiring. If it is awe-inspiring, it is worthy of awe. Things are valuable because of certain properties that they have. Something may be interesting because of its originality, or its complexity, or its importance. Something may be awe-inspiring in part because of its size.

To be clear, I do not intend a response-dependent account of value—a 'fitting attitude' account.[10] Perhaps fitting attitude accounts of value put the cart before the horse. A positive attitude, some might think, is an attitude that it is appropriate to have in response to something of value rather than the other way around. I take no stand on the cart and the horse. Regardless of whether a fitting attitude analysis of value is correct, we can learn a great deal about value by considering how things ought to be valued, or how it is appropriate to value them.

I have already introduced the building blocks of an understanding of personal and impersonal value in Section II(*iii*) of Chapter 10. There I introduced the idea that facts can be valuable because of their perspectival significance. Such facts are valuable for a conscious being, in a specific sense—they are valuable because of their role in the lives of conscious beings. Impersonal value lacks this kind of perspectival significance. It does not depend on the value that it has for conscious beings.

ii) Impersonal value and the lives of persons

Some find the idea that there is impersonal value puzzling. I should say immediately that the idea of impersonal value does not imply that there is value that is completely independent of the lives of beings with perspectives. It may depend on such lives, but not because the value is value for these beings.

Some examples make the idea of impersonal value less controversial. It is sometimes thought that equality is impersonally valuable.[11] On this view, the fact that X has the same amount of some relevant currency (such as well-being or resources) as Y is valuable in itself. It is valuable even if it is neither better for X nor better for Y that this is the case. But if equality is valuable in this way, it is valuable because of the importance of beings. In particular, its value depends on the value of the currency that we are concerned with for such beings. Equality for trees is not impersonally valuable.

There are many candidates for impersonal value of this kind, and it is a matter of judgement which candidates really are valuable in this way. For example, some people think that it is intrinsically valuable that bad people suffer—suffering is intrinsically good or valuable in some way if it is deserved. It is bad for the bad person that she

[10] Fitting-attitude accounts of value include T M Scanlon *What We Owe to Each Other* (Cambridge, Mass: Harvard UP, 1998) ch 2, M Smith 'Neutral and Relative Value after Moore' (2003) 113 *Ethics* 527, and T Ronnow-Rasmussen *Personal Value* (Oxford: OUP, 2011) chs 2 and 3.

[11] The most important defence of this view is L Temkin *Inequality* (Oxford: OUP, 1993).

suffers, and it may not be good for anyone. Yet it is good in itself. I deny that this is true, but it is difficult to demonstrate its falsity.[12]

We have so far considered two controversial cases of impersonal value: equality and deserved suffering. Whilst these candidates have their defenders, many people also deny that these things are impersonally valuable. I am undecided about the first case and I doubt the second.

But there are some cases of impersonal value that are less controversial, and indeed very hard to deny. One case concerns aggregation. Consider the obvious fact that when a disaster occurs it is worse that more people die rather than fewer. This seems true independently of any relationship between the people who die. Obviously, death is bad for each person who would have had a life worth living were she not to have been killed. But it is not bad for any of these people that more people die.

In order to explain the almost universally accepted intuition that it is worse that more people die rather than fewer, we rely on a principle of aggregation: if some event, E1, would be bad for X and some other event, E2, would be bad for Y, it is worse that both of these events occur rather than only one. But it is not worse for anyone that both events occur rather than only one. So any principle of aggregation is an impersonal principle. Although this principle is impersonal, it is dependent on personal value: the aggregation of personal value is impersonally valuable.

A similar case involves different levels of well-being that can occur in possible worlds, where the identity of those with these different levels of well-being is not held constant. Consider:

> *Two Worlds*. Compare the following one-person possible worlds:
>
> World 1: Only X exists and X lives a happy life.
>
> World 2: Only Y exists and Y lives a life that is just worth living.

All other things equal, World 1 is clearly better than World 2. We are right to value it more. Yet there is no person for whom World 1 is better than World 2.

Perhaps it might be argued that World 1 is better for X than World 2 because X exists in World 1 but not World 2. But this view has the implausible implication that our World is terrible for all of the potential people that could have existed in other possible worlds but don't exist. Think about it this way. Consider a person that might come into existence if my partner and I choose to have another child. It is not bad for this potential person that we choose not to have another child. There is no person who this is bad for. We should conclude that World 1 is not bad for Y and World 2 is not bad for X.

How, then, do we vindicate the powerful intuition that World 1 is better than World 2? We do not have a stronger reason to bring about World 1 than World 2 for X's sake. We have a stronger reason to bring it about because although World 1 is no better for anyone than World 2, it is nevertheless better than World 2. World 1 is impersonally better than World 2.[13]

[12] A wide array of views of this kind is imaginatively explored in S Kagan *The Geometry of Desert* (Oxford: OUP, 2011). Many philosophers are desert sceptics, including me. My doubts are outlined in *The Ends of Harm: The Moral Foundations of Criminal Law* (Oxford: OUP, 2011) ch 4; 'Responses' (2013) 32 *Law and Philosophy* 241 and 'Moving Mountains: Variations on a Theme by Shelly Kagan' *Criminal Law and Philosophy*, forthcoming. For an insightful discussion of the inconsistency of retributivism with the harm principle, see P Tomlin 'Retributivists! The Harm Principle is Not For You' (2014) 124 *Ethics* 272.

[13] The locus classicus for discussion of this problem is, of course, D Parfit *Reasons and Persons* (Oxford: OUP, 1984). There is an enormous, and rapidly growing, literature on the non-identity problem.

Some people deny this on the grounds that if something is better, it is always better for something or someone.[14] Those who think this need not deny that there is impersonal value—they might think that water is good for flowers, even though flowers lack a perspective. But it is not very plausible that happiness is 'good for the world', so these people deny that World 1 is better than World 2.

But the intuition that World 1 is better than World 2 is much more powerful than the intuition that claims such as 'good' or 'better' always imply 'good for' or 'better for'. It is powerfully intuitive that World 1 is better than World 2 simply because it has better things in it, even if there is no one or nothing who this is better for.

iii) The value of things

A second kind of impersonal value has a different kind of connection to conscious beings. Things of great beauty, complexity, and sophistication may have value in themselves. This category of impersonal value includes the natural environment, works of art, historically important artefacts and sites, and so on.

One controversy is whether the value of these things depends on people valuing them. We can consider this question by thinking about why it might be wrong to damage or destroy them. Suppose that I destroy something beautiful. One reason why this might be wrong is that there are people who could have appreciated the beauty of the thing who will now not be able to do so. I wrong these people by depriving them of the opportunity to value this beautiful thing.

But it seems wrong to destroy a beautiful thing simply because it is beautiful, and regardless of whether anyone finds it beautiful. Consider a giant redwood. The redwood is awe-inspiring. Its value seems independent of its actually being held in awe by anyone. To say that the giant redwood is awe-inspiring is to say that it ought to inspire awe, regardless of whether it does so. Imagine a one-person world. The person in this world is unmoved at the sight of a giant redwood. This fact does not make the redwood any less awe-inspiring. We can see this by imagining that the person later comes to find the redwood awe-inspiring. This person comes to see the value that it has. He does not invest it with value. This implies that its value is independent of his valuing it.

This idea is consistent with each of two contrasting conceptions of impersonal value:

1) *Dependent Impersonal Value*. The value of some things depends not on their actually affecting some agent, but it does depend on their potential to affect agents.
2) *Independent Impersonal Value*. The value of some things depends on their valuable properties independently either of the affect they have on agents or their potential to affect agents.

Some impersonal value is independent. Recall *Two Worlds*. The fact that World 1 is better than World 2 is independent not only of whether anyone values World 1 more than World 2, but also of whether it *could* be valued in that way. Even if no one could value the fact that World 1 exists rather than World 2, World 1 would nevertheless be better than World 2. This would be true, for example, if these worlds contained non-human animals who could not make comparisons of value.

The value of natural beauty, however, is probably better understood as dependent on its potential to affect well-disposed agents in the right way. We could imagine agents

[14] See, for example, J J Thomson *Normativity* (Chicago: Open Court, 2008); R Kraut *Against Absolute Goodness* (Oxford: OUP, 2011).

with a range of different cognitive capacities, and what is valuable in a particular world depends on which capacities agents have. Imagine a world where there have never been, and never will be, any sighted beings. There is no such thing as the value of natural beauty in such a world.

A complete version of the view that natural beauty is a dependent value involves a more precise understanding of what the value is dependent on. Once we rule out the idea that natural beauty is valuable in a world which never has any sighted beings in it, we have a range of options. For example, the value of natural beauty might depend on the existence of a being who could value the thing. Or it might depend only on the past or future existence of such a being. Alternatively, it might be necessary that some being actually comes into contact with the thing, or could come into contact with it, or would do so were she virtuous. Furthermore, it might depend on whether the relevant being has the capacities to value the thing, or on whether it would do so were it virtuous. I am not sure which amongst these views is right.

IV. Criminalization and Impersonal Value

In Chapter 6, we considered various versions of principles such as the harm principle and the sovereignty principle. These principles seem like person-affecting principles—they are concerned with ways in which one person's conduct can make another worse off, or interferes with their sovereignty. But they are not necessarily person-affecting principles. The harm principle can be formulated in a way that takes into account aggregate harm; the sovereignty principle can be formulated in a way that takes into account aggregate interference with sovereignty. But supporters of these principles might be uncomfortable with this idea. These principles seem to many plausible because they restrict criminalization to rights violations. But a mere set-back to impersonal value does not violate rights.

i) Aggregation

Those favouring these principles might thus prefer to explain cases which seem as though they are concerned with impersonal value by showing that rights are indeed violated in the relevant cases. And in some cases, at least, this is plausible.

Consider:

> *Kills*: Philip threatens Claudia that if she does not kill Manu or both Alfred and Christoph, Philip will kill all three and her. If she does either thing, everyone else will be spared. Claudia kills both Alfred and Christoph. Manu, Alfred, and Christoph are equal in all salient respects, and are completely independent of each other.

I have claimed that it is impersonally valuable that fewer people die: it is impersonally worse that Alfred and Christoph are killed rather than just Manu. But the aggregation principle on which this relies depends on the impersonal disvalue of more people being killed. It is not worse for anyone that two people are killed rather than one. It is worse for Manu that Manu is killed rather than Alfred and Christoph. It is worse for Alfred that Alfred and Christoph are killed rather than Manu. It is worse for Christoph that Alfred and Christoph are killed rather than Manu. But it is no worse for either Alfred or Christoph that *both* Alfred and Christoph are killed rather than Manu. So the idea that it is altogether worse that Alfred and Christoph are killed rather than Manu depends on the impersonal badness of more being killed.

Assume, as is plausible, that Claudia ought to have a duress defence if she kills Manu.[15] Intuitively, she ought not to be given a defence for killing Alfred and Christoph. She ought to have taken the option of killing only one person rather than two. The fact that it is impersonally worse that Alfred and Christoph are killed than Manu explains this judgement.

But it is not the only way of explaining the judgement. Some think that Alfred and Christoph each have a right that Claudia kills Manu rather than both of them. This has been defended on the ground that each person has a right to be taken into consideration in the decision whom to kill. Were Christoph not there, there would be nothing to choose between killing Alfred and killing Manu. If she kills Alfred and Christoph, she treats Christoph's presence as though it makes no difference to her decision whom to kill. It is wrong to treat Christoph thus. Therefore Christoph has a right not to be killed. The same thing is true, of course, of Alfred. Therefore, if Claudia kills Alfred and Christoph, she violates their rights: their rights to affect Claudia's decision whom to kill.[16] Thus, those who favour the criminalization of Claudia's conduct in *Kills*, as most will, need not rely on the idea that it is impersonally worse that Alfred and Christoph are killed.

Still, we should be suspicious about this proposal. Whilst the solution to the problem of aggregation is ingenious, it does not seem to be the best explanation of the wrongness of Claudia's conduct. Her conduct seems wrong simply because it is so much worse that two people are killed rather than one. And the fact that this is so much worse seems a good enough reason to criminalize her conduct.

Furthermore, it is not clear how the argument offered extends to all cases of aggregation. Consider:

> *Broken Arms*: Philip threatens Claudia with the deaths of her, her family, and everyone else in the problem. He gives her two options: 1) break both Manu's arms; or 2) break one arm of each of 10,000 people. If she does either thing, everyone else will be spared. Claudia chooses 2).

It seems wrong for Claudia to choose 2), given the number of people who will have a single arm broken. Yet if Claudia chooses 2) she does not treat anyone as having no importance. Were the other 9,999 not present, Claudia ought not to break Manu's arms, so in harming the 10,000, she does not treat anyone as though they make no difference to her decision. Perhaps some ingenious argument can be offered why Claudia violates the rights of the 10,000 without relying on the impersonal badness of aggregate harm. But the natural view is that Claudia would act wrongly by doing this because so many more people will be harmed if she does so.[17] This also seems sufficient to warrant criminalizing her conduct.

ii) Non-identity

Non-identity cases provide a more powerful threat to principles such as the harm principle and the sovereignty principle. Given the enormous philosophical attention

[15] For defence of this view, see, for example, G Rosen 'Culpability and Duress: A Case Study' (2014) 88 *Aristotelian Society Supplementary Volume* 69; V Tadros 'Duress and Duty' in S Bazargan and S Rickless *The Ethics of War: Essays* (Oxford: OUP, forthcoming).

[16] See, especially, F M Kamm *Morality, Mortality Volume 1: Death and Whom to Save From It* (Oxford: OUP, 1993) ch 6; T M Scanlon *What We Owe to Each Other*, 229–41.

[17] There are admittedly thorny problems on the horizon. For a brilliant and unsettling demonstration of just how thorny they are, see L Temkin *Rethinking the Good: Moral Ideals and the Nature of Practical Reasoning* (Oxford: OUP, 2012).

that the non-identity problem has received in moral philosophy since Derek Parfit's groundbreaking work in *Reasons and Persons*, it is surprising that this problem has not figured much in debates about criminalization.

The most obvious context to consider this problem is environmental damage. Consider:

> *Environment*: The government is taking a decision whether to adopt a systematic environmentally friendly policy. Such a policy includes the criminalization of acts unfriendly to the environment, such as pollution. No one in the current generation is helped by such a policy, but it has a profound effect on the happiness of future generations. The policy will give rise to higher levels of happiness for whoever lives in the society than would occur without it. However, the identity of members of future generations depends on whether such a policy is adopted.

This scenario is plausible because such a policy will affect human action in large and small ways, which will determine who has sex with whom and when, making a difference to the identity of members of the next generation.

Criminalizing the environmentally unfriendly acts, it might be argued, does not prevent harm. This is because the policy does not make anyone better off than they would have been were the policy not enacted. Suppose that the government decides not to enact the policy. Now consider a person, Eivind, who comes into existence after this decision is taken. The environment that Eivind lives in is worse than the environment that would have existed were the policy enacted. But, it might be argued, the policy does not protect Eivind from harm given that Eivind would not have existed were the policy to have been enacted. Someone else would have existed who would be better off than Eivind. But this does nothing to benefit Eivind.

Furthermore, Eivind's sovereignty does not seem to have been interfered with, and for a similar reason. Eivind cannot complain that his autonomy is eroded by the decision not to enact the policy, because he would not have existed were the policy enacted. Eivind has no interest in the policy being enacted, given that his existence depends on this not being so. Eivind might have an interest in such a policy if his life is not worth living as a result of the poor environment in which he lives. But it seems justified to adopt the policy even if all of the inhabitants of the world have lives worth living.

Some might object that the policy will indeed prevent harm. In Chapter 10 I defended a complex counterfactual account of harm. Some event, E, harms a person, V, if V is worse off in the actual world than she is in some relevant possible world. The relevant world, I argued, is not restricted to the nearest world in which E did not occur. This, I suggested, helps us properly to evaluate overdetermination cases such as:

> *Finger*: D chops off one of V's fingers, pre-empting that finger and another being chopped off by X.

D, I claimed, harms V but benefits him overall. He harms him by chopping off a finger, but benefits him overall because his chopping off a finger prevents an even greater harm.

One way to understand this case is that D's chopping has two causal effects that can be distinguished from each other. One is the chopping of V's finger; the other is the prevention of X chopping off two. Because these two causes can be distinguished, D both harms X and prevents him from suffering a greater harm.

Some might argue that something similar occurs in Eivind's case. Failing to enact the environmental policy benefits Eivind by bringing him into existence, but fails to protect him from harm by preventing his environment becoming polluted. So, they might conclude, although he is benefited overall, he is nevertheless harmed.

This kind of analysis does seem plausible in some cases. Consider this simpler case:

> *Bomb*: Jascha puts a time bomb in the basement of Mieko and Rainer's house. Jascha's friend warns them that he has done this. They search the house, but don't discover the bomb, and conclude that the warning was a hoax. The search alters the time when Mieko and Rainer have sex. Their child, Larry, is born, and he continues to live in the house after his parents die. The time bomb goes off, and Larry loses a leg.

It seems plausible that Jascha harms Larry. Certainly, the blast from the bomb harms Larry. The planting of the bomb is the cause of the blast. So Jascha causes the event that harms Larry. It might then be argued that Jascha causes Larry to come into existence and harms him with the same act. It is difficult to know whether this is right. That depends on whether there is a relevant counterfactual where Larry comes into existence but is not harmed by the blast. Some might think that *Environment* should be understood in the same way, and hence the harm principle can explain the case.

But even if the harm principle can explain *Environment*, it is not plausible that the principle can accommodate all non-identity cases. Not all decisions that affect identity have two causes, one of which brings a person into existence and the other of which results in harm to that person. Sometimes, a decision simply gives rise to a person coming into existence who is worse off than some other person would have been were they to have been brought into existence without harm being inflicted.

For example, suppose that some event results in the fertilization of an egg, which gives rise to a person with a genetic propensity to a painful disability that cannot be prevented. It is not plausible that the person who comes into existence is harmed if they have a life that is overall worth living. Yet a decision that gives rise to a large number of such events is surely wrong simply because of the reduction in welfare that occurs. Similarly, it is surely wrong to make all conscious creatures extinct simply because doing so gives rise to a world in which nothing valuable occurs. This is so even though no one need be harmed by extinction.

So whilst friends of the harm principle might find some arguments to show that the harm principle is consistent with criminalizing conduct in real world non-identity cases, they do not seem to have the right explanation. It seems sufficient to warrant criminalization that the policy will prevent conduct that contributes to impersonally worse states of affairs, regardless of whether anyone is harmed. Even if it can be shown that some people are harmed by the relevant policies, the case for criminalization need not rely on this idea.

iii) Dependent impersonal value

Dependent impersonal value also seems to provide good reason to criminalize conduct. Where such value exists, there is something that someone could value, or that she has good reason to value. But that is consistent with no one valuing the thing.

Consider a beautiful country inhabited by people who do not care at all for natural beauty. They cover the whole land with hideous buildings and road systems, leaving no natural beauty at all. No one cares that this has been done, because no one values natural beauty, and no one would have valued natural beauty had they not done this. Our question is: ought this society to have criminalized some of this destructive conduct? The answer, I think, is that it ought to have done so. People in this society ought to have valued natural beauty, and ought to have criminalized its destruction. The fact that they did not value natural beauty cannot deprive them of a duty to protect it.

Some might object that destruction of natural beauty, in such a society, is not wrong because no one would have valued it anyway. But the fact that no one would have valued natural beauty is irrelevant if they ought to have done so. They had a beautiful environment that they could have protected and valued. Criminalization would have been part of a policy to achieve this. The fact that they would not have valued the environment does not deprive them of a duty to protect it. This case is similar to the Nazi case considered earlier, except that case involved disrespect for actual people now dead.

V. Enforcement

Perhaps it might be argued that the intuitive case that I have presented for the role of impersonal value in a theory of criminalization fails, because this kind of value cannot justify the infliction of preventive or punitive force on wrongdoers. This might be argued on the grounds that impersonal value is typically, or always, trumped by the rights that people have against the use of force.[18]

Given that impersonal value can be very significant, though, this is very hard to believe. Aggregation cases are the clearest cases. It is obviously permissible to use force to ensure that harmful wrongdoing does not occur where the wrong depends on the aggregate of harms. But in such cases, as I have shown, the value that is set back is impersonal. Suppose that I am right that Claudia wrongly breaks 10,000 arms in *Broken Arms*. The facts that make this wrong are surely sufficiently important to justify interfering with Claudia to prevent her acting thus. The same thing is true in non-identity cases. The difference is that the government is surely permitted to force people not to pollute in *Environment*, even if enacting the policy does not prevent anyone from being harmed.

Cases involving dependent impersonal value may seem weaker. But again, it is difficult to believe that mild use of force to prevent the destruction of a great deal of natural beauty is unwarranted. There is room for a right to do wrong, I argued in Chapter 7. I suggested that if early abortion is wrong (which I doubt), women have a right to do wrong in this case. But the reasons I offered were not simply to do with the fact that the value at stake was impersonal, but with the fact that abortion concerns a value that is so deeply and intimately connected to the life of the person who performs the act. Obviously, the same thing is not true in the case of natural beauty.

Perhaps it might be argued that the duty view of punishment that I favour cannot support the criminalization of wrongdoing based on impersonal value. The duty view, it might be argued, justifies punishment on the basis of what wrongdoers owe to victims. In cases of impersonal value, there are no victims to whom duties are owed.[19]

[18] Ronald Dworking relied on something like this to justify liberal policies on abortion. See *Life's Dominion: An Argument About Abortion, Euthanasia, and Individual Freedom* (New York: Vintage Books, 1993). For doubts see M Clayton 'A Puzzle about Ethics, Justice, and the Sacred' in J Burley *Dworkin and His Critics* (Oxford: Blackwell, 2004).

[19] A range of commentators have pressed the idea that the duty view has implications for criminalization that are too restrictive. See, for example, K K Ferzan 'Rethinking *The Ends of Harm*' (2013) 32 *Law and Philosophy* 177; V Bergelson 'The Duty to Protect the Victim—or the Duty to Suffer

There are two responses to this. First, in some cases of wrongdoing grounded in impersonal value, duties may be owed to particular people, even if those people have not been harmed by the wrongdoing. To see this clearly, recall:

> *Bomb*: Jascha puts a time bomb in the basement of Mieko and Rainer's house. Jascha's friend warns them that he has done this. They search the house, but don't discover the bomb, and conclude that the warning was a hoax. The search alters the time when Mieko and Rainer have sex. Their child, Larry, is born, and he continues to live in the house after his parents die. The time bomb goes off, and Larry loses a leg.

It is debatable, I suggested, whether Jascha harms Larry. But even if we think that he has not, Jascha has obviously incurred a duty to respond to the fact that his bomb has blown Larry's leg off. It is not very plausible that such duties are vitiated by the fact that Larry would not have existed but for Jascha's act.

More importantly, the duty view does not depend on wrongdoers owing duties to anyone. It depends only on their incurring enforceable duties as a result of their wrongdoing. It seems plausible that they do incur such duties in the case of impersonal wrongdoing. A wrongdoer whose act is wrong because of some important value that constrains her freedom to act plausibly owes a duty to respond to the set-back in the value. A person who has destroyed a site of natural beauty, for example, might incur an obligation to restore that site of natural duty, or, failing that, to protect other beautiful sites. If the values are important enough, such duties might be enforceable. Harming the person for reasons of deterrence might, in that case, be warranted.

To show that the relevant conduct ought to be criminalized all things considered, it must be shown that two kinds of proportionality calculation are satisfied. The first is the narrow proportionality calculation. It must be shown that those who commit wrongs grounded in impersonal value are liable to be harmed to serve the ends of punishment. To do this, it must be shown that they incur duties to serve these ends that are sufficiently stringent to require them to bear the costs that punishment inflicts on them.

It seems to me plausible that this can be done. Remember that criminal sanctions need not inflict grave harm. Imprisonment might well normally be wrong in cases of dependent impersonal value. But the fine is the most common sanction used in the criminal law. Those who destroy natural beauty seem to me liable to suffer fines for the sake of protecting the environment from further damage.

Second, it must be shown that criminalization can meet the wide proportionality calculation: that the goods achieved by criminalization can outweigh its costs. Whether this is so, of course, depends on empirical considerations. But I doubt that we can rule out the possibility that this proportionality calculation can be satisfied as well. As I noted in Chapter 6, even though friends of the harm principle are right that the criminal law is a clumsy tool, it is not very plausible that harm prevention is always necessary for the wide proportionality requirement to be satisfied.

In order to know whether criminalization could be justified purely because of the benefits to impersonal value that would be secured, we need to know just how clumsy a tool criminal justice need be. I am not sure how to answer this question, but I have a hunch that fines for those who damage things of natural beauty should be on the table for consideration.

Punishment?' (2013) 32 *Law and Philosophy* 199; S Uniacke 'Punishment as Penalty' (2015) 9 *Criminal Law and Philosophy* 37. For replies, see V Tadros 'Responses' (2013) 32 *Law and Philosophy* 241; 'Answers' (2015) 9 *Criminal Law and Philosophy* 73.

VI. Conclusion

Because criminal law is concerned with aggregate harms, it is concerned with impersonal value. It is also concerned with impersonal value that has nothing to do with harm. Non-identity cases are one kind of case. Dependent impersonal value is another. There are difficult empirical questions about whether criminalization can ever be warranted in the last of these cases without showing any reduction in harm. I would not rule the possibility out.

16

Intentions and Inchoate Wrongdoing

Some conduct has been criminalized not because the conduct sets back something valuable in itself, but because of the relationship between that conduct and conduct that does set back something of value. Attempts are a central case. They are criminalized because of their relationship with completed crime. In standard cases, the completed crime is harmful but the attempt is not. Is the attempt wrong? And how do we justify criminalizing it?

Here we focus on one kind of case, but a central one. Suppose:

1) X performs an act, *n*, with the intention of facilitating another act, *v*.
2) If X *n*s, his *n*ing will causally contribute to his *v*ing if nothing intervenes between his *n*ing and his *v*ing.
3) It is wrong for X to *v*.
4) It is not wrong for X to *n* independently of its relationship with his *v*ing.
5) After having *n*ed, whether X *v*s remains completely within his control.

If *n*ing is a crime, it is what criminal lawyers call an incomplete inchoate crime. In this chapter, I am interested in a related moral idea: if *n*ing is wrong, it is an incomplete inchoate wrong. Incomplete inchoate wrongs, unlike incomplete inchoate crimes, have received relatively little philosophical attention. I leave an investigation into the criminalization of inchoate wrongs to the next chapter. Focusing on the moral issue first helps us better to understand the relationship between wrongs and crimes.

Focusing on cases where *v*ing is wrong in virtue of the harm it causes will help us to understand incomplete inchoate wrongs. If *n*ing is wrong, it is wrong in virtue of its relationship to *v*ing. If X *n*s and then goes on to *v*, X's *n*ing is causally involved in his *v*ing. But the wrongness of incomplete inchoate wrongdoing (if there is such a thing) does not depend on X *v*ing. Hence, X's *n*ing need not cause the harm that explains its wrongness. This exemplifies the fact that *n*ing is an inchoate wrong: *n*ing is insufficient to cause the harm that explains its wrongness.

Where X's inchoate wrongdoing is incomplete, X wrongly *n*s, *n*ing is wrong because of its relationship with a complete wrong, *v*, and whether X *v*s remains within X's control.[1] X commits a complete inchoate wrong if X acts wrongly because of the prospect of a certain result occurring, the result does not occur, and whether the result occurred was beyond X's control. For example, X commits a complete inchoate wrong if X shoots at Y with the intention to kill him, but misses. His wrong is inchoate—the

[1] This is not the only way to draw the contrast between complete and incomplete inchoate wrongs. Another way to draw the contrast distinguishes between cases where X needs to perform further acts in order to cause or risk bringing the relevant result about and cases where X needs to perform no further acts. See, for example, R A Duff *Criminal Attempts* (Oxford: OUP, 1996) 119. This conception makes it possible for X to commit a complete inchoate attempt, but have it in his power to prevent the relevant outcome.

harm that explains the wrongness of his conduct does not occur. But his inchoate wrong is complete: whether his bullet killed Y was beyond X's control.

Here is an illustration of an incomplete inchoate wrong: X points a gun at Y intending to kill Y, but is yet to pull the trigger. Another person stops him before he has a chance to do so. Plausibly, X acts wrongly. If so, X's wrong is both inchoate and incomplete. It is inchoate because X's act does not cause the harm that explains its wrongness. It is incomplete because the complete wrong of killing Y would have remained fully within X's control had the intervention not occurred.

Our question is: are there incomplete inchoate wrongs, and if so what explains them? I consider three views. *The Intentions View* is that *n*ing is wrong in virtue of the fact that *n*ing is performed with the intention to facilitate X's intention to *v*. Furthermore, it claims that the wrongness of *n*ing is non-derivatively explained by X's intention to *v*. It is X's intentions *as such* that explain the wrongness of X *n*ing, and not the fact that X's intentions increase the probability that *n*ing will have bad consequences.

This view is controversial: many people reject the significance of intentions to permissibility. They claim, roughly, that the difference between a permissible and a wrongful act cannot be merely the intentions with which the act is performed. Those who reject the significance of intentions to permissibility might favour one of two other views. *The Control View* is that *n*ing is not wrong. If X remains in control over whether she goes on to *v*, acts that facilitate *v*ing are not wrong. The bad intentions with which X *ns* cannot render *n*ing wrong directly. They also cannot render *n*ing wrong in virtue of the predictable consequences that *n*ing will have if X remains in control of these consequences. This might be thought true because X can make his complete course of conduct permissible by choosing not to bring about the relevant consequences.

The Prediction View, in contrast, is that *n*ing can be wrong because of the predictable consequences of *n*ing. It is predictable that we will execute our intentions. If X *vs*, and *v*ing is wrong, and *n*ing facilitates *v*, X can predict that his *n*ing facilitates his *v*ing. It is wrong to facilitate wrongdoing. Hence X wrongly *ns*. *The Prediction View* is consistent with the idea that intentions have derivative significance to permissibility: they render X's prediction that *n*ing will facilitate *v*ing secure. However, were X's prediction secure for other reasons, his *n*ing would be equally wrong.

I defend *The Intentions View*. My foil is T M Scanlon's discussion of inchoate wrongdoing in *Moral Dimensions: Permissibility, Meaning, Blame.*[2] Scanlon rejects the significance of intentions to permissibility. He recognizes inchoate wrongdoing as a challenge to this view, and considers both *The Control View* and *The Prediction View*. It is unclear which view he ultimately endorses. Neither view, I will suggest, is plausible. Furthermore, in the light of considering these views, we are well placed to respond to two more general arguments that have been mounted against the significance of intentions to permissibility.

The chapter is structured as follows. Section I clarifies the view that intentions are irrelevant to permissibility. Section II reveals the implausible implications of *The Control View*. It also highlights a puzzle concerning remote and innocuous acts. Section III considers *The Prediction View*. Section IV returns to the puzzle that remained at the end of Section II. It concludes that *n*ing with the intention of *v*ing is wrong even if *n*ing is on its own both remote from *v*ing and 'outwardly' innocuous. Section V responds to two arguments that have been offered against the relevance of intentions to permissibility in the light of our discussion of inchoate wrongdoing.

[2] (Cambridge, Mass: Harvard UP, 2008).

I. Clarifying the Irrelevance of Intentions

The view that intentions are irrelevant to permissibility (*the irrelevance of intentions*) claims that acts are neither permissible nor wrong just because of the intentions with which they are performed. Here is a way of understanding this view. Consider an act-type that a person can perform, including all of the morally salient features of any token of the type, but excluding the intentions that the person will have in performing it. Call this an 'intention-free act-type'. Let us suppose that there is a token of this type that it would not be wrong to perform. *The irrelevance of intentions* claims that tokens of this act-type that are performed with bad intentions are also not wrong.

The irrelevance of intentions is consistent with intentions having derivative importance for permissibility. Consider:

> *Admiration*: Yoshi wants to impress Xena. Yoshi will kill an innocent person if Xena *n*s with bad intentions. Yoshi will not kill an innocent person if Xena *n*s with good intentions.

It is permissible for Xena to *n* with good intentions, but wrong for her to *n* with bad intentions. However, this need not be due to anything about intentions as such. The causal effects of Xena *n*ing on Yoshi's behaviour are morally salient independently of her intentions. Were Xena's good intentions, but not her bad intentions, to have the relevant effect, *the irrelevance of intentions* implies, it would be wrong to perform the act with good intentions, but it may be permissible to perform it with bad intentions.

Here is a good heuristic device to determine whether it is permissible to perform a token of an intention-free act-type. Consider a token of an intention-free act-type where X acts with the best intentions. If X acts permissibly, *the irrelevance of intentions* implies, X also acts permissibly if he acts with the worst intentions. This is not true if X's intentions have different causal effects, but that is because these causal effects alter the intention-free act-type.

To illustrate, consider this familiar case:

> *Trolley*: A trolley is headed towards five innocent people. Xena can redirect the trolley towards Yoshi, who is on a different track. If Xena does so, the five will be saved, but Yoshi will be killed. Diverting the trolley is the only way for Xena to save the five. There are no other morally salient differences between each of the five and Yoshi.

If all of the morally salient facts other than Xena's intentions are included in this description of the case, the case describes the intention-free act-type of turning the trolley from the five to Yoshi.

Let us use our heuristic device to determine whether there is a permissible token of this intention-free act-type. Consider the best intentions with which Xena could act. She should have good intentions and lack bad intentions: she intends to save the five and does not intend to kill Yoshi. Many think that it is permissible for Xena to act with these intentions. If so, *the irrelevance of intentions* implies that Xena's bad intentions cannot render it wrong for her to perform the same intention-free act-type. Hence, Xena can permissibly turn the trolley intending to kill Yoshi, without intending to save the five. Some people find the idea that similar acts cannot differ with respect to permissibility simply in virtue of a person's intentions highly intuitive, and endorse *the irrelevance of intentions* on this basis.[3]

[3] See, for example, J J Thomson 'Self-Defense' (1991) 20 *Philosophy and Public Affairs* 283; J J Thomson 'Physician-Assisted Suicide: Two Moral Arguments' (1999) 109 *Ethics* 497; F M Kamm *Intricate Ethics: Rights, Responsibilities, and Permissible Harm* (Oxford: OUP, 2007) ch 5; and Scanlon *Moral Dimensions*.

Now consider incomplete inchoate wrongs. If *n*ing is wrong, it is wrong because of its relationship with *v*. Now consider the simple relationship that *n*ing is done with the intention to *v*. Were it not for X's intention to *v*, X could permissibly perform a token of the intention-free act-type, *n*. *The irrelevance of intentions* implies that bad intentions cannot directly make *n*ing wrong. Hence, it is not wrong for X to *n* because *n*ing is done with the intention to *v*.

To illustrate, consider:

> *Poison*: Xena buys rat poison in order to kill Yoshi, who is completely innocent. The poison would also be useful to kill the dangerous rats infesting Zelda's house.

To use our heuristic device for considering whether there is a permissible token of Xena's intention-free act-type of buying poison, consider the best intentions with which Xena could act: she buys it to kill Zelda's rats, and not to kill Yoshi. Assume this is permissible (animal lovers, shut your ears). *The irrelevance of intentions* implies that Xena's bad intentions do not directly make her conduct in *Poison* wrong.[4]

If Xena acts permissibly if she buys the poison to help Zelda, here are two options for defenders of *the irrelevance of intentions*. They could accept the view that Xena acts permissibly in *Poison*. Or they could aim to show that Xena's intentions have derivative significance in *Poison*, making her conduct wrong. The most obvious way to do this is to show that Xena's intentions alter the role that Xena's buying poison predictably has in Yoshi's death.

II. Rejecting The Control View

Here is the basic idea of *The Control View*. In putative cases of incomplete inchoate wrongdoing, there is an intention-free act-type that could be part of a course of conduct that it is wrong to perform, or a course of conduct that it is permissible to perform. Although X has bad intentions, performing the permissible course of conduct remains within X's control. The potential bad results of one's acts cannot make one's acts wrong if one has complete control over whether those results occur. X's bad intentions cannot non-derivatively render his acts wrong. Therefore, there are no incomplete inchoate wrongs.

To illustrate this view, consider Scanlon's argument to support the view that Xena acts permissibly in *Poison*.[5] If Xena buys the poison intending to kill Yoshi, she can decide not to kill Yoshi, but rather to help Zelda. Buying the poison and helping Zelda is a permissible course of conduct. Therefore, Scanlon argues, buying the poison to kill Yoshi is permissible.

This view might be reinforced as follows. Suppose that Xena buys the poison, abandons her intention to kill Yoshi, and helps Zelda. Insofar as anything is within our control, it is within Xena's control to do this. Xena would then perform a token of exactly the same intention-free act-type that she would have performed had she had good intentions throughout. Some might find the view that Xena acts wrongly in this

[4] Some who think that intentions are relevant to permissibility accept *the irrelevance of intentions* as stated here. They think that what matters is whether the person's act could have been performed without bad intentions, and not whether it was actually performed without bad intentions. See W J FitzPatrick 'Intention, Permissibility, and Double Effect' in M Timmons *Oxford Studies in Normative Ethics* vol 2 (Oxford: OUP, 2012). The arguments offered in this paper also challenge this view.

[5] *Moral Dimensions*, 43–4.

case no more intuitive than the view that Xena acts permissibly in *Trolley*, if she intends to kill Yoshi.

Scanlon reinforces the view further. It is implausible that all acts that are performed in order to facilitate wrongdoing are wrongful, he suggests. This would include acts that are, outwardly, remote and completely innocuous. He considers:

Get Up: Xena gets up early, as doing so is necessary to murder Yoshi.

Scanlon finds it implausible that it is wrong for Xena to get up early. *Get Up*, he thinks, is no different from *Poison*. Hence, Xena also acts permissibly in *Poison*.

The Control View, though, has counterintuitive implications.[6] First, Xena might perform all of the acts necessary to perform the complete wrong, with the intention of doing so, and yet Xena might be able to interfere before the wrong is complete. In such cases, it is hard to believe that the person has not yet acted wrongly.

Consider:

Last Act: Xena puts poison in tea that she is about to serve to Yoshi in order to kill Yoshi. Zelda realizes that Xena has done this, and pours the tea down the sink before Yoshi drinks it. Had Zelda not done this, X would have had time to pour the tea down the sink herself. As Xena firmly intended to kill Yoshi, she would not have done this.

Had Zelda not acted, Xena's poisoning of Yoshi remained completely within Xena's control. *The Control View* implausibly implies that Xena acts permissibly.

Perhaps it might be argued that Xena acts wrongly independently of whether she intends to pour the poison down the sink. This would explain the intuitive view that Xena acts wrongly. This need not be true, though. Suppose that others intend wrongfully to kill Yoshi. Yoshi thinks he is safe from these threats. Xena might have put poison into Yoshi's tea in order to demonstrate to Yoshi how vulnerable he is to being poisoned. The permissibility of her doing this cannot make her act permissible in *Last Act*.

Furthermore, one can sometimes render a complete *pro tanto* wrong permissible by performing a further act that would justify it. The argument offered for *The Control View* implausibly implies that such complete acts are not all things considered wrong even if they are not performed with the intention to do the further justificatory act, and only with bad intentions. Consider:

Hotwire: A pregnant woman down the street goes into labour and desperately needs a lift to the hospital. Xena knows this, but is not influenced by it. She hotwires Yoshi's car and starts driving it down the street to sell it to a shady local trader.

The fact that it would be permissible for Xena to hotwire the car in order to take the pregnant woman to the hospital does not plausibly make her conduct permissible in *Hotwire*. The explanation offered for *The Control View*, though, implies that Xena acts permissibly. It remains within Xena's control to take the pregnant woman to the hospital after taking the car. If she does this, she performs a course of conduct that is 'outwardly' identical to the course of conduct that a person with good intentions would perform.

Finally, whether an act is *pro tanto* wrong sometimes depends on the intentions with which it is done. Consider:

Sex Holiday: Xena lies to her husband that she is going on a business trip for a week, when really she is planning to go on a rampant drug fuelled sex holiday.

[6] For related discussion, see M Hanser 'Acting Wrongly by Trying' in M Timmons *Oxford Studies in Normative Ethics* vol 4 (Oxford: OUP, 2014) 149–53.

Xena wrongfully lies to her husband. This view is not plausibly vitiated by the fact that it would be permissible for Xena to tell exactly the same lie in order to devote the week to organizing a huge surprise party for her husband, and it remains completely within Xena's control to do this rather than going on the drug fuelled sex holiday. I doubt that it is even *pro tanto* wrong for Xena to lie to her husband in order to organize a surprise party for him.

Perhaps it might be argued that as cases like *Hotwire* and *Sex Holiday* are not cases of incomplete inchoate wrongdoing, they lack implications for *The Control View*.

This response would not explain the powerful intuition that Xena acts wrongly in *Last Act*. More importantly, *Hotwire* and *Sex Holiday* show that the explanation offered for *The Control View* fails. The fact that these acts can be part of a course of conduct that is within the person's control, and that would be permissible if done with good intentions, is insufficient to make them permissible. We then have no reason to accept that argument against incomplete inchoate wrongdoing.

Rejecting *The Control View* does leave us with a difficult question. Scanlon finds it implausible that Xena acts permissibly in *Get Up*. I would not put this as strongly as Scanlon, but I agree that it is somewhat intuitive that Xena acts permissibly. Scanlon's explanation of this intuition cannot be right, for the reasons offered. We are left with two possibilities: either accept the counterintuitive view that it is wrong for Xena to get up early, or find some principled distinction between *Get Up* on the one hand and cases such as *Last Act, Hotwire*, and *Sex Holiday* on the other. In Section V I will argue for the first possibility.

III. Rejecting The Prediction View

Before endorsing *The Control View*, Scanlon offers what he describes as the most plausible explanation for the significance of intentions to permissibility in cases where an action is done as part of a wider plan the execution of which would be wrong. About *Poison*, he writes:

> A person who intends to do something believes that he will do it, or at least that he will try and that he will have a reasonable chance of success … In buying the poison the man is facilitating a murder, in this case one that he has reason to believe that he himself will carry out. This seems to me the most plausible explanation of how intention is relevant to permissibility in the case of actions that are part of larger plans. In particular, it is more accurate to say that such actions are impermissible because they facilitate other wrongs than to say simply that they are impermissible because they are done for certain reasons. These two ways of explaining the impermissibility are closely related: the larger plan provides a reason for the smaller action *because* it facilitates that action. Nevertheless, the two explanations are distinguishable, and facilitation provides a better explanation of what makes these acts wrong. They are not wrong because of the reason for which *they* are done, but because the agent's larger intention changes their likely consequences. This is an instance of what I called … the *predictive* significance of intent.[7]

It is not clear whether Scanlon endorses the predictive significance of intent. *The Control View*, which Scanlon later seems to endorse, is in conflict with it: a person can be in complete control over an action that he predicts that he will perform. In both *Poison* and *Get Up*, Xena predicts that *n*ing will facilitate *v*ing. If intent has the predictive significance that Scanlon assigns to it, Xena acts wrongly in both cases. Scanlon

[7] *Moral Dimensions*, 42–3.

clearly rejects this view of *Get Up*—he finds it absurd. This suggests that intent lacks the predictive significance that Scanlon seems to assign to it in the passage quoted above. Later, though, Scanlon continues to treat intent as having predictive significance.[8]

Leaving aside the best interpretation of Scanlon's view, notice that *The Prediction View* can explain our intuitions about *Hotwire, Last Act*, and *Sex Holiday*. It is, in that way, superior to *The Control View*. I first explain *The Prediction View* more clearly. I offer a controversial argument against it: control normally vitiates the significance of prediction to permissibility. I then suggest that even if this argument fails, and *The Prediction View* is true, *The Intentions View* is also true.

i) Clarifying The Prediction View

The Prediction View is that *n*ing can be wrong in virtue of the fact that *n*ing predictably facilitates *v*ing, and facilitating a wrongful action, including one's own wrongful action, is wrong. It is not concerned with the fact that *n*ing increases the probability of *v*ing. This feature of the view is attractive—an act that facilitates future wrongdoing could be wrong even if it does not raise the probability of future wrongdoing. For example, it seems wrong to provide a killer with a gun even if, were I not to do so, another person would provide the killer with a gun. Facilitating the killing is wrong even though doing so, in this case, does not raise the probability of the wrongdoing. *The Prediction View* extends this idea to a person facilitating his own future action.

The controversial feature of *The Prediction View* is that it treats future actions that one is in complete control of in a similar way to future actions that one is not in control of. Facilitating one's future wrongful conduct that is without one's control is often wrong. For example, it would be wrong for Xena to buy poison knowing that she was about to go insane, and if she did so she would try to kill Yoshi. Doing this would be wrong with or without the intention of killing Yoshi: Xena's knowledge of her future conduct is clearly sufficient to make her act wrong.

The Prediction View treats future acts that the person is in control of in the same way. Facilitating one's future wrongdoing, on this view, is equally wrong whether the person knows or intends their future wrongdoing. Hence, *Poison* is morally equivalent to:

> *Poison (Knowledge)*: Xena buys rat poison because she thinks that there might be a rat infestation in her house in the future. However, she knows that she is likely to form the intention to murder Yoshi. She will use the rat poison to kill Yoshi if she does so.

The Prediction View implies that Xena acts wrongly in buying rat poison, even though she does not buy the poison with a bad intention. *Poison* and *Poison (Knowledge)* are explained in the same way. Hence *The Prediction View* is consistent with *the irrelevance of intentions*.

ii) The irrelevance of prediction to permissibility

The Prediction View implies that one's predictions about how one's current act affects one's future wrongdoing are relevant to permissibility, even when one is in control of whether one performs these actions. Here I offer an argument that such predictions are irrelevant to permissibility. The conclusion of the argument is highly controversial. It

[8] See *Moral Dimensions*, 45.

is worth emphasizing at the outset that if my argument succeeds, *The Prediction View* fails. If it does not succeed, *The Intentions View* may still be true—*The Prediction View* and *The Intentions View* are not in conflict. In the next subsection I argue that if *The Prediction View* is true, *The Intention View* is also true. The overall argument, then, does not rely on the success of the controversial argument in this section, though if the argument is successful, it substantially strengthens *The Intention View*.

Consider *Poison (Knowledge)*. *The Prediction View* implies that as Xena can predict that her buying of poison will, or might, facilitate her future poisoning of Yoshi, Xena wrongly buys poison. However, it remains possible for Xena not to poison anyone, and only to use the poison to kill rats. She could do so by refraining from forming and executing intentions wrongly to kill people. Whether Yoshi refrains from forming and executing such intentions remains completely within Xena's control. This, I argue, makes it permissible for Xena to buy poison.

Many will immediately be sceptical of this argument on the following grounds. When considering what we ought to do, we often rightly treat our future actions as a matter of prediction. We take decisions now on the basis that we will make fallible decisions later. When we do so, we do not imply that we are not in control of our future decisions. For example, I ought not to stuff the cupboards with cakes, on the basis of a prediction that I will stuff my face if I do. This judgement does not depend on the belief that stuffing my face is beyond my control. Similarly, it might be argued, Xena ought not to buy poison in *Poison (Knowledge)* because she predicts that if she does so, she will use it to kill Yoshi.

However, although it has some initial appeal, *The Prediction View* has unacceptable implications. The source of the problem is that a person's tendency to act wrongly cannot vitiate his duties if he is in control of whether he acts wrongly. An implication is that he may be required to *n* if *n*ing is necessary for him to fulfil his duties. This claim is not vitiated by the fact that he predicts that if he *n*s he will not fulfil his duties. But if he is required to *n*, he is permitted to *n*. As a person cannot be required to *n* and required not to *n*, he is not required not to *n*. Hence, it is not wrong for the person to *n* because of his prediction about his future wrongdoing if he *n*s.

I have space only for a condensed argument. Consider the following abstract scenario:

X has three options:

1) *a* and *b*.

2) *a* and *c*.

3) not *a* and neither *b* nor *c*.

X can do either *b* or *c* only if he *a*s. Only option 1) averts a grave harm. Option 1) is not costly to X. Although options 2) and 3) each fail to avert a great harm, option 2) causes much greater harm than option 3). Option 3) is thus much better than Option 2).

Suppose X is well disposed. Plausibly, X has a duty to *a* and *b* because doing so averts a great harm. Also, plausibly, were X to have only options 2) and 3) it would be wrong to choose 2) on the grounds that 2) causes great harm. Let us suppose these judgements are right.

Now consider the following case:

Tendencies: X can *b* if he *a*s. However, he predicts that he will *c* if he *a*s. He will be fully responsible for *c*ing if he *a*s. Refraining from *c*ing will be fully within his control.

Ought X to *a*?

Some claim X is required not to *a*. X is required to choose option 3) rather than option 2). If X *a*s, X will choose option 2) rather than option 3). Hence, X ought not to *a*. But now consider the following problem. Given that option 1) is far better than options 2) or 3), and is not costly to X, X has a duty to choose option 1). X's duty to *a* and *b* is not vitiated by his tendency to *c* rather than *b* if he *a*s. As *a*ing is necessary for X to *b*, X can fulfil his duty to *a* and *b* only if he *a*s. The view that X is required not to *a* thus implies that X is required to act in a way that makes conforming to his duty to *a* and *b* impossible.[9] This is hard to accept.

Here is another way to see the problem. We must pick one of the following, all of which seem at least somewhat unpalatable:

i. reject the claim that as X tends to *c* if he *a*s, X has a duty not to *a*; or
ii. reject the claim that X's tendency cannot relieve him of his duties, and hence reject X's duty to *a* and *b*; or
iii. endorse the claim that X has a duty to *a* and a duty not to *a*; or
iv. endorse the claim that X's duty to *a* and *b* does not imply a duty to *a*.

Of these options, i) seems to me best.

This option does, admittedly, come at a cost. If X has a duty not to *a* and *c*, it might be argued, X has a duty to prevent himself from doing *a* and *c*. The only thing that will in fact be effective in preventing him from doing *a* and *c* at the time, *t*, when he is deciding whether to *a* is to refrain from *a*ing. Yet i) implies that X may yet *a*.

In response, we are inclined to conclude that X is required not to *a* because we are inclined to treat refraining from *a*ing as necessary for X to avoid doing *a* and *c*. But all participants in this debate accept that X can refrain from doing *a* and *c* by refraining from *c*ing, even though this is not what X will in fact do if he *a*s. If X does *a* and *c* he was no more, and no less, able to refrain from *c*ing than from *a*ing. Once we reject our inclination to see X refraining from *a*ing as necessary for him not to *c*, the verdict that X lacks a duty not to *a* seems more palatable.

Nevertheless, let us accept that i) comes at a cost. This cost must be weighed against the costs of the other options. Of the remaining options, iv) is the most popular. Some claim that X has a duty to *a* and *b*, and also a duty not to *a*.[10] X's duty to *a* and *b* is not vitiated by his tendency to *c* if he *a*s, defenders of this view agree. Ought may imply can, but it does not imply will![11] However, defenders of this view claim, a duty to *a* and *b* does not imply a duty to *a*.

But, iv) violates the plausible principle that if one has an all things considered duty to do something, then one also has a duty to do the things that are necessary for one to do that thing. As X can *a* and *b* only if he *a*s, X has a duty to *a*.

To reinforce this view, notice that we can ask: what is X required to do at time *t*, when he can *a*, but before he can either *b* or *c*? X cannot *a* and *b* at *t* or *a* and *c* at *t*.

[9] For this problem, see J Ross 'Actualism, Possibilism, and Beyond' in R Schafer-Landau *Oxford Studies in Normative Ethics* vol 2 (Oxford: OUP, 2012) 83–4.

[10] See F Jackson and R Pargetter 'Oughts, Options, and Actualism' (1986) XCV *Philosophical Review* 233. See, also, J Louise 'Self-Prediction, Moral Obligation and Moral Deliberation' (2009) 146 *Philosophical Studies* 327, 330–1.

[11] See, also, D Estlund 'Human Nature and the Limits (If Any) of Political Philosophy' (2011) 39 *Philosophy and Public Affairs* 207.

So we can ask only whether X has a duty to *a* at *t* or a duty not to *a* at *t*. X's duty to *a* and *b* can be fulfilled only if X *a*s at *t*. Hence, if X does not *a*, X violates his duty to *a* and *b*. He violates this duty at *t*, for at *t* X has ensured that he cannot *a* and *b*. On pain of contradiction, X is not permitted to violate a duty. Hence, X has a duty to *a* at *t*. If X has a duty to *a*, X is permitted to *a*. If X is permitted to *a*, it is not wrong for X to *a*. Hence, the fact that X tends to *c* if he *a*s does not make it wrong for X to *a*.

Here is a further reason to doubt iv). The main motivation to accept iv) is that it can avoid the cost identified above in accepting i) without accepting the even heavier costs in accepting ii) or iii). But this turns out to be a very modest advantage of iv) over i). Friends of iv) are committed to accepting a very similar cost in another set of cases.

Consider:

Tendencies 2: X has three options:
1) Do nothing either now or later.
2) Harm Y seriously now.
3) Harm Y gravely later.

If X does nothing now, he will harm Y gravely later. If X harms Y seriously now, he will not harm Y gravely later. Whether he harms Y either now or later is completely within X's control.

It may seem that if the only way to prevent him from harming Y gravely later is to harm him seriously now, X ought to harm Y seriously now.

Friends of iv) are nevertheless committed to accepting that X is required to choose 1). They agree that our predictions about our future conduct do not vitiate our duties. The fact that X will harm Y gravely later if he does not harm Y seriously now does not vitiate his duty not to harm Y seriously now. As friends of iv) agree that X cannot have both a duty not to harm Y now and a duty to harm Y now, they must conclude that 2) is wrong.

But if it is wrong for X to harm Y seriously now, it is wrong for X to do the only thing that will avert him harming Y gravely later. This is a cost of iv) when compared with ii) and iii). Furthermore, this cost is similar to the cost that friends of i) must accept in cases like *Tendencies*. Friends of iv) are thus little better off than friends of i). Only friends of ii) and iii) are significantly better off with respect to this cost than friends of i). But, of course, ii) and iii) are extremely unpalatable in other respects.

Given that the main cost of i) is very similar to a cost that friends of iv) bear in other cases, we should prefer i) to iv). For iv) comes with a great cost that i) lacks. Friends of i) can endorse the highly intuitive idea that a person with a duty to *a* and *b* violates that duty by refraining from *a*ing at *t*, and thus acts wrongly at *t*. And they can endorse this without endorsing clashes of obligations.

This has all been a bit dense and technical. Let me clarify by applying the discussion to a variation on our *Poison* cases:

Poison (Required): as *Poison (Knowledge)*, except using rat poison is necessary to control the dangerous rats in Xena's house where Xena's children live.

Plausibly, Xena has a duty to control the rats in her house. This obligation is not vitiated by the fact that if she possesses the rat poison, she will tend to use it wrongly to kill Yoshi. She could refrain from doing this. In this way she could fulfil her obligation to her children whilst not violating any obligations. But she can fulfil his obligation to her children only by buying rat poison. Hence, she has an obligation to buy the rat poison. Hence, she is permitted to do so.

The Prediction View has the wrong implication. It is better for Xena not to buy rat poison and not kill anyone than it is for her to buy rat poison, control the rats, and then kill a person. If X buys rat poison, she will do the latter. Hence, *The Prediction View* implies that X ought not to buy rat poison. But X's tendency to act wrongly does not vitiate her obligation to buy rat poison, control the rats, and not kill anyone. It follows that X does not act wrongly in buying rat poison. Hence, *The Prediction View* is false.

Of course, if we compare what Xena will do if she doesn't buy poison with what she will do if she buys poison, it is preferable that she doesn't buy poison. But as Xena has the option of buying poison, killing the rats, and not killing anyone, this comparison isn't relevant to determining Xena's duties.

Some might claim: surely it makes sense for Xena to reason as follows. If I buy the poison, I will likely kill someone. So I ought not to buy the poison. Reasoning like this does make sense. It is just that the 'ought' claim does not refer to a duty, properly understood. It refers to what we might call a 'second-best duty': we can consider what our duties are, and what are duties are *given that we will violate one of our duties.* Between violating her duty to her daughter or her duty to Y, she ought to violate her duty to her daughter. She knows she will violate one of these duties, and she can reason about what she ought to do given this knowledge. But this does not imply that she ought, all things considered, to violate her duty to her daughter. As she can do something that violates neither duty, that is what she ought to do.

Some might claim that this argument, if it succeeds, shows only that intent lacks predictive significance in cases of a conflict of duties. We should not draw conclusions about the predictive significance of intent in cases where there is no such conflict. I think that the conclusion we should draw is more general than this. Our question is whether our duties are shaped by our predictions about actions we have full control over.[12] If we conclude that they are not, our conclusion should apply generally, regardless of whether we are concerned with cases of conflict of duty.

But I need not rely on that further claim. It would be easy to imagine variations on cases such as *Hotwire, Last Act*, and *Sex Holiday* where Xena acts with bad intentions, but has a duty to do the very same thing in order to execute good intentions that she is required to have. For example, we could easily imagine that Xena is required to hotwire the car in order to ensure that the woman down the street does not die in childbirth. This would not affect the intuitive verdict that it is wrong for Xena to hotwire the car where she does not act with such an intention. We would still have reason to prefer *The Intentions View* to *The Prediction View* as an explanation of these judgements.

iii) The independent significance of intentions

The argument against *The Prediction View* seems powerful. Yet as it has some implications that are hard to accept, some will not find it decisive. If we reject that argument, and accept *The Prediction View*, what conclusion should we draw about *The Intentions View*?

The truth of *The Prediction View* does not demonstrate the falsity of *The Intentions View*. These views are compatible. Xena's intentions might explain the wrongness of her actions in cases like *Last Act, Hotwire*, and *Sex Holiday* both derivatively and

[12] As Jacob Ross notes, we do hold fixed intentions that we will, in the future, be manipulated to form and act on. See 'Actualism, Possibilism, and Beyond', 81–2.

non-derivatively. The idea that *The Prediction View* does not supply a complete account of the wrongness in these cases is appealing.[13]

To consider whether *The Intentions View* is true, even if *The Prediction View* is also true, we should consider pairs of cases where we hold constant the prediction that *n*ing will facilitate *v*ing, but in one case the person acts in order to *v* whereas in the other, the person has good intentions. Intentions make a powerful intuitive difference to permissibility in such pairs of cases.

Compare these variations on *Last Act*:

> *Last Act 2*: Xena, who is Yoshi's chief of security, puts poison in tea that she is about to serve to Yoshi in order to kill him. Xena knows that there is a high chance that she will lose her nerve, and if she does so she will pour Yoshi's tea down the sink. If she does this, Yoshi will realize how vulnerable he is to being poisoned, and will better be protected from others who wish to murder him.

> *Last Act 3*: Xena, who is Yoshi's chief of security, puts poison in tea that she is about to serve to Yoshi in order to demonstrate that Yoshi is vulnerable to being poisoned by others who wish to murder him. He will then be better protected against being murdered. However, Yoshi has insulted Xena, and she knows that there is a small chance that she will decide to murder Yoshi. If she does so, she will refrain from pouring the tea down the sink, and Yoshi will be killed.

Suppose that the chance of Xena acting wrongly in *Last Act 3* is sufficiently small that even if *The Predictive View* is correct, Xena permissibly puts poison in Yoshi's tea. It is implausible that we should also conclude that Xena acts permissibly in *Last Act 2*. The fact that Xena is likely to change her mind, and act in a way that will benefit Yoshi, can hardly justify her attempt to poison Yoshi.

Similarly, compare the following variations on *Hotwire*:

> *Hotwire 2*: A woman down the street goes into labour and desperately needs a lift to the hospital. Xena knows that this has occurred. She hotwires Yoshi's car and starts driving it down the street to pick the woman up to drive her to hospital. However, she knows that there is a low chance that she will be tempted to ignore the woman, and drive the car to sell it to a shady local trader.

> *Hotwire 3*: A woman down the street goes into labour and desperately needs a lift to the hospital. Xena knows that this has occurred. She is not at all influenced by this fact. She hotwires Yoshi's car and starts driving it down the street to sell it to a shady local trader. However, she knows that there is a high chance that she will lose her nerve, and if she does she will use the car to drive the woman to the hospital.

Xena plausibly acts permissibly in *Hotwire 2*, even if we accept that her prediction that she might sell the car to the shady local trader has implications for the permissibility of her action. Surely we should not conclude, in the light of this, that she permissibly takes the car in *Hotwire 3*.

Finally, compare these two variations on *Sex Holiday*:

> *Sex Holiday 2*: Xena lies to her husband that she is going on a business trip for a week, when really she is planning to organize a large surprise party for him. However, she knows

[13] Scanlon himself concedes that the non-derivative explanation of the significance of intentions 'may seem forced': *Moral Dimensions*, 43. See, also, D Husak 'The Costs to Criminal Theory of Supposing that Intentions are Irrelevant to Permissibility' in *The Philosophy of Criminal Law: Selected Essays* (Oxford: OUP, 2010) 79–85.

that there is a low chance that she will be tempted to spend the week on a rampant drug fuelled sex holiday.

Sex Holiday 3: Xena lies to her husband that she is going on a business trip for a week, when really she is planning to go on a rampant drug fuelled sex holiday. She knows there is a high chance that she will lose her nerve, and if she does he will organize a large surprise party for her husband.

In each case, Xena reasonably predicts that if she lies to her husband, she will organize a large surprise party for him, and her lie will facilitate the surprise party. There is also some chance that her lie will facilitate a rampant drug fuelled sex holiday. Even if *The Prediction View* is right, intuitively Xena permissibly lies in *Sex Holiday 2*. But it is not plausible that she permissibly lies in *Sex Holiday 3*.

IV. Remoteness, Innocuousness, and Wrongdoing

Here is a summary of the argument so far. *The Intentions View* is that bad intentions play a non-derivative role in determining whether an act is permissible. Such a view either yields the right verdicts, or is compatible with those verdicts, in all of the cases considered so far, except perhaps *Get Up*, which I will consider in a moment.

Unlike *The Control View, The Intentions View* plausibly implies that Xena acts wrongly in *Last Act, Hotwire*, and *Sex Holiday* because her preparatory acts are performed in order to complete a wrong. It plausibly implies that Xena would act permissibly in such cases were she to perform a token of the same intention-free act-type for better reasons.

The Prediction View can also explain these intuitions. However, unlike *The Prediction View, The Intention View* is compatible with the view that Xena is required to buy poison in *Poison (Required)*, and I argued that this is the right view. It is also compatible with the view that she acts wrongly in that case.

Hence, even if my argument that Xena acts permissibly in *Poison (Required)* fails, and *The Prediction View* yields the right verdict, it does not follow that *The Prediction View* should be preferred to *The Intentions View*. To establish that, we should consider whether intentions make a difference to permissibility when we hold the predictive implications of our preparatory acts constant. We considered variations on *Last Act, Hotwire*, and *Sex Holiday*, and found that it is intuitive that intentions make a difference to permissibility when we do this. Hence, even if *The Prediction View* is true, it is more plausible when supplemented by *The Intentions View* than it is alone.

I conclude that *The Control View* is false. There are powerful arguments against *The Prediction View*. If *The Prediction View* is false, we have powerful reasons to believe *The Intentions View*. And even if *The Prediction View* is true, we nevertheless have powerful reasons to believe *The Intentions View*.

Now consider the problem that remained at the end of Section II. Rejecting *The Control View* leaves us with the challenge of evaluating cases where *n* is a typically innocuous act that is far removed from a complete wrong, but is performed with the intent to facilitate *v*.

Recall:

Get Up: Xena gets up early, as doing so is necessary to murder Yoshi.

Scanlon, recall, finds it implausible that Xena acts wrongly. He offers the explanation that getting up early is consistent with a permissible course of conduct. As Xena could get up early and abandon her plan to kill Yoshi, Xena acts permissibly. We have seen the implausible implications of this view.

I don't find the view that Xena acts wrongly in *Get Up* as implausible as Scanlon does—far less implausible than the view that Xena acts permissibly in *Hotwire, Last Act*, and *Sex Holiday*. If no attractive principled distinction between these cases can be found, I settle on the view that Xena acts wrongly in *Get Up*.

Get Up has at least two features that might be salient that the other cases lack: getting up is remote from the killing, and getting up is typically innocuous. Let us consider them in turn.

i) Remoteness

The idea that remoteness vitiates legal wrongness is familiar from the law of causation. Here is one way to understand the idea. If there is a sequence of events (E1, E2, E3, E4, E5 … E*n*) where each event in the sequence causes the next event, it does not follow that the first event causes the last event. Michael Moore attributes this view to the law of torts, claiming that liability doctrines in tort law 'presuppose that causation is the kind of relation that can "peter out"'.[14]

This is not very plausible as a moral view, at least in cases where a person intends the final result, and knows that it will occur. Consider:

> *Beelzebub*: Beelzebub flips a switch. This gives rise to a very long chain of diverse events, each of which causes the next. Yoshi's death is the last event in the chain. Beelzebub knows that Yoshi's death counterfactually depends on his flipping the switch.

The judgement that Beelzebub wrongly kills Yoshi is unaffected by the number of events in the sequence between pulling the lever and Yoshi's death.[15]

It might be thought more plausible that the permissibility of *n*ing depends on the number of actions that X needs to perform in order to commit a complete wrong. This view claims: if there is a sequence of actions (A1, A2, A3 … A*n*), and A1 is performed in order to facilitate the performance of A*n*, and A*n* is wrong, the fact that A1 is performed with the intention of performing A*n* makes A1 wrong only if the sequence from A1 to A*n* is sufficiently small.

This view still has counterintuitive implications. Consider:

> *Beelzebub 2*: Beelzebub has acquired a nuclear missile. He points it at London. In order to set it off, he needs to flip a number of switches in sequence. He can do this very quickly.

It is hard to believe that whether Beelzebub has acted wrongly depends in a significant way on the number of switches he still has to flip to set the missile off.

Perhaps it might be argued that what matters is the time between A1 and A*n*. To evaluate this, consider:

> *Beelzebub 3*: Beelzebub has acquired a nuclear missile. He points it at London. He intends to kill the maximum number of people that he can with it, which will occur if he sets it off during the Olympic games. He puts everything in place, and all that he has to do to kill all these people is to flip a switch at the time that the games are on.

[14] M Moore *Causation and the Law: An Essay in Law, Morals and Metaphysics* (Oxford: OUP, 2009) 121–3.

[15] For further discussion, see V Tadros 'Causation, Culpability, and Liability' in C Coons and M Weber *The Ethics of Self Defense* (Oxford: OUP, 2016).

Again, it does not seem plausible that whether Beelzebub acts wrongly depends in a significant way on whether the Olympic games is held today, tomorrow, or next year.

Finally, remoteness does not explain our intuition in *Get Up*. Xena might need to perform only very few acts in order to murder Yoshi in *Get Up*. The fact that getting up is not remote from the killing of Yoshi does not affect our intuition about the case.

The English law of criminal attempts offers a related view that might seem better. It distinguishes between acts that are merely preparatory to wrongdoing and acts that are more than merely preparatory.[16] A similar distinction is that between preparing to act wrongly and embarking on wrongdoing. Distinctions like this might be justified on the basis of the following principle:

> *Trying*: if it is wrong to *v*, it is also wrong to try to *v*.

This is what Gideon Yaffe calls a *transfer principle*—the moral wrongdoing of *v*ing transfers to other acts, such as trying to *v*.[17] Of course, as Yaffe also notes, the truth of such a principle does not imply that trying to *v* is as gravely wrong as *v*ing.[18] All that it implies is that the wrongness of *v*ing transfers in some measure to trying to *v*.[19]

Before making further progress, it is worth noting that *Trying* is not quite right. Sometimes a person's trying to *v* is not explained by his ambition to *v*. In such cases, *v*ing is not what he has in mind in his decision to *v*. Consider:

> *Instructor*: Yoshi is Xena's martial arts instructor. Yoshi wishes to show the class how to deflect an attack. Yoshi encourages Xena to try to break his arm. Xena tries with all her might to do this, but Yoshi immediately deflects the attack.

It would have been wrong for Xena to break Yoshi's arm. Suppose that unbeknownst to Yoshi, Xena has the skill. Clearly, Xena would act wrongly were she to exercise it. But it is not wrong for Xena to try to break Yoshi's arm if she lacks the skill to break it. This is because Xena's trying to break Yoshi's arm is not done with the aim of breaking the arm. This suggests that *Trying* needs amending. I will not attempt further progress with amending it here. Let us suppose a suitable amendment has been made.

In order to try to *v*, one must do something that is more than merely preparatory towards *v*ing—there is a difference between preparing and attempting. It might then be argued that the moral wrongness of *v*ing transfers to trying to *v*, but not to acts short of trying to *v*. This would explain why Xena does not act wrongly in *Get Up*.

However, if *Trying* is valid, why stop there? Further *transfer principles* seem true. For example:

> *Planning*: if it is wrong to *v*, it is also wrong to plan to *v*.
>
> *Preparing*: if it is wrong to *v*, it is also wrong to prepare to *v*.
>
> *Intending*: if it is wrong to *v*, it is also wrong to form an intention to *v*.

These principles seem no less attractive than *Trying*. For like trying, planning, preparing, and forming an intention are all to be understood by reference to another act that they will become—*v*ing. If the act that they are to become, *v*ing, is wrong, so are the acts that are to be understood with reference to the acts they will become.[20] These principles do not imply that the relevant acts are as gravely wrong as *v*ing, or even as

[16] Criminal Attempts Act 1981, s 1.
[17] For this transfer principle, see *Attempts* (Oxford: OUP, 2010) 25.
[18] See *Attempts*, 26–7.
[19] For an extended defence of *Trying*, see Hanser 'Acting Wrongly by Trying'.
[20] For this explanation of *Trying*, see Hanser 'Acting Wrongly by Trying'.

gravely wrong as trying to *v*. Nevertheless, it does often seem wrong to prepare to act wrongly, as in *Poison*. It also seems wrong to plan a murder, and even to form an intention to murder.

Finally, it is not difficult to find reasons in favour of the legal distinction between preparatory acts from those that are more than merely preparatory. The most obvious reasons, though, do not seem salient to the question whether it is morally wrong to perform the preparatory act. For example, the criminal law is concerned with averting harm. Criminalizing preparatory acts is less important in securing this goal than criminalizing acts that are more than merely preparatory. And a law prohibiting preparatory acts runs a greater risk of punishing the innocent, as it is more difficult to distinguish those who are genuinely preparing to commit a crime from those who are merely showing bravado. Factors like these do not plausibly have implications for the wrongness of preparing.

ii) Innocuousness

The contrast between preparatory acts that are typically innocuous and those that are not seems important. How can getting up early be wrong, we think, even if it is done in order to kill one's wife, given that getting up is in itself so innocuous? We have similar intuitions about less remote preparatory acts. For example, turning on the lights does not seem wrong, even if this is done in order to see the victim better to assist with my killing her. There is some intuitive contrast between this case and the loading of a gun in order to fire it—our intuition that the loading is wrong seems more powerful. These judgements support the view that whether a preparatory act is wrong depends on whether it is typically innocuous.

Furthermore, the acts in *Hotwire, Last Act*, and *Sex Holiday* are not typically innocuous. Whilst hotwiring another person's car can be done for innocuous reasons, hotwiring is normally done to steal cars. Whilst one can secretly put poison in another person's tea for innocuous reasons, this is typically done to poison others. Whilst one can lie to one's husband about a business trip for innocuous reasons, it is typically part of a plan to act wrongly. Furthermore, it is plausible that we have the intuition that Xena acts wrongly in these cases because the intention-free act-types involved are not typically innocuous. The fact that Xena could have put poison in Yoshi's cup in *Last Act* for a good reason, for example, seems insufficient to make her act permissible because putting poison in a cup is not normally innocuous.

Here is a closely related but distinct idea. It might be thought that *Get Up* is not a case of wrongful preparation because getting up is not precisely tailored to the end of killing. In contrast, the preparatory acts in *Hotwire, Last Act*, and *Sex Holiday* are precisely tailored to killing. An act is precisely tailored to an end if it is performed in a way that suits that end particularly well, and doesn't support many other ends particularly well. Getting up early suits a very wide range of ends equally well. Putting poison in someone's tea suits the end of poisoning the person especially well. It only suits a small range of alternative ends equally well.

Now imagine that Xena could kill Yoshi only if she gets up at precisely 4.35am: any earlier and her getting up would wake Yoshi; any later and she would miss her opportunity. The intuition that Xena acts permissibly is less secure in this variation compared with *Get Up*. This is so even though getting up at precisely 4.35am is typically innocuous. Perhaps that is because getting up early is precisely tailored to killing. This idea would also explain the wrongness of, for example, forming an intention to act wrongly and planning to act wrongly: these acts are precisely tailored to the complete wrongs to which they are related.

I think that one of these distinctions, or perhaps both together, explain our contrasting intuitions in cases like *Get Up* and cases like *Poison*. But should we accept these intuitions? I doubt it. Suppose that we conclude that the wrongness of *v*ing can render it wrong to prepare to *v*. Why should it make a difference to the wrongness of preparing to *v* whether the act involved in the preparation is typically innocuous or not, or is narrowly tailored to *v*ing or not? Once we accept that a token of an intention-free act-type can be wrong because it is performed in order to complete a wrongful action, there seems little reason to think that the range of actions that this is true of is restricted to those that are not innocuous or are narrowly tailored. At least, I can think of no explanation that plausibly has moral salience that would differentiate between these cases.

So although I think that our intuition that Xena acts permissibly in *Get Up* can be explained, I suspect that we ought to reject the intuition. The explanation of the contrast between our intuitions in *Get Up* and some of the other cases that we have been considering does not point to anything relevant to permissibility. It is worth noting, though, that although I favour an expansive version of *The Intentions View*, a narrower version is available that would have more intuitive implications.

V. Choice, Practical Reasoning, and Inchoate Wrongdoing

In the light of our discussion, we can address two more general arguments against the significance of intentions to permissibility.

i) Choice

The first concerns the relationship between wrongness, permissibility, and choice. Let *n* be some intention-free act-type that it is necessary for X to perform in order either to contribute to some future wrongful act, *v*, or to some future permissible act, *w*. Scanlon claims that whilst X can choose whether or not to *n*, X cannot choose the ultimate reasons for which he *n*s. We are responsible for determining what we think are reasons for action, Scanlon claims, but determining what we think those reasons are does not involve choice, because it lacks the requisite element of 'free play'.[21] But if it is wrong to perform an act, Scanlon believes, we must be able to choose not to perform it. Hence, as it is permissible for X to *n* in order to *v*, it is also permissible for X to *n* in order to *w*.

One way to resist this argument is to defend the view that it can be wrong to act with certain intentions even if we cannot choose the intentions with which we act.[22] It is not so clear that wrongness and permissibility always require choice. To see this, notice that it seems wrong to have racist beliefs. Yet we do not normally choose which

[21] See *Moral Dimensions*, 60.

[22] See J McMahan 'Intention, Permissibility, Terrorism, and War' (2009) 23 *Philosophical Perspectives* 345.

beliefs to have. Similarly, it might be argued that it could be wrong to act with certain intentions even if we do not choose which intentions to have.

Alternatively, it might be argued that we can choose whether to *n* with the intention to *v* or to *n* with the intention to *w*. I think that we can have these choices.[23] Scanlon claims that a person cannot choose her intentions. But he grants, as is obviously true, that a person can choose to abandon her wrongful plans. However, choosing whether to abandon one's wrongful plan can amount to a choice whether to act with the intentions that having such a plan involves. This already suggests that we can choose the intentions with which we act.

Notice that even if Scanlon's argument that we cannot choose our ultimate reasons is correct, it does not follow that we cannot choose the intentions with which we act. Choosing our further intentions need not involve choosing our ultimate reasons, for our further intentions may not refer to our ultimate reasons. X might be able to choose whether to *n* in order to *v* or to *n* in order to *w* because *v* and *w* are not X's ultimate aims. So any inability of X to choose his ultimate aims does not hamper his ability to choose whether he *ns* in order to *v* or to *w*.

Furthermore, it is highly plausible that X can choose his further intentions, or at least that X's further intentions are appropriately sensitive to his choices. Suppose that X has the intention to *v*. He is deciding whether to *n* in order to *v*. What ought he to do? As Scanlon himself suggests, he ought to abandon his plan to *v*. If he abandons his plan to *v*, he will not perform any acts in order to *v*. Hence, any acts that he performs will not be performed with the intention to *v*. If he ought to abandon his plan to *v*, by Scanlon's lights, he can choose to abandon his plan to *v*. He could also, of course, choose not to do this. It is highly plausible that he has this choice.

Suppose that X abandons his plan to *v*. What choices does he have left? He could choose to *w*. As *n*ing is necessary for him to *w*, he will then choose to *n*. If he chooses to *w*, he will choose to *n* in order to *w*. Hence, it is a matter of choice for X whether he *ns* in order to *v* or *ns* in order to *w*.

Now consider the claim that it is wrong for X to *n* with the intention to *v*, but permissible for X to *n* with the intention to *w*. This claim does not imply that X's duties apply to something over which he has no choice. X can choose to abandon his plan to *v*, choose to *w*, and choose to *n* in order to *w*. Hence, if it is wrong for X to *n* in order to *v*, X can refrain from *n*ing in order to *v*. He can do so by abandoning his intention to *v*. And that, as Scanlon suggests, is what X ought to do. X can nevertheless then choose to *n* in order to *w*. Hence, X can choose to refrain from *n*ing in order to *v*, and yet choose to *n* in order to *w*.

To illustrate this argument, recall:

> *Poison*: Xena buys rat poison in order to kill Yoshi, who is completely innocent. The poison would also be useful to kill the dangerous rats infesting Zelda's house.

Now consider the claim that it is wrong for Xena to buy the poison in order to kill Yoshi, but permissible to buy the poison to control Zelda's rats. Scanlon's argument suggests that this is false: whilst Xena can choose whether or not to buy the poison, she cannot choose her reason for buying it.

However, by Scanlon's own lights, Xena ought to abandon her plan to kill Yoshi. As Xena ought to do this, again by Scanlon's own lights, Xena can choose to abandon

[23] For related responses to Scanlon's argument, see V Tadros *The Ends of Harm: The Moral Foundations of Criminal Law* (Oxford: OUP, 2011) ch 7 and N Kolodny 'Scanlon's Investigation: The Relevance of Intent to Permissibility' (2011) 52 *Analytic Philosophy* 100.

this plan. Now suppose that Xena does what she ought to do. She can nevertheless choose to control Zelda's rats. If she does, she will form the intention to do this. And she can further that intention by choosing to buy the poison to kill Zelda's rats. Hence, whether she buys the poison to kill Yoshi or to control Zelda's rats is a matter of choice.

It follows that the claim that Xena ought not to buy the rat poison to kill Yoshi, but may buy it to kill Zelda's rats, does not imply that Xena's duties apply to things over which she lacks choice. Whatever the merits of Scanlon's view about our ability to choose our ultimate reasons, then, this view does not imply that intentions are irrelevant to permissibility. This is true even if our duties only apply to things over which we have choice.

ii) Reasoning about wrongness

Broadly the same idea counts against an argument against the significance of intentions offered by Judith Jarvis Thomson and endorsed by Scanlon.[24] This argument claims that when we consider whether it is permissible to *n*, we don't normally consider the intentions with which we will *n*. We normally consider other facts about *n*ing, such as whether *n* will harm a person, or will restrict her choices.

Now suppose that Xena has the intention to *v*, and is considering whether *n*ing is permissible. It is not unusual for her to consider the permissibility of *n*ing by considering whether *v*ing is permissible. Consider trying to *v*. Doing this may involve acts that would be permissible were Xena not trying to *v*. The difference between performing such acts and trying to *v* is in Xena's intentions in performing these acts. But there is nothing odd about concluding from the fact that it is wrong to *v* that it is wrong to try to *v*. A similar thing can be said about preparing to *v*.

More generally, if we are considering the permissibility of performing an action to secure some goal, it is not at all unusual to reflect on the permissibility of the goal. If we conclude that it is impermissible to pursue some goal, it is not at all unusual to conclude from this that it is also impermissible to plan to do it, take steps to further it, try to do it, and so on. If we conclude from the impermissibility of our goal that it is also impermissible to take steps to further it, we nevertheless leave open the possibility that we will perform the same intention-free act-type for a different purpose. For the same intention-free act-type might be instrumentally effective in securing more than one goal.

Recall *Poison*. Xena might consider the permissibility of killing Yoshi. Suppose that she concludes that this is wrong. If she does, she might also conclude that it is wrong for her to take steps to further her plan. Hence, she will conclude that it would be wrong to buy the poison in order to kill Yoshi. But this leaves open the possibility that she will nevertheless buy the poison. After abandoning her plan, she might choose to control Zelda's rats. In determining whether it is wrong for her to buy the poison for this reason, she might reflect on whether killing the rats is wrong. If it is not, and there is no other reason why buying the poison is wrong, she ought to conclude that she may permissibly buy the poison to kill Zelda's rats. Reasoning in this way does not seem unusual or forced.

Notice that Xena does not directly reflect on whether it is wrong to buy the poison with the intention of facilitating her killing of Yoshi, or to buy it with the intention

[24] 'Self-Defense' (1991) 20 *Philosophy and Public Affairs* 283, 293–6, endorsed by Scanlon in *Moral Dimensions*, 19–20.

of controlling the rats. This indeed would be odd. But the oddness is not explained by *the irrelevance of intentions*. It is explained as follows. The wrongness of buying the poison to kill Yoshi is inherited from the wrongness of killing Yoshi. It is thus odd to reason directly about the wrongness of buying poison to kill Yoshi. This conclusion will normally follow directly from the conclusion that it is wrong to kill Yoshi in virtue of a transfer principle such as *Preparing*.

VI. Conclusion

The view that intentions are irrelevant to permissibility has implausible implications for incomplete inchoate wrongdoing. Furthermore, two well-known arguments that have been offered to support the irrelevance of intentions to permissibility fail to establish that intentions are not relevant to permissibility in this context. Incomplete inchoate wrongdoing, I conclude, is often wrong non-derivatively in virtue of the intentions of the person acting wrongly. It remains to be seen whether incomplete inchoate wrongdoing can be criminalized.

17

Possession, Prohibition, and Protection

All modern systems of criminal law criminalize possession of offensive weapons, nuclear material, sensitive security information, and so on. They all do so, at least in part, in order to prevent harmful wrongdoing. Either the person possessing it, or another person, might use the material to perpetrate harmful wrongdoing. The ambition of governments that criminalize possession is to reduce instances of harmful wrongdoing.

I focus on one central case: criminalization of possession of firearms. Criminalization might prevent harm in more than one way. It makes the tools that are used for harmful wrongdoing less widely available, and it deters not only possession, but also the production and sale of the relevant material. Deterring possession may reduce the circulation of firearms, and hence gun violence in another way. A rigorously enforced prohibition on possession of firearms results in firearms only being available from unlicensed sources. Firearms are likely to be more expensive from such sources if participants in the market risk punishment. Hence, punishing those who possess firearms reduces the circulation of firearms by driving up transaction costs.[1] Effectiveness is, of course, a disputed empirical question that I do not attempt to answer.

Let us suppose that possession offences prevent harm. It does not follow that they are just. As I suggested in Chapter 6, it is often wrong to criminalize conduct that a person has a right to perform, even if doing so reduces the rate of harmful wrongdoing. But there I also suggested that there are exceptions. Rights can be overridden. When they are, the person's rights are infringed, but not violated. The person is wronged *pro tanto*, but wronging her is not wrong all things considered.[2] My strategy is to focus on how firearms prohibitions can be justified in the light of objections that might be made on behalf of different people who will be affected by them.

Sections I and II argue that two kinds of wrongdoer who possess firearms are liable to punishment: those whose possession increases the risks of others wrongly using the firearm and those who intend wrongly to use their firearm. Section III argues that those who permissibly possess firearms, but who are disposed wrongly to use them, are also liable to punishment. Section IV argues that firearms prohibitions can extend beyond the conduct explored in the first three sections to include those who neither act wrongly, nor are disposed to act wrongly.

The conclusions defended in Sections III and IV are worth highlighting. They conflict with a range of popular views about crime and punishment, including: the view that only wrongdoing may be criminalized (*The Strong Wrongness Constraint*); the view that only public wrongdoing may be criminalized (*Public Wrongdoing*); the view that

[1] See P J Cook, J Ludwig, S Venkatesh, and A A Braga 'Underground Gun Markets' (2007) 117 *The Economic Journal* 588. Gary Kleck reports that only 7.6% of imprisoned felons reported getting their guns from the black market or from a fence. See *Point Blank: Guns and Violence in America* (New York: de Gruyter, 1991) 46, drawing on J D Wright and P H Rossi *Armed and Considered Dangerous: A Survey of Felons and Their Firearms* (New York: Aldine, 1986). However, the analysis offered by Cook et al may well apply to other unlicensed sources.

[2] See, further, Chapter 6.

conduct may be criminalized only on condition that the conduct is wrong once it has been criminalized (*The Weak Wrongness Constraint*); and the view that only those who deserve punishment may permissibly be punished (what is sometimes called *Negative Retributivism*[3]).

I. Wrongful Use by Others

When is it wrong to possess firearms? It might be argued that possession is never wrong because possession is a status rather than an act or omission, and only acts or omissions can be wrong.[4] This objection does not seem powerful.[5] But even if it is, taking or retaining possession could nevertheless be wrong. For those who think that possession is not wrong on this basis, replace possession with 'taking or retaining possession' in what follows.

i) The Mantra

Possessing a firearm might be wrong because it might go off accidentally. This is quite rare, though perhaps sufficiently common to render possession wrong in some cases.[6] More commonly, possession might be wrong because others will wrongly use one's firearms. Many firearms that are wrongly used are stolen. Consider:

> *Kids and Guns*: Arnie possesses a firearm for recreational purposes. Wesley, a local kid, steals the firearm and wrongly shoots Sly.

Does Wesley's act make Arnie's possession wrongful?

Some might deny this if Wesley is fully responsible for his conduct. As the familiar gun-lobby mantra says: people, not guns, kill. Given that Wesley kills, Arnie does not kill. The mantra might be unpacked as follows:

The Mantra:

1) A gun cannot (except in unusual circumstances) kill a person without a person intentionally pressing the trigger.
2) D possessing a gun does not immediately cause the trigger intentionally to be pressed.
3) If X, a responsible adult, wrongly kills V with D's gun, X is fully responsible for killing V.
4) If X is fully responsible for killing V, the chain of causation between D's possession and V's death is broken.
5) Harm can only make an act wrong if the chain of causation between the possession and the harm is not broken.
6) Therefore, V's death does not make it wrong for D to possess the gun.

[3] For doubts about the aptness of this label, see V Tadros 'Response to Blumenson' (2015) 3 *Law, Ethics and Philosophy* 56

[4] Markus Dubber makes much of the parallel between status offences, such as vagrancy offences and possession offences, in 'The Possession Paradigm: The Special Part and the Police Power Model of the Criminal Process' in R A Duff and S P Green *Defining Crimes: Essays on the Special Part of the Criminal Law* (Oxford: OUP, 2005).

[5] For a nice defence of the idea that possession can itself be wrong, see G Yaffe 'In Defense of Criminal Possession' *Criminal Law and Philosophy*, forthcoming.

[6] It has been reported that 2% of firearms deaths in the United States were unintentional. See M Miller, D Azrael, and D Hemingway 'Firearms and Death in the United States' in D W Webster and J S Vernick *Reducing Gun Violence in America: Informing Policy with Evidence and Analysis* (Baltimore: John Hopkins University Press, 2013) 3.

This argument would not apply to *Kids and Guns* if Wesley is not a responsible agent. But as responsible agents perpetrate most wrongful killings this limitation of *The Mantra* is not very important.

Should we accept *The Mantra*? My doubts are about premises 4) and 5). These premises cannot be accepted together. The reason to consider them together is that it is difficult to determine the best way to understand their relationship. To simplify our discussion, let us suppose that Sly's death counterfactually depends on Arnie possessing the firearm. If Arnie had not possessed the firearm, Sly would not have been killed. I leave aside pre-emption and simultaneous overdetermination cases—for example, the case where Wesley would have secured a firearm from elsewhere had Arnie not possessed one.

Some claim that counterfactual dependence is insufficient to establish causation because the chain of causation can be broken by voluntary intervening acts. Others deny this. Whether Arnie wrongly possesses the gun, though, does not turn on this dispute. Those who believe that voluntary intervening acts break the chain of causation might believe that that counterfactual dependence of harm on one's act can make that act wrong even where harm is not caused. Whether this is true does not depend on the best theory of causation, but on the moral significance of counterfactual dependence. Let us consider two moral arguments that might support *The Mantra*.[7]

ii) The division of responsibility

The Responsibility Argument is that one person's responsibility for some event reduces or negates another person's responsibility for that event. This explains why Arnie is not responsible for Sly's death, and thus why Sly's death cannot make Arnie's possession wrong.

Against *The Responsibility Argument*, Wesley's responsibility for Sly's death has no implications for Arnie's responsibility. Responsibility is not 'zero-sum'. The responsibility of one person does not even reduce the responsibilities of others. Two people can each be fully responsible for causing the same harm. We can see this from the fact that groups of people can each be fully responsible for harm. This is true where the group execute a common plan to harm. Two people who together kick a person to death, for example, are each fully responsible for the death.

Friends of *The Responsibility Argument* might respond that the reason why responsibility is not zero-sum in cases of group action is that each person intends the others to participate in the plan. In this way, each becomes responsible for the actions of the others. They might argue that responsibility is zero-sum where each is not responsible for the actions of the others. But responsibility is not zero-sum in cases where people do not act with joint intentions.

Consider:

> *Two Killers*: Melinda puts a bomb on a plane in order to get the insurance money, knowing that there are passengers on board, but not knowing who they are. Katie knows that Melinda has done this. She is not working with Melinda. She forces Sandy onto the plane in order to kill Sandy. The bomb goes off, killing Sandy.

Melinda and Katie are each fully responsible for Sandy's death. Although Katie acts with the intention that Melinda acts, Melinda does not act with the intention that

[7] I further develop the brief arguments offered here in 'Permissibility in a World of Wrongdoing', Philosophy and Public Affairs, forthcoming.

Katie acts. Melinda might prefer Katie not to act in this way. Yet Melinda's responsibility for Sandy's death is not plausibly negated, or even diminished, by Katie's act. Melinda is not even less responsible for Sandy's death than she is for the deaths of the other passengers on the plane.

iii) Liberty and wrongdoing

The Liberty Argument is that one person's liberty cannot be restricted by another person's tendency to act wrongly. Andrew Simester and Andreas von Hirsch offer this argument. They write:

> The central question is whether we may be legitimately compelled to give up options merely because … others might later misbehave. Our answer is, no.[8]

They believe that more is required: the person must either affirm the wrongful conduct, or act in a way that is like affirming it, by assisting, encouraging, or otherwise endorsing it.

Simester and von Hirsch's quote can be understood in more than one way, as the options they refer to might be moral options or legal options. They could accept that Arnie wrongly possesses a firearm, but that he may not be coerced to deprive him of the firearm. Alternatively, they may believe that Arnie's right not to be interfered with is that he is permitted to possess the firearm.

First, let us focus on whether Wesley's wrongdoing makes Arnie's possession wrong. Against this, it might be argued that this allows Wesley's wrongdoing to determine the scope of Arnie's moral freedom, and this is objectionable. Here is an obvious response. If Arnie's liberty is not restricted in this way, and Arnie possesses a firearm, Wesley will wrongly kill Sly. It may be objectionable that Wesley's wrongdoing costs Arnie his liberty. It is much more objectionable that Wesley's wrongdoing costs Sly his life.

Here is a further problem. The argument that one person's wrongdoing cannot restrict another person's liberty in this way has wide implications. Simester and von Hirsch seem to believe that there is something especially objectionable about Arnie being constrained by Wesley's *future* wrongdoing. But it is not clear why. Wesley might also change the consequences of Arnie's actions as a result of his past wrongdoing. *The Liberty Argument* has equal force in such cases but its implications are clearly implausible in that case.

Consider:

> *Target*: Brenda likes shooting at targets in her back garden. Lisa wrongly ties Maria to the front of the target.

Obviously, Brenda is not permitted to shoot at the target with Maria tied to the front of it. But if she is not permitted to do this, Lisa's past wrongdoing has restricted Brenda's liberty. If *The Liberty Argument* lacks force in this case, why should it have force in cases of future wrongdoing?

[8] A P Simester and A von Hirsch *Crimes, Harms, and Wrongs: On the Principles of Criminalisation* (Oxford: Hart, 2011) 81. See, also, A Ashworth and L Zedner *Preventive Justice* (Oxford: OUP, 2014) 112. Husak, in contrast, is open to criminalization in cases where a person knows or risks others acting wrongfully. See 'The Nature and Justifiability of Nonconsummate Offences' in *The Philosophy of Criminal Law: Selected Essays* (Oxford: OUP, 2010) 139. In other work, Simester acknowledges that autonomy and liberty considerations of the kind involved here are not trumps, but are merely to be weighed in the balance. See 'Prophylactic Crimes' in G R Sullivan and I Dennis *Seeking Security: Pre-Empting the Commission of Criminal Harms* (Oxford: Hart, 2012) 61.

Perhaps it might be argued that when we are completely certain that some wrongful act has been performed, or will be performed, intervening agency is morally irrelevant, but it is relevant when we are uncertain about how a person will act. This might be supported on the grounds that we are entitled to presume that morally responsible agents won't act wrongly when we are uncertain that they will.

The implications of this view are not much better. Consider:

> *Drone*: Bill is testing out a new drone. It is flying over an area that is normally unpopulated. He targets the drone's weapon on a house that he believes to be empty when he receives information that Kathy, a suspected terrorist, was hanging around the house the day before, and might have hidden hostages inside the building.

Obviously, the risk of killing the hostages makes it wrong for Bill to destroy the house. The idea that he should presume that Kathy is morally innocent is not plausible.

Perhaps defenders of *The Liberty Argument* might just rely on the intuitive difference between the effects of past wrongdoing and the effects of future wrongdoing. Those who act wrongly in the future are intervening agents, where those who act wrongly in the past are not. But whilst many people have the intuition that intervening agency makes a difference to permissibility, this intuition does not seem very robust when we hold other things equal.

Consider:

> *Prime and Launch*: Barak and George are in separate booths. Each has an identical button in front of him. If Barak and George both press their buttons, a weapon will be primed and launched, which will kill four. The first press, whichever button it is, primes the weapon. The second, whichever it is, launches the weapon. Barak can rescue five people, but as a side effect he will press his button. He knows that George will certainly press his button either immediately before Barak or immediately afterwards, because George wants the four dead. Barak does not know which.

If Barak presses before George, George will be an intervening agent. If Barak presses after George, George will not be an intervening agent. Barak will directly launch the missile. The view that intervening agency is inherently morally significant implies that Barak has a reason to find out whether George has pressed to determine whether he is permitted to save the five. If George has pressed, Barak would wrongly save the five. If George has not pressed, Barak would permissibly save the five. It is difficult to believe, though, that Barak has a reason to find out whether George has pressed. Whether Barak is permitted to save the five does not plausibly depend on whether he primes or launches the weapon.

Furthermore, suppose that Barak can save more lives if he presses later than if he presses earlier. He is certain, either way, that the weapon will be launched at the four. The view that intervening agency is inherently morally significant implies that Barak has a reason to press now rather than later, even though he will save fewer lives if he does so, in virtue of the fact that if he waits, George is less likely to be an intervening agent, and hence it is less likely that the moral significance of the harm to the four will be discounted in the proportionality calculation. This is also hard to believe.

iv) Criminalization

Suppose that I am right that intervening agency does not negate, or even diminish, the significance of harm for wrongdoing. Arnie thus acts wrongly in *Kids and Guns*. It does not follow that it is permissible for the state to restrict Arnie's liberty to possess a firearm. Arnie might have a right to do wrong. And it does not follow from the state's permission to interfere with possession that the state may criminalize possession. A person may lack a right to do wrong, but have a right not to be punished for it.

Once we see why Arnie's act is wrong, though, enforceability seems uncontroversial. Cases like *Prime and Launch* suggest that the explanation of the wrongness of acting in a way that will lead to others inflicting harm is just the same as the explanation of the wrongness of acting in a way that will inflict harm on others as a side effect of one's acts. Duties not to seriously harm others, including the duty not to seriously harm others as a side effect, are normally enforceable through the criminal law.

To reinforce this view, the main reason why duties might be unenforceable has to do with freedom from interference by others. A person who is required to *v* already lacks the freedom to *v* in the moral sense outlined in Chapter 3. As we saw in Chapter 8, a person who is not free in this way may have reason to value freedom from interference. But even if gun-possessors have some reason to value freedom from interference by the state, perhaps because of their cultural attachment to guns, it is difficult to believe that this reason decisively rules out criminalization, at least if possession substantially increases the risk of wrongful harm by others.

II. Criminalizing Inchoate Wrongdoing

Can criminalization be justified to those who do not run a substantial risk that others will wrongly use their firearms, but who intend wrongly to use them themselves?

Consider:

> *Buy to Kill*: Pistol Pete buys a firearm to kill Andy. There is no chance of the firearm being wrongfully used by others.

The arguments in the previous chapter show that Pistol Pete's intentions make it wrong for him to buy the firearm. Here I offer two arguments to support the view that this makes him liable to punishment.

i) The Direct Argument

The Direct Argument is that a person with bad intentions directly forfeits her right not to be harmed to avert threats posed by others. Some claim that a person is liable to be harmed as a means only to avert threats that she is responsible for posing or causing.[9] *The Direct Argument* rejects this view.

To see the issues clearly, consider:

> *Unread Letter*: Veronica and Wilma each wish to kill Dan. Independently, each sends a letter to Kev, a hit man. Each letter instructs Kev to kill Dan using a pistol at noon. Dan receives Veronica's letter. Wilma's letter gets lost in the post. Kev immediately acts on Veronica's instructions, finds Dan and, just before noon, attempts to kill him. Had he received Wilma's letter and not Veronica's, he would have acted in exactly the same way. When Kev finds Dan, Veronica, Wilma, and Irene, an innocent bystander, are standing nearby.[10]

[9] Jeff McMahan has influentially defended this view. See, for example, 'The Basis of Moral Liability to Defensive Killing' (2005) 15 *Philosophical Issues* 386 and *Killing in War* (Oxford: OUP, 2009).

[10] I discuss this case in more detail in 'Causation, Culpability, and Liability' in C Coons and M Weber *The Ethics of Self Defense* (Oxford: OUP, 2016).

Veronica is liable to be used to avert the threat that Kev poses to Dan. It would be permissible for Dan to use Veronica as a shield to protect himself against Kev if this was the only way of doing so. This is so even if using Veronica would harm her significantly. This much seems uncontroversial.

Now suppose that Dan cannot use Veronica to protect himself. He could use either Wilma or Irene. Only Veronica, and not Wilma, caused the threat that Dan faces. If a person is only liable to be harmed to avert threats that she is responsible for posing or causing, Wilma is no more liable to be harmed than Irene. This implies that if it is wrong for Dan to use Irene as a shield to avert Kev's threat, it is also wrong for him to use Wilma as a shield.

Assuming the stringent prohibition on harmfully using a person that I supported in Chapter 4, it would be wrong for Dan to use Irene to protect himself were this to cause her significant harm. But it is not plausible that this is true of Wilma. It may be wrong for Dan to use Wilma as a shield to protect himself if Wilma will be killed.[11] Wilma and Veronica may not be equally placed with respect to their liabilities given that Veronica and not Wilma caused the threat. But Wilma and Irene are surely not equally placed.

Now consider whether Pistol Pete makes himself liable harmfully to be used to avert threats that others pose by acting on his intention to kill Andy. There are several differences between this case and *Unread Letter* that might count against this view. In *Unread Letter*, Wilma intended to harm the very victim that she is used to protect. And she intended to pose exactly the same threat that he currently faces. If Pistol Pete is harmfully used to avert the threats posed by other potential possessors of firearms, in contrast, Pete is used to avert threats to other victims, who would otherwise be harmed at different times, and in somewhat different ways. Furthermore, in *Unread Letter* Wilma has done everything that she believed necessary to execute her wrongful intention. This is not true of Pistol Pete in *Buy to Kill*.

Even if these facts are morally significant, I doubt that they are sufficiently significant to make Pistol Pete's liabilities identical to those of innocent bystanders. If we could impose a modest cost either on Pete or an innocent bystander to avert a lethal threat another faces, we would have reason to use Pete. And there are costs that it would be permissible to impose on Pete for this end that it would be wrong to impose on innocent bystanders.

Some might claim that if Pistol Pete is liable to be harmed more than an innocent bystander, this is true only because of Pete's intention to kill, and not because he buys a firearm. I doubt this. The fact that Pete has taken a substantial step towards executing his intention makes a significant difference to his liabilities. If Pete formed an intention to kill but did nothing to advance it, I think his liability to be harmed would be significantly weakened, though even in that case perhaps it would not be eliminated altogether. Hence, the objection to Pete being punished to some degree for reasons of general deterrence can be met. Now suppose that punishing many people in Pete's circumstances could significantly reduce the homicide rate. Doing this may be permitted even if punishing the same number of innocent people would be wrong.

[11] McMahan tentatively endorses this verdict in a somewhat similar case in 'The Moral Basis of Liability to Defensive Harm'. He does not consider whether attempters are liable to suffer lesser harm to avert the threats posed by others.

ii) The Indirect Argument

Here is *The Indirect Argument*. As Pistol Pete intends to kill Andy, and has a lethal weapon with which to execute this intention, Pete poses a significant threat to Andy. Consequently, Pete is liable to be harmed to avert that threat. It would not wrong him to restrict his liberty to do so. It is also permissible to take Pete's weapon from him and to threaten him with harm to deter him from securing a new firearm. Pete could also be harmed for reasons of special deterrence—to deter him from taking substantial steps towards the execution of his intention to harm Andy. He would be harmed as a means, but only as a means to avert a threat that he himself poses. This, it is generally acknowledged, is much easier to justify than harming a person to avert threats posed by others, as we noticed when considering Veronica in *Unread Letter*.

This argument helps to justify inflicting harm on Pete, but only to avert threats that he poses. Now suppose that harming him in one of these ways is necessary to avert the threat he poses. He then lacks a powerful complaint against being used for general deterrent purposes. Given that the state does not wrong Pete by harming him to avert threats that he poses, it is unproblematic for state officials to act with further good aims in mind, such as the aim to deter others.

To see this clearly, suppose that Pete's liberty may be restricted in order to prevent him from killing Andy in one of two ways. If it is done in one way, other potential offenders will not be deterred from harming their victims. If it is done in a second way, the harm that is inflicted on Pete will have additional deterrent effects. The choice does not affect Pete's interests. As benefits to others are secured at no additional cost to Pete, the state may pick the second way. Hence, if Pistol Pete is liable to be harmed to avert a threat that he poses, he is also liable to be punished for reasons of general deterrence.

III. Violent People and Gun Control

So far I have defended the view that two groups of people are not wronged by firearms prohibitions: those whose firearms will be wrongly used by others, and those who intend to use them to act wrongly. In both cases, the person acts wrongly by possessing the firearm, and so these arguments do not conflict with familiar views about criminalization, such as various wrongness constraints. However, many people acquire firearms for recreational or defensive reasons.[12] They lack bad intentions, and the risk that they pose through others wrongly using them is modest, especially if they keep them secure. My arguments so far thus support only a narrow prohibition on possession: one that would be unlikely to be very effective.

Here is another group to consider: some who possess guns for recreational or defensive reasons and have dispositions wrongly to use their guns. Do they have a legitimate objection to criminalization of possession? Consider:

> *Confrontation*: Dan purchases a firearm to defend his family. Dan does not have bad intentions, but he is disposed to be violent. If there is a firearm within reach, Dan is quite likely to use it wrongfully to harm others when such confrontations occur. If he does so, he will fulfil standard compatibilist conditions of responsibility.[13]

[12] See Kleck *Point Blank*, 25–6.

[13] We explored some such conditions in Chapter 5.

If Dan possesses a firearm there is a higher risk that others will suffer death or severe injuries during Dan's violent confrontations.

Evaluating *Confrontation* is important. One plausible reason why the homicide rate in the US is much higher than the homicide rate in many other developed countries is the availability of firearms. This conclusion has been supported in the following way. The difference in the rate of violent confrontations between the US and other countries is much smaller than the difference in the rate of homicides between the US and other countries. One explanation is that easy access to firearms makes it more likely that violent confrontations result in death.[14] When these deaths occur, the perpetrators who kill are normally fully responsible for killing.

To take just one important context, levels of domestic abuse are not significantly higher in the US than in other developed countries. However, domestic abuse is far more likely to lead to homicide if the abuser possesses a firearm than if he does not.[15] Were the criminal law only to prohibit possession of a firearm if the possessor intends to commit a crime, a restriction that Andrew Ashworth, for example, supports,[16] the criminal law would be unable to protect potential victims of domestic abuse from being shot. Few domestic abusers purchase firearms with such intentions, and it would be extremely difficult to prove that they have them even if they do.

Many will believe that Dan wrongly possesses a firearm in *Confrontation* because his act facilitates his future wrongdoing. But we saw serious problems with this view in the previous chapter: he may be required to possess a firearm to protect his family, and if so his bad dispositions cannot make this wrong. Although Dan's dispositions do not make it wrong for him to possess a firearm, these dispositions do give others good reason to restrict his liberty to do this. Dan's family may have good reason to restrict his liberty to possess a gun. This is because Dan has an option—the option to possess the gun, protect his family, and not wrongly harm anyone—that his family cannot get him to take. Hence, although Dan has a duty to possess a gun, others ought not to let him have one.

Some might object that this view is disrespectful. Even if it is predictable that Dan will wrongfully harm others if he possesses a gun, it is within his control not to do so. The state ought to respect Dan as an autonomous agent, and respect requires the state

[14] See, further, F Zimring and G Hawkins *Crime is Not the Problem: Lethal Violence in America* (Oxford: OUP, 1998); Miller, Azrael, and Hemingway 'Firearms and Death in the United States'. Of course, any empirical claim about firearms, especially in the US, will be hotly contested. For a very well-known, and highly controversial, defence of the striking claim that an increase in the number of guns reduces the crime rate, see J R Lott Jr. *More Guns Less Crime: Understanding Crime and Gun Control Laws* (Chicago: University of Chicago Press, 2010). Lott's findings have been widely questioned. For the claim that there is a strong correlation between weaker firearms laws and higher homicide rates, see E W Fleegler, L K Lee, M C Monuteaux, D Hemenway, and R Mannix 'Firearm Legislation and Firearm-Related Fatalities in the United States' (2013) *JAMA Internal Medicine* 732. It is also worth noting here that one of the reasons cited for the ineffectiveness of prohibitions in the US—that those who possess guns will violate the law rather than giving them up—does not apply to jurisdictions outside the US. See D N Husak 'Guns and Drugs' (2004) 23 *Law and Philosophy* 437, 457. Compliance levels with firearms prohibitions across Europe are high. For the claim that wider availability of firearms leads to higher levels of serious violence (though lower levels of non-serious violence), see J N van Kesteren 'Revisiting the Gun Ownership and Violence Link' (2014) 54 *British Journal of Criminology* 53.

[15] For an overview of the evidence concerning domestic abusers and firearms, as well as policy recommendations to restrict the possession of firearms by abusers, see A M Zeoli and S Frattaroli 'Evidence for Optimism: Policies to Limit Batterers' Access to Guns' in Webster and Vernick *Reducing Gun Violence in America*.

[16] 'The Unfairness of Risk-Based Possession Offences' (2011) 5 *Criminal Law and Philosophy* 237.

not to act on the accurate predictions that it can make about the wrongful autonomous actions of others. This might be understood as an extension of the presumption of innocence—we should presume that a person will not act wrongly, even if we accurately predict that she probably will.[17] I doubt that this idea has any moral force. As I have addressed it in some detail elsewhere,[18] I will keep my comments here brief.

The view that we should act on the presumption that others will not act wrongly is often defended on the grounds that were we not to do this we would treat the person as incapable of acting permissibly.[19] Some also claim that acting on the prediction that a person will act wrongly treats her like a child.[20] These claims are false. A person can herself recognize that she is likely to *v* whilst acknowledging that she is capable of not *v*ing. Indeed, this is a perfectly familiar idea. When a person predicts that she will act wrongly, she does not treat herself like a child. Others no more treat her like a child when they act on similar predictions.

Furthermore, it is false that predicting that I will *v* implies that I am incapable of refraining from *v*ing. We can see this from the fact that predicting that I will not act wrongly does not imply that I am incapable of wrongdoing. Why not endorse the same conclusion about a person's ability to act permissibly?

Finally, the view that we have stronger reason not to act on our predictions of wrongdoing when they are made about the actions of autonomous agents has counter-intuitive implications. Consider:

> *Childcare*: I am suddenly called away on urgent life-saving business and I must leave my child with one of two relatives. Both would like her to visit. Chris is a kind person, but is subject to uncontrollable bouts of mental illness which cause him irrationally to harm others. Desmond is often kind, but he has a short temper, so he often wrongly harms others, and is fully responsible for doing so.

Suppose that I assess the chances of my child being harmed if I leave her with Chris and Desmond, and conclude that Chris is less likely to harm her. The view that respect for autonomy should lead us not to act on our predictions, seems to imply that I ought nevertheless to leave her with Desmond. This view is hard to believe. If anything, there is stronger reason to discount the harm that Chris might inflict—he is not responsible for his tendency to inflict harm, and so we should be more reluctant to restrict his opportunities on this basis.[21]

Some might think that this is because of my special relationship with my child. But things are no different were we concerned with someone else's child. The explanation is rather that, as long as my predictions are accurate, there is nothing disrespectful about

[17] Something like this view is defended in K K Ferzan 'Beyond Crime and Commitment: Justifying Liberty Deprivations of the Dangerous and Responsible' (2011) 96 *Minnesota Law Review* 141; A Walen 'A Unified Theory of Detention, With Application to Preventive Detention for Suspected Terrorists' (2011) 70 *Maryland Law Review* 871 and 'A Punitive Precondition for Preventive Detention: Lost Status as a Foundation for a Lost Immunity' (2011) 48 *San Diego Law Review* 1229; A Ashworth and L Zedner *Preventive Justice*, 111–2.

[18] In V Tadros 'Controlling Risk' in A Ashworth, P Tomlin, and L Zedner *Prevention and the Limits of the Criminal Law* (Oxford: OUP, 2013). The next three paragraphs are a brief sketch of the argument offered there. For an excellent parallel argument in the case of the use of bad character evidence in criminal trials, see M Redmayne *Character in the Criminal Trial* (Oxford: OUP, 2015) ch 4.

[19] See, for example, Walen 'A Unified Theory of Detention', 46.

[20] For an argument of this sort in the context of criminalization, see A P Simester and A von Hirsch *Crimes, Harms, and Wrongs*, 62.

[21] See, also, my discussion of *Hostel* in 'Controlling Risk'.

refraining from leaving her with Desmond on the grounds that he is more likely than Chris to harm her.

Is Dan liable to punishment in *Confrontation*? In the previous section I offered two arguments to support the liability of inchoate wrongdoers to punishment. *The Direct Argument* does not apply to Dan. His bad tendencies do not render him liable to punitive harm to protect others. However, *The Indirect Argument* does apply. Dan is liable to be harmed to avert the threat he poses to others. As he is liable to preventive harm, this harm may also be inflicted on him with the intention of deterring others with similar dispositions from possessing firearms. The argument in the previous chapter suggests that possessing an offensive weapon cannot be wrong in virtue of the tendency that the possessor has to act wrongly if she does so. Even if this argument is sound, though, Dan is nevertheless liable to be punished in pursuit of general deterrence.

In this case, then, Dan's liability to be punished is not dependent on his acting wrongly. It is dependent only on his acting in a way that facilitates his future wrongdoing. And facilitating one's own future wrongdoing is not wrong where one lacks the intention to do so.

IV. Punishment Without Liability

To recap, subject to empirical considerations about the effectiveness of the law, we have justified a criminal prohibition on possession of firearms that includes the following groups: those who possess firearms that will wrongly be used by others; those who possess firearms with the intent to act wrongly; and those who possess firearms who are disposed to act wrongly.

However, a prohibition that is restricted to only these groups may still be insufficiently effective in tackling gun violence. A broader prohibition seems better—as the prosecution would not be required to prove that the defendant had the relevant intentions or tendencies, fewer people would possess firearms, and fewer firearms would be in circulation. A broad prohibition of this kind might include exceptions under a licensing scheme. Prohibitions of this kind are found, for example, in the UK. Can such broader prohibitions be justified if they are more effective? I think so.

I consider two arguments in favour of these broader prohibitions. Some might argue that a broader prohibition can be justified because we all have obligations to protect each other from harm. If a broad prohibition is effective, it is wrong to breach the prohibition. Because those who breach the prohibition act wrongly, they are liable to punishment. This argument is an instructive failure. Seeing why it fails helps us better appreciate a more powerful argument: one that justifies punishing the innocent.

i) *Mala prohibita*

The term *mala prohibita* is used in more than one way. I use it in the following strict way: a *mala prohibita* offence is an offence the creation of which makes the conduct that it prohibits wrongful.

Defending the existence of *mala prohibita* offences, so understood, is especially attractive to those who endorse either retributivism or forfeiture theories of punishment. *Mala prohibita* offences promise to justify extending the criminal law to secure important state aims, such as protection from harm, whilst conforming to the requirement that only those who act wrongly are liable to, or deserve, punishment.

But how does criminalizing conduct make it wrong? One way this can occur is that a criminal prohibition alters people's conduct, and the alteration of that conduct alters the moral status of the conduct prohibited by the law. This idea applies in this context. Take a person who possesses a firearm for defensive reasons, creating a risk that the firearm will be stolen and wrongly used. Possessing the firearm might be permissible if many other people possess firearms, but not if possession is rare. The conduct is permissible only if the defensive reasons to possess outweigh the risks of wrongful use by others. And the strength of the former set of reasons depends on the likelihood of violent attack by others, especially with firearms. But the strength of defensive reasons thus depends on whether possession is criminalized. For if possession is criminalized, fewer people will possess firearms, weakening the person's defensive reasons to possess. So it can be permissible for a person to possess a firearm where this is not criminalized, but criminalization can make doing so wrong. Elsewhere, I argue that this shows that we should reject *The Strong Wrongness Constraint*: the view that conduct should be criminalized only if it is wrong independently of its being criminalized.[22]

This is a good argument for *mala prohibita* offences. But it does not fully meet the challenge that prohibitions that are carefully tailored to ensure that only those who are liable are captured are unworkable given the impossibility of distinguishing those who are liable from those who are not. It only applies where criminalization makes possession wrong. But criminalization makes possession wrong only if it alters the facts in the ways suggested above. This may not make it wrong for many people to possess firearms, even where criminalization is effective in reducing the homicide rate. Even where the homicide rate is reduced, some people may have defensive reasons to possess that are sufficiently powerful to outweigh the risks that possession imposes on others, given that they lack the intentions and dispositions that make a person liable to punishment.

An argument of the following kind is commonly offered in response to this problem:[23]

1) Reducing the rate of homicide and serious injury is a legitimate state purpose.
2) Deterring those with certain intentions and tendencies from possessing firearms advances this purpose.
3) The state cannot adequately distinguish those who have the relevant intentions and tendencies from those who do not.
4) Therefore, a broad prohibition on firearms possession is necessary for the state to advance its goal of reducing the rate of homicide and serious injury.
5) Such a prohibition would not impose heavy costs on citizens. They could avoid criminal liability simply by refraining from possessing firearms.

[22] See V Tadros 'Wrongness and Criminalization' in A Marmor *The Routledge Companion to Philosophy of Law* (London: Routledge, 2012). For responses, see R A Duff 'Towards a Modest Legal Moralism' (2014) 8 *Criminal Law and Philosophy* 217; M S Moore 'Responses and Appreciations' in K K Ferzan and S J Morse *Legal, Moral, and Metaphysical Truths: The Philosophy of Michael Moore* (Oxford: OUP, 2016). For what it's worth, I think these responses either obliterate, or at least make trivial, the contrast between the *Weak Wrongness Constraint* and the *Strong Wrongness Constraint*.

[23] See, for example, R A Duff 'Perversions and Subversions of Criminal Law' in R A Duff, L Farmer, S E Marshall, and V Tadros *The Boundaries of the Criminal Law* (Oxford: OUP, 2010); C H Wellman 'Rights Forfeiture and *Mala Prohibita*' in R A Duff, L Farmer, S E Marshall, M Renzo, and V Tadros *The Constitution of the Criminal Law* (Oxford: OUP, 2013).

6) Therefore a broad prohibition on firearms possession is just.
7) Therefore the state is permitted to create a broad prohibition on firearms possession.
8) Citizens owe an obligation to their fellow citizens to do their fair share to advance the goals secured by just prohibition.
9) Abiding by just prohibitions is required in order to discharge this obligation.
10) Therefore, citizens who violate a just prohibition on firearms violate the rights of their fellow citizens.
11) Citizens who violate the rights of fellow citizens forfeit their right not to be punished.
12) Therefore, it is permissible to enforce the prohibition on possession of firearms with the threat of punishment.
13) Therefore, criminalizing possession of firearms is permitted.

One attractive feature of this argument is that it does not rely on the idea that citizens have an obligation to obey unjust laws. It is very controversial, and I think false, that citizens have such an obligation.[24]

But the argument nevertheless fails. Step 9) is the problematic step. To see this, suppose the state creates a prohibition on firearms possession. Now suppose that D possesses a firearm in violation of that prohibition but lacks the intentions or tendencies wrongfully to use the firearm. *Ex hypothesi*, the risk that others face of suffering death or serious injury is not increased by D's possession of a firearm. How, then, has D failed to discharge his obligation to do his fair share to advance the goal of reducing the rate of homicide and serious injury?

One possibility is that by possessing a firearm, D makes it more difficult for the state to ensure that those who possess firearms with the relevant intentions or tendencies are convicted and punished. Hence, it is more difficult for the state to protect other citizens from these people.[25]

But, in reply, the state's task is made more difficult in this way only if it refrains from convicting and punishing those in D's circumstances. If the state convicts and punishes those who possess firearms irrespective of whether they have the relevant intentions and tendencies, D's possession has not made the state's task of ensuring that those who have the relevant intentions and tendencies more difficult. What, then, makes possession wrong under these circumstances?

To see the problem clearly, consider this simplified two-person case:

Two Possessors: Duane and Eddy possess firearms. Duane possesses a firearm for recreational purposes, and does not tend to use it wrongly. Eddy possesses a firearm in order to kill Vince. Duane and Eddy appear identical to the state in all salient respects. It knows that either Duane or Eddy intends to kill Vince. If the state punishes Duane and Eddy, Eddy will not kill Vince. If the state punishes neither Duane nor Eddy, Eddy will kill Vince.

[24] The idea that punishing those who violate *mala prohibita* offences can be justified even if these offences are unjust is rightly criticized in D N Husak '*Malum Prohibitum* and Retributivism' in *The Philosophy of Criminal Law: Selected Essays*. For a good refutation of the view that an obligation to obey just laws is redundant, see Wellman 'Rights Forfeiture and *Mala Prohibita*', 89.

[25] See Wellman 'Rights Forfeiture and *Mala Prohibita*', 87–8, for defence of this idea in the related context of specified speed limits on roads.

Given that the state has no way of distinguishing between Duane and Eddy, either it is permitted to punish both or neither, relative to the evidence that it has.[26] If the state refrains from convicting and punishing Duane and Eddy for possession on the grounds that it cannot determine who has the relevant intentions or tendencies, it fails to protect Vince from Eddy.

Perhaps it might then be argued that Duane's possession has made the state unable to protect citizens from Eddy by making it true that the state cannot tell whether Eddy has the relevant intentions and tendencies or not. Hence, Duane has violated his obligation to other citizens to ensure that the state can advance its goal of protecting citizens from Eddy. But this argument relies on the state not punishing Duane and Eddy. Duane sets back the state's ability to protect Vince only on condition that it convicts and punishes only those who it can identify as having the relevant intentions and tendencies. If it adopts a policy of convicting all those who possess firearms, without attempting to determine whether these people have the relevant intentions and tendencies, Duane's possession of firearms has no impact on the state's ability to secure its aims.

It might be argued that Duane has acted wrongly because the state can achieve its aim of protection only by bearing the costs of convicting and punishing him. But it is not very plausible that it is wrong to possess a firearm because of the costs of enforcement. And even were this so, these wrongdoers would be liable only to receive trivial sentences.[27] Furthermore, the increased deterrent effects of punishing him might offset any costs to the state of punishing Duane. If Duane's punishment deters others from possessing firearms, the state is saved the cost of convicting and punishing those who are deterred.

Now suppose that a broad general criminal offence prohibiting possession of firearms is created and enforced. Those who possess firearms, but who lack the relevant intentions and tendencies, have done nothing to hamper the state's ability to secure the conviction and punishment of those who have the relevant intentions and tendencies. Hence, the argument that they have violated their duty to support the state in pursuit of its goal of reducing the rate of homicide and serious injury fails.

ii) Punishing the innocent

This failure nevertheless points us to a justification for a broad prohibition on possession. It seems that a broad criminalization offence is overinclusive and hence unjust—it warrants the punishment of those who are not liable to be punished.[28] The argument in the previous section aimed to show that possessing a firearm is wrong if possession is criminalized. It failed because when such an offence is created and enforced against all who violate it, those who possess firearms, but who lack the relevant intentions and dispositions, do not act wrongly. However, the conclusion that they do not act wrongly is true *only on condition that the broad offence is enforced.* This fact can help to justify a broad offence.

[26] I leave aside the possibility that the state may punish one of the two but not both. Some arguments can be mounted in favour of this view—for example, that punishing one but not the other maximizes the chance that the state fulfils its duty. Overall, though, this view is not very plausible.

[27] Wellman attempts to meet this concern in 'Rights Forfeiture and *Mala Prohibita*', 90–5. I lack the space to evaluate his proposal.

[28] This is, I think, the most forceful objection to broad possession offences. It is developed most powerfully in Husak 'Guns and Drugs' 476–87. Meeting it thus goes a long way to justifying such offences.

Recall *Two Possessors*. Suppose that the state punishes both Duane and Eddy in order to protect Vince. Duane might object to being punished on the grounds that he poses no threat to Vince, and hence is not liable to be punished. Part of the response to the objection is that Duane could have avoided punishment simply by refraining from possessing a firearm. This imposes some cost on him—he cannot pursue his recreational purposes as effectively. But this cost seems relatively modest compared with the importance of protecting Vince's life.

This part of the response, though important, is not sufficient. The fact that punishment is avoidable cannot on its own justify punishment, even when punishment is effective in deterring crime. A second part of the response is that non-liable possessors of firearms could ensure that only liable possessors of firearms are punished by not possessing firearms. Were Duane (and all other non-liable possessors) not to possess a firearm, the state could punish all possessors without violating anyone's rights.

We have already seen that Duane does not act wrongly by possessing a firearm. But it would be wrong for Duane to claim that the state must not punish either him or Eddy. For if Duane makes this demand, he demands that the state does not protect Vince in order to avoid punishing him. It would be wrong for Duane to possess a firearm if possessing the firearm would make protecting Vince from Eddy impossible. Similarly, it would be wrong for Duane to possess a firearm if possessing the firearm would make protecting Vince from Eddy unjust. If it did so, Duane's possession of a firearm would restrict the freedom of the state to protect Eddy.

For this reason, either:

1) It is wrong for Duane to possess the firearm; or
2) It is permissible for Duane to possess a firearm, but it is not unjust for the state to protect Vince from Eddy by punishing both Duane and Eddy.

2) is right. As long as the state does not refrain from punishing Duane and Eddy in the light of Duane's claim, it is not wrong for Duane to possess the firearm. The permissibility of Duane's possession, then, depends on the state not refraining from punishing Duane and Eddy. The state ought not to refrain for were it to refrain on the basis of Duane's claim, Duane's innocent possession of the firearm would lead to Vince's death. Duane is liable to be harmed to prevent him from making Vince vulnerable in this way. Hence, Duane's claim that punishing him is wrong lacks force.

Firearms prohibitions are, in this way, the converse of *mala prohibita*. Possessing firearms is permissible because of a criminal offence that warrants punishment for doing so.

iii) The complaint of self-defence

The argument just offered relied on the idea that it is not costly for citizens to refrain from possessing firearms. This is true where firearms are possessed for recreational reasons. However, some citizens claim to need a firearm for self-defence, and some such claims may be valid. *Two Possessors* should be evaluated differently, it might be argued, if Duane could defend himself against a lethal attack only by possessing a firearm.[29]

It is sometimes argued that gun possession increases rather than decreases the risk that one will be a victim of serious violence.[30] These findings are difficult to interpret,

[29] John van Kesteren reports that 23% of handgun owners possess firearms for prevention or protection reasons. See 'Revisiting the Gun Ownership and Violence Link', 59.

[30] Van Kesteren supports this claim. See 'Revisiting the Gun Ownership and Violence Link', 69.

for gun possession may be coincidentally, rather than causally, linked with an increased risk of victimization. Furthermore, even if the average person is more likely to be a victim of violent crime in virtue of possessing a firearm, possession may increase the security of some people.

Perhaps it might be argued that the criminal law could accommodate such concerns by creating a defence to the offence of possessing a firearm for those who can demonstrate the need to possess firearms for self-defence. But it is very difficult to distinguish those who will use a firearm to defend themselves against would be attackers and those who would wrongly use it to attack. One reason is that some fall into both categories—they need firearms for self-defence and have the intentions or tendencies wrongly to use them. The high proportion of deaths from gunshot wounds amongst those processed in the juvenile justice system in the United States illustrates the problem—those juveniles who have been convicted of criminal offences are also much more likely to be victims of gun crime.[31] Any defence that is readily available to those who need firearms for defensive reasons is also likely to be available to those who are liable to punishment for possession, making the prohibition on possession much less effective in preventing deaths and serious injuries through the use of firearms.

If firearms prohibitions are to be effective in reducing the rate of homicide and serious injury, then, these offences must prohibit possession of firearms by some people who need them for self-defence. This is difficult to justify to these people. They are faced with the following dilemma. Either they refrain from possessing a firearm, increasing the risk that they will be unable to deter attacks on them, or to defend themselves if they are attacked, or they possess a firearm and risk conviction and punishment for possession.

One response is that firearms prohibitions can be justified to these people because the prohibitions reduce the risks that these people face overall. A person might be more secure with a firearm than without one, whether or not possession of firearms is prohibited. But that person might be more secure without a firearm if possession of firearms is prohibited than she is with a firearm if possession of firearms is not prohibited. Criminalization improves her security overall whether or not she abides by the prohibition.

But the law will have uneven effects on neighbourhoods and communities. Police resources may be targeted in reducing gun violence in some neighbourhoods at the expense of others. The police may not act wrongly in targeting their resources in this way. Some people may be made worse off overall by criminalization.

The fact that some people are worse off overall as a result of criminalization is not necessarily decisive, though. However, in order to justify criminalization, it is insufficient to show that criminalization improves aggregate security. The reason is as follows. Criminalization of possession is morally analogous of depriving a person of the ability to defend himself. Depriving a person of the ability to defend himself infringes his rights. Aggregate improvements in security are not sufficient to justify rights infringements.

To see the problem clearly, consider:

Triple Attack: Xavier, Yoshi, and Zane wrongfully attack Al, Bert, and Chris respectively. Xavier, Yoshi, and Zane have firearms. Al has a firearm and will be able to defend himself

[31] See L A Teplin, J A Jakubowski, K M Abram, N D Olso, M L Stokes, and L J Welty 'Firearm Homicide and Other Causes of Death in Delinquents: A 16 Year Prospective Study' (2014) 134 *Pediatrics* 63.

against Xavier if nothing is done. Bert and Chris will not be able to defend themselves against Yoshi and Zane if nothing is done. I can either do nothing or deprive Yoshi, Zane, and Al of their firearms. I cannot deprive Xavier and Zane of their firearms without depriving Al of his as well. If I act, Xavier will kill Al. However, the lives of Bert and Chris will be saved.

Removing the firearms of Yoshi, Zane, and Al reduces the homicide rate overall. Al's murder will be caused, but the murders of Bert and Chris will be prevented. Nevertheless, it might be argued that it is impermissible to act. If I refrain from acting I allow the deaths of Bert and Chris. If I act I causally contribute to the death of Al by depriving him of the means of defending himself. This, it might be argued, is morally analogous to harming Al.

Some will respond that non-consequentialist constraints such as the *Doctrine of Doing and Allowing* apply in interpersonal morality, but not to the state.[32] This is hard to believe. The standard rationale for the *Doctrine of Doing and Allowing* is that we are more deeply involved in what we do than what we allow. This idea seems no less important when applied to individuals acting in their capacity as state officials than it is when applied to individuals in ordinary interpersonal settings. It is hard to believe that the appropriate judgement in *Triple Attack* depends on whether I am a state official acting in that capacity or an ordinary civilian.[33]

The argument from *Doing and Allowing* is nevertheless difficult to evaluate. I can only gesture at some of the relevant arguments. There might be important moral differences between *Triple Attack* and more standard cases discussed in the context of the *Doctrine of Doing and Allowing*. One such difference is that if I deprive Al of his gun, I do not directly kill him. Depriving Al of the means of preventing himself from being killed might be thought easier to justify than directly killing a person.

Another difference is that in more standard cases, the victim is not killed with ill will. In this case, I create the circumstances in which Xavier kills Al with ill will. It might be thought that creating the conditions where a person is killed with ill will is more difficult to justify than creating the conditions where a person is harmed without ill will—for example, if I made Al unable to defend himself against a tiger rather than a villain. I doubt that either of these differences is very important.

A further difference between this case and standard cases discussed under the *Doctrine of Doing and Allowing* is that in this case I intend to affect all members of a group of people by removing their guns, knowing that some will wrongfully be harmed. Whilst I do not use those who are wrongfully harmed, I do intend to affect them in a way that results in them being harmed. This may make my harm-causing action more difficult to justify.

A further question concerns the stringency of the *Doctrine of Doing and Allowing*. Most commentators think that the *Doctrine of Doing and Allowing* is not as stringent as the *Doctrine of Double Effect*. It is common to claim that even if it is wrong to kill one person as a side effect of saving two, it is permissible to kill one as a side effect of saving five. This implies that criminalization of gun possession might be justified even if it makes some people less secure, as long as it renders five times as many people more secure.

[32] See, for example, C Sunstein and A Vermeule 'Is Capital Punishment Morally Required? Acts, Omissions, and Life-Life Tradeoffs' (2005) 58 *Stanford Law Review* 703.

[33] For a fuller argument, see A O Hosein 'Doing, Allowing, and the State' (2014) 33 *Law and Philosophy* 235.

Some people, though, distinguish between cases where a threat is diverted and cases where a new threat is created. They think that the prohibition on diverting a threat is much less stringent than the prohibition on creating new threats.[34] If this view is right, it might be argued, firearms prohibitions are more difficult to justify. For such prohibitions do not merely divert threats. They make threats that could otherwise be averted more potent.

I doubt that it is distinctively wrong to create new threats, though.[35] The view that it is implied that the state's efforts to provide security to its citizens is severely hampered. For it is very often true that the state prevents threats to some but in the process causes threats to others. This is typical of policing and of military action. For example, police officers are often justified in engaging in high-speed chases to arrest dangerous criminals even though their actions increase the risk of harm to pedestrians. The permissibility of doing this does not depend on demonstrating that the civilians who are made less secure from being harmed in the high-speed chase are also potential future victims of the criminal being chased. Similarly, bombing a munitions plant is permissible even if doing so will kill some civilians as a side effect, as long as significantly more lives will be saved by doing so. This is so even if the civilians who are killed are not made more secure overall by the bombing.

Overall, criminalization of possession of firearms can be justified even if it makes some people less secure overall. It can be justified as long as a significantly greater number of people are rendered more secure overall by the policy. How many lives must be saved in order to justify such prohibitions depends on the stringency of the non-consequentialist principles such prohibitions engage.

V. Conclusion

I have argued that broad firearms prohibitions are warranted. But the conclusion that I have drawn rests on rejecting a very popular view about criminalization: that it is permissible to criminalize conduct only if that conduct is wrong. It may be wrong to condemn those who possess firearms, for it is normally wrong to condemn those who have not acted wrongly. But it may be permissible to punish them for the sake of general deterrence. Citizens may have a right to bear arms, but the state is nevertheless permitted to punish them for doing so.

[34] Those who find this idea morally significant include J A Montmarquet 'On Doing Good: The Right and the Wrong Way' (1982) 79 *The Journal of Philosophy* 439; P Foot 'Killing and Letting Die' in P Foot *Moral Dilemmas* (Oxford: OUP, 2002); and J J Thomson 'The Trolley Problem' in J J Thomson *Rights, Restitution, and Risk: Essays in Moral Theory* (Cambridge, Mass: Harvard UP, 1986).

[35] Warren Quinn and Frances Kamm concur. See Quinn 'Actions, Intentions, and Consequences: The Doctrine of Doing and Allowing' in *Morality and Action* (Cambridge: CUP, 1993) 159–60; Kamm *Morality, Mortality Volume II: Rights, Duties and Status* (Oxford: OUP, 1996) 162–6.

Bibliography

Adams, R M (1999) *Finite and Infinite Goods* (Oxford: OUP)
Alexander, L (1980) 'The Doomsday Machine: Proportionality, Punishment and Prevention' 63 *The Monist* 199
Alexander, L (1991) 'Self-Defense, Punishment, and Proportionality' 10 *Law and Philosophy* 323
Alexander, L (1996) 'The Moral Magic of Consent II' 2 *Legal Theory* 165
Anderson, M (2005) 'Negotiating Sex' 78 *Southern California Law Review* 1401
Archard, D (1998) *Sexual Consent* (Oxford: Westview)
Ashworth, A (2011) 'The Unfairness of Risk-Based Possession Offences' 5 *Criminal Law and Philosophy* 237
Ashworth, A and Zedner, L (2014) *Preventive Justice* (Oxford: OUP)
Baker, L R (2006) 'Moral Responsibility without Libertarianism' 40 *Noûs* 307
Barry, C and Øverland, G (2014) 'The Implications of Failing to Assist' 40 *Social Theory and Practice* 570
Bedke, M (2011) 'Passing the Deontic Buck' in R Schafer-Landau *Oxford Studies in Metaethics* vol 6 (Oxford: OUP)
Bergelson, V (2013) 'The Duty to Protect the Victim—or the Duty to Suffer Punishment?' 32 *Law and Philosophy* 199
Berman, M (2008) 'Punishment and Justification' 118 *Ethics* 258
Berman, M (2011) 'Two Kinds of Retributivism' in R A Duff and S P Green *Philosophical Foundations of Criminal Law* (Oxford: OUP)
Berman, M (2011) 'Blackmail' in J Deigh and D Dolinko *Oxford Handbook of Philosophy of Criminal Law* (Oxford: OUP)
Brink, D O (2013) *Mill's Progressive Principles* (Oxford: OUP)
Chiao, V (2016) 'What is the Criminal Law For?' 35 *Law and Philosophy* 137
Christiano, T (2015) 'What is Wrongful Exploitation?' in D Sobel, P Vallentyne, and S Wall *Oxford Studies in Political Philosophy* (Oxford: OUP)
Clayton, M (2004) 'A Puzzle about Ethics, Justice, and the Sacred' in J Burley *Dworkin and His Critics* (Oxford: Blackwell)
Coates, D J and Tognazzini, N A (2013) *Blame. Its Nature and Norms* (Oxford: OUP)
Cohen, J (1993) 'Freedom of Expression' 22 *Philosophy and Public Affairs* 207
Cook, P J, Ludwig, J, Venkatesh, S, and Braga, A A (2007) 'Underground Gun Markets' 117 *The Economic Journal* 588
Cowan, S (2007) 'Choosing Freely: Theoretically Reframing the Concept of Consent' in S Cowan and R Hunter *Choice and Consent: Feminist Engagements With Law and Subjectivity* (London: Routledge)
Darwall, S (1977) 'Two Kinds of Respect' 88 *Ethics* 36
Darwall, S (2002) *Welfare and Rational Care* (Princeton: Princeton University Press)
Darwall, S (2006) *The Second-Person Standpoint: Morality, Respect, and Accountability* (Cambridge, Mass: Harvard UP)
Demetriou, K (2010) 'The Soft-Line Solution to Pereboom's Four-Case Argument' 88 *Australasian Journal of Philosophy* 595
Dempsey, M M (2011) 'Public Wrongs and the "Criminal Law's Business": When Victims Won't Share' in R Cruft, M H Kramer, and M R Reiff *Crime, Punishment, and Responsibility: The Jurisprudence of Antony Duff* (Oxford: OUP)
Dougherty, T (2013) 'Sex, Lies, and Consent' 123 *Ethics* 717
Dougherty, T (2015) 'Yes Means Yes: Consent and Communication' 43 *Philosophy & Public Affairs* 224

Dubber, M D (2005) 'The Possession Paradigm: The Special Part and the Police Power Model of the Criminal Process' in R A Duff and S P Green *Defining Crimes: Essays on the Special Part of the Criminal Law* (Oxford: OUP, 2005)
Duff, R A (1996) *Criminal Attempts* (Oxford: OUP)
Duff, R A (2001) *Punishment, Communication, and Community* (Oxford: OUP)
Duff, R A (2007) *Answering for Crime: Responsibility and Liability in the Criminal Law* (Oxford: Hart)
Duff, R A (2010) 'Perversions and Subversions of Criminal Law' in R A Duff, L Farmer, S E Marshall, and V Tadros *The Boundaries of the Criminal Law* (Oxford: OUP)
Duff, R A (2014) 'Towards a Modest Legal Moralism' 8 *Criminal Law and Philosophy* 217
Duff, R A (2016) 'Legal Moralism and Public Wrongs' in K K Ferzan and S J Morse *Legal, Moral, and Metaphysical Truths: The Philosophy of Michael S Moore* (Oxford: OUP)
Duff, R A and Marshall, S E (2006) 'How Offensive Can You Get?' in A von Hirsch and A P Simester *Incivilities: Regulating Offensive Behaviour* (Oxford: Hart)
Duff, R A and Marshall, S E (2010) 'Public and Private Wrongs' in J Chalmers, F Leverick, and L Farmer *Essays in Criminal Law in Honour of Sir Gerald Gordon* (Edinburgh: EUP)
Duff, R A, Farmer, L, Marshall, S E, and Tadros, V (2007) *The Trial on Trial* vol 3 (Oxford: Hart)
Dworkin, G (1982) 'Is More Choice Better than Less?' 7 *Midwest Studies in Philosophy* 47
Dworkin, R (1993) *Life's Dominion: An Argument About Abortion, Euthanasia, and Individual Freedom* (New York: Vintage Books)
Dworkin, R (2006) *Is Democracy Possible Here? Principles for a New Political Debate* (Princeton: Princeton University Press)
Edwards, J (2014) 'Harm Principles' 20 *Legal Theory* 253
Edwards, J Forthcoming 'Master Principles of Criminalisation' *Jurisprudence*
Ellis, A (1995) 'Thomson on Distress' 106 *Ethics* 112
Enoch, D (2002) 'A Right to Violate One's Duty' 21 *Law and Philosophy* 367
Enoch, D (2013) 'The Disorder of Public Reason' 124 *Ethics* 141
Enoch, D (2014) 'Authority and Reason-Giving' LXXXIX *Philosophy and Phenomenological Research* 296
Enoch, D (2015) 'Against Public Reason' in D Sobel, P Vallentyne, and S Wall *Oxford Studies in Political Philosophy* (Oxford: OUP)
Estlund, D (2011) 'Human Nature and the Limits (If Any) of Political Philosophy' 39 *Philosophy and Public Affairs* 207
Farmer, L (2016) *Making the Modern Criminal Law: Criminalization and Civil Order* (Oxford: OUP)
Feinberg, J (1984) *Harm to Others* (Oxford: OUP)
Feinberg, J (1985) *Offense to Others* (Oxford: OUP)
Feinberg, J (1986) *Harm to Self* (Oxford: OUP)
Feldman, F (2010) *What is This Thing Called Happiness?* (Oxford: OUP)
Ferzan, K K (2011) 'Beyond Crime and Commitment: Justifying Liberty Deprivations of the Dangerous and Responsible' 96 *Minnesota Law Review* 141
Ferzan, K K (2013) 'Rethinking *The Ends of Harm*' 32 *Law and Philosophy* 177
Fine, K (1995) 'Ontological Dependence' 95 *Proceedings of the Aristotelian Society* 269
Fischer, J M (2006) 'Responsibility and Manipulation' in J M Fischer *My Way: Essays on Moral Responsibility* (Oxford: OUP)
Fischer, J M and Ravizza, M (1998) *Responsibility and Control: A Theory of Moral Responsibility* (Cambridge: CUP)
FitzPatrick, W J (2012) 'Intention, Permissibility, and Double Effect' in M Timmons *Oxford Studies in Normative Ethics* vol 2 (Oxford: OUP)
Fleegler, E W, Lee, L K, Monuteaux, M C, Hemenway, D, and Mannix, R (2013) 'Firearm Legislation and Firearm-Related Fatalities in the United States' *JAMA Internal Medicine* 732
Foot, P (2002) 'Killing and Letting Die' in P Foot *Moral Dilemmas* (Oxford: OUP)

Frankfurt, H (1988) *The Importance of What We Care About* (Cambridge: CUP)
Fricker, M (2016) 'What's the Point of Blame?' 50 *Noûs* 165
Frowe, H (2014) *Defensive Killing* (Oxford: OUP)
Gardner, J (2007) 'Justifications and Reasons' in J Gardner *Offences and Defences: Selected Essays in the Philosophy of Criminal Law* (Oxford: OUP)
Gardner, J (2011) 'Relations of Responsibility' in R Cruft, M H Kramer, and M R Reiff *Crime, Punishment, and Responsibility: The Jurisprudence of Antony Duff* (Oxford: OUP)
Gardner, J (2011) 'What is Tort Law for? Part 1: The Place of Corrective Justice' 30 *Law and Philosophy* 1
Gardner, J and Shute, S (2007) 'The Wrongness of Rape' in J Gardner *Offences and Defences: Selected Essays in the Philosophy of Criminal Law* (Oxford: OUP)
Gardner, J and Tanguay-Renaud, F (2011) 'Desert and Avoidability in Self-Defense' 12 *Ethics* 111
Gaus, G (2011) *The Order of Public Reason: A Theory of Freedom and Morality in a Diverse and Bounded World* (Cambridge: CUP)
Gibbard, A (1990) *Wise Choices, Apt Feelings: A Theory of Normative Judgement* (Oxford: OUP)
Goldberg, J and Zipursky, B (2005) 'Accidents of the Great Society' 64 *Maryland Law Review* 364
Graham, P (2014) 'A Sketch of a Theory of Moral Blameworthiness' 88 *Philosophy and Phenomenological Research* 388
Green, L (2013) 'The Nature of Limited Government' in J Keown and R P George *Reason, Morality, and Law: The Philosophy of John Finnis* (Oxford: OUP)
Haji, I (1998) *Moral Appraisability* (Oxford: OUP)
Hanser, M (2008) 'The Metaphysics of Harm' 77 *Philosophy and Phenomenological Research* 432
Hanser, M (2011) 'Still More on the Metaphysics of Harm' 82 *Philosophy and Phenomenological Research* 459
Hanser, M (2014) 'Acting Wrongly by Trying' in M Timmons *Oxford Studies in Normative Ethics* vol 4 (Oxford: OUP)
Herstein, O (2012) 'Defending the Right to Do Wrong' 31 *Law and Philosophy* 343
Hieronymi, P (2011) 'On Metaethics and Motivation: The Appeal of Contractualism' in R Jay Wallace, R Kumar, and S Freeman *Reasons and Recognition: Essays on the Philosophy of T M Scanlon* (Oxford: OUP)
Hitchcock, C (2011) 'Counterfactual Availability and Causal Judgment' in C Hoerl, T McCormack, and S R Beck *Understanding Counterfactuals, Understanding Causation: Issues in Philosophy and Psychology* (Oxford: OUP)
Hosein, A O (2014) 'Doing, Allowing, and the State' 33 *Law and Philosophy* 235
Hurd, H (1996) 'The Moral Magic of Consent' 2 *Legal Theory* 121
Husak, D N (2000) 'Retribution in Criminal Theory' 37 *San Diego Law Review* 959
Husak, D N (2004) 'Guns and Drugs' 23 *Law and Philosophy* 437
Husak, D N (2008) *Overcriminalization: The Limits of the Criminal Law* (Oxford: OUP)
Husak, D N (2010) 'Paternalism and Consent' in F G Miller and A Wertheimer *The Ethics of Consent: Theory and Practice* (Oxford: OUP)
Husak, D N (2010) *The Philosophy of Criminal Law: Selected Essays* (Oxford: OUP)
Jackson, F and Pargetter, R (1986) 'Oughts, Options, and Actualism' XCV *Philosophical Review* 233
Jacobson, D (2013) 'Regret, Agency, and Error' in D Shoemaker *Oxford Studies in Agency and Responsibility* vol 1 (Oxford: OUP)
Kagan, S (1989) *The Limits of Morality* (Oxford: OUP)
Kagan, S (2009) 'Well-Being as Enjoying the Good' 23 *Philosophical Perspectives* 253
Kagan, S (2011) *The Geometry of Desert* (Oxford: OUP)
Kamm, F M (1992) *Creation and Abortion: A Study in Moral and Legal Philosophy* (Oxford: OUP)

Kamm, F M (1993) *Morality, Mortality Volume 1: Death and Whom to Save From It* (Oxford: OUP)
Kamm, F M (1996) *Morality, Mortality Volume II: Rights, Duties, and Status* (Oxford: OUP)
Kamm, F M (2007) *Intricate Ethics: Rights, Responsibilities, and Permissible Harm* (Oxford: OUP)
Kavka, G (1982) 'The Paradox of Future Individuals' 11 *Philosophy and Public Affairs* 93
Kleck, G (1991) *Point Blank: Guns and Violence in America* (New York: de Gruyter)
Kolodny, N (2011) 'Scanlon's Investigation: The Relevance of Intent to Permissibility' 52 *Analytic Philosophy* 100
Korsgaard, C (1996) *Creating the Kingdom of Ends* (Cambridge: CUP)
Kraut, R (2011) *Against Absolute Goodness* (Oxford: OUP)
Lacey, N (1998) *Unspeakable Subjects: Feminist Essays in Legal and Social Theory* (Oxford: Hart)
Lacey, N (2016) *In Search of Criminal Responsibility: Ideas, Interests, and Institutions* (Oxford: OUP)
Larmore, C (2015) 'Political Liberalism: Its Motivations and Goals' in D Sobel, P Vallentyne, and S Wall *Oxford Studies in Political Philosophy* (Oxford: OUP)
Lazar, S (2012) 'Necessity in Self-Defense and War' 40 *Philosophy and Public Affairs* 3
Levy, N (2011) *Hard Luck: How Luck Undermines Free Will & Moral Responsibility* (Oxford: OUP)
Lewis, D (2000) 'Causation as Influence' 97 *Journal of Philosophy* 182
Lippert-Rasmussen, K (2015) 'To Serve and Protect: *The Ends of Harm* by Victor Tadros' 9 *Criminal Law and Philosophy* 49
Lott Jr, J R (2010) *More Guns Less Crime: Understanding Crime and Gun Control Laws* (Chicago: University of Chicago Press)
Louise, J (2009) 'Self-Prediction, Moral Obligation and Moral Deliberation' 146 *Philosophical Studies* 327
Marshall, S E and Duff, R A (1998) 'Criminalization and Sharing Wrongs' 11 *Canadian Journal of Law and Jurisprudence* 7
Matravers, M (2013) 'Political Neutrality and Punishment' 7 *Criminal Law and Philosophy* 217
McKenna, M (2012) *Conversation and Responsibility* (Oxford: OUP)
McKenna, M (2008) 'A Hard-Line Reply to Pereboom's Four-Case Argument' (2008) 77 *Philosophy and Phenomenological Research* 142
McKenna, M (2014) 'Resisting the Manipulation Argument: A Hard-Liner Takes It on the Chin' 89 *Philosophy and Phenomenological Research* 467
McMahan, J (1994) 'Self-Defense and the Problem of the Innocent Attacker' 104 *Ethics* 252
McMahan, J (2002) *The Ethics of Killing: Problems at the Margins of Life* (Oxford: OUP)
McMahan, J (2005) 'The Basis of Moral Liability to Defensive Killing' 15 *Philosophical Issues* 386
McMahan, J (2009) *Killing in War* (Oxford: OUP)
McMahan, J (2009) 'Intention, Permissibility, Terrorism, and War' 23 *Philosophical Perspectives* 345
McMahan, J (2010) 'Humanitarian Intervention, Consent, and Proportionality' in N A Davis, R Keshen, and J McMahan *Ethics and Humanity: Themes from the Philosophy of Jonathan Glover* (Oxford: OUP)
McMahan, J (2013) 'Causing People to Exist and Saving People's Lives' 17 *Journal of Ethics* 5
Mele, A R (2001) *Autonomous Agents: From Self-Control to Autonomy* (Oxford: OUP)
Mele, A R (2006) *Free Will and Luck* (Oxford: OUP)
Menzies, P (2011) 'The Role of Counterfactual Dependence in Causal Judgements' in C Hoerl, T McCormack, and S R Beck *Understanding Counterfactuals, Understanding Causation: Issues in Philosophy and Psychology* (Oxford: OUP)
Mill, J S (1991) J Gray (ed), *On Liberty and Other Essays* (Oxford: OUP)

Miller, M, Azrael, D, and Hemingway, D (2013) 'Firearms and Death in the United States' in D W Webster and J S Vernick *Reducing Gun Violence in America: Informing Policy with Evidence and Analysis* (Baltimore: John Hopkins University Press)
Montmarquet, J A (1982) 'On Doing Good: The Right and the Wrong Way' 79 *The Journal of Philosophy* 439
Moore, M S (1997) *Placing Blame: A Theory of Criminal Law* (Oxford: OUP)
Moore, M S (2009) *Causation and the Law: An Essay in Law, Morals and Metaphysics* (Oxford: OUP)
Moore, M S (2014) 'Liberty's Constraints on What Should Be Made Criminal' in R A Duff, L Farmer, S E Marshall, M Renzo, and V Tadros *Criminalization: The Political Morality of the Criminal Law* (Oxford: OUP)
Moore, M S (2016) 'Responses and Appreciations' in K K Ferzan and S J Morse *Legal, Moral, and Metaphysical Truths: The Philosophy of Michael Moore* (Oxford: OUP)
Nance, D A (1997) 'Guidance Rules and Enforcement Rules: A Better View of the Cathedral' 83 *Virginia Law Review* 837
Nelkin, D K (2011) *Making Sense of Freedom and Responsibility* (Oxford: OUP)
Nelkin, D K (2016) 'Difficulty and Degrees of Moral Praiseworthy and Blameworthiness' 50 *Noûs* 356
Nozick, R (1974) *Anarchy, State, and Utopia* (Oxford: Blackwell)
Otsuka, M (1994) 'Killing the Innocent in Self-Defense' 23 *Philosophy and Public Affairs* 74
Owens, D (2012) *Shaping the Normative Landscape* (Oxford: OUP)
Parfit, D (1982) 'Future Generations: Further Problems' 11 *Philosophy and Public Affairs* 113
Parfit, D (1984) *Reasons and Persons* (Oxford: OUP)
Parfit, D (2011) *On What Matters* vols 1 and 2 (Oxford: OUP)
Pereboom, D (1995) 'Determinism *al Dente*' 29 *Noûs* 21
Pereboom, D (2001) *Living Without Free Will* (Cambridge: CUP)
Pereboom, D (2014) *Free Will, Agency, and Meaning in Life* (Oxford: OUP)
Pereboom, D (2015) 'A Notion of Moral Responsibility Immune to the Threat of Causal Determination' in R Clarke, M McKenna, and A M Smith *The Nature of Moral Responsibility: New Essays* (Oxford: OUP)
Perry, S (2003) 'Harm, History, and Counterfactuals' 40 *San Diego Law Review* 1283
Pundik, A (2015) 'Coercion and Deception in Sexual Relations' 28 *Canadian Journal of Law and Jurisprudence* 97
Quinn, W (1993) 'Actions, Intentions, and Consequences: The Doctrine of Doing and Allowing' in W Quinn *Morality and Action* (Cambridge: CUP)
Rosen, G (2014) 'Culpability and Duress: A Case Study' 88 *Aristotelian Society Supplementary Volume* 69
Quong, J (2009) 'Killing in Self-Defense' 119 *Ethics* 507
Quong, J (2011) *Liberalism Without Perfection* (Oxford: OUP)
Quong, J and Firth, J (2012) 'Necessity, Moral Liability and Defensive Harm' 31 *Law and Philosophy* 673
Radzik, L (2009) *Making Amends: Atonement in Morality, Law, and Politics* (Oxford: OUP)
Raz, J (1986) *The Morality of Freedom* (Oxford: OUP)
Raz, J (1999) 'Facing Diversity: The Case of Epistemic Abstinence' in J Raz *Ethics in the Public Domain: Essays in the Morality of Law and Politics* (Oxford: OUP)
Raz, J (1999) 'Morality and Self-Interest' in J Raz *Engaging Reason: On the Theory of Value and Action* (Oxford: OUP)
Raz, J (1999) *Practical Reasons and Norms* (Oxford: OUP)
Raz, J (2001) *Value, Respect, and Attachment* (Cambridge: CUP)
Rawls, J (1999) *A Theory of Justice*, revised edn (Oxford: OUP)
Rawls, J (2001) *Collected Papers* (Cambridge, Mass: Harvard UP)
Rawls, J (2005) *Political Liberalism: Expanded Edition* (New York: Columbia University Press)

Redmayne, M (2015) *Character in the Criminal Trial* (Oxford: OUP)

Renzo, M (2012) 'Crimes Against Humanity and the Limits of International Criminal Law' 31 *Law and Philosophy* 443

Renzo, M (2013) 'Responsibility and Answerability in Criminal Law' in R A Duff, L Farmer, S E Marshall, and V Tadros *The Constitution of the Criminal Law* (Oxford: OUP)

Ripstein, A (2006) 'Beyond the Harm Principle' 34 *Philosophy and Public Affairs* 215

Ripstein, A (2009) *Force and Freedom: Kant's Legal and Political Philosophy* (Cambridge, Mass: Harvard UP)

Ronnow-Rasmussen, T (2011) *Personal Value* (Oxford: OUP)

Ross, J (2012) 'Actualism, Possibilism, and Beyond' in R Schafer-Landau *Oxford Studies in Normative Ethics* vol 2 (Oxford: OUP)

Sartorio, C (2016) *Causation and Free Will* (Oxford: OUP)

Scanlon, T M (1998) *What We Owe to Each Other* (Cambridge, Mass: Harvard UP)

Scanlon, T M (2008) *Moral Dimensions: Permissibility, Meaning, Blame* (Cambridge, Mass: Harvard UP)

Scanlon, T M (2013) 'Interpreting Blame' in D J Coates and N A Tognazzini *Blame: Its Nature and Norms* (Oxford: OUP)

Scanlon, T M (2013) 'Giving Desert Its Due' 16 *Philosophical Explorations* 1.

Scanlon, T M (2015) 'Forms and Conditions of Responsibility' in R Clarke, M McKenna, and A M Smith *The Nature of Moral Responsibility: New Essays* (Oxford: OUP)

Schaffer, J (2001) 'Causation, Influence, and Effluence' 61 *Analysis* 11.

Scheffler, S (2001) 'Relationships and Responsibilities' in S Scheffler *Boundaries and Allegiances: Problems of Justice and Responsibility in Liberal Thought* (Oxford: OUP)

Scheffler, S (2013) *Death and the Afterlife* (Oxford: OUP)

Schulhofer, S (1998) *Unwanted Sex: The Culture of Intimidation and the Failure of Law* (Cambridge, Mass: Harvard UP)

Sherwin, E (1996) 'Infelicitous Sex' 2 *Legal Theory* 209

Shiffrin, S (1999) 'Wrongful Life, Procreative Responsibility, and the Significance of Harm' 5 *Legal Theory* 117

Shiffrin, S (2012) 'Harm and Its Moral Significance' 18 *Legal Theory* 357

Simester, A P (2012) 'Prophylactic Crimes' in G R Sullivan and I Dennis *Seeking Security: Pre-Empting the Commission of Criminal Harms* (Oxford: Hart)

Simester, A P and Sullivan, G R (2005) 'On the Nature and Rationale of Property Offences' in R A Duff and S P Green *Defining Crimes: Essays on the Special Part* (Oxford: OUP)

Simester, A P and von Hirsch, A (2002) 'Rethinking the Offense Principle' 8 *Legal Theory* 269

Simester, A P and von Hirsch, A (2011) *Crimes, Harms, and Wrongs: On the Principles of Criminalisation* (Oxford: Hart)

Singer, P (2010) 'Bystanders to Poverty' in N A Davis, R Keshen, and J McMahan *Ethics and Humanity: Themes from the Philosophy of Jonathan Glover* (Oxford: OUP)

Slavny, A (2014) 'How Eventful is the Event-Based Theory of Harm?' 48 *Journal of Value Inquiry* 559

Smith, M (2003) 'Neutral and Relative Value after Moore' 113 *Ethics* 527

Smith, M and Strabbing, J T 'Moral Obligation, Accountability, and Second-Personal Reasons' (2010) 81 *Philosophy and Phenomenological Research* 237

Snedegar, J (2015) 'Contrastivism about Reasons and Ought' 10 *Philosophy Compass* 379

Spinoza, B (1996) *Ethics* (London: Penguin)

Stanton-Ife, J (2010) 'Horrific Crime' in R A Duff, Lindsay Farmer, S E Marshall, M Renzo, and V Tadros *The Boundaries of the Criminal Law* (Oxford: OUP)

Sunstein, C and Vermeule, A (2005) 'Is Capital Punishment Morally Required? Acts, Omissions, and Life-Life Tradeoffs' 58 *Stanford Law Review* 703

Tadros, V (2005) *Criminal Responsibility* (Oxford: OUP)

Tadros, V (2009) 'Poverty and Criminal Responsibility' 43 *Journal of Value Inquiry* 391

Tadros, V (2011) 'Consent to Harm' 64 *Current Legal Problems* 23

Tadros, V (2011) 'Harm, Sovereignty, and Prohibition' 17 *Legal Theory* 35

Tadros, V (2011) 'Independence Without Interests?' 31 *Oxford Journal of Legal Studies* 193

Tadros, V (2011) *The Ends of Harm: The Moral Foundations of Criminal Law* (Oxford: OUP)

Tadros, V (2012) 'Replies' 5 *Jerusalem Review of Legal Studies* 89

Tadros, V (2012) 'Wrongness and Criminalization' in A Marmor *The Routledge Companion to Philosophy of Law* (London: Routledge)

Tadros, V (2013) 'Controlling Risk' in A Ashworth, P Tomlin, and L Zedner *Prevention and the Limits of the Criminal Law* (Oxford: OUP)

Tadros, V (2013) 'Responses' 32 *Law and Philosophy* 241

Tadros, V (2014) 'Orwell's Battle with Brittain: Vicarious Liability for Unjust Aggression' 42 *Philosophy and Public Affairs* 42

Tadros, V (2014) 'Resource Wars' 33 *Law and Philosophy* 361

Tadros, V (2014) 'What Might Have Been' in J Oberdiek *Philosophical Foundations of the Law of Torts* (Oxford: OUP)

Tadros, V (2015) 'Answers' 9 *Criminal Law and Philosophy* 73

Tadros, V (2015) 'Response to Blumenson', 3 *Law, Ethics and Philosophy* 56

Tadros, V (2015) 'Wrongful Intentions Without Closeness' 43 *Philosophy and Public Affairs* 52

Tadros, V (2016) 'Causation, Culpability, and Liability' in C Coons and M Weber *The Ethics of Self-Defense* (Oxford: OUP)

Tadros, V (2016) 'The Wrong and the Free' in K K Ferzan and S J Morse *Legal, Moral, and Metaphysical Truths: The Philosophy of Michael S. Moore* (Oxford: OUP)

Tadros, V Forthcoming 'Doing Without Desert' *Criminal Law and Philosophy*

Tadros, V Forthcoming 'Duress and Duty' in S Bazargan and S Rickless *The Ethics of War: Essays* (Oxford: OUP)

Tadros, V Forthcoming 'Moving Mountains: Variations on a Theme by Shelly Kagan' *Criminal Law and Philosophy*

Tadros, V Forthcoming 'Permissibility in a World of Wrongdoing' Philosophy and Public Affairs

Tadros, V Forthcoming 'Punishment and the Appropriate Response to Wrongdoing' *Criminal Law and Philosophy*

Tadros, V Unpublished 'Anarchic War'

Tadros, V Unpublished 'Overdetermination and Obligation'

Tasioulas, J (2006) 'Crimes of Offence' in A von Hirsch and A P Simester *Incivilities: Regulating Offensive Behaviour* (Oxford: Hart)

Temkin, L (1993) *Inequality* (Oxford: OUP)

Temkin, L (2012) *Rethinking the Good: Moral Ideals and the Nature of Practical Reasoning* (Oxford: OUP)

Teplin, L A, Jakubowski, J A, Abram, K M, Olso, N D, Stokes, M L, and Welty, L J (2014) 'Firearm Homicide and Other Causes of Death in Delinquents: A 16 Year Prospective Study' 134 *Pediatrics* 63

Thomson, J J (1986) 'The Trolley Problem' in J J Thomson *Rights, Restitution, and Risk: Essays in Moral Theory* (Cambridge, Mass: Harvard UP)

Thomson, J J (1990) *The Realm of Rights* (Cambridge, Mass: Harvard UP)

Thomson, J J (1991) 'Self-Defense' 20 *Philosophy and Public Affairs* 283

Thomson, J J (1999) 'Physician-Assisted Suicide: Two Moral Arguments' 109 *Ethics* 497

Thomson, J J (2008) *Normativity* (Chicago: Open Court)

Thomson, J J (2011) 'More on the Metaphysics of Harm' 82 *Philosophy and Phenomenological Research* 436

Thorburn, M (2011) 'Criminal Law as Public Law' in R A Duff and S P Green *Philosophical Foundations of Criminal Law* (Oxford: OUP)

Tomlin, P (2014) 'Retributivists! The Harm Principle is Not For You' 124 *Ethics* 272

Uniacke, S (2015) 'Punishment as Penalty' 9 *Criminal Law and Philosophy* 37
van Kesteren, J N (2014) 'Revisiting the Gun Ownership and Violence Link' 54 *British Journal of Criminology* 53
Velleman, J D (2008) 'Persons in Prospect' 36 *Philosophy and Public Affairs* 221
Walen, A (2006) 'The Doctrine of Illicit Intentions' 34 *Philosophy and Public Affairs* 39
Walen, A (2011) 'A Punitive Precondition for Preventive Detention: Lost Status as a Foundation for a Lost Immunity' 48 *San Diego Law Review* 1229
Walen, A (2011) 'A Unified Theory of Detention, With Application to Preventive Detention for Suspected Terrorists' 70 *Maryland Law Review* 871
Wallace, R J (2011) 'Dispassionate Opprobrium: On Blame and the Reactive Sentiments' in R Jay Wallace, R Kumar, and S Freeman *Reasons and Recognition: Essays on the Philosophy of T M Scanlon* (Oxford: OUP)
Watson, G (2004) 'Two Faces of Responsibility' in G Watson *Agency and Answerability: Selected Essays* (Oxford: OUP)
Wedgwood, R (2011) 'Defending Double Effect' 24 *Ratio* 384
Wellman, C H (2012) 'The Rights Forfeiture Theory of Punishment' 122 *Ethics* 371
Wellman, C H (2013) 'Rights Forfeiture and *Mala Prohibita*' in R A Duff, L Farmer, S E Marshall, M Renzo, and V Tadros *The Constitution of the Criminal Law* (Oxford: OUP)
Wertheimer, A (2003) *Consent to Sexual Relations* (Cambridge: CUP)
West, R (1996) 'A Comment on Consent, Sex, and Rape' 2 *Legal Theory* 233
Westen, P (2004) *The Logic of Consent* (Aldershot: Ashgate)
Williams, A (2000) 'The Alleged Incompleteness of Public Reason' 6 *Res Publica* 199
Williams, B (1981) 'Moral Luck' in B Williams *Moral Luck* (Cambridge: CUP)
Wolf, S (2011) 'Blame, Italian Style' in R Jay Wallace, R Kumar, and S Freeman *Reasons and Recognition: Essays on the Philosophy of T M Scanlon* (Oxford: OUP)
Wolf, S (2015) 'Above and Below the Line of Duty' in S Wolf *The Variety of Values: Essays on Morality, Meaning, and Love* (Oxford: OUP)
Woodward, J (2003) *Making Things Happen* (Oxford: OUP)
Wright, C (1992) *Truth and Objectivity* (Cambridge, Mass: Harvard UP)
Wright, J D and Rossi, P H (1986) *Armed and Considered Dangerous: A Survey of Felons and Their Firearms* (New York: Aldine)
Yaffe, G (2010) *Attempts* (Oxford: OUP)
Yaffe, G (2016) 'In Defense of Criminal Possession' 10 *Criminal Law and Philosophy* 441
Zaibert, L (2013) 'Instruments of Abolition, or Why Retributivism is the Only Real Justification of Punishment' 32 *Law and Philosophy* 33
Zeelenberg, M and van Dijk, E (2005) 'On the Comparative Nature of Regret' in D R Mandel and D J Hilton *The Psychology of Counterfactual Thinking* (London: Routledge)
Zeoli, A M and Frattaroli, S (2013) 'Evidence for Optimism: Policies to Limit Batterers' Access to Guns' in D W Webster and J S Vernick *Reducing Gun Violence in America: Informing Policy Evidence and Analysis* (Baltimore: John Hopkins University Press)
Zimring, F and Hawkins, G (1998) *Crime is Not the Problem: Lethal Violence in America* (Oxford: OUP)

Index of (Mostly Hypothetical) Cases

Index of Names

Subject Index

Printed and bound by CPI Group (UK) Ltd, Croydon, CR0 4YY